A Companion to Contemporary Art since 1945

BLACKWELL COMPANIONS TO ART HISTORY

These invigorating reference volumes chart the influence of key ideas, discourses, and theories on art, and the way that it is taught, thought of, and talked about throughout the English-speaking world. Each volume brings together a team of respected international scholars to debate the state of research within traditional subfields of art history as well as in more innovative, thematic configurations. Representing the best of the scholarship governing the field and pointing toward future trends and across disciplines, the *Blackwell Companions to Art History* series provides a magisterial, state-of-the-art synthesis of art history.

A Companion to
Contemporary Art
since 1945

Edited by

Amelia Jones

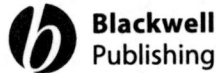

Blackwell
Publishing

BLACKWELL PUBLISHING
350 Main Street, Malden, MA 02148-5020, USA
9600 Garsington Road, Oxford OX4 2DQ, UK
550 Swanston Street, Carlton, Victoria 3053, Australia

The right of Amelia Jones to be identified as the Author of the Editorial Material in this Work has been asserted in accordance with the UK Copyright, Designs, and Patents Act 1988.

First published 2006 by Blackwell Publishing Ltd

1 2006

Library of Congress Cataloging-in-Publication Data

A companion to contemporary art since 1945 / edited by Amelia Jones.
p. cm. — (Blackwell companions in art history)
Includes bibliographical references and index.
ISBN-13: 978-1-4051-0794-5 (hardback : alk. paper)
ISBN-10: 1-4051-0794-4 (hardback : alk. paper)
ISBN-13: 978-1-4051-3542-9 (pbk. : alk. paper)
ISBN-10: 1-4051-3542-5 (pbk. : alk. paper) 1. Art, Modern—20th century—History.
2. Art, Modern—21st century—History. I. Jones, Amelia. II. Series.
N6490.C65615 2006
709.04′5—dc22
2005034704

A catalogue record for this title is available from the British Library.

Set in 10.5/13pt Galliard
by Graphicraft Ltd, Hong Kong

The publisher's policy is to use permanent paper from mills that operate a sustainable forestry policy, and which has been manufactured from pulp processed using acid-free and elementary chlorine-free practices. Furthermore, the publisher ensures that the text paper and cover board used have met acceptable environmental accreditation standards.

For further information on
Blackwell Publishing, visit our website:
www.blackwellpublishing.com

Contents

Figures

Notes on Contributors

Dore Bowen received her PhD from the University of Rochester's Visual and Cultural Studies Program. Besides publishing widely she has received grants and fellowships from the Getty Research Library, the National Endowment for the Arts, the College Art Association, the Photography Institute, the Susan B. Anthony Institute for Gender and Women's Studies, and the School for Criticism and Theory at Cornell. She is currently Assistant Professor of Contemporary Art and Theory at San Jose State University.

Gavin Butt teaches in the Department of Visual Cultures at Goldsmiths College, University of London. He is author of *Between You and Me: Queer Disclosures in the New York Art World 1948–1963* (2005), and editor of *After Criticism: New Responses to Art and Performance* (2004).

Mark Crinson published *Modern Architecture and the End of Empire* (2003), and he edited *Urban Memory: History and Amnesia in the Modern City* (2005). He has published on several aspects of contemporary art and is an occasional contributor to *Mute*. He teaches in Art History and Visual Studies at the University of Manchester.

Neil Cummings and **Marysia Lewandowska** have collaborated together since 1995. They have published the books *Lost Property* (1996) and *The Value of Things* (2000). Their art projects include a series of events entitled *Documents* (2000), which marked the culmination of a year-long residency at the Design Council Archive; *Capital* at the Tate Modern, in cooperation with the Bank of England Museum (2001); *Free Trade* at the Manchester Art Gallery (2002); and most recently, *Enthusiasts*, an exhibition involving amateur film clubs, at the Centre for Contemporary Art in Warsaw (2004) and the Whitechapel, London (2005). The website *liverpoolcommons.org* documents their contribution to the Liverpool Biennial in November 2004. Cummings is Reader in Theory and Practice at Chelsea College of Art and Design, London, and Lewandowska is Professor in Fine Art at Konstfack, Stockholm. For more information on their projects visit http://www.chanceprojects.com.

Pauline de Souza is Senior Lecturer of Art History at the University of East London. She is also Director of the African and Asian Visual Artists Archive at the same institution.

Anna Dezeuze is Research Fellow at the AHRB Research Centre for Studies of Surrealism and its Legacies, University of Manchester. In 2003, she obtained her PhD from the Courtauld Institute of Art, London, with a thesis on the topic of spectator participation in the 1960s. She has published articles on Fluxus and on the Brazilian artist Helio Oiticica and writes exhibition reviews for *Art Monthly*.

Jennifer Doyle is an Associate Professor of English at the University of California, Riverside. She is co-editor of *Pop Out: Queer Warhol* (1996), and has published several articles on sexuality and art, including "Sex, Scandal, and Thomas Eakins's *The Gross Clinic*" (*Representations* 1999). Her book *Sex Objects: Art and the Dialectics of Desire* is forthcoming from University of Minnesota Press.

María Fernández teaches in the Department of the History of Art at Cornell University. She has published essays on electronic media and postcolonial studies in *Third Text* and *Art Journal*, in the book *Alzado Vectorial/Vectorial Elevation* (2000), and in the anthology *Domain Errors: Cyberfeminist Practices* (2002).

Sam Gathercole lives in London and works at University of Essex and University of Liverpool. He completed his PhD, *The Constructionist Environment: Abstract Art and Architecture in Britain 1951–1969*, at the University of Manchester in 2000. He has had work published in a number of books and journals, including *Visual Culture in Britain*.

Jennifer González is Associate Professor of Contemporary Art and Visual Culture at the University of California at Santa Cruz. Her writing has appeared in numerous periodicals including *Frieze*, *World Art*, *Bomb*, and *Art Journal*, and in anthologies such as *The Encyclopedia of Aesthetics*, *With Other Eyes: Looking at Race and Gender in Visual Culture*, and *Race in Cyberspace*.

David Hopkins is Professor of Art History and Theory at the University of Glasgow. His most recent books are *After Modern Art 1945–2000* (2000), and *Dada and Surrealism: A Very Short Introduction* (2004).

Amelia Jones is Professor and Pilkington Chair in Art History and Visual Studies at the University of Manchester. She has written numerous articles in anthologies and journals and has organized exhibitions with accompanying catalogues, including *Sexual Politics: Judy Chicago's* Dinner Party *in Feminist Art History* (1996). Jones co-edited the anthology *Performing the Body/Performing the Text* with Andrew Stephenson (1999), edited the volume *Feminism and Visual Culture Reader* (2003), and has published the books *Postmodernism and the En-Gendering of Marcel Duchamp* (1994), *Body Art/Performing the Subject* (1998), and *Irrational Modernism: A Neurasthenic History of New York Dada* (2004). Jones has received ACLS, NEH, and Guggenheim fellowships.

Caroline A. Jones teaches in the History, Theory, and Criticism Section of the Department of Architecture at MIT. Producer/director of two documentary films and curator of many exhibitions, her books include major museum publications, such as *Bay Area Figurative Art, 1950–1965* (1990), the award-winning *Machine in the Studio: Constructing the Postwar American Artist* (1996/98), and the co-edited volume *Picturing Science, Producing Art* (1999). Her most recent book, *Eyesight Alone: Clement Greenberg's Modernism and the Bureaucratization of the Senses* is forthcoming from the University of Chicago Press.

Jonathan D. Katz is Visiting Associate Professor at the State University of New York at Stony Brook. Formerly the director of the Larry Kramer Initiative for Lesbian and Gay Studies at Yale University, and the founding chair of the Department of Lesbian and Gay Studies at City College of San Francisco, he was the first tenured faculty in gay and lesbian studies in the US. Katz's newest book, *The Collective Closet: Jasper Johns, Robert Rauschenberg and the Queering of American Art*, is in final pre-paration. A committed activist, as well as academic, Katz co-founded Queer Nation San Francisco, founded and chaired the Harvey Milk Institute, and founded the Queer Caucus of the College Art Association.

Grant Kester is Associate Professor of Art History at the University of California, San Diego, and the author of *Conversation Pieces: Community and Communication in Modern Art* (2004).

Liz Kotz teaches in the Department of Cultural Studies and Comparative Literature at the University of Minnesota, and was a 2004–5 Getty Fellow. She is completing a book on uses of language in 1960s American art, and preparing a collection of essays entitled *Aesthetics of the Expanded Screen*.

Johanne Lamoureux is Professor and Chair of the Department of Art History and Film Studies at the Université de Montréal. She has published essays in *Parachute, October, Cahiers du Witte de With, Word and Image*, and other periodicals, and has contributed to many catalogues for exhibitions of contemporary art. She published a book of essays on site specificity and the rhetoric of contemporary exhibitions, *L'art insituable. De l'in situ et autres sites* (2001). She is also an independent curator and has organized *Seeing in Tongues. A Narrative of Language and Visual Arts in Québec* (1995), and two exhibitions (with bilingual catalogues) at the Musée national des beaux-arts du Québec: *Irene F. Whittome. Bio-Fictions* (2000), and *Doublures. Vêtements de l'art contemporain* (2003).

Carol Mavor is Professor of Art History at the University of North Carolina. Her

publications include *Pleasures Taken: Performances of Sexuality and Loss in Victorian Photographs* (1995), and *Becoming: The Photographs of Clementina, Viscountess Hawarden* (1999). In addition to her books, Mavor has published in such journals as *Cultural Studies, Genre* and *Periskop*. Mavor has just completed a book on Proust, J. M. Barrie, Jacques-Henri Lartigue, and D. W. Winnicott (*Reading Boyishly*), and *Full*, an attempt at the "novelesque."

Laura Meyer is Assistant Professor of Art History and Theory at California State University, Fresno. She has written several essays on the feminist art movement in California, including essays in *Sexual Politics: Judy Chicago's* Dinner Party *in Feminist Art History* (1996); *Art/Women/California: Parallels and Intersections, 1950–2000* (2002); and *The Sons and Daughters of Los: Culture and Community in L.A.* (2004). She is currently completing a book on Louise Bourgeois.

Nick Mirzoeff is Professor of Art and Art Professions at New York University. He is the author of *Watching Babylon: The War in Iraq and Global Visual Culture* (2005) and *An Introduction to Visual Culture* (1999), as well as editor of the *Visual Culture Reader* (2002). He is working on a project called "1977."

Margaret Morgan is an artist living in Los Angeles whose practice includes video, photography, drawing, and writing. For the past 12 years her work has explored the residues of the twentieth, "American," century and its fascination with hygiene. As a consequence she is included in exhibitions with titles such as *Orifice, Hygiene, Bathroom, Trash, Out of Order*, and *A Pictorial Guide to Sanitary Defects*. Her work is exhibited internationally, most recently in Zürich, Amsterdam, Los Angeles, and Melbourne. Her writing has appeared in *Plumbing, Sounding Modern Architecture,*

Women in Dada, and as "The Plumbing of Modern Life" in *The Journal of Postcolonial Studies*.

Steven Nelson, Assistant Professor of African and African American Art History at UCLA, is former Reviews Editor for the College Art Association's *Art Journal*. He recently completed a book-length manuscript, entitled *Site and Symbol: Mousgoum Architecture, Race, and Modernity*, and is working on an urban history of Dakar titled *Dakar: The Making of an African Metropolis*.

Adrienne Posner received her BA in Art History at the University of California, Santa Cruz in 2003, where her research on contemporary art was distinguished with a Dean's and Chancellor's award.

Christine Ross is Associate Professor and Chair of the Department of Art History and Communication Studies at McGill University. She is a regular contributor to *Parachute*, to journals such as *Art Journal* and *October*, and to anthologies on contemporary art, and is a curator of exhibitions in media arts (notably at the Art Gallery of Ontario, YYZ Artist's Outlet, Oboro Gallery, and Optica Gallery). Ross is the author of *Images de surface: l'art vidéo reconsidéré* (1996), and *The Aesthetics of Disengagement: Contemporary Art and Depression*, forthcoming from the University of Minnesota Press.

Henry M. Sayre is Distinguished Professor of Art History at Oregon State University, Cascades Campus in Bend, Oregon. He is producer and creator of the ten-part television series, *A World of Art: Works in Progress*, aired on PBS in the fall of 1997, and author of seven books, including *The Object of Performance: The American Avant-Garde since 1970* (1989).

Howard Singerman, Associate Professor, McIntire Department of Art, University of Virginia, is the author of *Art Subjects: Making Artists in the American University* (1999), and has contributed to numerous exhibition catalogues including *Public Offerings* (2001), *Mike Kelley: Catholic Tastes* (1993), and *A Forest of Signs: Art in the Crisis of Representation* (1989). His essays have also appeared in *Artforum*, *October*, *Oxford Art Journal*, and *RES*.

Marquard Smith is Senior Lecturer in Visual Culture in the School of Art and Design History, Kingston University, London. He is a founder and editor-in-chief of *journal of visual culture*, the co-editor of the four-volume *Visual Culture* (2005), and a founding editor of the cultural theory journal *parallax*. He is also editor of *Stelarc: The Monograph* (2005), co-editor of *The Prosthetic Impulse: New Essays from the Humanities*, forthcoming from the MIT Press, and author of the forthcoming book *Moving Bodies: Perverse Visions of Prosthetic Culture*.

Sarah Wilson is Reader in the History of Art at the Courtauld Institute of Art, University of London, and has taught at Paris-Sorbonne IV. She curated and edited the catalogue for *Paris, Capital of the Arts, 1900–1968*, an exhibition at the Royal Academy of Arts, London, and the Guggenheim Museum, Bilbao, in 2001. She has published extensively on twentieth-century European art, including three edited volumes on the links between contemporary French philosophy and art, and has collaborated frequently with the Centre Georges Pompidou, Paris. She is currently preparing two books, *Red Paris* and *The Visual World of French Theory*. She is preparing a Pierre Klossowski retrospective for the Whitechapel Art Gallery, London, in 2006.

Series Editor's Preface

Blackwell Companions to Art History is a series of edited collections designed to cover the discipline of art history in all its complexities. Each volume is edited by specialists who lead a team of essayists, who represent the best of leading scholarship, in mapping the state of research within the sub-field under review, as well as pointing toward future trends. This volume examines *Contemporary Art since 1945* and through its very structure recognizes one of the principal concerns of a survey of this period: How to reconcile chronological coverage with broader thematic issues? The multiple but coherent structures of the sections of the book – Decades, Aesthetics, Politics, Identity/Subjectivity, Methods/Theories, Technology – offer a new and innovative way of presenting the key issues under review. Together, the chapters offer the reader a solid investigation of contemporary art in Britain and the United States, complemented by an analysis of the political and conceptual issues involved in the formulation of its histories. Indeed, the problematic nature of the relationship between contemporary art and its existence as an historical phenomenon is a fundamental theme in the volume.

A Companion to Contemporary Art since 1945 is a lively and original survey which will be essential reading for students and teachers of contemporary art, postwar culture, gender, and feminism, as well as critical issues in visual culture. As one of the initial volumes to be published it is an important standard-bearer for the *Blackwell Companions to Art History* series.

Dana Arnold, 2005

Acknowledgments

First and foremost I must thank, with a depth of gratitude that cannot be fully expressed in words, the authors who have patiently and laboriously worked with me over the past two-and-a-half years to complete these amazing and original essays. My thanks also go to Jayne Fargnoli, my brilliant, supportive, and far-sighted commissioning editor at Blackwell, who dealt patiently with my queries and complaints as the book progressed, and to the series editor of the *Blackwell Companions to Art History*, Dana Arnold, who was generous enough to invite me to edit this volume and who has been continually patient and supportive throughout the editorial process. My research assistant, Elisa Oliver, is a goddess for working patiently with authors and with me to get the volume in shape.

My colleagues at UC Riverside and then at the University of Manchester provided the intellectual dialog that kept this project alive – and my students (bright, hardworking, and always inquisitive) at these two institutions were an inspiration. It is the younger generations coming behind me (pushing ahead inexorably with that productive impatience) that make the hard work necessary to complete such a project seem worthwhile. In addition to the authors of the chapters in this book, colleagues and friends around the world to whom I'm particularly grateful – not the least for the vital inspiration that their brilliant work and conversation about politics, art, and the visual has provided – include Ron Athey, Sutapa Biswas, Judy Chicago, Kevin Dalton Johnson, Jane Chin Davidson, Vaginal Davis, Laura Doan, Jennifer Doyle, Rebecca Duclos, Tom Folland, Andrew Gellatly, Rachel Garfield, Jonathan Harris, Adrian Heathfield, Tam Hinton, Emil Hrvatin, Kathy Huffman, Jennie Klein, David Joselit, Caroline Jones, Carrie Noland, Lorraine O'Grady, Osseus Labyrint (Hannah Sim and Mark Steger), Tej Purewall, Joanna Roche, David Ross, Moira Roth, Carolee Schneemann, Susan Silton, Adrien Sina, Jackie Stacey, Andrew Stephenson, Robert Summers, and The Toxic Titties (Julia, Clover, and Heather).

I could not have survived the turmoil in my personal life, nor the pressures of completing a complex project such as this while making an international move, running a department, and being a newly minted single parent, without the love and support of my family (Ginnie on down; without your visits abroad . . .) and friends. In particular, Toni, Vanessa, Jennifer, Ananda, Laura, Mary, Andrew S., Veronica, and Phil, Neil, and Marysia.

This book is dedicated to my children, Evan (resolute, empathetic, tough and soft at the same time), and Vita (strong in the best ways, beautiful and smart). Evan and Vita have taught me how to live, not to mention how to love. Contemporary art works in their own right, they are vibrant examples of hope for future worlds of creativity, moxey, and political agency, those things that artists have striven to enact over the last 50 years.

Amelia Jones, 2005

PART I

Introduction

Introduction: Writing Contemporary Art into History, a Paradox?

Amelia Jones

How can what is defined as *in existence now* – the contemporary – be written into (a) history? Is the notion of "contemporary art history" or a "history of contemporary art" a contradiction in terms?

This book accepts the challenge of exploring the complexities both of contemporary art as a now "historical" phenomenon (as the years between "now" and 1945 expand in number) and of contemporary art as potentially the cutting edge of what people calling themselves artists (or understood by others as such) are making and doing in this increasingly complex and globalized economy of cultural practices.

Certainly since at least the mid to late 1970s departments of art history, visual culture studies, or visual studies in Britain and North America have at least explored the possibility of teaching courses on art practices dating from the end of WWII onward[1] – with 1945 taken as a key turning point in Euro-American history because of the shift of cultural, political, and economic power from Europe to the US that took place during and after the war, and because of the way in which the war marked the tortuous death of European colonialism.[2] The growing number of survey books on art since 1945 (or, in some cases, art since 1960 – another convenient cutting off point, due to the emergence around this time of new generations of artists interested in overturning dominant modes of modernist practice) testifies to the general acceptance of the importance of developing specific tools for studying and talking about contemporary art practices in Europe and North America.[3] Largely due to the vitality of the innovations in the visual arts over the past 60 years, as well as to the explosive growth of what Guy Debord in 1967 called the "society of the spectacle," the visual arts are now arguably one of the most crucial areas of cultural practice in terms of understanding what and how people convey, contest, or otherwise negotiate aspects of contemporary life.

Given that "contemporary art history," as it were, now has a 60-year life span – a span of time characterized in part by the increasing rapidity and density with which historical events have come to occur – the need for developing new ways of understanding the complexities of visual art practices since 1945 is acute. To that end, this volume is conceived as an alternative and crucial supplement to the standard survey texts in English covering the chronological, social, and aesthetic history of the development of contemporary art. These available surveys, as the author of one of them (David Joselit) has noted, make a "tacit, if impossible, promise: to represent the totality of art produced within a particular set of temporal and geographical boundaries," narrating a more or less coherent story of developments in Euro-American art since the end of WWII.[4] This book, in contrast, offers both a more comprehensive and a more focused set of stories about art since 1945. (It should be noted that, as with these surveys, the focus of the chapters here is on developments in Great Britain and North America, with some attention paid to global or non-Euro-American art trends and movements.) It is more comprehensive in that it explores a range of topics from multiple points of view, with 27 different authors from across the French- and English-speaking worlds of art history and visual studies, and more focused in that each author takes a particular topic and explores it in some depth.

Contemporary Art is thus intended to be both complementary to and different from the available surveys, which are generally filled with numerous illustrations, written by single authors, and cover the established chronological progression of mediums, movements, and themes in the visual arts since 1945. This book has relatively few illustrations, is of course multiply authored, and addresses a vast range of media (from painting and sculpture to performance and body art, video, digital art, and live political activism presented as art). It is organized through a dual logic, covering decades as well as major themes. So as to address the complexity of contemporary art from a historical perspective, the book begins with a section of chapters focusing on developments within specific periods (based loosely on the decades since 1945). Following these chronologically oriented chapters, the thematic sections are meant to provide multiple lenses through which to view the extremely complex debates and developments in Euro-American art and art discourse since the mid-twentieth century.

Eschewing the rigidity of the conventional narratives of contemporary art history, which generally adhere to overdetermined groupings by "movement" (i.e., "abstract expressionism," "pop art," etc.), this volume thus addresses major historical, conceptual, theoretical, and aesthetic issues that have informed contemporary visual art practices and debates about the visual arts; these thematic issues, which are further subdivided into the topics of the individual chapters, are loosely organized according to their chronological appearance in these debates (i.e., "aesthetics" is the first broad thematic category because it was central to 1940s–50s discussions about abstraction versus realism; at the same time, within the category of aesthetics, the chapters bring the reader up to the present moment – the final chapter in this section addresses "Beauty," a recent "hot" issue in art criticism).

In organizing the book in this way, and commissioning authors from diverse pedagogical, scholarly, or artistic traditions (from art historians to scholars of visual culture studies to practicing artists) and cultural backgrounds, I have attempted to bring together a book that will provide a fresh approach to the study (and potentially the making) of contemporary art. Each author was urged both to cover the bases – to address canonical figures and note generally understood historical trajectories – and to rethink the topic at hand in order to provide an original take on it. Rather than inviting the scholar best known for addressing a topic or decade, I commissioned chapters from relatively unexpected writers, encouraging them to push their thinking in new directions complementary to their known published work. To that end, each of these chapters explores well-known as well as previously marginal works, movements, and cultural pressures, forging into new territory by addressing the visual arts and art discourses from the post-WWII period from a fresh perspective.

My high expectations regarding the richness and range of chapters I would receive were not disappointed. To that end, I believe and hope that *Contemporary Art* can become an indispensable handbook for any student or practitioner of art criticism, art history, or the visual arts themselves, as well as a crucial book for anyone interested in twenty-first century ways of thinking about the visual arts since 1945. Covering the most important historical and theoretical issues and debates that have conditioned our understanding of the contemporary visual arts, as well as offering new approaches to old problems, the book points the reader to future trends, as well as offering multiple, and often interdisciplinary, perspectives on past movements and conceptual issues.

Organization of the Book

Decades

As noted, the first section of the book after this Introduction includes five chapters, each of which addresses one of the decades since 1945, loosely construed (with the first obviously covering a decade and a half). Gavin Butt's chapter, "'America' and its Discontents: Art and Politics 1945–60," thus covers the rise of US cultural dominance in this period; noting the tendency to historicize art from the 1950s purely through dominant practices of painterly abstraction, Butt offers a vital counter-narrative of, in his words, "how in the fifties we witness the development and consolidation of a Modernist 'center' at precisely the same time that this gets undone in the various 'alternative' practices to it and to American Abstract Expressionism."

Covering the 1960s, Anna Dezeuze, in her chapter "The 1960s: A Decade Out-of-Bounds," notes the tendency to understand the art history of this period as achieving a "systematic dismantling of modernist media," exploring the decade's art practices as seeking to "open" the art work to chance, the everyday, language, the body, and its social and political context. Addressing practices by artists from Britain to the US to Brazil, Dezeuze's chapter also points to the rapid development of an increasingly globalized art world in the 1960s.

In his chapter, "'I'm sort of sliding around in place . . . ummm . . .': Art in the 1970s," Sam Gathercole uses a phrase spoken by Dan Graham in his 1977 performance and video piece *Performer/Audience/Mirror* to evoke the slipperiness of 1970s culture as well as the difficulties of the decade in political and social terms, especially (with state and market both increasing their hold on culture in all its forms) for creative people interested in working *outside* or *against the grain* of these forces. Even as Graham "slides around," Gathercole argues, artists of the 1970s "fumbl[e] for a next move as previously held assumptions of meaning fragment and collapse all around (and through) the work."

Howard Singerman's "Pictures and Positions in the 1980s" charts the rise of "simulation" theory, and the concomitant explosion of "appropriation" art, particularly in New York City, the heart of the Euro-American art world during this period (and, arguably, since 1945). Noting the parallel emergence of AIDS, which had an enormous impact on the creative arts during the 1980s and following, and of the politics of the Reagan–Thatcher era, Singerman turns to the writings of art historians Hal Foster and Douglas Crimp to argue that dominant art practices and discourses during this decade were characterized by a drive to critique and dismantle both the traditions associated with artistic modernism and the conservative, even deadly (considering the cost of AIDS to the creative communities of Western culture) assumptions about identity and meaning informing broader social and political structures and beliefs during this period.

The final chapter in the "Decades" section, Henry Sayre's "1990–2005: In the Clutches of Time," traces the explosive transformation in visual cultures with the rapid rise of digital culture in this period. Making note of the decade's "culture wars" (more expansively discussed by Katz in chapter 12), Sayre explores the tendency for issues of identity to pressure and inform 1990s art practices, as well as the expansion of the art world to embrace international and global trends and works, and the expansion of durational and new media practices during this vital period of development in the visual arts. Like many other contemporary critics, Sayre sees Matthew Barney's *Cremaster* series, which he argues meshes all of these developments into one complex project, as epitomizing the cutting edge of these trends.

Aesthetics

The first thematic section of the book addresses issues of aesthetics – generally speaking, taken here to comprise issues of meaning and value as these have been determined and understood since the rise of aesthetic theory in the eighteenth century. These issues were taken to be paramount in modernist formalist theory (particularly the writings of Clement Greenberg and Michael Fried), but fell into disfavor in the 1960s and following with the rise of pop, conceptual, and performance art and of the identity-based cultural movements. Questions of aesthetics, however, rose to prominence again with the burgeoning of "beauty discourse" spearheaded by the 1990s writings of west coast US-based art critic Dave Hickey.[5]

Caroline Jones's chapter "Form and Formless" maps the development of modernist formalist art critical models from the early twentieth century through the return of formalism in the guise of the "formless" (*informe*) exhibition organized in 1996 at the Centre Georges Pompidou in Paris. Jones examines the historical pressures informing the particular kinds of formalist criticism, as well as the artistic practices that have either responded to, or been addressed by, these models. Because formalism (she notes) is the "theoretical tool bequeathed to art writing by the search for universally significant form" (and is thus related to certain anthropological assumptions), it can easily become (and has done in the past) a means for stigmatizing and denigrating practices that are viewed not "universally significant" (i.e., non-European art, etc.). The rapid globalization of visual and other cultures points ultimately to the (at best) useless and (at worst) dangerous assumptions guiding the application of simplistic models of form or formless and yet, Jones suggests, the core understanding of visual art works always comes back to *form* in some way – we cannot communicate visually without it.

David Hopkins' chapter, "Re-Thinking the 'Duchamp Effect'," addresses one of the key trajectories developing in resistance to certain rigidities perceived in modernist aesthetics – the conceptualist critique of the idea of *form* as the primary basis of artistic creation and aesthetic interpretation. Citing conceptual artist Joseph Kosuth, Hopkins makes the argument, which became standard in 1980s accounts of postmodern art, that Marcel Duchamp's readymades from the 1910s initiated a shift toward the "function of art as a question." Hopkins also notes the role of the formalist criticism of Greenberg and Fried, which became so dominant in the New York-based contemporary art world by 1960 that younger generations of artists began to look to alternative – idea-based – modes of making art as a way of questioning or attempting to overthrow this dominant force.

In "Regarding Beauty," Margaret Morgan discusses the discourse of beauty as it developed in abstract expressionism (via Greenberg's use of Kantian aesthetics), went underground in the 1960s through the early 1990s, and reemerged through the "beauty" discourse of Dave Hickey and his associates on the west coast of the US (with broad international influence). She astutely interrogates the politics of this reemergence, exploring which practices have been legitimated by it and thus have benefited from the return of "beauty" precisely at a time in which artists previously excluded from the canons of art history had been making inroads into making their work seen and appreciated in the Euro-American art world.

Politics

This section includes chapters addressing debates about the political roles and efficacy of particular types of contemporary art practice, tracing historical links to earlier modernist models of artistic intervention in the political sphere. Collectively, these chapters make the strong point that, although it would be impossible (as David Joselit notes in the quotation above) to narrate a coherent or unified story of Euro-American contemporary art, on some level all art since 1945 has been pressured and inflected by political demands and exigencies and, in many cases, has explicitly responded to them. If anything Euro-American contemporary art has taught us that there is no way to separate art from the social and political realms (as the romantics and to some extent modernist formalist critics would have it).

In her chapter, entitled "Avant-Garde: A Historiography of a Critical Concept," Johanne Lamoureux traces the notion of the avant-garde as it was borrowed from nineteenth-century French military parlance, adopted as a label for artists working "in advance of" mainstream bourgeois culture, and transported to contemporary art debates from the 1940s and beyond (from the art criticism of Greenberg to the work of British cultural theory in the 1960s and 1970s, to the writings of the group of art critics associated with the highly influential journal *October* in 1980s New York and following). Noting that any term that proposes to label what is "advanced" will inevitably *exclude* what is not deemed such, Lamoureux probes the historical ways in which "avant-garde" has in fact functioned to marginalize important kinds of art practice (for example, by women) even as it has also proved its usefulness in encouraging a politicized notion of visual arts practice.

Jennifer González and Adrienne Posner deal with the intersection of activist and artistic practices in contemporary art in their chapter entitled "Facture for Change: US Activist Art since 1950." Their chapter expands on the inevitably *political* and *social* nature of all artistic practices, noting that art discourse now generally acknowledges the fact that "aesthetics . . . does not exist without politics." Drawing on the important work of art historian Lucy Lippard, they explore the complexities of the relationship between art and politics both in a general sense (viewing works from the 1950s as implicitly political), and through the lens of activist art projects (from GranFury's performative and visual protests relating to the AIDS crisis to Internet activism) that attempt to make the connection direct, explicit, and overt.

Further exploring the art–politics intersection, Jonathan Katz's chapter " 'The Senators Were Revolted': Homophobia and the Culture Wars" explores the violent "wars" between artists and art institutions and the increasingly powerful forces of right-wing politics in the US in the 1980s and following. Katz begins by noting how difficult it is to remember a time when "avant-garde art and conservative politics were not sworn enemies in the United States," and the chapter explores the intricacies of the right wing's manipulation of culture (and particularly the visual arts) as a way of articulating their political position and agency. Tracing the various permutations of these debates, he argues persuasively that the culture wars represent a more or less covert attempt to associate the visual arts with gay culture – itself viewed through a tainted lens colored by assumptions that AIDS is a "gay" disease and so a sign of the pathology of gay sexualities ("art/gay/AIDS") – and thus to discredit art as morally suspect, while simultaneously confirming negative beliefs about gay men.

Grant Kester's "Crowds and Connoisseurs: Art and the Public Sphere in America," the last chapter in this section on politics, deals with the debates and practices relating to "public art." Addressing the question of what or who comprises the public sphere, debates about public funding, and a range of practices from official corporate-sponsored monumental sculpture to earth art, Kester traces the increasingly complex relationships between the artist and the public sphere since 1945 and attends to the political and social shifts paralleling these relationships. Finally, he notes the crucial shift away from "official" public art (due in part to an awareness on the part of artists of the inevitably compromised nature of its sponsorship structure) to a *critical* public practice that would produce (citing artist Krzysztof Wodiczko) "aesthetic-critical interruptions, infiltrations and appropriations that question the symbolic, psycho-political and economic operations of the city."

Identity/Subjectivity

Chapters in this section address the ending of European colonial empires in the post-WWII period, the development of a "postcolonial" consciousness, and the rise of identity politics in the 1960s and beyond, tracing its roots and discussing its impact on discourses and practices of contemporary art. Collectively these chapters make a strong argument for aspects of identity formation and subjectivity as being absolutely central to all contemporary art, whether explicitly acknowledged by the artist and her/his art critical and institutional supports or not. They also address the burgeoning of art practices during the post-1970 period in particular that emphasize questions of subjectivity and the body in its specific identifications.

In her chapter, "The *Writerly* Artist: Beautiful, Boring, and Blue," Carol Mavor explores the shifting conceptions of the artistic author from the modernist to the postmodernist period (particularly after the late 1960s), through a text that is itself "writerly." Exploring the interchanges between the work of novelist Marcel Proust and filmmaker Chantal Akerman (with detours into poststructuralist and feminist theories of authorship and subjectivity), Mavor thus enacts the very opening of the text or work of art to the interpreter that characterizes one of the most significant shifts in postmodernism. Her chapter is a meditation on the dispersal of authorial agency which differentiates art since 1960 from its precursor movements, which tended to continue to rely on the modernist idea of the artist as a fixed and coherent origin for the meaning (and the value) of the work of art.

In "Diaspora: Multiple Practices, Multiple Worldviews," Steven Nelson grapples with the complex effects of colonialism and its legacy. By addressing this crucial (if not *the* crucial) aspect of globalization – the diasporic shift of populations away from their native lands and into new places (often the very nations that initially had colonized their native cultures) – Nelson unsettles the conventional accounts of contemporary art as a singularly "Western" product. Examining a range of works by diasporic artists and various crucial exhibitions addressing diaspora and globalization, he traces the effects and influences of diaspora *in both directions.* Ultimately Nelson argues that, "[i]n a world that is increasingly interdependent, and increasingly structured by international flows of capital, technology, information, and media," diaspora is a crucial – if also impossibly complex – signifier that pressures every aspect of the way in which contemporary art is made, displayed, marketed, and written about.

While the civil rights movement was the first post-WWII identity-based political movement in the US, until the 1990s it had less purchase in the visual arts than feminism, which was the first identity discourse to develop as a coherent institutional force within academia and the art world (by 1970, the feminist art movement was going strong in New York, London, and Los Angeles). This chapter by Laura Meyer, entitled "Power and Pleasure: Feminist Art Practice and Theory in the United States and Britain," traces the historical rise of the movement and its debates from the late 1960s to the present, including conflicts within the movement. Meyer addresses the dualisms that have haunted feminist art discourse and practice – the "British" versus the "US" models; issues of essentialism vs. anti-essentialism; class issues and national differences; and debates about the movement's assumption of whiteness and heterosexuality – and ultimately complicates these oppositions by showing how many of these themes overlap in complicated ways in single artworks or artists' oeuvres within the feminist movement.

Jennifer Doyle, in "Queer Wallpaper," traces the parallel rise of queer activism in the art world after the Stonewall uprising in New York City in 1969 and examines how queerness has been articulated in art and its discourses. As Doyle argues in contrasting two situations – a particular Andy Warhol print hung in a particular site in Los Angeles (a gay bar), where it is viewed as "queer wallpaper," versus the normalizing presentation of Warhol's work in an official museum retrospective – the former example forces us to question the very nature of how visual images come to mean and come to have social, political, and personal value. Thinking about the queer (that which relates to "deviant" or non-normative sexual behaviors and identifications) in contemporary art has enabled a radical unsettling of how we think about art. *Queer*, rather than the more essentializing terms "gay" and "lesbian", Doyle argues, affords an understanding of the subtle and complex ways in which sexuality pressures the making, displaying, and reception of visual culture.

Pauline de Souza's chapter "Implications of Blackness in Contemporary Art" charts the increasing pressures of racial and ethnic difference on visual arts discourses and practices over the past four decades. With the diasporic immigration of formerly colonized populations to Europe and the rise of Civil Rights and other racial identity discourses in the US and Britain (including postcolonial theory and various modes of activism), the visual arts have been inexorably transformed. No longer can art institutions pretend that race and ethnicity have nothing to do with aesthetics, or that whose art gets shown where is a neutral issue untempered by preconceptions about artists' identities and social positionalities. Artists such as Kara Walker and Roshini Kempadoo produce works that, for de Souza, exemplify the trend toward explicit exploration of the history of racial oppression and aspects of racial and ethnic identification in Euro-American art in the contemporary period.

If aspects of identity as they are articulated, experienced, and understood in contemporary life deeply inform (if not entirely condition) contemporary art discourses and practices, then the exploration of how identity *takes place* must in some way be central to the study of these discourses and practices. In her chapter "The Paradoxical Bodies of Contemporary Art," Christine Ross thus explores the veiling of the body in modernism, and its reemergence as a major trope and medium in art since the 1960s – in practices from performance art to Minimalism to "cyborg" practices. Ross argues that the role and significance of the body in contemporary art is still little understood – although recent practices exploring *affectivity* via the enactment of the body provide the best means of getting to the bottom of how the body *means* in contemporary visual practice and so ultimately how it is experienced in other aspects of contemporary life.

Methods/Theories

This section includes chapters addressing major theoretical influences and shifts in contemporary art discourse and pointing to the ways in which art practices and visual culture have both informed and responded to these methodological shifts. Pivoting around the 2001 performative public event by Jeremy Deller – called *The English Civil War Part II*, and colloquially known as the *Battle of Orgreave* – Neil Cummings and Marysia Lewandowska's chapter "A Shadow of Marx" thus explores the various roles played by Marxist theory in contemporary art practices and critical theories of the visual arts.

As Cummings and Lewandowska suggest, projects such as Deller's, which involved the elaborate reenactment of the epochal miner's strike in Britain in the 1980s that was viciously suppressed by the Thatcher administration, insist on art as an explicitly political cultural act and one that is always already caught up in (and even in many cases reproductive of) the forces of capital. As Cummings and Lewandowska note, such works put into play the Marxist recognition that we are all "enacting a text written elsewhere. And this text, whether we like it or not and whether we can name it or not, is called ideology." Artists and art theorists in the contemporary period can thus either embrace their own inexorable commodification (like the "Young British Artists," or YBAs have done), or attempt to move out from the comforts provided by official art institutions producing performative works like Deller's – works that both re-mind us that the history of capitalism is a specific one with various events marking its triumphant development, and provide ways of thinking against the grain of its structures.[6]

Examining another key theoretical development closely related to develop-ments in the visual arts, Sarah Wilson's chapter, entitled "Poststructuralism and Contemporary Art, Past, Present, Future . . ." provides an overview of the devel-opment of poststructuralism in continental philosophy (from semiotics to Lacanian and French feminist psychoanalytic theory), and its links to art practice and theory. Noting that poststructuralism as such was largely invented by Anglo-Americans enamored of complex theories of meaning and identity taking shape in France after WWII, Wilson points to the relative disinterest in Britain and the US in French contemporary art practices. She examines as well links between poststructuralist philosophy and literary theory, feminism, and other disciplinary models of cultural analysis relating to the visual arts.

Similarly, in the chapter " 'Fragments of Collapsing Space': Postcolonial Theory and Contemporary Art," Mark Crinson notes the crucial intersection between contemporary art and postcolonial theory from the 1980s onward. Beginning with the collapse of the European empires after WWII (in particular the break-away of India from Britain (1947) and of Algeria from France (1962)), develop-ing in tandem with identity politics, and inaugurated by the 1952 publication of Frantz Fanon's crucially influential *Black Skins, White Masks*, postcolonial theory began to have a major impact on art debates and practice in the 1980s. Crinson examines closely the work of artists such as Sonia Boyce, Yinka Shonibare, and Chris Ofili to explore how artists have drawn on aspects of postcolonial theory to produce works critically invested in notions of hybridity and globalization.

Driven by the impulse to break down disciplinary boundaries, and informed by ideas from cultural studies (a British interdisciplinary mode of cultural criti-cism developing in the 1960s), the sub- or anti-discipline of visual culture has arisen out of the desire to break down the boundaries staged by traditional art history in order to define high art as an ontologically separate field of objects intended for special (art historical) analysis. Marquand Smith's chapter, "Visual Culture Studies: Questions of History, Theory, and Practice," explores the rise of visual culture, its development as an (anti- or cross-)disciplinary model for examining visual imagery, and the impact of this discourse on the understanding and making of contemporary art. Smith discusses the important texts and insti-tutional sites relevant to the rise of visual culture studies, as well as the debates between more traditional art historians (who tend to be threatened by the concept of visual culture) and avatars of visual culture, ending with an exploration of the project he himself is involved in developing. Called "The Poetics of Place," this project exemplifies the ways in which contemporary art practices can usefully respond to the challenges posed by visual culture theory.

Technology

Ever since the rise of photography and the development of mass reproductive techniques from the mid-nineteenth century onward, technologies of image making have increasingly eroded traditional conceptions of art and aesthetics. With contemporary art, technologies of image making, reproduction, and dissemination (whether acknowledged or not) have become increasingly and unavoidably central to our understanding and experience of visual imagery. This final section of *Contemporary Art* addresses technological shifts in relation to visual culture and the ideological as well as new artistic strategies that have accompanied them.

Debates about the division between high and low culture emerged at the very beginnings of contemporary art discourse with Clement Greenberg's epochal 1939 essay "Avant-Garde and Kitsch." The first chapter in this section on technology, Nick Mirzoeff's " 'That's All Folks': Contemporary Art and Popular Culture," traces the trajectory of these debates and the impact of mass cultural modes of producing and disseminating images on contemporary art. Mirzoeff discusses the crucial role of Andy Warhol in emphasizing art making as inexorably tied to mass cultural production, the rise of postmodern theory, and the significance of the arguments made by Antonio Negri and Michael Hardt in their influential 2000 book on globalization (*Empire*). Paralleling the arguments made in other chapters in *Contemporary Art*, he ends by pointing to the crucial impact of decolonization on globalization.

Photography and photographic technologies became increasingly central to contemporary art practice from the 1960s onward. With conceptual art work (by artists such as John Baldessari, Douglas Huebler, and Dan Graham) the incursion of semiotic theory, and, in particular, the important 1977 essay by Rosalind Krauss on the photographic index, artists and theorists began recognizing the profound implications of this incursion of the photographic mode of seeing into our relationship with visuality. In "Image + Text: Reconsidering Photography in Contemporary Art," Liz Kotz addresses these theoretical concerns and focuses on the work of artists who explored or interrogated the photographic index as a means, in her words, "to move beyond the object to work directly on representation and cultural sign systems," examining as well the links between official conceptual art and photo-based work from the 1970s and 1980s.

Dore Bowen's "Imagine There's No Image (It's Easy If You Try): Appropriation in the Age of Digital Reproduction," also explores the ongoing impact of photographic technologies, as well as digital media, on contemporary art. Tracing the development of discourses addressing the rise of what Guy Debord called "the society of the spectacle" with the explosion of the mass media in the twentieth century (and its acceleration after WWII), Bowen also analyzes a range of art practices exploring the spectacle and its effects in relation to the screen, from Fluxus performative works commenting on the vicissitudes of mass reproduction, to the works of Vietnamese-American photographer Binh Danh, and the melodramatic video installations of Bill Viola. In closing, Bowen notes that the *screen* has become the locus and metaphor for artists dealing with the crucial contemporary obsessions of perception, imagination, and a specific kind of memory ("third memory") particular to our current highly technologized image culture.

The final chapter of the book, María Fernández's "'Life-like': Historicizing Process and Responsiveness in Digital Art," charts the history – now over half a century long – of digital arts, from telematic and robotic works developed in the overlapping terrain between the sciences and arts during and after WWII, to recent artistic projects using artificial life, genetic, and cybernetic technologies to explore the boundaries of life itself. Fernández examines the growing body of art and visual theory that examines or enacts the erosion of boundaries between "the organic, the inorganic, the material, and the virtual," ultimately questioning the very meaning and existence of the human subject.

In Conclusion. . . . What is Contemporary Art?

Contemporary art can be understood, of course, as any work produced in the context of official visual arts institutions and discourses in Europe and the US (and, increasingly, beyond) in the post-WWII period. As noted, the author of the survey book on contemporary art is constrained by the necessity of pulling together some kind of coherent narrative, addressing a range of interrelated themes, in order to produce a viable handbook for students and other non-specialist readers.

In contrast, the 27 authors of the chapters in this book – coming from France, Britain, Canada, and the US – articulate multiple narratives about contemporary art and its attendant discourses. Their points of view range widely from the explicitly historicist or social art historical framework to the more cultural studies (or visual culture studies) oriented model, informed by Marxist, queer, feminist, postcolonial, and anti-racist theory. What this book offers that is unique, then, is precisely the diversity of point of view, which comes together only in the loosest possible way through intersecting arguments emphasizing a varied and heterogeneous range of characteristics associated with art made since 1945. (Although, of course, it must not be glossed that *I* certainly have a very particular editorial point of view, and that I am solely responsible for having commissioned the authors whose work is represented here.)

The few thoughts that might pull the book together as a whole, without violating its vitality (precisely sparked by its lack of unified point of view), would revolve around very broad concepts. In closing, then, let me just note that the excitement and richness of viewing and studying contemporary art resides, for me, precisely in the way, in its most interesting forms, it continually unsettles understandings of and expectations about the way art functions and means in our culture. From Jackson Pollock flinging paint on a vast plain of canvas spread horizontally across the floor of his studio around 1950, to Robert Morris's and Eva Hesse's elegant yet sloppy "process art" (anti-)sculptural installations from around 1970, to Carolee Schneemann pulling a scroll from her vaginal canal in the mid 1970s, to Shirin Neshat's elegant video installations from c.2000 narrating the complexities of male/female relationships in Iranian Islamic culture, to Jeremy Deller's recent restaging of the "battle of Orgreave" or Sutapa Biswas's ongoing interrogations of postcolonial Indian-British identity – the best things artists have done in the post-WWII period have revolved around finding ways to open our eyes to what otherwise *would or could not be seen*. Perhaps most profoundly, art since 1945 has insistently, in ways varying as widely as the kinds of people making it, explored the *contingency* of the visual arts (like any form of expression) – the way in which works of art (including performances, live events, etc.) exist and come to mean within circuits of meaning, economic and social value, and personal and collective desire that are far more complex than we can ever fully understand.

But *that* – fortunately – will never keep us from trying. This book joins, humbly but with optimism, in that ongoing attempt.

Notes

1 When I attended Harvard University and studied art history in the early 1980s there was already in place a section on art since 1945 in the primary survey course. Granted, this section stopped more or less with the work of Morris Louis from the 1960s, included no work by women artists or artists of color, and addressed the work in a traditional way (using formalist models of analysis and anecdotal historical accounts), but at least the course addressed the contemporary.

2 For the best short overview on this and other related shifts see West (1990).

3 See Archer (2002); Fineberg (1995); Hopkins (2000); Joselit (2003); Lucie-Smith (2001); Wheeler (1991); Wood (1993).

4 Joselit (2003), 6. Joselit's is among the most nuanced of the available surveys, though it only addresses *American* art since 1945.

5 See Hickey (1994).

6 Notably, since Cummings and Lewandowska completed their essay, Deller was chosen as the Turner Prize winner in Britain for 2004. The Turner Prize is the single greatest honor given to contemporary artists in Britain (but also the most institutionalized form of recognition, with the work of Turner Prize finalists exhibited at the Tate Britain, and the whole process obsessively covered by the mainstream media). Deller's designation as Turner Prize winner further reinforces Cummings and Lewandowska's point about the inexorability of capitalism's incorporation of all forms of culture, even those that ostensibly contest its machinations; but also, of course, his triumph testifies to the significance of his work.

References

Archer, Michael (2002). *Art Since 1960*, new edn. London: Thames and Hudson.

Debord, Guy (1967). *Society of the Spectacle*. Originally trans. into English 1977. Entire text available at: http://www.marxists.org/reference/archive/debord/society.htm

Fineberg, Jonathan (1995). *Art Since 1940: Strategies of Being*. New York: Harry Abrams.

Hickey, Dave (1994). *The Invisible Dragon: Four Essays on Beauty*. Los Angeles: Art Issues Press.

Hopkins, David (2000). *After Modern Art: 1945–2000*. Oxford: Oxford University Press.

Joselit, David (2003). *American Art Since 1945*. London: Thames and Hudson.

Lucie-Smith, Edward (2001). *Movements in Art Since 1945*. London: Thames and Hudson.

West, Cornel (1990). "The New Cultural Politics of Difference." In *Out There: Marginalization and Contemporary Cultures*, ed. Russell Ferguson, Martha Gever, Trinh T. Minh-ha, and Cornel West. Cambridge, MA: MIT Press. 48–64.

Wheeler, Daniel (1991). *Art Since Mid-Century, 1945 to the Present*. New York: Vendome Press.

Wood, Paul, Francis Frascina, Jonathan Harris, and Charles Harrison (1993). *Modernism in Dispute: Art Since the Forties*. New Haven: Yale University Press.

PART II

Decades

2

"America" and its Discontents: Art and Politics 1945–60

Gavin Butt

Histories of the art of the immediate postwar years, and in particular of the 1950s, have been largely dominated by stories of the rise of US art in a world transformed by the emergence of the cold war. Such narratives have largely fallen into two camps: one, modernist and celebratory of the rise to prominence of US art, the other socio-historical and critical. Perhaps these tendencies are best represented by two now famous art historical studies, the titles of which fairly transparently telegraph the differences between them: Irving Sandler's 1970 book *The Triumph of American Painting* and Serge Guilbaut's *How New York Stole the Idea of Modern Art*, published in 1983. Both of these studies take abstract expressionist painting as the focus of their deliberations, principally because it was this movement that had come to represent most prominently the character and value of "American" painting in the immediate postwar years.

Sandler charts the emergence of this art out of the crucible of debates about the avant-garde during the years of WWII. Most profoundly, the artists who were to become famous as the abstract expressionists – including Jackson Pollock, Willem de Kooning, Barnett Newman, and Clyfford Still – are shown struggling to produce a new art befitting the changed realities of the postwar age, and, since this age was seen to be emerging as decidedly American, it was to be discovered by working through and surpassing the existing forms of the pre-war European avant-garde, most notably surrealist automatism and late variants on cubism. Sandler's book is at pains therefore to carefully elaborate the novelty of American art's new painterly techniques: the "gestural" work of, for example, Jackson Pollock – produced by movements of the artist's hand and body over the canvas – and the "color field" painting of Barnett Newman and others, characterized by the all-over application of pigment on large canvases creating expansive "fields" of color.

In departing in such a manner from European art, New York abstract art in particular came to be seen by some as the most "advanced" art of the day. Given the premium placed on being at the forefront of progressive artistic developments by the discourse of avant-gardism, New York generally came to replace Paris as the recognized center for contemporary art production. This American "triumph," seen by Sandler as a function of the quality and conviction of New York art, is accounted for in very different terms by Serge Guilbaut, one of a group of social art historians that has drawn attention to the importance of abstract expressionism's symbolization of freedom in establishing its cultural dominance at this time.[1] This was very important to a postwar US state for which ideas of freedom – of expression, of the market – were to be central in distinguishing its imperial ambitions from those of its cold war enemy the Soviet Union. From a socio-historical perspective then, the success of abstract expressionist painting is seen to reside less in any "inherent" aesthetic quality of the work itself, and rather more in how its informal, non-traditional style lent itself to being deployed as representative of specifically "American" freedoms – as opposed to the prescriptive forms of art in totalitarian states, particularly of Soviet Socialist realism in the USSR.

In beginning with these two historical accounts relating radically different stories about the emergence of US art at this time, I want to make it explicit from the outset that the concerns of this chapter are as much historiographical as they are historical. This means that, in what follows, I shall, of necessity, be concerned with (re)telling the different stories that have been told about the art of this period – as well as their critical relations to one another – rather than attempting (naively) to write from any notional position of neutrality or objectivity. But also, even though I start my chapter with reference to these established studies, I want to make it clear that I do not think it sufficient to satisfy ourselves with simply choosing one account over the other in our approach to fifties art. This is because, despite their very real differences, in some respects these narratives amount to simply two different versions of the *same* story: that of US abstraction. In contrast what follows will attempt to eschew such an exclusive focus by signposting other histories – of differing artistic and cultural practices both inside and outside the United States – which serve to displace the centrality of this narrative stream. For what is truly *my* story here is how in the fifties we witness the development and consolidation of a modernist "center" at precisely the same time that this gets undone in the various "alternative" practices to it and to American abstract expressionism.

This (de)centering of "American" art and its histories has to be understood not only in relation to cold war politics but also in relation to the massive social, legal, and cultural changes that were brought about in the west by the processes of European decolonization on the one hand, and the birth of the US-based black civil rights movement on the other. From the granting of independence to

India in 1947, European states faced large and effective independence movements across the colonized world, which led them gradually to loosen their hold on third world countries. The success of such movements emboldened the development of the US civil rights movement, which made significant advances over the politics of segregation throughout the fifties. This, alongside the large-scale immigration into Europe of people from former colonized countries, brought about huge challenges, and slow changes, to established western cultural forms and identities. And it wasn't just the international migration of non-white peoples that drove this process: the fifties also saw the initial development of the postwar politics of gender and sexuality. From the publication of Simone De Beauvoir's *The Second Sex* in English in 1953, to the birth in the early 1950s of lesbian and gay rights groups the Daughters of Bilitis and the Mattachine Society, a decade often renowned for its conservatism in matters of society and culture on closer inspection can be seen to have harbored some very radical and transformative energies indeed.

All of these energies, as we shall see, are played out within emergent forms of art practice at this time. In particular, I will be concerned to draw out how such world historical developments come to be productive of multiple new ways in which the very idea of "politics" comes to be understood and practiced in cultural terms. This may seem to be odd given that it is during these years that we come to witness the rise to power of an institutionally and critically sanctioned modernist view of art, in which any discussion of the political is seen to be deeply irrelevant to considerations of the aesthetic value of works of art. But it is the contention of this chapter that the emergence of the idea of an "a-political" art, is, in itself, deeply political – being only one form in which various economic, institutional, and political interests come to forge their ideological articulation at this time. It can be taken alongside other discourses and practices which variously attempt to reformulate the relations between "art" and "politics," and the precise ways in which these terms might be understood. I will consider, therefore, amongst other things, the "queer" silences of so-called Neo-Dada art, the participatory activism of Neoconcrete art and Happenings, as well as the ambivalent reflections on mass culture evident within emergent pop art, with a view to illuminating the various generative models of critical culture produced well before the artistic rebellions of the 1960s and 1970s.

Sometimes, for the agents of such alternative cultural activities, abstract expressionism seemed so culturally dominant, so all-pervasive, that, as the artist Robert Rauschenberg has recalled: "Jasper [Johns] and I used to start each day by having to move out from abstract expressionism."[2] For Rauschenberg and others in the 1950s, then so too for me as I write this chapter in the early years of the twentieth-first century. For in what follows I too shall endeavor to "move out" from abstract expressionism, both in the sense of taking it as my starting point, as well as in terms of going beyond it in my attention to other artistic and cultural practices. Insofar as I do this, my chapter will hopefully mime some of the strategic maneuvering of 1950s artistic practices. It will take abstract expressionism as starting point only in order that – as beginning – it might be deconstructively undermined and dispersed by the other, multifarious aesthetic and political possibilities provided within fifties culture.

Stories of A-Political Painting

It was during the 1950s that modernist discourse came to be established as the pre-eminent, and institutionally sanctioned, discourse of art in the western world. Spearheaded by US art critics Clement Greenberg and (in the 1960s) Michael Fried, and supported by the Museum of Modern Art in New York as well as journals like *Partisan Review*, modernist criticism exhibited a formalist approach to art which held the "integrity" of the individual mediums of painting and sculpture, above all, to be sacrosanct. This meant that painting, for example, should concern itself only with that taken to be "proper" to itself: its flatness and two-dimensionality. The most "advanced" art, wrote Clement Greenberg in 1955, was that which tested "the limits of the inherited forms and genres, and of the medium itself."[3] The work of Still, Newman, and Mark Rothko was taken to be most advanced by Greenberg at this time by dint of the "emphatic" flatness of their paintings, derived from the "all-overness" of their surface design. This was brought about by the relative lack of tonal variation across the canvas field and resulted in a comparatively undifferentiated, and expansive, whole.

This strict valorization of an art that stayed close to the "essence" of its medium came to be the dominant way of accounting for the value of "a-political" painting in the postwar years – *a*-political because its value as art was deemed to be purely aesthetic and autonomous from all other systems of worth. Such a modernist view was in many ways in stark contrast to art critic Harold Rosenberg's perspective on abstract expressionist art. For Rosenberg, writing in 1952, the value of abstract expressionist work accrued less to its formal character as painting, and rather more to its status as artistic *action*. Indeed, writing in an article significantly entitled "The American Action Painters," Rosenberg helped usher in a shift in conceptions about the ontology of the postwar artwork by approaching abstract expressionist works in terms of an *event*: "At a certain moment the canvas began to appear to one American painter after another as an arena in which to act. . . . What was to go on the canvas was not a picture but an event."[4] This not only inaugurated an understanding of the work of Pollock et al. which would be important for the subsequent development of Happenings and performance art in the late 1950s and early 1960s, but was also important in thinking through the *political* importance of such artistic actions: "The big moment came when it was decided to paint . . . just TO PAINT. The gesture on the canvas was a gesture of liberation, from Value – political, esthetic, moral" (30). Although this may seem of a piece with the formalist appreciation of the autonomous value of the modernist artwork above, especially in its characterization of action painting's distance from political and moral values, Rosenberg's reference to action painting's "gesture of liberation" clues us in to the ways in which he understands it as a fundamentally political kind of act – an *originary* and *revolutionary* one, freeing the artist from all conventional structures of meaning and value.[5]

This reading of action painting's revolutionary ethos has been subject to much criticism by art historical accounts produced within the past few decades informed by feminism and post-colonial theory. Both Amelia Jones (1998) and Rebecca Schneider (2004) have variously criticized the idea of action painting's singular "originary" gesture as a patriarchal trope designed to style the masculine subject as creative and generative of culture, whilst relegating its presumptive feminine Other to the realm of nature and the *pro*creative. This draws our attention to the ways in which representations and evaluations of the action painter's gesture were often coded with stultifyingly conventional gender meanings, making it difficult for women to take up the brush as abstract expressionist artists. Not only were the paintings of Pollock, for instance, as T. J. Clark has argued, "clearly implicated in a whole informing metaphorics of masculinity" ("the very concepts that seem to apply to them – space, scale, action, trace, energy . . . are all, among other things, operators of sexual difference"), but women artists were also limited by the expectation that they act as wives and mothers within the conventional frameworks of mainstream heterosexual culture.[6]

Various photographs from the period testify to the biases women faced, showing female artists like Lee Krasner and Elaine de Kooning as passive wives to their active and creative male husbands, as does the recent biopic *Pollock* (2000), directed by and starring Ed Harris in the leading role, with Marcia Gay Harden, literally and diegetically in a supporting role as "Pollock's wife" Krasner.[7] Female artists, in order to survive and be recognized *as artists* therefore, had to do all they could to suppress their identities as women. The art historian Anne Wagner discusses, for example, how Lee Krasner would invariably sign her work as "L.K." – or not sign her work at all – in a bid to escape her critical interpellation as a "woman artist" and all the stereotypical expectations that such a phrase brought in its wake (Wagner 1989).

It was a similar story too for black artists attempting to enter into the western mainstream of modernist abstraction. Ann Gibson, for example, has written of the prejudice faced by African-American abstract artists such as Norman Lewis and Beauford Delaney whose work, though visible at the time, was often viewed in stereotypical racial terms and seen to be of lesser value than that of their white male peers (Gibson 1997). This was equally true for black artists working in Europe. Aubrey Williams, born in Guyana but working in London from 1952 onwards, was – like other (white) artists in Britain including Patrick Heron – heavily impressed by a show of American abstract expressionist painting held at the Tate Gallery in London in 1956.[8] This was to have an effect on the development of the abstract style of Williams' painting during the 1950s, perhaps bringing it closer to the work of Arshile Gorky than to Jackson Pollock. However, as Rasheed Araeen argues, despite Williams' attempt to work in the manner of his American heroes, his paintings were repeatedly viewed in primitivizing terms by British critics. Araeen cites Jan Carew, writing in 1959 in the *Art News and Review*:

> These paintings . . . express in essence a sense of being which differs from that of the European in the same way that the music of a spinet differs from the rhythm of a drum. . . . His art reflects the instinctive sense of rhythm of the Negro fused with the mytho-poetic imagination of the Indian-Voodoo and the image of gods and man, the dreams born in cradles of a forest and brought to the city where twentieth-century man paces the pavements of destruction.[9]

Thus Williams' work is seen to be the product of some essential, unchanging ethnic culture, born of a place alien to the western "center" and remaining fundamentally distinct from it. We shall see later how such constructions of "the Negro" get played out in fifties Beat culture, but for now it will suffice to consider the colonialist ironies of modernist abstraction at this time. For, as the art historian David Craven has argued, while it was acceptable for white abstract expressionist artists to borrow freely from the forms of Native and Latin Ameri-

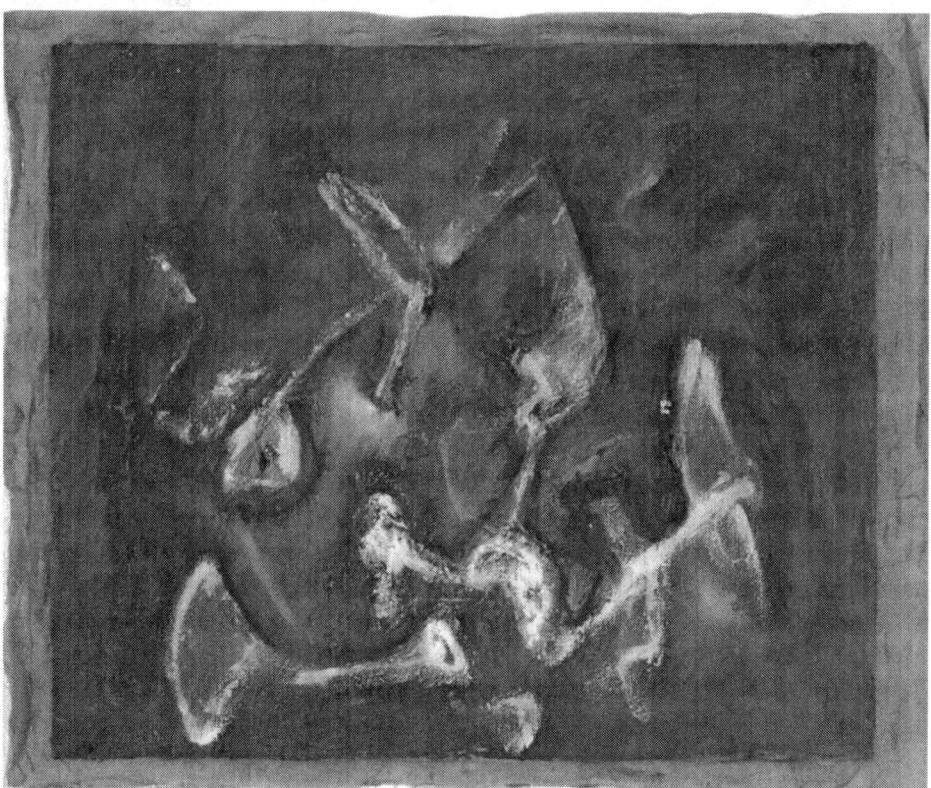

FIGURE 2.1 Aubrey Williams, *Bone Heap*, 1959. Courtesy of the Institute of International Visual Arts, London, © 2005. All rights reserved, DACS

can painting (Pollock's art, for instance, was indebted to the work of Navajo sand painters and Mexican muralists such as David Siqueiros), it was not deemed acceptable to the western art establishment for colonial subjects to traffic in the techniques of modernist art and hope to be treated with the same degree of seriousness and accorded the same value.[10] Which is to say that, whilst artistic practice in the western metropolis was undeniably transformed by the influx of artists from (increasingly former) colonies during the 1950s, artistic discourse was largely mired in US- and Eurocentric understandings, and was therefore largely unable to respond in a productive manner to the post-colonial challenges provided by the art of the day. This, alongside my comments about gender above, make of the discourses of 1950s abstract painting a curious amalgam of revolutionary and reactionary values and attitudes.

Not everyone in the fifties, however, wanted to get on the bandwagon of modernist abstract art. Many viewed the development of abstraction as the cultural arm of US imperialism and much debate took place in European circles, particularly on the Left, about its viability as artistic form. As Brendan Prendeville has written in a very useful account of realist art during this time (Prendeville 2000), in 1947 Soviet Socialist Realism was forcibly asserted as the official artistic credo for the USSR, paying great attention to the value of figurative – as opposed to abstract – art in representing the "realities" of life under communism. This view of an explicitly political art was also taken up by numerous left-wing artists outside the Eastern bloc countries, despite Stalin's show-trials and the Nazi–Soviet pact of the late 1930s, which had caused many Soviet sympathizers in the west to turn away from communism in general, and Stalinism in particular. Artists as varied as Renato Guttuso in Italy and André Fougeron in France practiced their own versions of social realism, whilst in Britain the critic John Berger took up the cause of art for society's sake by debating the merits of abstraction vs. figuration with the painter Patrick Heron in the pages of the *New Statesman*. Instead of the abstract expressionists, or indeed the abstract canvases of Heron himself, Berger championed the work of British artists like John Bratby instead, a so-called "kitchen sink" painter famed for his representations of everyday, mundane urban scenes. In addition to such Left critiques, abstraction also had its reactionary right-wing detractors, particularly in the US. Thomas Hart Benton, for example, a leading member of the American regionalist school of painting in 1930s, remained a vociferous critic of abstraction well into the early 1950s. For Benton, as for Berger and others, abstraction offered nothing but "an academic world of empty pattern" as opposed to an art that could claim to represent the everyday realities of people's lives.[11]

Silence and the Politics of Contingency

What I would like to turn to now, however, is the contemporary development of a set of artistic practices that eschewed the strict either/or of the aesthetic politics of the cold war. Rather than plump for the priorities of one camp or the other – of abstraction *or* figuration – a number of artists either worked across both simultaneously and/or weaved between the two, appearing seemingly unconcerned for the vested interests that held them as opposing alternatives to one another. I am thinking here, principally, of the work of the so-called Neo-Dada artists, Jasper Johns and Robert Rauschenberg – "Neo-Dada" because of their use of "found" imagery in the manner of a Duchampian practice of the ready-made. Johns and Rauschenberg worked with images and icons culled from everyday visual culture – such as flags, newspaper clippings, and photographs – and combined them in various technical ways with the gestural styles of postwar abstraction. But this way of working comprised much more than mere stylistic hybrid, and can be seen as promoting a very different kind of aesthetic politics, avoiding the either/or opposition of aesthetic autonomy versus a socially committed, representational art.

Johns and Rauschenberg drew much of their inspiration from the composer John Cage. Cage eschewed the ethos of self-expression that was so important to abstract expressionism. In responding to Willem de Kooning's avowed desire to be a great artist, Cage comments that "it was this aspect of wanting to be an artist . . . who had something to say, who wanted through his work to appear really great . . . which I could not accept."[12] This idea of not being an artist "with something to say," indeed of being one with *nothing* to say, was starkly set out in Cage's "Lecture on Nothing" which he delivered to members of the abstract expressionist circle in 1949. During this lecture he famously proclaimed the statement which might stand as a totem of Cage's aesthetics of silence: "I have nothing to say, and I am saying it." This was to announce succinctly Cage's investment in a non-expressive musical practice, one that was not about the communication of ideas or the expression of the composer's feelings, but rather an exploration of the "silence" left by the stripping away of authorial presence. This was borne out by his most famous composition, *4'33"*, first performed in 1952, which comprises four minutes and thirty three seconds without any conventional musical composition as such – a piece "composed" of silence. However this was no "simple" silence but rather one which worked to foreground other kinds of ambient *noise* in the auditorium. As Caroline Jones writes, "[t]he only body acoustically present in *4'33"* is the body of sound; the withdrawal of the performer's body from action paradoxically authorises our recognition of ambient noise."[13]

Cage himself has acknowledged that such a recognition of ambient sound was in part derived from first seeing Rauschenberg's *White Paintings* in 1952. In looking at these white canvases vacated of all expressive marks, Cage was impressed by the degree to which they were nevertheless animated by the changes of light and shadow that played across their surfaces and described them as "airports for lights, shadows and particles," leading him to suggest further that, while white, they weren't *without* color at all, but were continually dappled by differing hues and shades brought about by the chance passage of the painting's spectator(s).[14] And this goes right to the heart of the Cagean interest in silence

– and to Rauschenberg's attempt at painting "nothing": namely, that once one composes "silence" or paints "nothing" one ends up producing *something* in its stead: whether it be the ambient noise from the street or the auditorium, or the shapes and forms of cast and reflected light. The negation of an expressive act, then, the erasure of a subjective presence, brings about the creation of something else, something *new*. As Cage himself has said, "no silence / exists / that is not / pregnant / with / sound."[15]

But how might the politics of such an aesthetics of "silence" be construed? Some recent queer art historians have argued for the significance of sexuality in taking into account such artistic developments. Jonathan Katz, for example, has argued that Cage moved away from making expressive music in order to free himself from the artistic imperative of placing his homosexual self at the center of his art, which would otherwise have made him visible and vulnerable as a gay man – especially within the homophobic contexts of McCarthyite America and the macho circles of 1950s bohemian culture. Cage's composed pieces of silence could therefore be understood as self-imposed forms of "closeting" behavior, albeit rather complex ones which drew upon Cage's interest in Zen Buddhism. Zen had taught the composer that transcending individual feeling and emotion was a more desirable way of dealing with "personal" issues than with talking endlessly about them through the confessional or the psychoanalytical talking cure. This Zen-like approach to homosexuality, directed into an art of detachment, makes Cage's silences pregnant with queer meaning – a queerness made present, paradoxically, through the performance of its very absence.

Similarly perhaps for the painter Agnes Martin, who, though not strictly speaking part of the Cagean circle at this time, can be seen to perform a comparable closeting maneuver in her paintings of the late fifties. Martin also took silence to be an important part of her aesthetic enterprise. As were many artists at this time, she too was interested in Asian thought – including Taoism as well as Zen Buddhism – in "experience that is wordless and silent" and in expressing this experience "in art work which is also wordless and silent."[16] Such an interest set her apart from artists who were interested in making themselves the autobiographical subject of their art and instead led her to make an art of apparent self-negation. Her canvases are made up, one might almost say, of "nothing," save for a delicately pencil-lined grid formation which is more or less visible depending upon the spectator's proximity to, or distance from, the painting's surface. These have been readily understood as forms of self-erasure: "So suppressed or subtle were the traces of Martin's hand that there was a sense almost, as one critic put it, that "the painter has disappeared."[17] In contrast, then, to the "presence" of the artist's body announced by the gestural marks on an abstract expressionist canvas, Martin's paintings can be seen instead to register the withdrawal of her (lesbian) body from the field of meanings that one might ascribe to her work.

But is it enough to say that such forms of "silencing" – whether in music or in painting – resulted in a simple *negation* of their gay or lesbian creators? For the art historian Kenneth Silver, the answer to this question is "no." For even though Johns and Rauschenberg have been generally loath to speak of their relationship, which lasted from the mid-fifties until the early 1960s, historians such as Silver have been concerned to elaborate upon how their art can be viewed alongside the development of the 1950s gay rights movement in beginning to "speak" of gay love in more positive terms than silence and nothingness. Silver, for example, reads Johns' 1955 painting *Target with Plaster Casts* – made up of human body casts and a painted target – in order to understand it as a latter-day version of that homoerotic staple of western painting: the martyrdom of Saint Sebastian. In reading the painting thus, Silver purports to unveil *Target*'s gay significance – to "out" it – by drawing our attention to its buried homoerotic iconography (the male body as target of hostile fire). He thus claims, grandly, that Johns' painting can be understood as the "first portrait of the homosexual man of the postwar period."[18] In Silver's hands Johns' work appears to be less about a queer silence or invisibility – a queerness that can't quite be represented – but one which is available to be *read* once one knows how to crack the codes.

For yet other historians, however, like Branden Joseph, a reading like Silver's misses the point of Johns', and particularly of Rauschenberg's, art: that, if anything, their work attacks the very idea of art *as representation* – of sexual identity or anything else. In various ways, Joseph argues that the work of Rauschenberg resists the very logic of representation itself: the way in which the world is made to appear as an object of knowledge to be apprehended by a classically distanced observer. The point, as far as Joseph is concerned, is therefore *not* to read Rauschenberg's painting from this vantage point – to try to comprehend, for example, what meanings may lie encoded within the various scraps of iconography of one of his *Combine* paintings – but rather to engage in a mode of looking that keeps the eye mobile and active whilst keeping the determination of any "final" meaning in play. This is to highlight the importance of Neo-Dada art in creating the conditions for the emergence of a performative, *activated* form of spectatorship in postwar art. For, as the body of the spectator of Rauschenberg's *White Paintings* moves before such supposedly "blank" canvases it becomes the body of a *participant-observer* – occasioning chance passages of light and shade across their surfaces, and serving, in the process, to recreate the works anew in, and as, the moment of spectatorial engagement.

Experience and Participation: From Angst to Happenings

This activated spectatorship finds echoes in other forms of art and culture in the 1950s: from the reliance on existentialism and the interest in engaging the urban environment in European art, to the participatory ethos of Neoconcrete art and early Happenings in the Americas. Existentialism, as a philosophical outlook, influenced many different kinds of art practice throughout the period covered by this chapter, as did the important phenomenological work of Maurice Merleau-Ponty. Jean-Paul Sartre's existentialist novel *Nausea*, originally published in French in 1938, was translated into English in 1949, making its tenets available to a wider English-speaking world, and Merleau-Ponty's *Phenomenology of Perception* was published in 1945. Both books contributed to an artistic culture that valorized the profundities and transformative possibilities of perception, of being able to apprehend the world differently, perhaps even more intensively, by means of individual sensory and kinetic experience. Such a valorization should be understood as often interweaving with a latter-day postwar surrealism, whose energies were directed toward a defamiliarization of conventional perceptions of everyday life.

All of these intellectual tendencies derived their critical force in the context of a postwar consumer society in which the potentialities of individual perception were being increasingly reduced to the simple recognition of one's identity in terms of the social role prescribed by what social theorists Theodor Adorno and Max Horkheimer had termed the "culture industry" – whether as national citizen, executive, housewife, etc. (Adorno and Horkheimer 1997). Such instrumentalized representations as those found in postwar advertising were subject to an early critique in *The Mechanical Bride* (1951) by Marshall McLuhan, who was to become world famous for his analysis of media culture in the 1960s.

Set against what some would see as the "false consciousness" of capitalist society, artists such as Alberto Giacometti in France and Francis Bacon in Britain set about making works that sought to visualize the perceptions of existential Being. In Giacometti's studies of lone human figures, the image is wrought either through a multiplicity of drawn and painted lines, as if "hard-won," or through fragile, elongated sculptural bodies which seem to carry the sheer metaphysical weight of existential "nothingness" on their shoulders. Francis Bacon's figural paintings, on the other hand, such as *Study for Crouching Nude* (1952), appear in semi-clinical, almost mythically "modern" surroundings. They evoke individual angst in the face of the terrors – the Holocaust, Hiroshima – perpetrated in the name of rationalist modern society. His horribly mutilated figures scream, but silently; their terror lies in the fact that they are not heard. But above all, they strike the spectator in all their fleshy materiality, evoked by the power and texture of Bacon's painterly handling (the intention was, as Bacon was to relate some years later, to get his paintings to "come across directly onto the nervous system").[19]

This attempt to utilize the power of painting and sculpture to produce alternative perceptions of the modern world is underlined in a slightly different way by the so-called *décollagistes* in France and Mimmo Rotella in Italy. In the late 1950s, artists such as Rotella, and *décollagistes* such as François Dufrêne, worked with the physical site of the advertising billboard, ripping away the glossy images and surfaces of the capitalist commodity, to reveal a hidden archaeology of formlessness. Such work formed part of a wider range of artistic practices across

Europe that, working through the heritage of pre-war Marxist-informed surrealism, began to produce work that critically intervened in what Guy Debord would call, in his 1967 book, "the society of the spectacle."

The Situationist International, of which Debord became the leading intellectual figure, was formally established in 1957, though had its artistic roots partly in a Northern European artistic group called Cobra. This was named after the cities from whence its members hailed (COpenhagen–BRussels–Amsterdam), and had amongst its legion the Danish painter Asger Jorn. Jorn, and others like Karel Appel, were experimenting with surrealist automatism throughout the period but, by 1959, Jorn turned to producing paintings out of "modified" thrift store pictures. It is in such works that we begin to glimpse the beginnings of what would later be recognized as Situationist aesthetics. By crudely painting imagery onto such "found," and degraded paintings, Jorn signaled the potential for the creative revivification of capitalist detritus through what the Situationist International would later call "détournement": the critical and creative re-use of preexisting visual elements. This reanimating of capitalist culture owed less intellectually to Sartre and Merleau-Ponty and rather more to the Marxist writings of Henri Lefebvre, whose book *Critique de la Vie Quotidienne (Critique of Everyday Life)* was published in 1947. The symbolic violence of Jorn's creative interventions was echoed by others, such as Arman and Niki de Saint Phalle, who in France and the US in the late fifties and early 1960s produced works that entailed latter-day Dada-esque acts of destructive creation.

Whereas much European art valorized existentialist experience or a Marxist–Surrealist intervention in everyday life, some Latin American art was moving toward a considered exploration of the phenomenological engagement of artist and artwork. The Neoconcrete group based in Rio de Janeiro in the late 1950s, for example, worked with constructivist form and included the artists Hélio Oiticica and Lygia Clark amongst others. Works such as Oiticica's *Spatial Reliefs*, which hung low from the ceiling, and Clark's painted wooden reliefs, which were attached vertically to the gallery wall, took abstract form and attempted to instantiate it as present in an active interrelationship with the viewer.

As Anna Dezeuze has written, Oiticica's art in particular "sought to transform the spectator into a 'discoverer [*descobridor*] of the work' by setting up an intimate relation between [it] and the viewer," commenting upon how his reliefs were hung in such a way as to allow the spectator to move around them and peer into them from various different angles.[20] This engagement of work and spectator in interactive, dynamic relation in time and space was a key feature of the "experiential" nature of Neoconcrete work, and presaged the move toward minimalism in US art in the 1960s. The embodied conditions of spectatorship called for by such works also, as Dezeuze notes, signaled the shift toward installation and performance that would take place in both Oiticica's and Clark's work in the 1960s.

This emphasis upon the importance of an embodied experience was also variously important in US art and culture at this time. In so-called "Beat" culture, the first sub-cultural movement of the postwar world, there was a revalorization of the condition of being exhausted, sleepless, and emptied out – as in "I'm too beat." For this also suggested being wide-eyed, open, and receptive to new experiences – especially those beyond the parameters of mainstream American culture. Indeed it wasn't just experience per se that was celebrated within Beat culture, but those particular experiences undergone by bodies rejected by respectable society – in particular black bodies. Another usage of the term "beat" refers to being without money and a place to stay, and to a life lived on one's wits on the streets. Beat culture saw this life as that of the black man, subject as he was in fifties culture to poverty and racism, and it was taken to be exemplary of a more "authentic" and "vital" existence – one lived on the margins of respectable white culture. As Norman Mailer wrote at the time, many white beatniks thereby came to view themselves as "white negroes," drifting out "at night looking for action with a black man's code to fit their facts."[21] Beat is largely known as a literary movement and associated with the writers and poets Allen Ginsberg, Jack Kerouac, and William Burroughs, though it was also a much wider cultural attitude adopted by "beatnik" artists such as Larry Rivers and others.

Beat's stereotypical, primitivized image of the black man's experiences demonstrates the cultural importance ascribed to non-normative experiences within avant-garde and sub-cultural circles in the US at this time. It formed part of a culture seeking for direct, "authentic" experience of the world as opposed to the purportedly illusory and mediated experiences served up to the masses by consumer culture. Such a quest was given artistic form in the late fifties in the shape of the first "Happenings" which took place in New York. Allan Kaprow produced his now legendary *18 Happenings in 6 Parts* at the Reuben Gallery in 1959, in 1960 Jim Dine staged his *Car Crash*, and Claes Oldenburg's *The Store* took place in 1961.

Happenings were not like conventional theatrical productions but were more akin to spontaneous and unruly "events," often blurring the boundaries between art and life and incorporating spectators as participants. The point was to stage "authentic" actions that would activate spectators as participants, and empower them to open their eyes to, and see afresh, the world around them. As Kaprow put it in 1958, "[n]ot only will these bold creators [of the new art] show us, as if for the first time, the world we have always had about us but ignored, but they will also disclose entirely unheard-of Happenings and events, found in garbage cans, polices files, hotel lobbies; seen in store windows and on the streets; and sensed in dreams and horrible accidents."[22] From this we can derive the general politics of the "experiential" and "participatory" arts of the fifties, one based upon enlivening the perceptions of the spectator to the everyday realities of capitalist society – of detritus, of crime, of the hidden political maneuverings of power – as well as to the repressed contents of the unconscious mind. In many ways this is an anticipation of the liberatory politics of sixties culture which was to put great store by a Marxist–Freudian unmasking of "one-dimensional" society, and an uninhibited emancipation of human drives and desire.

Pop's Ambivalences

The 1950s were the years in which the "mass-media" of postwar consumer society came to be firmly established and widely distributed: mass circulation magazines, such as *Life* and *Time*, enhanced the reach of corporate advertising, whilst the spread of television ownership and the consolidation of Hollywood cinema's global reach meant that lens-based technologies came to have a hugely transformative effect upon the visual environment of western culture. This change has been seen by some as indicative of a gradual economic shift in the west from societies organized around industrial production to those structured more expressly around the rituals of consumption which, in turn, has been seen to herald a move from "modern" to "postmodern" culture. Such transformations of the economic, social, and cultural fields have also been told as the story of an increasing "Americanization" of the postwar world, as the "vulgar" forces of corporate culture come to encroach upon the older, established traditions of European "civilized" culture. Thus it marks the era in which "the great divide" (as Andreas Huyssen (1988) has put it) between "high" and "low" cultures – between the fine arts of painting and sculpture, for instance, and the forms of mass culture – came to be an important issue for artists to deal with.

For many artists working at this time, as we have seen, mass culture was to be either ignored as trivial or critiqued as the false consciousness of capitalist society. For members of the London-based Independent Group in the 1950s, it was not the artist's job simply to dismiss or criticize it; the point, rather, was to see the relations between fine art and mass culture less in hierarchical and judgmental terms (the former being above, and superior to, the latter), and more in terms of a horizontal continuum of equal values. As Richard Hamilton, one of the leading members of the group, noted: "Instead of Picasso sitting on top of an ever-widening heap of inferior activity, with Elvis Presley and Henry Hathaway somewhere below him . . . Elvis was to one side of a long line while Picasso was strung out on the other side." For the budding pop artist the strategy was then "to pull things out from one point along the continuum and drop them at another, then stir well – the fine/pop soup alternative" (Hamilton's own description here taking the parodic form of a "recipe" for art production).[23]

This "mixture" was evident in an Independent Group exhibition held at the Whitechapel Gallery in London in 1956 entitled This is Tomorrow. In many ways, the title echoes the futural programs and manifestoes of the avant-garde at the same time as riffing on the rhetoric of postwar reconstruction evident in national exhibitions such as the Festival of Britain, held in London in 1951. The exhibition brought together artists, photographers, interior designers, architects, and critics and reflected the interdisciplinary nature of the Independent Group's

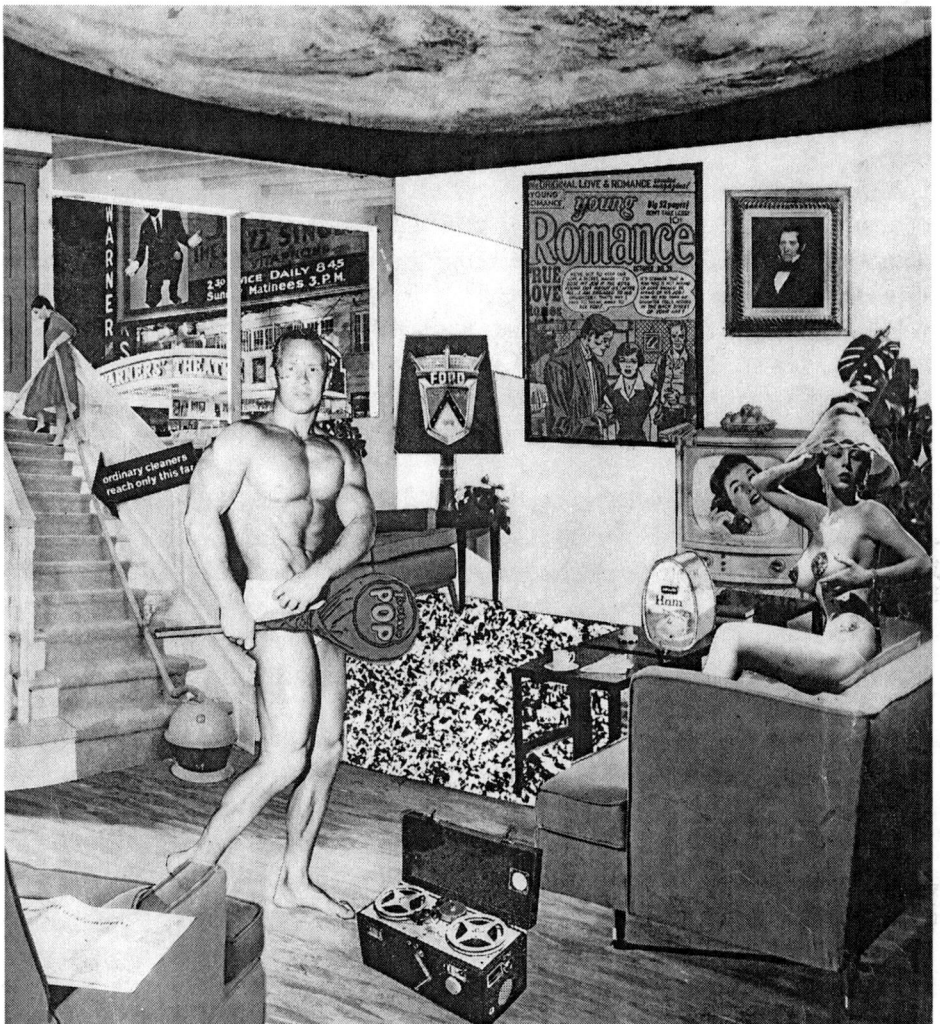

FIGURE 2.2   Richard Hamilton, *Just what is it that makes today's homes so different, so appealing?* 1957. Courtesy of Kunsthalle Tübingen. © Richard Hamilton 2005. All rights reserved, DACS

work. It attempted to reflect the rich heterogeneity of postwar culture, incorporating high art imagery as mass object (a print of Van Gogh's *Sunflowers*); cinematic imagery (a billboard style painting of Marilyn Monroe alongside Robbie the Robot from *Forbidden Planet*); pop music; photography; and modernist architectural spaces.

One of Hamilton's contributions was a small 1956 photo-collage entitled *Just what is it that makes today's homes so different, so appealing?*, which, like Eduardo Paolozzi's work around this time, was made up of imagery culled from the mass media. It represented a paradigmatic modern postwar domestic interior, complete with modernist furniture, various appliances (vacuum cleaner, reel-to-reel tape player), mass information and entertainment (television, newspaper), convenience foods, and a parody of an idealized, presumptively heterosexual, pair of inhabitants – one culled from a "beefcake," the other a "cheesecake," magazine.

But the question raised by such works is this: if not a categorical criticism of mass culture, then what? Does it celebrate – as opposed to criticize – the commodification of postwar living? Another work by Hamilton from 1958 seems to pose this question directly by means of its title: *Hommage à Chrysler Corp.* Based on various magazine advertisements for cars, the painting consists, as Hamilton himself has written, of a veritable "anthology of presentation techniques." "One passage," he goes on, "runs from a prim emulation of in-focus photographed gloss to out-of-focus gloss to an artist's representation of chrome to ad-man's sign meaning chrome."[24]

Hamilton's almost analytical approach to the semiotics of advertising extends to the sexualization of the image too. He utilizes a few iconic features (lipsticked lips, curvaceous and bra-enhanced breasts) to signal the sexually-available woman attendant within the *mise-en-scène* of most automobile advertising of the time – "available" that is, at least at the level of fantasy, to the presumptively heterosexual male buyer of a Chrysler car. Here Hamilton can be seen to lay bare the codes by which advertising interpellates (Althusser 1977) its prospective buyers, and the values implicit within its modes of address – not least those of gender, which Hamilton would explore further in later paintings such as *Hers is a Lush Situation*, *$he*, and *AAH!*

But this analysis focuses on only one aspect of Hamilton's artistic practice, turning him into a "critical" artist concerned to expose the workings of commodity culture. For Sarat Maharaj, the point is rather to comprehend the ways in which Hamilton's work, and pop art in general, challenges our binary expectations of critical/celebratory attitudes. For pop engenders a relation to both mass culture and high culture which keeps their differences in play without making a value judgment of the one over the other. Drawing upon the philosopher Jacques Derrida, Maharaj argues instead that works such as *Hommage à Chrysler Corp* might better be understood as "undecidable" hommages – ones which stage a paradoxical dilemma for the viewer by appearing *neither* to celebrate *nor* to critique their subjects whilst, still yet, appearing to do *both* at the same time. For though Hamilton's work can be seen to engage in some form of "critical" address to mass cultural products as we have seen above, it also, simultaneously, embraces those characteristics seen by many as proof of its worthlessness. Hamilton lists these features (approvingly?) as follows: "popular, transient, expendable, low cost, mass produced, young, witty, sexy, gimmicky, glamorous, big business."[25]

As we alight upon Hamilton's words here, particularly upon "big business," we find ourselves quickly returned to where I began this chapter: with the cultural influence of corporate America. This was an influence, as I said at the beginning, which was felt in many different ways and in many different corners of the world: from the corporate underpinning of the international promotion of abstract expressionism to the development of mass culture and pop art. It was also an influence that artists worked hard to escape, to undermine, or to work with playfully. Some of the artistic forms and strategies adopted to achieve this have formed the subject of this chapter.

But by returning to the force of US capitalism as I close this chapter I hope to exemplify not only how, in the late 1940s and throughout the 1950s, it was a force to be reckoned with by artists but also how, as we write histories of art from the vantage point of the present, we are brought to reckon with its heritage today. If I began with what I was suggesting was a false choice between either celebratory or critical narratives of US art, then – if pop tells us anything – it might suggest the importance of writing complex histories which catch the *multifarious* ways in which the economic, technological, and cultural power of the US informed the developing art of this time.

Notes

1   In addition to Guilbaut's book, see essays by Max Kozloff, Eva Cockcroft, David and Cecile Shapiro, and Fred Orton and Griselda Pollock, in Frascina (1985).
2   Cited by Katz (1993), 197.
3   Greenberg (1955), 196.
4   Rosenberg (1959), 25.
5   For more on the relations between action and revolution in Rosenberg's reading see Orton (1996).
6   Clark (1990), 229.
7   For a useful analysis of such "artist and wife" photographs see Jones, C. A. (1996), 36–41.
8   For more on Williams' art see Brett (1999).
9   Cited in Araeen (1989), 32.
10 For more on this see Craven (1991).
11 Benton (1951), 9.
12 Cited in Sandler (1970), 164.
13 Jones, C. A. (1993), 650.
14 Cited in Sandler (1970), 174.
15 Cited in Jones (1993), 646.
16 Martin (1992), 89.
17 Chave (1992), 139.
18 Silver (1993), 190.
19 Sylvester (1975), 18.
20 Dezeuze (2004), 62.
21 Mailer (1961), 273.
22 Kaprow (1993), 9.
23 Hamilton (1982), 31.

24 Ibid.
25 Ibid., 28.

References and further reading

Adorno, Theodor W., and Max Horkheimer (1997). *Dialectic of Enlightenment.* London: Verso.

Althusser, Louis (1977). "Ideology and Ideological State Apparatuses (Notes Towards an Investigation)." In *"Lenin and Philosophy" and Other Essays.* London: New Left Books.

Araeen, Rasheed (1989). *The Other Story: Afro-Asian Artists in Post-war Britain.* London: Hayward Gallery.

Benton, Thomas H. (1951). "What's Holding Back American Art?" *Saturday Review of Literature*, December 15:9–11, 38.

Brett, Guy (1999). "A Tragic Excitement: The Work of Aubrey Williams." *Third Text*, no. 48:29–44.

Chave, Anna C. (1992). "Agnes Martin: 'Humility, the beautiful daughter . . . All of her ways are empty'." In *Agnes Martin*, ed. Barbara Haskell. New York: Whitney Museum of American Art.

Clark, T. J. (1990). "Jackson Pollock's Abstraction." In *Reconstructing Modernism: Art in New York, Paris, and Montreal 1945–1964*, ed. Serge Guilbaut. Cambridge and London: MIT Press. 172–238.

Craven, David (1991). "Abstract Expressionism and Third World Art: A Post-Colonial Approach to 'American' Art." *Oxford Art Journal*, vol. 14, no. 1:1–32.

Dezeuze, Anna (2004). "Tactile Dematerialisation, Sensory Politics: Hélio Oiticica's Parangolés." *Art Journal*, vol. 63, no. 2:59–71.

Frascina, Francis, ed. (1985). *Pollock and After: The Critical Debate.* London: Harper and Row.

Gibson, Ann E. (1997). *Abstract Expressionism: Other Politics.* New Haven and London: Yale University Press.

Greenberg, Clement (1955). "'American-Type' Painting." *Partisan Review*, vol. XXII, no. 2:179–96.

Guilbaut, Serge (1983). *How New York Stole the Idea of Modern Art: Abstract Expressionism, Freedom, and the Cold War.* Chicago and London: University of Chicago Press.

Hamilton, Richard (1982). *Collected Words.* London and New York: Thames and Hudson.

Huyssen, Andreas (1988). *After the Great Divide: Modernism, Mass Culture, Postmodernism.* Basingstoke: Macmillan.

Jones, Amelia (1998). *Body Art: Performing the Subject.* Minneapolis and London: University of Minnesota Press.

Jones, Caroline A. (1993). "Finishing School: John Cage and the Abstract Expressionist Ego." *Critical Inquiry*, vol. 19, Summer:628–65.

—— (1996). *Machine in the Studio: Constructing the Postwar American Artist.* Chicago and London: University of Chicago Press.

Joseph, Branden W. (2003). *Random Order: Robert Rauschenberg and the Neo-Avant-Garde.* Cambridge, MA and London: MIT Press.

Kaprow, Allen (1993). *Essays on the Blurring of Art and Life.* Los Angeles and London: University of California Press.

Katz, Jonathan (1993). "The Art of Code: Jasper Johns and Robert Rauschenberg." In *Significant Others: Creativity and Intimate Partnership*, ed. Whitney Chadwick and Isabelle de Courtivron. London: Thames and Hudson. 188–207.

Maharaj, Sarat (1992). "Pop Art's Pharmacies: Kitsch, Consumerist Objects and Signs, the 'Unmentionable'." *Art History*, vol. 15, 3:334–50.

Mailer, Norman (1961). "The White Negro: Superficial Reflections on the Hipster." In *Advertisements for Myself*. London: Panther. 269–89.

Martin, Agnes (1992). *Writings*. Winterthur: Kunstmuseum Winterthur.

Orton, Fred (1996). "Action, Revolution and Painting." In *Avant-Gardes and Partisans Reviewed*, Fred Orton and Griselda Pollock. Manchester and New York: Manchester University Press. 177–203.

Prendeville, Brendan (2000). *Realism in 20th Century Painting*. London and New York: Thames and Hudson.

Rosenberg, Harold (1959). "The American Action Painters." In *The Tradition of the New*. New York: Horizon Press. 23–39.

Sandler, Irving (1970). *The Triumph of American Painting: A History of Abstract Expressionism*. New York and London: Harper and Row.

Schneider, Rebecca (2004). "Solo Solo Solo." In *After Criticism: New Responses to Art and Performance*, ed. Gavin Butt. Oxford: Blackwell. 23–47.

Silver, Kenneth E. (1993). "Modes of Disclosure: The Construction of Gay Identity and the Rise of Pop Art." In *Hand-Painted Pop: American Art in Transition, 1955–1962*, ed. Russell Ferguson. Los Angeles: Museum of Contemporary Art. 179–203.

Sylvester, David (1975). *Interviews with Francis Bacon 1962–1979*. London: Thames and Hudson.

Wagner, Anne M. (1989). "Lee Krasner as L.K." *Representations*, no. 25:42–57.

3

The 1960s: A Decade Out-of-Bounds

Anna Dezeuze

The development of art in the 1960s has often been described as a systematic dismantling of modernist media such as sculpture and painting and the explosion of hybrid forms of art drawing on, and often combining, photographs, texts, performances, industrial and natural materials, and everyday objects. For example, Jean Tinguely's 1960 *Homage to New York* (Figure 3.1) is a motorized sculpture made out of junk programmed for self-destruction, while Yayoi Kusama's 1965 *Infinity Mirror Room – Phalli's Field* (Figure 3.2) is an "environment," a form that originated with the expansion of painting into a three-dimensional space the viewer can enter (in this case, viewers access the environment by peeping through holes and their heads are reflected on its mirrored walls). In *Situation T/T* (Figure 3.3), Artur Barrio scattered his *Bloody Bundles*, made up of soiled pieces of cloth, toilet paper, bandages, and newspapers, in the streets of Rio de Janeiro in 1970; snapshots of the bundles lying in various locations document this action.

Descriptions of these new types of works and the various artistic movements that emerged and developed during this period – from Happenings to performance art, from kinetic art and *nouveau réalisme* to conceptual art, from minimalism to process art – cannot, however, solely account for the significance of 1960s art. For specific practices raise other kinds of questions. What myths were being literally exploded by Tinguely's useless machines? In what ways was it radical to involve the viewer's body in the perception of an environment as Kusama did? What did it mean to scatter bloody bundles in Brazil in 1970? By sketching out answers to some of these questions, I hope to demonstrate in this chapter how the radical questioning of the art work's status in 1960s artistic practices was indissociable from the social and political concerns of the time.

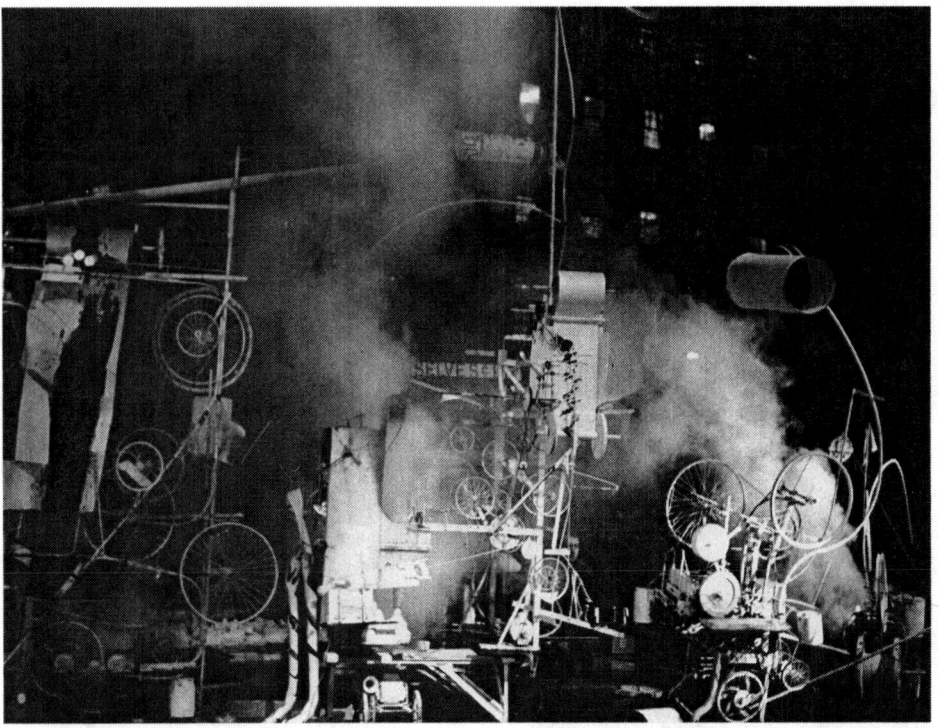

FIGURE 3.1   Jean Tinguely, *Homage to New York*, 1960. Photograph: David Gahr.
Courtesy of the Tinguely Museum, Basel. © ADAGP, Paris and DACS, London 2005

Rather than starting with Clement Greenberg's formalist theories of modern art, which continued to be influential in the North American art world during the 1960s – even as something to explicitly reject, in many cases – my reading of the 1960s starts from Umberto Eco's discussion of "the open work," developed in an eponymous book first published in Italian in 1962. Reflective rather than prescriptive, Eco's book maps out a common desire amongst contemporary artists to explore the ambiguity of meaning and the plurality of interpretations of the art work by introducing disorder, chance, mobility, and indeterminacy within its structure. Expanding on Eco's account, I will suggest that many artists in the 1960s sought to "open" the art work – not only to chance and disorder, but also to everyday objects, and to language (part I), to the body (part II), and to its social and political context (part III). Rather than giving a chronological account of the period, I will examine the motivations and implications of these "openings" in relation to specific contextual issues: consumption, labor, and technology in late capitalism (I), the 1960s "sexual revolution" and counterculture (II), and the decade's massive political upheaval, which culminated in student revolts and widespread demonstrations in the late 1960s and early 1970s (III).

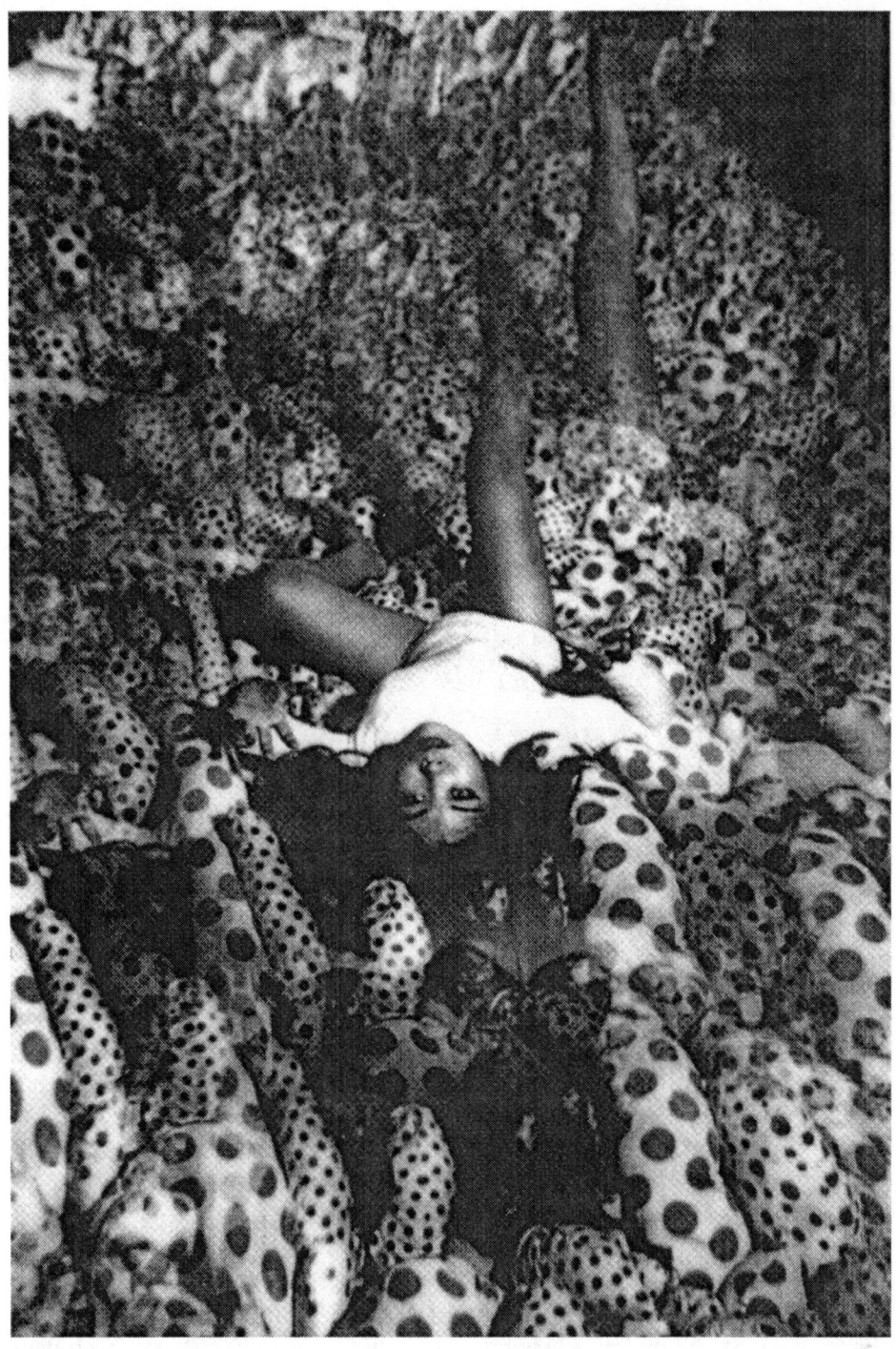

FIGURE 3.2 Yayoi Kusama posing in her *Infinity Mirror Room – Phalli's Field*, 1965.
© Yayoi Kusama

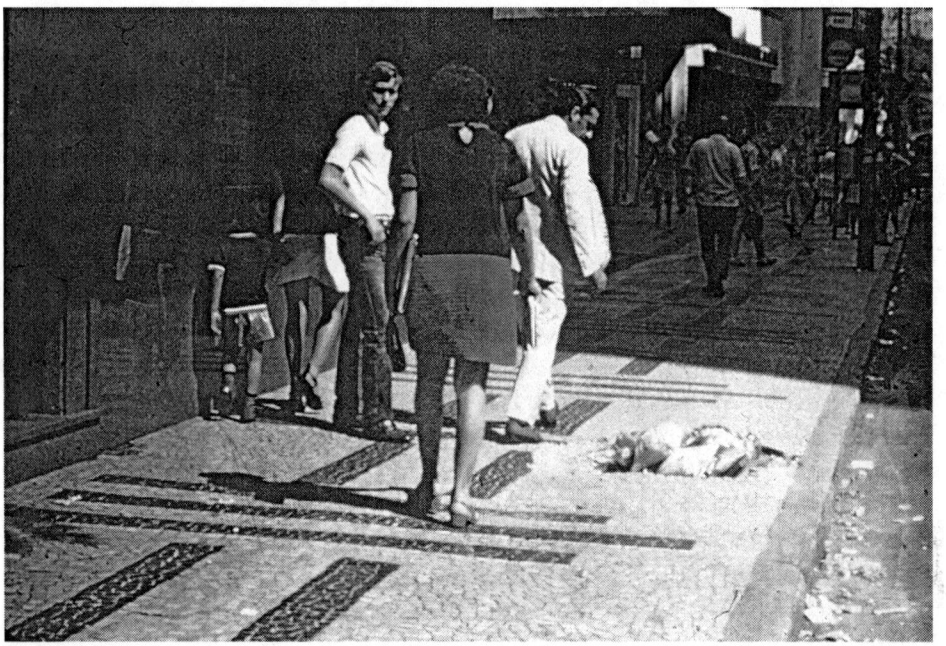

FIGURE 3.3   Artur Barrio, *Defl . . . – Situação . . . + s + . . . Ruas . . . Abril . . . 1970,*
1970. Photograph: César Carneiro. © Artur Barrio

I   Objects

Matter, immateriality, movement
Through colour I feel a total identification with space; I am truly free!
Yves Klein[1]

[T]he artist has achieved total freedom: pure matter is transformed into pure
energy.

Piero Manzoni[2]

For the French artist Yves Klein and the Italian Piero Manzoni, both working
in the late 1950s and early 1960s, freedom was to be found in the exploration
of space, matter, and energy. Inspired by the sky of his native Riviera, Klein
captured this feeling of space by uniformly applying an intense blue pigment
on small rectangular canvases. Manzoni responded to Klein's *Blue Monochromes*
by creating his *Achromes*, or "colorless" paintings, which consist only of white
materials – from the creases of the canvas itself, dipped in white china clay, to
fake white fur and painted bread-rolls. While Klein's smooth and sensual monochromes invite viewers to plunge metaphorically into the infinite spaces of the

sky and the sea, the *Achromes*' dynamic "energy" lies in the tension between the static rectangle of the painting and the organic, sagging, yellowing, decaying materials with which it is filled.

The most immediate inspiration for Manzoni, Klein, and many other artists at the time interested in notions of space, energy, and matter, was no doubt the race which was taking place between the US and the USSR to colonize outer space. Four years after the first satellite was launched by the USSR in 1957, both countries were able to send their first astronauts into space. For a few seconds in 1960, Takis, a Greek Paris-based artist who had introduced magnets in his paintings and sculptures from 1958, partook in this conquest of space by launching his friend, the poet Sinclair Beiles, into the air (a huge magnet was attached to his belt). The space race also encouraged popular interest in nuclear and quantum physics. What struck many artists above all was the idea that matter was always in movement. This led to a general desire to introduce movement in art, and the development of two of the 1960s' most successful international artistic trends: op and kinetic art. Op art suggested movement virtually by using optical devices such as retinal aftereffects to destabilize the viewer's perception of lines, shapes and colors. Kinetic art often used electric lights and motors to create robot-like machines. Kinetic artists such as the German Hans Haacke and the London-based Filipino David Medalla combined in their work electric current and natural forces such as wind and water. For artists such as the Brazilian Lygia Clark, movement was provided by the spectator's gestures: in her *Bichos*, or *Beasts*, started in 1960, viewers are invited to arrange the hinged, geometrical planes of three-dimensional metal sculptures.

Movement in space and time became crucial concerns for a range of artists working in a variety of media and styles. In 1957, the American artists Allan Kaprow, Robert Watts, and George Brecht planned a collective project drawing on scientific concepts and new technologies in order to better embrace the ideas of change, spontaneity, and randomness in everyday life.[3] All three used junk materials and everyday objects, and their experiments with chance were encouraged by composer John Cage, whose classes at the New School for Social Research in New York City were attended by Brecht and Kaprow. While Watts created humoristic motorized assemblages, Kaprow, who wanted work in "real space" rather than the "suggested space" of painting, simultaneously developed, from 1958, his first environments which people could enter and encounter directly, and his first "Happenings," in which a scripted profusion of real-time activities was performed in front of an audience. In 1959, George Brecht put on an exhibition in which he displayed cabinets and other containers filled with objects that could freely be taken out, handled, and placed back by visitors.

The enthusiasm many artists of the 1960s showed toward scientific and technological progress is often difficult to comprehend today. After all, it is clear that the space race was only the echo of another, more frightening cold war reality: the threat of an annihilating nuclear conflict. Rather than celebrating a blind faith in progress, the most successful explorations of movement in real time and space in 1960s visual art were in fact the ones that emphasized that very precarious balance between construction and destruction, appearance and disappearance. In one of the darkest kinetic works, Gustav Metzger, denouncing "the increasing stockpiling of nuclear weapons" in his 1960 "manifesto of auto-destructive art," donned a gas mask and sprayed acid on nylon tarpaulins on London's South Bank.[4] Within fifteen seconds, the nylon had dissolved.

Consumption and destruction

It is significant that Metzger had been sent away to England as a child when his family was arrested in 1939 by the Gestapo – his "auto-destructive art" recalled the rockets and bombs of the past as well as the then current nuclear threat. For many artists working in Europe in the late 1950s and early 1960s, the ghosts of the Second World War were still very present. Benjamin Buchloh has argued that European artists often participated in the collective amnesia of their countries by burying this tragic past within works more evidently concerned with another manifestation of technology: the tidal wave of consumer goods from the United States which was washing over Europe in the 1960s.[5]

The nouveaux réalistes, for example, were never a politicized group, unlike the situationists in Paris, who announced the impossibility of creating art in the face of Europe's shameful past and France's compromised present – in particular, the country's role in the violent conflicts accompanying decolonization in Asia and Algeria. The 1960 "Nouveaux Réalistes' Declaration of Intention," written by the critic Pierre Restany, is a enthusiastic manifesto echoing the optimism of the early twentieth-century avant-gardes and celebrating "the thrilling adventure of the real perceived in itself."[6] While Restany's claims and the artists' embrace of found and ready-made objects posited the dominant presence of consumer goods and advertising as a source of inspiration for new painting and sculpture, nouveaux réalistes' work nevertheless suggested an ambivalence about this new economic boom.

For example, the "*décollagistes*," a sub-group of nouveau réalisme, including Raymond Hains, Jacques de la Villéglé, and François Dufrêne, collected and exhibited used billboards covered with layers of lacerated posters evoking the endless cycle of emergence and oblivion characterizing capitalist production. Similarly, when Arman filled with trash every available space of the Iris Clert gallery in Paris in 1960, thus condemning the spectator to look through the window instead of entering the building, he was not only referring to the huge quantities of waste produced by consumer societies, but also a general "condition of catastrophe" evoking scenes of horror and destruction of the Second World War.[7]

Analyzing the unconscious desires and fears embodied in consumer goods in the 1960s, Jean Baudrillard remarked that the "suicide" or "murder" of the mechanized object was a recurrent trope of the capitalist unconscious. An instance of this, he suggested, were contemporary "Happenings" in which objects are destroyed in an "orgiastic" manner during a "hetacomb whereby our whole satiated culture revels in its own degradation and death"[8] – as in Tinguely's spectacular *Homage to New York* (Figure 3.1) and his 1961 *Study for the End of the World*, in which complex machines with pyrotechnic self-destructive properties gradually exploded with hiccups and puffs of smoke in front of an audience. In different ways, then, many nouveaux réalistes created works speaking to us about our own mortality. Similarly, in the United States in 1964, the same year in which Andy Warhol shifted away from his dark "Disaster" silk-screens and exhibited his squeaky clean *Brillo Boxes* in New York, the Los Angeles County Museum threatened to close down Edward Kienholz's retrospective because of the inclusion of his *Backseat Dodge '38*, a life-sized assemblage in which the door of a wheel-less car opened to reveal two drunken lovers, crafted out of chicken-wire and plaster, awkwardly groping each other. For many Americans, Kienholz's piece would have been, as Thomas Crow put it, "an all-too-contemporary allegory of stunted lives and hopes."[9]

Production

If the nouveaux réalistes perceptively sounded the increasing role of consumer goods in late-capitalist society, their reflection on art's position as yet another consumer good was often uncritical. Yves Klein was an exception within the group, and both he and Piero Manzoni demonstrated, with flourish and humor, the ambivalent role of the artist and his products in the current economic situation. Constantly oscillating between lofty spirituality and outrageous publicity stunts, Klein, for example, invited an audience to watch him direct naked women as they applied blue paint on their thighs and torsos and dragged each other on canvases placed on the floor in order to create his *Anthropométries* in 1960. In a 1960 exhibition, Manzoni ritually distributed hard-boiled eggs stamped with his thumb print; he also sold balloons filled with the *Artist's Breath* and, most notoriously, cans of *Artist's Shit*: in all cases, Manzoni played on the quasi-religious faith in art, which placed a unique value on the artist as a person, as well as on the use of packaging as an omnipresent device for marketing and advertising even the artist as a commodity.

In the United States, artists' doubts about their roles focused on the notion of artistic labor. As Helen Molesworth has suggested, artists were responding to late capitalism's radical mechanization and distribution of labor which had resulted in an unprecedented rise in middle-class managers.[10] It was indeed the position of a manager that Warhol occupied in his aptly-named Factory, where he delegated the production of many of his silk-screened works to his assistants, and focused on the development of astute marketing strategies to appeal to popular and critical tastes instead.[11] Another group of artists who would come to be known collectively as the minimalists turned to industrial materials instead of popular images, but shared with pop art an attraction to serial production.

Produced from the mid- to late-1960s, works such as Donald Judd's metal cubic structures, Dan Flavin's neon sculptures, Carl Andre's floor works consisting of juxtaposed bricks or flat squares of lead or copper, and Robert Morris's early plywood beams were made of industrial materials and could be fabricated according to the artist's instructions and assembled at the site of the exhibition. Many minimalist works relied on either an orderly, repeated sequence of identical units, or a single, unified regular shape which could be grasped immediately by the viewer – all features of mass-produced goods. As in pop art, all traces of the artist's "touch" or skills as a craftsperson were erased. Unlike pop artists, however, the minimalists did not highlight their relationship to mass culture, but instead developed complex theoretical discourses that have been at the center of all discussions of the work ever since.[12] Indeed, minimalism embodied a historical shift during which, for the first time, artists were obtaining university degrees and acquiring verbal skills as part of their training, encouraging a professionalization of the artist and creating a situation that paralleled the late-capitalist separation between mental labor and manual labor.

While pop and minimal art were quickly embraced by dealers, museums, and collectors, another group of artists, Fluxus, passed more or less unnoticed. Fluxus was a truly international grouping of artists who staged performances together from 1962 and produced various kinds of collective publications. At the core of both performances and publications lay the "event score," verbal instructions written by artists which could be performed not only by the artist or another artist during Fluxus concerts, but also by any potential reader, anywhere. Modeled on the musical score, Fluxus scores poked fun at concert conventions, as well as encouraging readers to find poetry, humor, and food for thought in everyday activities ("Make a salad," states Alison Knowles's 1962 *Proposition*). As the organizer of Fluxus concerts and the producer of Fluxus objects, the Lithuanian artist and impresario George Maciunas played a key role in printing, packaging, and designing labels for the event scores and other small objects made according to the artists' ideas, as well as advertising and distributing them by mail-order, independently from galleries and institutions. The playful aspect of these boxes and their lack of material value parodied both the exchange of packaged consumer goods and the high-minded world of art (Figure 3.4). Fluxus, according to Maciunas, was considered above all as an "art-amusement," which would demonstrate that anything can be art, and that artists would eventually become dispensable.[13]

Conceptual art and the "aesthetics of administration"

In 1968, Lawrence Weiner decided to formulate his sculptural proposals as verbal descriptions of the action to be realized; a statement could read for example: "one quart exterior green enamel thrown on a brick wall." This was a logical extension of the minimalists' emphasis on conception to its most extreme point – the final object was not only secondary, it "need not be built" at all,

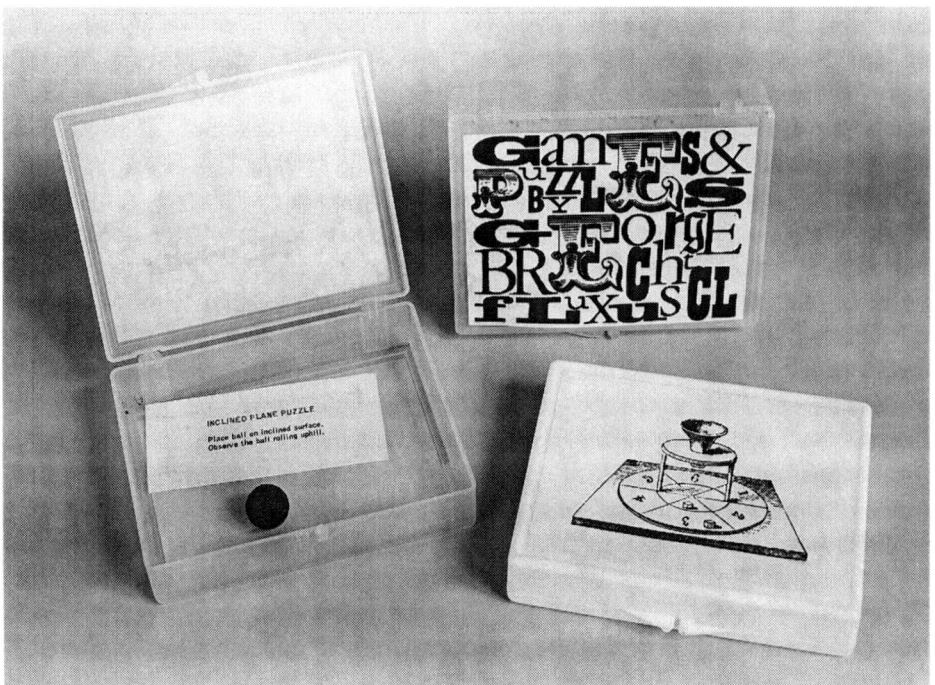

FIGURE 3.4   George Brecht, *Games and Puzzles/Inclined Plane Puzzle*, 1965–76 (three versions). Fluxus Editions. Photograph: Brad Iverson. Courtesy of the Gilbert and Lila Silverman Fluxus Collection, Detroit

according to Weiner.[14] Conceptual works, produced in the late 1960s, and consisting of text, photographs, and other forms of documentation, were mistakenly believed by some at the time to be "freed from a commodity status and market orientation" because no one "would actually pay money, or much of it, for a Xerox sheet referring to an event past" or "a group of photographs documenting an ephemeral situation or condition."[15]

Conceptual art did, indeed, seek to negate the purely visual attractiveness of painting and sculpture and the idea of the art work as a unique work existing independently from its context. In contrast, it emphasized other forms of information in order to direct viewers' attentions toward the processes involved in artistic practice. These processes – often couched as tasks to be carried out – could occur in the artist's studio, in the gallery, or outside these traditional spaces. In 1970, in New York, Douglas Huebler photographed forty people "at the instant exactly after the photographer [had] said, 'You have a beautiful face.'" Since 1966, On Kawara has painted canvases consisting solely of the date on which the work is made (if the painting is not completed by midnight on that day, it is destroyed); in 1968 Bruce Nauman, for his part, made a series of short films of himself performing useless activities in his studio, such as *Bouncing*

Two Balls between the Floor and the Ceiling. The visual object presented by the artist as the end of this task is visually different in each case: forty individual photographic portraits and a typed text that "join together to constitute the form" of Huebler's *Variable Piece #34*; a monochrome painting; a nine-minute film; and, in Weiner's work, green enamel paint thrown against a wall. What all these works do share, however, is that the object is either the product or the document of a simple task, and that neither the process nor the object sheds light on the artist's emotions, tastes, or traditional skills as a sculptor, painter, or photographer.

Rather than producing objects, like pop or minimalist artists, most conceptual artists sought to generate, classify, and transmit information. Thus, in terms of labor, they seemed to mimic the position of consultants, administrators, and the white-collar employees of the service industry. According to Benjamin Buchloh, conceptual art, instead of questioning late-capitalist society, developed instead a new "aesthetics of administration" which directly mirrored the rise of the bureaucratic middle-class.[16] Rather than seeking to transform society, this new aesthetics contented itself with reporting, often with humor, wit, poetry, or melancholy, on things as they were. Much of conceptual art, indeed, emphasizes the constraints of the artist's role in society and highlights the partiality and limitations of all forms of documentation – whether linguistic or visual.

II   Bodies

Consumerism, technology, shifts in the labor market, and the rapid expansion of the art market and cultural institutions were only some of the social phenomena with which artists were confronted in the 1960s. One of the paradoxes of the decade, in fact, is that the climate of economic growth and apparent stability of late capitalism was *precisely* what allowed for a steadily growing dissent. Art's relation to these unprecedented social and economic phenomena is complex. As I will discuss in section III, in some cases, artists or critics declared their allegiance to a specific political agenda. In other cases, general analogies can be made between the attitude of an artist, or the implicit critiques suggested by certain art works, on the one hand, and, on the other hand, a general social trend. For example, Tony Godfrey has argued that conceptual art probed what became known as the "credibility gap" between gung-ho governmental rhetoric about the Vietnam War and the gruesome images of murder and suffering through its general "emphasis on truth- and lie-telling" in works which promoted a transparency of process and encouraged viewers to question accepted notions of art and art-making.[17]

A third perspective on the relations between art and politics in the 1960s is suggested by Tom Crow in his notion of art as a "laboratory of a future politics" in which a new "sensibility" or "attitude" can be developed at the same time, and even before, it becomes explicitly political.[18] A "sensibility" may be difficult to describe, but, in fact, many aspects of the 1960s social "revolution" were vague. Although there were very clear, and urgent, battles to be fought – against the war, against racism, for the promotion of civil rights, women's liberation, and gay rights – other forms of protests were more general. The main activist political force in the 1960s was the New Left, which defined itself in its abandonment of some of the traditional beliefs and most strategies of the old socialist and communist left. As the New Left expanded into a mass movement, "revolution" came to equate for some anything from rock music to public nudity or the use of hallucinogenic drugs. With these political developments in mind, this section will focus on two aspects of this "sensibility" in relation to 1960s artistic practices: first, a renewed interest in the body as the site of sexual revolution, desire, and pleasure, and, second, the idea of community.

"Liberating" the body

In 1964, New York-based artist Carolee Schneemann staged her first performance of *Meat Joy*, a loosely scripted happening in which men and women clad in skimpy bikinis touched and painted each other, rolled around heaps of crumpled paper, and finally threw raw fish and meat at each other. The inspiration for the piece derived from her painting, collage, and assemblage practice, but the rocking Motown soundtrack, strong smells of decaying fish and chickens, sensuality of the contact between half-naked adults, and casual juxtaposition of animal and human flesh were undoubtedly shocking at the time: one journalist described it simply as an "orgy."[19] The notion of sexuality as a taboo subject had been inherited from the 1950s, a quasi-Victorian period of social conservatism in Europe and the United States; for this reason, the promotion of practices such as sex before marriage, contraception, and sexual experimentation is probably one of the most enduring legacies of the 1960s. For Schneemann, and many of the thousands of young people who rejected the lifestyles of their parents, this "sexual revolution" involved a celebration of sensuality, pleasure, and freedom from conventions. The joyful corporeality of her performances was carried over into film in her intimate *Fuses* (1964–7), which shows herself and her partner making love. Fluxus artist Yoko Ono's *Film no. 4* exhibited a similar sexual frankness in a simple sequence of close-ups of walking naked bottoms of all sizes and shapes, which caused outrage when it was first shown in London in 1966.

In contrast to Schneemann and Ono, the Viennese Actionists, a group of Austrian artists working in the 1960s, created shocking and disgusting collective performances in which bodies were mingled with blood, urine, excrement, and the carcasses of slaughtered animals. These performances combined a politicized refusal of the repression of sexual perversions such as sado-masochism with consensual, but disturbing, violence against women's bodies. In the arch-conservative context of 1960s Austria, the Viennese Actionists seemed to have been exorcising nationally-specific ghosts such as the violence of Nazism and the complicity between the Catholic Church and the Austrian State. Nevertheless, they shared a desire with Schneemann and other 1960s "art-events and Happenings" to "bring into the open," as Udo Kultermann put it in 1971, "the hidden, forgotten, or buried *ur*-experiences that determine the elemental existence of man," and explore the taboos related to "the basic human symbols and constants" of death, sexuality, and food.[20]

While it was widely acknowledged that the pill and abortion rights (granted in the United Kingdom in 1967) were crucial for women's liberation, other aspects of the "sexual revolution" such as the rise of pornography and *Playboy* clubs inspired vigorous activism and critique on the part of the burgeoning feminist movements in the late 1960s and early 1970s. Another Viennese artist, Valie Export, tackled the issues of women's freedom and enslavement dramatically in works such as her 1968 *Touch and Taste Cinema*. In this work, she paraded in the street with a curtained box around her bare chest and invited passers-by to reach through the curtains and touch her breasts while she gazed at them, thus simultaneously inviting and frustrating the traditional objectification of the female body in patriarchal society.

Abstraction and desire

In his popular *Eros and Civilisation* (1955), the US-based Frankfurt School philosopher Herbert Marcuse proposed that the revolutionary potential of play and sexuality was actively repressed by a capitalist society bent on channeling these libidinal energies into productivity. In order to counter this repression, Marcuse advocated in particular a return to instinctual behavior and a reversal of the guilt and purification involved in "sublimating" these drives. Marcuse's emphasis on "desublimation" was echoed in the works of certain artists investigating notions of form and formlessness in painting and sculpture in the later 1960s.

"The makers of what I am calling . . . eccentric abstraction," explained Lucy Lippard, "refuse to eschew imagination and the extension of sensual experience while they also refuse to sacrifice the solid formal basis demanded of the best in current nonobjective art."[21] *Eccentric Abstraction* was the name of the exhibition curated by Lippard at the Fischbach Gallery in New York in 1966, and the "current nonobjective art" which she referred to was the then-dominant form of sculpture in the United States: minimalism. The "imagination" and "sensual experience" of "eccentric abstraction" were defined in opposition to the minimalists' claims to have evacuated from sculpture all but the most basic geometric shapes in order to emphasize the spatial situation staged by and around the works.

Eccentric Abstraction, for example, included Eva Hesse's 1965 *Ingeminate*, a pair of long balloons. Bound in cord, sprayed with black enamel paint and hooked together with a rubber tube, the balloons evoke, without actually representing, bloated penises or elongated breasts linked by an umbilical cord. In her later works, Hesse subjected minimalism's relentless production-line repetitions to the slight irregularities and organic textures of her serial arrangements of latex forms, which evoke the messiness of bodily relations. This critique of the repression of the body in minimalism implicit in Lippard's text and Hesse's works was nowhere clearer than in Robert Morris's turn away from his earlier minimalist work in favor of soft sculptures made of limply hanging felt strips hooked to the wall, or detritus scattered on the gallery floor. For Morris, himself influenced by Marcuse, a refusal of the definite forms of minimalism was deemed subversive because it suggested openness, spontaneity, and a rejection of the stability of repression.[22]

Both the Japanese artist Yayoi Kusama, based in New York in the late 1960s, and the Brazilian Lygia Clark shared with Hesse and Morris an interest in abstraction combined with soft, pliable organic shapes that resonate with the body. Rather than sculpture, however, Kusama and Clark were associated with late 1950s–mid-1960s trends of painting which explored a vocabulary affiliated with the geometric abstraction of Mondrian and constructivism. Where Kusama obsessively covered canvases with repeated patterns of proliferating dots, circles, and spirals, Clark sought to highlight the instability of forms in rigorously geometric paintings whose incised lines suggest that they could be dis-assembled like puzzles.

In their subsequent works, this contrast was translated in the immersive atmosphere of Kusama's all-encompassing environments on the one hand, and, on the other, Clark's quest to create forms of dialog between the spectator, and between two or more spectators. Kusama's motifs – soft phallic protrusions made up of stuffed canvas, but also real macaroni, red polka dots, silver plastic spheres – seemed to cover objects and environments like a disease (Figure 3.2). Abandoning the metal of her kinetic *Bichos*, Clark's 1966 *Sensory Objects* all consisted in everyday objects such as stones, shells, and plastic bags filled with air or water, which solicited the touch of the viewer. Whereas Clark became increasingly involved in the psychological aspect of these interactions in her group experiments, Kusama became more interested in taking her work into the street. For example, in 1969, she caused a scandal by bringing in eight naked people to step into New York's Museum of Modern Art pond and mime the poses of its decorative sculptures.

Imagined communities

The collective nature of performances organized by Schneemann, the Viennese Actionists, Clark, or Kusama was a recurrent motif of 1960s Happenings or "art-events," and the site of significant crossovers between art and New Left politics during this period. From the first civil rights groups led by Martin Luther King in the 1950s US, and the influential radical protest movement Students for a Democratic Society (SDS), an egalitarian image of community based on collective decision-making became the motivating force behind New

Left thought and protest activity. Termed "participatory democracy," it was associated with love, non-violence, and solidarity, and became an immediate model not only for the organization of the protest groups but also for many hippie communes which spread across the United States.

Group exercises were encouraged within experimental theater, in the New York-based Living Theater for example, as well as in contemporary dance. The Judson Dance Theater organized performances and weekly workshops at the Judson Memorial Church in New York City which were open to anyone, even those without any dance training. Collective works such as Yvonne Rainer's 1963 *We Shall Run*, in which participants dressed in ordinary street clothes performed simple, repeated actions like running across the stage, with tasks distributed among performers on equal terms, embodied, according to Crow, the very "anti-hierarchical model of consensus fostered among pacifist groups."[23]

Outside the theater context, collective activities were means of conjuring temporary communities. Allan Kaprow for example moved away from the rigid codes of participation of his earlier Happenings with his 1967 *Fluids*, in which a group of people built a wall with ice bricks together; one year later former kinetic artist David Medalla invited participants in *A Stitch in Time* to sew anything they wished on long sheets of cotton. In contrast with these work-based collaborations, other 1960s manifestations set up a festive context for meetings and interactions. One of the key cultural events of the 1960s was the Woodstock music festival in the summer of 1969, which gathered 500,000 people in a joyful, non-violent, and cooperative atmosphere that became for some the model of an ideal community.

Artists throughout the decade sought to bring together people in a similar way by erecting pneumatic structures outdoors, by organizing events in parks, or by placing their works in unusual city spaces during group exhibitions. In Brazil, Hélio Oiticica and Lygia Pape, who participated with Lygia Clark in the Neoconcrete group in the early 1960s, infused their abstract geometric work with the celebratory mood of the Rio carnival. Inspired by samba dancing, in 1964 Oiticica started creating his *Parangolés*, colorful capes, flags, and tents made out of jute and plastic bags, painted or printed fabrics, and pockets filled with objects. The capes are made to be slipped into by the viewer, and presuppose movement and display; they were often worn by Oiticica's friends from the Rio shanty-town neighborhood of Mangueira. Lygia Pape's 1968 *Divisor* (*Divider*) (Figure 3.5) consisted of a huge white thirty-by-thirty-square-meter piece of cotton punctuated with evenly spaced holes through which people could put their heads. In the Brazilian climate of the time – an increasingly policed society under dictatorship – street agitation of a collective nature could easily become a subversive action. New Left movements and hippie communes across Europe and North America also promoted the power of what Daniel Cohn-Bendit, one of the leaders of the May 1968 uprisings in France, called "insurrectional cells."[24]

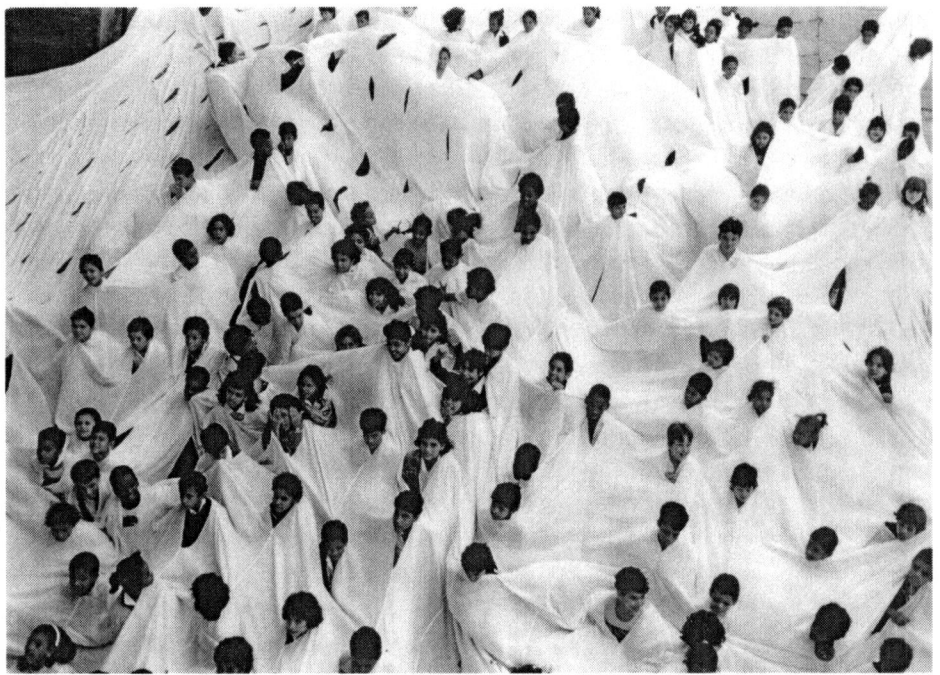

FIGURE 3.5   Lygia Pape, *Divisor*, 1968. Photograph: Paula Pape. © Projeto Lygia Pape

III   Contexts

If you are an artist in Brazil, you know of at least one friend who is being tortured; if you are one in Argentina, you probably have had a neighbor who has been in jail for having long hair (. . .); and if you are living in the United States, you may fear that you will be shot at, either in the universities, in your bed, or more formally in Indochina. It may seem too inappropriate, if not absurd, to get up in the morning, walk into a room, and apply dabs of paint from a little tube to a square of canvas.[25]

This quote from Kynaston McShine's introduction to the catalog for the 1970 exhibition *Information* at the Museum of Modern Art (MoMA) in New York clearly reveals the darker mood of the last years of the decade. The Nixon administration was actively repressing rebellion in the United States, and some pacifists turned to more violent means of protest, sometimes expressing solidarity with the guerrilla movements in Asia, Africa, and Latin America. Activists had risked their lives from the 1950s civil rights protests onward, but the threat of arrest or murder at the end of the decade led to a more bitter politicization which contrasted with the idealism of the mass youth movements across the world. If many artists had abandoned painting long before 1968, the effect of these social shifts was an increasing pressure to take political stances in relation to these events. In some cases, the political claims made by artists or critics lay in the connotations and implications of the works, rather than in their obvious message or content. Other artistic practices adopted more direct forms of political protest such as demonstrations and other interventions that took place either within institutions or in alternative spaces, including the street and other less tangible arenas such as the media.

Deconstructing painting and sculpture

It may seem surprising that Arte Povera, a movement comprised of Italy-based artists brought together by the Genoese critic Germano Celant from 1967, was seen by some as radically political in the late 1960s. What could be political about a large 1968 wicker cone by Mario Merz, Giovanni Anselmo's 1968 structure made up of a lettuce held by a wire between two vertical blocks of granite, or a 1967 installation in which Jannis Kounellis filled steel boxes with earth and cacti, placed a live macaw against a blackboard on the wall, and showed a roughly cubic metal structure overflowing with white cotton? Celant, however, explained that such works were "revolutionary" because their use of "poor" materials (i.e. everyday materials and objects that were perishable or of low value) opposed not only the industrial aesthetic of American pop and minimalism, but also all forms of systematic, and hence authoritarian, thinking, celebrating instead individual, lived experience through a "new humanism" in tune with the work of guerrilla heroes such as Che Guevara.[26]

A less romantic and more intellectually sophisticated intersection between art and politics occurred in the work of two groups of French artists: the short-lived BMPT (named after its four members, Daniel Buren, Olivier Mosset, Michel Parmentier, and Niele Toroni) and Supports-Surfaces, a group whose members developed their works from the mid-1960s onward but that only came together officially in 1970. If Arte Povera was primarily three-dimensional, the work produced by BMPT and Supports-Surfaces was resolutely based in the practice of painting. Having reduced their styles to one single motif each, Buren, Mosset, Parmentier, and Toroni staged collective events, such as a 1967 event in which their works were hung above the stage in a lecture theater at the Musée des Arts Décoratifs in Paris filled with an invited audience that was, after an hour's wait, informed that "it was simply a matter of looking at the paintings."[27] After their involvement with BMPT, both Buren and Toroni would continue to use their signature patterns (painted vertical stripes 8.7 cm wide, and small squarish marks with a number 50 brush at regular intervals of 30 cm, respectively) as simple pointers to draw attention to the architectural, institutional, and, by extension, the ideological contexts in which art works are viewed.

Although they shared a desire to demystify painting and its traditional tropes of unique authorship and autonomy, Supports-Surfaces started from the opposite perspective to BMPT by aiming toward the systematic deconstruction of the basic components of painting. While Daniel Dezeuze's 1967 stretcher covered with a transparent plastic sheet seems programmatic, other works such as Claude Viallat's wall-hung woven grids or André Valensi's floor-bound knotted cord intersections evoke the weave of the canvas more obliquely. In their writings, the Supports-Surfaces artists enrolled a wide range of theoretical references developed in France at the time to make highly political, and utopian, claims for their work. Drawing on Louis Althusser's writings about Marx, for example, they defined painting as an "object of knowledge" – as opposed to a commodity object. Subjecting this "object" to an intense critical analysis similar to the Marxist critique of capitalist ideology would, according to them, provide positive bases for a new revolutionary culture.[28]

Protest by artists

It is perhaps surprising that few artists responded directly to the Vietnam War, which dominated American culture from 1964 to 1973. The rare exceptions include Carolee Schneemann's 1967 *Snows*, a Happening in which the performers' bodies were overlaid with filmed images of the conflict, Edward Kienholz's life-sized tableau of five soldiers straining to plant an American flag on the terrace of a non-descript fast-food bar (*The Portable War Memorial*, 1968), and Martha Rosler's 1967–72 series of photomontages called *Bringing the War Home*, which introduced unbearable images of Vietnamese suffering into pictures of the pristine interiors of the American house. Collective, activist efforts on the part of artistic communities were, however, more widespread. After the 1966 Artists' Tower of Protest in Los Angeles and the Angry Arts Week in New York, one year later the Art Workers' Coalition (AWC), which was formed in 1969, called a Strike Against Racism, Sexism, Repression, and War in 1970. That same year, the AWC printed and distributed 5,000 posters of a color photograph which had first been published in newspapers in November 1969 and showed a pile of bodies lying in a ditch in Vietnam. Shortly before, an unknown discharged soldier, Paul Meadlo, had described on American television how he had participated, in 1968, in the spree of destruction, rape, and shooting of these peaceful villagers of My Lai. Meadlo's platoon commander, Lieutenant William Calley, was tried and charged with killing 109 people. What struck most Americans with horror was the casualness with which such violence had been inflicted. The tragic image on the poster printed by the AWC was overlaid by a laconic extract from Meadlo's television interview as transcribed in the *New York Times*: "Q: And babies? A: And babies."[29]

Art as intervention

Artists who refused to create works within an art world they perceived to be politically compromised were faced with the issue of finding alternative spaces to

exhibit. Adrian Piper, a conceptual artist who had worked as a gallery reception-
ist, decided in 1970 that any mediation between the artist and her public was
harmful, and chose to develop her *Catalysis* series in the streets of New York. In
Catalysis III, for example, she casually strolled down the street and went shopping in a shirt painted in wet paint with the hand-written logo "Wet Paint."
While Piper's self-identification as an African-American woman conferred an
implicit political dimension to her public self-presentations, Barrio's 1969–70
street interventions in Rio de Janeiro deployed objects, instead of the artist's
body, to address the issue of political violence in dictatorial Brazil, as he abandoned his disturbing *Bloody Bundles* soiled with blood, spit, excrement, hair,
bones, and fingernails, in streets and on river banks (Figure 3.3). In Argentina,
Victor Grippo's 1972 *Construction of a Traditional Rural Oven for Making
Bread* in the center of Buenos Aires was a more optimistic gesture aimed at
drawing people's attention to the lost rural community ritual of collective baking and sharing bread. Just as Barrio's actions were interrupted by the police,
the police smashed Grippo's clay and brick oven, thus confirming these works'
potential for subversion.

The process of "drawing attention" was perceived as the first step to political
action by artists as well as political activists. The street had always been an ideal
space to communicate with a non-art-going public through interventions, demonstrations, and the distribution of leaflets. In addition, one of the characteristics of many late 1960s protests was their savvy use of the media as a means to
address a wider audience. Most famously, Fluxus artist Yoko Ono teamed up
with her Beatles husband to broadcast their political beliefs. Together, Ono and
Lennon conceived in 1969 huge white billboards bearing in enormous black
capitals the words "WAR IS OVER!" and in smaller letters, "if you want it."
When, that same year, they stayed in bed to demonstrate their belief in peace in
their highly-publicized *Bed-in*, they effectively brought together the idealism of
art Happenings, the model of mass pacifist sit-ins, and a strategic use of the
media cult of star personalities.

In a decidedly less glamorous context, members of the Argentinean Grupo de
Artistas de Vanguardia (Group of Avant-Garde Artists) worked to counter the
government media propaganda about one of the country's poorest provinces,
Tucumán, in which the sugar refineries had been shut down, leading to an
economic disaster that the dictatorial regime was covering up by promoting a
sham development plan. The group's 1968 action, entitled *Tucumán Arde
(Tucuman Burns)*, involved distributing posters and flyers in the city, mounting
an exhibition of the data they had researched in the meeting place of the
workers' union, and giving a press conference. Drawing media attention was a
means of feeding information back into the "informational circuit" they were
contesting.[30]

Developing a similar idea, the Brazilian Cildo Meireles investigated in 1970
what he called Brazil's "ideological circuits."[31] On recyclable Coca Cola bottles,
for example, he silk-screened the motto "Yankees go home!" which only became

visible when the bottle was empty. Although they are specific responses to the Brazilian dictatorship and its American support, Meireles's strategies to short-circuit censorship through mass-circulated supports could be developed elsewhere. Indeed, when his Coca Cola bottles were exhibited in *Information*, they slipped into other "circuits," pointing not only to the consumption of commodities, and the commodification of culture, but also to American interventions in international politics in general. Irrupting into an art world controlled by America and Western Europe, works in *Information* such as Meireles's or Oiticica's reflected nascent postcolonial concerns pioneered in the 1960s by writers, film-makers, and artists outside the dominant geographical locations.

Conclusion

The "various displacements and rethinkings of materiality," which many artists, according to Michael Newman, carried out in their practices, constitutes one of the most significant shifts in 1960s art.[32] These "rethinkings," which Lippard misleadingly described at the time as a "dematerialization," involved an exploration of the processes and materials of painting and sculpture, the introduction of everyday objects and actions in art, and an investigation of other less tangible means of conveying meaning, such as language and the documentation of ephemeral actions.[33] While in the early 1960s this rethinking of materiality was often accompanied by reflections on polarities such as matter and the immaterial, form and formlessness, creation and destruction (Klein, Manzoni, kinetic art), the later 1960s focused more particularly on the material value of the art work. Within these phenomena, new forms of materiality came to be identified with a liberation of the body (Hesse and "eccentric abstraction" or "Process Art," the work of Kusama and Lygia Clark) and politics (Arte Povera, BMPT, Supports-Surfaces). Alternative modes of production could bypass, at least temporarily, institutional and commercial structures, but also risked mimicking existing forms of late-capitalist labor as artists took the positions of managers or administrators. For some artists, performances and interventions replaced the production of objects and opened new spaces of freedom and protest, from group exercises and collective activities, to direct political actions against the Vietnam War, street interventions, and insertions into the ideological circuits of the media and commodity capitalism.

One of the crucial links between heterogeneous practices during the 1960s was the recurrent equation between the boundaries of art and the limits imposed by authority, whether this authority was the rule of the businessman or the adman, the ideological language of the state and its institutions, the straitjacket of social norms and conventions, or the patriarchal system denounced by feminists. Emancipation, liberation, spontaneity, freedom, revolt were words which could be found in the writings of artists and critics as much as in the wall graffiti of Paris students in May 1968; criticizing dominant discourses, raising consciousness, and encouraging dissent were objectives shared by many artists with the emerging New Left thinkers. As we have seen, the relation between art and politics in the 1960s often remained implicit, playing a role at the level of general beliefs, attitudes, and moods. Only in the last years of the decade were artists really faced with urgent political decisions. Artists and critics reacted in different ways – some emphasized a clear separation between their work as artists and their political beliefs, while others made often impossible political claims for their works. The bottom line for many art historians has been whether (and for how long) those works escaped from the machinations of an art market avid for novelty and the speedy institutionalization of art movements in the second half of the twentieth century. Another, maybe more fruitful question may be: how can artistic practices offer effective models of interaction between people and objects, and among human beings? From this perspective, it will become clear that 1960s art has still a great deal to offer.

Notes

1   "My Position in the Battle between Line and Colour" (1958) in Brett (2000), 242.
2   "Free Dimension" (1960) in Brett (2000), 247.
3   "Project in Multiple Dimensions" (1957–8), in Marter (1999), 153–9.
4   "Manifesto of Auto-Destructive Art" (1960), in Selz and Stiles (1996), 402.
5   Benjamin Buchloh, "Plenty or Nothing: From Yves Klein's *Le Vide* to Arman's *Le Plein*" (1998) in Buchloh (2000), 257–83. For a different account of the latent violence of nouveau réalisme, cf. Maurice Berger, "Forms of Violence: Neo-Dada Performance," in Hapgood (1994), 66–83.
6   Pierre Restany, "The Nouveaux Réalistes Declaration of Intention" (1960), in Selz and Stiles (1996), 306.
7   Arman, quoted in Buchloh (2000), 269.
8   Baudrillard (1996), 122.
9   Crow (1996), 76.
10 Helen Molesworth, "Work Ethic," in Molesworth (2004), 25–51.
11 Cf. Jones (1996).
12 Cf. Donald Judd, "Specific Objects" (1965); Robert Morris, "Notes on Sculpture Part I" (1966) and "Notes on Sculpture Part II" (1966) in Meyer (2000), 207–10, 217–20.
13 George Maciunas, "Art/Fluxus Art-Amusement" (1965), in Hendricks (1981), 9.
14 Weiner, "Declaration of Intention" (1968) cited in Crow (1996), 157.
15 Lippard (1973), 263.
16 Buchloh (1990).
17 Godfrey (1998), 190.
18 Crow (1996), 170.
19 Cited in Kristine Stiles, "Uncorrupted Joy: International Art Actions," in Schimmel (1998), 253.
20 Kultermann (1971), 137.
21 Lucy Lippard, "Eccentric Abstraction" (1971), quoted in Williams (2000), 43.

22 Cf. Williams (2000), 70–7.
23 Crow (1996), 127.
24 Daniel Cohn-Bendit and Gabriel Cohn-Bendit, as quoted by Stephens (1998), 29.
25 Kynaston McShine, "Introduction to *Information*" (1970), in Alberro and Stimson (1999), 212.
26 Cf. Williams (2000), 140–9.
27 BMPT, quoted by Godfrey (1998), 175.
28 For a brief but useful discussion of Supports-Surfaces, cf. Singerman (2003), 125–9, 142–50.
29 For more information on all these protests, cf. Frascina (1999).
30 María Teresa Gramguglio and Nicolás Rosa, "Tucumán Burns" (1968), in Alberro and Stimson (1999), 79.
31 Cf. "Insertions into Ideological Circuits" (1970), and "Statements" (1981), in Alberro and Stimson (1999), 232–3, 410–12. On Latin American art and politics in general, cf. Guy Brett, "Life Strategies: Overview and Selection, Buenos Aires/London/Rio de Janeiro/Santiago de Chile, 1960–1980," in Schimmel (1998): 196–225; Mari Carmen Ramírez, "Tactics for Thriving on Adversity: Conceptualism in Latin America, 1960–1980," in Camnitzer et al. (1999), 53–71.
32 Michael Newman, "The Material Turn in the Art of Western Europe and North America in the 1960s," in Kalinovska (2000), 73.
33 Cf. Lippard (1973).

References and further reading

Alberro, Alexander, and Blake Stimson eds. (1999). *Conceptual Art: A Critical Anthology*. London and Cambridge, MA: MIT University Press.

Baudrillard, Jean (1996). *The System of Objects* (1968), trans. James Benedict. London and New York: Verso.

Brett, Guy (2000). *Force Fields: Phases of the Kinetic*. London: Hayward Gallery.

Buchloh, Benjamin (1990). "Conceptual Art 1962–1969: From the Aesthetic of Administration to the Critique of Institutions." *October*, vol. 55:104–43.

—— (2000). *Neo-avantgarde and the Culture Industry: Essays on European and American Art from 1955 to 1975*. London and Cambridge, MA: MIT Press.

Camnitzer, Luis et al., eds. (1999). *Global Conceptualism: Points of Origin, 1950–1980*. New York: Queens Museum of Art.

Crow, Thomas (1996). *The Rise of the Sixties: American and European Art in the Era of Dissent 1955–69*. London: The Everyman Art Library.

Eco, Umberto (1989). *The Open Work* (1962), trans. Anna Cancogni. Cambridge, MA: Harvard University Press.

Frascina, Francis (1999). *Art, Politics and Dissent: Aspects of the Art Left in Sixties America*. Manchester and New York: Manchester University Press.

Godfrey, Tony (1998). *Conceptual Art*. London: Phaidon.

Hapgood, Susan, ed. (1994). *Neo-Dada: Redefining Art 1958–62*. New York: American Federation of Arts and Universe Publishing.

Hendricks, Jon, ed. (1981). *Fluxus Etc.* Bloomfield Hills, MI: Cranberry Academy of Art Museum.

Jones, Caroline (1996). *Machine in the Studio: Constructing the Postwar American Artist*. Chicago: University of Chicago Press.

Kalinovska, Milena, ed. (2000). *Beyond Preconceptions: The Sixties Experiment*. New York: Independent Curators International.

Kultermann, Udo (1971). *Art-Events and Happenings*, trans. John William Gabriel. London: Mathews Miller Dunbar.

Lippard, Lucy (1973). *Six Years: The Dematerialization of the Art Object From 1966 to 1972*. London: Studio Vista.

Marcuse, Herbert (1969). *Eros and Civilization: A Philosophical Inquiry into Freud* (1955). London: Sphere Books.

Marter, Joan, ed. (1999). *Off Limits: Rutgers University and the Avant-garde, 1957–1963*. Newark: Newark Museum.

Meyer, James, ed. (2000). *Minimalism*. London: Phaidon.

Molesworth, Helen, ed. (2004). *Work Ethic*. Baltimore: Baltimore Museum of Art.

Osborne, Peter, ed. (2002). *Conceptual Art*. London: Phaidon.

Schimmel, Paul, ed. (1998). *Out of Actions: Between Performance and the Object, 1949–1979*. Los Angeles: Museum of Contemporary Art, and London: Thames and Hudson.

Selz, Peter, and Kristine Stiles, eds. (1996). *Theories and Documents of Contemporary Art: A Sourcebook of Artists' Writings*. Berkeley and London: University of California Press.

Singerman, Howard (2003). "Noncompositional Effects, or the Process of Painting in 1970." *Oxford Art Journal*, vol. 26, no. 1:125–50.

Stephens, Julie (1998). *Anti-Disciplinary Protest: Sixties Radicalism and Postmodernism*. Cambridge: Cambridge University Press.

Williams, Richard J. (2000). *After Modern Sculpture: Art in the United States and Europe, 1965–70*. Manchester and New York: Manchester University Press.

4

"I'm sort of sliding around in place . . . ummm . . .": Art in the 1970s

Sam Gathercole

The 1970s lack the clear identity that the decades on either side of it are thought to possess. The radical, progressive 1960s and the reactionary backlash of the 1980s frame a decade of disappearance, disintegration, and fragmentation. Toward the end of Bruce Robinson's film *Withnail and I* (1987), set in 1969, the character Danny remarks, with a sense of disappointment and failure, on one decade's closure and the dismal prospects for the next: "They're selling hippy wigs in Woolworth's." A decade of promise and optimism was to give way to one of disillusion; its political signifiers were to be marketed as products, their radical significations deflated.

The title of this chapter, a phrase uttered by Dan Graham while performing in his 1977 piece *Performer/Audience/Mirror* (discussed later in this chapter), points to the uncertain position in which art, and particularly avant-garde art, found itself in the 1970s.[1] In 1976, Rosalind Krauss could thus write of a "diversified, split, factionalised" moment, "proud of its own dispersal."[2] A more recent account, concerned specifically with the history of terrorism, describes the 1970s as "the age of the 'groupuscules', the tiny, fissiparous radical activist groups which spread across Western Europe."[3] What follows suggests that such an observation might be applied more broadly; that this model of fragmentation might be useful in making sense not only of the various Red Army Factions in Europe, but also of radical cultural responses to the period such as those of the "Anarchitecture" group in New York.[4] Things got nasty and scrappy in the 1970s, as the state and the market attempted to reassert an authority that had been lost, or at least questioned, in the late-1960s, and as political activism faced up to a shifting climate. Positions became both entrenched and more difficult to sustain in the face of dramatic political events. Nineteen seventy saw the United States extend its offensive from Vietnam into Cambodia, and the American National Guard shoot four student-protesters at Kent State University. Nineteen seventy-two witnessed the "Bloody Sunday" shootings on the part of the British army in Northern Ireland. The 1970s were dark, with the effects of oil crisis-induced power cuts being ameliorated only occasionally by glitter balls and disco lights.

One key event is often evoked in summarizing what the beginning of the decade symbolized in cultural as well as political terms. On July 15, 1972 a mass housing scheme, Pruitt Igoe in St. Louis, Missouri, was demolished. For the architectural commentator, Charles Jencks, this was the "precise moment in time" (3:32 pm to be exact) that "the death of modern architecture" occurred. Dating from the early-1950s, Pruitt Igoe had been "constructed according to the most progressive ideals" and had won awards, but had nevertheless come to represent a "failure in planning and architecture."[5] Jencks points out that Pruitt Igoe had been an unhappy place of residence to the point where it was the sustained target for vandalism by its own inhabitants, and that the authorities finally succumbed to this spontaneous public protest and blew up several of the slab blocks in a well-publicized and documented demolition. That "activism" of this sort (spontaneous acts of vandalism) forced the hand of the officials is significant: the 1970s can be seen as being characterized by this shift from the 1960s notion of coordinated and organized collective groups, trusting ideologies and agitating for social change, to the subsequent decade's stress on localized points of protest, and the power of the individual act.

In another text, Jencks celebrated the "plural counter-culture" of the decade. The visual arts might have lacked the single moment of rupture that architecture endured/enjoyed on a July afternoon in 1972, but Jencks noted an "open pluralism, both political and cultural" as "one of the great accomplishments of the 1970s."[6] Not everyone celebrated this pluralism, however; many of a more explicitly political mind than Jencks noted that it veiled a tendency to ignore class issues and that it could also be seen in negative terms as a troubling fragmentation. All the same, it also pointed to the tendency to localize political concerns in specific acts and subjects in order to realize change (both legislative and in wider social attitudes) – a tendency I will argue is central to understanding art practices from the 1970s.

This chapter is concerned, above all, with the decade's most advanced and progressive art practice – its "avant-garde" work – and the debates surrounding it. I focus on art in Europe and the United States, where the dominant responses to modernism were being articulated. I propose in this chapter that it is in facing the complexities and contradictions arising at the cutting edge (or avant-garde) of visual culture that a sense of the issues and responses of the 1970s might best be approached. This is not a decade of easy assumptions.

An Avant-Garde Impasse

In 1977, the Marxist intellectual Fredric Jameson reflected on a debate that had been played out in the 1930s between critical theorists Bertolt Brecht and Georg Lukács, in which they had argued about what kind of artistic practice would best serve to encourage awareness and criticism of social categories and class structures. The particular terms of the debate between Brecht and Lukács (with the former arguing in support of avant-garde experiment as the most effective way of seeing reality properly by rejecting convention and the complacency of established terms; the latter insisting on a realism of the pure signified, in which form gives direct access to content), had been somewhat lost in the ideological mists of the cold war. Still, while Brecht's ideas appeared to retain some credence, Lukács's ideas had been dismissed or forgotten largely because of their association with the much-maligned Socialist realism of the Eastern Bloc.

The 1960s and 1970s saw a renewed interest in such debates, and Brecht's position in particular became central to much of the writing about radical visual practice in the British journals *Screen* and *Block*. These journals contributed to a growing awareness of a politically engaged work of the early-twentieth-century European avant-gardes, and even the terms of their various opponents. Ideas became available after decades of having been buried under the dominant language of modernist formalism, which had promoted the idea of art as being necessarily autonomous from the political and social realms. Whether it was in the dynamic, energized visual, social, and political work of the Russian constructivists of the 1920s (knowledge of which we might now take for granted, but which was virtually unavailable to Western Europeans and Americans for 30 or 40 years), or the possibility that avant-garde advances had been, in the 1930s, intimately bound up with a realist social agenda, aspects of history reappeared (in a decade of disappearances).

In his text, Jameson revives an idea of culture as involving the "collective re-education of all the classes."[7] Toward this end, both Socialist realism as advocated by Lukács *and* the avant-garde modernism promoted by Brecht appeared to Jameson as being respectively "inadequate" and "inappropriate" for the 1970s.[8] An impasse is here identified, with modernism "and its accompanying techniques of 'estrangement'" dominating, and with the audience, the "consumer," now "reconciled with capitalism." The idea of a "totality" through which society and its culture might be critically understood was presented as having been "systematically undermined by existential fragmentation."[9]

The question that preoccupied Jameson is thus one of how to reestablish "a more totalizing way of viewing phenomena" leading him, surprisingly perhaps, to turn to Lukács – "wrong as he might have been in the 1930s" – for an appropriate model. Insisting that "the fundamental structure of the social 'totality' is a set of class relationships," and that "reification necessarily obscures the class character of that structure," Jameson recommended "the forcible reopening of access to a sense of society as a totality, and of the reinvention of possibilities of cognition and perception that allow social phenomena once again to become transparent, as moments of the struggle between classes."[10]

The first images of the period that come to mind in reading such recommendations are those of the American painter, Leon Golub (Figure 4.1). He, as much as anyone, was pushing toward a new realism that accorded with the terms outlined by Jameson. In the 1960s, against the background of American involvement in Vietnam, Golub had used art as a means of protest, as a means of criticizing state power and authority. In 1970, he started painting heroically-scaled works called *Assassins*, and, in 1976, another series, *Mercenaries*. State-commissioned violence is the subject here, but Golub did not specify the national identity of his subjects, noting that he saw his "problem" as being one of "the reconstruction of a generic type" whilst "trying to retain a raw, brute look so that the events do not become over-synthesised."[11]

The insistent flatness of Golub's work does not conceal a determined alternative to formalist abstraction. Indeed, Golub described his work as "objective realism": "it is a realist art because it essays to show power, to make power manifest as it is frequently encountered. [. . .] This is how it is, this is how power is configured in events and actions, and perhaps this is how it's abstractly structured in our society."[12] With such statements Golub, whether knowingly or not, echoes Lukács' call for "a depiction of objective reality with its real driving forces and real development tendencies" in which "there is no space for an 'ideal,' whether moral or aesthetic."[13]

While Jameson surely would have approved of Golub's project, it was not widely appreciated in the 1970s. In fact, his work received significant critical attention and acclaim only in the early 1980s. It is ironic, what with the nature of the work and its correlation with Jameson's arguments, that it would find a place at a time when the objects of art in the form of painting and sculpture (what Lukács called "the fetishized forms of capitalist society"[14]) were being reasserted by both a critical framework and the art market. There is insufficient space here to deal in any detail with the significance of Golub's stubborn pursuit of an appropriately politicized mode of painting in the 1970s. But it would be all too easy, given the current status of artists such as Golub or, more clearly, the German painter Gerhard Richter, to rewrite history by assuming that their practice has been consistently recognized as significant throughout the last 40 years when, in fact, in the 1970s conceptualist modes of visual practice were dominant and critically celebrated, and painting was generally marginalized, at least in major Western art centers.

Jameson is not alone in his recognition of the "failure" of the modernist avant-garde and, indeed, that of the established terms of a realist art. We will come to how others interpreted and located this failure, but also to how an idea of a "single shared objective reality" came under attack in the 1970s. Jameson's need to locate a totality was one that increasingly few intellectuals and artists

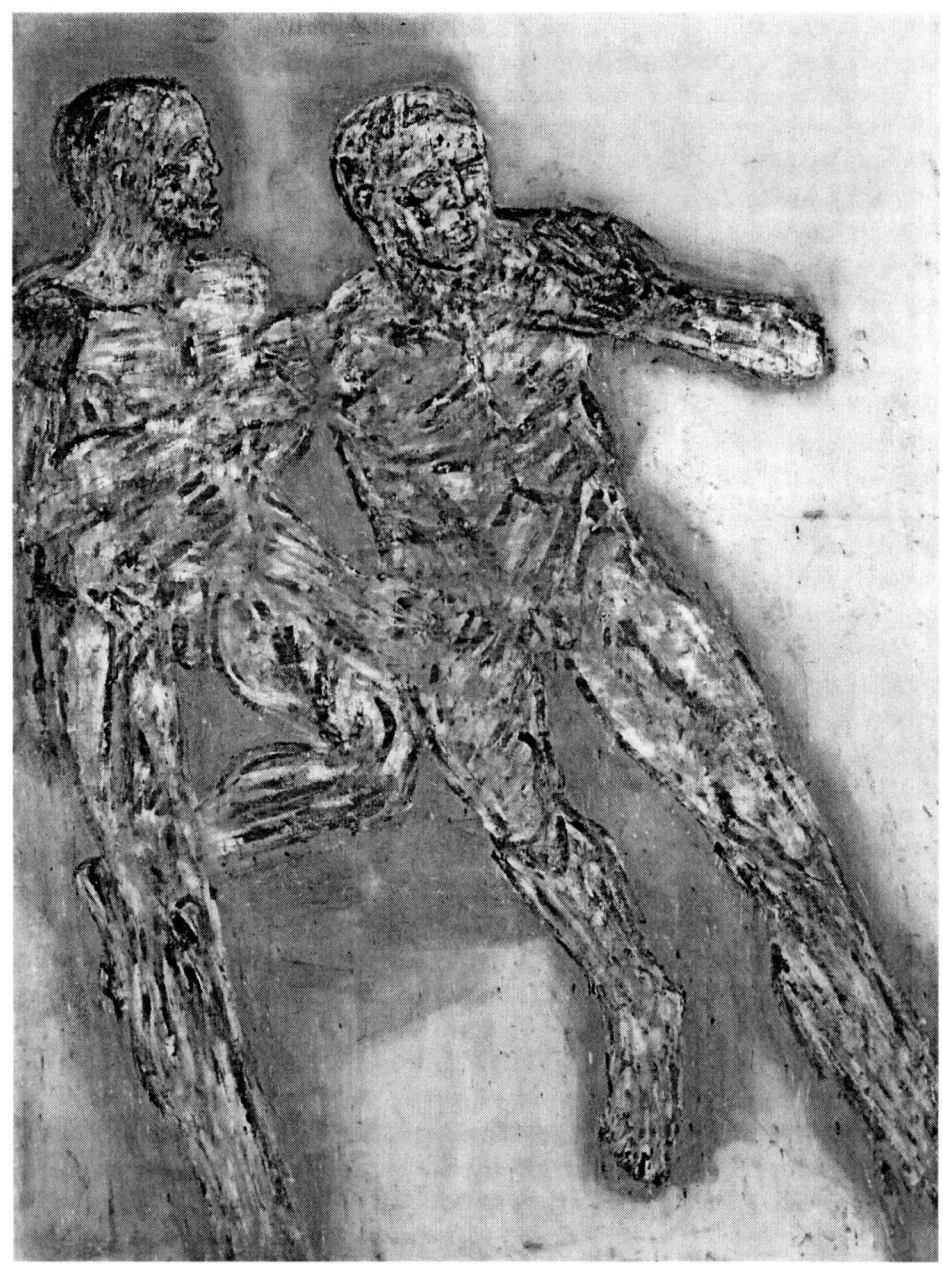

FIGURE 4.1   Leon Golub, *Assassins*, 1970. Courtesy Ronald Feldman Fine Arts, New York. © DACS, London, VAGA, New York 2005

were to share as the 1970s progressed. Instead, we will see that, rather than turning to realism as Golub continued to do, artists in the 1970s were more likely to embrace a deliberate fragmentation of wholeness as a legitimate (Brechtian) response to the pressures of the moment. Before this tendency is further developed, however, it is worth briefly consulting another highly influential text from the time, a text that, like Jameson, revisited history in order, in part, to understand the then present.

In 1974, the German literary theorist, Peter Bürger, published *Theorie der Avantgarde*, which would be translated into English a decade later as *Theory of the Avant-Garde*. In his book, Bürger distinguishes an early- to mid-twentieth-century "historical avant-garde" from a postwar "neo-avant-garde."[15] The historical avant-garde's project (exemplified in Bürger's book by Dada and surrealism) is to attack art as an institution "such as it has developed in bourgeois society." Bürger tells of the "failure" of the avant-gardist intention of reintegrating art into "the praxis of life." Given this failure, the neo-avant-garde's continued use of radical artistic strategies such as montage becomes a futile means of criticizing cultural convention – a failure that, for Bürger, is exemplified in the work of Andy Warhol.

Bürger's central claim, then, was that what had been a "historical" anti-artistic intent had been inverted by the neo-avant-garde; that many of the same procedures (such as the rejection of individual artistic techniques) were being maintained, but toward *artistic* ends. In spite of the perceived "failure" of the historical avant-garde, it had, nevertheless, made "art recognisable as an institution and also reveal [art's] inefficacy in bourgeois society as its principle." Bürger goes on to say that "post-historical-avant-garde" work "must come to terms with this fact in bourgeois society."[16] This is a clear and provocative challenge to artists, one to which many responded in the 1970s, whether they were explicitly aware of Bürger's text or not.

A New Avant-Garde in the Gallery

Let us start to explore the limits of Jameson's and Bürger's frameworks by looking at attitudes of artists in 1970s Europe and North America to the physical institution: the museum or gallery. A quick glance at a number of avant-garde statements tells us much, and confirms Bürger's "historical" and "neo" distinctions. As early as 1909, Marinetti had insisted that the Italian futurists would "destroy the museums, libraries, academies of every kind."[17] Eleven years later, Rodchenko would shout that constructivists in Russia would "[w]ork for life and not for palaces, cathedrals, cemeteries and museums."[18]

By 1970, the tone had changed: the Art Workers' Coalition in America issued a "Statement of Demands" that replaced the revolutionary (or terrorist communiqué) language of Rodchenko with that of trade union negotiations.[19] "All means should be explored in the interest of a more open-minded and democratic museum," the AWC suggested. A list of 13 "demands" included the proposition that artists should form a one-third part of boards of trustees in museums, that admission should be free (with evening openings to "accommodate working people"), that museums should "decentralize" to be inclusive of multi-racial, multi-ethnic communities, that gender equality must be achieved in exhibitions, collection policy, and staffing, and that artists should "retain a disposition over the destiny of their work, whether or not it is owned by them."[20] For the AWC the institution, rather than being destroyed, was to be reformed.

Robert Morris, one of the key figures within the AWC, attempted to rethink modernist gallery display techniques in his 1971 exhibition at the Tate Gallery, London. Organized into three sections, the exhibition invited varying degrees of physical interaction with structures of wood and metal, with the idea of affecting the behavior of those within the gallery spaces. In a reversal of the terms on which a formalist modernism had been understood, the viewer was treated as anything but disinterested, the gallery space anything but neutral, and the experience of the work – much more than simply being a visual, aesthetic one – as involving performance by the audience itself. Within four days, however, the exhibition was closed because of damage to works and injury to visitors.

Morris was not alone in his perhaps deliberately disruptive attempts to expose the problematic relationship between production and the conditions of distribution or display. The German artist Hans Haacke's attentions were directed toward social systems, including those of the museum. Very aware of points such as Bürger's argument that "art as an institution neutralises the political content of the individual work,"[21] Haacke set out to force the issue by producing work that would resist such neutralization. Here, the institutional site of the exhibition becomes its subject.

In 1971, Haacke thus produced a work for display at the Guggenheim Museum in New York entitled *Shapolsky et al. Manhattan Real Estate Holdings, a Real-Time Social System, as of May 1, 1971*. This was a bold, knowingly provocative and uncompromising piece that, like Morris's, downplayed aesthetic interest, this time in favor of a direct exposure of the power of capital and the commercial interests that supported the museum's institutional structure. The work consisted of a series of panels of photographs, maps, charts, and texts that documented the involvement of members of the museum's board of directors in property speculation in the city's slum districts. The museum's director, Tomas Messer, cancelled the exhibition and sacked the curator responsible for working with Haacke on the piece.

Clearly, for Haacke, it was crucial to encourage awareness (both in the public and in museums themselves) of the cultural climate in which art was produced and of the politics behind the institutions in which it was encountered. As Haacke himself admitted though, "[s]o-called 'avant-garde art' is at best working close to the limitations set by its cultural/political environment, but it always operates within that allowance."[22] In his determination to remain *within* the institutions he is attempting to critique, Haacke reveals his commitment to Brechtian ideas of avant-garde practice.[23] In his theory of the avant-garde, Bürger notes that, whilst he was clearly an avant-gardist, Brecht's arguments were not wholly consistent with the tenets of the historical avant-garde in that he did not share their intention of destroying art as an institution.[24] Brecht's pragmatic goal of seeking to change rather than destroy the institutions of art became central to avant-garde practice in the 1970s, as is evident in Haacke's work.

Like Haacke, French conceptual artist Daniel Buren focused attention on the gallery as a framing structure. In a Paris exhibition in 1967, Buren had started making "images" consisting only of 8.7 cm vertical stripes.[25] Initially on canvas (and in red and white), but subsequently applied to a variety of surfaces and in a variety of contexts both inside and outside the gallery, the work was repeated without variation. Through this repetition of his signature stripes, the situation or context in which his single intervention was made became the content of the work. On the troubled streets of Paris in 1968, Buren's stripes could be seen on sandwich boards, but – per Brecht's model, and Haacke's practice – by the 1970s the work was placed almost exclusively within an art institutional framework in order "to reveal the 'container' in which the work is sheltered."[26]

Haacke's and Buren's provocations of art institutions can be seen as successful critiques of sorts, but there is also a sense of failure inherent in these examples. Buren's work ultimately, if not quickly, assumed its place within the art system, rather than against it. That he goes on making such work to this day, and is invited to do so as part of an international art scene, raises questions about the sustainable power of the work as critique and suggests that, more than anything, his work signals the success of the institution in accommodating the work of even its most fervent critics.

A sense of failure and disappointment regarding the potential of critique, so central to 1960s art and activism, to change the system emerges as something characteristic of the cultural climate of the early 1970s. By 1973, Lucy Lippard was already reflecting on conceptual art's inability to resist "the general commercialisation" of art and the mechanisms of the market – "the tyranny of commodity status and market-orientation."[27] She noted the high prices paid for work that only a few years before seemed immune to the very idea of commercial exchange, and the place that the artists associated with it had found in prestigious galleries. Haacke and Buren were included in a list of "exceptions," but it was noted (with some regret) that these artists had "been confined to art quarters, usually by choice."[28]

A New Avant-Garde Outside of the Gallery

There were others less interested in or convinced of the possibilities of change in galleries and museums; turning away from the art institution altogether, they were thus less preoccupied with the sense of failure associated with such attempts.

The American artist Robert Smithson produced land art works through which he hoped to bypass notions of art as commodity and a reliance on a museum and gallery structure. In 1972, reviving the terms of assault employed by Marinetti and Rodchenko, Smithson described museums as "asylums and jails" in which art is "confined." In confluence with the motivation behind the work of artists such as Haacke and Buren, Smithson suggested that "it would be better to disclose the confinement rather than make illusions of freedom,"[29] but he also sought a more independent alternative.

In April 1970, Smithson started the construction of his best-known work, *The Spiral Jetty*, at Great Salt Lake in Utah. He described searching for a site and finding, in Utah, "evidence of a succession of man-made systems mired in abandoned hopes." On deciding the particular site of the work, Smithson later wrote of his recognition of its "immense roundness" and suggestion of "rotary" movement: "From that gyrating space emerged the possibility of the Spiral Jetty. No ideas, no concepts, no systems, no structures, no abstractions could hold themselves together in the actuality of that evidence."[30] This "actuality" appeared to the artist to be a reality beyond human control and corruption, and the work conceived for it is one that he apparently ("no ideas, no concepts") imagined to be unmediated by the intellect. Reading his "The Spiral Jetty" text is, paradoxically (given his position as the darling of scholars interested in promoting work critical of modernism) to encounter the heroic language of American high modernism, and the language associated with Jackson Pollock in particular.[31] There is a sense of natural "essence" here, but Smithson is aware of the work's contingency and its place in relation to cultural space (no matter its conceptual and physical distance from that space's more familiar locations).

A still bigger work was Christo and Jeanne Claude's 18-foot high, 24-mile long *Running Fence*, which linked two counties in California in September 1976. *Running Fence*, unlike *Spiral Jetty*, made no claim toward achieving a natural, environmental harmony. This is a confrontational, excessive art, on an absurd scale. There is no sublime here, no "land myth" such as that conjured-up in Smithson's work. *Running Fence* crossed 23 roads, including two highways (disappointingly though, leaving gaps for access on the roads), and cut through the town of Valley Ford. The work both made visible the contours of the rolling landscape and disrupted it physically and functionally. This is an event more than an object; while Smithson hints at a prehistory, Christo and Jeanne Claude thus emphasize a transient present.

Gordon Matta-Clark's 1974 work *Splitting Four Corners*, actualized in Englewood, New Jersey, was equally disruptive in physical terms, as well as being psychologically disruptive in its violent approach to domestic space. Christo and Jeanne Claude divided and ruptured with a material barrier, Matta-Clark achieved much the same by cutting: in this example, literally slicing a suburban house in half. Matta-Clark's vertical cut was narrow at ground level and opened toward the roof as gravity pulled the two halves apart, thus shifting, if not fundamentally undermining, the structure of the building. The house had been

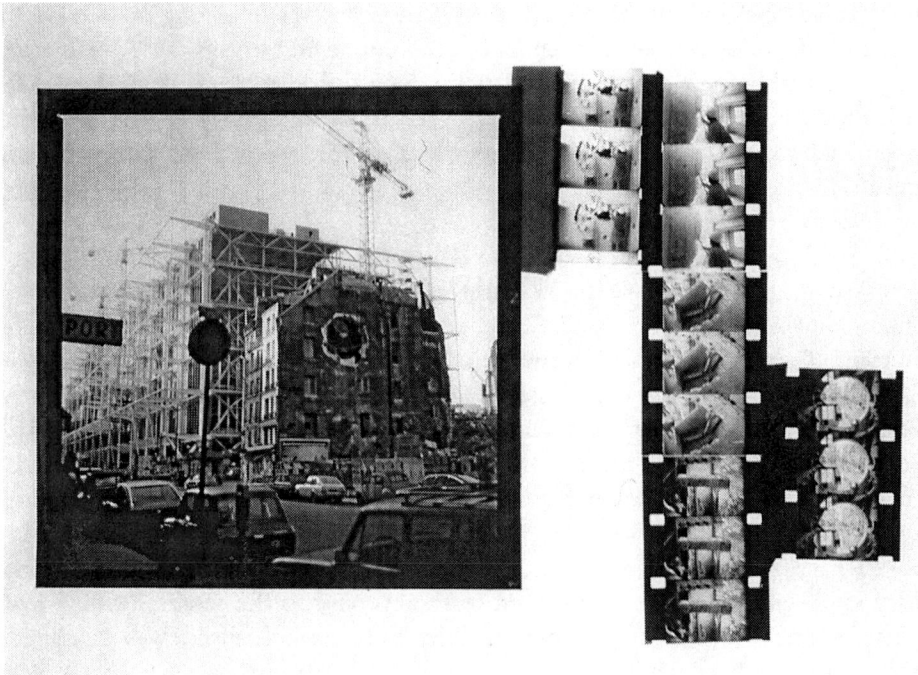

FIGURE 4.2   Gordon Matta-Clark, *Conical Intersect*, 1975. Cibachrome photograph. 76.2 × 101.6 cm, 30 × 40 in. GMCT2147. Courtesy of David Zwirner, New York. © ARS, New York and DACS, London 2005

forcibly vacated to make way for a planned urban renewal project, but more than being a simple comment on displacement in the modern age, the work challenged basic assumptions about the home as a safe and stable place.

Matta-Clark's work revives a dialogue between inside and outside that had been a feature of modern architecture, but to a different end. His interventions appear more as wounds, as ruptures to the rational articulation and division of space, and the logic of shelter. In 1975, his *Conical Intersect* (Figure 4.2) removed sections of houses that were to be demolished to make way for the Centre Pompidou development in Paris (ironically, the Pompidou itself was to become one of the most visible examples of "deconstructive" architecture, in which a building's interior mechanisms are placed on the outside). Matta-Clark's project interrogates the conventional notion of improvement and progress through construction by means of a *literal* deconstruction of building structures, linking back to the cultural impact of the Pruitt Igoe demolition in 1972.

In a 1973 work, *A W-Hole House: Datum Cuts* in Genoa, Italy, Matta-Clark puns on the opposition between completeness and void. Around this time, he had written that to achieve "the perfect structure" it was necessary or desirable to "erase all the buildings for a clear horizon."[32] Matta-Clark's illustration of this idea of "erasing" undesirable buildings with reference to the Twin Towers of the World Trade Center (which had been completed in April 1973) resonates very differently today, after their destruction in a terrorist attack in 2001. At the time though, his was an antagonistic response to the arrogance of such symbols of bloated capitalist excess that had survived at the expense of more utopian social schemes like Pruitt Igoe.

The Woman Question

In 1972, Grégoire Müller published his book *The New Avant-Garde: Issues for Art of the Seventies*. The list of artists featured in the book is long, but for a reason that will soon become apparent, is worth presenting in full: Carl Andre, Joseph Beuys, Walter De Maria, Dan Flavin, Michael Heizer, Sol LeWitt, Mario Merz, Robert Morris, Bruce Nauman, Richard Serra, Robert Smithson, and Keith Sonnier. Müller writes of a "fluid" art scene, of art that foregrounds the work's "actual physical presence . . . in time and space." For Müller, "the primary importance of what is proposed to the eye and to the senses," which had been dismissed or sidelined in minimalism and conceptualism, was being re-asserted in art of the 1970s.[33]

But Müller's claimed priority for artists of the decade that had just begun left out many. In thinking of what artists he privileged through this "totalizing" theory of 1970s art trends, one has to ask, "Why are there no women artists among those he features in the book?" Just a year earlier, the question had been put slightly differently in what remains one of the most important essays of the decade: "Why Have There Been No Great Women Artists?" In this landmark text, Linda Nochlin articulated an idea of art history – previously "the white Western male viewpoint, unconsciously accepted as *the* viewpoint of the art historian" – in line with the feminist movement that had been developing for some years in Western Europe and North America. However, the impact of this new approach to art history was not intended to be limited within an academic framework. Rather, its implications were to resonate much more broadly: Nochlin wrote of the necessity of the "so-called women question" becoming "a catalyst, an intellectual instrument, probing basic and 'natural' assumptions" and extending to other fields, to other questions.[34]

Nochlin's agenda was clearly feminist, but the very idea of the "women question" was something that required careful consideration, and was not to be seen in isolation. For Nochlin, the privileging of the white male was institutionalized and normalized to the point of being systematically accepted and overlooked. Nochlin did not seek to address this by invoking "examples of worthy or insufficiently appreciated women artists throughout history." Nor did she postulate a "subtle essence of femininity." To suggest such a thing, she argued, was to remain bound up in the "naïve idea that art is the direct, personal expression of individual emotional experience." Art is a language, a construct with its own rules and conventions, and it is here that the real problem resides: the language of art privileges the male.[35]

Like Nochlin, Lucy Lippard was keen to lay bare the discrimination that underpinned a social and institutional structure. In the early 1970s she was, however, prepared strategically to localize attentions, to limit discussion to art and women's art practice. Lippard noted that women were excluded from art world systems, but her focus on those that had "made it" was at odds with Nochlin's insistence that simply finding a space within the cultural category "art" was not enough. Lippard was also, in contrast to Nochlin, "convinced that there is a latent difference in sensibility" particular to women's art, and one that should be acknowledged and celebrated. She hesitated to define this sensibility, pausing when presented with terms like "earthiness," "organic images," "curved lines," and "a central focus," but was prepared to concede that if "art comes from the inside, as it must, then the art of men and women must be different too."[36] For Lippard, the establishment of an "essential" form of feminist art was a necessary stage toward asserting a female practice, and correcting the injustice of women's exclusion from visual culture and, by extension, the terms on which society was structured.[37]

Lippard's reference to a "central focus" characteristic of women's images was developed and elaborated in the artwork and writings of feminist artist Judy Chicago, one of the main figures, with Miriam Schapiro, leading the Los Angeles-based arm of the feminist art movement. Performing just the kind of recuperative history Nochlin repudiated, Chicago sought to recover figures from history, to rethink their work according to new terms that went beyond the dominant (male) language of formalist criticism. Georgia O'Keeffe, sidelined in formalist models, was said to be "the first great female artist because she bases her work on the experience of a female. What that brings us to is, first of all, the nature of 'cunt' as an image." As did Lippard, Chicago promoted an art of authentic self-expression, claiming that a woman artist "is intent on arriving at an art that grows out of her experience."[38] Whilst rejecting formalist terms, she nevertheless implied that art was something approaching a "pure" realm of activity, and could be seen to transcend the limitations of society.

Throughout the 1970s, Chicago worked "to forge a new kind of art expressing women's experience," culminating in 1979 with the exhibition of an installation piece, *The Dinner Party* (Figure 4.3), consisting of a triangular table with places set for 39 female guests, taken either from history or mythology (with a further 999 invitees, important women from the past, named on floor tiles).[39] Each place setting includes an individualized but abstracted portrait in the form of a decorated ceramic plate and an embroidered runner.

Much might be said about Chicago's strategy of collaborating with large groups of assistants, and about her rescuing of traditional female craft activities such as china painting and needlepoint from their conventional low position within the cultural hierarchy. Too, a great deal could be said about the debates

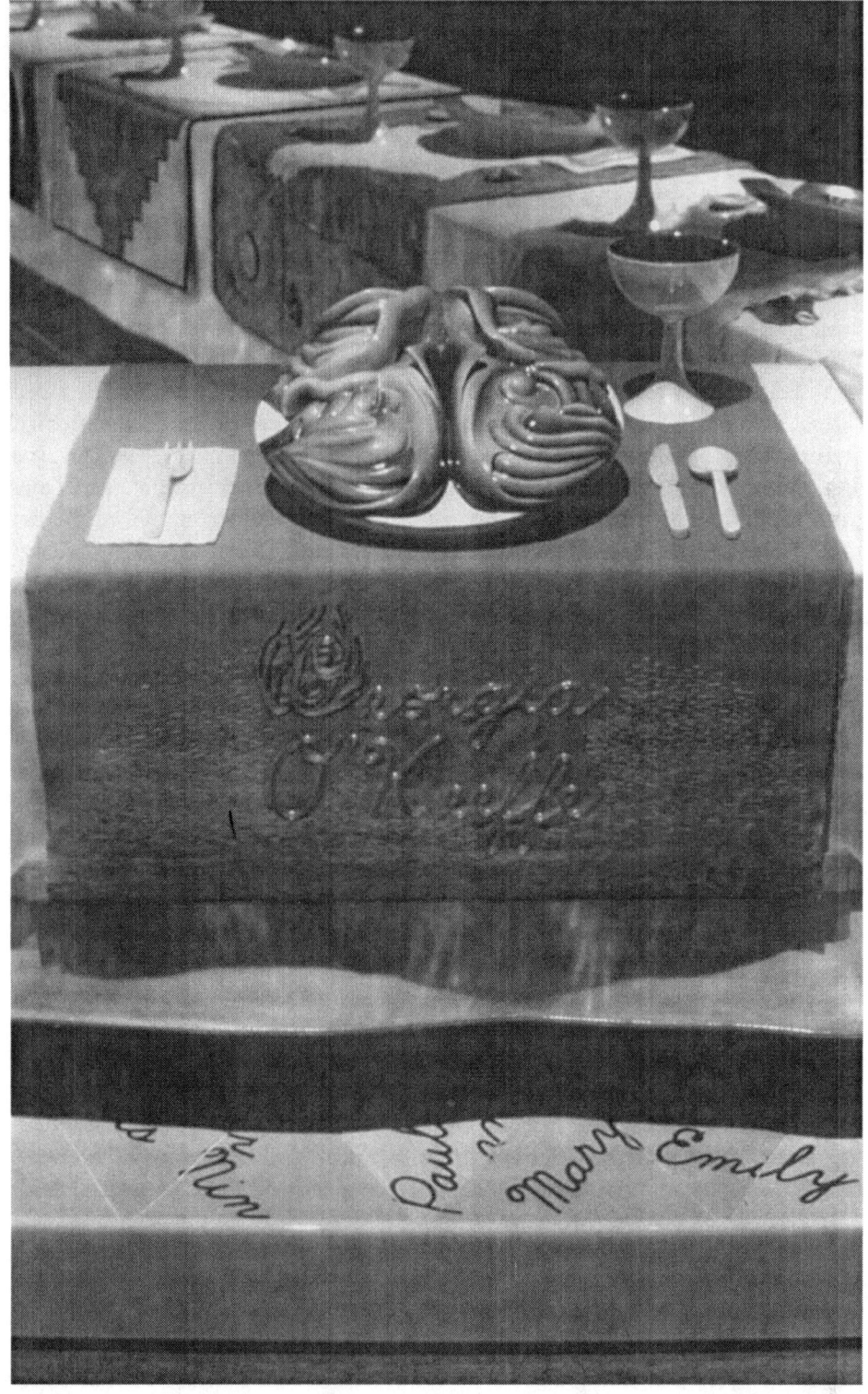

FIGURE 4.3   Judy Chicago, Georgia O'Keeffe place setting, from *The Dinner Party*, 1979. Mixed media. Collection of the Brooklyn Museum of Art, gift of The Elizabeth A. Sackler Foundation. © Judy Chicago 1979. Photograph © Donald Woodman

within and beyond feminism over the art historical importance and aesthetic as well as political success of this controversial piece. The imaging of female as an abstract essence through the sculpted, stylized, and painted renditions of female sexual organs (reclaimed "cunts") at each place setting, however, has been the most controversial aspect of the piece and is most pertinent to the discussion here.[40]

Variations on the theme of female essence can be found in the work of Ana Mendieta and Carolee Schneemann. The Cuban-born Mendieta produced work that dealt with absence and presence in a different way from Chicago. Her 1970s *Siluetas* were earthworks of sorts, but on a wholly different scale from that of either Smithson's or Christo and Jeanne Claude's work. Using natural materials, Mendieta modestly (and temporarily) marked the earth with silhouettes of her own body, or, as Lippard has written "that of Everywoman or the goddess."[41] In Schneemann's 1975 *Interior Scroll* performance, the artist undressed, painted her body, and produced a scroll from her vagina, which she proceeded to read to the audience. The female body here becomes a producer and source of truth and knowledge.[42]

Other feminist artists exploded stereotypes of female subjectivity rather than celebrating positive aspects of female experience. In Martha Rosler's 1975 video work, *Semiotics of the Kitchen*, the female body is present, but as a site of violence. Filmed in black and white with a fixed single-point camera, the video shows Rosler behind a counter demonstrating the use (or mis-use) of various kitchen utensils: for example, demonstrating a "ladle," Rosler stirs, scoops, but then tosses away the imaginary contents. Again, with the "chopper," the repeated plunging of her arm into an empty metal bowl indicates the growing sense of hardly repressed violence in the performance (even if she ends with a "tenderizer"!).

Rosler clearly refused to indulge the idea of a natural female essence, preferring instead to consider "female" as a social and political construction, and one that, because defined through patriarchal, masculine language, had to be rejected. Laura Mulvey's 1975 essay, "Visual Pleasure and Narrative Cinema," proposed that psychoanalytic theory offered the means toward an analysis of that language; that it (although being another "male" language) "can at least advance our understanding of the status quo, of the patriarchal order in which we are caught." Reference to Freudian and Lacanian models revealed that in the "patriarchal unconscious" woman symbolizes castration and nothing else, and thus functions "as bearer of meaning, not maker of meaning."[43]

Mulvey's attention was directed particularly toward the language of cinema, and between 1977 and 1980, the American artist Cindy Sherman also took film conventions as the subject of a series of 69 *Untitled (Film Stills)*. Like Rosler, Sherman eschewed the notion of a natural essence of womanhood; in this series of pseudo-filmic representations Sherman plays out an idea of femininity as masquerade, adopting poses that imply filmic narratives and societal expectations of the female character.

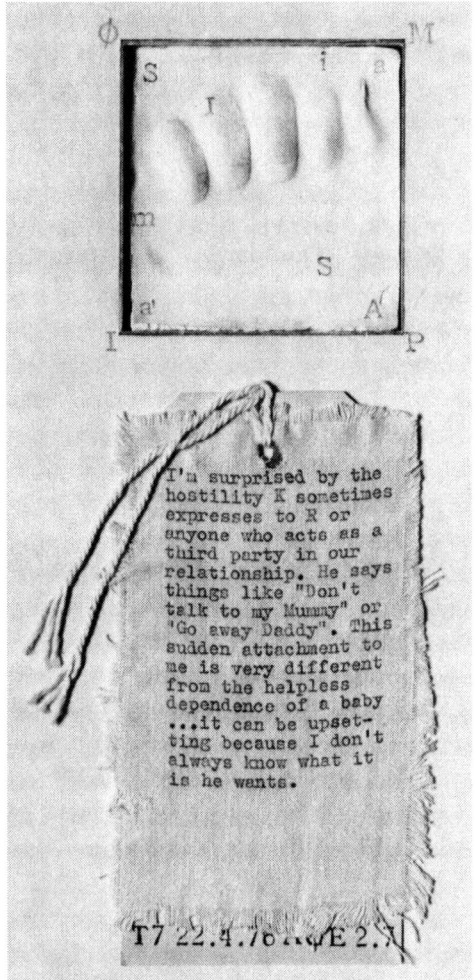

FIGURE 4.4 Mary Kelly, *Post-Partum Document*, 1973–9. Documentation IV, transitional Objects, Diary, and Diagram, 1976. Detail, one of eight units. Plaster, cotton. 11 × 14 in. Collection: Zurich Museum, Switzerland. Photograph © Ray Barrie. Courtesy of the artist

Another American, Mary Kelly, shared this "anti-essentialist" position. Kelly describes her six-part installation *Post-Partum Document* (Figure 4.4) – which documents her own relationship with her male child between 1973 and 1979 through "the juxtaposition of found objects and commentary with a series of diagrams" – as having been "conceived as an on-going process of analysis and visualisation of the mother-child relationship." Drawing extensively on psychoanalytic theory like Mulvey, Kelly explores with this work "the possibility of female fetishism" and attempts "to articulate the mother's fantasies, her desire, her stake in that project called 'motherhood,'" seeking to foreground motherhood's "social construction as a representation of sexual difference within specific discourses."[44]

The Personal and the Political

Kelly's work exemplifies the way in which the political framework for art was foregrounded in art and art theory from the 1970s. As Lippard noted: "the feminist insistence that the personal is political has, like a serious flood, interrupted the mainstream's flow, sending it off into hundreds of tributaries."[45] But, as Nochlin warned, there is a danger in disassociating the "woman question" from a broader field of historical inquiry. The feminist claim that "the personal is political" runs the risk of reducing those issues to the level of the individual struggle. In 1980, Martha Rosler posed the question, "Well, *is* the personal political?" To which she replied herself that only with a "consciousness of a larger, collective struggle" in relation to personal life, and the recognition of the two being both "dialectically opposed and unitary," could the answer be positive. If the focus is limited to "the privatised tinkering with one's solely private life, divorced from any collective effort or public act, and simply goes on to name this personal concentration as political," then the answer would have to be "no."[46] Ultimately, control or influence over the direction of society as a whole had to be the aim.

Such a principle was central to the feminism advocated by Nochlin, but it was not confined to those engaging issues of gender. The German artist, Joseph Beuys, had his own version of the relationship between the individual and society, between the personal and the political. Beuys believed that art – "only art" in fact – was "capable of dismantling the repressive effects of a senile social system," promoting "free individual productive potency" toward a concept of "direct democracy."[47] Beuys's performance works maintained a social relevance, whilst employing a highly personalized and symbolic ritual content.

While Beuys's ideals point back toward the early twentieth-century avant-gardes' interest in inviting participation from the audience, his refusal to trust in fixed ideologies signals a different, more suspicious attitude in the 1970s toward the viability of such ideologies. Still, in locating authentic meaning only within the individual yet maintaining a critical stance toward power, artists such as Beuys ran the risk of promoting the reactionary individualism of the 1980s and 1990s. As British critic Richard Cork argued in 1980: "Subjectivity, when abused, can deteriorate rapidly into a species of self-indulgence which is invariably indistinguishable from narcissism." Cork noted that in shows such as the 1975 Paris Biennale, which housed contributions by over 120 young artists from 19 nations, "subjectivity looked as if it had been reduced to a mere travesty of its rightful function: a subtle and questioning investigation by the self, but not necessarily of the self."[48]

An Expanded Field

Art practice in the 1970s comes in various forms – photography, film, performance, installation, and book – each with its own implications for redefining function, production, and reception and for reaching new audiences in new ways. Rosalind Krauss famously wrote of "sculpture in the expanded field" in the 1970s. For Krauss, secure categories of practice such as "sculpture" were either lost altogether, or were forced "to become almost infinitely malleable."[49]

What was certainly necessary was an acceptance that these new forms would find no easy place within the institutional structures as they existed, and an acknowledgment that this was more often than not deliberate on the part of artists. Lippard, writing in the early 1970s, had maintained the idea that art was a legitimate cultural category; in spite of the fact that many (all but white males) had been excluded from it, once access had been gained the category would hold. Others, including Nochlin, were unconvinced; for her, local reform would not suffice. Artists such as Smithson, Christo and Jeanne Claude, and Matta-Clark sought alternatives to the gallery context. For others, the idea of "alternative" spaces meant something other than seeking out sites as remote as Smithson's Great Salt Lake.

For American feminists, the anti-hierarchic alternative exhibition space was particularly important and, for all that has been said here about the individual, these spaces were often organized by anonymous groups and collectives. An offshoot from the Art Workers' Coalition, WAR (Women Artists in Revolution) was one such group.[50] Others included WSABAL (Women, Students and Artists for Black Art Liberation), WIA (Women in the Arts), WCA (Women's Caucus for Art), and AIR (Artists In Residence). Such groups, and the spaces that they reclaimed for exhibitions and events (most commonly redundant buildings), provided essential networks for artists who found themselves either excluded from the mainstream museums and galleries, or who had little interest in entering them on the terms they offered.

Britain too had its groups and exhibitions and increased funding from the Arts Council of Great Britain freed artists from absolute dependence on commercial galleries.[51] The Art Net Gallery in London acted as a point of contact for European and North American artists. In 1977, an exhibition, *Radical Attitudes to the Gallery*, was staged there. For this exhibition, Mary Kelly, clearly aware of the limits of the idea of the "personal as political," wrote, "[a] political commitment is primarily a collective social practice as opposed to an individual attitude," while Martha Rosler warned of independent organizations' potential for assimilation: "Those artist-run ['alternative spaces'] tend to espouse anarchism, while resting on state support, and to proclaim freedom from commodification while serving as testing-grounds for dealers."[52] And again, as with the issue of the 1970s individual in relation to 1980s individualism, it is interesting to note the transformation of the spaces of former alternative galleries into upmarket galleries in 1980s–90s New York and London. What independent spaces remain act above all as the very "testing-ground" for dealers that Rosler warned of.

Dan Graham's work – which made use of video, performance, architecture, and text – sums up many of the aspects of 1970s I have explored here, testing the limits of the alternative space, and examining the tension between the individual and the collective, the personal and the political, by drawing from Lacanian psychoanalysis.[53] In particular, Graham's use of mirrors and other reflective surfaces refers to Lacan's "mirror stage," a complex model for explaining the conflicted formation of the self in infancy through reflected image as a split or alienated subject, who learns to identify her/himself always *as* a reflection and/or in relation to others.[54] Responding to this, for Graham, mirrors act as "metaphors for the Western concept of the 'self.'"[55]

Expanding on this model, a recurring theme in Graham's work is the negotiation of one's individuality, but a relocation of that individuality in relation to a collective (in relation to others). Participation in his work – and thus in the social interaction with others – is an obligation; at the very least, the spectator is forced to be aware of him/herself as a participant in the work, in relation to other spectators. In Graham's structural and performance works, unstable circuits of objective and subjective experience are presented to the audience members, who are constructed as both viewers and viewed.

Take Graham's *Performer/Audience/Mirror* of 1977 (Figure 4.5). The "performer" (Graham himself) faces an audience with a mirror covering the wall behind him. In a four-stage work, he begins by describing his movements and "the attitudes he believes are signified by this behaviour."[56] He then describes the audience's external behavior. Then, he turns his back to the audience to face the mirror and returns to a description of himself and his actions. Audience members can see him and themselves in the same mirror-view that he has. Finally, he again describes the audience, but still with his back to them, thus relying on the reflected image. Graham noted: "Through the use of a mirror the audience is able to instantaneously perceive itself as a public body (as a unity), offsetting its definition by the performer. This gives it a power within the performance equivalent to that of the performer."[57]

Returning to the themes introduced at the beginning of this chapter, Graham's work indicates the appeal of a low-tech Brechtian model of avant-garde experimentalism structured according to the terms of social engagement. An understanding of the "whole" (to which Lukács aspired) is here located according to Lacanian thought: the "whole" consists of reflections, of fragments. With the project of totalizing shown thus to be ultimately impossible, the artist-as-individual became an active purveyor of personal experience transformed into collective significance, and the artist's corollary, the viewer/interpreter, was shown to be an active participant in an art work (image, object, performance, text, film, etc.) understood to be open and contingent, rather than constitutive. We find Graham "sliding around," describing his every self-conscious gesture and those of his audience. Here is the avant-garde of the 1970s fumbling for a next move

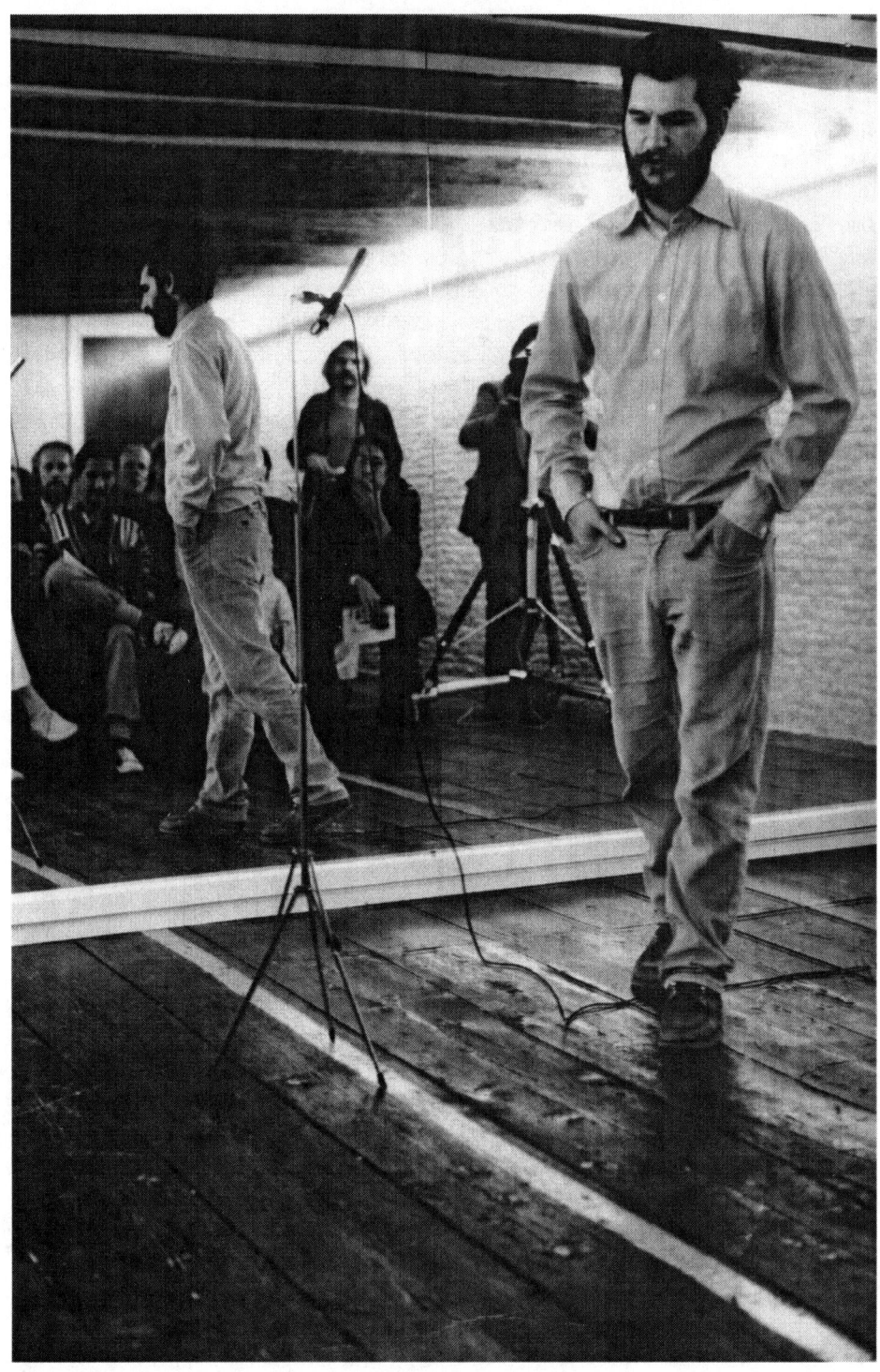

FIGURE 4.5   Dan Graham, *Performer/Audience/Mirror*, 1977. Courtesy of the artist and Marian Goodman Gallery, New York

as previously held assumptions of meaning fragment and collapse all around (and through) the work.

Notes

1 Graham (1977), 125.
2 Krauss (1976), 196.
3 Townshend (2002), 68.
4 The "Anarchitecture" group was formed in 1973 by Gordon Matta-Clark, Suzanne Harris, and Tina Girouard. See Lee (2000), 104.
5 Jencks (1977), 9.
6 Jencks (1992a), 23.
7 Jameson (1977), 977.
8 Ibid.
9 Ibid., 978.
10 Ibid.
11 Golub (1981), 243.
12 Ibid.
13 Lukács (1932), 399.
14 Ibid., 398.
15 Bürger writes: "The concept of the historical avant-garde movements used here applies primarily to Dadaism and early Surrealism but also and equally to the Russian avant-garde after the October revolution." Bürger (1984), 109, n.4. By "neo-avant-garde" Bürger is referring to work made in Western Europe and the United States during the fifties and sixties.
16 Bürger (1984), 57.
17 Marinetti (1909), 147.
18 Rodchenko (1920–1), 315.
19 The AWC was a group of American artists and critical commentators that included Carl Andre, Robert Morris, and Lucy Lippard. It can be seen to reflect the mid-1960s to the mid-1970s tendency of artists and their supporters to organize themselves in collective groups based on political beliefs.
20 Art Workers' Coalition (1970), 901–2.
21 Bürger (1984), 90.
22 Haacke (1974), 905.
23 Haacke quotes from Brecht directly in ibid.
24 See Bürger (1984), 88.
25 The exhibition at the Musée d'Art Moderne featured the work of four artists. Buren, who took stripes as his image; Olivier Mosset, who presented a black circle on white as his image; Michel Parmentier, who presented grey and white horizontal bands; and Niele Toroni, who made square blue marks with a flat brush on a white ground.
26 Buren (1969–70), 147.
27 Lippard (1973), 895.
28 Ibid.
29 Smithson (1972a), 947.
30 Smithson (1972b), 532.

31 Indeed, Smithson himself thinks of Pollock in responding to the intensity of the site and being "enveloped in a flaming chromosphere": ibid., 533.
32 Matta-Clark (1973), quoted in Lee (2000), 107.
33 Müller (1972), 8.
34 Nochlin (1971), 146.
35 Ibid., 147–9.
36 Lippard (1971), 50–3.
37 Indeed, Lippard herself would revise this position by 1980, arguing that any temptation to "pin down a specific formal contribution" of women's art was "useless." Lippard (1995a), 172.
38 Chicago (1972), 294.
39 Chicago (1979), 360.
40 See Jones (1996).
41 Lippard (1973), 56.
42 See Schneemann (1975), 718.
43 Mulvey (1975), 964–5.
44 Kelly (1982), 858–61. The work was published as a book in 1983.
45 Lippard (1995a), 172.
46 Rosler (1980), 95–6.
47 Beuys (1974), 903.
48 Cork (1980), 15.
49 Krauss (1978), 277 and 290.
50 WAR sponsored the first all-women's exhibition in New York in 1970, *X to the 12th Power*, at Museum, an alternative space that had been the venue for another exhibition the same year, *Artists' Strike Against Racism, Sexism, Repression and War*.
51 For example, the 1979 *Art For Whom?* exhibition at the Serpentine Gallery, London, organized by artists Conrad Atkinson and Stephen Willats and the critic Richard Cork, maintained some of the issues that concerned the AWC in the US.
52 Kelly (1977) and Rosler (1977), 40 and 46. Kelly's commitment to a collective social practice is first apparent in her joining the Berwick Street Film Collective in London in the early 1970s. An example of the collective's work is *Night Cleaners*, a film documenting the conditions of low-waged women office workers and their struggle to unionize themselves.
53 Graham argued that "through performance discussion, social groups could effect social change through personal change"; Graham (1979), 143.
54 See Krauss (1976), 197.
55 Graham (1979), 55. He goes on to describe Lacan's mirror stage in detail.
56 Graham (1977), 124.
57 Ibid., 125.

References

Alberro, Alexander, ed. (1999). *Two-Way Mirror Power: Selected Writings by Dan Graham on his Art*. Cambridge, MA: MIT Press.

Art Workers' Coalition (1970). "Statement of Demands." In *Art in Theory 1900–1990: An Anthology of Changing Ideas*, ed. Charles Harrison and Paul Wood. Oxford: Blackwell. 901–2.

Beuys, Joseph (1974). "I am Searching for Field Character." In *Art in Theory 1900–1990: An Anthology of Changing Ideas*, ed. Charles Harrison and Paul Wood. Oxford: Blackwell. 902–4.

Buren, Daniel (1969–70). "Beware!" In *Theories and Documents of Contemporary Art: A Sourcebook of Artists' Writings*, ed. Kristine Stiles and Peter Selz. Berkeley and London: University of California Press. 140–9.

Bürger, Peter (1984). *Theory of the Avant-Garde*. Minneapolis: University of Minnesota Press.

Chicago, Judy (1972). "Woman as Artist," In *Feminism-Art-Theory: An Anthology 1968–2000*, ed. Hilary Robinson. Oxford: Blackwell. 294–5.

—— (1979). "The Dinner Party: A Symbol of Our Heritage." In *Theories and Documents of Contemporary Art: A Sourcebook of Artists' Writings*, ed. Kristine Stiles and Peter Selz. Berkeley and London: University of California Press. 360.

Cork, Richard (1980). "Collaboration Without Compromise" *Studio International*, vol. 195, no. 990:4–19.

Golub, Leon (1981). "The Mercenaries: Interview with Matthew Baigell." In *Theories and Documents of Contemporary Art: A Sourcebook of Artists' Writings*, ed. Kristine Stiles and Peter Selz. Berkeley and London: University of California Press. 241–4.

Graham, Dan (1977). "Performer/Audience/Mirror." In *Two-Way Mirror Power: Selected Writings by Dan Graham on his Art*, ed. Alexander Alberro. Cambridge, MA: MIT Press. 124–35.

—— (1979). "Essay on Video, Architecture, and Television." In *Two-Way Mirror Power: Selected Writings by Dan Graham on his Art*, ed. Alexander Alberro. Cambridge, MA: MIT Press. 52–61.

Haacke, Hans (1974). "Statement." In *Art in Theory 1900–1990: An Anthology of Changing Ideas*, ed. Charles Harrison and Paul Wood. Oxford: Blackwell. 904–5.

Harrison, Charles, and Paul Wood, eds. (1992). *Art in Theory 1900–1990: An Anthology of Changing Ideas*. Oxford: Blackwell.

Jameson, Fredric (1977). "Reflections on the Brecht-Lukács Debate." In *Art in Theory 1900–1990: An Anthology of Changing Ideas*, ed. Charles Harrison and Paul Wood. Oxford: Blackwell. 976–9.

Jencks, Charles (1977). *The Language of Post-Modern Architecture*. London: Academy.

—— (1992a). "The Post-Modern Agenda." In *The Postmodern Reader*, ed. Charles Jencks. London: Academy. 10–39.

——, ed. (1992b). *The Postmodern Reader*. London: Academy.

Jones, Amelia, ed. (1996). *Sexual Politics: Judy Chicago's* Dinner Party *in Feminist Art History*. Berkeley: University of California Press.

Kelly, Mary (1977). "Statement." *Studio International*, vol. 195, no. 990, 1980:40.

—— (1982). "Preface to *Post-Partum Document*." In *Theories and Documents of Contemporary Art: A Sourcebook of Artists' Writings*, ed. Kristine Stiles and Peter Selz. Berkeley and London: University of California Press. 858–61.

Krauss, Rosalind E. (1976). "Notes on the Index Part 1." In *The Originality of the Avant-Garde and Other Modernist Myths*. Cambridge, MA: MIT Press, 1985. 196–209.

—— (1978). "Sculpture in the Expanded Field." In *The Originality of the Avant-Garde and Other Modernist Myths*. Cambridge, MA: MIT Press, 1985. 277–90.

Lee, Pamela M. (2000). *Object to be Destroyed: The Work of Gordon Matta-Clark*. Cambridge, MA: MIT Press.

Lippard, Lucy (1971). "Twenty-Six Contemporary Women Artists." In *The Pink Glass Swan: Selected Feminist Essays on Art*. New York: The New Press. 50–3.

—— (1973). "Postface" to *Six Years: The Dematerialization of the Art Object*. In *Art in Theory 1900–1990: An Anthology of Changing Ideas*, ed. Charles Harrison and Paul Wood. Oxford: Blackwell. 895–6.

—— (1995a). "Sweeping Exchanges: The Contribution of Feminism to the Art of the 1970s." In *The Pink Glass Swan: Selected Feminist Essays on Art*. New York: The New Press. 171–82.

—— (1995b). *The Pink Glass Swan: Selected Feminist Essays on Art*. New York: The New Press.

Lukács, Georg (1932). "'Tendency' or Partisanship?" In *Art in Theory 1900–1990: An Anthology of Changing Ideas*, ed. Charles Harrison and Paul Wood. Oxford: Blackwell. 395–400.

Marinetti, Filippo Tommaso (1909). "The Foundation and Manifesto of Futurism." In *Art in Theory 1900–1990: An Anthology of Changing Ideas*, ed. Charles Harrison and Paul Wood. Oxford: Blackwell. 145–52.

Müller, Grégoire (1972). *The New Avant-Garde: Issues for Art of the Seventies*. London: Pall Mall Press.

Mulvey, Laura (1975). "Visual Pleasure and Narrative Cinema." In *Art in Theory 1900–1990: An Anthology of Changing Ideas*, ed. Charles Harrison and Paul Wood. Oxford: Blackwell. 963–70.

Nochlin, Linda (1971). "Why Have There Been No Great Women Artists?" In *Women, Art, and Power and Other Essays*. London: Thames and Hudson, 1988. 145–78.

—— (1988). *Women, Art, and Power and Other Essays*. London: Thames and Hudson.

Robinson, Hilary, ed. (2001). *Feminism-Art-Theory: An Anthology 1968–2000*. Oxford: Blackwell.

Rodchenko, Alexander (1920–1). "Slogans." In *Art in Theory 1900–1990: An Anthology of Changing Ideas*, ed. Charles Harrison and Paul Wood. Oxford: Blackwell. 315–16.

Rosler, Martha (1977). "Statement." *Studio International*, vol. 195, no. 990, 1980:46.

—— (1980). "Well, *is* the Personal Political?" In *Feminism-Art-Theory: An Anthology 1968–2000*, ed. Hilary Robinson. Oxford: Blackwell. 95–6.

Schneemann, Carolee (1975). "Woman in the Year 2000." In *Theories and Documents of Contemporary Art: A Sourcebook of Artists' Writings*, ed. Kristine Stiles and Peter Selz. Berkeley and London: University of California Press. 717–18.

Smithson, Robert (1972a). "Cultural Confinement." In *Art in Theory 1900–1990: An Anthology of Changing Ideas*, ed. Charles Harrison and Paul Wood. Oxford: Blackwell. 946–8.

—— (1972b). "The Spiral Jetty." In *Theories and Documents of Contemporary Art: A Sourcebook of Artists' Writings*, ed. Kristine Stiles and Peter Selz. Berkeley and London: University of California Press. 530–3.

Stiles, Kristine, and Peter Selz (1996). *Theories and Documents of Contemporary Art: A Sourcebook of Artists' Writings*. Berkeley and London: University of California Press.

Townshend, Charles (2002). *Terrorism: A Very Short Introduction*. Oxford: Oxford University Press.

5

Pictures and Positions in the 1980s

Howard Singerman

According to theorist Sylvère Lotringer, what we think of as "the 1980s began in 1983, with the publication of John Baudrillard's *Simulations*." *Simulations* is his starting point not just because his journal, *Semiotext(e)*, was its publisher,[1] but also because such trademark Baudrillardian phrases as "the 'precession of the simulacra' and 'the desert of the real' perfectly described the new landscape: The mirage preceded the image."[2] Baudrillard's writing seemed to map the postindustrial west – or the lived experience of its urban intellectuals – across an increasingly digitized landscape, one marked not by the centrality of power figured in Foucault's panoptical eye, but by spread, the newly felt effects of networks and webs. America's actor-president stood as the perfect Baudrillardian figure: Reagan was the triumph of the virtual, but there were other triumphs as well. On Wall Street in 1983, over a third of all corporate bond issues were so-called "junk bonds," and just uptown in Soho the reputations of artists and dealers seemed equally inflated, running on pure hype and sheer circularity: Mary Boone graced the pages of *Esquire, Life,* and *People*; Julian Schnabel, those of *Forbes*: "I think Mary is famous because I'm famous and I'm famous because Leo [Castelli] is famous."[3] In this context, in particular, Baudrillard offered a useful theoretical tool; he and Schnabel spoke the same language: "It is no longer necessary that anyone produce an opinion, all that is needed is that all reproduce public opinion, in the sense that all opinions get caught up in this kind of general equivalent. . . . For opinions as for material goods: production is dead, long live reproduction."[4]

Lotringer's origin story situates the 1980s in English (albeit, and tellingly, in translation) and in New York; this chapter shares that geographical bias. While significant scenes and practices coalesced in Germany and Italy at the beginning of the decade, and in Los Angeles and London at its close, New York was the art world's imperial capital in the decade: those other sites were validated in its art magazines, shown in its galleries, and sold in its auction houses. Lotringer's story also recognizes the faddishness of theory in the 1980s art world, its value not only as a way to describe or understand, but, and continuous with that, as a way to sell. As Thomas Crow wrote near the end of the decade: "This vocabulary, which is largely French in origin, has become part of the everyday, informal processes by which artists explain their work to others and to themselves; it is part of the dealer's helpful explanations and the collector's proud account of his acquisitions."[5] For the moment the theorist was an art world celebrity: between 1983 and 1987, *Flash Art* published interviews with Baudrillard (which appeared alongside an extensive interview with Schnabel), Felix Guattari, Han-Georg Gadamer, Frederic Jameson, Julia Kristeva, Jean-François Lyotard, Louis Marin, Peter Sloterdijk, Phillippe Sollers, and Cornel West. Baudrillard's own writing spoke to the conflation of culture and the commodity, to that "stage where the commodity is immediately produced as a sign, as sign value, and where signs (culture) are produced as commodities,"[6] but what he, in particular, was seen to be proffering was not so much a critique of an increasingly networked and capitalized art world, but the terms with which to embrace the collapse of the historical project of the avant-garde.

If the 1980s began in 1983, at least one version of the decade might have been over by 1987. Baudrillard appeared to a packed house at the Whitney as a "distinguished lecturer" on American art in March of that year; in response, the artists' collective Group Material organized an exhibition at White Columns entitled *Resistance (Anti-Baudrillard)*, accusing the theorist – at least as he had been read in the art world – of "disarming the idea of culture as a site of contestation/resistance."[7] *Semiotext(e)* published a translation of a ten-year old essay of his entitled "Forget Foucault" that year, as well, but they packaged it with an interview between Baudrillard and Lotringer that the latter named "Forget Baudrillard."[8] Nineteen eighty-seven ended other things as well: the junk bond bubble that began to inflate in earnest in 1983 burst on October 19, in the greatest single-day loss Wall Street had ever suffered. The month before the "Black Monday" crash, *Art in America*'s "Artworld" column covered an "exodus" from the East Village and offered a list of galleries closing in Soho as well. The stock market would bounce back, regaining all the ground it had lost by September 1989, and the auction prices for art continued to climb even during the two-year dip, as money pulled from the stock market came into the secondary market for art: some of those nomadic East Village galleries were in search of larger spaces in Soho. Still, and against that rather unreal backdrop, the year was marked by a closing down, by mourning and by what Hal Foster later described as "the return of the real" – a particularly cruel and Lacanian real, one marked by missed encounters and ruined, repeated representations. "This shift in conception – from reality as an effect of representation to the real as a thing of trauma – may be definitive in contemporary art."[9]

In 1987, that shift was not yet primarily a theoretical one: it seemed quite present and palpable. The sense of trauma was intimately linked to the emergence of AIDS, Acquired Immune Deficiency Syndrome, first diagnosed in New York and San Francisco in 1981, and named by the Centers for Disease Control in 1982. According to the scrolling LED timeline that the artists' group Gran Fury installed in the window of the New Museum in November 1987 as part of its installation *Let the Record Show*, "by Thanksgiving 1982, 1,123 known dead . . . AIDS . . . no word from the President." By Thanksgiving 1987, the count continued, "25,644 dead."[10] The installation attacked mainstream discourse and political demagoguery on AIDS and gay sexuality, and even more, the US administration's refusal to recognize the epidemic, its insistence on ghettoizing the disease and its supposed targets, its reliance on their shame or silence: the work's capstone was a large neon sign, beneath a pink triangle was the equation Silence=Death. Nineteen Eighty-Seven saw that silence broken in a number of more or less effective ways in the gay community, from the Gran Fury installation to the formation of Act-Up, the AIDS Coalition to Unleash Power, which held its first action in March of that year against pharmaceutical companies on Wall Street, to the initial unfurling of the Names Project Memorial Quilt in October at the National March on Washington for Gay and Lesbian Rights (Figure 5.1).

Foster argued for the "shift in conception" from representation to trauma in a 1996 essay on Andy Warhol, but his argument for Warhol's "traumatic realism" would have been very unfamiliar a decade earlier. Warhol in the 1980s was the model media artist; his work trafficked in images without referents and "reproducing public opinion," to return to Baudrillard's words, was at the center of his project. As the painter Peter Halley said at the time, "Reading Baudrillard is the equivalent for me of looking at a painting by Andy Warhol." "Ah, Warhol!" responded Baudrillard to his *Flash Art* interviewer, "For me he meant a great deal as well."[11] It is only coincidence that Warhol died in February 1987, but one could take his death, or the revision it provoked, as another marker of the end. His work would be significantly rewritten afterwards, and not only by Foster; beginning that May with Thomas Crow's "Saturday Disasters: Trace and Reference in Early Warhol," it would return to the real, figuring death and trauma, on the one hand, and identity and sexuality on the other.

Pictures

From 1983 to 1987 is a very short decade, and one could construct it in other ways. The ground for Baudrillard, after all, had been well prepared beginning in the late 1970s, and the "substituting of signs of the real for the real itself"[12] was already a familiar effect in 1983. As early as 1977, the young art historian Douglas Crimp had made it the subject of *Pictures*, an exhibition he curated at Artists Space. Indeed, ten years later in his review of *Resistance (Anti-Baudrillard)*, artist Ronald Jones linked Baudrillard's arrival directly to Crimp's show: "The

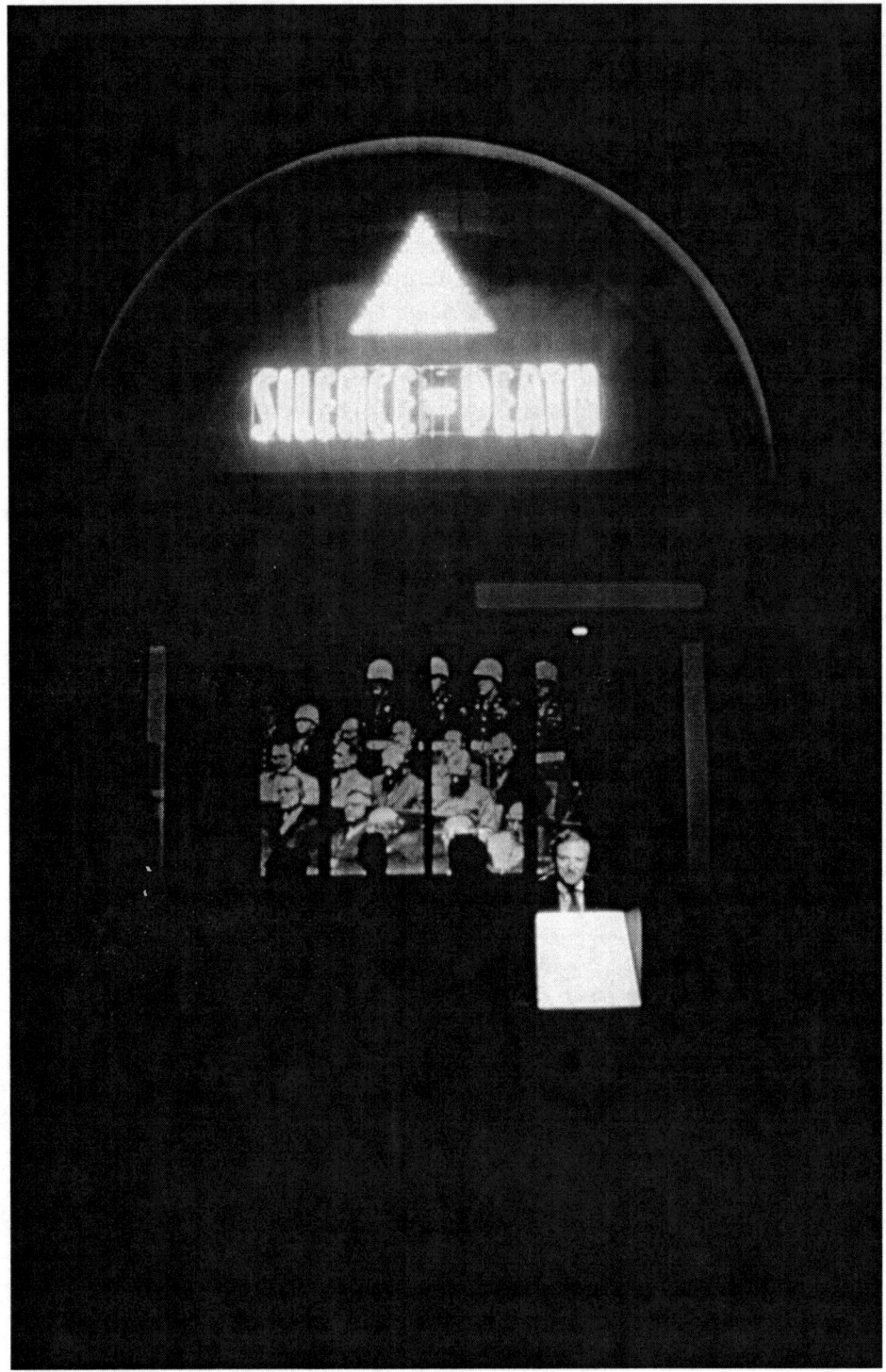

FIGURE 5.1   ACT-UP (Gran Fury), *Let the Record Show* . . . . Installation at the New Museum of Contemporary Art, New York, November–December 1987. Image courtesy of the New Museum of Contemporary Art

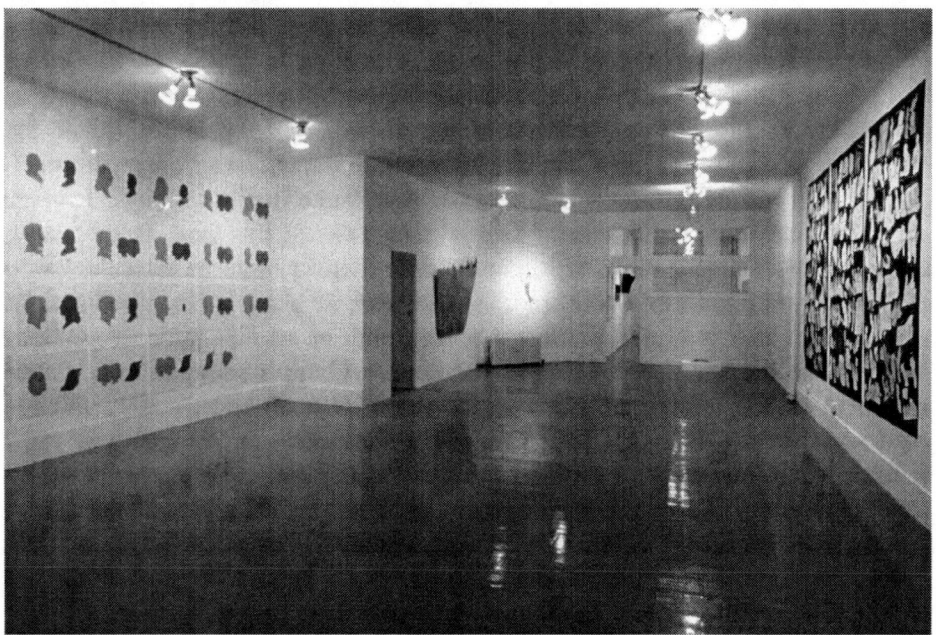

FIGURE 5.2　*Pictures* exhibition. Installation view at Artists Space, New York, September 24 to October 29, 1977, with works by (l–r) Sherrie Levine, Robert Longo, and Philip Smith. Image courtesy of Artists Space

timing was such that Baudrillard's essays inflated just after the Pictures exhibition in 1977 and began to fill an existing theoretical abyss"[13] (Figure 5.2). How large that theoretical gap was isn't clear; Crimp's catalogue essay cited texts by Walter Benjamin, Jacques Lacan, Ferdinand de Saussure, and others that would become quite familiar across the 1980s. But Jones is right that Crimp's argument pointed toward the space Baudrillard would come to fill: "While it once seemed that pictures had the function of interpreting reality, it now seems that they have usurped it," Crimp wrote; in response, a group of younger artists has returned to representation "not in the familiar guise of realism, which seeks to resemble a prior existence, but as an autonomous function that might be described as 'representation as such'."[14] By 1977, the language that would mark the 1980s was already falling into place, as were some of the artists and critics whose trajectories would limn the decade: Crimp would be an editor of the journal *October* across the decade and an early member of Act-Up; Helene Winer, the director of Artists Space, would found the Metro Pictures, one of the decade's two most important galleries internationally, in 1980; and three of the five artists Crimp included – Jack Goldstein, Sherrie Levine, and Robert Longo – would wind up showing at Metro and becoming the art world equivalent of household names.

I would like to take 1977 as an opening for the 1980s, but it is a genesis with a stutter: Crimp's "Pictures" is a familiar place to start, but the version that is by far the best known appeared not in the catalogue in 1977, but in *October* in 1979, and it is significantly different from the initial essay. One can situate in that difference the first construction of the discourse of the 1980s. While the earlier essay contains a now familiar theoretical frame, its closing paragraph invokes not postmodernism – the name of that frame in the art world – but a particular version of modernism: "The primary issue in this work is, of course, the structure of signification, with that distance that separates us from the world and that constitutes our desire. In this, the work of these artists maintains an allegiance to that radical aspiration that we continue to recognize as modernist."[15] While the issue would remain the same – Crimp's summation is a clear statement of the interest of much art of the 1980s: distance, desire, and the psychoanalytic and linguistic structures of signification – by the spring of 1979 in what is now the essay's canonical form, he would recognize the work somewhat differently. While acknowledging that it might still be addressed as a "modernism conceived differently," Crimp argues for its postmodernism: it is "useful to consider recent work as having effected a break with modernism and therefore as postmodernist. But if *postmodernism* is to have theoretical value, it cannot be used merely as another chronological term; rather it must disclose the particular nature of a breach with modernism."[16]

Much of the second version of "Pictures" is devoted to constructing that break. The terms in which Crimp outlined the concerns of recent art, and with which he theorized its postmodernism, were drawn in specific opposition to the modernism Michael Fried adumbrated in his 1967 essay "Art and Objecthood." The tenets of Friedian modernism were aesthetic autonomy, medium specificity, and what he called "presentness," the sense that, as Crimp quotes Fried, "at every moment, the work is wholly manifest." Against the modernist work that strove to both encapsulate a synoptic historical present and culminate the medium's past, Crimp championed work that was, to use a phrase with which Fried had dismissed minimal art, marked by a "preoccupation with time." But while minimalism's time was situational and experiential, the work in "Pictures" pointed to a different, and more specifically representational sense of time, a "psychologized temporality" embedded in the language of narrative: "foreboding, premonition, suspicion, anxiety." In the place of presentness, finally, Crimp offers the absence that is a corollary to both representation and narrative expectation: "Needless to say, we are not in search of sources and origins, but structures of signification: underneath each picture is always another picture."[17]

Crimp's invocation of postmodernism is not his last word in "Pictures"; the essay was rewritten not only against Fried's late-sixties modernism, but against other readings of the return of representation in its own moment. The *October* essay's combative closing paragraphs single out the Whitney's 1978 exhibition *New Image Painting* and, one could say, work to separate "pictures" from "new images," around the issue of painting. The Whitney's show was just one of a number of attempts to address the avalanche of new representational work, mostly deliberately schematic or cartoonish painting, that broke in the late seventies: between 1977 and 1980, curators and critics hazarded not only *Pictures* and *New Image Painting*, but *Abstract Images, Primary Images, Visionary Images, Bad Painting, Emblematic Figuration*, and more. The sudden return of representational imagery was taken by most writers as Crimp had taken it, as evidence of a break with modernism, but most often that "postmodernism" was figured as pluralism, either as the end of modernism as a style or – and this is always only implicit – as the end of modernism as a critical historical project. Marcia Tucker set the bargain this way in her 1978 catalogue for *Bad Painting*: "the freedom with which these artists mix classical and popular art-historical sources, *kitsch* and traditional images, archetypal and personal fantasies, constitutes a rejection of the concept of progress per se."[18] Along with the deliberate personalism and idiosyncrasy of the images, the sense of being after history would be one of the hallmarks of the new painting, and of the sort of postmodernism that Crimp ended "Pictures" arguing against.

Place

Crimp's final move in the *October* version of "Pictures" was to link painting as a moribund medium to the institution of the museum. The questions raised by a critical postmodernism must necessarily be asked elsewhere, he wrote, in places like Artists Space: "So if we now have to look for aesthetic activities in so-called alternative spaces, outside the museum, that is because those activities, those *pictures*, pose questions that are postmodernist."[19] By the time Crimp wrote those words, however, alternative spaces themselves were well on their way to being institutionalized. When they began at the very end of the 1960s and in the early 1970s, such spaces were often the direct outcome of an increasingly politicized awareness on the part of artists of the situation of art and of the boundaries of the museum-gallery system. In the US, they were founded with widely varying levels of innocence or savvy to address a number of art world ills, and the demands of a number of new constituencies: they spoke to the increasing size and geographical spread of the art world nationwide and the overproduction of artists in new and often far-flung MFA programs; and supported not only new forms such as installation, video, performance, or artists' books, but also new artists, artists whose gender or color or sexuality had rendered them invisible in mainstream arts institutions.[20]

Nineteen seventy-seven may well have marked the apex of the alternative space movement, and feature articles in the mainstream art press – *Artnews* and *Art in America* – announced the "rise of the alternative space."[21] Money flowed into and through such spaces not only from the National Endowment for the Arts – the NEA had funded non-profit artist-run galleries since 1972 under the heading "workshops," and updated the name in 1976 to "workshops/alternative spaces" – but also, by the last years of the 1970s, through the newly reformulated programs of the Comprehensive Employment and Training Act, which under the Carter administration became the largest federal arts program in history. CETA's training programs and residencies were often administered through alternative spaces, which were increasingly reshaped by the bureaucratic work necessary to secure ever-larger grants and administer government programs.

The Reagan administration slashed CETA funding in its first budget in 1980, and ended the program in 1982; it reduced crucial aspects of the NEA's budget as well, singling out funding for alternative spaces. In 1977 the head of the NEA's Visual Arts Program had assured readers of *Artnews* that "there is such enthusiasm for the alternative spaces program that we are not about to change that funding category";[22] by 1983, the sense was very much the opposite: "No one at the NEA is saying that alternative spaces are slated en masse for some Endowment scrap heap," reported Gerald Marzorati in *Art in America* on the new Reagan appointees, "but no one is exactly defending them either." Those in command at Reagan's NEA argued for privatization, and for making artists' organizations more responsive to the private sector. "We need more input at the Endowment from the galleries," Marzorati quoted Reagan's NEA director Frank Hodsell. "In my view, most artists would like to have a commercial gallery. We need to help artists get gallery representation."[23]

The attack on increasingly institutionalized alternative spaces came not only from Reagan's NEA, but also from the Left, and the Lower East Side. In 1980, the artists of Group Material opened a storefront space on East Thirteenth Street with the paired goals of supporting art for social change and building a relationship between artists and the community by including their neighbors as exhibitors and participants. By September 1981 they had abandoned the storefront; according to a manifesto circulated around the Lower East Side, the group's "energies were swallowed by the space, the space, the space." Entitled "Caution! Alternative Space!" the statement was a heartfelt critique of the way that the vision with which they had opened the space had succumbed to the pragmatic, bureaucratic demands of running it, as well as a scathing rejection of the sort of alternative space Reagan's NEA might have wanted, a "farm team" for the commercial gallery system. "We hated the association with 'alternative spaces' because it was clear to us that most prominent alternative spaces are, in appearance, policy, and social function, the children of the dominant commercial galleries in New York."[24] The impetus behind politicized artists' groups like Group Material or Fashion Moda or Collaborative Projects (CoLab) was a critical examination of the social and economic place of the artist in the political geography of the city. Group Material's storefront, Fashion Moda's space in the South Bronx (Figure 5.3), CoLab's temporary spaces for exhibitions like the Times Square Show (in June 1980 in an ex-massage parlor on West Forty-first) and the Real Estate Show (illegally installed in a city-owned tenement at 123 Delancey Street) suggest a different kind of mapping, and a different art world; they took place not in the imaginary art world space of the "clean white cube," but at a

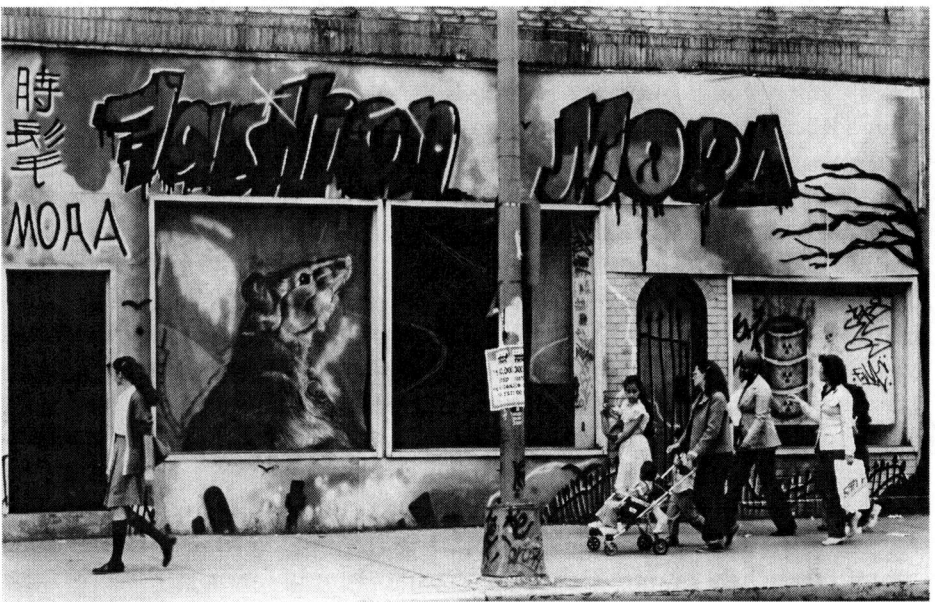

FIGURE 5.3 Fashion Moda gallery, 149th Street and 3rd Avenue, Bronx, New York. Exterior murals by Crash. Photograph © Lisa Kahane, 1982

particular address, and about it. Painter Bobby G described ABC No Rio's site on Rivington Street in the Lower East Side in terms intended to mark its distance from the white-walled lofts and galleries of Soho: "It's not a space, it's a place,"[25] a distinction that echoes in Group Material's repeated, disdainful, "the space . . .".

The shows organized by CoLab or mounted at Fashion Moda featured an unequal mix of local, usually self-taught artists drawn from the graffiti and punk scenes, and young, newly arrived art school and university graduates who tended to work with the same pop art sources: graffiti, album covers, television cartoons, and comic books. Beginning in 1981, that same mix and sensibility would characterize the East Village gallery scene; as Craig Owens noted: "the youth of the new avant- or, rather, 'enfant-garde,' indicates that Youth itself has become an important subcultural category."[26] The East Village's first gallery, the appropriately-named Fun, was opened that summer by Patty Astor, one of the stars of Charlie Ahearn's 1982 hip-hop documentary *Wild Style*. The work that Fun and most of the first wave of East Village galleries supported shared the same aesthetic politics as those artists involved in the new, more explicitly political collectives in the South Bronx and the Lower East Side; it was often the same cast of characters. According to a 1984 survey of an East Village scene already nostalgic for its origins, openings at Fun in the early days were "minifestivals of the slum arts, featuring rap music and break-dancing along with the graffiti paintings exhibited on its walls."[27]

Astor opened Fun as a commercial gallery rather than an alternative space because, she said, she "wanted a place to show art and didn't want to bother filling out grant forms."[28] But with the multiplication of similarly entrepreneurial gallery spaces over the next two seasons, the scene began to look as though it had taken up the challenge to privatize issued by Reagan's NEA. Early on, the East Village's galleries were often miniaturized, tongue-in-cheek versions of the commercial galleries of Soho and 57th Street, as though those involved were simply posing as artists and gallerists. In 1985, at the height of the East Village's heyday, a number of neighborhood art celebrities sat for a series of pictures for *Arts Magazine*, in which (by category) artists, dealers, critics, and collectors were posed as "The Irascibles," after Nina Leen's famous 1950 *Life Magazine* photograph of the abstract expressionists. The images insisted on their irony and reiterated the sense of play-acting, but by then what Owens (1984) – playing on the relation between artistic "pluralism" and the market – called their "puerilism" was only an alibi for very real commerce. The photographs were accompanied by excerpts from critic Robert Pincus-Witten's diary recounting the discussions and arguments that surrounded their making and the kind of "adieu" they marked. April 2, 1985: "The dissolution of the early East Village continues apace. . . . 'Last year at this time we were having fun. Now it's just business'." By mid decade, the East Village was one of the symbols of the triumph of the eighties' art market; and it was held accountable in ways Soho was not, not only for the "new entrepreneurial mode and unrepentant careerism" that emerged so quickly after its initial communalism, but for gentrification, the imbrication of art and real estate.[29] "The story of the East Village's newest bohemian efflorescence," wrote Walter Robinson and Carlo McCormick in 1984, "can also be read as an episode in New York's real-estate history – that is, as the deployment of a force of gentrifying artists in lower Manhattan's last slum."[30]

Painting

"It is possible that the triumphs of Ronald Reagan and Julian Schnabel have some deeper connection," speculated Marzorati in his *Art in America* essay on Reagan's NEA and the push toward privatization. "There are those who would argue, say, that the renewed interest in conventional painting modes reflects a general conservative shift. . . . Whatever the explanation, the gallery boomlet for this new painting exists, and those setting the agenda for visual arts at the NEA are watching it."[31] Marzorati could have had Crimp's *October* colleague Craig Owens in mind. In a scathing 1982 critique of a triumphal alumni show at the California Institute of the Arts, the alma mater of a number of artists whose work addressed the issues of representation Crimp had surveyed in "Pictures" – and some of whom now made paintings – Owens linked the turn to painting directly to the new conservatism. Against the backdrop of CalArts' progressive, conceptualist history in the seventies, "their return to the tangible – and, what is

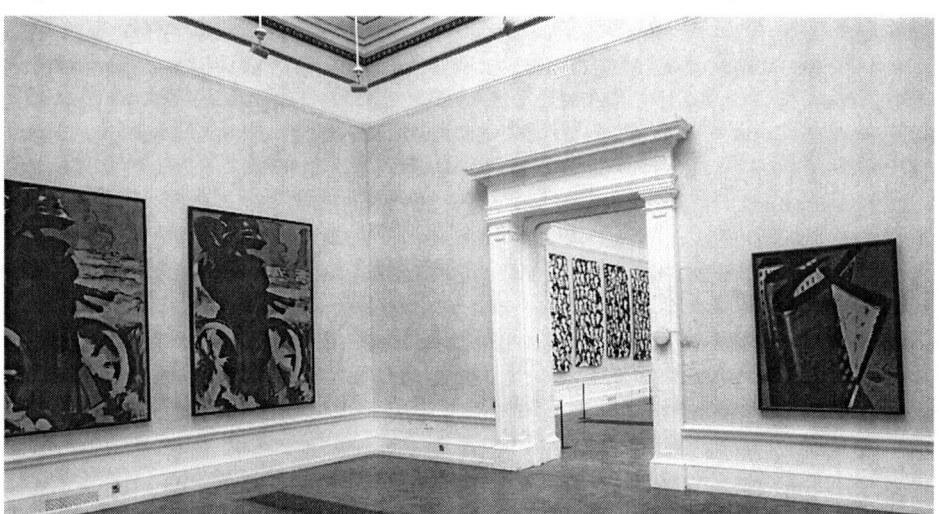

FIGURE 5.4   *A New Spirit in Painting* exhibition. Installation view at the Royal
Academy of Arts, January 15 to March 18, 1981, with works by (foreground) Markus
Lupertz and (through doorway) Jannis Kounellis. Image courtesy of Royal Academy
of Arts, London

more important, marketable – object" must be seen as part of a "widespread
backlash against the '60s counterculture that motivates the Neo-conservative
platform for the economic and spiritual 'renewal' of the U.S., and which culminated in November 1980 in the election of the celebrity-commodity to the
Presidency."[32] Owens's accusation – and his sense of betrayal – seems far out of
proportion, but his target was not only the exhibition at hand, and perhaps not
even just the truckloads of painting that were suddenly filling galleries worldwide. It was cast in response in particular to the language that accompanied the
new painting, a discourse that sounded very much like that coming from Reagan's
White House, Helmut Kohl's chancellery, and Margaret Thatcher's 10 Downing Street. Indeed, in Thatcher's case, the language of her program for a new
"cultural regeneration" was crafted in part by Charles Saatchi, a partner in the
public relations firm that managed her campaign, and a major collector of the
new painting.

Painting's return was heralded in London in early 1981 by *A New Spirit in
Painting*, an international exhibition at the Royal Academy curated by the academy's Norman Rosenthal, along with Nicholas Serota of London's Whitechapel
Gallery, and the Berlin-based art critic Christos Joachimides, who wrote the
catalogue's title essay (Figure 5.4). His opening line placed readers back in the
studio and before the easel: "the artists' studios are filled with paint pots again. . . .
Wherever you look in Europe or America you find artists who have discovered
the sheer joy of painting."[33] There was nothing particularly new about most of

the 38 artists in *A New Spirit*: the average age was 50, and most of the British painters – a roster that included Francis Bacon, Lucien Freud, and Frank Auerbach – were even older. And there was nothing spiritual about such Americans as Andy Warhol and Robert Ryman. It was the curatorial rhetoric rather than the individual selections that proved most provocative: the curators' language echoed quite intentionally, it seems, the language of the new right in America and Western Europe. "Our times, wherever you look, are pervaded by a reassessment of traditional values," wrote Joachimides, and his call for an art that "conspicuously asserts traditional values, such as individual creativity, accountability, [and] quality," rhymed to the public pronouncements of Thatcher's Tory government and Reagan's Republican one.[34] There is more than a passing resemblance between the continually repeated curatorial rejection of historical modernism or progress in art, and the Thatcherite rejection of Marxian economic analysis, and the championing of individual creativity matched her promotion of entrepreneurialism and the attack on the welfare state.

In the US the link between creativity and the free market economy would be made crystal clear: by the middle of 1982, the "Pressure to Paint" – to borrow the title of a show at Marlborough Gallery that included many of the "New Spirit" artists – came not only from the urgings of the spirit, but from the sales floor. "The new market/new painting has underneath its layers of materialism, opportunism, and ambition, a poetry so radical that to my eye it is clearly the most significant art of this time," wrote curator Diego Cortez. Cortez also noted: "It is good marketing in bed with the best art . . . a strategy of soul. My admiration and respect for the new dealers . . . is at least equal to that of the artists and their work."[35]

The complete conflation of the new spirit and the capitalist one would take a little longer in Britain than it did in New York, despite the efforts of the Royal Academy. While public funding for the arts in Britain, particularly that which came through the national system of art schools, was squeezed dry by Thatcher's attack on "dependency culture" and the "nanny state" across her reign, the kind of artistic entrepreneurship that spurred the East Village in the early 1980s – and that answered to New York's new speculators and developers – did not emerge in London until late in the decade, in conjunction with an aggressively cold artistic practice modeled after sixties' minimalism as it had been updated by New York Neo-Geo in the mid eighties; that is, by the art highlighted in the gallery Charles Saatchi opened in an old warehouse on Boundary Road in north London. In March 1988, a group of young artists from Goldsmith's College pitched themselves to the real-estate and stock market moguls who had benefited from Thatcher's monetary policies in the now infamous *Freeze* exhibition; organized by Damien Hirst, it was housed in yet another building vacated by the collapse of Britain's traditional industrial economy – this time in the Docklands – and ripe for the investments of a new one.[36]

"We need him in a risky world, to risk for all of us the humiliation, the frustration, and the mighty exhaustion of self-expression," wrote Charles' wife,

Doris Saatchi in 1982, at a moment when the Saatchis were still heavily invested in the new expressionist painting (according to an accounting in *Artnews* in 1985, the collection included "23 Kiefers, 24 Clementes and 27 Schnabels"). "We need him to show us how to feel."[37] Whether in New York or London or on the continent, the supporters of the new painting all dismissed the ideas of historical progress and the experimental that had characterized modernism; they were worn out, damaging, unbelievable, and in their place the new painting offered the power of the subjective and the artist's vision. As theorized by Achille Bonito Oliva and pushed hard by *Flash Art*, the work of the Italian "transavanguardia" marked – again – an end to the linear, temporal trajectory of historical avant-gardes in favor of a synchronic or topographical move across history's spatialized end. "Today to make art means having everything on the table in a revolving and synchronous simultaneity," wrote Bonito Oliva in 1979, and he too offered artistic subjectivity – a "non-stop 'immaginario' without anchorage or reference points" – in history's place. But his artist is not quite Doris Saatchi's hero: the singularity of the artist comes at the cost of his dispossession, and of the ego. Trans-avantgarde painting "intentionally lacks character, it does not hold heroic attitudes," and its pastiched and cobbled together surfaces are the mirrors of a concomitant "shattering [of] the myth of the unity of the ego."[38]

These are "bewildered images," Bonito Oliva writes in terms are borrowed from Gilles Deleuze and Felix Guattari, marked and disheveled by their "nomadism" and their explicit "minority." Like the French theorists' "minor literature," trans-avantgarde painting could only appear as "a mixture, a schizophrenic mélange, a Harlequin costume."[39] Compared to the theorizations of postmodernism that appeared in *October* and *Art in America* or *Screen*, which valued artistic practice after Lacan or the Frankfurt School as cultural critique, Deleuze and Guattari were minor literature; they imagined practice not as cultural, the work of signification, but in figures of deterritorialization, lines of flight, flows and intensities, as creative or, rather, "productive." Theirs was a more romantic version of the possibility of the work of art, and however different it might be from the romance proposed by *A New Spirit in Painting*, it was easy enough to read them together, and to see this painting, too, as it hung in the Saatchi collection or at Mary Boone as official language.

The collapse of the historical, the palpable sense that people and events were no longer tied together by a single, common story of progress or enlightenment or salvation that could support "the idea of a unitary end of history and a subject" – a master narrative, in Jean-François Lyotard's oft-quoted phrase – played differently, and more bleakly, in Germany.[40] The abandonment by history and the shattering of the ego are tropes of German criticism as well, but the breach is far more Manichean: it runs through the Second World War and along the Berlin Wall. Divided from a "usable past" by the unassimilable nightmare of the Holocaust and by the Third Reich's usurpation of Germany's past and its heroes, as well as of its social and cultural institutions, West German art in the postwar years was characterized by a deliberately international focus and the cosmopolitanism of minimal and conceptual art.[41] The question posed by the reemergence of painting – the championing, beginning in the late 1970s, of an older, but still working generation of German painters like Georg Baselitz, Karl-Heinz Hödicke, and Bernd Koberling – tended to be phrased in one of two ways: on the one side, usually the left, how to face and acknowledge that past; and on the other, particularly after the election of Helmut Kohl's Christian Democratic Party in 1982, how to repair "our loss of a cultural identity in the postwar era," or to redeem it.[42] The question of sides was debated most insistently around the paintings of Anselm Kiefer, whose iconography returned insistently to the mythic figures of Germany's past, to a German landscape mapped by both ancient legend and modern battles, and to the possibility of a redemptive culture, a salvational art. Subjectivity, the visionary, myth, grace: all the terms of the new painting appear in his paintings as questions. "Here, then, is the dilemma," wrote Andreas Huyssen: "whether to read these paintings as a melancholy fixation on the dreamlike ruins of fascism that locks the viewer into complicity, or, instead, as a critique of the spectator, who is caught up in a complex web of melancholy, fascination, and repression."[43] Huyssen's 1989 essay on Kiefer was subtitled "The Terror of History, the Temptation of Myth," a choice that rephrases his dilemma and directs it not only to Kiefer, but to the reemergence of German nationalism and its own investment in myth, in its calls for a restored cultural identity, and its claims for the power of art to redeem: the myth of painting is an ongoing theme for Kiefer, figured as a palette that is variously winged or burning or chained or, indeed, crucified.

Positions

"To paint today is an act of faith," announced Sandro Chia from the cover of the April 1983 issue of *Artnews*; "Painting today is invariably about the possibility of painting," concluded the German art historian Wolfgang Max Faust.[44] The repeated claim for painting is that something is at stake, something about the continuity of feeling or value or connection, the possibility of humanity or individual freedom against the technological state. However damaged its surfaces, however achingly ironic its pastiches of art history and popular culture, painting must continue. "We still need heroes," wrote Doris Saatchi, "and artists who are grappling with life's weighty problems will do."[45] The problem with heroes, though, is that, as Teresa de Lauretis noted, glossing a structuralist theory of narrative, is that they are always masculine: "In the mythical text, then, the hero must be male regardless of the gender of the character. . . . As he crosses the boundary and 'penetrates' the other space, the mythical subject is constructed as human being and as male; he is the active principle of culture, the establisher of distinction, the creator of differences."[46]

The absence of women in the role of the artist-hero was not simply theoretical – though theory was certainly one of the primary ways in which it would be unpacked; rather it was quite literal, and insistently ideological. When Roberta Smith reviewed *A New Spirit in Painting* in 1981, her complaint was not only that it slighted Italian and American painters in favor of German ones, but that "it omitted a number of excellent, mostly American painters who happen to be women. Which is to say: there were *no women* among the show's 38 participants." Smith's italicized her exasperation in no small part because of how glaring the omission was: the most important painters to emerge in the States at the end of the seventies were women; she singles out Jennifer Bartlett, Elizabeth Murray, and Susan Rothenberg. "The nasty message implicit in the complete absence of women painters from this show, a message which also seemed to be reflected in many of the overblown canvases, is that painting is once again 'man's work.' . . . Sexism is certainly not dead in the American art world, but the European version, as seen here, takes one's breath away."[47] The link between masculinity and painting as an "act of faith" would be imported, and joined quite clearly to the American market. In a discussion of the onslaught of figurative expressionism in New York in the 1981–2 season, Corinne Robins noted that none of the 18 European and American artists included in *The Pressure to Paint* were women: "Big-deal art marketing, Mary Boone observed . . . , has neither time nor space for women artists. 'It's the men now who are emotional and intuitive. . . . Besides, museums just don't buy paintings by women artists'."[48]

The alignment of painting, subjectivity, gender, and the market was a target for feminist critics, and for the direct tactics of the Guerrilla Girls, whose posters and magazine ads beginning in 1985 made the absence of women and artists of color in museums, commercial galleries, and criticism a matter of public record. The primary issue for an increasingly theoretically informed feminism in the 1980s, however, was not a demographic one, where the work of painters like Rothenberg and Murray might fill the canon of artist-heroes differently; rather, the task was to challenge the very terms in which works of art – and paintings in particular in the modern period – were valued, as unique objects and authentic expressions. It was a position that 1980s feminism shared with postmodernism as it was adumbrated in the pages of *October* and *Art in America* in the first years of the decade. Crimp, Owens, and Rosalind Krauss, among the earliest critical champions of artists such as Sherrie Levine and Cindy Sherman, pitted the postmodern tactics of appropriation, citation, and recoding against the promises of an autonomous art; in the place of painting as singular and unique – and the unified subject of humanist philosophy figured in its image – they offered the repetitions and dispersals of the text after Roland Barthes and photography after Walter Benjamin. But *October*'s critical project, and that which they imputed to the work they discussed in relation to photography and allegory, was not initially, nor even now necessarily, aligned with the politics of feminism.

In 1982, Jenny Holzer and Barbara Kruger were among a group of younger New York-based artists discussed in Benjamin Buchloh's "Allegorical Procedures: Appropriation and Montage in Contemporary Art," an essay that read them in relation to Barthes's *Mythologies* and a practice of ideological unveiling that had its roots in Dada; the following year they were included in Joanna Isaak's exhibition *The Revolutionary Power of Women's Laughter* in New York in January of 1983, alongside Mary Kelly's *Post Partum Document*, a hanging that situated the works quite differently. Reviewing the exhibition, Jane Weinstock suggested that the context had indeed changed, and offered just such "a different reading of Holzer and Kruger": one that seemed quite insistently directed against Buchloh's. "I will not mention 'appropriation,' nor will I historicize the work in question. While I am indebted to Roland Barthes, my argument will not take the form of a Barthesian analysis. Rather, my reading will address the blind spot of the current critical discourse – the question of sexual difference."[49] That same year, Craig Owens' "The Discourse of Others: On Feminism and Postmodernism" also took feminism as a context for rereading; he revisited not only Buchloh's "Allegorical Procedures," noting that what Buchloh had not noticed was that all the artists he addressed were women (along with Holzer and Kruger, he had discussed Dara Birnbaum, Louise Lawler, Sherrie Levine, and Martha Rosler), but also his own 1979 "Allegorical Impulse," and his discussion there of the work of Laurie Anderson. What Owens had failed to see there – his "blind spot," in Weinstock's words, or, as he puts it, his "remarkable oversight" – was that famous "greeting" Anderson had appropriated from the National Aeronautic and Space Administration was an "image of sexual difference or, rather, of sexual differentiation according to the distribution of the phallus." Insofar as it "aspires to the status of a general theory of contemporary culture," Owens concluded, postmodernism must take into account that "among the most significant developments of the past decade – it may well turn out to have been *the* most significant – has been the emergence, in nearly every area of cultural activity, of a specifically feminist practice."[50]

The feminist practice to which Owens referred was not the same one that had emerged in the US, particularly on the West Coast, in the first years of the 1970s. Rather, its roots are in a psychoanalytically driven, post-Lacanian feminism that emerged in the 1970s in France in the writings of Hélène Cixous, Luce Irigaray, and Julia Kristeva, and differently in Britain around the journal *Screen*. Where French feminism tended to thematize writing, *Screen* took film and the scene of seeing and being seen as its object. Against an earlier feminism accused of assuming sexuality "as a quality or attribute, innate, essential and liberating," *Screen* developed a discourse on sexuality "compositely fashioned from the Lacanian rereadings of Freud . . . and the historical project of Michel Foucault in which the potentially oppressive socio-psychic production of sexuality is stressed. Sexuality is perceived as an effect of social discourses and institutions."[51] Lacan's dividing, castrating gaze and his subject constructed in language were wedded to – or conflated with[52] – Foucault's panoptical, situating gaze and his subject

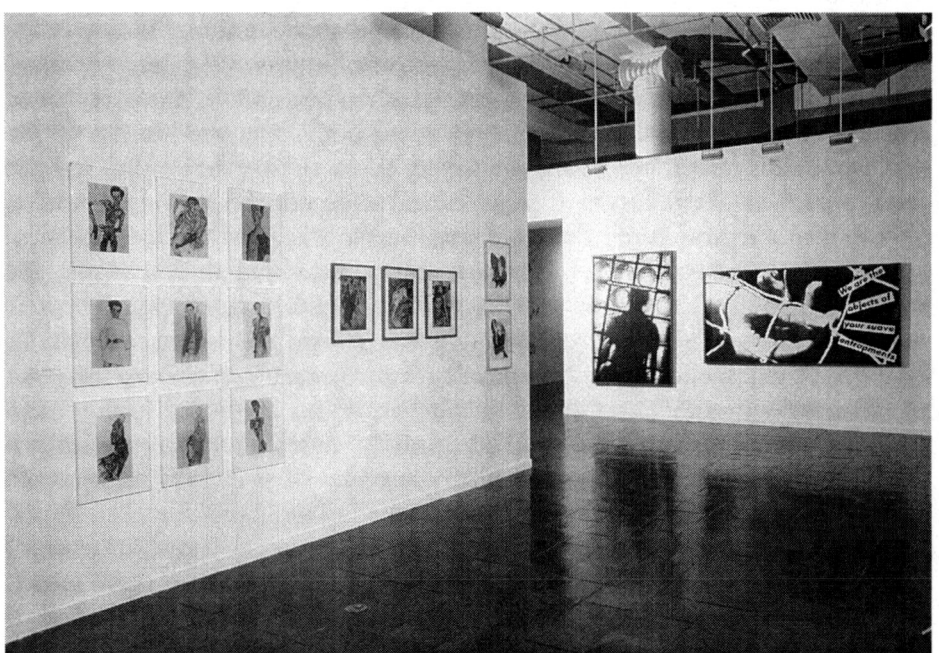

FIGURE 5.5 *Difference: On Representation and Sexuality* exhibition. Installation view at the New Museum of Contemporary Art, New York, December 8, 1984 to February 10, 1985, with works by (l–r) Sherrie Levine and Barbara Kruger. Image courtesy of the New Museum of Contemporary Art

positioned by language as the theoretical underpinnings of an art practice that refused contemplative immersion (and here the texts were Brecht and the Frankfurt School debate on realism and politics) in order to foreground the gendered dynamics of vision. Mary Kelly put the argument for the political effectivity of a theoretically-engaged feminism directly: "What's discovered in working through the *Post-Partum Document* is that there is no preexisting sexuality, no essential femininity; and that to look at the processes of their construction is also to see the possibility of deconstructing the dominant forms of representing difference and justifying subordination in our social order."[53]

In 1984 the exhibition *Difference: On Representation and Sexuality*, curated by Weinstock and Kate Linker at the New Museum in New York, expanded the roster and the project of *The Revolutionary Power* show, bringing together the work of a number of the British artists associated with *Screen* – Kelly, Yve Lomax, and Marie Yates, and others – with works by American artists such as Holzer, Sylvia Kolbowski, Kruger, and Levine. The exhibition also included the work of Ray Barrie, Victor Burgin, Hans Haacke, and Jeff Wall, since "the question of difference is not a question for women only, of course. . . . [I]t is now becoming increasingly urgent that men undertake the task of examining the construction of their own sexuality and its effects."[54] Earlier feminism, particularly in America, tended to privilege the bonds of narrative over the presentation of theory or the attractions of the image; it was built around consciousness raising and the story-based project of bringing women together, often exclusively, through shared accounts of sexism or identity in relation to the body. The work in the *Difference* show was situated in and for the gallery in a way that that earlier feminist practice was not; it was also in a strong critical sense not about women. Rather, it worked to foreground the gendered system of looking and the implication of the art object and its viewer within that scene. According to Hal Foster, the project of feminism at the intersection of Lacan and Foucault was to unveil visual desire's "conventional captures (e.g. voyeurism, narcissism, scopophilia, fetishism)," and, by doing so, "to reflect back the (masculine) gaze to the point of self-consciousness."[55] By the end of the decade, the theoretical and political power of feminist discourse had worked, in oddly contradictory ways, to institutionalize it, to install it both in the gallery system – Kruger and Levine would both be given one-person shows at Mary Boone in 1987, and few older feminists missed the irony – and at the site of the superego. As Mary Kelly would remark to Foster in a 1990 interview, the "psychic consequence of the historical existence of the women's movement [is] the word of the 'other' internalized in the place of the Law and the father. She sees you seeing."[56]

"Looking, Freud tells us, is not indifferent; it is always implicated in a system of control," writes Linker of the psychoanalyst's insistence on "connecting sexuality to the *situation* of the subject." The "role of 'places' here is essential," since "what constitutes, or differentiates the drive is the way the subject positions itself within its circuit." Later in the same essay, in a discussion of Kruger's work, Linker gives language that same power to situate individual subjects, and to fix their desires: "'Position' is an effect of language."[57] Over and over again the subject is situated in and as a system of determinants, pinioned in position; as Barbara Kruger fashioned it in a 1982 work: "We have received orders not to move." The positioned subject, precisely in contrast to the heroic "subject" of painting, characterized a politics of art in the 1980s. "There are no fixed or generic subjects in political art," theorized Hal Foster: "historical specificity, cultural positioning is all."[58] Knowing that one is positioned, and marking it, making it knowledge and then making work out of that knowledge: this might be a formula for art in the 1980s, even art whose political possibilities are far from clear.

"Existence is defined only in terms of position," wrote the painter Peter Halley. "If position is lost, existence vanishes."[59] Halley's sheer positionality continues the reduction of the subject produced by the conjunction of Foucault and Lacan, but its effects have been cranked up and streamlined by Baudrillard. Language and ideology no longer fix the conjunction of subject and subjected body; power is no longer accounted for, or rather, it surges. The subject "can no longer produce the limits of his own being, can no longer play nor stage himself, can no longer produce himself as a mirror. He is now only pure screen, a switching center for all the networks of influence."[60] Halley's "cell" paintings updated Mondrian's utopian geometry and Donald Judd's industrial one, and replaced them with the geometry of switching centers and circuit board. They shared their stuccoed surfaces with street after street of suburban houses, as though at once models for and instances of what Baudrillard called

satellitization of the real, . . . of the two-room-kitchen-and-bath put into orbit. That was the most familiar reading of Halley's paintings at the time, but one could see his interconnected, plugged-in rectangles as figuring not only a satellitized home on the net, but as an image of his own practice, produced in relation to the system of its consumption: crossed through by "connections, contact, contiguity, feedback and [the] generalized interface that goes with the universe of communication.[61]

The art world in the second half of the eighties was an increasingly globalized and wired branch of that universe, one that offered little resistance – to continue the electrical metaphor – to the flows of information or of capital. "As an artist," writes Peter Halley, "I am very much aware of myself as a construct."[62] The art world positions Halley as an artist, situates him within the market, produces him as a package, as coming in relation and after, occupying a space. Or as Barbara Kruger told *Artnews* just before her first show at Mary Boone: "I wanted [any works] to enter the marketplace because I began to understand that outside the market there is nothing – not a piece of lint, a cardigan, a coffee table, a human being. . . . Signed, sealed and delivered."[63]

On a panel sponsored by *Flash Art* in 1986, the East Village gallerist and painter Peter Nagy asked Halley and his fellow panelists for a position: "In what ways does this new work depart from or elaborate upon the work done by the Pictures generation of appropriators (that being the group associated with Metro Pictures . . .)?"[64] Nagy's question asked the panelists to historicize their work, but more than that, to situate it as product: his direct identification of a theoretical project with a commercial outlet suggests once again a scene, and a present, where, as Baudrillard wrote, "the commodity is immediately produced as a sign, as sign value, and where signs (culture) are produced as commodities."[65] Certainly, the work of most of the artists represented on the panel – in addition to Nagy and Halley, Levine (being asked to supersede herself), Ashley Bickerton, Haim Steinbach, Jeff Koons, and Philip Taaffe – could be seen as enacting that commutation of the cultural and the economic. Levine's "check" paintings and Taaffe's recasting of Barnett Newmans after Gucci insisted that the work of painting acknowledge its fungibility, its function as commodity; and Steinbach's product-topped Formica shelves and Koons' Plexiglas encased vacuum cleaners, in turn, were predicated on the flexibility and depth of the commodity as sign.

Bickerton's response to Nagy's question suggested that the work done by the "Pictures" artists did indeed still cling, in Crimp's now decade-old invocation, to that "radical aspiration we continue to recognize as modernist"; their work was still "essentially deconstructive and task oriented." The artists and critics of "Pictures" were still involved in a project of ideological critique, of unveiling corruption, Bickerton continued, "whereas at this point I feel we are utilizing that process of corruption as a poetic form."[66] Fiction covers over nothing, he suggests; it is all we have. Or, as he might have read in *Simulations*, "ideology only corresponds to a betrayal of signs; simulation corresponds to a short-circuit of reality and to its reduplication by signs."[67] Bickerton's decaled, packaged works figured just that sort of reduplication – "These are not paintings. They are paradigms of painting" – as they plotted their own circulation within the system of the art world, their own connections on the grid: "every station of its operational life, i.e., storage, shipping, gallery access, rack, reproduction, and on the wall."[68] They enact, if not the precession of the simulacrum one more time, then certainly that of the market.

Notes

1 *Simulations* was among the first of Semiotext(e)'s Secret Agent series, which included titles by Deleuze and Guattari, Michel Foucault, Jean-François Lyotard, Paul Virilio, and others.
2 Lotringer (2003), 194.
3 Schnabel, cited in McGuigan (1982), 93–4.
4 Baudrillard (1983a), 126.
5 Crow (1988), 20.
6 Baudrillard (1981), 147.
7 Miller (1987), 49.
8 For the story of Baudrillard's visit and, more broadly, his reception in the art world in the US, see Lotringer (2003); for a longer version of how French theory enters the art world in New York, see Lotringer (2001).
9 Foster (1996), 146.
10 Crimp (1987), 11.
11 Baudrillard and Halley, cited in Francblin (1986), 54.
12 Baudrillard (1983a), 4.
13 Jones (1987), 88.
14 Crimp (1977), unpaginated.
15 Ibid.
16 Crimp (1979), 186.
17 Ibid., 176–7, 180, 186.
18 Tucker (1978).
19 Crimp (1979, 1987).
20 This section is indebted to Ault (2003), as well as research by Margaret Owen Guggenheimer.
21 Patton (1977), 80.
22 Larson (1977), 38.
23 Marzorati (1983), 9.
24 Goldbard (2002), 186–7.
25 Cited in Moore (2002), 333.

26 Owens (1984), 162.

27 Robinson and McCormick (1984), 136.

28 Ibid.

29 Pincus-Witten (1987), 402, 403.

30 Robinson and McCormick (1984), 135.

31 Marzorati (1983), 13.

32 Owens (1982), 101–2.

33 Joachimides (1981), 14.

34 Ibid., 15.

35 Cortez is cited in Robins (1982), 100 and Sandler (1998), 225.

36 See Thompson (2001).

37 Cited in Hawthorne (1985), 72, 78.

38 Bonito Oliva (1979), 16, 18, 20.

39 Deleuze and Guattari (1986), 26.

40 Lyotard (1984), 73.

41 Faust (1981), 34.

42 Diederichsen (1992), 66. This phrase is from the cover of Hans Jürgen Syberberg's *Vom Unglück und Glück der Kunst im Deutschland nach dem letzten Kriege* (1990), cited in ibid.

43 Huyssen (1989), 39.

44 Faust (1981), 37.

45 Cited in Hawthorne (1985), 81.

46 de Lauretis (1987), 43.

47 Smith (1981), 71, 75.

48 Robins (1982), 101.

49 Weinstock (1983), 8.

50 Owens (1983), 60–1.

51 Pollock (1988), 161.

52 In a footnote to her discussion of the formation of *Screen*, Pollock adds that "these two formulations are not necessarily compatible and indeed Foucault's analysis implicated psychoanalysis in the historical construction of social regulation of persons via the constructions of sexuality"; Pollock (1988), 221, n.19.

53 Kelly, cited in Weinstock (1983), 9.

54 Smith (1985), 195.

55 Foster (1985), 8.

56 Kelly (1990), 58.

57 Linker (1983), 395, 407, 415.

58 Foster (1985), 149.

59 Halley (1988), 165.

60 Baudrillard (1983b), 133.

61 Ibid., 128, 127.

62 Halley, in Wei (1987), 121.

63 Kruger, cited in Squiers (1987), 84.

64 Nagy (1986), 46.

65 Baudrillard (1981), 147.

66 Bickerton, in Nagy (1986), 46.

67 Baudrillard (1983a), 48.

68 Foster (1996), 104, 101.

References and further reading

Ault, Julie (2003). *Alternative Art New York, 1965–1985*. Minneapolis: University of Minnesota.

Baudrillard, Jean (1981). *For a Critique of the Political Economy of the Sign*, trans. Charles Levin. St. Louis: Telos Press.

—— (1983a). *Simulations*, trans. Paul Foss, Paul Patton, and Philip Beitchman. New York: Semiotext(e).

—— (1983b). "The Ecstasy of Communication." In *The Anti-Aesthetic: Essays on Postmodern Culture*, ed. Hal Foster. Port Townsend: Bay Press. 126–34.

Bonito Oliva, Achille (1979). "The Italian Trans-avantgarde." *Flash Art*, nos. 92–3 (October–November):17–20.

—— (1982). *The International Trans-avantgarde*, trans. Dwight Gast and Gwen Jones. Milan: Giancarlo Politi Editore.

Crimp, Douglas (1977). *Pictures*. Exhibition catalogue. New York: Artists Space. Unpaginated.

—— (1979). "Pictures." In *Art after Modernism: Rethinking Representation*, ed. Brian Wallis. Boston: David R. Godine, 1984. 175–87.

—— (1987). "AIDS: Cultural Analysis: Cultural Activism." *October*, no. 43 (Winter):3–16.

Crow, Thomas (1988). "Versions of Pastoral in Some Recent American Art." *The BiNational: American Art of the Late 1980s*. Exhibition catalogue. Organized by David A. Ross and Jürgen Harten. Boston: Institute of Contemporary Art and Museum of Fine Arts; and Cologne: DuMont Bucherverlag.

Deleuze, Gilles, and Félix Guattari (1986). *Kafka: Toward a Minor Literature*, trans. Dana Polan. Minneapolis: University of Minnesota Press.

Diederichsen, Dietrich (1992). "Spiritual Reactionaries After German Reunification: Syberberg, Foucault, and Others." *October*, no. 62 (Fall):65–83.

Faust, Wolfgang Max (1981). "'Du hast keine Chance. Nutze sie!' With It and Against It: Tendencies in Recent German Art." *Artforum*, vol. 20, no. 1 (September):33–9.

Foster, Hal (1985). *Recodings: Essays on Art, Spectacle, Cultural Politics*. Port Townsend, WA: Bay Press.

—— (1996). *The Return of the Real*. Cambridge, MA: MIT Press.

Francblin, Catherine (1986). "Interview with Jean Baudrillard." *Flash Art*, no. 130 (October–November):54–5.

Fried, Michael (1967). "Art and Objecthood." *Artforum* 5 (June): 12–23.

Goldbard, Arlene (2002). "When (Art) Worlds Collide." In *Alternative Art New York, 1965–1985*, ed. Julie Ault. New York: The Drawing Center; and Minneapolis: University of Minnesota Press. 183–200.

Halley, Peter (1988). *Peter Halley: Collected Essays, 1981–1987*. Zurich: Galerie Bruno Bischofberger.

Hawthorne, Don (1985). "Saatchi & Saatchi Go Public. *Artnews*, vol. 84, no. 5 (May):72–81.

Huyssen, Andreas (1989). "Anselm Kiefer: The Terror of History, The Temptation of Myth." *October*, no. 48 (Spring):25–45.

Joachimides, Christos M. (1981). *A New Spirit in Painting.* Exhibition catalogue. Organized by Christos M. Joachimides, Norman Rosenthal, and Nicholas Serota. London: Royal Academy of the Arts.

Jones, Ronald (1987). "Group Material: White Columns." *Flash Art,* no. 134 (May):88–9.

Kelly, Mary (1990). *Interim.* Exhibition catalogue. New York: New Museum of Contemporary Art.

Larson, Kay (1977). "Rooms with a Point of View." *Artnews,* vol. 76, no. 8 (October):32–8.

de Lauretis, Teresa (1987). *Technologies of Gender: Essays on Theory, Film, and Fiction.* Bloomington: Indiana University Press.

Linker, Kate (1983). "Representation and Sexuality." In *Art after Modernism: Rethinking Representation,* ed. Brian Wallis. Boston: David R. Godine, 1984. 391–415.

Lotringer, Sylvère (2001). "Doing Theory." In *French Theory in America,* ed. Sylvère Lotringer and Sande Cohen. New York: Routledge. 125–62.

—— (2003). "My 1980s: Better than Life." *Artforum,* vol. 41, no. 8 (April):194–7, 252–3.

Lyotard, Jean-François (1984). *The Postmodern Condition: A Report on Knowledge.* Trans. Geoff Bennington and Brian Massumi. Minneapolis: University of Minnesota Press.

Marzorati, Gerald (1983). "Issues and Commentary: The Arts Endowment in Transition." *Art in America,* vol. 71, no. 3 (March):9–13.

McGuigan, Cathleen (1982). "Julian Schnabel: I Always Knew It Would Be Like This." *ArtNews* (Summer):88–94.

Miller, John (1987). "Baudrillard and his Discontents." *Artscribe International,* no. 63 (May):48–51.

Moore, Alan, with Jim Cornwell (2002). "Local History: The Art of Battle for Bohemia in New York." In *Alternative Art New York, 1965–1985,* ed. Julie Ault. New York: The Drawing Center; and Minneapolis: University of Minnesota Press. 321–65.

Nagy, Peter, moderator (1986). "*Flash Art* Panel: 'From Criticism to Complicity.'" *Flash Art,* no. 129 (Summer):46–9.

Owens, Craig (1982). "Back to the Studio." *Art in America,* vol. 70, no. 1 (January):99–107.

—— (1983). "The Discourse of Others; Feminists and Postmodernism." In *The Anti-Aesthetic: Essays on Postmodern Culture,* ed. Hal Foster. Port Townsend, WA: Bay Press. 57–82.

—— (1984). "Commentary: The Problem with Puerilism." *Art in America,* vol. 72, no. 6 (Summer):162–3.

Patton, Phil (1977). "Other Voices, Other Rooms: The Rise of the Alternative Space." *Art in America,* vol. 65, no. 4 (July–August):80–9.

Pincus-Witten, Robert (1987). *Postminimalism into Maximalism: American Art, 1966–1986.* Ann Arbor: UMI.

Pollock, Griselda (1988). *Vision and Difference: Femininity, Feminism and the Histories of Art.* London: Routledge.

Robins, Corinne (1982). "Ten Months of Rush-Hour Figuration." *Arts Magazine,* vol. 57, no. 1 (September):100–3.

Robinson, Walter, and Carlo McCormick (1984). "Report from the East Village: Slouching Toward Avenue D." *Art in America,* vol. 72, no. 6 (Summer):134–61.

Sandler, Irving (1998). *Art of the Postmodern Era: From the Late 1960s to the Early 1990s*. Boulder: Westview Press.

Smith, Paul (1985). "Difference in America." *Art in America*, vol. 73, no. 4 (April):190–9.

Smith, Roberta (1981). "Fresh Paint?" *Art in America*, vol. 69, no. 6 (Summer):70–9.

Squiers, Carol (1987). "Diversionary (Syn)Tactics: Barbara Kruger has her Way with Words." *Artnews*, vol. 86, no. 2 (February):76–85.

Thompson, Jon (2001). "The Economics of Culture: The Revival of British Art in the 80s." In *Public Offerings*. Exhibition catalogue. Organized by Paul Schimmel. Los Angeles: Museum of Contemporary Art; and London: Thames and Hudson. 208–19.

Tucker, Marcia (1978). *Bad Painting*. Exhibition catalogue. New York: New Museum of Contemporary Art. Unpaginated.

Wallis, Brian (2002). "Public Funding and Alternative Spaces." In *Alternative Art New York, 1965–1985*, ed. Julie Ault. New York: The Drawing Center; and Minneapolis: University of Minnesota Press. 161–81.

Wei, Lilly (1987). "Talking Abstract, Part Two." *Art in America*, vol. 75, no. 12 (December):112–29.

Weinstock, Jane (1983). "A Lass, A Laugh, and a Lad." *Art in America*, vol. 71, no. 6 (Summer):7–10.

6

1990–2005:
In the Clutches of Time

Henry M. Sayre

The 1990s were the decade in which the Internet came into being, that electronic agora that has changed how we (understanding that by "we" here I refer to a global elite) interact. In 1992, the world had fifty websites; by 2001 it had over 28 million, and as of July 22, 2004, Google listed 4,285,199,774. In 1992, the University of Minnesota's Gopher was the preferred system for navigating the Internet, but in August 1993 the first World Wide Web browsers were released, initiating the dominance of the Web. By 1995, 16 million people were online worldwide; by 2001, over 513 million, or close to 9 percent of the world's population, were connected.[1] Today, the collections of most of the world's museums are increasingly available to be viewed online and galleries and artists host their own websites, some creating works designed exclusively for the Web, all to such a degree that André Malraux's famous "Museum without Walls" has thus, in the past decade, taken on an entirely expanded meaning.[2] The question, of course, is – has the Internet, or the sensibilities it has generated, changed the way we think about art?

Censorship

Certainly, some things have not changed. The 1990s were bracketed by censorship and iconoclasm. In the United States, they opened, in April 1990, with the arrest of Dennis Barrie, director of the Cincinnati Arts Center, charged with pandering and the use of a minor in pornography in the exhibition of Robert Mapplethorpe's "X Portfolio" – he was later acquitted – and they concluded with the controversy surrounding the exhibition *Sensation: Young British Artists from the Saatchi Collection* at the Brooklyn Museum of Art, October 2, 1999–

January 9, 2000. Ironically in the last months of 1990, the Brooklyn Museum had hosted an installation inspired by the events in Cincinnati and the concomitant attack on the NEA by the United States Congress, created by Joseph Kosuth and called *The Play of the Unmentionable*. Drawing on works from the Museum's collection, the show juxtaposed works of art from throughout history that had been deemed politically, religiously, or sexually objectionable, with statements about the role of art in society by writers the likes of Oscar Wilde, Adolf Hitler, and Jean Jacques Rousseau. Hitler's proclamation that "The artist does not create for the artist; he creates for the people and we will see to it that henceforth the people will be called in to judge the artists" was, for instance, set beside congressional arguments to restrict NEA funding.

Now, a decade later, at the center of the controversy in Brooklyn was a 1996 painting called *The Holy Virgin Mary*, by Chris Ofili, a British-born artist who was raised by Catholic parents born in Lagos, Nigeria (their first language was Yoruba). Perhaps because the Virgin is portrayed here as a black woman, perhaps because the *putti* surrounding her are bare bottoms cut out of porn magazines, certainly because two balls of elephant dung, acquired from the London Zoo, support the painting (they are inscribed with the words "Virgin" and "Mary" and a third clump defines one of her breasts), many were offended. The Catholic League for Religious and Civil Rights chose to ignore their own name and called for people to picket the museum. Calling Ofili's painting "sick stuff," New York Mayor Rudolph W. Giuliani threatened to cut off the museum's city subsidy and remove its board if the exhibition were not cancelled – the courts forced him to back down. And, finally, Dennis Heiner, a seventy-two-year-old Christian, managed to smear the painting with white paint – consciously or not symbolic of both religious "purity" and his own race.[3] Even as the painting embodied the twilight zone in which so many in the new global society find themselves, it found itself immersed in the power politics of a resurgent conservative nationalism.

Feminist Retrospectives

The mood of the decade was, in fact, both nostalgic and apocalyptic, and both the longing for a lost, golden era and the prognostication of imminent disaster tend to feed the kind of conservative nationalism epitomized, at the onset of the Iraq War in 2002, by America's jingoistic boycott of all things French, from French fries to "R.S.V.P." (from the French *répondez s'il vous plaît*). But not all nostalgias are conservative. Sometimes they are productive. The 1990s were, in fact, a decade of important retrospective exhibitions that seemed more forward-looking than sentimental. This was especially the case with feminist art.[4] Lucy Lippard probably summed it up best in the introduction to her 1995 *The Pink Glass Swan*: "It's not just nostalgia that keeps calling me back to the pioneering feminist art of the seventies but the ever-more-obvious affinities with what's going on in the 1990s. It seems politically and aesthetically crucial that the work done then not be forgotten now, and that its connections to the succeeding decades be clarified" (15–16). German Artist Rebecca Horn's *Inferno-Paradiso Switch* twenty-year retrospective at the Guggenheim – the *Inferno* at the downtown Soho branch, the *Paradiso* in the top three rings of Frank Lloyd Wright's Dantesque uptown building – clarified the roots of the mechanical/biological metaphor so central to art in the 1990s, to say nothing of the importance of film and performance to her sculptural work. Carolee Schneemann's *Up To And Including Her Limits* retrospective at the New Museum and Hannah Wilke's two posthumous shows at Ronald Feldman Gallery in New York – the *Intra-Venus* photographs, shown in 1994, charting the devastation wracked on her body by lymphoma, and *Performalist Self-Portraits and Video Film Performances 1976–85*, exhibited in 1996, embodying the comic pathos of Wilke as Jewish daughter and femme fatale, victim and vamp – established the powerful place of the female body in feminist practice, while Eleanor Antin's 1999 retrospective at the Los Angeles County Museum underscored the ways in which the body is an effect of social mores and discourses as much as it is essentialist in its corporeality.

The exposition of the tension in feminist practice between biological determinism and social conditioning – the so-called "essentialist/deconstructivist" dichotomy – became the site not of debate but interrogation, especially in the 1996 exhibition curated by Amelia Jones at the Armand Hammer Museum in Los Angeles, *Sexual Politics: Judy Chicago's* Dinner Party *in Feminist Art History*.[5] The relevance of this interrogation to contemporary feminist practice is probably nowhere better embodied than in Italian Vanessa Beecroft's series of performances (Figure 6.1), which have been exhibited internationally. Beecroft asks her "armies" – her word – of live models, dressed in meager g-string outfits, panties, bras, or nothing at all save high heels, to stand at attention (or sometimes move according to prescribed dictates) through museum or gallery spaces. Her work openly defies those deconstructivist feminists who would argue that feminist art must specifically resist the "male gaze," the visual pleasure that patriarchal culture takes in representations of the female body.[6] In fact, by exercising authoritarian control over her "armies," Beecroft herself becomes a surrogate figure for patriarchal culture. In that role, she addresses the culture that prescribes the bodies she puts on display – her earliest work consists of drawings of young women variously caught up in eating disorders that date from 1993 when she was living with a model in Milan and keeping a food diary – exposing the way in which the culture, specifically the fashion industry, has constructed that body. The essence of Beecroft's feminine is no longer the breast or the vulva (the foci of much 1970s feminist art); it is no longer the body but high heels. They become a symbol of social subjugation and physical (self-)abuse entirely comparable to ballet's *pointe* shoes. Here the body as object of the gaze and the sexual politics that constructed it as such are entirely conflated. Beecroft underscores the essential sameness of her models' bodies even as she exposes them as culturally and psychically constructed phenomena.

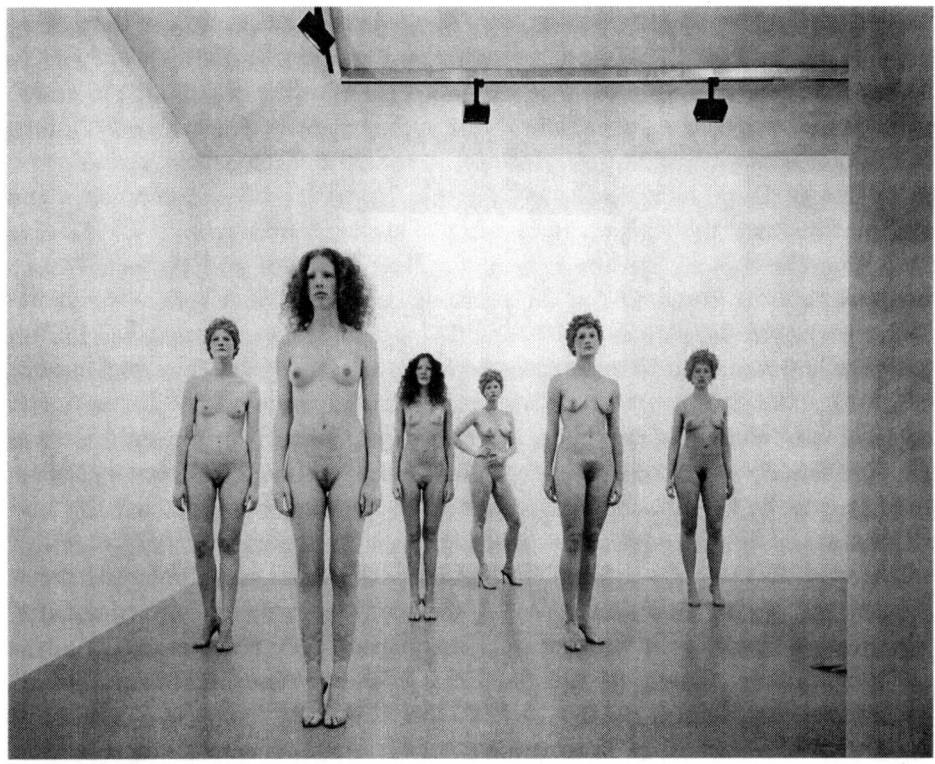

FIGURE 6.1 Vanessa Beecroft, *VB 43 2000*, 2000. Photograph: Todd Eberle.
Courtesy of the artist and Gagosian Gallery, London

Identity

By and large, nonetheless, the feminist project in the 1990s was subsumed
under larger questions of the intersection of construction of gender, sexual, and
ethnic identity. Photographer Nan Goldin's career, leading up to her 1993
exploration of the transsexual community, *The Other Side*, follows this trajectory.
So does the work of Japanese artist Yasumasa Morimura, whose on-going series
of self-portraits as great European masterworks and, beginning in the mid-
1990s, as Hollywood stars like Marilyn Monroe and Elizabeth Taylor destabilize
the representation of both gender and ethnicity – they simultaneously feminize
the masculine and masculinize the feminine, Orientalize the Occident and
Occidentalize the Orient.

The complexities of cultural identity became the special focus of many black
artists in the 1990s, epitomized perhaps by the simultaneity of Chris Ofili's
many identities – British, black, Catholic, Nigerian, postmodern, winner of the

Turner prize in 1998, the baddest of Sensation's bad boys. The work of Fred Wilson has been an especially potent force in this development, culminating in his retrospective, *Fred Wilson: Objects and Installations, 1979–2000*.[7] Originally a freelance museum educator, Wilson's medium is the museums themselves and the hidden biases about race, class, and gender that their collections embody. In the 1993 *Mining the Museum* show at the Maryland Historical Society, in an act of what he calls "interrogative archeology," he juxtaposed items from the Historical Society's collection – a "punt gun" ostensibly used for hunting birds on Chesapeake Bay beside reward notices for runaway slaves; a set of iron shackles in the middle of a display of silver *repoussé* objects made by Maryland craftsmen before 1800; a whipping post used at the Baltimore city jail until 1938 next to the museum's collection of antique cabinetry. In this way, his installations often juxtapose what he labels as "Mine" and "Yours." The photograph of the black family ("Mine") in the 1995 *Mine/Yours* (Figure 6.2) is not literally his family – he is the son of an international consulting civil engineer and a school teacher – but they represent the idea of the black family with which he identifies, as opposed to the stereotyped ceramic figurines that are labeled "Yours." His work, he says, is an effort, he says, "to root out . . . denial." At the same time, creating such exhibitions, he says, is "a healing process . . . a lot of what I do is about healing myself."[8]

More disturbing – and certainly more controversial – was the work of Kara Walker, whose work was first exhibited in 1994 in New York at the Drawing Center. That show consisted of a single piece *Gone: An Historical Romance of a Civil War as it Occurred Between the Dusky Thighs of One Young Negress and Her Heart*, a wall-size installation of black silhouettes on a white wall. The piece is notable, first, for its totally low-tech technique – as if standing adamantly in opposition to the mechanical/technological impulses of "new media." It is even more notable for the boldness of its imagery, its absolutely forthright equation of slavery as an institution with sexual assault and scatological degradation. As the title *Gone* suggests, it seemed to many to be a kind of *Gone with the Wind* gone porno, so much so that Betye Saar, one of the two or three most established African-American artists of the day, initiated a letter-writing campaign calling for a boycott of the work which she felt demeaned African-Americans.[9] But for Walker hers is a slave narrative, if previously repressed, that goes directly to the horrific heart of what it means, psychologically, to be black.

Tied directly to the question of racial identity is yet another – national identity, a concept challenged by the Westernization of world culture even as Palestinians, Kurds, Sikhs, American Indian tribes – all nations without states – as well as Africans, Asians, and Eastern Europeans struggle to affirm the viability of their languages and cultures. From the 1995 exhibition *Seven Stories about Modern Art in Africa* at the Whitechapel Art Gallery to the emergence of new Biennale exhibitions worldwide – perhaps most notably Korea's Kwangju Biennale, inaugurated in 1995, the first show of its size in Asia – and Nigerian-born Okwui Enwezor's appointment as director of the 2002 globalization-focused

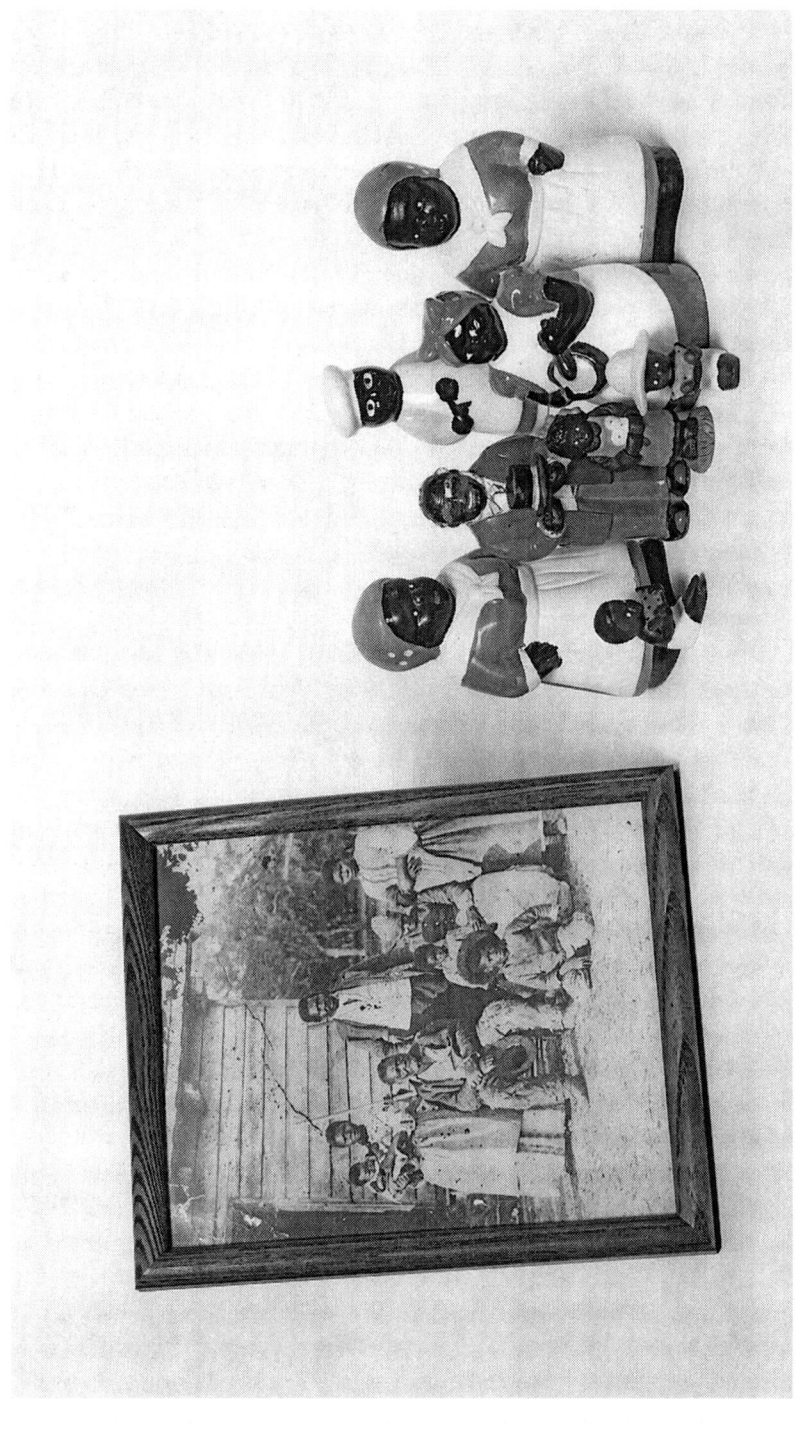

FIGURE 6.2 Fred Wilson, *Mine/Yours*, 1995. Framed photograph, seven painted ceramic figures, one plastic and painted tin figure and wood stand, overall installed, 11 × 24 × 11 in. Whitney Museum of American Art, New York. Purchase, with funds from Joanne Leonhardt Cassullo, The Dorothea L. Leonhardt Foundation Inc., and the Katherine Schmidt Shubert Purchase Fund. 96.52a–j

Documenta XI, the tension between the monocultural impetus of the new global art market and global capitalism in general and what Lucy Lippard has called "the lure of the local" has been played out over and over again. As Lippard herself has defined the problem:

> We are living today on a threshold between a history of alienated displacement from and longing for home and the possibility of a multicentered society that understand the reciprocal relationship between the two. . . . And in the case of a restless, multitraditional people, even as the power of place is diminished and often lost, it continues – as an absence – to define culture and identity. It also continues – as a presence – to change the way we live.[10]

What might the world look like once we step over this threshold? One model is offered by the film and video work of Iranian-born New York artist Shirin Neshat, which explores what might be called the political territory of the head-to-toe black chador worn by Iranian women initially as a protest of Western modernization, but in post-1983 Iran increasingly a symbol of the repression of individual sexuality and identity. In her 1999 film *Rapture*, Neshat juxtaposes, on two screens, one hundred men in an old fort (tradition) to one hundred women in chadors on the desert (freedom). At first, the men sing and chant while the women appear passively to look on. But then things change – as a woman dances barefoot on a drum, others hike up the chadors, climb into a boat and push out to sea. Not without a certain equivocation, Neshat's work equates freedom with exile, and exile with a forever divided self.

Performance artists Guillermo Gómez-Peña and Roberto Sifuentes, aka El Mad Mex and CyberVato, offer another model for debunking the normative identities connected to ideas of nation, as evident in their following dialogue:

> EL MAD MEX (trance-like): The nation-state will collapse in 2000, immediately after the Second U.S./Mexico War, which, in fact, Mexico will win. The ex-U.S.A. will fragment into myriad micro-republics loosely controlled by a multiracial junta, and governed by a Chicano Prime Minister. The White House will become the Brown House. Washington will become Wa-chingón. Spanglish will be the official language. Other accepted linguas francas will include frangle, japañol, and computer talk. Anglo militias and rabid teens will desperately attempt to recapture the Old Order, which paradoxically they are contributing to overturn as we speak. The newly elected government will sponsor interactive ethnographic exhibits to teach the perplexed population of the United States of Aztlan how things were before and during the Second U.S./Mexico War.
>
> CYBERVATO: Our presence here is a foreshadowing of the inevitable future. The global Mextermination Project is an example of the future official hybrid culture. Our performances/installations present real-life posthuman specimens as well as unique archeological artifacts, which are both residues of our dying Western civilization, and samples of an emerging Nueva Cultura, a culture in which the margins have fully occupied the center. Enough.[11]

This dialogue is based on Gómez-Peña and Sifuente's *Temple of Confessions* performance installation, in which they exhibited themselves for five to ten hours a day in 1994 and 1995 inside Plexiglas booths in front of which a church pew equipped with a microphone allowed the audience members to confess their "intercultural fears and desires." Earlier, beginning in 1992, Gómez-Peña had collaborated with Coco Fusco in a series of performance pieces called *Two Undiscovered Amerindians . . .* , in which he and Fusco were exhibited in a cage as recently discovered, wholly uncivilized "natives" of the fictitious island of Guatinaui in the middle of the Gulf of Mexico. In London, Madrid, Minneapolis, and New York nearly half of their audience assumed they were real, and that there was nothing unusual about keeping such "barbaric" specimens locked up.[12] But always, in addressing stereotypes, Gómez-Peña tears them down and begins to create the kind of Nueva Cultura of which he speaks.

Blockbuster Retros

But if a Nueva Cultura was beginning to assert itself in the 1990s, the mechanisms of traditional culture were securely in place, as a series of mega-retrospectives dedicated to the work of Sigmar Polke, Robert Ryman, Cy Twombly, Jasper Johns, Robert Rauschenberg, and Gerhard Richter, toured the Western world. They were nostalgic tributes to an older male generation, pulling the last half of the century all together in a narrative of masculine artistic achievement, even as they catapulted us apocalyptically forward into, as it turned out, catastrophe – Y2K (the panic ensuing over the supposed computer meltdown that was feared at the turn of the century), 9/11 (the attack on the World Trade Centers and Pentagon in the USA by Al Qaeda on September 11, 2001), the war in Iraq.[13] As sometimes predictable as these shows were, over the course of the decade they revealed that our habits of viewing were undergoing a process of transformation. Raised under the sign of modernist formalism, trained to regard the work of art as a self-contained whole, the viewer, a century after Henry Adams had experienced something of the same feelings in the Gallery of Machines at the Great Exposition of 1900, "found himself lying in the galleries of the Museum of Modern Art, his historical neck broken by the sudden irruption of forces totally new."[14] Douglas Crimp had noted in his book *On the Museum's Ruins*, in a chapter called "The End of Painting," that in the eighties "the dimension that had always resisted even painting's most dazzling feats of illusionism – time – now became the dimension in which artists staged their activities, as they embraced film, video, and performance. And, after waiting out the entire era of modernism, photography reappeared, finally to claim its inheritance" (93).

But at the Pace Gallery and then the Museum of Modern Art in 1992 and 1993, Ryman's new painting seemed anything but exhausted. In fact, it seemed to aspire to the conditions of film, video, performance, and photography – that is, to the conditions of time. The new Rymans, at the Pace, were airy, almost ethereal, topped, as they were, by a band of wax paper that seemed to dissolve not only the paintings' uppermost edges but the wall as well. And the paintings themselves consisted of fields of marks, bounded by, or bounding, other fields of unmarked canvas, the borders between these areas seeming to melt or dissolve into each other, as the light from the paintings seemed to melt or dissolve into the space of the room. Viewing them was like walking in a fog through which the sun is about to break.

In the 1990s, too, the retrospective began to take on the characteristics of narrative. For example, New York artist Nan Goldin's 1996 retrospective at the Whitney, *I'll Be Your Mirror*, made it clear that each individual photograph only became legible in relation to all the others, as image to image, room to room, they began to spell out a life. It became possible to think of the display as a precise instance of Roland Barthes' "text," and it seemed right to substitute the word "retrospective" for "text" in Barthes' famous analysis of the nineteenth-century novel in his book *S/Z*: "The text is a galaxy of signifiers, not a structure of signifieds; it has no beginning; it is reversible; we gain access to it by several entrances, none of which can be authoritatively declared to be the main one; the codes it mobilizes *extend as far as the eye can reach*, they are indeterminable" (5–6). The individual work of art is an example of what Barthes calls a *lexia*, or unit of reading in a larger narrative. These "blocks of signification" cut the narrative into

> a series of brief, contiguous fragments [think of paintings in an exhibition] . . . the best possible space in which we can observe meanings. . . . The text, in its mass [the exhibition], is comparable to a sky, at once flat and smooth, deep, without edges and without landmarks; like the soothsayer drawing on it with the tip of his staff an imaginary rectangle wherein to consult, according to certain principles, the flight of birds, the commentator traces through the text certain zones of reading, in order to observe therein the migration of meanings, the outcroppings of codes, the passage of citations (13–14).

What is most remarkable about American artist Cy Twombly's painting, for instance, as his 1994 retrospective at the Museum of Modern Art made clear, is that it ignores, even exorcizes, any sense of wholeness. The four paintings that make up the 1993–4 suite *The Four Seasons, Il Quattro Stagione* include snatches of poetry, as in so much of his work in the 1990s, evidently translated by Twombly himself from George Seferis's *Three Secret Poems*. Like the fragments of poetry, often barely legible, each individual painting functions as a (self-)critique of its own autonomy. Twombly's painting is always announcing its fragmentary nature, the fact that each work is a part of something much larger than itself, just as his quotations are part of larger texts, his references part of a larger history, a larger series. It is, indeed, through a consideration of the painting's place in series, experienced as a time-oriented medium such as film, video, or photography – painting as a series of "stills," as a cyclical, sequential, *serial* activity – that painting's possibilities began to (re)emerge.

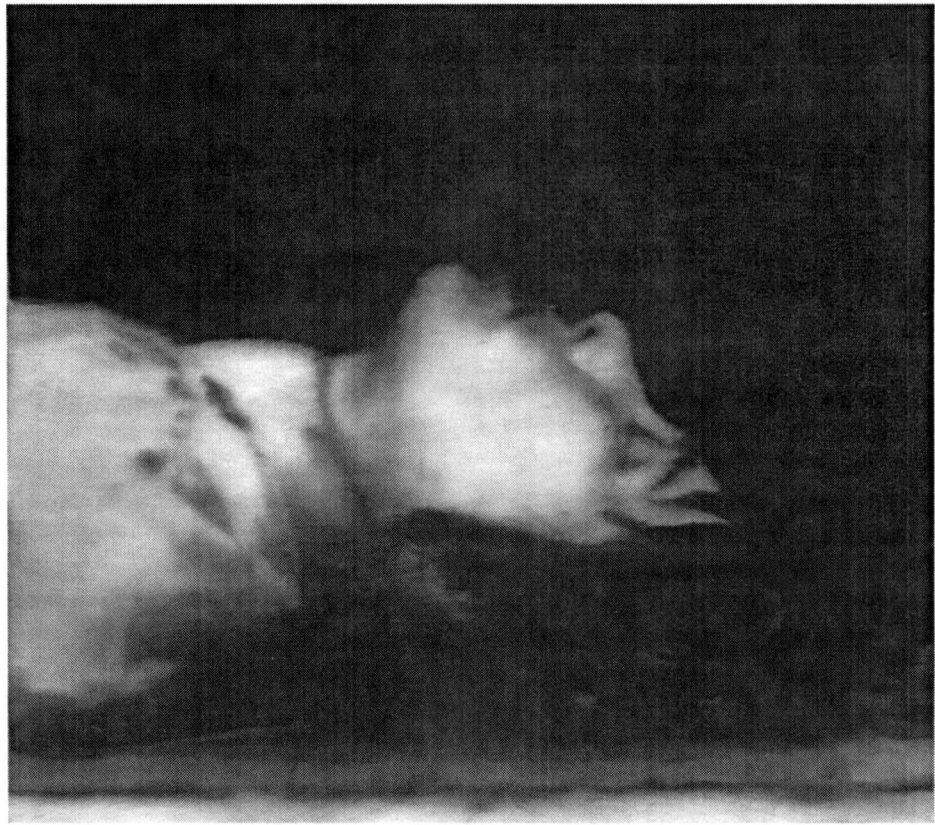

FIGURE 6.3   Gerhard Richter, *Dead (1)* [*Tote (1)*], from *October 18, 1977*, 1988.
Oil on canvas. 24¹/₂ × 28³/₄ in. The Sidney and Harriet Janis Collection, gift of Philip
Johnson, and acquired through the Lillie P. Bliss Bequest (all by exchange); Enid A.
Haupt Fund; Nina and Gordon Bunshaft Bequest Fund; and gift of Emily Rauh
Pulitzer (169.1995.i). The Museum of Modern Art, New York. © copyright the artist.
Digital Image © The Museum of Modern Art/Licensed by SCALA/Art Resource,
New York

And it is, of course, a consideration of painting as a series of "stills" that most
informs German artist Gerhard Richter's painting. And the series depends upon
memory. Photographs are icons of memory, of the persistence of the past in the
imagination. As Roland Barthes reminds us in *Camera Lucida*, what we discover
"more or less blurred beneath the abundance and the disparity of contemporary
photographs" is death: "In front of the photograph of my mother as a child, I
tell myself: she is going to die: I shudder . . . *over a catastrophe which has already
occurred*. Whether or not the subject is already dead, every photograph is this
catastrophe."[15] Richter's series of paintings *October 18, 1977* (Figure 6.3) is
based on documentary photographs depicting the suicides (or perhaps murders)

on October 18, 1977 of three members of the Red Army Faction's Baader-Meinhof Group at Stammheim prison just outside Stuttgart, and other aspects relating to these events. The paintings, black and white, smeared and smudged, are precisely Barthes' blurred images of death, paintings that announce blurring as the very condition of memory. Painted in 1988, they are technically a product of the eighties, but because they were first exhibited in the United States at New York University's Grey Art Gallery in March and April 1990, subsequently purchased by the Museum of Modern Art in 1995, and given central place in Richter's 2002–3 retrospective, it is in the 1990s and in the new century that they have insisted on their authority, at least with US-dominated versions of contemporary art discourse.

In Richter's work we are always at the edge of the image's disappearance. The image itself is blurred, as if caught in the viewfinder of a cameraman passing by in an automobile. The object does not move, the gaze does. The fluidity of the paint does not so much slow down the act of looking as draw the look across the field of the painting, to the corner of your eye, lending the image the quality of the just-having-been-seen-and-not-fully-taken-in. Visual reality, in Richter's paintings, is always something we have just moved beyond. It lags just behind us, over our shoulder, as if we just missed it. If, as Freud reminds us, the uncanny, the *unheimlich*, is "something repressed which *recurs*. . . nothing new or alien, but something which is familiar and old-established in the mind and which has become alienated from it only through the process of repression,"[16] then it is in death, death depicted in the photograph, and the photograph as death, that the uncanny is most at home (*heimlich*). And it is uncanny that the deaths Richter depicts took place at *Stammheim* prison, the name of which translates literally as the "family home."

The Arts of Duration: From Painting to Video

The authority that Richter's work asserts over Euro-American art since 1990 rests in its insistence that painting is not so much a spatial medium as it is time-based – that all work in series is time-based – and, by extension, that the central characteristic of all time-based media is that they reside in that imprecise, un-reliable, and endlessly mutable zone, the condition of memory. If memory is the "family home" where we come to rest, it is also what drives us, even as the repressed, forward. The singular force of Richter's work is that he sensed that our memories of October 17, 1977 – not our literal memories but the cultural exercise of repression that our forgetfulness of the events of that day epitomize – would come home to roost, as indeed they did on 9/11. Our deeds possess a certain duration, even if when they recur as an instance of the uncanny we can't quite recognize them as durational.

If it suddenly seemed natural to regard painting in terms of time rather than space – or rather, to see it as something of a time–space continuum – it was also apparent that something had changed, or was changing, that had broader implications. It is safe to say that by the end of the century, duration had begun to assert itself as one of the primary "dimensions" of art, taking its places beside the traditional spatial dimensions of height, width, and depth. In his influential essays on postmodernism, written between 1984 and 1990 and collected in his book, *Postmodernism, or, The Cultural Logic of Late Capitalism*, Fredric Jameson first articulated many of the themes developed here. He speaks of the emergence of a new space that "makes it impossible for us to use the language of volume or volumes any longer ... [a space] without any of that distance that formerly enabled the perception of perspective" (43). The dominant site of this new space, he recognized, was video, both commercial television and experimental video, or "video art," because, he says, "it is the only art or medium in which ... [the] ultimate seam between space and time is the very locus of the form" (76).

While Jameson's descriptions are compelling, it is interesting to note how much has changed over the course of the last decade, throwing the rest of Jameson's approach into question. In the first place, Jameson chooses to approach video through the filter of experimental video, though another route, he admits, might be through "that new form or genre called MTV, which I cannot deal with here" (71). Jameson thus chose to ignore what would become the dominant model for video art, the form in which many if not most video artists learned their trade, especially anyone under the age of, say, thirty-five. Furthermore, MTV is arguably late capitalism's preeminent cultural gesture, turning every video into an advertisement for a CD, every entertaining moment into a commercial for the musical product. But by approaching video through the filter of experimental video in 1991, Jameson ends up saying things like this: "Memory seems to play no role in television, commercial or otherwise. . . . Nothing here haunts the mind or leaves its afterimages in the manner of the great moments of film" (70–1), missing the point that MTV exists solely to create a visual space for music, a memory site, if you will, that the viewer can take to the store and the recording company to the bank.

Describing quite accurately the kind of video art produced in the seventies and eighties, Jameson links its primary temporal quality to aesthetic boredom:

> Imagine, a face on your television screen accompanied by an incomprehensible and never-ending stream of keenings and mutterings: the face remaining utterly without expression, unchanging throughout the course of the "work." . . . It is an experience to which you might be willing to submit out of curiosity for a few minutes. When, however, you begin to leaf through your program in distraction, only to discover that this particular videotext is twenty-one minutes long, then panic overcomes the mind and almost anything else seems preferable. (72)

Given this description, it must have seemed obvious enough to Jameson that one of the primary roles of video art was to critique commercial television. But the 1990s are marked by a gradual withdrawal away from this kind of video. Consider Douglas Gordon's 1993 *24 Hour Psycho*, an extreme slow-motion

(2 frames per second as opposed to the standard 24) video projection, lasting twenty-four hours, of Alfred Hitchcock's 1960 classic film *Psycho* onto a free-standing translucent screen. What Gordon does is, indeed, threaten the viewer with boredom, but at this pace every Hitchcockian strategy of framing, dissolve, shot change, camera angle, and so on is revealed in excruciating detail, so that the film we all know and love is remade before our eyes. It is as if memory itself slows down, not quite to a series of frozen stills such that, for instance, the famous shower scene would seem frozen in time, but into a fabric of slow motion dissolves that have the effect of extending memory, stretching it out. The work is not so much an attempt to establish a pace for video art that distinguishes it from film (or television) as it is an exploration of the sources of film's very power as a medium.

Bill Viola's *The Greeting*, created for the 1995 Venice Biennale, where Viola was the American representative, is similarly an extreme slow-motion projection shot with a special high-speed 35-millimeter camera capable of exposing an entire role of film in about 45 seconds at a rate of 300 frames per second. Viola thus filmed 45 seconds of three women coming together in a recreation of Jacopo Pontormo's 1528 painting *The Visitation*.[17] When projected at regular speed, the film lasts over ten minutes. "I never felt more like a painter," Viola said in a video documenting the making of the piece. "It was like I was moving color around, but on film. . . . I added what painting can never possess but only intimate – time."[18]

Both Gordon's and Viola's pieces draw attention to duration as a key component of their work, but in neither is duration necessarily equated with boredom. By the time Viola created his video installation *Five Angels for the Millennium*, first exhibited in 2001,[19] duration had in fact become not the source of boredom but of suspense. Five individual video sequences show a clothed man plunging into a pool of water. The duration of each video is different, with long sequences of peaceful aqueous landscape suddenly interrupted by the explosive sound of the body's dive into the water. Viola turned the image upside down so that his angel seemed to be rising upwards instead of sinking down, or he ran the footage backwards so that the angel seemed to be drawn up and out of the water like some aqueous bird. Because the videos are continuously looped and projected onto the gallery walls, their different durations make it impossible to predict which wall will suddenly become animated by the dive, the one behind you, the one in front of you, the one around the corner. What the installation does is spatialize time. As Viola explains:

Time is the ultimate invisible world. It's all around us. It literally is our life. We live in it like fish in water, yet we can't taste it, see it, touch it, smell it. If your interest is to hold onto time, then you regard it as something slipping away, that's being lost. But if your interest is transformation, growth and change – wanting to ride the wave as it's cresting – then there is no problem. You are immersed within the flow of time, and you are dripping wet![20]

Both Gordon and Viola employ video as an extended form, one in which duration is foregrounded. But more and more, and especially as artists who have grown up with MTV begin to emerge on the scene, a short, roughly 3½-minute format, the length of your average pop song, has come to the fore. (MTV was founded in August 1981, so roughly anyone born after 1970 grew up as a teenager with the works like Peter Gabriel's 1987 *Sledgehammer*, the most screened music video ever, etched in their consciousness.) A pop rocker as well as artist, Pipilotti Rist not surprisingly makes video installations and individual video works that are overtly MTV-inspired. "I have the greatest respect for some MTV clips," she says, "since they have a power of innovation and spirit of discovery that really surpasses video art."[21] Rist's 1997 *Ever is Over All*, projected onto two walls, shows a young woman strolling down a street smashing car windows with a long-stemmed flower, picked evidently from the garden of brilliantly colored blossoms projected on the other wall, all to an hypnotic musical score.

At the 2001 Venice Biennale, one of the more popular video presentations was by Englishman Chris Cunningham, born in 1970. Cunningham presented the actual MTV video he shot and directed for the 1999 Björk pop song *All is Full of Love*. The video reenacts a classic modernist theme, the mechanization of human sexuality, harking back to the WWI-era machine-body images of Marcel Duchamp and Francis Picabia. But especially in its narcissism, the video indulges in the modernist myth of the self-love of Narcissus. As the symbolist poet Paul Valéry put it: "Narcissus: Is it not at all to think of death to regard oneself in a mirror? Does not one see there one's perishable part? . . . A mirror takes us out of our skin, of our face. Nothing resists one's double."[22] The face here is Björk's own, literally taken out of her skin, transplanted onto a cyborg, doubled, then redoubled again just as precisely as the mechanical means of reproduction have doubled and redoubled her performance, reified her, commodified her art, marketed it and distributed it, and arguably stripped her of her own humanity.

New Media

The opening up to popular culture represented in the video works of Rist, Cunningham, and others like them, defies the aesthetic positioning – or is it posturing? – of postmodern art. The fact that their work traffics as easily as it does in contemporary mass media culture is, for Jameson and others like him, a sure sign of their lack of quality. If for Jameson, the postmodern work of video art "systematically sets out to short-circuit traditional interpretive temptations," then "new criteria of aesthetic value then unexpectedly emerge from this proposition: whatever a good, let alone a great videotext might be, it will be bad or flawed whenever such interpretation proves possible" (91–2). But by engaging, precisely, the rhetoric and structure of popular cultural practice, by entering into the new digital society of the spectacle, appropriating its methods and techniques, and exposing its clichés and assumptions, these artists create entirely legible works that are simultaneously extraordinarily powerful self- and social critiques.

In fact, the rise of video in the 1990s foregrounds the singular formal feature of new media from digital photography, internet-based art, to video, film, and performance – that is, the ways in which these media migrate more or less seamlessly between and among one another. It is not that we have entered so much a multimedia world as an intermedia constellation.[23] There is nothing unusual about performance artists making video works, as for instance, Tim Etchells, known for his performance work with England's Forced Entertainment group, explores the play between real and recorded time in the 2001 video *Down Time*. He first video-taped himself for ten minutes "thinking about good-byes," then added a voice-over trying to remember, as he watches the tape, what he was thinking at each instant. Nor does it seem unusual for a performance artist like Eleanor Antin to "direct" rather than perform in constructing the large format photographic *tableaux vivants* that make up her 2001 *Last Days of Pompeii*. Similarly, Jeff Wall's cinematographic photographs are digitally manipulated performance pieces that position Wall as something of a filmmaker of the still, while the monumental photography of Thomas Struth and Andreas Gursky aspire, seemingly, to the conditions of painting. Since the early 1990s, South African artist William Kentridge has been making short, animated films out of charcoal and pastel drawings that he alters, erases, and changes over the course of filming – "drawings for projection," he calls them – which chronicle his country's transition from apartheid in an attempt, reminiscent of Richter's *October 17, 1977* series, to forestall forgetting even as they represent the vicissitudes of memory.

Perhaps no work more embodies the intermedia impulse of the era than Matthew Barney's *Cremaster Cycle* (Figure 19.1), which originated out of his earlier works such as the 1991 video *Blind Perineum*. Here, wearing a full body harness and climbing gear, but otherwise naked, and anally penetrated by an ice screw, Barney negotiated the walls and ceilings of his studio – a space described by Nancy Spector in the *Cremaster* retrospective catalogue as a "hybrid version of Gold's Gym and an S/M fetish club" (4–5). (The name Cremaster itself, which suggests a pop culture super-hero, in fact refers to a small muscle in the male scrotum.)

Barney's exploration of the male body as at once a narcissistic and abject place became the basis for the five films in the *Cremaster Cycle*; made, rather like the *Star Wars* cycle, out of order, they are set in a number of locales: from *Cremaster 1*, in Boise, Idaho; *Cremaster 2*, back and forth between the Columbia Icefield in Canada and the Bonneville Salt Flats in Utah; *Cremaster 3*, in the Chrysler Building in New York City; *Cremaster 4*, on the Isle of Man in the Irish Sea; and *Cremaster 5*, in Budapest. In the same order, they represent the development height of the gonads in the male body, from their embryonic "ascended" state in *Cremaster 1*, to their most fully "descended" state in *Cremaster 5*. They are respectively 40 minutes in duration, one hour and nineteen minutes, three hours and two minutes, 42 minutes, and about 55 minutes. Over the nearly decade-long process of making these films, Barney created a whole array of other related but independent works – drawings, photographic collages, sculptures, and installations. All of these, together with the films, compose what amounts to Barney's *Gesamtkunstwerk*, the "total work of art" that bridges all media and forms and pushes the very idea of "media" to the limits, even as the *Cremaster Cycle* itself seems to push to their very limits the possibilities of pleasure, both carnal and aesthetic. Such a project enfolds, even as it summarizes, the aspirations as well as the limits of the Euro-American art world 1990–2005.

Notes

1   These statistics are from Gromov (2001) and from Google.com.
2   See André Malraux, *Museum Without Walls* (1967).
3   For a copiously complete survey of news coverage of the events surrounding the Sensation exhibit in Brooklyn see the website www.ArtsJournal.com/issues/Brooklyn.
4   The retrospectives of the women artists discussed here were first shown at the following venues: *Rebecca Horn: The Inferno-Paradise Switch*, Guggenheim/Soho Guggenheim, 1993; *Carolee Schneemann: Up To And Including Her Limits*, New Museum, New York, 1997; *Hannah Wilke: Intra-Venus*, Ronald Feldman Gallery, New York, 1994, and *Performalist Self-Portraits and Video/Film Performances*, Ronald Feldman Gallery, 1996; *Eleanor Antin*, Los Angeles County Museum of Art, 1999.
5   When Jones exhibited *The Dinner Party* in 1996, it had been in storage since its last exhibition in Melbourne, Australia in 1988. Since the 1996 show it has been acquired by Brooklyn Museum of Art trustee Elizabeth Sackler and donated to the museum, where beginning in 2006 it will be permanently displayed in the BMA's Sackler Center for Feminist Art.
6   The now classic essay on the subject is Laura Mulvey's 1975 "Visual Pleasure and Narrative Cinema."
7   *Fred Wilson, Objects and Installations 1979–2000*, first shown at the Center for Art and Visual Culture, University of Maryland, Baltimore County, Maryland, 2001–2.
8   Leslie King-Hammond, "A Conversation with Fred Wilson," in Corrin, ed. (1994), 34.
9   For a brief discussion of this controversy see Wagner (2003), 92.
10 Lippard (1997), 20.
11 Gómez-Peña et al. (2001), 38–9.
12 For a detailed discussion of this piece, see Fusco (1994).
13 The status of the venues of these major male artists' retrospectives makes a strong contrast to the relatively modest venues where, with the exception of Rebecca Horn, the work of the women artists discussed here was exhibited. For example, *Polke* was held at the San Francisco Museum of Modern Art, the Hirshhorn Museum, Washington, D.C., the Museum of Contemporary Art, Chicago, and the Brooklyn Museum from 1990–2. *Robert Ryman* was held at the Tate Gallery, London, the

Museum of Modern Art, and other important international venues in 1993–4. *Cy Twombly: A Retrospective* appeared at the Museum of Modern Art, New York in 1995. *Jasper Johns: A Retrospective* was held at the Museum of Modern Art, New York, the Museum Ludwig, Cologne, and the Museum of Contemporary Art, from 1996 to 1997. *Robert Rauschenberg: A Retrospective* was shown internationally at venues including the Guggenheim Museum, New York, and the Museum Ludwig, Cologne from 1997 to 1999. And *Gerhard Richter: Forty Years of Painting* showed around the US at prestigious venues, originating at the Museum of Modern Art, New York in 2002, and ending at the Hirshhorn Museum, Washington DC in 2003.

14 The phrase is actually "found himself lying in the Gallery of Machines at the Great Exposition of 1900, his historical neck broken by the sudden irruption of forces totally new"; from Henry Adams (1918), 382.

15 Barthes (1981), 96.

16 Freud (1955), 241.

17 The Pontormo is in the Pieve di S. Michele in Carmignano, Italy.

18 "A World of Art: Works in Progress: Bill Viola." Produced by Oregon Public Broadcasting in association with Oregon State University, 1997. Distributed by the Annenberg Project.

19 It was first exhibited at Anthony d'Offay Gallery in 2001, and later as the culminating work to the exhibition *Bill Viola: The Passions* which began at the J. Paul Getty Museum in 2003 and traveled to London and Munich.

20 Gayford (2003), 24–5.

21 Quoted Ziegler (1998), 80. Rist is a member of the all-female rock group *Les Reines Prochaines*.

22 Quoted in Levine (1994), 138–9.

23 Fluxus artist Dick Higgins described the "intermedia condition" long before anyone else. See, for instance, his 1965 essay, "Synesthesia and Intersenses: Intermedia."

References

Adams, Henry (1910). *The Education of Henry Adams*. Boston: Houghton Mifflin Co.

ArtsJournal.com: The Daily Digest of Arts and Cultural Journalism (2004). "Guiliani vs. Brooklyn," www.artsjournal.com/issues/Brooklyn.htm.

Barthes, Roland (1974). *S/Z*, trans. Richard Miller. New York: Hill and Wang.

—— (1981). *Camera Lucida: Reflections on Photography*, trans. Richard Howard. New York: Hill and Wang.

Berger, Maurice (2001). *Fred Wilson: Objects and Installations, 1979–2000*. Baltimore County: Center for Art and Culture, University of Maryland.

Corrin, Lisa G., ed. (1994). *Mining the Museum: An Installation by Fred Wilson*. New York: The New Press.

Crimp, Douglas (1993). *On the Museum's Ruins*. Cambridge, MA: MIT Press.

Freud, Sigmund (1955). "The Uncanny." In *The Standard Edition of the Complete Psychological Works*, vol. 17. London: Hogarth Press.

Fusco, Coco (1994). "The Other History of Intercultural Performance." Originally published in *The Drama Review* (1994); from *English is Broken Here: Notes on Cultural Fusion in the Americas*. New York: The New Press, 1995.

Gayford, Martin (2003). "The Ultimate Invisible World: Interview with Bill Viola." *Modern Painters*, no. 16 (Autumn):22–5.

Gómez-Peña, Guillermo (in collaboration with Roberto Sifuents and Matthew Finch) (2001). "Aztechnology." *Art Journal*, no. 60 (Spring):33–9.

Higgins, Dick (1965). "Synesthesia and Intersenses: Intermedia." Originally published in *Something Else Press Newsletter* (1965); republished in *Horizons, the Poetics and Theory of the Intermedia*. Carbondale, IL: Southern Illinois University Press, 1984.

Hopps, Walter, and Susan Davidson (1997). *Robert Rauschenberg: A Retrospective*. New York: Guggenheim Museum Publications.

Jameson, Fredric (1991). *Postmodernism, or, The Cultural Logic of Late Capitalism*. Durham, NC: Duke University Press.

Jones, Amelia, ed. (1996). *Sexual Politics: Judy Chicago's* Dinner Party *in Feminist Art History*. Berkeley: University of California Press.

Kosuth, Joseph (1992). *The Play of the Unmentionable: An Installation by Joseph Kosuth at the Brooklyn Museum*. New York: The New Press.

Levine, Steven Z. (1994). *Monet, Narcissus, and Self-Reflection: The Modernist Myth of the Self*. Chicago: University of Chicago Press.

Lippard, Lucy R. (1995). *The Pink Glass Swan: Selected Essays on Feminist Art*. New York: The New Press.

—— (1997). *The Lure of the Local: Senses of Place in a Multicentered Society*. New York: The New Press.

Malraux, André (1967). *Museum Without Walls*, trans. Stuart Gilbert and Francis Price. London: Secker and Warburg.

Mulvey, Laura (1975). "Visual Pleasure and Narrative Cinema." First published in *Screen* (1975). Repr. in *Visual and Other Pleasures*. Bloomington: Indiana University Press, 1989.

Spector, Nancy (2002). *Matthew Barney: The Cremaster Cycle*. New York: Guggenheim Museum.

Storr, Robert (1993). *Robert Ryman*. London: Tate Gallery Publications.

—— (2000). *Gerhard Richter: October 18, 1977*. New York: Museum of Modern Art.

—— (2002). *Gerhard Richter: Forty Years of Painting*. New York: Museum of Modern Art.

Sussman, Elizabeth, and David Armstrong (1996). *Nan Goldin: I'll Be Your Mirror*. New York: Whitney Museum of Art.

Varnedoe, Kirk (1994). *Cy Twombly: A Retrospective*. New York: Museum of Modern Art.

—— (1996). *Jasper Johns: A Retrospective*. New York: Museum of Modern Art.

—— (2002). *Cy Twombly: Lepanto*. New York: Gagosian Gallery.

Wagner, Anne M. (2003). "Kara Walker: The Black-White Relation." In *Kara Walker: Narratives of a Negress*, ed. I. Berry, C. English, V. Patterson, and M. Reinhardt. Cambridge, MA: MIT Press.

Walsh, John, ed. (2003). *Bill Viola: The Passions*. Los Angeles: J. Paul Getty Museum.

Ziegler, Ulf Erdmann (1998). "Rist Factor," *Art in America*, no. 86 (June):80–3.

PART III

Aesthetics

7

Form and Formless

Caroline A. Jones

Few oppositions have organized post-1960s art as completely as form versus formless (or, more pretentiously, *informe*). Both are accompanied by critical methods that continue to have purchase on the contemporary art world. The brief hegemony of the method called "formalism" came in the 1950s and early 1960s, and its reign is the crucial backdrop for contemporary antagonisms between form and formless. If the revival of "formless" in the 1990s was accompanied by a method, it was deconstructive in nature, committed to process and naturalized in contemporary art discourse at least since the postmodern turn against art writer Clement Greenberg in the 1980s. Yet both modes have longer histories. Form and *informe* have been particularly crucial discourses in Anglo-American art worlds, but the antinomy has its sources in Continental philosophies as old as modernism itself.

Formalism was a compelling but always embattled component of aesthetic theory in a disjunctively modernizing Europe, and theories attending to the "formless" were, in several interesting respects, less a rejection than an extension of formalism's earliest motivations. In brief, "form" has been identified as modernist, "formless" as a process beyond the postmodern divide – yet this chapter will claim that theorists of the *informe* have not moved beyond form as much as they have returned to a lost future rescued from formalism's complex past.

The history of formalism reveals enclaves of fierce supporters, but no widespread success until after World War II. At that moment, the US art world was propelled into prominence by the *pax Americana*, and formalism emerged as the most appropriate method for the bureaucratic optimism of the age. But formalism's much longer prior history shows that the method is strongly identified with modernity itself. Appearing in several countries simultaneously in the first decades of the twentieth century, and affecting fields as diverse as anthropology, music composition, literary analysis, and the visual arts, it grew from an extraordinary mix of post-Enlightenment positivism and the romantic cult of the individual. Both reached their apogee in industrializing France, but required promoters elsewhere to spread the news. On the one hand, there was the brisk secular positivism initiated by Auguste Comte and popularized by John Stuart Mill; on the other, the work of romantic and symbolist poets (Paul Verlaine, Arthur Rimbaud, Stephan Mallarmé), who followed Baudelaire in exploring extreme sensations through new poetic forms. These seemingly oppositional cultural formations each required an educated individual with a finely-tuned *sensibilité*, and it was in such *receptive* terms that formalism staked its claims.

Rather than form/formless, early binaries coalesced around questions of *form versus content*. In this early twentieth-century pairing, *form* was taken to be the radical term – unconcerned with biography, unfettered by religion, unconstrained by subject matter, free of national or linguistic boundaries – form offered the equivalent of a critical "Esperanto" in a world beset by class warfare, rapid industrialization, and the often violent birth of nation-states. To take only one example, the group of linguists and literary theorists who developed the "new formal method" in revolutionary Russia (roughly 1905 to 1924) drew from Comtean models of positive knowledge to produce a rational, scientific approach that would focus on the texts themselves rather than their biographical, historical, or cultural "envelopes."[1] Roman Jakobson articulated their goals this way in 1921: "The old literary historians remind us of policemen who, in order to arrest a certain individual, arrest everybody and carry off everything from his lodgings, and arrest also anyone who passed by on the street."[2]

Jakobson's metaphor referenced formalism's own embattled status in the Soviet system at the time, where concerns with "pure form" had triggered suspicion in a new Soviet power elite, which increasingly viewed the method as a screen for bourgeois indulgence. Formalism's emphasis on a receptive individual, and the method's lack of concern with declarative "content," meant that it was less amenable to control by a centralized authority; as a result, formalism as such was deemed dangerously reactionary. The outcast pioneers of formalism defended their method by arguing that it transcended politics to become a value-free science: "We are not 'Formalists' but, if you will, specifiers."[3]

Early twentieth-century formalism was given a more romantic slant by British art writers Roger Fry and Clive Bell. Developing along different lines from some of the same European sources, these writers in the London Bloomsbury group downplayed the Russians' Comtean scientism, emphasizing the sensate individual that "specification" might imply. Adopting "form" and "formalism" from the Soviets, Fry and Bell transposed these terms to visual genres; they also shifted attention even further to the reception of abstract elements within a given artwork. Fry's preference for post-impressionist volumes and plasticity (over impressionist or Whistler-type "decorations") ensured that reception entailed a certain moral position (e.g., some forms were better than others). As Clive Bell distilled such formulations, aesthetic inquiry implied judgments of value, based on the sensitive human's emotionally affective perception of "significant form."[4]

Such value judgments rendered the Bloomsbury group's formalism as political as the Eastern Europeans' – although that might not seem obvious at first. Fry and Bell worked with exotic objects that had become available through imperial expansion, and their politics lay in an attempt to reverse (or at least inflect) the conquerors' cultural valuations. Bell, in particular, took up formalism in order to neutralize two contemporary poisons: Germanic notions of historical progress, and Enlightenment denigrations of "the savage." He located examples of "significant form" throughout human history – in an ancient Chinese sculpture, a Persian dish from the Middle Ages, a Byzantine mosaic, and a Peruvian pot (all, along with Cézanne and Picasso, illustrated in his 1914 book *Art*).[5]

A larger programmatic goal reveals itself in Bell's theory, where he describes *absence of representation* as crucial to the formalist dream. This utopian telos would be taken up again by champions of the *informe* – but in both cases, art that "denies representation" proved to be a shifting and chimerical goal. In the case of Fry and Bell, it could only have been sheer late-Victorian ignorance that imagined non-Western (or non-modern) art forms to be absent of representation; what seemed non-representational merely hied to a system of signs and practices that were utterly alien to the codes developed by the entrenched art academies of modern Europe. "Formal significance loses itself in preoccupation with exact representation and ostentatious cunning,"[6] Bell insisted, but of course he knew next to nothing about the savvy systems of ostentation that ruled Nazca Peru.

By the same token, modernists' ignorant celebration of non-Western forms as being free of representational significance meant that those same forms were available for Western appropriation, and appreciation, in potentially any work of art. The effects of this were simultaneously arrogant and generous. Modernists had a field day appropriating West African sculpture, for example, but by the same token their attention to tribal art dealt a fatal blow to the academic trivium and its affiliation with the upper class. This gave the Bloomsbury group's formalist project its political valence, as decades of Ruskinian indoctrination (which had insisted that a deep knowledge of Christian culture was necessary to appreciate Gothic cathedrals, for instance) were bumptiously ignored. In the place of a white Christian background and equally white aristocratic privilege, they plumped for a receptive individual sensibility that could connect with *any* object from *any* culture to find "significance" in its form.

Fry's formalism aimed to be a democratic discipline, available to all – but in the eyes of some Marxists, it remained irredeemably bourgeois. As Raymond Williams could later argue:

What emerged in bourgeois economics as the "consumer," . . . emerged in cultural theory as "aesthetics" and the "aesthetic response." All problems of the multiplicities of intention and performance could then be undercut, or bypassed, by the transfer of energy to this other pole. Art, including literature, was to be defined by its capacity to evoke this special response.[7]

The art was privileged for its capacity to evoke response, but the individual needed training in order to *have* that response.

British formalism *did* open the field of aesthetics to non-white practitioners, such as Ananda Kentish Coomaraswamy (1877–1947), who enlisted formalism's utopian universalism on behalf of the form-making traditions of Hindu and Buddhist religions. Seeking a foundational formal tradition (notably non-abstract) that would pre-date the perceived "error" of Greek rationalist thought, Coomaraswamy produced an architectural formalism that was frankly metaphysical, linking European and non-European artifacts in essays such as "Usnisa and Chatra: Turban and Umbrella" (1938). Coomaraswamy's use of formalism suggests the suppleness of the tool in the earlier decades of the twentieth century, before later developments rendered such approaches mere cul-de-sacs in formalism's otherwise technocratic and progressivist path.

That latter path was laid down primarily by scholars in the German-speaking universities (some in Vienna or Switzerland), who were eager to organize world history and culture via formalisms that grouped objects according to visible qualities. Such groupings ("linear," "painterly," etc.) could then be given racial, national, psychological, or historical significance, and because of their material basis, they could be aligned with scientific positivism. These Germanic scholars approached form in ways that were philosophical (as in Ernst Gombrich and the Vienna School of logical positivists), psychological (as in Aloïs Riegl and Wilhelm Worringer), and philological (exemplified by Heinrich Wölfflin). This last was the most influential in the American case, where Wölfflin's easy binaries (painterly versus linear, etcetera) became codified as a kind of comparative philology (the profession of Wölfflin's father), described by art historian Donald Preziosi as "pre-eminently formalist in the sense that each object would be classified primarily according to its morphological or stylistic properties, used to discriminate different artists, area or period patternings, or the signs of different national or ethnic groups."[8]

Against such sortings of form-types and invariant structures (deeply historical, racial, and national in their thrust), the French offered anti-metaphysical, body-based, universalist phenomenologies emerging from the work of Henri Bergson. The German emphasis on stable typologies and genre-specific boundaries met Bergson's vehemently anti-spatial philosophy and produced some curious hybrids. Bergson students such as Élie Faure (*The Spirit of the Forms* [1927]) and Henri Focillon (*The Life of Forms in Art* [1935]) were propounding a vitalist formalism in which historical or social context (place and race) had far less to do with a given work of art's form than did epistemological structures of human thought (described as conformity and originality, stability and change). In this respect, their work resembled the psychological formalism of Austrian theorist Aloïs Riegl, but departed from Riegl's interests in defining the essentials of a given genre. These sometimes amateur French art historians were much more likely to group objects on the basis of their peculiar psychological effects, emphasizing their ultimate uniqueness as works of art.

Not surprisingly, via this focus on the felt mystery of the artistic object, the French formalists of the 1920s and 1930s could be connected with the first surrealists and their "operations," emerging at the same moment in the same cultural milieu. But the goals of these two groups were very different. While Faure and Focillon were arguing that form alone provided the tools for its own decoding, surrealist philosopher Georges Bataille was declaring war on form itself. These were not unrelated moves; both sides pursued an anti-rational suspicion of grand metaphysical explanations, pitting Bergson, as it were, against Hegel's dialectics (exemplified by Wölfflin, whose influential "scientific" formalism from 1915, *Principles of Art History*, was even at that moment being translated into French and English). Broadly speaking, the Continent was divided into French, Bergsonian formalisms (phenomenological), and Germanic Wölfflinian formalisms (dialectical).[9]

Surrealism, particularly in the hands of Georges Bataille, attempted to demolish them both. Bataille's writing spanned the interwar period, stretched into the early 1960s, and was then revived in the US beginning in the 1980s. Bataille and the artists with whom he was associated provide a key focal point for the form/formless debate.

The Great War had stimulated various moves against positivism and empiricism (such as Bataille's), but the Second World War codified and institutionalized such antagonisms. In the aftermath of fascism and the dark dawn of the nuclear age, Europeans celebrated a surrealist legacy of *informe* while the US came to certify a technocratic formalist abstraction. This bifurcation was conducted largely in rhetoric; it was not always evident in the appearance of the art works themselves. Paintings classed in Paris as "*informe*," "*Tachist*," or "*l'art autre*" ("other art"), sometimes linked with artifacts from the Japanese Gutai groups, appeared visually to have strong connections to US abstract expressionism in its spread immediately after the war. Turbid color dulled to mud, roughly handled paint incorporating all sorts of foreign materials, and increasing levels of abstraction linked these manifestations formally, even as their justifying philosophical frameworks diverged. The shards and debris of this painting were parsed for underlying order in the US, while Europeans continued to insist on the traumatic performance and abysmal pulverization offered by "formless" works of art.

Informe helped Paris, the center of modernist art, position itself after WWII as having been either an innocent victim of Vichy or the primary source of resistance to fascist rule. Although the city itself was largely undamaged by the war, a pervasive sense of trauma could be felt in its arts and letters; *informe* spoke to that condition. Bataille's brilliant 1930s theorization of capitalism had encompassed sacrifice, desire, and excess, with dollops of Sadean nihilism and eroticized violence; his ideas seemed appropriate to the postwar 1940s, fueling a widespread Parisian interest in images of trauma and abjection that were eventually packaged in the 1950s as "l'art informel."[10] Exemplary of the complications that came with this *informel* packaging were the works of Wols.

Born Alfred Otto Wolfgang Schulze in Berlin in 1913, Wols worked in Paris primarily as a photographer. Many of his photographs appeared in Bataille's important surrealist publication *Documents*; these were primarily straightforward images of animal meat (lungs, tasty cutlets) posed on banal surfaces on which they seemed inappropriate or uncanny (rose-patterned oilcloth, or a worn carpet floor). Wols's wartime turn to canvas produced a very different kind of work. Characterized by splattered or roughly applied paint, their smallish surfaces were then fiercely scratched or jabbed, sharing Bataille's celebration of formlessness and *bassesse* (baseness). At least they were interpreted that way at the time. Although later theorists of *informe* (Yves-Alain Bois and Rosalind Krauss) eliminate Wols's paintings from their privileged category of the Bataillean "operation," Wols emerged after the war with a whole set of artists (Jean Dubuffet, Alberto Giacometti, Jean Fautrier, even Antonin Artaud) whose treatment of the canvas surface clearly registered the widespread attempt to violate or stigmatize "form."

"Stigmatize" is just the right term to characterize these operators in Catholic France, for the canvas was rendered *a body* that then suffered for inexpressible sins. The explosion of anti-form in Paris was perhaps a result of the collapse of optimistic Enlightenment ideals of perfectibility, which had become linked to ideologies of "pure form." The formal tradition of geometric abstraction had built on Cubo-Futurism, evolving in Germany and Eastern Europe during the twenties (as suprematism, de Stijl, constructivism, and finally the Bauhaus). These practitioners had positioned "form" as a universal language, linked with the progressive values of engineering and science, a broad tendency that was specifically targeted by fascism and survived the Second World War only in exile. Even as fascism made sure that few practitioners remained in Europe to rescue this tradition in the postwar period, the geometers were castigated by the surrealists as naive and depthless. The exiled purveyors of optimistic, technophilic "formalist" values became influential in the US (where Ilya Bolotowsky cofounded the American Abstract Artists group in 1936, the New Bauhaus opened in Chicago in 1938, and Mondrian produced a vigorous new set of works in New York in the early 1940s, his "Boogie-Woogie" paintings). The modernizing countries of South America had their own appetite for the scientific yet spiritual language of pure form. So if the rationality of form seemed untenable in Europe, it was taken up elsewhere.

Bataille's prewar campaign against form merged with existentialism in post-WWII Paris (only in the 1980s would he be extricated from this enabling mix). Yet existentialism produced an inherent contradiction that would haunt the future uptake of Bataillean anti-form. Within the Sartrean context, anti-compositional *informe* was doomed to be interpreted as a "gesture," an existential Act. (Even Bois's attempt at a radical revival of the formless in the late '90s is tinged with that vocabulary.[11]) Harnessed to such "actions," formlessness became the witness or trace of something in time. Its spatialization could only become representational, as capable of reproduction and exchange as any iconography.

Wols reveals how the intention to make "anti-compositional" art can paradoxically produce a convention of unconventionality (the "form" of *informe*
acts). Like the works of Fautrier and Dubuffet with which they hung, Wols'
anti-images are centered in rectangular frames, often biaxially symmetric, signed
and dated. Roughly spherical shapes (perhaps bodies, or heads?) convey themselves through pigment that seems to have crept, slithered, or been violently
propelled onto the canvas, never stroked by a sable brush. This type of formlessness was not worked out through a refusal to organize matter; rather, the
informe appearing in postwar Paris seems to have required that the canvas
maintain its integrity as a coherent body covered by a "skin" of paint. This
requirement was maintained precisely so that the implied body and its skin could
be violated by the male artists of the *informe* – through punctured paint surfaces
in Wols, gouged and sliced impasto in Fautrier, sgraffito, pebbles, and dirt in
Dubuffet – stigmatically marking the paint skin to register the suffering of the
informe.

Accompanied by revivals and reinterpretations of Bataille, these attempts to
instantiate *informe* were bolstered by the rhetoric of Wols, Dubuffet et al. These
artists insisted, as Dubuffet put it, on their "Anti-Cultural Positions."[12] On the
one hand, baseness and formlessness participated in the grand avant-garde project,
serving to *épater les bourgeoises* and confound academic conventions of narrative,
classical design, and "*fini.*" On the other, existentialist surrealism rejected the
technocratic progressivism that geometric abstraction seemed to exemplify, finding
such brisk professionalism inadequate to the technological war's dark revelations
about human capacities for evil.

Initially, the shocking crudeness of this art did function to express the absolute cultural nadir that Europeans experienced immediately after the war. With
perfect hindsight, existentialism and surrealism seemed to have prophesied that
condition all too well. Writing in 1929, Bataille had observed that "the universe
resembles nothing and is only *formless . . .*, something like a spider or spit."
"Revived" once in the existentialist 1940s, and again by the post-structuralists
around *October* magazine in the 1980s, Bataille outlined a cultural and social
program of intentional debasement: "*informe* is not only an adjective having a
given meaning, but a term that serves to bring things down in the world, [a
world which otherwise requires] that each thing have its form."[13] Of course, like
any other perceptible reality, *informe* would come to have its "significant" form.

But this formalism of *informe* was easier to identify at the end of the twentieth
century. In the immediate postwar period, the *perception* of form versus formlessness could be quite local, affecting the fate of specific objects in material
ways. Painting emerging from New York in the 1940s, for example, seemed raw,
crude, and shockingly unformed to critics weaned on European art. At first, this
shock was welcomed by the US artists as a sign of their chthonic uniqueness.
Despite their grudging acceptance of the rubric "The New York School" (self-
consciously named in emulation of the *école de Paris*), they railed against what
they saw as European-type "relational compositions" made with mahlsticks,

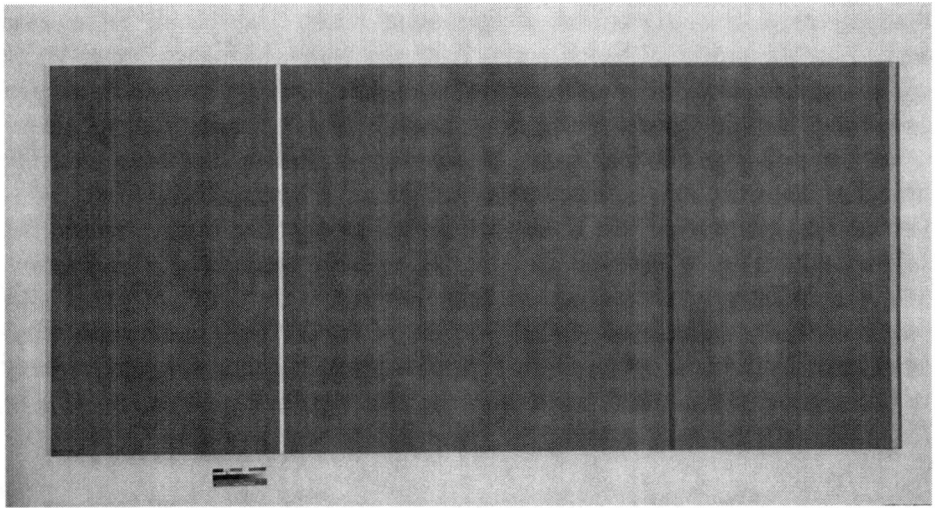

FIGURE 7.1   Barnett Newman, *Vir Heroicus Sublimis*, 1950–1. Oil on canvas. 7 ft
11⅜ in × 17 ft 9+ in. Gift of Mr and Mrs Ben Heller, 240.1969. Collection Museum
of Modern Art, New York. Digital image © The Museum of Modern Art, licensed by
SCALA and Art Resource New York. © 2005 Barnett Newman Foundation/Artists
Rights Society (ARS), New York

palettes, and expensive brushes. They, too, were enamored of the uncontemplated
"Act." "Free from the weight of European culture," Barnett Newman wrote in
1948, "we are making . . . cathedrals . . . out of our own feelings . . ."[14] These
sentiments resonate with the painter's own expansive canvases, saturated as they
were with a single, barely inflected hue (his field paintings *Cathedra* and *Vir
Heroicus Sublimis*, for example, from 1951), punctuated with a vertical "zip" of
a muted color (often white or black) (Figure 7.1). Alternatively, the new attributes of an abstract spirituality "out of our own feelings" could be taken to
describe the turbulent palimpsests of gestures found in a Jackson Pollock skein
painting (such as the similarly titled *Cathedral*, from 1947).

Only a culture obsessed with relating form to feeling could find "formal" links
between two such different works of art. A more significant point of commonality
appeared to be the works' participation in the discourse (and formal language)
of the sublime. The sublime builds in a temporal component – an oscillation in
narrative and/or experience – that uses the move from form to formlessness, or
alternatively, from chaos to order, to fuel its very dynamic. Pollock's seemingly
chaotic skein paintings were seen by many to activate the moment of ego-
dissolution in the trajectory toward an oceanic sublimity (formlessness), while
Newman's minimally inflected field paintings were used to put that subject back
together again (as form). Per Newman: "[The viewer] relates to me when I

made the painting because in that sense I was there. . . . I hope that my painting has the impact of giving someone as it did me, the feeling of his own totality, of his own separateness, of his own individuality, and at the same time of his connection to others, who are separate."[15]

Early readings of Pollock's painting as formless or disordered, even violently so, circulated widely in the popular press – particularly in those conservative US media outlets that were most concerned with America's foreign reputation. *Time* magazine, for example, reported on European receptions of Pollock in one 1950 article with the title "Chaos, Damn It!"[16] As the 1950s unfurled within the art world proper, critics lined up on either side of the polemic. Pollock's works either had order, or they didn't; they had form, or were as formless as the godless universe itself.

Those holding onto Sartrean existentialism saw Pollock's non-objective drip paintings as heroic gestures against the void, inchoate thrashings against annihilation. Such readings were captured by Harold Rosenberg's essay on "American Action Painters" in 1952, which seemed to be describing Pollock (without naming him) as producing "events" rather than paintings. This strain would fuel an "underground" of anti-form that would return, with a vengeance, after the collapse of 1950s formalism in the US.

The mainstream, however, soon adopted readings of an ordered Pollock that had their source in the criticism of Clement Greenberg. This enormously influential art writer became closely identified with Pollock, yet he drew no weighty distinction between the painted and dripped Pollocks. The drips, far from inaugurating a suddenly "anti-form" Pollock in 1947, were simply more of the same, confirming a painter of "classical" order. As the term *skeins* implies, Pollock's webs of paint were *woven* from back and forth movements that eschewed the wrist in favor of the arm, allowing Greenberg his idiosyncratic but ultimately determinative reading of the drip paintings' rational urban order. For Greenberg, Pollock's actions were only the beginning. The painter responded in bodily ways to the implicit order of the urban grid, producing results that were ultimately industrial, the canvas's textured "all-overness" providing the unity Greenberg demanded in modernist form.[17]

After Greenberg had begun to be important for Pollock, numerous canvases were given the title *Number One* – as if in obeisance to Greenberg's formalist demand for "unity" in these works. Admittedly, "Oneness" also tracked with the American-style existentialism wielded by Rosenberg, exemplifying how the split between form and formless could be maintained at almost every point (right up to the present). The raw, base, "formless" Pollock of Rosenberg co-existed with the cool, classic, "formalist" Pollock forwarded by Greenberg (an ambiguity that still oscillated in the 2000 Hollywood film *Pollock*). It was all a matter of scale – while Rosenberg celebrated the heroic individual, Greenberg bypassed the individual as such, urging that the material arrangement of pigment and canvas was accessible to anyone willing to apprentice him/herself to formalist viewing protocols. Form's cool rational leveling, available to all, was contrasted by Greenberg to formlessness and its romantic extremity, suitable (in his view) only to a hysterical individual out of touch with urban order and its future promise. And yet, interesting vestiges of formlessness were maintained within this system, as Greenberg connected the all-over painting epitomized by Pollock with the polyphonic nuances of new music:

> So these painters render every element, every part of the canvas equivalent; and they likewise weave the work of art into a tight mesh whose principle of formal unity is contained and recapitulated in each thread. . . . But these painters go even beyond Schoenberg by making their variations upon equivalence so subtle that at first glance we might see in their pictures, not equivalences, but an *hallucinated uniformity.* . . . This very uniformity, this dissolution of the picture into sheer texture, sheer sensation, into the accumulation of similar units of sensation, seems to answer something deep-seated in contemporary sensibility. It corresponds perhaps to the feeling that all hierarchical distinctions have been exhausted . . .[18] [Emphasis added]

Greenberg was experiencing the same postwar "ground zero" condition that his peers in Paris had identified. Even his conclusions were similar to those celebrated by theorists of the *informe* (both then and in postmodernism): "the future of the easel picture . . . has become very problematical; for in using the easel picture as they do – and cannot help doing – these artists are destroying it."[19] Yet the compelling aspect of Greenberg's project was that such evident formlessness *necessarily became* the grounds for formalism's apotheosis. From the antithesis of exhausted distinctions and collapsed hierarchies, a set of new distinctions and far more subtle hierarchies would emerge, as if "hallucinated," from the ashes. As in previous formalist systems, Greenberg's demanded a cultivated observer as sensitive and experienced as the critic himself – but the training for that viewer would be available to all, based on "experience" and what he terms "eyesight alone."[20]

The terms for Greenberg's reading of modern art as formally ordered were in place as early as the fall of 1943, when Greenberg reviewed one of Mondrian's New York boogie-woogie paintings and articulated a kind of credo that would be mapped onto Pollock and his inheritors over the decades to come:

> Something of the harmony of the original white square of canvas should be restored in the finished painting. But harmony a thousand times more intense, because it is the result of the successful resolution of a difficult struggle. The simplest way almost of accounting for a great work of art is to say that it is a thing possessing simultaneously the maximum of diversity and the maximum of unity possible to that diversity.[21]

Not only does the "resolution of . . . struggle" posited by Greenberg provide the means to rescue form from formlessness, but it sets up the thinly veiled terms of a political morality. In an epoch characterized by Americans' self-image as the "Vital Center" between totalitarian socialism and a putatively vanquished fascist threat, the "maximum of unity possible" could be read in political terms – suggesting the totalizing imperative and hallucinated uniformity of democratic capitalism itself.

Scholars have bemoaned the "depoliticization" that postwar American formalism effected on postwar painting, yet the hidden politics of this formalism can now be seen. Formalism found a way for "formless" paintings to become aligned with an *ideology of no ideology* crafted by the abstract expressionist artists themselves. In this respect, Greenberg only made programmatic what many New York School artists already professed. The abstract painter Adolph Gottlieb spoke directly to the issue in 1948, commenting that New York School artists were attacked by both the right *and* the left: "The black sheep, it seems, are neither white enough nor red enough.... With the cry of unintelligibility the critics attack ..."[22] In this context, abstraction and the formalism that would theorize it were specific alternatives to the representational and political requirements of regionalism, social realism, and fascist realism. The feint of depoliticization was, in fact, a precise political tool, allowing the art's mobilization as "unity," and permitting it to be interpreted as a statement of maximum individual freedom within a smooth technocratic apparatus – via formalist criticism and its universal claims.

The channeling of sensation Greenberg advocated (paintings for eyesight alone) let form obey a pervasive logic that linked the high-keyed, hard-edged, Color Field painting favored by US formalists in the 1960s with Hi-Fi listening and other "narrow-bandwidth" modes of addressing (and commodifying) the body's portals in a bureaucratization of the senses. Extraordinarily, this narrowing could be experienced as an exhilarating fecundity. US art historian Michael Fried, one of the most erudite and effective of Greenberg's interpreters, accepted the art writer's linkage of formalism to modernism, and went one step further, insisting that modernist form and its protocols (inherently abstract) were the *only* viable paradigm for postwar artists. What had been a spectrum of quality judgments from Fry to Bell to Greenberg became, in Fried, programmatic. The results Fried obtained from this intensely channeled perceptual phenomenology were profound. As he argued in his famous polemic against minimalism (the essay "Art and Objecthood" from 1967), form was by necessity form *within a specific genre convention*. Pictorial form was distinct from sculptural form, just as poetry had rules that distinguished it from prose. Form wrested from modernist pictorial conventions had "presence" and "presentness," versus artworks that flirted with the boundaries between painting and sculpture (minimalism, which he called "literalism" and stigmatized as theatrical). In the essay's well-known conclusion, formalism's restrictions conveyed a seriousness of purpose that was moral and, ultimately, religious: "Presentness is grace."[23]

Fried's denigration of "literal" art in favor of transcendental modernist form appears now to have been a narrow doctrinal dispute – for surely minimalism was just as obsessed with modernist form as the objects Fried celebrated. Yet Fried's formulation, which pitted "presence" (good forms) against theatrical "duration" (bad forms) galvanized artists. Durational process art, theatrical body art, and aggressive "anti-form" artworks were dialectically re-positioned and given a new political valence – the countermand to modernist "unity" and "pure form" could be analogized, for example, to the unruly opposition to the American war in Vietnam. Even the minimalists' concerns with "good gestalt" were driven so far that they came out the other end – as formlessness. For erstwhile minimalist Robert Smithson, the anti-gestalt theories of psychologist Anton Ehrenzweig became useful in undermining the conventions of Greenbergian modernism. Ehrenzweig's de-differentiated vision replaced Greenberg's foveal eye; duration, formless entropy, wandering, peripheries, and dirt replaced instantaneous presence, formal unity, primary structures, urban centers, and the white cube. Modernism, in some sense because Fried was willing to give it such paradigmatic status, became replaceable; Smithson was only one of the artists who began to flirt with an odd oxymoron in the *seventies*: "Post-modernism."

Another symptom of the turn against Greenbergian formalism came when high minimalist sculptor and theorist Robert Morris (under Smithson's influential peddling of Ehrenzweig) turned from "good gestalt" to *Anti-Form* in his influential essays on sculpture published in *Artforum* in the late 1960s.[24] With works such as *Untitled (Threadwaste)* from 1968, Morris reframed the industrial order Greenberg held to be implicit in modernist form, replacing positivist certainty with messy *waste* (Figure 7.2). The lint, fabric scraps, animal hair, plant fiber, grease, and wire in Morris's piles constituted the paradoxical form of the *informe* in Greenberg's wake.[25]

The rest, as they say, is history – a history we still periodize as "contemporary art." In the post-1960s pluralist scene, form and formlessness recur, but as partial and nostalgic formations. Performance and body art, installation art, and the new millennium's "lounge art" are part of a delta spreading out from the late 1960s to the present, posed against the channeled sensory regimes Greenberg had used to organize "form" during the apogee of high modernism in the 1950s. Yet if the rebellious energies of *informe* are routinely summoned to code for avant-gardism, it is also true that form and formalism remain at hand, offering their utopian promise of universal accessibility (if one is willing to apprentice oneself to the implicit conventions that are always required).

The first few years of the twenty-first century have witnessed the invention of "New Formalisms" in various disciplines. In poetry, "new formalism" is a rebellion against the anti-form free verse of the 1960s and 1970s; in architecture, it is instead a continuing strain of corporate-identified design that has remained with us since the postwar popularization of International-style modernism. Inflecting the austere formal vocabulary of the International Style with richer materials (travertine facings, for example) and classical allusions (the arch, the pediment, the colonnade), architecture's "new formalism" continues to tempt designers with dreams of a comforting and rigorous universalism in a multicultural age.

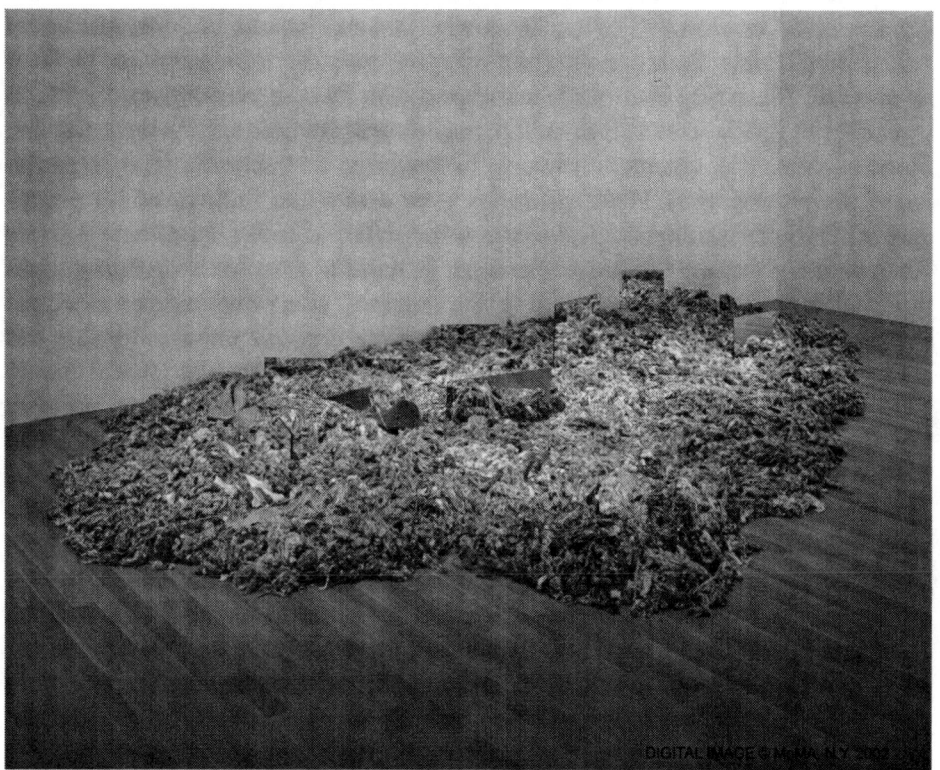

FIGURE 7.2   Robert Morris, *Untitled (Threadwaste)*, 1968. Felt, asphalt, mirrors, wood, copper tubing, steel cable, and lead. $21\frac{1}{2}$ in × 21 ft 11 in × 16 ft 9 in; variable. Collection Museum of Modern Art, New York. Gift of Philip Johnson, 504.1984. Digital image © The Museum of Modern Art, licensed by SCALA and Art Resource New York. © 2005 Robert Morris/Artists Rights Society (ARS), New York

The most direct attempt to clarify the post-1960s muddle of form, formalism, and formlessness, at least in terms of visual art practice, was the *Informe* exhibition produced by Bois and Krauss at the Centre Georges Pompidou in 1996 (accompanied by a similarly titled book translated into English as *Formless: A User's Guide*). The Pompidou installation was part of a series of "signed" exhibitions whose frankly personal and opinionated nature was to be contrasted with an earlier "positivist" pose of neutrality in museum praxis. In place of the professional codes of conduct claimed by Greenberg's generation, the "signed" exhibition was meant to be transparent to the interests guiding its displays – consistent with a poststructuralist, postmodern turn.

In *Formless*, Bois and Krauss used the Pompidou's late modernist frame to produce a polemic against modernism's misreadings of the *informe*. Bois's introduction argues that *informe* can only be understood by "locating certain operations that brush modernism against the grain" while refusing to counter modernism's "formal certainties by means of the more reassuring and naive certainties of meaning."[26] That is to say, *informe* would be revealed as an "operation" rather than a stable iconography, resisting representation in favor of process. The artists historically associated with *l'art informel* from the 1930s through the 1950s were sifted, culled, and sometimes ignored. As with the first blush of formalism, abstraction was to be preferred to figuration (the exception being the photograph). Wols' paintings were denigrated in favor of his photographs; Dubuffet's mineralogical works were preferred to his figurative portraits; Rauschenberg's more Cagean works were featured in place of his pre-pop combines. The personal passions guiding the curators' selections became clear, yet the proclamation of a "User's Guide" implied the demotic universality that had always been formalism's domain.

Formless hardly penetrated the contemporary scene in which it was situated, but the curators' active role in art criticism made their selections salient. Mike Kelley, Cindy Sherman, and Allan McCollum were the few artists from the 1990s who were invited into the core *informe* group; the rest of the catalogue featured works from the 1950s (Pollock, Rauschenberg), 1960s and 1970s (Robert Morris, Andy Warhol, Bruce Nauman, Gordon Matta-Clark, Robert Smithson, Cy Twombly) and a few certified forebears from the 1930s (Marcel Duchamp, Wols, Brassaï, et al.). Kelley and Sherman were carefully preserved from the discourses of abjection so characteristic of that decade (and of their work), because, unlike the hoped-for emphasis on "operations," the abject (in Krauss's conclusion) produced "a thematics of essences and substances," placing it "in absolute contradiction to the idea of the *formless*."[27] Cindy Sherman could be salvaged because her photographs insistently reference horizontality; Mike Kelley could be saved if his assemblages of soiled, cast-off children's toys were understood as part of a process: "because the 'low' occurs here not as a substance (excrement) or as a theme (abjection understood as gender and degradation), but as the functional factor in an operation."[28] Ironically, of course, the authors' hopes "of liberating our thinking from the semantic [and] the servitude to thematics"[29] could hardly avoid either, since the genre of the exhibition object and its catalogue constituted the unacknowledged form of this *Informe*.

At the turn of the millennium, installation art (not the photograph, and certainly not "painting" or "sculpture") became the genre to contend with. Is there "form" implied and encoded in the conventions of the installation? Formalism's long alliance with the modernist white cube is the explicit target of postmodern installation art, and installations implicitly position themselves on the "formless" side of the binary. Where sensory purification was Greenberg's aim, one might expect that sensory miscegenation would be the postmodern rule. Obeisance to this rule is evident in proliferating global biennials, which present artists' hanging nets of spices, formless piles of coffee, or spreads of pollen. The intention is to overwhelm any visual or sculptural associations with waves of invisible aroma and the mathematical sublime (where do you get *that much pollen?*). Smell in particular subverts formal hierarchies, entering the viewer's body in airborne molecules that bypass conscious cognition.

Sound, too, is a favored tool of the anti-form installation artist. One can characterize the wheeling lights, psychedelic revival, and blaring funk loops of the 2004 installation by artist group Assume Astro Vivid Focus as blatant sensory mixing (if not sheer pop culture overload). AAVF's installation for the Whitney Biennial presented a mesh of sonics and optics that could not be unraveled by formalism as such; it could only be "experienced" (as an operation . . .). By the same token, their display depended on a nostalgia for the anti-formalist events staged by Warhol and his Factory "workers," as in the "Exploding Plastic Inevitable" performance/cinematic Happenings presented in the 1960s to accompany the Velvet Underground rock band.

Balancing these efforts at sensory miscegenation is a strain of neo-conceptual installation art that could be emblematized by Janine Antoni's *Slumber* (1994 and ongoing). The museum label for this piece indicates something of its "formlessness"; it reads: "Loom, yarn, bed, nightgown, EEG machine, and artist's REM reading; dimensions variable." During the day, Antoni labors at a loom, where she weaves a simple meandering design based on the recording of her rapid-eye-movement sleep during the previous night. The fabric she weaves serves as the blanket over her body, which sleeps in the gallery through the night while hooked up to the electro-encephalograph machine. Such a work builds on conceptual protocols from minimalism, feminist body art, and process art of the 1970s, but rather than reviving psychedelia or invoking *informe*'s avant-garde tropes, Antoni's performance and installation put the binary of form/formless itself under pressure, by ostentatiously removing conscious artistic will from the process of form, and relocating it to the surrealist's prized plane of the "unformed" unconscious.

Yet the formless here is subjected to two abstracting operations: scientific inscription (EEG) and traditional female labor (weaving). This is neither formalism nor the ideology of *informe*. Such a third way embraces the connections between form (intentional, designed) and formless (accidental, habitual, unconscious). Formal design in *Slumber* occurs on a purely conceptual plane outside the form-generating process itself, yet the work's very "formless" qualities are generated by a form-making concept (which, when understood, can even be opened to formal analysis). The "formless" Pollockian gesture that crawls into the warp and woof of Antoni's weaving attains meaning only when the *concept* is parsed as a graph of points on the EEG of Antoni's brain during sleep. There is nothing universal about such "form" (indeed, it is as unique as a similarly-graphed voiceprint would be), yet its formlessness turns out to carry meaning. In such neo-conceptual works, the fantasized universality of pure form, and the liberation signified by *informe*, both give way to what one could call discursively determined form. Only a neurologist can properly read the "form" that otherwise appears so "formless." Such artworks acknowledge that the making of meaning can never be global and universal, and can never be detached from an intersubjective frame that is necessarily both local and specific.

If form has lost its purity in the postwar period, "formless" conveys an even more intractable period air. Only the derivative term, "formalism," retains its viability in contemporary art. As the theoretical tool bequeathed to art writing by the search for universally significant form, formalism designates those structures or typologies that characterize a given genre and construct its conventions as universal. "Formalism" becomes both the tool for articulating the hidden assumptions undergirding cultural communication, and the way to stigmatize those practices as false in their universal claims. The new vernacular of biennial culture offers a useful case in point. The collapse of the old-world antagonism between capitalism and communism has fueled, on the one hand, an explosion of biennials and global cultural offerings that purport to be unformed architectures of discourse.[30] On the other hand, those very architectures presume the global possession of a postmodern patois that must exist in order to ensure communicability within the exhibition's discursive frame. As one scholar has recently identified the underlying conventions guiding curator Okwui Enwezor's 2002 Documenta XI, the contemporary cultural field is ruled by "platform formalism" – the unacknowledged formal constraints that a series of decentered yet tightly designed "platforms" impose on local discourse.[31]

Such constraints can hardly be avoided. Cultural practitioners in the twenty-first century must simply acknowledge the local limits and presumptions that subtend their attempts to be global and universal. In philosophical terms, formlessness will always lurk as the stubborn residue or necessary adumbration to cultural form. Likewise, form is the "hallucinated" common structure that constitutes the precondition for culture itself (the culture of *informe* no less than others). The useful antinomy of form and formless has long produced a generative relation between these foundational cultural concepts. The best contemporary art acknowledges both the artifice of that relation, and the mutually constitutive role that "form" and "formless" continue to play in the visual culture of our time.

Notes

1 Russian Formalism is arguably the most important source for art world usage. Beginning with the English translation and publication of four formalist essays by Lemon and Reis (1965), articles began to appear with greater frequency, and the term began to be used with some precision. "Formalism" appears as an item in *Art Index* in 1965, with articles specifically addressing the Russian movement as well as conventional US usage.
2 Roman Jakobson, quoted by Rene Wellek in Gibian and Tajalsma (1976), 44.
3 Participants in *Opoyaz* (The Society for the Study of Poetic Language), quoted in Steiner (1984), 17.
4 See Bell (1914), 11.
5 Ibid., 23.
6 Ibid.
7 Williams (1977), 150.
8 Preziosi (1989), 83.
9 See Molotiu (2004).

10 Famously, Bataille's thoughts on the libertory potential of extreme states were stimulated by a black and white photograph of a criminal being flayed alive in colonial China, "Slow Death by Leng-Tch'e (cutting into pieces)." See Bataille (2004).
11 Bois, "The Use Value of 'Formless'," in Bois and Krauss (1997), 13–40.
12 This was the name of Dubuffet's touring lecture, which he gave at the Arts Club of Chicago in 1951, and later in New York.
13 Bataille, "*Informe*," in *Documents* 1:7 (1929): 392, translated in Bataille (1985), 31, and cited by Bois and Krauss (1997), 5 (translation slightly modified here). Bois and Krauss draw a sharp distinction between abjection and the *informe*, but I argue that "spit," for example, draws them rhetorically together – and that bodily abjection accompanies the formless in many of its aesthetic forms.
14 Newman (1948), 53. Words reordered for syntax.
15 Barnett Newman to David Sylvester, "Easter 1965," cited in Auping (1987):140.
16 *Time*, November 20, 1950; cited Naifeh and Smith (1991), 650.
17 This argument is articulated in my "Talking Pictures" (2004).
18 Greenberg, April 1948, reprinted in Greenberg (1986–93), CEC v. 2, 224.
19 Ibid., 225.
20 Greenberg in CEC v. 4, 59. I expand considerably on this theme in my *Eyesight Alone* (2005).
21 Reprinted in Greenberg (1986–93), CEC v. 1, 153.
22 Adolph Gottlieb from 1948, anthologized in Ross (1990), 53.
23 Fried (1967/1998), 168.
24 Morris (1966–9). The final number of his four-part "Notes on Sculpture" was titled "Beyond Objects." There is no escape from this condition. To the extent Morris's *Threadwaste* can enter the world as art, it is formed (the representational form of *informe*). Bois and Krauss present a lovely, rectangular illustration of a detail in *Formless* (p. 33) that also serves to illustrate my point. With a coil of copper wire singled out, the detail is beautifully ordered within the book-object *Formless* – the coil spirals the gaze out from the book's gutter and leads smoothly to the next page.
25 Peggy Deamer, Dean of the Yale School of Architecture, in a conference on architectural pedagogy at MIT in 2003, commented that it was time for a new formalism to come back into the studio.
26 Bois, "Introduction: The Use-Value of Formless," in Bois and Krauss (1997), 16.
27 Krauss, "Conclusion: The Destiny of the Informe," Bois and Krauss (1997), 245.
28 Ibid., 249.
29 Ibid., 252.
30 In contemporary curatorial practice, where professional boundaries between artistic "expression" and curatorial "presentation" are challenged, the open-ended frameworks that result are described as "architectures of discourse," per artist/curator Ute Meta Bauer (2001).
31 Albrethsen (2004).

References and further reading

Albrethsen, Pernille (2004). "Platform Formalism." *Nordic Review*, 16 April; archived at http://www.16beavergroup.org/mtarchive/archives/00873.php

Auping, Michael (1987). *Abstract Expressionism: The Critical Developments.* Buffalo, NY: Albright-Knox Art Gallery.

Bataille, Georges (1985). *Visions of Excess: Selected Writings, 1927–1939.* Minneapolis: University of Minnesota Press.

—— (2004). Entry in "PopSubculture[dot]Com's Biography Project, an Independent Reference Resource." http://www.popsubculture.com/pop/bio_project/georges_bataille.html, accessed June–July 2004.

Bauer, Ute Meta (2001). *Architectures of Discourse.* Barcelona: Fundacio Antoni Tapies.

Bell, Clive (1914). *Art.* New York: Frederick A. Stokes Co.

Bois, Yve-Alain, and Rosalind Krauss (1997). *Formless: A User's Guide.* Cambridge, MA: Zone Books and MIT Press.

Coomaraswamy, Ananda Kentish (1938/1995). "Usnisa and Chatra: Turban and Umbrella." In *Essays in Architectural Theory.* Ed. and with an introduction by Michael Meister. Oxford: Oxford University Press.

Fried, Michael (1967/1998). "Art and Objecthood." Originally published in *Artforum*, reprinted in M. Fried, *Art and Objecthood.* Chicago: University of Chicago Press. 148–72.

Gibian, George, and A. W. Tajalsma, eds. (1976). *Russian Modernism.* Ithaca: Cornell University Press.

Greenberg, Clement (1986–93). *Collected Essays and Criticism* [CEC]. Vols. 1–4. Edited by John O'Brian. Chicago: University of Chicago Press.

Hildebrand, Adolf von (1893). *Das Problem der Form in der bildenden Kunst.* Trans. as *The Problem of Form in Painting and Sculpture.* New York: G. E. Stechert, 1907.

Jameson, Frederic (1972). *The Prison-House of Language: A Critical Account of Structuralism and Russian Formalism.* Princeton: Princeton University Press.

Jones, Caroline A. (2004). "Talking Pictures." In *Things that Talk*, ed. Lorraine Daston. New York: Zone Books.

—— (2005). *Eyesight Alone: Clement Greenberg's Modernism and the Bureaucratization of the Senses.* Chicago: University of Chicago Press.

Lemon, Lee, and Marion Reis, comp. (1965). *Russian Formalist Criticism: Four Essays.* Lincoln: University of Nebraska Press.

Molotiu, Andrei (2004). "Focillon's Bergsonian Rhetoric and the Possibility of Deconstruction." In *Visible Culture: An Electronic Journal for Visual Studies*, http://www.rochester.edu/in_visible_culture/issue3/molotiu.htm (accessed 2004).

Morris, Robert (1966/1967/1969). "Notes on Sculpture," parts 1–4, *Artforum*, vol. 4, no. 6 (February 1966):42–4; vol. 5, no. 2 (October 1966):20–3; vol. 5, no. 10 (Summer 1967):24–9; and vol. 7, no. 8 (April 1969):50–4.

Naifeh, Steven, and Gregory White Smith (1991). *Jackson Pollock: An American Saga.* New York: Harper Perennial.

Newman, Barnett (1948). "The Sublime is Now." *Tiger's Eye* 6 (December 15).

Preziosi, Donald (1989). *Rethinking Art History: Meditation on a Coy Science.* New Haven: Yale University Press.

Ross, Clifford, ed. (1990). *Abstract Expressionism: Creators and Critics, An Anthology.* New York: Harry N. Abrams.

Steiner, Peter (1984). *Russian Formalism.* Ithaca: Cornell University Press.

Twitchell, Beverly H. (1976). *Cézanne and Formalism in Bloomsbury.* Ann Arbor: UMI Research Press.

Williams, Raymond (1977). *Marxism and Literature.* Oxford: Oxford University Press.

8

Re-Thinking the "Duchamp Effect"

David Hopkins

In 1969 Joseph Kosuth, at that time an emergent figure in conceptual art, published an article in which he asserted that "[t]he function of art as a question was first raised by Marcel Duchamp," following this up with the statement: "All art after Duchamp is conceptual (in nature)."[1] He was giving voice here to an idea that, by the end of the 1980s, would be one of the most tenaciously held assumptions about post-World War II avant-garde art: namely that this art represented a sequence of conceptual footnotes to Duchamp. For Kosuth and other commentators the sheer intelligence of Marcel Duchamp, embodied most acutely in "unassisted readymades" such as *Fountain* of 1917, had in some sense altered the trajectory of art history, and stood behind the self-questioning nature of much post-1945 art (particularly movements such as Neo-Dada, pop and conceptualism).

It should be said straight away that many would see the lineage set up by Kosuth as far too narrow. The conceptualist tradition can just as easily be understood as a broad-based reaction originating in the later 1950s and 1960s to the formalist emphasis on visuality in the criticism of Clement Greenberg and Michael Fried. One consequence of such a reaction was the attempt to depart from traditional painterly and sculptural practices, to the extent that "thought" became as much a material in art as anything else. But Kosuth's formulation has been remarkably influential, and the "Duchamp Effect" is a topic in postwar art that demands to be looked at in its own right.[2]

My purpose in this chapter will thus be twofold. Firstly I will plot the entire unraveling of Duchamp's reception since 1945 in broadly chronological terms. At the same time, however, I will take issue with the idea that Duchamp's legacy can in any case be neatly reduced to the Kosuthian "art-as-idea" formulation. In doing so I hope not to lessen the sense of Duchamp's importance, but to detract from the mythologization of his intellect, which surely vies with the way in which Roland Barthes once discussed the myth of Einstein's brain.[3] Other commentators have also perceived a necessity to de-idealize – and subsequently to re-embody – Duchamp. In 1994 Amelia Jones criticized the one-dimensionality of what she termed "the readymade Duchamp" by arguing that "[t]he obsessive focus on the readymades instantiates the reduction of the 'man-and-his-work' to the 'man-as-a-work-of-art,' with the 'readymade Duchamp' then mobilized to support an avant-gardist and authoratitive notion of criticality in post-modernism."[4] Jones is surely correct to criticize the simplistic equation between Duchamp and the idea of the readymade, which is ultimately the source for characterizations of him as a conceptual guru, but there still remains a need to properly re-historicize the range of Duchamp's postwar reception, particularly in its European dimension (which is largely neglected by Jones) in order to achieve a balanced view of just how well it dovetails with the tradition of "art-as-idea."

Marcel Duchamp (1887–1968) produced the larger part of his artistic (or, in his terms, anartistic) output, prior to 1924. This output consisted of a heterogeneous collection of items: paintings, photographs (usually in collaboration with Man Ray), "readymades" of various kinds (including "unassisted readymades" such as the urinal titled *Fountain* of 1917 and "assisted readymades" such as the bird cage containing chunks of marble and a thermometer titled *Why Not Sneeze* of 1921), and, most famously, his *Large Glass* (full title *The Bride Stripped Bare by Her Bachelors, Even*) of 1915–23. These objects had in various ways fulfilled Dada and surrealist tenets, with the Frenchman's activities in New York between 1915 and 1923 representing the fulcrum for proto-Dada manifestations in that city. But Duchamp had largely sidestepped "membership" of either Dada or surrealism. This independence of spirit was exemplified by the way that, after 1924, he acquiesced to rumors that he had given up art in favor of chess (which he played at an international level), although in fact he still occasionally dabbled in artistic activity. For instance, between 1935 and 1941 he quietly and painstakingly assembled his *Bôite-en-Valise*, an edition of "suitcases" in which some 69 items from his previous oeuvre were reproduced or miniaturized in a cross between a portable museum-cum-catalogue and a traveling salesman's display case. When the Second World War broke out, Duchamp, who had spent much of the late 1920s and 1930s in France, escaped back to New York.

The story of Duchamp's reception in the postwar period must, of necessity, be presented schematically here, but it is important to appreciate how very differently each artistic generation viewed him. The immediate postwar years were ones in which modernist painting (as defined by the critic Clement Greenberg) was dominant in the USA, and it is not surprising that Duchamp maintained a relatively low public profile, given the opposition to a purely optical or "retinal" art that works such as his readymades or *Large Glass* had earlier embodied.[5] From the viewpoint of the rising abstract expressionist painters in New York, the work of surrealist artists such as Max Ernst had greater intrinsic interest than Duchamp; however, figures such as Arshile Gorky and even Willem de Kooning looked to Duchamp. De Kooning, who would later praise Duchamp as a "one-man movement . . . open to everybody,"[6] made unexpected use of the ex-Dadaist's work. His important *Pink Angels* of 1945 bears a distinct affinity with Duchamp's studies for *King and Queen Surrounded by Swift Nudes* (1912). The final version of that work had been reproduced in the special issue of the surrealist journal *View* of 1945, which had far greater significance in disseminating Duchamp's reputation than is generally acknowledged.

In terms of American art, it was the post-abstract expressionist generation, who emerged between the mid 1950s and the mid 1960s and were in retreat from the intense subjectivity of artists such as De Kooning, who most comprehensively "rediscovered" Duchamp. With few of his works on display in major collections, he was an almost unknown quantity. It is relatively straightforward, therefore, to track the stages of his historical rediscovery. The main catalyst here was the composer John Cage, who had been a friend of Duchamp since 1942 and who, by the early 1950s had cross-fertilized Dada ideas and aspects of Eastern mysticism to produce experimental musical compositions predicated on chance and the denial of artistic will (such as the notorious *4'33"* of 1952).

In 1952 Cage was teaching at Black Mountain College in North Carolina, where he collaborated with the young Robert Rauschenberg, who was later to be instrumental, along with his friend, Jasper Johns, in first translating full-blown Duchampian concerns – the implications of the *Large Glass* and the readymades for instance – into the terms of 1950s art practice. In the 1960s Cage was to describe Rauschenberg's first concerted departures from abstract expressionist aesthetics – his *White Paintings* of 1951 – as "airports for the lights, shadows and particles,"[7] a quotation which goes a long way to pinpointing how Rauschenberg's works departed from pictorial conventions. The pictures were primarily "receptors," registering external events or activity, rather than imposing any particular "artistic vision" on the viewer. In many ways a more active role was implied for the works' spectators, and Cage's later understanding of Rauschenberg was broadly informed by Duchamp's 1957 lecture "The Creative Act," in which he asserted that the role of the viewer was as fundamental to the creative act as that of the artist. This represented an extremely significant downplaying of the authorial position which had wide repercussions in postwar art.

If the earlier-mentioned 1945 issue of *View* was crucial in bringing about Duchamp's rediscovery in America, Robert Motherwell's 1951 anthology *The Dada Painters and Poets* was also key in setting in motion a reconsideration of Dada, but it devoted relatively little space to Duchamp. However, in 1954 Walter Arensberg's important collection of the French artist's work, including the *Large Glass*, went on show permanently at the Philadelphia Museum of Art, and in 1959 the first monograph on Duchamp, by Robert Lebel, complete with an extensive catalogue *raisonné*, became widely available, in French and English. Actual exhibitions of Duchamp's work had to wait until the 1960s, with Walter Hopps's Pasedena Art Museum retrospective of 1963 being the key American event. Two early European showings were Serge Stauffer's 1960 *Dokumentation über Marcel Duchamp* at the Kunstgewerbemuseum, Zurich, and Richard Hamilton's much more comprehensive *The Almost Complete Works of Marcel Duchamp* at the Tate Gallery, London, of 1966.

In 1960 Jasper Johns can also be found responding to the first publication in English of Duchamp's *Green Box* notes, a crucial means of understanding Duchamp's thought processes in relation to the *Large Glass*, by writing in a review of the "the revelation of the extraordinary qualities of Duchamp's thinking."[8] This modest text provides a marker for the reception of Duchamp as a preeminently "cerebral" figure which became so dominant later in the twentieth century, although the British artist Richard Hamilton, to be discussed later, was also promoting a view of the idea-based nature of Duchamp's output around this time. In the years immediately preceding this the work of Johns, like that of his associate Rauschenberg, had been remarkable for the way the most fugitive aspects of Duchamp's visual output were appropriated and re-energized. Even Johns' "breakthrough work" *Flag* of 1954–5, which undercut the emphasis on interiority in abstract expressionism, can also be seen as responding to a relatively obscure work by Duchamp, *Allégorie de Genre* (1943), which Johns may merely have glimpsed in a 1944 issue of the surrealist journal *VVV*. However, if Duchamp's "allegory" – consisting of a blood-stained bandage doubling as the American flag – had had political connotations as the Second World War came to a close, Johns' later painting of the stars and stripes opted for formal ambiguity rather than political or social comment at a time when America, then in the grip of McCarthyist anti-Communism, was intensely xenophobic.

Duchamp is customarily thought of as an essentially apolitical artist, and this is one of the reasons that Marxist-orientated art historians have tended to downplay his role in postwar art. It is striking for instance that T. J. Clark has made little secret of the fact that he sees Duchamp as a minor figure.[9] This account of the background to Johns' *Flag* suggests, however, that the subtle political inflections of Duchamp's practice – which admittedly often amounted to equivocation itself being raised to the level of an ethical imperative rather than any distinct "position" being held – were often lost sight of by his respondents, who, as Moira Roth has noted, tended to assume his posture of "indifference" rather literally.[10]

By the mid 1960s Johns' allusions to Duchamp were overt. His painting *According to What* of 1964 responds directly to Duchamp's peculiar final painting, the enigmatic *Tu m'* of 1918, cataloguing modes of representation and painterly allusions, such as a color chart, in a knowing echo of the French artist's work. One of the most remarkable features of *Tu m'* is the incorporation of an actual bottle brush which juts out disconcertingly into the viewer's space. Duchamp's physical incorporation of a (readymade) object into what is otherwise a flat, painted surface adumbrates many of Johns' works of the early 1960s (notably *Fool's House* of 1962), in which actual objects are attached to the canvas. Johns' works were in turn related to Rauschenberg's "Combines" of the late 1950s, such as *Monogram* (1955–9), in which a painting acted as plinth for a free-standing stuffed Angora goat with a car tyre around its middle. Such works militated against the Greenbergian injunction, which by then had become dominant in American cultural circles, that the distinguishing attribute of modernist art was disciplinary "purity." On this view painting and sculpture should investigate their own defining attributes and avoid promiscuous cross-fertilization.[11] Rauschenberg's and Johns' works clearly reveled in transgressing Greenbergian proprieties, but it is important to see the impetus for their anti-modernism as fundamentally Duchampian. Greenberg certainly perceived Duchamp as a threat. Seeing the French iconoclast as someone who wished to "transcend" questions of "quality" in art, to go beyond "good and "bad," Greenberg tended to dismiss Duchamp merely as an exponent of the "far out."[12]

In the late 1950s and early 1960s American critics began to use the term "Neo-Dada" to characterize the post-Duchampian productions of Johns, Rauschenberg, and other artists drawn to techniques of "assemblage" (or mixed media).[13] This tendency was also discernible in Europe, notably in the French "Nouveau Réaliste" movement formed in 1960. It is interesting here that, to some degree, Duchamp himself engineered the international spread of Neo-Dada. On returning briefly to France in 1959 he met two of the major Nouveau Réaliste artists, Daniel Spoerri and Jean Tinguely. Over the next year or so, with Duchamp as a common reference point, these young French artists engaged in a spate of collaborative projects with their American counterparts, including a performance at the theater attached to the US Embassy in Paris in which, after a recital of Cage's music by David Tudor, Johns and Rauschenberg joined forces with Tinguely and the French-American artist Niki de Saint Phalle.

This international phase of Neo-Dada was relatively brief. Much as art historians tend to generalize about the all-pervasive nature of Duchamp's influence on the early 1960s avant-garde in Europe and the US, it is useful to draw some distinctions between the character of his take-up in these two contexts. Two representative examples will suffice to make the point. An important European respondent to Duchamp was the Italian Piero Manzoni, whose work in many ways echoes that of another key European figure, the French Nouveau Réaliste artist Yves Klein. Aware of Duchamp's readymades, but obviously more interested in the way in which the French artist's works had often made use of physical substances or residues (such as the use of dust as a means of "coloring" a portion of the *Large Glass*), Manzoni used his bodily resources as a "material" within certain of his works. His *Artist's Breath* works of 1960, for instance, involved the artist blowing up balloons, in an allusion to the classical notion of the "divine pneuma" whereby the artist "breathes life" into the work of art. The brief lives of Manzoni's balloons were subsequently memorialized with their wrinkled remains being affixed to plaques (Figure 8.1). There is a direct Duchampian allusion here, namely to his ampoule of *Paris Air* of 1919, but it is clear that Manzoni has expanded the idea to encompass the "life" of the art work, which is keyed to his physical expenditure.

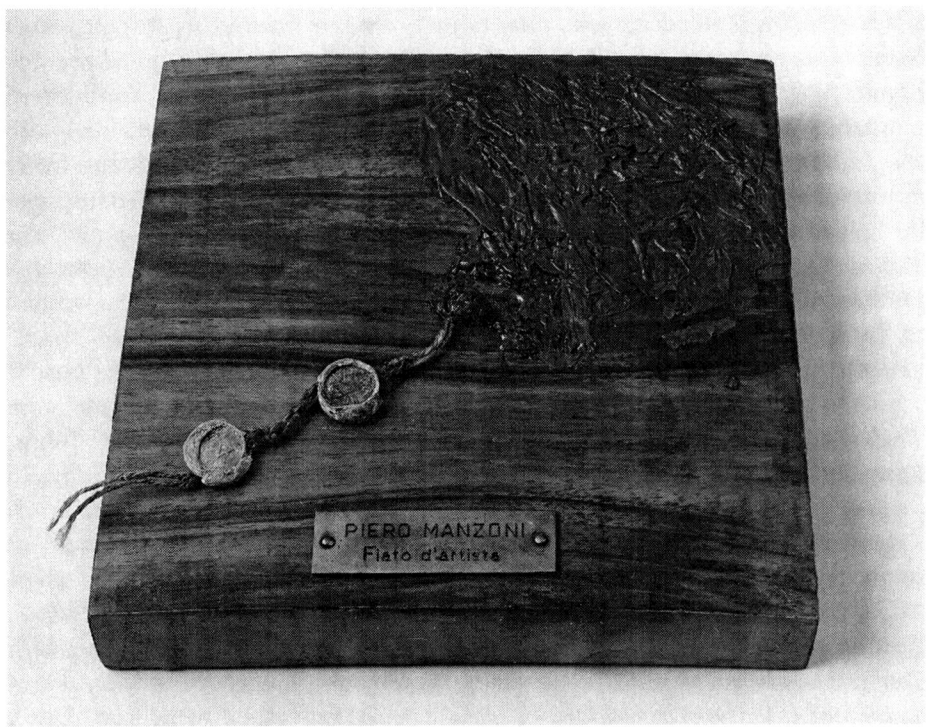

FIGURE 8.1   Piero Manzoni, *Artist's Breath* [*Fiato d'artista*], 1960. Balloon, wood and lead seals. Tate Collection, London. Photo © Tate, London 2005. © DACS 2005

A fairly direct comparison can be drawn between this and the work of an American artist, Robert Morris, produced three years later. In many ways, Morris was concerned with bringing together his two primary role models, Duchamp and Jasper Johns, at this time, and produced a sequence of works in 1960–3 that not only subtly engage with Duchamp, but do so in a way that takes account of Johns' own ongoing commentary. It is *Metered Bulb* of 1963 which bears direct comparison with Manzoni. The work consists quite simply of a light bulb which hangs from an inverted L-shaped armature directly above an electric meter. Should the light/work of art be "turned on" its output will thus be monitored. In many ways this work correlates with the erotic/mechanical closed-circuit represented by the Bride and the Bachelors of Duchamp's *Large Glass*, but it hints more broadly at Duchamp's ironical attitude toward the expressive outpourings of the artist, which are shown to be self-referential and routinized. (Morris may also have been aware of a note in Duchamp's *Green Box* of notes for the *Large Glass*, where the French artist speculates mordantly on the possibility of a regime where people are fitted with "air meters," the penalty for non-payment of bills being "simple asphyxiation"). Morris is concerned with ironically anthropomorphizing the art object, rather like Manzoni, but his work is strictly materialist in spirit, with none of the metaphysical associations that haunt Manzoni's gesture.

Many of the European respondents to Duchamp in fact had some inkling of the esoteric, alchemical interpretations of his work that were beginning to take hold in academic circles, and their own cultural backgrounds sensitized them to the Catholic allusions in Duchamp's oeuvre, however much he had sought to undercut religion.[14] A case in point is the German artist Joseph Beuys. On the one hand, Beuys asserted in an action of 1964 that "The Silence of Marcel Duchamp is Overrated," obviously expressing frustration at the way in which the very enigma of the inactive ex-Dadaist was capturing the imaginations of his artistic peers, but also implying, with some justification, that Duchamp was withdrawing aristocratically from the social consequences of his readymades. On the other hand, Beuys relied heavily on the Duchampian readymade in works such as his 1964 *Fat Chair*; works that were often imbued with esoteric symbolism relating to belief systems such as alchemy or anthroposophy.

This distinction between a materialist American attitude toward Duchamp and a metaphysically-tinged European one by no means holds for all examples, but it is a useful way of rethinking the topic. For the present, it is the American take-up that I wish to concentrate on. To return to Robert Morris, around 1964 he began to move toward the production of simplified geometrical forms, usually in highly specific spatial situations, that would be seen by critics as part of a growing "minimalist" trend. Numerous commentators have come to see minimalism as a crucial departure from modernist artistic principles, particularly insofar as the works concerned often shifted attention from the intrinsic properties of the art object to the object's necessary relation to a spectator or setting and, in that sense, the tendency owed a generic debt to Duchamp's emphasis on the work of art's "completion" by the spectator. Beyond this, however, Duchamp tends to be seen rather too routinely as a reference point for minimalism This is partly a legacy of the text which supplied minimalism with its name: Richard Wollheim's essay "Minimal Art" of 1965, in which, using the Duchampian readymade as a key exemplar, he painstakingly enumerated the minimal conditions under which an object might legitimately qualify as a "work of art." However, this philosophical exercise detracted from the fact that minimalists such as Morris and Judd were not so much reducing art to its basic conditions as isolating properties of objects which might, in their terms, lead to a more unified or "whole" art experience.

Whatever its limitations in illuminating the vagaries of actual art practice, something of the logic of Wollheim's argument was reprised when, in 1969, the artist Joseph Kosuth signaled the emergence of conceptualism as minimalism's avant-garde successor with the publication of the text that was quoted at the opening of this chapter. Focusing attention, as Wollheim had, exclusively on the example of the "unassisted readymade" Kosuth argued that:

The event that made conceivable the realization that it was possible to "speak another language" and still make sense in art was Marcel Duchamp's first un-assisted Ready-made. With the unassisted Ready-made, art changed its focus from the form of the language to what was being said. Which means that it changed the nature of art from a question of morphology to a question of function. This change – from "appearance" to "conception" – was the beginning of "modern" art and the beginning of "conceptual" art. All art (after Duchamp) is conceptual (in nature) because art only exists conceptually.[15]

It has frequently been pointed out that, much as Kosuth aimed to signal a definitive rupture from modernism, he was in fact highly reliant on Greenberg's thought. He even went so far as to say that "the 'value' of particular artists after Duchamp can be weighed according to how much they questioned the nature of art,"[16] which amounts to a reiteration of Greenberg's modernist teleology, with the goal of optical purity being replaced by conceptual rigor. The art historian Benjamin Buchloh has been particularly scathing about Kosuth's narrow emphasis on the tautalogical (self-defining) nature of conceptual art, predicated as it is on the act of nomination (the conferral of art status on an object by the artist). Buchloh himself asserts the importance of the Duchampian readymade for con-ceptualism, but argues that artists such as Daniel Buren or Marcel Broodthaers astutely moved on from the institutional critique suggested by the readymade gesture – and here it is the way in which the urinal titled *Fountain* of 1917 was plucked out of everyday circulation and exhibited in an art context that is at issue – to a position where not just the traditional status of the art object but the very framing conditions for art's social existence would be opened to question.[17]

However much it offers a corrective to Kosuth, Buchloh's critique still leaves the image of a prescient, conceptually preeminent Duchamp very much intact, and it has been left to other commentators and participants in conceptualism to question the constant harking back to the image of the all-knowing Dada that underpins early critical constructions of conceptual art. Seth Siegelaub, a former gallerist, has attacked Buchloh's historicism, noting that the "fixation" on an "omnipotent" Duchamp has resulted in a skewed history of conceptualism being fabricated around the "armature of the Duchamp idea." The overall effect, he claims, is exclusionary; leaving out of the historical picture artists – such as Carl Andre or Robert Barry – who owed little to Duchamp.[18] Similarly the historian of the British Conceptual group Art & Language, Charles Harrison, discussing the exemplary denial of the authorial position supposedly enacted by Duchamp (via the act of nomination rather than the artisanal fabrication of art objects), argues that "the suppression of the artist as author was all too often during the 1960s and 1970s treated not as a matter of ethical necessity but as a form of avant garde opportunism. In the Duchampian tradition, the artist as author died only to be resurrected as a dandy."[19]

Harrison's invocation of Duchamp's dandyism – and thus his self-declared roots in symbolist writers such as Mallarmé – is a powerful antidote to the more prevalent conceptualist veneration of Duchamp as intellectual guru (and the

French artist's dandyism would be seen in positive terms by someone such as Andy Warhol, to be discussed shortly). Ironically, Harrison's was a critique that was rarely voiced among an artistic generation that claimed strong Marxist sympathies. An exception is the Land artist Robert Smithson who, like Joseph Beuys, was exercised by the alienated relationship to labor represented by the Duchampian model: "Duchamp is trying to transcend production itself in the Readymades when he takes an object out of the manufacturing process and then isolates it. He has a certain contempt for the work process, and here, I think, he is sort of playing the aristocrat."[20]

Smithson's critique of Duchamp is unusual for its historical acuity; it is a criticism that might easily have been leveled at Duchamp by his Berlin-based, Dada contemporaries in 1918. But few other conceptualist commentators seemed able to move beyond an incipient philosophical idealism with regard to Duchamp. The physical substance of Duchamp's readymades (including here the assisted readymades) were routinely dissolved by this artistic generation into a notion of disembodied conceptual purity. This is admittedly something Duchamp partly encouraged. In the later 1960s we find him stating: "It's not the visual question of the readymades that matters. . . . Visuality is no longer a question: the Readymade is no longer visible, so to speak. It is completely grey matter. It is no longer retinal."[21] But Duchamp in fact adjusted his ideas about his readymades regularly, often as a wry response to trends occurring around him (witness his production of replica readymades in 1964). He never subscribed to a fixed view of his own works. By contrast even conceptualists who were suspicious of the Duchamp cult, such as Art & Language, seem to have taken the readymade-as-idea as their conceptual horizon, thus submitting to an idealist logic in spite of their materialist commitments in other respects.[22]

The specter of the "unassisted" readymade presided over other artistic tendencies of the early 1960s, especially pop art, but pop eschewed intellectualism in favor of a realist emphasis on the burgeoning mass production and consumerism of the period, in a spirit that was often celebratory. Hence, in 1964 Andy Warhol blithely had readymade commercial logos from products such as Brillo Pads or Heinz Tomato Ketchup silk-screened onto minimalist-style wooden boxes in his "Factory." In many ways, pop's accessibility meant that it overshadowed other avant-garde tendencies of the period such as Fluxus, where a more incisive critique of consumerism was underway. Deriving partly from Cage, with his in-depth appreciation of Duchamp, Fluxus owed as much to Dada in general as Duchamp in particular, but, at its most Duchampian, it took its impetus not so much from the readymade as from the iconoclast's *Boîte-en-Valise*, his ironic repackaging of his oeuvre in a suitcase. On one level, Fluxus was dedicated to a sophisticated undermining of the capitalist-backed gallery system via what amounted to pointedly anachronistic "cottage industry" modes of production and distribution. Portable boxes containing editioned games, kits, or textual works thus became emblematic of Fluxus. By contrast to this tradition, pop's response to the readymade can often be read as capitulation to the sheer spectacle of mass consumption. There is a sense, though, in which the extended dialogue with the readymade in the postwar period can actually be understood as an ongoing critique of art's relation to commodity production.

The opening gambit in this dialogue would be Jasper Johns' *Painted Bronze (Ale Cans)* of 1960 in which Johns effectively metamorphosed the readymade back into the terms of traditional sculpture by bronze-casting replicas of two beer cans and hand-painting commercial brand labels onto them. The next step, fittingly, was taken by Duchamp himself. He had been happily consenting to the production of one-off replications of his readymades for some time, but in 1964 he authorized Arturo Schwarz to produce replicas of 14 of his readymades in editions of ten, scandalizing those who saw his original Dada gestures as sacrosanct by submitting the readymades to a subtle combination of (severely limited) mass production and aestheticization. Warhol aside, the next moves in this dialogue, whose terms slid capriciously between questions of originality, replication, mass production, and artistic value, had to wait until the 1980s and a sequence of works by Jeff Koons, Robert Gober, and Sherrie Levine. Reflecting postmodern ideas about the impossibility of "originality," and employing appropriative strategies in terms of the use not only of existing "readymade" objects but also of other artists' productions, these artists also exploited the increasingly sophisticated semiotic codings (often sexual in basis) that had become current in advertising.

For instance in 1991 Sherrie Levine, ironizing her position as a woman artist who specialised in "re-presenting" works by modernist "Masters," turned her attention to the most overtly "masculine" of Duchamp's readymades, the urinal. Telescoping together the Johnsian reading of the gesture and knowledge of Duchamp's decision to edition the readymades (as well as an awareness that Duchamp had at one time indulged in a degree of art world speculation by acting as an agent for Brancusi) she bronze-cast a series of shiny urinals, emphasizing their "feminine" characteristics to the point of hyperbole. In her hands they become glossily seductive, curvaceous objects – tarted-up ready maids. Levine's main achievement was possibly the preservation of something of Duchamp's acidic humour (something remarkably rare in the playing-out of his reception), but the most significant point at present is the way in which, in its post-pop manifestations, the readymade slips from encapsulating conceptual "purity" to tracking social production and semiotic currency. The delayed historical unraveling of the readymade's implications thus serves to "infect" the idealist presuppositions inherent in the reading of the gesture as "conceptual."

Staying with the sexualization of the Duchampian legacy, it is appropriate here to backtrack briefly to the beginnings of pop, and shift attention from America to Britain. Strictly speaking pop as a movement had begun in Britain with the activities of the Independent Group around 1952–6. The group took an almost academic approach to the analysis of popular culture and one of its artistic leaders, Richard Hamilton, looked to Duchamp not only out of admiration for the "dry," diagrammatic style of the French artist's work, which Hamilton duly emulated, but also for Duchamp's ironic openness to technological and commercial iconography. Hamilton was instrumental in promoting a more scholarly awareness of Duchamp both amongst artists and academics, and produced the typographic version of the notes for the *Large Glass* that stimulated Jasper Johns' earlier-mentioned review. By the same token, Hamilton undertook a painstaking reconstruction of the *Large Glass* (as did Ulf Linde in Sweden) and organized the seminal Tate retrospective mentioned earlier.

What is not often appreciated, however, is the extent to which Hamilton set in motion an analysis of the gendered aspects of Duchamp's iconography at pronounced variance to the emphasis at that time on the "readymade Duchamp" in America. Taking its lead from the *Large Glass*, in terms of a blurring of mechanical and biologistic imagery, Hamilton's *$he* of 1958–61 addressed the phenomenon of housewife celebrities on American television, mordantly revealing how early 1960s conceptions of female sexuality were dependent on metaphors at play in advertising. As we have seen, it was not until the 1980s that this emphasis on the semiotic underpinnings of gender would play a larger part in post-Duchampian discourse, and Hamilton's formative role in this area merits some reconsideration.

In certain respects, however, the "postmodern" emphasis on issues of gender of the 1970s and 1980s focused more on issues of the "performative" nature of gender identity – taking its lead from Duchamp's creation of his female alter-ego Rrose Sélavy in a sequence of photographs produced in 1921/24 in collaboration with Man Ray – than with femininity or masculinity as such; feminist debates of the period centered, after all, on the "constructed" nature of gender rather than any supposedly "essential" attributes. In this context, an important revision of the American Neo-Dada reception of Duchamp took place, largely among scholars, predicated on the realization that Duchamp's attraction for the likes of Johns and Rauschenberg was based on his dandyish persona as much as his actual works. Given that Johns and Rauschenberg were, by the early 1990s, understood to have had a lengthy homosexual relationship, it became possible to think of Duchamp as appealing to "camp" sensibility, and this certainly makes explicable the way that Warhol, the very embodiment of camp in terms of the 1960s avant-garde, understood Duchamp.[23] In 1973 Warhol had himself photographed surrounded by glamorous women and drag queens in an image explicitly dedicated to "Rrose Sélavy and Belle Haleine" (two of Duchamp's female pseudonyms).[24] In 1981 Warhol was himself to pose wearing female wigs and male attire in the "Altered Image" photographs produced in collaboration with Christopher Makos.

Just as Duchamp, along with the underground film culture prevalent in 1960s New York, provided Warhol with the license to investigate aspects of gay transvestite fantasy, so certain heterosexually-identified artists also began to reinterpret Duchamp around this time. Performance art, which flourished in particular through the 1970s and early 1980s, offers some key instances. In *Seedbed* (1972) the American artist Vito Acconci masturbated under a ramp in a gallery whilst his verbal fantasies and mutterings were amplified through a loudspeaker in the space above. To a degree Acconci saw this exploration of male identity as Duchampian in origin; he saw his "planting of seed" as analogous to the function of the *Large Glass* as, in Duchamp's terms, an "agricultural machine," and thus identified with the onanistic activities of the Bachelors in Duchamp's work (the notes for the *Large Glass* had asserted that "The Bachelor grinds his chocolate for himself").[25] Beyond this, the very frankness of Duchamp's interest in sexual mechanics opened up the possibility for intensive male self-questioning on Acconci's part. Disempowering himself, insofar as he was literally "walked over," Acconci set up a pointed dialectic between the (hidden) authority he exercised over the gallery as generative male and the passivity of his actual position.[26]

All of this supplies the cerebral, "disembodied" Duchamp of the conceptualist tradition with a much more palpable, embodied persona. In the late 1980s the discovery of certain works by Duchamp that had previously been overlooked – including the notorious *Wayward Landscape* of 1946, consisting of a semen stain on a ground of black silk – further consolidated this sense that he had indeed had distinctly visceral preoccupations, and the way was thus paved for Duchamp to have yet further relevance for a generation of artists concerned with issues of bodily abjection, such as Robert Gober and Mike Kelley.[27] Gober's important 1989 installation at Paula Cooper's New York gallery took Duchamp's "bride" as its central reference point. In Gober's installation a satin bridal gown stood upright and disturbingly "empty" in a larger environment in which simulated cat-litter bags leant against the walls. The walls in turn were wallpapered with graffiti-style depictions of male and female genitalia interspersed with inset drainage holes, or with the juxtaposed images of a sleeping white male and a hanging black man. Although multiple associations were activated, the conceptual nexus pointed to the way in which socially-prescribed norms of domestic hygiene and heterosexual marital bliss are predicated on blocking out external realities such as racial inequality or disruptive and dangerous manifestations of sexuality; the AIDS epidemic was a major issue of the 1980s and 1990s.

Such developments might appear to sit well with the identitarian preoccupations of postmodern artistic discourse, but in one of the central organs of postmodern debate, the American journal *October* (founded 1976), attention often continued to be placed on a quasi-Kosuthian view of Duchamp as an intellectual fount or point of origin for postwar art. Several *October* contributors – notably Benjamin Buchloh, Hal Foster, and Thierry de Duve – were heavily affected by the publication of the German theorist Peter Bürger's *Theory of the Avant-Garde* of 1974 (translated into English 1984). Writing from a Marxian viewpoint, Bürger saw Duchamp's readymades as paradigmatically "avant-garde" insofar as they represented a "radical negation of the category of individual creation."[28] He further regarded Duchamp's "neo-avant-garde" heirs as dismally colluding in a capitulation to the (capitalist) status quo, observing that under the aegis of the neo-avant-garde "the protest of the historical avant garde against art as institution is accepted as art."[29] The *October* critics acknowledged Bürger's importance, but saw his conclusions as hobbled by a limited knowledge of post-war art. Hal Foster, for instance, preserved the central importance of Duchamp but saw his reception by the neo-avant-garde as a part of a "deferred action" whereby a psychological "working through" of the French artist's legacy took place, characterized by unconscious resistances to or even productive misconstruals of the works themselves.[30] Foster's argument has the advantage of admitting to the symptom-like characteristics of the readymade fixation, but nevertheless leaves Duchamp's guru-like status firmly in place; indeed more so to the extent that Foster sees the full realization of the Duchampian heritage as effectively postdating its unconscious assimilation on the part of the neo-avant-garde.

Other *October* critics were remarkably astute at identifying shifts in 1980s–1990s artistic dialogue, largely as an outcome of their attention to the historical Duchamp. The work of the journal's co-founder, Rosalind Krauss, is import-ant in this respect, notably the two-part essay on the "Index" of Spring and Fall 1977. Here, via an analysis of the *Large Glass* in terms of photography, she drew attention to Duchamp's recurrent emphasis on indexical signs – usually in the form of physical traces or deposits of the real world – in works such as *With My Tongue in my Cheek* (1959). Krauss simultaneously pinpointed a tendency toward the indexical in the post-conceptualist art of the period which, in her terms, substituted "the registration of sheer physical presence for the more highly articulated language of aesthetic conventions."[31] Her argument served to re-focus attention on the 1960s use of body casts by artists such as Bruce Nauman. At the same time it tacitly conceded that conceptualism's heirs were beginning to read Duchamp more as embodied being rather than disembodied intellect. It might be argued, however, that the social disjunctions that artists such as Gober would make vivid in re-embodying Duchamp were strangely smoothed-over via the sophisticated structural maneuvers of Krauss's writing.

This talk of embodiment provides a suitable note on which to move from discussing Duchamp's legacy historically to reflecting, albeit briefly, on art of the recent past. If this chapter has tracked a multiplicity of readings of Duchamp – whether in terms of anti-Greenbergian discourse, the metaphysical preoccupa-tions of European artists, the idealist focus on "art as idea" in conceptualism, the analysis of the commodity in mass culture, or the performative utilization of camp – my emphasis throughout has been to point out the limitations of pigeon-holing Duchamp as a primarily intellectual figure and thus to consolidate the shift away from the "readymade Duchamp" model. The narrative I have constructed has reinforced this reading, not least by "ending" with indexicality. Current artists certainly seem to be exercised by a more complex, and more physically palpable Duchamp. This is not to say that he is any less enigmatic. In many ways it is the Duchamp of the "infra-thin" notes – the series of reflections he jotted down in the late 1930s on states of "in-betweeness" or liminality – who currently holds sway. Such ideas were realized most directly in Duchamp's visual output by the *Female Fig Leaf* sculpture of 1950, a "positive" cast taken from the pudendum of the mannequin in his final installation, *Etant Donnés* (1946–1966), in an attempt to pinpoint the interface between solid and void. In line with such works, Duchamp is perhaps best approached as someone who is never fully "retinal" or "conceptual" in approach, but something in between. As he said: "my art would be that of living . . . each breath is a work which is inscribed nowhere, which is neither visual nor cerebral."[32] The work of several contem-porary artists encourages a rereading of him in these terms. The British sculptor Rachel Whiteread, for example, interrogates the implications of casting. In the case of the notorious *House* of 1993, she obtained a cast from the "empty" interior space of a condemned house in Bow, East London. The piece made the sense of human absence uncannily present.

It might also be asserted that certain areas of current art imply a reaction against the feminist-informed understanding of Duchamp of the 1980s. Arguably Duchamp's thematization of his masculinity – his ironic attitude toward his own "essential" gender characteristics in terms of the male iconography developed in works such as *Fountain* (as opposed to the experiments with indeterminate sexual identity in the Rrose Sélavy gesture) – has broad connections with the vogue for "laddishness" in recent art, particularly that of the "young British artists" (yBas). (Interestingly, it is the early 1990s self-images of a female yBa – Sarah Lucas – that seem to echo Duchamp most directly.) To a degree this represents a recovery of Dada irreverence in the wake of the emphasis in 1980s art on critical theory. The most overt contemporary exploration of masculinity in Duchampian terms, however, has a fundamentally serious and self-reflexive quality, in the tradition of Acconci. This is *The Cremaster Cycle* (1994–2002) by the American artist Matthew Barney. Whilst the visual characteristics of this project owe much more to the florid imagery of surrealism than to Duchamp, Barney's images of narcissistic or dandyish male types (especially in *Cremaster 4*), along with a strong thematic interest inherited from his pre-*Cremaster* work in self-contained biological systems, set up interesting connections with the masturbatory "Bachelor Machine" of Duchamp's *Large Glass* (see Figure 19.1).[33]

A recent project by the American sculptor Saul Melman also merits attention in this context. Melman's 2003 *Johnny on the Spot* was an enormously enlarged version of Duchamp's *Fountain*, in which the shiny porcelain of the original was replaced with a white translucent material called Tyvek stretched over a scaffolding of wood (Figure 8.2). Measuring 32 feet in width and 24 feet at its highest point, the piece was conceived as a public art work and located in the Nevada Black Rock Desert. The artist himself has talked of wishing to extend the issue of context addressed by the original urinal, but the piece also has interesting connotations for male artistic discourse. One significant area of 1970s art that this chapter has failed to address is land art, mainly because Duchamp had little direct impact on it. However, given that American land art has frequently been characterized as inherently masculinist, largely due to its obsession with dominating scale, Melman's public art work, which can be entered and explored like a

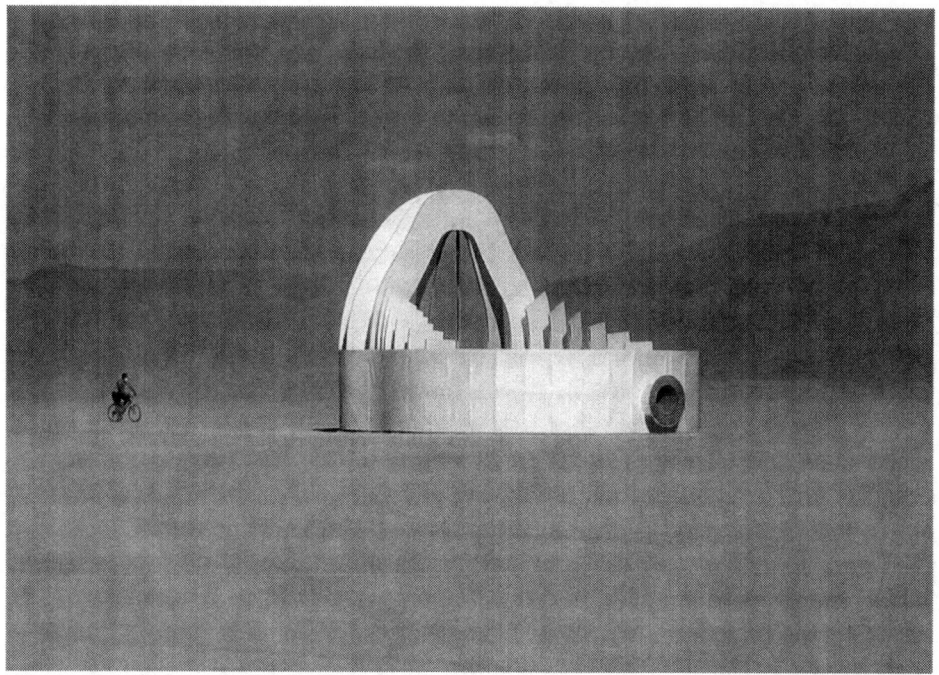

FIGURE 8.2 Saul Melman, *Johnny on the Spot*, 2003. Wood, tyvek steel, fluorescent lights, in Black Rock Desert, Nevada, US. Photograph courtesy of Saul Melman

shrine, could be seen as representing an ironic oasis for the male traveler in an otherwise arid landscape.

It is clear, then, that artists are still very much involved in a dialogue with Duchamp. In saying this, however, one inevitably runs the risk of reinstating the kind of heroic, omnipotent Duchamp that commentators such as Seth Siegelaub have found so distasteful. However much one seeks to replace the "disembodied" Duchamp with one who is more materially "graspable" one ends up positing Duchamp, to quote Amelia Jones, as "the paradoxical origin . . . of a movement critical of artistic authority."[34] This paradox is an intractable one, and in the end it stems from Duchamp himself, who both orchestrated and side-stepped the consequences of his output with consummate skill; as, for instance, with his careful "holding-back" of his final work *Etant Donnés*, which was not publicly revealed until after his death.

So how does the historian escape Duchamp's seduction? This is surely the burning methodological issue for scholars and students of the Duchampian art-as-idea legacy. One strategy would be to drop the "influence model" completely – however much Duchamp, perversely, obliges us to adopt it – and to think of "the Duchamp effect" as more fundamentally generic and related to larger shifts in industrial production and mass media. Dieter Daniels, for instance, asserts that the readymades must be considered in a context which extends far beyond the context of art. It is a context which begins in the mid-19th century with the invention of photography and the simultaneous staging of industrial products in a new form of "public commodities" in department stores, obliging the customer to choose from products with fixed prices, without the option to haggle. It ends with the mass media perversion of the utopian equation between art and life . . .[35]

Is there a need, therefore, to jettison the art historical trope of the supremely intelligent Duchamp and his avant-garde progeny and to develop an alternative model of his reception predicated on the structural logic of modernity and late capitalism? The methodological consequences of this might include the strategic downplaying of the importance of the whole "avant-garde" framework for Duchamp and his legacy, which I have found it convenient to preserve in this chapter. But it might be another way of re-politicizing Duchamp, given earlier points about the silence of social art historians on the Duchamp question.

In the final analysis, beyond rethinking questions about the subtle differences between European and American receptions of Duchamp, it would seem that the time is ripe for a quite different conceptualization of the Duchampian legacy, and of the art-as-idea tradition that is bound up with it, to be undertaken. In clarifying the historical outlines and range of the topic as it stands, I hope at least to have helped clear the way for that project.

Notes

1 Kosuth (1969), 80.
2 One attempt to do so is by Buskirk and Nixon (1996).
3 Barthes (1957), 68–70.
4 Jones (1994a), 38. See also chapter 2 for an overall discussion of this point.
5 For Duchamp's anti-retinal stance see his statements in Pierre Cabanne (1971).
6 De Konning, cited in D'Harnoncourt and McShine (1973), 196.
7 Cage (1961), 102.
8 Johns (1960/1996), 20.
9 Clark (1999), 167, 314. Significantly, in one of the finest Marxist-informed general readings of post-1940s art (see Wood et al. [1993]), Duchamp is mentioned only once.
10 Roth (1977). See also Hopkins (2003), 60–6 and passim.
11 The key text here is Greenberg: "Modernist Painting" (1961) in O'Brian (1993), 85–93.
12 Greenberg: "Avant Garde Attitudes" (1970), in O'Brian (1993), 301–2.
13 The term was first used by Rosenblum (1957), 33.
14 The most notorious alchemical interpretations of Duchamp were developed in the 1960s by Arturo Schwarz, and published in 1969. From 1954 Schwarz ran a bookshop and later a gallery in Milan, with which Manzoni among others would have been familiar.
15 Kosuth (1969), 80.

16 Ibid., 80–1.
17 Buchloh: "From the Aesthetics of Administration to Institutional Critique" in *L'Art Conceptuel* (1990), 51 and passim.
18 Siegelaub, "Addendum" in *L'Art Conceptuel* (1990), 258 and passim.
19 Harrison (1991), 93.
20 Smithson (1973), 47.
21 Duchamp, interview with Philippe Collin (1967), cited in *Marcel Duchamp* (2002), 38.
22 For Art & Language on Duchamp see Atkinson (1969) and (1970).
23 On Johns, Rauschenberg and Warhol in relation to gay sensibility see Silver, "Modes of Disclosure: The Construction of Gay Identity and the Rise of Pop Art" in Ferguson (1992), 178–203.
24 See d'Harnoncourt and McShine (1973), 227.
25 For Acconci on Duchamp see Pincus-Witten (1972), 47–9.
26 See Jones (1994b).
27 For a discussion of "Wayward Landscape" see Hopkins (1992), 330.
28 Bürger (1974/1984), 51.
29 Ibid., 53.
30 Foster (1994), 11, 23, 30 and passim.
31 Krauss (1977/1985), 209.
32 Duchamp in Cabanne (1971), 72.
33 See Spector (2002), 4–7.
34 Jones (1994a), 50.
35 Daniels (2002), 38.

References and further reading

Ades, Dawn, Neil Cox, and David Hopkins (1999). *Marcel Duchamp*. London: Thames and Hudson. (See "Postscript: Duchamp after Duchamp.")
Atkinson, Terry (1969). "Introduction." *Art-Language*, vol. 1, no. 1.
—— (1970). "From an Art and Language Point of View." *Art-Language*, vol. 1, no. 2.
Barthes, Roland (1957). *Mythologies*. Paris: Editions de Seuil.
Battcock, Gregory, ed. (1968). *Minimal Art: A Critical Anthology*. New York: Dutton.
Berger, Maurice (1989). *Labyrinths: Robert Morris, Minimalism, and the 1960s*. New York: Harper and Row.
Blessing, Jennifer, ed. (1997). *Rrose is a Rrose is a Rrose: Gender Performance and Photography*. New York: Guggenheim Museum.
Bürger, Peter (1974/1984). *Theory of the Avant-Garde*, trans. Michael Shaw. Minneapolis: University of Minnesota Press.
Buskirk, Martha, and Mignon Nixon (1996). *The Duchamp Effect*. Cambridge, MA: MIT Press.
Cabanne, Pierre (1971). *Dialogues with Marcel Duchamp*. London: Thames and Hudson.
Cage, John (1961). "On Robert Rauschenberg, Artist and his Work." In *Silence: Lectures and Writings*. London: Marion Boyars.
Clark, T. J. (1999). *Farewell to an Idea*. New Haven: Yale University Press.

Cooke, Lynne (1990). "Reviewing Francis Picabia, Man Ray, Marcel Duchamp, Rrose Sélavy, Marchand Du Sel." In *The Readymade Boomerang: Certain Relations in 20th Century Art*. Sydney: Eighth Biennale of Sydney.

Daniels, Dieter (2002). "Marcel Duchamp: The Most Influential Artist of the Twentieth Century." In *Marcel Duchamp*. Basel: Museum Jean Tinguely and Hatje Cantz.

Daniels, Dieter, and Alfred Fischer (1988). *Übrigens sterben immer die anderen. Marcel Duchamp und die Avantgarde seit 1950*. Cologne: Museum Ludwig.

D'Harnoncourt, Anne, and Kynaston McShine, eds. (1973). *Marcel Duchamp*. New York: Museum of Modern Art; Philadelphia: Philadelphia Museum of Art.

Duchamp, Marcel (1957). "The Creative Act." Available at http://members.aol.com/mindwebart3/marcel.htm.

—— (1960). *The Bride Stripped Bare by her Bachelors, Even (The Green Box Notes)*. Typographic version by Richard Hamilton, trans. George Heard Hamilton. Stuttgart, London, and Rekjavik: Edition Hansjorg Mayer.

Ferguson, Russell, ed. (1992). *Hand-Painted Pop: American Art in Transition 1955–62*. Los Angeles: Museum of Contemporary Art.

Foster, Hal (1994). "What's Neo about the Neo-Avant-Garde?" *October*, no. 70 (Fall).

Hamilton, Richard (1982). *Collected Words 1953–1982*. London: Thames and Hudson.

Harrison, Charles (1991). *Essays on Art and Language*. Oxford: Blackwell.

Hopkins, David (1992). "Questioning Dada's Potency: Picabia's *La Sainte Vierge* and the Dialogue with Duchamp." *Art History*, vol. 15, no. 3 (June).

—— (2000). *After Modern Art 1945–2000*. Oxford: Oxford University Press.

—— (2003). "The Politics of Equivocation: Sherrie Levine, Duchamp's 'Compensation Portrait' and Surrealism in the USA 1942–45." *Oxford Art Journal*, vol. 26, no. 1.

Johns, Jasper (1960/1996). "Duchamp." As reprinted in Jasper Johns, *Writings, Sketchbooks. Interviews*. New York: Museum of Modern Art.

Jones, Amelia (1994a). *Postmodernism and the En-Gendering of Marcel Duchamp*. Cambridge: Cambridge University Press.

—— (1994b). "Dis/playing the Phallus: Male Artists Perform Their Masculinities." *Art History*, vol. 17, no. 4 (September).

Kosuth, Joseph (1969). "Art After Philosophy, part 1." *Studio International* (October).

Kozloff, Max (1964). "Johns and Duchamp." *Art International*, vol. VIII, no. 2.

Krauss, Rosalind (1977/1985). "Notes on the Index, part 1." Reprinted in *The Originality of the Avant-Garde and Other Modernist Myths*. Cambridge, MA: MIT Press.

Lebel, Robert (1959). *On Marcel Duchamp*, trans. George Heard Hamilton. New York: Grove Press.

L'Art Conceptuel (1990) (2nd edn.). Paris: Musée d'art moderne de la ville de Paris.

Maharaj, Sarat (1992). " 'A Liquid Elemental Scattering': Marcel Duchamp and Richard Hamilton." In *Richard Hamilton*. London: Tate Gallery.

Marcel Duchamp (2002). Exhibition Catalogue. Basel: Museum Jean Tinguely and Hatje Cantz Publishers.

Motherwell, Robert, ed. (1951/1989). *The Dada Painters and Poets*. Cambridge, Mass.: Harvard University Press.

O'Brian, John (1993). *Clement Greenberg: The Collected Essays and Criticism*, vol. 4. Chicago: University of Chicago Press.

Pincus, Robert L. (1991). " 'Quality Material:' Duchamp Disseminated in the Sixties and Seventies." In *West Coast Duchamp*, ed. Bonnie Clearwater. Miami Beach FL: Grassfield Press.

Pincus-Witten, Robert (1972). "Vito Acconci and the Conceptual Performance." *Artforum* (April).

Rosenblum, Robert (1957). "Castelli group." *Arts Magazine*, vol. 31, no. 8.

Roth, Moira (1977). "The Aesthetics of Indifference." *Artforum* (November).

Schwarz, Arturo (1969/2000). *The Complete Works' of Marcel Duchamp*. New York: Delano Greenridge Editions.

Smithson, Robert (1973). "Interview with Moira Roth." *Artforum* (October).

Spector, Nancy (2002). "Only The Perverse Fantasy Can Save Us." In *Matthew Barney: The Cremaster Cycle*, ed. Nancy Spector. New York: Guggenheim Museum.

Tancock, John (1973). "The Influence of Marcel Duchamp." In *Marcel Duchamp*, ed. Anne D'Harnoncourt and Kynaston McShine. New York: Museum of Modern Art; Philadelphia: Philadelphia Museum of Art.

Wollheim, Richard (1965/1968). "Minimal Art." *Arts Magazine*. As reprinted in *Minimal Art: A Critical Anthology*, ed. Gregory Battcock. New York: Dutton.

Wood, Paul, Francis Frascina, Jonathan Harris, and Charles Harrison (1993). *Modernism in Dispute: Art Since the Forties*. New Haven: Yale University Press.

9

Regarding Beauty

Margaret Morgan

The term *beauty* has been much back in play in the Anglophone art world of the past ten years or so. Beauty is variously invoked in the name of good art; the "purely" aesthetic; the pleasurable; the pretty; the well-designed; the elegant; the sublime; as antithesis to the conceptual, the analytic, the narrative, the didactic, the political, the abject; or as an absence of overt content in reaction to a perceived overly instrumentalized content. What is actually *meant* by the term beauty needs more carefully to be examined.

My task in this chapter is to put the vagaries of beauty's changing status in the context of two competing drives: the first, a drive toward order and truth in the face of dispersal, doubt, and chaos; the second, the drive toward and through pleasure. Hegelian and Kantian by degrees, these drives are neither pure nor abstract, but are, rather, situated in, and structured by, the social spaces and times in which they operate. In tracing beauty's rise in the 1940s to its decline in the 1960s and 1970s, to its recuperation in the early nineties and its dispersal in the new millennium, one can identify at once the very labile nature of beauty *per se*, as well as the shifting ideologies of American cultural practice in the light of larger political movements and ideological changes concerning gender, nationalism, and the roles art plays in social life.

The Avant-Garde and the Aversion to Beauty

What is beauty? A most shifting and provocative term, a veritable Trojan Horse of meaning and Hel(l)enian to a fault, beauty has been the cause of certain strife in the history of art.[1] Beauty, goes the centuries old argument, is that which causes us to experience sensate pleasure: if, when we see or hear something, our senses are pleased, we must be in the midst of beauty – like a beautiful landscape or a beautiful woman or a beautiful piece of music, that which is harmonious, synthesized, balanced, neither jarring nor disturbing, but somehow moving, and stirring to behold, is, beautiful. And therein lies the rub. Tautological arguments – *a beautiful woman is beautiful* – and *we know beauty because it pleases us* – make it difficult to reply to beauty's invocation in art criticism. Beauty is obviously not as simple as the fantasy of immediacy would have it. There is a hierarchy of senses – if we taste something pleasing it is not beautiful but *delicious*, and, were we to bend down and *smell* beauty, well, our experience might not be described in terms of the beautiful: lingering about the sense of smell are the connotations of baseness, bestiality. To sniff at beauty, then, would be to denigrate *she* who operates in some higher realm associated with the aesthetic and with taste.

Under the avant-garde modernism of late nineteenth- and early twentieth-century European art, taste is the enemy and beauty is suspect; the avant-garde typically celebrated the ugly, the raw, the common, the everyday – all the kinds of culture that went against bourgeois notions of propriety and taste (that is, notions of what was *beautiful*). This kind of modernism would rather play in the sewer than the salon. Beauty and truth have been in dialectical torsion at least since the middle of the nineteenth century. I am thinking here of European modernist painting, impressionism and fauvism being the most obvious cases in point. In the 1865 Parisian salon, for example, Édouard Manet's *Olympia* was critically panned (by all but his friend, the poet and art critic Charles Baudelaire) as grotesque, monkey-like, sallow, and unbeautiful – as the *anti-Odalisque*.[2] Because he – the artist – dared speak the "truth" of contemporary Parisian culture, she – the figure in the frame – was declaimed as ugly. And if the figure in the frame is ugly, then the art (or so this brand of avant-gardism would have it) is true and great. The early nineteenth-century expectation that works of art should "enchant us, not because they are so natural but because they have been *made* so natural" no longer applied.[3] Art should not enchant but startle, challenge, disgust, and that gloss called "naturalism" was the cost readily paid for this new attitude.

If artifice and the cosmetic world of appearances are on the side of the feminine, then the new avant-garde art was assuming the trappings of masculinity. In relinquishing mimesis and beauty, this kind of art also relinquished the privileged position of the viewer and the immediate pleasure he might once have had. Any residue of that immediacy, once associated with the viewer's apprehension of the beautiful, came to reside in the point of view of the artist himself. That is, "truth" is situated in the artist's access to the "real world" and in the headlong rush of experience brought to bear in the painting of his pictures. Niceties like mimesis, beauty, contemplation, have no place in this new economy. As such this shift from the point of view of the bourgeois consumer to the bohemian producer complicates relations of exchange and service in ways that continue into the twentieth century as the privileging of artistic intent and of artistic sensibility. Simultaneously, but this is not to suggest causally, the aesthetic value of applied art increased – which is to say design became an art.

Indeed, by the early twentieth century, applied art was at the very forefront of the Soviet avant-garde. And by 1929, the *brand new* Museum of Modern Art (MoMA), under Director Alfred H. Barr, was to be home of the "visual arts of our time,"[4] from civil engineering and industrial design to film, fashion, furniture, and architecture as well as to the more familiar arts of painting and sculpture. In short, art became one among many visual forms and no longer *the* form by which, like philosophy and religion, "man" once distinguished himself.

Beauty, Modernism, Totalitarianism

So where in these discursive shifts, is beauty? In the Soviet Union it was in the ideological dustbin. At MoMA it resided in chairs, lamps, and eggbeaters, as much as in paintings. In modernist Vienna, with Adolf Loos, intellectual forebear of Alfred Barr, beauty had, for decades, been unabashedly ascribed to the applied arts of architecture and design. Loos, happily ignoring distinctions made by philosophers and politicos alike, noted: "The Indian says, 'This woman is beautiful because she wears gold rings in her nose and ears.' The man of high culture says, 'This woman is beautiful because she does not wear gold rings in her nose and ears.' To seek beauty only in form and not in ornament is the goal toward which all humanity is striving."[5]

Under Loosian modernism, functional objects – and women – could aspire to the *beautiful* (in the modernist sense) but only if their form was efficiently purposive and devoid of decoration. Here Loos positions modernist design, and fashion, as distinct from pre-modern design and craft and from non-western cultures, as the site of beauty par excellence (that place once reserved for fine art). Pleasure lies in the immediate apprehension of the modern object: we are pleased by its good design, its clever solutions, its elegance, its simplicity, the way its properties *make sense*. If "sense" in Enlightenment terms of philosopher Immanuel Kant concerned the auditory and the visual, a kind of disembodied thrall, then *making sense* in modern terms presupposed a whole concert of sensate faculties that have as much to do with the intellect as with any discrete organ of vision or hearing. That is, the modern beauty of utilitarian forms following their functions presupposes an active, rather than contemplative, viewer, a viewer who might actually be *doing something*, and whose cognitive faculties allow her to understand and organize the vernacular world of ordinary life. Under this brand of modernism, beauty and utility are intertwined; beauty is hardly standing still long enough to be contemplated.

And this intertwining prefigures the persistent and more general pleasure bound up in organization, in finding pattern, in making order, that is a seemingly irresistible part of contemporary culture and ordinary life. Witness, at least in California where I live, if I may digress to the first person for a moment, the proliferation of chains of stores dedicated solely to helping one organize one's life: Hold Everything, California Closets, Organize Everything, Home Depot, Office Depot, to name but a few. More ways to purchase an organizational strategy for *all that accumulated stuff* – it's like getting junk mail about how to stop junk mail. These companies tap into a wellspring of desire, seeming all the more to swell up in recent years, and to that desire attaches a psycho-political register: This proliferation of stores seems in inverse proportion to the overwhelming perplexity of the nation-state; individual order a buttress against the larger disarray, against the absurd and antidemocratic machinations of the not so United States. Thus within the home and the home-office, the TV news turned down low, those small filings of things, labelings of boxes, arrangements of colors, alphabetizing of CDs, become tiny victories to which one might cling in the midst of the chaos of a nation, hurtling like *a rocket out of control*, toward who knows what. In short those chain stores seem to enact the travesty of the American people failing, in the political sense, *to get organized.*

A child on the threshold of speech arranges a group of objects. – Meticulously, with a studiousness akin to an artist's consideration, the child studies and composes a still life consisting of book, cloth, object – her poodle, Miss Pink, as it happens to be (Figure 9.1). To observe this child one might imagine the aesthetic impulse already at work in the development of nascent personhood. One might also observe in the child, at around the same age, an acceding to language in the expression of words like "clean," "dirty," "nice," "art." In these inchoate utterances appears the rudimentary formation of subjectivity: the dividing of self and other, clean from dirty, order from chaos, the pairing of Truth and Beauty. Her knowledge of aesthetics or her understanding of the words she enunciates must be more limited than her skillful mimicry belies, but an observer, her mother, might catch herself interpreting these signs as an advanced aesthetic sense, and furthermore a projection of the primacy of the aesthetic impulse in the formation of subjectivity.

We scrutinize the child's arrangement of objects, and in our impulse to order, we make of the child's arrangement an intelligibility, allowing us to find meaning in the still life before us, indeed allowing us to understand the child's play as still life. And in that meaningfulness we find "beauty." This "beauty" appears to derive from pleasurable, sensate experience, but also from the pleasure of the putting together of random forms, like the stacking of children's blocks, the sorting of colored pencils, into a coherent whole, the primary desire to order, arrange and thereby comprehend the world, inextricably bound up with a desire to aestheticize it: ordering and tidying is beautifying. If "cleanliness is next to godliness," as the saying goes, then tidying is next to art. "Art" the child can say pointing at a photograph of a woman's cut and bleeding back, the bloody lines forming a childlike rendering of a girl-girl family, as the image sits in its frame upon a wall in her home (Figure 9.2).

"Ah yes," the mother replies mostly to herself, smugly, knowingly, of the superior aesthetic sense of her child and, given that, the superiority of the aesthetic in a hierarchy of cognitive developments. But the little girl will also point and say "art" when passing an aisle of picture frames for sale in the local Target™ store, and thereby deflate the mother's optimistic analysis of the superior insights of her infant daughter. Yet herein lies the revelation: the child responding to rows of empty frames for sale, with the same word "art," as to her own arrangements of

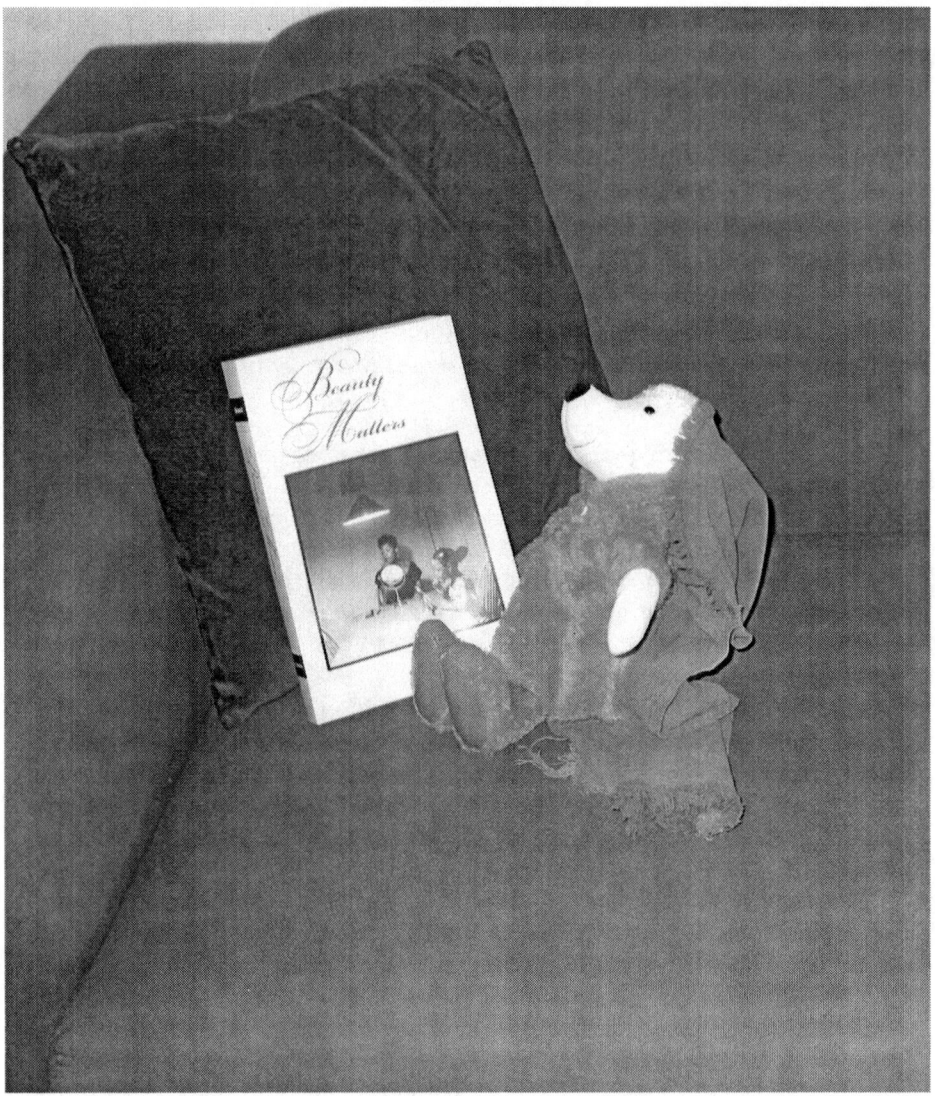

FIGURE 9.1   Margaret Morgan, untitled still life, 2005. Digital photograph © and courtesy of the author

found objects, and to the art upon the walls within which she lives, speaks of that drive to order, the containing within a frame, the specificity of an arrangement, the hanging upon a wall, and to the relation between order and art. In Orwellian speak it might simply be put: Order is truth, and truth is beauty.

Allow me now to zoom out from interpersonal subjectivity in order to situate Beauty's twentieth-century incarnations by briefly recounting, in Rube Goldberg fashion, what is now a very familiar history of art.[6]

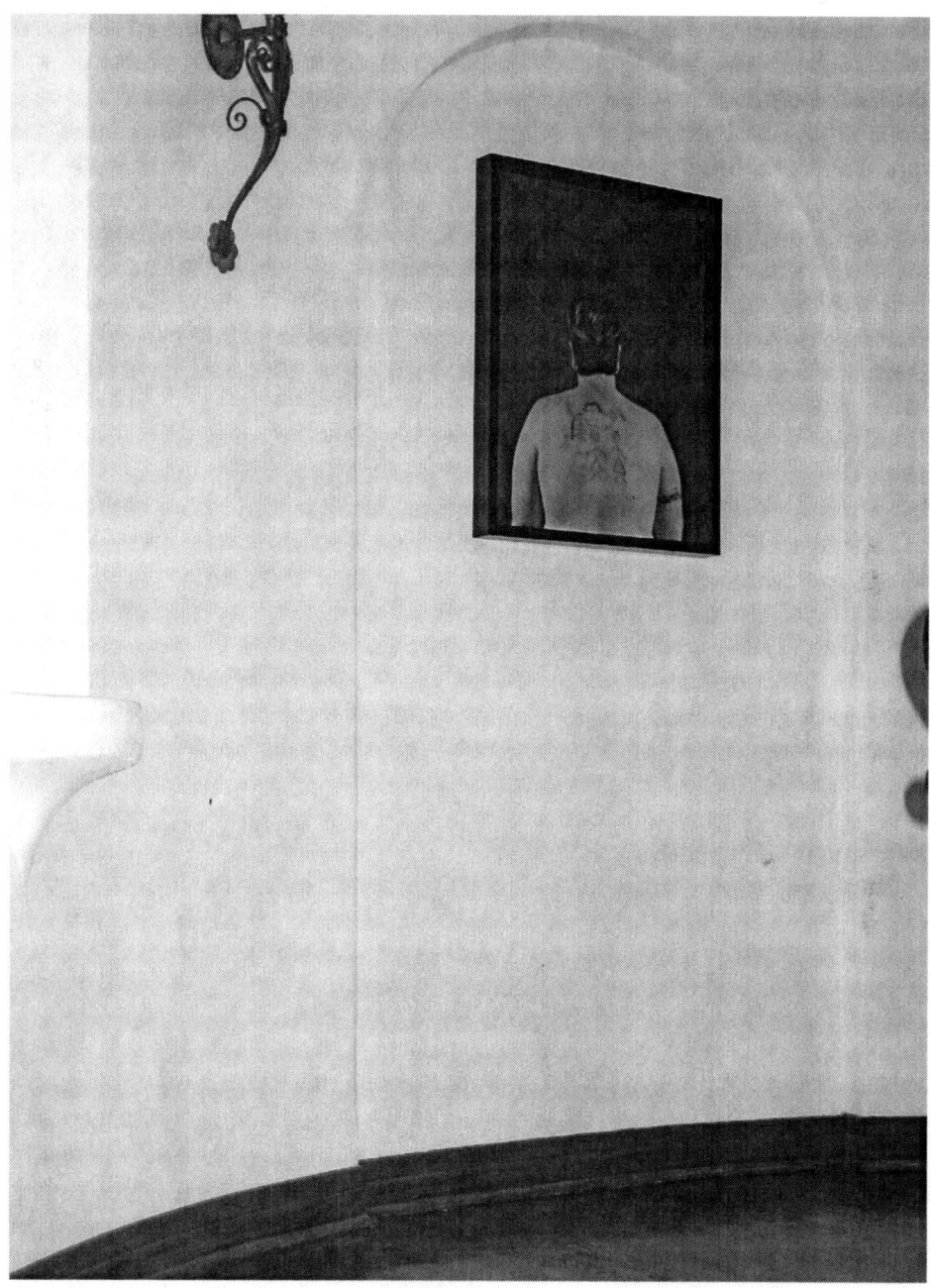

Figure 9.2 Margaret Morgan, untitled still life, 2005. Digital photograph © and courtesy of the author (Visible is Cathy Opie's *Self Portrait*, 1993.)

The Bolshevik Revolution, in the interlude from 1917 to 1923, advanced the remarkable coupling of an artistic avant-garde with the needs of a nascent socialist state, such that an artist like Gustav Klutsis could promote the idea of the electrification of the Soviet Union by employing the most radical of avant-garde typographic designs. Allow me to note here that beauty survived in the modernisms of Adolf Loos and Alfred Barr, as applied arts, which grew like ducklings into beautiful and fully-fledged artistic phenomena, whereas in the Soviet Union, photography and design's ascendance as the dominant avant-garde forms put beauty squarely on the sidelines, an ideological has-been, an anachronistic excess in relation to the lean and efficient form of the future. Be that as it may, the early Soviet example gave political inspiration to many progressive movements in western, democratic-capitalist states, and impetus to the leftward leanings of the intelligentsia.

Indeed by the 1930s in the United States many on the cultural left were card-carrying members or affiliates of the Communist Party, which was then a significant third party and viable political option.[7] As evidenced in the proliferation of John Reed Clubs and in the more enduring *Partisan Review*, for which art critic Clement Greenberg then wrote, the cultural left was a dominant and lively participant in contemporary cultural discourse.[8] If political inspiration came from the Soviet Union, aesthetic inspiration came from Western Europe, as well as the Mexican mural traditions of Diego Rivera, José Clemente Orozco, and David Alfaro Siqueiros. During the depression of the 1930s, American artists, under the auspices of President Roosevelt's federally funded arts programs (part of his massive Works Progress Administration [WPA] project), explored both overt political content and formal invention through mural painting and documentary photo programs.

Contemporaneous news of the Soviets' stringent and often violent suppression of artistic as well as political dissent (particularly by 1938 with news of Stalin's pact with Hitler) became increasingly difficult to ignore. Under an increasingly authoritarian regime, modernist avant-garde practice was being overtaken by Socialist realism. The Kasimir Malevich of *Black Square*, for example, was reduced by 1934 to a peasant-painter whose only autonomy could be expressed in the tiny black square with which he signed his late, state-sanctioned pictures.

A disillusioned American cultural left began to turn away from the Soviet experiment that had, under Stalin, gone terribly wrong. War in Europe put more pressure on progressive America. The split widened over participation in World War II, viewed, on one hand, as a war to defend democracy and the seat of modern culture against fascism, and on the other, to quote Dwight McDonald, as a war about "political and cultural submission to the ruling class at home."[9] Leon Trotsky's declaration – and here is where Beauty raises her ugly head – that "art can become a strong ally of revolution only in so far as it remains faithful to itself" became the cultural left's rallying cry, pushing toward the "autonomy of art" that was to become Greenbergian formalism.[10] By the mid-

1940s Clement Greenberg's invocation of Kantian immediacy dovetailed neatly with this turn away from Lenin and toward Trotsky. And though Greenberg's position vis-à-vis the Soviet Union was at that time quite nuanced – "the pathos of Stalinism has been remembered, but hardly any of the ideas connected with the revolution"[11] – the autonomy of the work of art and its independence from the state had begun its seemingly irrevocable slide toward art for art's sake.[12]

The twin stories of the ascendancy of Pollock's generation of abstract expressionists in the international art world and the promotional uses to which the US government and its agencies put their dominance, will be familiar to readers of cold war cultural criticism.[13] Allow me however briefly to recount the role of beauty, wearing her mask of abstraction, in this narrative: "Some day it will have to be told how 'anti-Stalinism' which started out more or less as 'Trotskyism' turned into art for art's sake and thereby cleared the way, heroically, for what was to come."[14]

The "Triumph of American Painting" and Beyond[15]

The heroism to which Greenberg here refers was that of the "triumph" of American abstraction, a narrative in which working-class guys, most famously Jackson Pollock, had found work painting murals for the WPA in the 1930s but by the 1940s had turned away from figuration and political content under the influence of surrealism, moving toward the automatic, the unconscious and, ultimately, the abstract. To forego "good works" and overt content then, and, instead, to focus upon the material stuff of painting was deemed to be a gesture of solidarity to those artists in the Soviet Union for whom there was no such choice. Abstraction was a political act, the value of which lay in its lack of constraint by arbitrary and external rules (including those of totalitarian regimes).[16] "[A]ccording to Kant (and this reviewer agrees with him)," wrote Greenberg in 1947, "art gives one the sensation of the thing without necessarily including its meaning."[17] Art, free from the constraints of content or meaning could, working through an internal logic, give over to sensate immediacy – to that which, by any other name, might be called, "beauty."

However, even with the rise of abstraction, "beauty," that thing we feel before we figure out what it is that is pleasing us, was important to Greenberg only in as much as it paralleled other concerns. Writing in *The Nation* in 1943, Greenberg argued that the impact of (Van Gogh's) art may have less to do with art than with that "emotion or quality or strikingness which Kant distinguishes as analogous to the beautiful, but only analogous, in that its presence makes us linger on the object embodying it because it keeps arresting our attention."[18] Kant's beauty, as understood by Greenberg, shares with art, or at least any art worthy of the name, the property of making us linger, of arresting our attention. But that is not to say that the art is, precisely, *beautiful*. Rarely does Greenberg mention beauty as such, and certainly Greenberg, unlike Kant, is more interested in the aesthetics of art than the beauty of nature. It is as if Greenberg cannot bring himself explicitly to speak of beauty, lest his invocations of heroism, hard work, philosophy, greatness, and importance be tainted with the feminine.

Historically, beauty was cast as feminine, as can be traced through the references in this chapter, and as such beauty's apprehension, the fantastical notion that we experience beauty directly and without consideration, lay in the purview of cultivated and sensitive *men*. Of course the gendering of beauty is more complex than this. I think of the actor and long-term male lover of Cocteau, Jean Marais, who played the titular beast in Cocteau's 1946 interpretation of Beauty and the Beast: Marais was also known to French cinephiles as *the most beautiful man in the world*. Or of the myriad advertising campaigns of recent times, Calvin Klein the first and most obvious, in which young beautiful men sell products to gay men and straight women at least as much as to straight men.[19] Suffice to say, then, that beauty's apprehension is value-laden, acculturated like any appreciation of fine things, as much as it is gendered.

So although Greenberg privileges art over beauty, Greenberg shares Kant's appreciation of appreciation: Greenberg argues that the ability to distinguish good art from bad – aesthetic judgment in Kant's terms – comes "through experience, and through reflection upon experience. Quality in art can be neither ascertained nor proved by logic or discourse."[20] While subjective judgment lies at the core of Greenberg's aesthetic pronouncements, he also argues, in the same breath, that "quality in art is not just a matter of private experience. There is a *consensus* of taste."[21] This consensus is among connoisseurs and those willing to experience art using "a certain exertion."[22] Here, down to the same contradictions, Greenberg's position echoes that of Kant: aesthetic pleasure then is distinct from other sensory pleasure, because, as Kant would put it, it "immediately connects satisfaction or dissatisfaction to the mere consideration of the object without respect to a use or an end";[23] and because, contradictorily, judgments of aesthetic value are not *a priori* but are the product of living in society.

Greenberg's was a career-long fascination with Kant, despite the fact that, Greenberg willingly acknowledges, "Kant had bad taste."[24] Indeed Kant's aesthetic highpoints resided in sunsets, waterfalls, and marching bands. Toward the end of his career, Greenberg argues that one cannot predict the future of art – but goes on to do just that. He predicts the continued primacy of painting, arguing that "neither [pop nor minimalism] has yet shown itself as capable of major art" and that both are "very small stuff . . . small, quite small."[25]

This is where Greenberg's address undoes itself, his very disavowal a harbinger of what was to come: above all a proliferation of "small art" in the fracturing of modernist modes of artistic practice that began with pop and minimalism, through earth art (if not physically small, then remote), performance, video, conceptual art, installation, post-conceptual art, digital art, and the multiplicity of media and styles of address that constitute art practice today. Perhaps, then, in spite of himself, Greenberg's invocation of Kant was prescient, revealing more about the direction of contemporary art than he could have imagined, a direction in which pretty sunsets and gorgeous thunderclouds can be had in earthworks and lightning fields; and in which marching bands are integral to an art-event-performance-fashion show;[26] a direction in which ephemera, trivia, transient projections, readymades, and random events, things precisely other than heroic painting, proliferate – that is, a direction toward beauty's dispersal, as initiated in the anti-aesthetics of the 1960s and 1970s. If for Greenberg being "small" was to be neither "major" nor "great," neither singular nor unique, then most art post-1960 – and I would say the best of it – is *tiny*.

If beauty were simply that which is pleasingly apprehended, directly and without mediation, one might imagine that it is akin to the "gestalt" invoked by Robert Morris in the mid-1960s.[27] Yet minimalist art is not typically described as "beautiful," for in the culture of the 1960s beauty was that which mystified and obscured and which maintained an elite class of connoisseurship, those things with which Greenbergian formalism was happily associated: *If art could really get off the pedestal and onto the streets*, the argument went, *then whether it was pleasing to the eye or not would become moot.* And in this aspect, even the rear-garde could be recuperated.

Indeed, in a stroke of brilliant intellectual perversity, Robert Morris argued in 1970, when the dismissal of Pollock had become an orthodoxy, that Pollock's use of paint, his dripping and pouring, had more in common with a post-minimalism of the order of Barry Le Va's broken glass and Richard Serra's molten lead than it did with high modernist aesthetics. Nor do those associated with minimalism like the word "beauty" to be linked to their practice – Serra, for example, deplores its invocation when discussing his work, particularly the 1998 *Torqued Ellipses* at MoCA's Geffen Contemporary that were so stirring, striking, evocative – all those qualities that Kant associated with the beautiful, and which Greenberg argued were analogous to beauty and associated with "major art." Rather, Serra speaks of the historic influence of contemporary dancers such as Yvonne Rainer:

> [Her work prompted] ways of relating movement to material and space, allowing me to think about sculpture . . . in a way that is precluded when dealing with sculpture as an autonomous object . . . I found very important the idea of the body passing through space, and the body's movement not being predicated totally on image or sight or optical awareness, but on physical awareness in relation to space, place, time, movement.[28]

This embodied experience of the work of art described by Serra, via Rainer's work, is antithetical to the Kantian experience of auditory and visual beauty, and seems to have more sympathy with what in nineteenth-century aesthetics is: "the moment . . . of delicious recoil from the flood of water in summer heat," that "exquisite interval" of sensate being, at once physically embodied, intelligent, and pleasured.[29] Yet the longer excerpt of Pater's tract, from which I here draw, is tinged with the dispersal of embodiment, a passing, like meteors through space:

> Fix upon it [our physical life] in one of its more exquisite intervals, the moment, for instance, of delicious recoil from the flood of water in summer heat. What is the whole physical life in that moment but a combination of natural elements to which science gives their names? But those elements, phosphorus and lime and delicate fibres, are present not in the human body alone: we detect them in places most remote from it. Our physical life is a perpetual motion of them – the passage of the blood, the waste and repairing of the lenses of the eye, the modification of the tissues of the brain under every ray of light and sound – processes which science reduces to simpler and more elementary forces. Like the elements of which we are composed, the action of these forces extends beyond us: it rusts iron and ripens corn.[30]

For in that immediacy of embodiment, we are also aware of the limit of our physical selves that, ultimately, is death – as Pater elsewhere puts it, "*that strange, perpetual, weaving and unweaving of ourselves.*"[31] For if we are directly to address our embodied sensate selves then we must also acknowledge the limits of our senses – their failings, our endings, the rusting of iron, and ripening of corn. And so too, if we conceive of an art that seeks out the point zero of connection to the material world, as one might argue has been the impetus of the avant-garde for more than a century, then one must also entertain the possibility of the success of that enterprise and the concomitant dissolution, or unweaving, of art's dominance in visual culture. In an avant-garde striving more and more closely to resemble – no, *to be* – real life, success is tinged with failure, as life with death. The beauty of such success has its saturnine cast, a "delicious recoil."

Beauty and Death

I recall an unlimited print from the late 1980s, a collaboration by New York artists Louise Lawler and Felix Gonzalez-Torres (Figures 9.3 and 9.4), displayed as a stack of prints from which viewers could take samples. The piece consisted of a juxtaposition: above, a faint, square image of a cloud trailing a rocket spinning out of control, and, below, in small italicized letters, the word *Beautiful*. In my creative misinterpretation, I had thought of it as an image of the Challenger space shuttle disaster from 1986, and in my exquisite image of an unraveling cloud bearing death and disaster in its wake, I saw an anti-monument to the failure of beauty to compensate, or to stand in for, or to connect, or to exchange – a failure to be *enough*. It spoke to me of deaths of many kinds, explicitly the Challenger disaster; and then, in the context of the New York art world of the 1980s, the loss of a generation of artists to HIV-AIDS; and, in the context of the postwar generation's fantasy of the expanding possibilities of

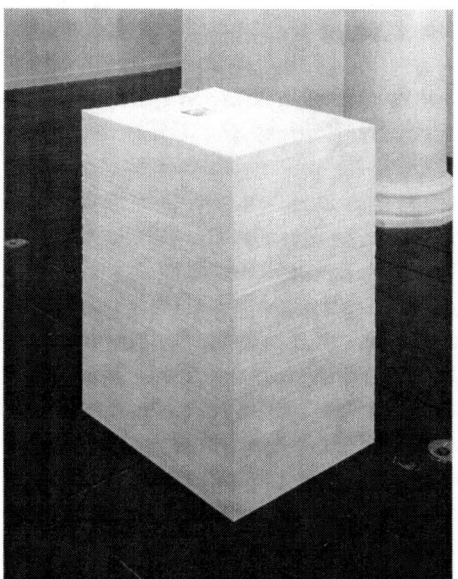

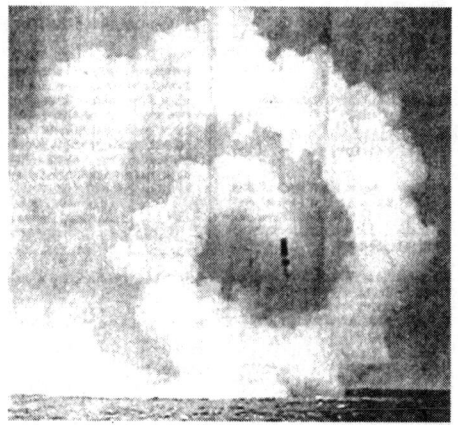

FIGURE 9.3 Felix Gonzalez-Torres in conjunction with Louise Lawler, Untitled (Beautiful), 1990. Offset print on paper, endless copies. 36 in. at ideal height × 23 × 29 in. © The Felix Gonzalez-Torres Foundation and Louise Lawler. Courtesy of Andrea Rosen Gallery. Photograph: Peter Muscato, New York

FIGURE 9.4 Detail of figure 9.3. Digital photograph © and courtesy of Margaret Morgan

political enfranchisement, the symbolic death of space exploration at the nether edge of that "final frontier." And in each connoted death could be apprehended the delicious residue of having deferred death – and in so doing, having lived. And therein was a kind of beauty – to be felt, touched, eaten, consumed, experienced, embodied – even up to its very moment of dissolution, like the spiraling vapors trailing a burning brand, moments before plunging into the ocean.[32] The Lawler/Gonzalez-Torres piece *contains* sublimity, holds it in check, and in the delicacy of its understatement, the faintness of its image, the scale of its inscription, is, itself, beautiful. And beautiful is a stack of cheap sheets, non-archival to be sure, freely to be taken and in the taking dispersed.

Beauty is always in an endless and futile struggle against death. That is the great appeal of art, its seeming fixity the promise of something more. For even the most ephemeral of works persist in documentation and in the minds of those who remember and misremember the stunning spiral, its evanescent stream on the verge of ceasing to be. I kept my copy of that print, shunting it around the globe, putting it up in one grungy office after another, its edges more and more tattered and discolored as the years went by. At some point I no longer had the work in my possession, but the image has stayed with me, if not the precise details of its maker or context.

When I called Louise Lawler to verify my recollection, however, I found that I had got it all wrong: the image was in fact, the Trident II Ballistic missile in the midst of self-destructing in August of 1989 – a very expensive way to make a pretty cloud effect. The saturnine pleasure had been of my own invention, though this exquisite failure to understand iconography was itself if not beauty, then (as Greenberg states in the quote above) "analogous to it."

On the stunningly bright blue morning of September 11, 2001, Al Qaeda made the most powerful use of the iconography of American hegemony since Neil Armstrong walked on the moon. In the felling of the Twin Towers Al Qaeda made mass murder a spectacle and beauty an accomplice. As if with the magic of comic book heroes, the pulverizing of two enormous buildings and thousands of civilians and their computers and papers and coffee cups and phones and brooms and bags became one of the most savvy visual statements in the history of media. It is more potent a symbol than the simultaneous attack on the Pentagon, though the Pentagon is arguably at least as powerful an institution as the financial markets. It has been repeated like psychosis, reiteratively discussed, represented, and used as metonym for the whole. It has been deployed to so many competing ends – by radical Islamists, by the current US Administration, by non-ideologues and ideologues of all stripes – small wonder there have been so many transformations of the event into logos (the affirming anchor of the word).

And so each time I see a tiny plane near a building I think of the image, and so too, on those exquisite clear days bursting on occasion from the darkness of a New York winter, or on cool mornings before the haze of late summer, that crystalline light, so perfect for lifting one's head towards, from the shadowed canyons of Manhattan, so perfect for seeing, so perfect for inexperienced pilots, that delicious daylight will forever be charged with the memory of the event. And the plumes of cumulous smoke, and the glow of white light in the evenings thereafter, as crews kept digging in the near futile search for survivors, these forms, these gorgeous forms – were they not part of the shorthand for Nine Eleven (itself a shorthand), they would be viewed with awe as if in the presence of great beauty.

There are those, Karlheinz Stockhausen and Damien Hirst among them, who labeled this event "the greatest work of art."[33] This is the moment when beauty, this formal thing, which I here conflate with art, has no morality but is instead apprehended in a flash of majesty, trust, and then in this case – recoil. In the post-Nine Eleven US there is no room for the amorality of form – all things visual are to be assessed *morally* – a badge of "good" or "bad" ascribed indelibly to the image, a waving flag, good (*stick it to your bumper*), a burning building, bad (*bomb someone into oblivion*) – images, like allies, are either "with us or against us." Beauty has no place here, for beauty is a small thing and nice, pleasing, a way to describe pots and baskets on bookshelves, and ordinary things, one of which is art. But majestic? Spectacular? No, that is not beauty's realm, but that of the sublime.[34]

Hirst and Stockhausen, who were both immediately vilified for daring to trivialize unspeakable horror, quickly thereafter retracted or complicated their initial responses. And yet each, in that first impulse, spoke to the mechanism by which one might, through art, if not apprehend, then contain the power of the image and all it implied, all that was actually too difficult to comprehend, the magnitude of which was too great fully to take up lest one be overwhelmed by that *apprehension*.

Apprehension: to take up and understand; apprehension, an anxious anticipation. Perhaps then we might suggest that part of the reason for the vociferous rejection of Hirst's and Stockhausen's complex positions, is precisely that art – for Hirst, it was to do with the way the attack changed how we see – is now more trivial than horror. That is to say, that art is no longer big enough, sublime enough, beautiful enough to be able to house or even address an event like Nine Eleven. If someone painted a *Guernica* about Nine Eleven, would anyone care?[35] This is not to say that a painting *should* be able to encapsulate so much, but rather simply to say that it doesn't. For better and worse art, if not architecture, is definitionally minor, or at least thoroughly quotidian, and to describe horror as art is unspeakable.

Perhaps this belief system partly explains the success of the Belgian artist Luc Tuymans, whose strategy when addressing the horrors of modernity (from the extreme viciousness of Belgian colonial rule in the Congo to the gas ovens at Auschwitz) is to paint the most modest of paintings. Tuymans' works are faint images, fragmentary, chalky, discontinuous scenes of the hinges of political history juxtaposed with the most inconsequential of subjects (wall papers, patches on an insomniac's ceiling, water jugs and fruit), as if to attest to the impossibility of painting a *Death of Marat* or a *Raft of the Medusa* for the twenty-first century[36] – as if to broach the enormity of historical change, or to represent the enormity of political terror, can only be with a sideways glance, a sense of movement, a darker shadow in the periphery of one's vision; as if such scale and weight can only be achieved inversely, and with the greatest of humility, modesty, an almost breathless smallness.

I am reminded of the images in Georges Bataille's 1961 book *Tears of Eros*, photographs documenting China's last public flaying and execution. The images are horrific, filling the pages of the book so that it seems almost physically to swell and drag with their power. But the issues the images raise in the author's dignified analysis are thoughtful, provocative. I am not sure that such a use would be condoned in the current climate in the US. Art is no longer the representative form in contemporary American culture – US tax dollars no longer support individual artists, art is no longer taught in the public schools of most of the 50 states, the US Pavilion at the Venice Biennale has lost most of its state and private funding. Would that the US Government's arsenal still consisted of art as a major (propaganda) weapon! Art, indeed images in general, are seen as guilty, or at least put indefinitely under detention. Internalized censorship, long the goal of the hounds of the art world like Senator Jesse Helms, seems to have taken root in the culture at large, as if relinquishing the role of art has cast its spell over the entire nation.[37]

The suppression of images of the war dead and wounded from the US occupation of Iraq (ongoing in 2005) has an obvious political function of withholding incriminating information; but it may have the ancillary effect of teaching a generation that death is unapproachable, disturbing images best avoided, jingoistic substitutions the better option. Art may be beautiful, but only like a pretty woman is beautiful. Art can be media savvy like Damian Hirst's, but only to pecuniary ends and not toward the ends of subversion or the unsettling of power. Art, it would seem, lacks the profundity to compete with the threat, terror, and death that is the Bush administration's mandate in 2005. Art is tamed, beauty contained. And I think this was part of the appeal of my interpretation of the Gonzalez-Torres/Lawler piece. *Beautiful*. For if we cannot speak of the form of death, how can we fix it in our memories as a promise of something more?

Beauty's Return

Which brings me, albeit obliquely, to Dave Hickey, a figure who has had such appeal in the Anglophone art world of recent years. I say figure because I think it is the idea of Dave Hickey, a Hickeyness, if you like, and what his ideas seem to suggest, that circulates so powerfully in conversation, in anecdote, in invocation, as much as in any close reading of the actual texts, themselves often slim and out of print. It is the idea of a "return" to pleasure, a return to beauty, which makes Dave Hickey – his beautiful and often funny formal plays of words and ideas as if for play's own sake – so appealing. I say "return" in quotes because it is clear both from this analysis and from Hickey's own invocations of beautiful painting under the Counter-Reformation, for example, that beauty is always, ineluctably, for better or worse, in the service of something, even and including beauty "for its own sake." Ask Oscar Wilde.[38] So that a return, as if to the good old days, is a fantasy that is produced out of the invocation of "Hickeyness."

Published in 1993, *The Invisible Dragon*, arguably most well known of Hickey's publications, speaks to the rise in the late 1980s of concerns with appearance and sensual appeal (what one might call the attributes of *beauty*), as defining features of contemporary art. The text begins with an anecdote in which Hickey, on the dais for a panel discussion, is broken from his doodling, unconscious reverie to find himself addressed from the audience with a solicitation of his opinion on what the "Issues of the Nineties" would be, to which he replies, "Beauty" – spontaneously, without contemplation or consideration, an off-the-cuff remark, so to speak, which thereby enacts (at least in the retelling) a fantastical moment wherein is had an immediate, direct experience of "beauty."

The moment is quite Kantian. If, for Kant, beauty resided in immediate and unmediated sensual pleasure it is, for Hickey, an immediate and unmediated premonition of beauty's rise from the philosophical dead. For Hickey, beauty (in images) is the agency that causes visual pleasure in the beholder.[39] But this returns us to Kant's quandary: that one may feel aesthetic pleasure in observing an object (a pleasure that, drawn through the subject's senses, is obviously *subjective*), but that one also expresses that feeling "objectively" as a judgment of the properties of the object: *It is Beautiful!* This dynamic then paradoxically situates one's subjective pleasure as objectively valid, as it does for Hickey, such that "the judgment of taste is based upon concepts . . . for otherwise there could be no room even for contention in the matter or for the claim to the necessary agreement of others."[40]

To paraphrase Hickey, the orthodoxy of the time, 1988, was such that if one were to speak of beauty it was only as the handmaiden of commerce, the grease on her pretty hands to smooth the way for the exchange of money and pictures.[41] Beauty was a slut, and the market corrupt. This hegemony was subscribed to by those in what Hickey calls, the "therapeutic institution . . . a loose configuration of museums, universities, bureaus, foundations, publications and endowments."[42] These institutions saw as their purpose, and here again I paraphrase, to support art that was good for you rather than art that was good, "picture-watching as a form of 'grace' that by its very 'nature' is good for both our spiritual health and our personal growth."[43] His corollary is that the institution believes that if beauty sells, it must be bad. This takes us back to the nineteenth-century avant-garde and its reception in the twentieth, which is to reiterate that if Hickey is right beauty is, and has been for a long time, suspect.

Hickey goes on to paint a picture of fat bureaucrats opining on art that is dull, obvious, and intended to edify those poor souls in need of education. His tone might be populist but it is underpinned by a refrain that sounds a lot like: "I and people who agree with me know good (beautiful) art when we see (feel) it." In other words, a refrain that sounds a lot like Kant via Greenberg. Except that Hickey's intertextuality updates the argument with more than a smattering of theoretical invocation drawn from feminism, poststructuralism, queer theory, and the like – the very discourses that he implies debase the pure production and apprehension of beauty in art, taught to graduate art students in the very therapeutic institutions he derides (although he himself teaches in one of them). Hickey's ideological agenda floats just below the shimmering surface of his argument.[44]

If his argument totalizes art's contemporary institutional frames – lumping MoMA in with the local university, with public art spaces and art journals – his position vis-à-vis *beauty incarnate* is more nuanced. Hickey's prime example of the failure of the therapeutic institution is the National Endowment for the Arts' response in 1988 to the charge led by Senator Helms against their support of (that is, use of tax-payers' money for) an exhibition of Robert Mapplethorpe's work that included some graphic homoerotic material.[45] The NEA's capitulation to the terms set up by Helms became the touchstone by which funding, already on the downward slide, could all the more dramatically be reduced. For this Hickey damns all publicly-funded arts organizations – and this in spite of the fact that there were numerous artists and institutions alike who, like Hickey, deplored the NEA's response, as can be attested by the vociferous protests of the time. Yet here, in spite of the limits of his critique of publicly-funded arts institutions, Hickey speaks eloquently to pleasure and control in the apprehension of art itself:

> Why do I submit to this gritty, baroque image of a man's arm disappearing up another man's anus? And choose to speculate upon it? And why must Robert [Mapplethorpe] have submitted to the actual, intimate, aromatic spectacle? And chosen to portray it? And why, finally, did the supplicant kneel and submit to having a lubricated fist shoved up his ass? And choose to have himself so portrayed?
>
> The answer, of course, in every case, is pleasure and control – but deferred, always deferred, shunting upward through concentric rituals of trust and apprehension, glimmering through sexual, aesthetic, and spiritual manifestations, resonating outward from the heart of the image through every decision to expand the context of its socialization . . . where the rule of law meets the grace of trust.[46]

"Pleasure and control, deferred though trust and apprehension . . . where the rule of law meets the grace of trust. . . ." Curiously, this sounds remarkably similar to that by which Hickey decries his "therapeutic institution": "picture-watching as a form of 'grace' that by its very 'nature' is [patronizingly deemed to be] good for both our spiritual health and our personal growth." For surely the description of his experience of the Mapplethorpe photograph, *Helmut and Brooks, N.Y.C.*, 1978, is, by Hickey's own account, nothing if not an experience of growth and trust, a form of grace.

Art as an Act of Giving

What is of import here is pleasure and control, beauty and order, grace and trust. These lie at the heart of the matter. If the image, the beautiful image, has been swung, pendulum-like, from side to side, from one ideological end to another, there are those artists for whom beauty really is moot and for whom pleasure is not the pleasure of looking but of *giving*.

What obtains if artist and viewer alike relinquish authority, mastery, grandiloquence, elitism, permanence? Wherein lies their pleasure? The drive toward art's increasing accessibility ultimately means its merging with or disappearance into ordinary life, the fruition of its egalitarian promise. From meals cooked for the audience (Rirkrit Tiravanija), to gardens grown (Robert Irwin), to histories unfolded (Fred Wilson), to lectures held (Andrea Fraser), to shelter provided (*Utopia Station*, Venice Biennale, curated by Molly Nesbit, Hans-Ulrich Obrist, and Rirkrit Tiravanija), art has increasingly turned toward the provision of service.[47] Indeed, part of the popularity of Hickeyan beauty could be attributed to its usefulness as a reaction formation against the partial decline in dominance of the art of images and objects as we have known them.

In the avant-garde contest between the aesthetic and the anti-aesthetic, beauty has been inversely proportional to a perceived degree of democratization – the more beautiful the art, the less democratic and vice versa. To call art "beautiful" in this context is almost pejorative.

In the 1990s, artists who had trained in the rigors of conceptual art graduated from art school with their critical faculties honed and took up their brushes, their watercolor brushes no less, and painted. That is, with the perversity of children rejecting their parents: *voila!* pretty pictures. These pictures had none of the bravura of Greenbergian painting; they were on the smallish side – illustrative, pictorial, and with the wit and sympathy of the works included in the germinal Pictures exhibition curated by Douglas Crimp back in 1977.[48]

The images in this late art are predominantly found, borrowed, copied and, under current copyright law, stolen – those now familiar appropriationist strategies of postmodernism. Painting in this incarnation is itself used instrumentally in concert with other media. For of course the artists of whom I speak inflect not only their conceptual training but the illustrative impulse as well: thus they make pictures that somehow document a web of artistic relations and influences (Dave Muller); or the psychodynamics between artist and dealer (Delia Brown); or they address the spectacle of viewership as a second degree turn in the couch-potato world of live-feed television sports (Andrea Bowers) (Figure 9.5); or they draw traces of photographs, as parts of larger treatises on the relations between art and popular culture (Şam Durant) (Figure 9.6). In each instance the pictures are part of a larger *messier* project often incorporating video, photography, sculpture, performance, and so on. And in each instance, the works are pretty, witty but rarely, and only then in the most obtuse of ways, beautiful.

And if beauty were once the privileged domain of art, contemporary attitudes toward beauty nudge it toward the prosaic. In just the past ten years we've gone from Cindy Crawford to Jennifer Anniston. Indeed, if, at an opening of contemporary art, we remark that "the work is beautiful" it may be construed as meaning "I don't understand it," or "I haven't really looked at it, I've been chatting to my friends," or "I think it's really vacuous." And when beauty is invoked sincerely and not as euphemism, it is much more likely to be about design than about art per se – a kind of reinforcement of the old adage that *a good drain implies as much as a beautiful statue.*[49]

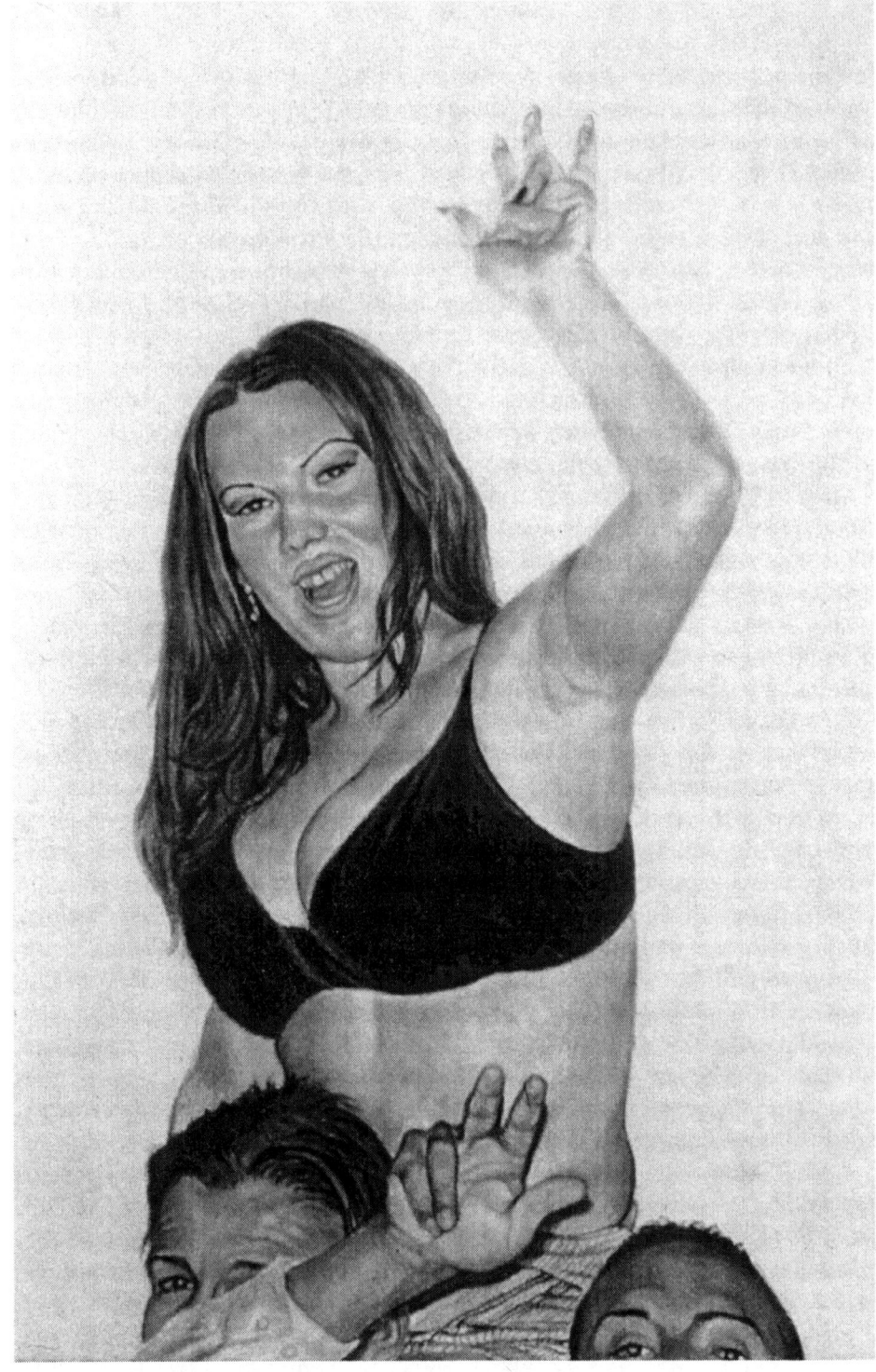

FIGURE 9.5   Andrea Bowers, *Crowd Drawing: LA Club Kid, Girl Waving* (detail), 1998/2004. Colored pencil on paper. 24 × 20 in. Courtesy of private collection and Sara Meltzer Gallery, New York

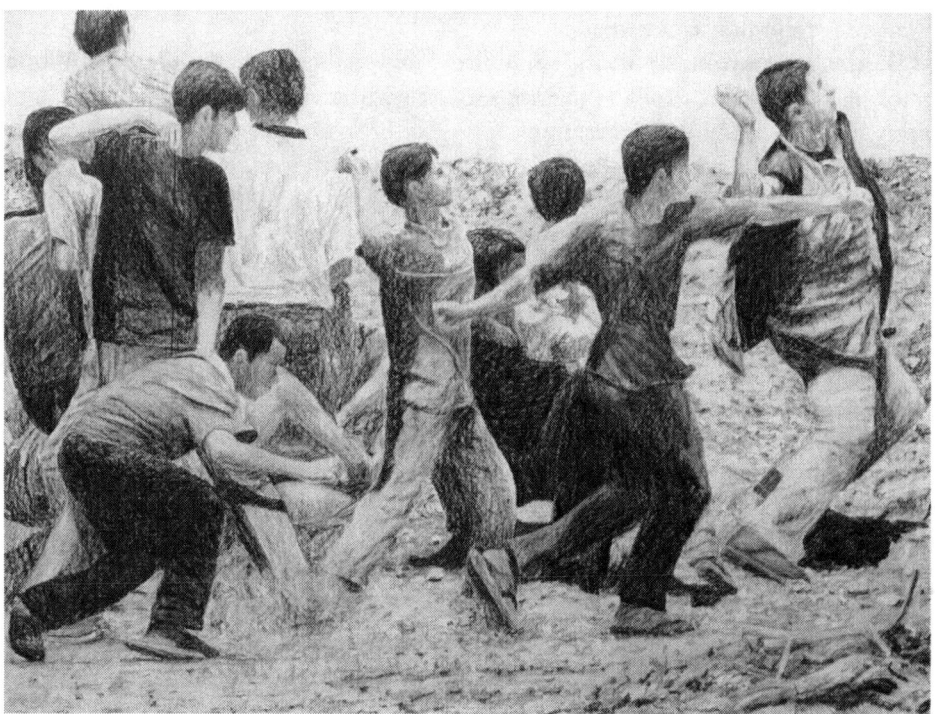

FIGURE 9.6 Sam Durant, *Palestinian Youths Throw Stones Toward Israeli Army Positions, Gaza, 2004*, 2004. Graphite on paper. 22 × 30 in. Location: Beit Hanoun, Gaza Strip. Based on a photograph by Kevin Frayer called "Palestinian Youths Throw Stones Toward Israeli Army Positions, Gaza." Courtesy of the artist and Blum & Poe, Los Angeles. Photograph: Joshua White

> I am driving, late to pick up my daughter, talking on the phone to a friend, carping about art, and suddenly in the cool grey dusk of a Los Angeles winter I see, all bloody carmine and glittering, the last of the day flickering, beautiful, like reptilian scales, on the sides of the lone tall building in my view – our conversation is arrested (if not the driver, phone in hand) – an evanescent flash of dying sunlight that in moments is gone. The light turns green.

Does beauty produce passivity? At least an inwardness, for it is in the moment of the pleasurable taking up of that which is before us – the sunset for example – that beauty resides, and this requires a contemplativeness that is in contradistinction to activity, to "busyness" and to *being in the world*. We must stop a while. But is that wakeful, cognitive, eye-shining, thinking state passive? I think not, she said.

Instead of the heady rush of singularity – the sunset – we have the noise of busy competition, a world bursting to the seams with images, from art schools and magazines and the back seats of cars and from digital cameras and phones and iPods and the sides of buildings and screens of our computers. To my two-year-old everything is a camera.

Beauty, meanwhile, is adrift, subliminal, impossible, a flicker like old film, a trace like the smell of milk – and we are left with horror, trivia, censorship, and petty quarrels among the remaining.

Notes

1 Helen of Sparta's legendary beauty, and her kidnapping by Paris of Troy, precipi-tated the Trojan war (the climax of which involved the Greeks infiltrating Troy with the "peace" offering of a giant wooden horse; once accepted inside the gates of Troy, the horse's hollow belly revealed Greek soldiers who snuck out and opened the gates for the Greek army). Hellenistic Greek art, from around 300 BC, is generally viewed in traditional art history as the earliest pinnacle marking, in its great beauty and psychological realism, the nascent dominance of European visual arts across the world.
2 See Clark (1984).
3 Hegel (1835/1997), 195.
4 See http://www.moma.org/about_moma/history/index.html on the history of the museum.
5 Loos (1898/1982), 40.
6 See Guilbaut (1983), and Frascina (1985).
7 This was also true in other Anglophone nations including Britain and Australia.
8 Named after the radical journalist and revolutionary, John Reed, whose 1920 *Ten Days That Shook the World* documented the October revolution and the formation of the USSR. Like many John Reed Clubs across the United States, the New York chapter established a journal. The journal survived the demise of the clubs, and was called the *Partisan Review*.
9 McDonald (1939), 3–20, cited in Frascina (1985), 172.
10 "Art, like Science, not only does not seek orders, but by its very essence, cannot tolerate them. Artistic creation has its own laws – even when it consciously serves a social movement. . . . Art can become a strong ally of the revolution only in so far as it remains faithful to itself." Trotsky (1938), 10.
11 Greenberg (1941/1988), 46.
12 Indeed it had been a long time coming: "In point of fact," Walter Benjamin writes, "the theory of *l'art pour l'art* assumes decisive importance around 1852 at a time when the bourgeoisie sought to take its cause from the hands of writers and poets." Benjamin (c.1935/1983), 59.
13 See Max Kozloff, "American Painting in the Cold War," and Eva Cockcroft, "Abstract Expressionism, Weapon of the Cold War," in Frascina (1985) and Guilbaut (1983).
14 Greenberg (1961), 230, cited in Frascina (1985), 180–1.
15 See Sandler (1970).
16 See Greenberg (1946/1988), 64–6.
17 Greenberg (1947/1988), 159.
18 Greenberg (1943/1988), 161.

19 See Bordo (2000), 112–54.

20 Greenberg (1961/1988), 118.

21 Ibid., italics original.

22 Ibid., 119.

23 Kant (1790/2001), 103.

24 Greenberg (1955/1988), 249.

25 Greenberg (1969/1988), 308, 310.

26 See Walter De Maria's 1977 *Lightening Field*; the latter to which I allude was organized largely single-handedly by artist Mark Bradford, while a student at California Institute of the Arts, Valencia, in the late 1990s.

27 See Morris (1970/1993), 71–93.

28 Serra (1997), 26.

29 Pater (1873/1998), 150.

30 Ibid.

31 Ibid., 152, my italics.

32 For Kant, fine feeling either relates to the sublime *or* the beautiful. That which awes and terrifies the viewer (like the explosion of the Challenger) is sublime, while the beautiful (as noted) can be small and ornamented.

33 In an interview, Hirst told BBC News Online: "The thing about 9/11 is that it's kind of an artwork in its own right. It was wicked, but it was devised in this way for this kind of impact. It was devised visually. . . ." Referring to how the event changed perceptions, he added: "I think our visual language has been changed by what happened on September 11: an aeroplane becomes a weapon – and if they fly close to buildings people start panicking. Our visual language is constantly changing in this way and I think as an artist you're constantly on the lookout for things like that." Hirst (2002).

34 See note 32.

35 Picasso painted *Guernica* (1937) in response to the fascist bombing of the eponymous town during the Spanish Civil War, and it has since come to symbolize the potential for art to act as political protest.

36 Jacques-Louis David's 1793 *Death of Marat* and Théodore Gericault's 1819 *Raft of the Medusa* were both major political paintings, each commenting on crises of the French state.

37 See Katz in this volume.

38 That Wilde was a staunch advocate of the autonomy of the work of art, of art for art's sake, stands in bitter contradistinction to the way in which his own oeuvre was vilified because of his private life – his public avowal of his homosexuality and his consequent imprisonment.

39 Hickey (1993), 11.

40 Immanuel Kant, as quoted in Scruton (2001), 101.

41 Hickey (1993), 13.

42 Ibid., 53.

43 Ibid.

44 On the ideological underpinnings of Hickey's neo-Kantian aesthetics, see Jones (2002).

45 See Katz in this volume.

46 Hickey (1993), 36.

47 On the paradoxical anti-democratic nature of the act of giving as it relates to the visual arts, see Bishop (2004), 51–79.
48 Crimp's *Pictures*, 1977, Artists Space, New York, included the work of Troy Brauntuch, Jack Goldstein, Sherrie Levine, Robert Longo, Cindy Sherman, and Philip Smith. See Singerman in this volume.
49 See Stobart (1915).

References

Benjamin, Walter (c.1935/1983). *Charles Baudelaire: a Lyric Poet in the Era of High Capitalism*, trans. Harry Zohn. London: Verso.

Bishop, Claire (2004). "Antagonism and Relational Aesthetics." In *October*, vol. 110 (Fall).

Bordo, Susan (2000). "Beauty (Re)Discovers the Male Body." In *Beauty Matters*, ed. Peg Zeglin Brand. Bloomington: Indiana University Press.

Clark, T. J. (1984). *The Painting of Modern Life*. New York: Princeton University Press.

Frascina, Francis, ed. (1985). *Pollock and After: The Critical Debate*. New York: Harper and Row.

Greenberg, Clement (1988). Essays in *The Collected Essays and Criticism*, vols. 1–4, ed. John O'Brian. Chicago: University of Chicago Press.

—— (1941/1988). "The Renaissance of the Little Mag." Vol. 1.

—— (1943/1988). "Review of Exhibitions of Van Gogh and the Remarque Collection." Vol. 1.

—— (1946/1988). "'Americanism' Misplaced." Vol. 2.

—— (1947/1988). "Pessimism for Mass Consumption." Vol. 2.

—— (1955/1988). "Review of *Piero della Francesca* and *The Arch of Constantine*, both by Bernard Berenson." Vol. 3.

—— (1961/1988). "The Identity of Art." Vol. 4.

—— (1969/1988). "Interview Conducted by Lily Leino." Vol. 4.

—— (1961). "The Late Thirties in New York." *Art and Culture*. Boston: Beacon Press.

Guilbaut, Serge (1983). *How New York Stole the Idea of Modern Art*. Chicago: University of Chicago Press.

Hegel, G. W. F. (1835/1997). "Art, Nature, Freedom." Repr. in *Aesthetics*, ed. Susan Feagin and Patrick Maynard. Oxford: Oxford University Press.

Hickey, Dave (1993). *The Invisible Dragon*. Los Angeles: Art Issues Press.

Hirst, Damien (2002). "9/11 Wicked But a Work of Art, says Damien Hirst," reported by Rebecca Allison. *The Guardian* (Wednesday September 11).

Jones, Amelia (2002). "'Every man knows where and how beauty gives him pleasure:' Beauty Discourse and the Logic of Aesthetics." In *Aesthetics in a Multicultural Age*, ed. Emory Elliott. Oxford: Oxford University Press.

Kant, Immanuel (1790/2001). *Critique of the Power of Judgment*, 5:242. Cambridge: Cambridge University Press.

Loos, Adolf (1898/1982). "The Luxury Vehicle." In *Spoken Into the Void*, trans. Jane Newman and John Smith. Cambridge, MA: Oppositions Books, MIT Press.

McDonald, Dwight (1939). "This Quarter – War and the Intellectuals: Act Two." *Partisan Review*, vol. 6, no. 3 (Spring).

Morris, Robert (1970/1993). "Some Notes on the Phenomenology of Making." *Continuous Project Altered Daily*. Cambridge, MA: MIT Press.

Pater, Walter (1873/1998). *The Renaissance: Studies in Art and Poetry*. Oxford: Oxford University Press.

Sandler, Irving (1970). *Triumph of American Painting: A History of Abstract Expressionism*. New York: Praeger.

Scruton, Roger (2001). *Kant, A Very Short Introduction*. Oxford: Oxford University Press.

Serra, Richard (1997). Interview by Lynne Cooke and Michael Govan. In *Richard Serra: Torqued Ellipses*. New York: Dia Center for the Arts.

Stobart, J. C. (1915). *The Glory that was Greece*. London: Sidgwick and Jackson.

Trotsky, Leon (1938). "Art and Politics." *Partisan Review*, vol. 5, no. 3 (August–September).

PART IV

Politics

10

Avant-Garde:
A Historiography of a
Critical Concept

Johanne Lamoureux

"Metaphor with a moustache": The French Origins and Development of the Notion of the Avant-Garde

Jürgen Habermas's opening remarks on the avant-garde in his important 1983 essay "Modernity – An Incomplete Project" recall the domain of emergence of the term in military parlance:

> Aesthetic modernity is characterized by attitudes which find a common focus in a changed consciousness of time. This time consciousness expresses itself through metaphors of the vanguard and the avant-garde. The avant-garde understands itself as invading unknown territory, exposing itself to the dangers of sudden, shocking encounters, conquering an as yet unoccupied future. The avant-garde must find a direction in a landscape into which no one seems to have yet ventured.[1]

In referring back to the military roots of the notion of the artistic avant-garde, Habermas stresses how the prefix of the expression doesn't just refer to precedence in time ("coming before" or "going first"); "*avant*" also implies the movement of an army marching in front of the rest of the troops, into disputed territory. It evokes spatial, and not necessarily legitimate, ambitions as well as temporal progress(ion).

Indeed, well before the twentieth-century use of the term in the cultural fields of literature and the visual arts, the notion of the avant-garde had twice migrated. From the military domain, it was first transplanted in the writings of Henri de Saint-Simon, a former soldier of the French revolutionary army.

Saint-Simon's vision for the renewal of society centered around the propelling role of a three-fold avant-garde, constituted by the scientist (*savant*), the engineer (*industriel*), and the artist, all working in concert to advance progress and prosperity in society. Considered more as a mere propagandist for the views designed by the two other activators of avant-gardism, artists were at first not given the same transformative efficiency as they are in the Saint-Simonian trilogy. Within a few years however, the artist was promoted to the same status as the *savant* and the *industriel*.[2]

In the 1820s and following, then, under the impulse of Saint-Simon's disciples, an alliance of political and artistic forces was developed in France. The equation between progress and avant-garde received a defining formulation in that context and so did the conception that political and artistic progress work hand in hand. This latter belief was to be echoed all through the nineteenth century in the utopian writings of Charles Fourier and the socialist and anarchist discourse of Pierre Paul Proudhon (to whom both Gustave Courbet and Charles Baudelaire were politically close in the late forties).

The thrust behind the Saint-Simonian vision was, however, at odds with the separation between art and politics or between aesthetics and everyday experience postulated in the aesthetic philosophy of Immanuel Kant and Friedrich von Schiller, both of whose models of aesthetics were increasingly dominant in the context of romanticism and later in institutionalized conceptions of modernism. Consequently, the notion of the avant-garde initially competed with the romantic conception that the artist had to be free from political and social constraints (a purveyor of "art for art's sake"). And in the course of the nineteenth century the paradigm of artists committing to the integration of a political ideal with their art practices came to be depreciated as simplistic while art with an explicit politics was viewed negatively as betraying the necessary "freedom" of artistic expression from political exigencies and social pressures. The dominance of such romantic and then modernist ideals partly explains, according to Neil McWilliam, why there are no "great Saint-Simonian artists" in the canons of European modernism.[3]

Between 1862 and 1864 Charles Baudelaire was planning his autobiography under the tentative title of *My Heart Laid Bare*. In the fragmentary notes for the never-completed book, Baudelaire elliptically writes: "On the Frenchman's passionate predilection for military metaphors. In this country, every metaphor wears a moustache." The poet then lists a few of these metaphors – the poets of combat, the vanguard of literature – and he continues with a comment that is most often omitted from quotes, probably because of its embarrassing xenophobic undertone: "This weakness for military metaphors is a sign of natures that are not themselves militant, but are made for discipline – that is to say, for conformity – natures congenitally domestic, Belgian natures that can only think in unison."[4]

This excerpt, scribbled at the very moment when Manet was making his entrance into the Parisian art world with the scandals related to the 1860s salon exhibition of his incendiary paintings *Olympia* and *Déjeuner sur l'herbe*, indicates that the term "avant-garde" was at the time still narrowly tied to the practice of literature (rather than to the visual arts) and viewed as inextricable from political commitment. Too, the term avant-garde clearly remained infused with military meaning. For today's reader, perhaps familiar with Carol Duncan's early 1970s feminist critique of the tropes of "virility and domination" characterizing the early twentieth-century pictorial avant-garde, it is tempting to misread Baudelaire's denunciation of the avant-garde as one of those "metaphors with a moustache" that the French cherish, and to project into it a clairvoyant protest against the masculinist gendering of the militant avant-garde (Figure 10.1).

But what Baudelaire targets in the military does not explicitly revolve around gender (the virility of the army, the testosterone of the moustache). Romantics such as Baudelaire despised the army as an institution that imposes uniforms and conformity (the moustache is the fashion convention of a group). To Baudelaire's eyes, such conformity is the common denominator between the military and the militant artistic avant-gardes. Moreover, the poet links this *esprit de corps* to a form of innate domestication (a term whose Latin root *domus* [home] can be heard to imply not only the sense of something being *tamed* – no longer wild – but also the connotation of being house-bound, of belonging to a depreciated domestic sphere that was increasingly gendered in the feminine during the nineteenth-century reshaping of boundaries between public and private domains).

Baudelaire's remarks also articulate an ambiguous gendering of the term around spatial references. Contrary to current associations, which intertwine the avant-garde with the cosmopolitanism and attraction of the metropolis, for Baudelaire, who wrote these notes in the midst of his voluntary but disenchanted exile in Brussels, the avant-garde does not seem to be a phenomenon of the capital.[5] In Baudelaire's text, the expression "Belgian minds," with its denunciation of a taste for conformity and unison, serves two functions. First, it acknowledges that the avant-garde, as a military term, refers to a *group* action, an aspect of the artistic avant-garde that will often be neglected and obliterated in modernist art history in order to enrich the cult of individual originality. (But the proliferation of artistic manifestoes between 1886 and 1930 shows how the avant-garde indeed involved group actions that promoted and prescribed a "collective form of singularity."[6]) Second, the expression also acts as a surrogate designation of the bourgeois. As Raymond Williams observes in *The Politics of Modernism*: "The bourgeois was *the mass* which the creative artist must either ignore and circumvent, or increasingly shock, deride or attack."[7] Williams also remarks that this class antagonism tended to focus on the bourgeois family, which, "with all its known characteristics of property and control, is often in effect a covering phrase for those rejections of women and children which take the form of a rejection of 'domesticity.'"[8]

Baudelaire's contemptuous perspective, and the distance between what it proposes and what became the enduring doxa of avant-garde-as-metropolitan, should

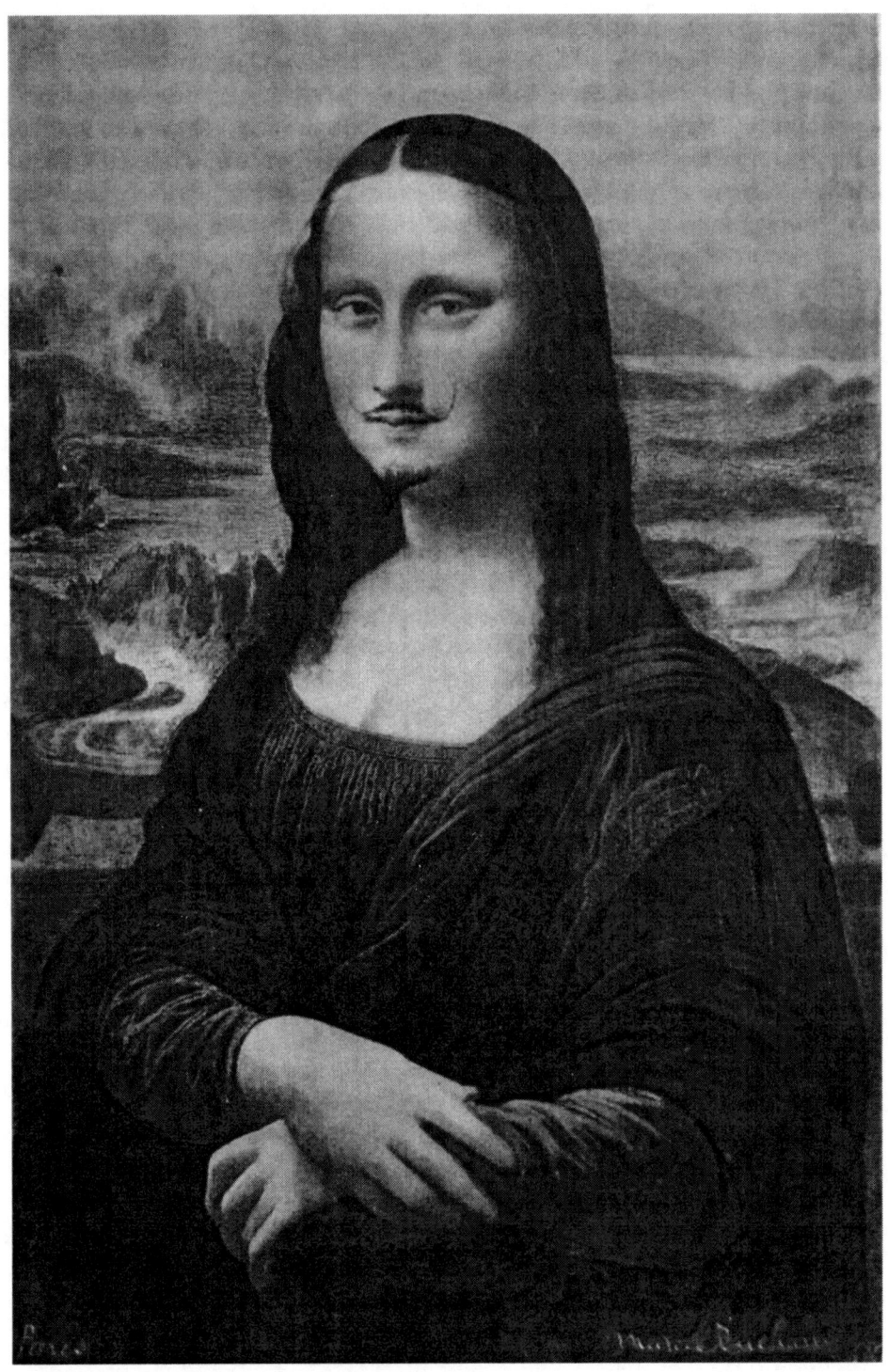

FIGURE 10.1 Marcel Duchamp, *LHOOQ*, 1919. © Succession Marcel Duchamp, 2005. ARS/NY, ADAGP/Paris

suffice to convince us that the notion of the avant-garde was from its inception a conflicted and contradictory term, never universally held as a site of originality or metropolitanism. Certainly the avant-garde was not "born" original but was reiteratively constructed as such, even if that construction happened rather early on.

"Everyone's gambit": The Avant-Garde as a "Form of Social Climbing"

In the 1860s Baudelaire had abandoned his political commitment of the late 1840s, when he had fought with the insurgents during the 1848 revolution. British social art historian T. J. Clark sheds some light on the poet's resentment of and suspicion regarding the avant-garde when he reminds us that the avant-garde and the Bohemians (among whom Baudelaire counted himself) "fought on different sides of the barricades in June; the Bohemians with the insurrection and the avant-garde with the forces of order."[9]

In *Image of the People*, his important 1973 book on Gustave Courbet and the 1848 Revolution, Clark is extremely critical of the notion of the avant-garde, with its double litany of "heroic history" and its "movement away from literary and historical subject matter."[10] Clark writes of the 1850s Parisian art world as one where

> being avant-garde was just an institutionalized variant of everyone's gambit. It was a kind of initiation rite – a trek out into the bush for a while, then a return to privileged status within the world you had left. It was a finishing school, an unabashed form of social climbing. [. . .] In this light, the real history of the avant-garde is the history of those who by-passed, ignored, rejected it; a history of secrecy and isolation; a history of escape from the avant-garde and even from Paris.[11]

With such descriptions, Clark, however, is retrospectively shifting the meaning of the term, clearly referring to "avant-garde" as it had come to be crystallized in the formalist version of modernism developed by influential American art critic Clement Greenberg in the post-WWII period (on which more below).

Due to this retroactive reasoning, Clark's list of avant-garde artists in *Image of the People* tends to favor artists who managed to escape the metropole and its feverish artistic milieu. The list includes Rimbaud, Stendhal, Lautréamont, Van Gogh, and Cézanne, and Clark also argues the case for Millet, Daumier, Courbet, and . . . Baudelaire. Manet, who was to become the canonical figure of modernist origins and artistic originality in the formalist narrative of the avant-garde refined in the twentieth century, does not figure on Clark's list at this point.[12]

It is worth noting that in his early Marxist texts on modernism from the late 1930s and early 1940s Clement Greenberg did not care much about Manet either: the 1939 article "Avant-Garde and Kitsch" does not mention him; the 1940 essay "Towards a Newer Laocoon" elects Courbet as "the first real painter of the avant-garde and mentions Manet only once, stressing how he is "indifferent to his subject."[13] Greenberg also focuses on Manet's abandonment of traditional sculptural modeling as a necessary attempt at finding a solution for the problems of the medium (problems that, Greenberg was to argue in his post-Marxist, formalist criticism from the mid-1940s onward, were at the core of all great modern art practices). From then on, the avant-garde, which according to Greenberg had evolved away from historical consciousness toward the goal of protecting high culture against industry, debased cultural production, and commodification, will be seen as a tradition opening with a Manet construed in formalist terms (or often, with the formulaic construct Manet-and-the-impressionists – artists who supposedly aimed to purify painting by reducing it to its core "formal" essence of flatness and abstraction).[14]

Reconsidering Clark's harsh characterization of being avant-garde as an "institutionalized variant of everyone's gambit" and a mode of "social climbing," British Marxist feminist art historian Griselda Pollock expands upon the usual concerns with class issues insisted upon and elaborated by social art history in order to address "avant-garde gambits" as a locus inextricably laden with gender and race issues.[15] Pollock focuses on the years 1888–93, when the term avant-garde was not yet a current one to designate the new art but when, according to her, the institutional conditions for the twentieth-century modernist notion of the avant-garde were already in place. She analyzes the racial and gender politics at work in Paul Gauguin's painting *Manao Tupapau* (1893), and its reworking of Manet's *Olympia*. Pollock notes that Gauguin, proudly returning from the French colonies, exhibited *Manao Tupapau* in his 1893 one-man show at Durand-Ruel's Paris gallery as a way to claim a dominant place in the metropolitan art world: "Gauguin's gambit is exemplary of the avant-garde strategy of reference, deference and difference which appear to stage a typically Oedipal formation: reference to the Father, deference to his coveted place, and difference the deadly blow by which his place is appropriated or usurped."[16]

As Pollock demonstrates, Gauguin's gambit, the formulation of his aesthetic difference, revolves around the issue of color. Whereas in *Olympia* Manet had depicted a white and an Afro-Caribbean woman at work in the modern and prosaic context of the "service" industry, Gauguin's Tahitian model, despite being given the "avant-garde bed" of Olympia, is shown as frightened and superstitious, afraid of the Spirit of the Dead; she is deprived of any historical specificity and recovered by a "Eurocentric discourse which slides from Blackness to Darkness and Death."[17] Thus the aesthetic difference in Gauguin's game of avant-gardism proceeds from a sexist, racist, and colonial perception of projected difference: an operation that avant-garde practices of the early twentieth century will maintain as they begin to appropriate artifacts and representational codes from outside the European canon in order to disrupt and challenge its traditions.

Difference and/or Repetition: Avant-Garde and the Repression of its Mechanical Other

Avant-Garde, noun:
   A French word meaning "vanguard," used to describe art or artists depart-ing from accepted tradition or the academic norm to explore techniques or concepts in an original way.[18]
   Those artists, whether literary, visual or musical, whose works are unconven-tional and experimental. Also refers to the works themselves.[19]
   A term describing art that departs from the norm in an original or experi-mental way.[20]

Art dictionaries' entries on the avant-garde all insist on presenting originality and innovation as the most enduring characteristics of the avant-garde. These values figure among the most resilient beliefs attached to the term, which in this form is more emblematic than a view of the avant-garde understood as a line of *progress* (of social and formal advancement converging or coexisting in strategic indifference), as an acceleration of art history through multiple ruptures and movements (avant-garde as a dynamic structure), or as a defensive strategy against the pervasiveness of the culture industry. A belief in originality and innovation is, in fact, embedded in all these variations of the avant-garde. But, unfortunately for the avid believer in a stable art lexicology, originality and innovation no longer survive unscathed.

In the late 1960s into the 1970s in the US, beset by the upheavals caused by the civil rights and various other identity-based rights movements and the on-going horrors of the Vietnam war, many artists attempted to revitalize the con-nection between art production and pressing political issues, denouncing the Greenbergian notion of a formalist avant-garde that had become dominant. Feminist art theorists and artists began to tackle the mythology of the vanguard. Looking at the depiction of women produced by avant-garde painters of the first decade of the twentieth century, for example, American art historian Carol Duncan exposed how fauves, cubists and German expressionists had so often depicted their female models as "powerless, sexually subjugated beings."[21] Duncan pointed out how art history has consistently stressed certain qualities in valuing the avant-garde at the expense of other qualities associated with the feminine: "One idea in particular is always emphasized: that the avant-garde consists of so many moments of individual artistic freedom, a freedom evidenced in the artist's capacity for innovation."[22] In case one might view her concern as well intended but anachronistic, she reminds us:

The same era that produced Freud, Picasso and D. H. Lawrence – the era that took Nietzsche's superman to heart – was also defending itself from the first

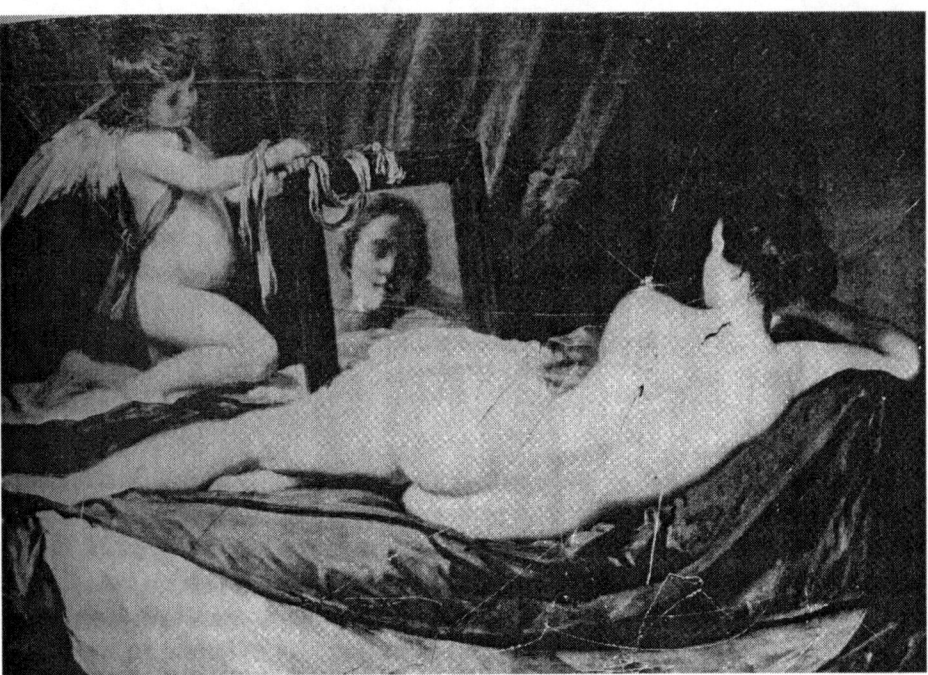

Figure 10.2 Diego Velasquez's *Rokeby Venus* as slashed by suffragette Mary Richardson in 1914

feminist challenge in history (the suffragette movement was at its height). Never before had technological and social conditions been so favourable to the idea of extending democratic and liberal-humanistic ideals to women.[23]

Ultimately Duncan argues that, whereas avant-garde is cherished as the embodiment of progressive values, the male painters of vanguard "gave voice to one of the most reactionary phases in the history of sexism."[24] In fact, Duncan is pointing to what can be seen as a fracture in the Saint-Simonian ideal of an alliance existing between political and artistic avant-gardes, both aiming toward ideals of social progress. (It is a fracture that could have been detected elsewhere – around, for example, the ideological convergence between Filippo Marinetti's futurism and fascism in the 1920s.) Duncan is quick to blame the willingness of art historians to uphold the myth of innovation and to use the notion as a screen to camouflage the perpetuation of a well established game involving historical precedence in formal devices, a narrative of outstanding individuals and a litany of "seminal" works (that is, works made by white male avant-garde artists). But if she questions a reactionary complacency in promoting the value of innovation, beyond setting that notion as part of a mythology, she does not radically question that innovation was indeed the crux of avant-garde practices.

The critical project of postmodernism would address these issues in more depth in the following decade. In her influential 1981 essay "The Originality of the Avant-Garde," American art historian Rosalind Krauss proposed that, with its obsession with origins, originals, and originality, the avant-garde represses its corollary: repetition. Krauss notes: "If the very notion of the avant-garde can be seen as a function of the discourse of originality, the actual practice of vanguard art tends to reveal that 'originality' is a working assumption that itself emerges from a ground of repetition and recurrence."[25] Her demonstration begins with the problem raised by a 1978 cast of Auguste Rodin's *Gates of Hell* and shifts to the grid, a trope of modernist painting "that can only be repeated," and to the category of the picturesque, wherein the copy is shown to be the underlying, condition of the original.

Krauss's essay was developed in a moment of conflict in the New York art world in the early 1980s – a moment in which the gestural figuration of neo-expressionist painting was posed in antagonism to the allegorist trend of appropriation art making use of reproducible materials and mass-media reproduction techniques.[26] It also appeared within a context that witnessed the rise of Walter Benjamin as an icon of critical theory and a new, complex father figure for the postmodernist project of rewriting the narratives of mainstream modernism.[27] Benjamin's 1936 essay, "The Work of Art in the Age of Mechanical Reproduction," became for postmodernist discourses a critical antidote to Greenberg's almost contemporaneous "Avant-Garde and Kitsch" and the rallying point for this change in father figures. Benjamin's perceptive insistence on the shift brought about by new technologies (photography, cinema) and their consequences for the prevailing conception of the work of art's authenticity stands in radical counterpoint to Greenberg's assertion that avant-garde must *resist* the debased images of mass production and the commodification of culture, and that "kitsch is mechanical."[28]

Typically, in her analysis of the avant-garde repression of repetition and mass culture, Krauss does not render explicit her concept of the avant-garde, using the term more or less as a synonym of a radical permutation of modernism. There is not a clear sense of any historicity to the avant-garde in her text, which is not surprising given its structuralist overtones. Krauss implicitly maintains Greenberg's timeline for the avant-garde, although she eschews his negative views on dada, surrealism, and constructivism.

However, after having construed repetition as the obverse and corollary of originality, Krauss in turn represses another corollary of repetition: difference. And such a blindness allows her to ignore what is at stake in a rethinking of "the hidden dialectic" between mass culture and the avant-garde – a topic brilliantly explored by Andreas Huyssen in his 1986 book *After the Great Divide: Modernism, Mass Culture, Postmodernism*.[29] Huyssen explores here how mass culture has been produced as the feminine Other of avant-garde culture, especially in the Frankfurt School tradition of Theodor Adorno and Max Horkheimer (whose ideas about the mass-media "culture industry" are close in spirit to Greenberg's notion of kitsch as the debased underside of high art).[30] In particular, as Amelia Jones has pointed out, Huyssen's book has been deeply influential in its articulation of a feminist critique of such hierarchies as resting on *gendered* assumptions posing the high art produced by the avant-garde in opposition to a debased and feminized mass culture, in turn embraced by a potentially "feminine" or "feminist" postmodernism.[31]

That Greenberg's art criticism percolates with sexist metaphors privileging the virility of avant-garde art is, through the work of feminists such as Duncan and Jones, well-established evidence by now. But other subtleties in Greenberg's account are lesser known. For example, in 1946, for an article in the French periodical *Les Temps modernes* edited by Jean-Paul Sartre, Greenberg produced a singular account (for which the English text no longer exists) of the tortuous path taken by the avant-garde in traveling from France in the period of the heroic avant-garde around the time of WWI to the United States, in the post-WWII period.[32] And his narrative implies that the radicality of French avant-garde art traveled to America via the Trojan horse of German avant-gardism, a more sentimental and expressive (and therefore less threatening) form of radical artistic practice. Through this mediation, avant-gardism thereby corresponded better "to that tendency to the minuscule, the delicate, to the sensory and the accessory that is so characteristic of the feminine side of the American temperament."[33]

Ultimately, then, Greenberg suggests that avant-gardism gained access to American soil in a travesty. He concludes rather pessimistically:

> Our incapacity to produce major art in XXth century America comes, I believe, from our repugnance to welcome or produce aesthetic positivism. [. . .] Whereas in France, vigorous materialists and sceptics have mostly expressed themselves through art, at home, they have confined themselves to business, politics, philosophy and science, abandoning art to the mid-brow, the credulous, the spinsters and the outdated visionaries.[34]

This view, however surprising (and ephemeral, since Greenberg was to regain confidence in the future of the American avant-garde by 1948), predictably imputes the compromised situation of the avant-garde in the United States to the corrupted taste of a gendered audience whose old-maid's taste for kitsch threatens the very survival of modernist avant-garde art. This oppositional hierarchy between the young, implicitly virile and male, avant-garde artist and the kitsch-loving spinster is predicated on gender but also on age, which is revealing inasmuch as it echoes the structural problem of constant ruptures and attempted rejuvenation within the accelerated dynamics of the avant-garde. But despite Greenberg's call for avant-garde to retreat in an ivory tower in order to eschew the pervasiveness of mass culture, his advocacy remained problematic both because such a retreat was increasingly untenable and because his description of the articulation of high and low in contemporary art and culture proved inaccurate. There has always existed a porous – albeit often denied – relationship between mass culture and avant-garde art.[35]

It is precisely this porous relationship that Huyssen, in fact, calls the "hidden dialectic" of modernism. Returning to terms reminiscent of Benjamin's in the "Work of Art" essay, Huyssen acknowledges the role of developing technologies of reproduction in this "hidden dialectic":

> no other single factor has influenced the emergence of the new avant-garde art as much as technology [. . .] The invasion of the very fabric of the art object by technology and what one may loosely call the technological imagination can best be grasped in artistic practices such as collage, assemblage, montage and photo-montage; it finds its ultimate fulfillment in photography and film, art forms which can not only be reproduced, but are in fact designed for mechanical reproducibility.[36]

But the relation of avant-garde to repetition cannot be reduced to this technological imagination. For repetition is not just something that the avant-garde addresses as it encounters technology; it is also the means through which it has maintained itself. The avant-garde has not only been seen as using reproducible materials, promoting the reproducible work of art: it has also been accused of repeating itself *through the logic of reproducibility*. This is where we encounter the impact of Peter Bürger's *Theory of the Avant-Garde*.[37]

Theory of the Avant-Garde: Resetting the Timeline and Reframing the Brief

Bürger's book was translated into English in 1984, a decade after its initial publication in German. Pending the availability of Bürger's essay in English, the most influential "theory of the avant-garde" had been that of Renato Poggioli, initially published in 1962 and made available in English in 1968.[38] Poggioli acknowledged the sociological dimensions of the avant-garde but his pervasive insistence on the role of romanticism as a condition of possibility of the avant-garde diluted the concept to a point where it lost its complex historical connections to the rise of industrial capitalism and to the dominance of the bourgeoisie in nineteenth-century politics. It also deflated the issue of its intended function (the transformation of society and a resistance to bourgeois values).

Poggioli's portrayal of the concept was thus limited to a typology of the quasi-psychological tendencies informing the project of the avant-garde: *activism, antagonism, nihilism, and agonism*. The first advocates gratuitous and blind agitation, the "sheer joy of dynamism";[39] the second relies on a focused oppositional stance whose target may vary (bourgeois society, the academic tradition, or a previous vanguard); the third is an all-out impulse to negate and destroy all conventions and barriers; and the fourth involves a willingness to self-ruin ("an obscure and unknown sacrifice to the success of future movements"),[40] and thereby bows to the *topos* of the avant-garde as the Phoenix's never-ending endgame.

In contrast to Poggioli, Bürger concisely defines the avant-garde as the last of three phases in the development of art history within bourgeois society.[41] According to his view, a relative autonomization of the aesthetic sphere occurred during the eighteenth century, triggered by the severance of the economic link between patrons and artists: a severance that submitted the latter group to the anonymous pressures of market economy. However, this cleavage did not right away compromise the capacity and willingness of art to reflect upon society, nor did it impose the fiction of aesthetic autonomy. It is only later, at the end of the nineteenth century, with the rise of symbolism, that this process of autonomization entered an autotelic phase that Bürger calls aestheticism wherein art retreated into a pursuit of formal issues as an end unto itself, and thereby lost its social connections and relevance.

With the emergence, during and after WWI, of movements such as dada, surrealism, and the productivist project in the Soviet Union, the advent of what Bürger calls the historical avant-garde marked the third phase of this process. Bürger sees these latter movements as animated with the deliberate mission to dissolve the bound-aries between art and practical life, to attack the institution of art and the artistic autonomy it both promotes and renders possible. Notably, Bürger's conception totally obliterates the mythic point of rupture of the modernist avant-garde, located in the mid-nineteenth century and emblematized under the name "Manet." In Bürger's view, if avant-garde introduces a rupture, it is precisely because it performs an about-face in relation to aestheticism and does not prolong the false autonomy of art ingrained in the first two phases of this art historical timeline.

Thus, Bürger's avant-garde is situated in a much narrower timeframe, the second decade of the twentieth century, and is characterized by its social function – the critique of the institution of art – that could not be more antagonistic to the aim Greenberg had defined for avant-garde: to oppose kitsch through a modern formalist tradition of elitist culture that deeply relied on the preservation of the institution of art. Moreover, Bürger's avant-garde is also embodied by practices that are precisely those excluded from the Greenbergian mainstream pantheon on the ground that they were, like constructivism and productivism, tainted by a political project, or, like Dada, concerned with the porous bound-aries between art and practical life, or, like surrealism, dependent upon literary considerations, exterior to the ontology of the medium.

The impact of Bürger's essay on American critical discourses in the visual arts is certainly connected to the coincidence of its publication with the on-going debate on postmodernism during the early and mid-1980s. Whereas the articulation of modernism and postmodernism had been an issue in literature and architecture from the sixties and seventies on, the polemic was still raging in the visual arts scene of the 1980s, especially in New York, because the economic boom seemed to have revivified an art market promoting a list of reactionary comebacks: the return to traditional practices (the medium of painting), formats (the grand picture), and notions (the distinctive style, the heroic artist). In such a context, Bürger's theory appeared both stimulating and challenging.

It was stimulating insofar as it gave back the avant-garde its political edge at a time when activism (the only one of Poggioli's four tendencies that Bürger's notion of the avant-garde seems to validate) was an important project of artistic production in the United States. It also reinforced the relevance of Walter Benjamin's critical contributions: his acceptance of the reproducible work of art; his lucid and complex embrace of technological media; his concepts of ruin and allegory. It was consonant with the project of postmodernism, understood not only as a terminal exit from modernism but as a rewriting of its origins, that would challenge its official timeline and Greenberg's formalist doxa.

But that is also how Bürger's conception proved challenging for postmodernist discourse. It narrated the development of the avant-garde as a monolithic, linear, and Manichean story at the very moment when such performances had become suspicious, following Jean-François Lyotard's characterization of the postmodern condition as one in which grand narratives had lost their legitimating power.[42] Moreover, Bürger's narrative was entirely dismissive of what he called the neo-avant-garde, a label he coined to describe the European and American sequels to Dada practices in the 1950s and 1960s (although *not* the American abstraction of this period but, rather, the work of artists interested in troubling the boundaries between art and mass culture, such as Robert Rauschenberg and Jasper Johns). Bürger condemned these practices in which he merely saw an impotent and farcical repetition of the strategies of the historical avant-garde. In its repetitiveness, the neo-avant-garde confirmed and underlined the tragic failure of the historical avant-garde to critique and even overturn the institutions of art – a failure Bürger saw as being reinforced by the uncritical reliance of late twentieth-century practices by artists such as Warhol on precisely these institutions.

Avant-Garde and Neo-Avant-Garde: The Performative Deceleration of the Avant-Garde

One of the most ambitious answers to Bürger was formulated by American critic and art historian Hal Foster in his 1994 essay "What's Neo about the Neo Avant-garde?" republished two years later in a modified version entitled "Who's Afraid of the Neo-Avant-Garde?"[43] Seeking to rethink the temporality, the narrative tendencies, and the performativity of the avant-garde, Foster impeccably locates many blind spots in Bürger's construction: a blindness to the historicity of *all* art, a neglect of the art of Bürger's own time (notably the institutional critiques of Michael Asher, Daniel Buren, and Hans Haacke) and, most importantly, a conception of the historical avant-garde as both the climax of an evolutionary and linear narrative of art history and as a point of absolute origin in relation to which all later cultural production appears depleted and repetitive. Thus, Bürger provides his own breed of the cult of origins and originality and Foster astutely exposes the pervasive romanticism of this heroic vision.

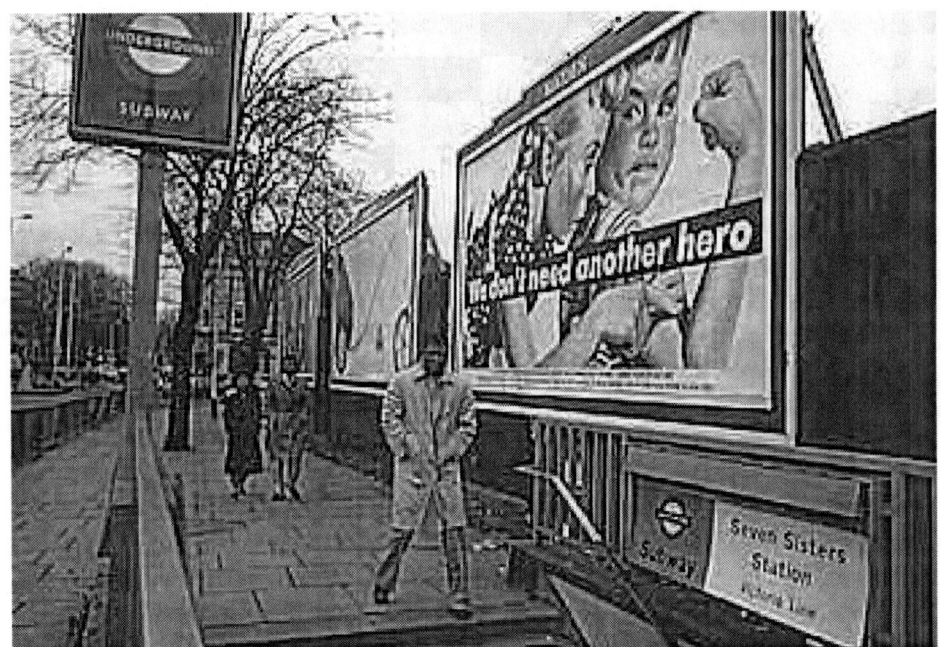

FIGURE 10.3   Barbara Kruger, *We Don't Need Another Hero*, billboard installation view, Artangel project, Jan–Feb 1987. Courtesy of the Mary Boone Gallery, New York

Foster's reading of the neo-avant-garde makes use of the psychoanalytical notion of deferred action (*nachträglich*), according to which the full elaboration of a trauma is always delayed.[44] It is only through repetition, through the occurrence of a second trauma that a subject is able to process and comprehend the initial but generally repressed trauma. Such a take on the avant-garde represents a significant shift in the historiography of the concept: it centers on the temporality of an *après-coup* (the French translation of deferred action) rather than on the spatial and differential *coup* implied in the "gambit" theory of the avant-garde.

Foster's recourse to psychoanalysis in order to complicate the temporality of the avant-garde is part of the author's dialogue with art historian Benjamin Buchloh, like Foster a critic associated with *October* magazine.[45] In his 1986 essay on the reiterative practice of the monochrome, Buchloh had proposed a Freudian explanation of repetition in the practices of the neo-avant-garde.[46] He saw repetition as a marker of the neo-avant-garde's authenticity insofar as it functioned as a symptom of the institutional repression and disavowal imposed on the historical avant-garde during the 1930s by the totalitarian regimes such as the Third Reich in Germany and the Stalinist program of the Soviet Union.

Following up on Buchloh's discussion of Alexander Rodchenko's 1921 series of three monochromes (each of them done in one of the three primary colors),

singulier dans ces tableaux ? Peut-être les deux. Mais alors, comment expliquer cet autre grand phé-nomène de masse dans l'art du XXe siècle : la conver-gence vers le Louvre de légions de Français, hommes, femmes et enfants, pour voir non pas une peinture, mais l'absence d'une peinture ? C'était l'espace laissé vide par la disparition de *La Joconde* que les foules recherchaient. Il s'agissait donc d'aller voir une œuvre d'art moins parce qu'elle était là que, justement, parce qu'elle n'était pas là.

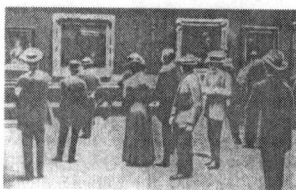

Le vol d'une banque n'a pas pour effet de faire de cette banque une attraction touristique, et il serait difficile d'imaginer l'invasion de la Tour de Londres par une foule avide de voir l'absence de la Couronne royale après quelque ingénieux cambrio-lage. Cela n'arriverait-il que lorsque l'objet dérobé est une œuvre d'art ? Et l'œuvre d'art en question devrait-elle avoir atteint une célébrité sans pareil ? Il est vrai que la Joconde est moins une peinture que le symbole de la peinture même. C'est pourquoi elle a toujours été la cible favorite des caricaturistes

FIGURE 10.4   Press photograph from *Le Matin*, August 30, 1911, showing a queue at the Louvre in front of the empty spot of the stolen *Mona Lisa*

Foster insists on the gap between what artists of the historical avant-garde claimed they did and what they actually achieved (a nuance generally overlooked in Bürger's essay). Rodchenko, he argues, did not end painting with his series; he demonstrated the conventionality of painting as a medium. In 1917, Marcel Duchamp, with the *Fountain*, a manufactured urinal he signed with the pseudo-nym R. Mutt and attempted to exhibit at the Society of Independent Artists' exhibition in New York City, had performed a similar task in relation to the category of art. But, Foster insists, in both cases "nothing explicit is demon-strated about the institution." He continues: "The modern status of painting as made-for-exhibitions is preserved by the monochrome [. . .] and the museum-gallery nexus is left intact by the ready made."[47] (Although, one could argue that the critique of conventionality was at least perceived and received as a potential threat on the institution: after all, when Leonardo's *Mona Lisa* was stolen from the Louvre in 1911, at the time of the cubist experiments with the codes of pictorial representation, the theft resulted in a line-up of visitors eager to contemplate its empty space on the museum wall (Figure 10.4), and Pablo Picasso and Guillaume Apollinaire, the poet who defended cubism, were briefly suspected of the deed, as if the radicality of the cubist movement could have been easily equated with a literal crime against the art institution.)

Foster corrects Bürger's dualistic model with the introduction of a third moment in the unfolding of the avant-gardes. He splits the neo-avant-garde in two phases: a first one, in the 1950s, that recovers the historical avant-garde, and especially Dada practices, and a second, from the 1960s onward, which was critical of the operation by which the first neo-avant-garde had transformed the avant-garde into an institution. It would be incumbent upon that second neo-avant-garde to expand the critique of conventions into an investigation of the institution of art. Thus, the project of the historical avant-garde is "enacted for the first time – a first time that, again, is theoretically endless."[48] As this statement implies, Foster's project is traversed by a deconstructive vein, rendered all the more obvious by a quote from French philosopher Jacques Derrida: "It is thus the delay which is in the beginning."[49]

But the way in which Foster construes the role of deferred action in the temporality of the avant-garde resonates with Hans Robert Jauss's aesthetic of reception,[50] a model of literary analysis that also addresses the incessantly delayed process through which art practices are historically redefined. This is what Foster acknowledges when he asks: "Did Duchamp *appear* as Duchamp? Of course not. [...] The status of Duchamp [...] is a retroactive effect of countless artistic responses and critical readings."[51] The emergence of Duchamp as the emblematic figure of twentieth-century avant-garde art was construed through the pivotal role the artist was gradually granted in a long series of paradigm shifts: the neo-Dada works of Jasper Johns and Robert Rauschenberg during the 1950s; the indexical category analyzed in Rosalind Krauss's "Notes on the Index" during the late 1970s;[52] and more recently in the redefinition of artistic judgment in Thierry de Duve's *Kant after Duchamp*[53] or in the critical model proposed by Amelia Jones in *Postmodernism and the En-gendering of Marcel Duchamp*.[54]

Among the authors of *October* magazine, Foster is certainly the one voice that attempts to rescue the value and validity of the avant-garde for contemporary cultural production. For Krauss, the avant-garde is strictly speaking a modernist project: quite surprisingly given her past inclination toward structuralism, she envisages the notion chronologically rather than as a structure or set of strategies that changes depending on the historical situation. Buchloh, despite his lucid criticism of Bürger's theory, also considers the avant-garde project as bound to fail because it addresses social contradictions that cannot be reconciled.[55] But Foster eschews the view of the avant-garde as *aporia* and insists on its *utopian* dimension: he takes into account the tension between the avant-garde's structural incapacity to effectuate change and the oblique but nevertheless performative efficiency of its resolution to attempt what cannot be done.

Foster's elaboration of the avant-garde stands out in the recent historiography of the notion wherein, to return to Poggioli's categories, activism and agonism generally prevail. Agonism, with its obsessive reiteration on the failures of the historical avant-garde, is a topos that runs from Dada's pronouncements about the abolition of culture and creation through the 1989 publication of Paul Mann's "theory-death of the avant-garde."[56] It is ingrained in the fabric of the concept, due to the Marxist conviction that art and culture are subsidiary (superstructural) actors in the transformation of society. Since Marxism informed most of the discourses that shaped the notion of the avant-garde (from the Frankfurt School to T. J. Clark's social history of art), few historians and critics of the avant-garde have argued, like Foster, for the current relevance of the notion, except perhaps in the United States.[57] Yet Foster's characterization of the contemporary avant-garde does not rely on the same oppositional stance inherent to the activism of earlier avant-gardes. Instead it accentuates "subtle displacements and/or strategic collaborations."[58]

So how are we to articulate and assess the relevance of the avant-garde for contemporary art practices? Features that once seemed structurally part of the notion (a constant renewal of movements and trends, an elitist circle of receivers, discriminatory pronouncements) certainly proved insufferable, but it turns out they are not the invariable traits they once seemed to be. However, there has been no theory of avant-garde without a critical project. All discourses on the avant-garde acknowledge the central role of criticality, even if they do not agree on the object or target of that criticality – including Greenberg's self-referentiality of the medium, Bürger's critique of the institution of art, and Foster's testing of institutional boundaries.

Of course, this latter form of criticality in contemporary art production has not collapsed or dissolved the institutions of art, but it has begun, under the pressures of feminism and postcolonial theory, to question non-artistic institutions. It thus participates in a reconfiguration of social and artistic spaces and practices; it precipitates the visibility and precarious inscription of new hybrid and fluid identity positions within those spaces. And whether or not these effects are indeed credited to the performativity of a contemporary avant-garde, whether or not they are labeled as avant-garde at all, ultimately matters less than the vitality of the critical project they formulate in relation to the socio-political conditions of the present.

Notes

1 Habermas (1983), 5.
2 For the best introduction to Saint-Simonianism, see McWilliam (1993).
3 Ibid., 116–22. Linda Nochlin's important contribution to early feminist discourse (her 1971 essay "Why have there been no great woman artists?") is echoed in McWilliams' book with a section entitled "Why were there no great Saint-Simonian artists?" Nochlin also wrote an informative article on the formation of avant-garde in relation to the social art of Saint-Simonians. Nochlin (1968), 1–24.
4 Baudelaire (1951), 188–9. Undoubtedly, Baudelaire's dislike of the military is also related to his hatred of his stepfather General Aupick. See T. J. Clark (1983), 141.
5 Baudelaire had gone to Brussels hoping to escape his debtors and to publish without further harassment from the censorship he had already endured under the

regime of the Second Empire. Reading Baudelaire's recriminations against Belgium in his 1864 text *Pauvre Belgique* confirms that the poet saw his country of chosen exile as a site of conformity.

6 Heinich (1994), 49.
7 Williams (1989), 53 (italics are mine).
8 Ibid., 57.
9 Clark (1973), 14.
10 Ibid., 18.
11 Ibid., 14.
12 When, a decade later, Clark published his *Painting of Modern Life*, he was to focus on Manet. However, Clark here construes Manet's works according to a broader and socio-political history as well, drawing on a broad series of images and discourses different from the litany of masterpieces: Clark's purpose in broadening the context in which Manet's works could be discussed was not a "demotion of artists" but a critique and refutation of modernism's heroic and triumphant litany about them. Clark (1984).
13 Greenberg (1985a), 25, and Greenberg (1985b), 39, 40.
14 See T. J. Clark on Greenberg's move away from "eliotic trotskysm" and his later anti-communism in the context of the cold war; Clark (1981), 169–87. For an analysis of how the avant-garde was constructed, during the cold war, as an emblem of freedom in capitalist society, see Guilbaut (1983).
15 Pollock (1992).
16 Ibid., 20.
17 Ibid., 13.
18 Piper (1988), 30.
19 Ehresmann (1979), [n.p].
20 Meyer (1969), 25.
21 Duncan (1982), 293.
22 Ibid., 294.
23 Ibid., 308.
24 Ibid., 308.
25 Krauss (1986), 157.
26 See Buchloh (1982), 43–56.
27 Jones (1993).
28 Greenberg (1985a), 25.
29 Huyssen (1986). As a defense mechanism, repression does not involve difference, but it is, like the construction of alterity and otherness, fueled by the combined affects of unacceptable attraction and repulsion.
30 Adorno and Horkheimer (1972).
31 Jones (1994), 18–21.
32 Greenberg (1993), 5–12 (translations into English are mine).
33 Ibid., 9.
34 Ibid., 12.
35 A brilliant account of the dialectic relations between high and low culture in modern art can be found in Crow (1983). Crow demonstrates that, from its beginnings, the artistic avant-garde worked with "degraded materials from capitalist manufacture" (215), but he shows how these appropriations were generally reduced to a one-way exchange that merely confirmed the ancillary status of mass culture.

He also, in a dialectical argument, underlines the role of the avant-garde "as a kind of research and development arm of the culture industry." For as he reminds us: "It was only a matter of a few years before the Impressionist vision of the spaces of commercial diversion became the advertisement of the thing itself [. . .]" (253).

36 Huyssen (1986), 9.
37 Bürger (1984).
38 Poggioli (1968).
39 Ibid., 25.
40 Ibid., 26.
41 See Bürger (1984), x–xv.
42 Lyotard (1984). The book was initially published in French in 1979 and was published in English by the same press that published Bürger's *Theory of the Avant-Garde*, and the very same year.
43 Foster (1996).
44 Laplanche (1989), 88.
45 For Buchloh's review of Bürger's *Theory of the Avant-Garde*, see Buchloh (1984).
46 Buchloh (1986).
47 Foster (1996), 17, 20.
48 Ibid., 32.
49 Ibid.
50 Jauss (1982).
51 Foster (1996), 8.
52 Krauss (1977).
53 De Duve (1996).
54 Jones (1994). See also Hopkins' essay in this volume.
55 Buchloh (1984), 234.
56 Mann (1991), 3.
57 As Andrea Huyssen has suggested, the absence of a first-hand experience of the historical avant-garde in the United States and the consequent rise of political art from the 1970s onward might explain this situation and the enduring currency of the avant-garde in that country. Huyssen (1981).
58 Foster (1996), 25.

References and further reading

Adorno, Theodor W., and Max Horkheimer (1972). "The Culture Industry: Enlightenment as Mass Deception." In *Dialectic of Enlightenment* (1944), trans. John Cumming. New York: Herder and Herder.

Baudelaire, Charles (1951). *My Heart Laid Bare and other Prose Writings* (c.1865), trans. Norman Cameron, introduced by Peter Quennell. New York: Vanguard Press.

Benjamin, Walter (1969). "The Work of Art in the Age of Mechanical Reproduction" (c.1935). In *Illuminations*, ed. Hannah Arendt. New York: Schoken Books. 217–51.

Buchloh, Benjamin (1982). "Allegorical Procedures: Appropriation and Montage in Contemporary Art." *Artforum*, vol. 21, no. 1, September:43–56.

—— (1984). "Theorizing the Avant-Garde." *Art in America*, vol. 72, no. 10, November:19, 21.

—— (1986). "The Primary Colors for the Second Time: A Paradigm Repetition of the Neo-Avant-Garde." *October*, no. 37, Summer:41–52.

Bürger, Peter (1984). *Theory of the Avant-Garde* (1974), trans. Michael Shaw, foreword by Jochen Schulte-Sasse. Minneapolis: University of Minnesota Press.

Clark, T. J. (1973). *Image of the People. Gustave Courbet and the 1848 Revolution.* London: Thames and Hudson.

—— (1983). "More of the Differences between Comrade Greenberg and Ourselves." In *Modernism and* Modernity, ed. Benjamin Buchloh, Serge Guilbaut, and David Solkin. Halifax: The Press of Nova Scotia College of Art and Design. 169–87.

—— (1984). *The Painting of Modern Life. Paris in the Art of Manet and his Followers.* Princeton: Princeton University Press.

Crow, Thomas (1983). "Modernism and Mass Culture in the Visual Art." In *Modernism and Modernity* (The Vancouver Conference Papers, 1981), ed. Benjamin H. D. Buchloh, Serge Guilbaut, and David Solkin. Halifax: Press of the Nova Scotia College of Art and Design.

Duncan, Carol (1982). "Virility and Domination in Early Twentieth-Century Vanguard Painting." In *Feminism and Art History. Questioning the Litany*, ed. Norma Broude and Mary D. Garrard. New York: Harper and Row. 292–313. Originally published in an earlier version in *Artforum*, vol. 12, no. 4, December 1973:30–9.

de Duve, Thierry (1996). *Kant after Duchamp.* Cambridge and London: MIT Press.

Ehresmann, Julia M., ed. (1979). *The Pocket Dictionary of Art Terms.* 2nd rev. edn. Boston: New York Graphic Society.

Foster, Hal (1996). "Who's Afraid of the Neo-Avant-Garde?" In *The Return of the Real.* Cambridge and London: MIT Press. 1–32. An earlier version of this text appeared under the title "What's Neo about the Neo-Avant-Garde?" *October*, vol. 70, Fall 1994:5–32.

Greenberg, Clement (1985a). "Avant-Garde and Kitsch." In *Pollock and after the Critical Debate*, ed. Francis Frascina. London: Harper and Row. 21–33. Originally published in *Partisan Review*, vol. 6, no. 5, Fall 1939:34–49.

—— (1985b). "Towards a Newer Laocoon." In *Pollock and After: The Critical Debate*, ed. Francis Frascina. London: Harper and Row. 35–45. Initially published in *Partisan Review*, vol. 7, no. 4, July–August 1940:296–310.

—— (1993). "L'art américain au XXe siècle." *Les Cahiers du Musée national d'art moderne*, nos. 45–6, Fall/Winter 1993:5–12. Originally published in *Les Temps modernes*, vol. 11, nos. 11–12, August–September 1946:340–52.

Guilbaut, Serge (1983). *How New York Stole the Idea of Modern Art. Abstract Expressionism, Freedom and the Cold War.* Trans. Arthur Goldhammer. Chicago: Chicago University Press.

Habermas, Jürgen (1983). "Modernity – An Incomplete Project." In *The Anti-Aesthetic. Essays on Post-Modern Culture*, ed. Hal Foster. Seattle: Bay Press. 3–15.

Heinich, Nathalie (1994). "Les manifestes et l'avant-garde artistique. Comment être plusieurs quand on est singulier." In *Le texte, l'œuvre, l'émotion.* Bruxelles: La lettre volée. 49–64.

Huyssen, Andreas (1981). "The Search for Tradition: Avant-garde and Postmodernism in the Seventies." *New German Critique*, no. 22, Winter:160–78.

—— (1986). *After the Great Divide: Modernism, Mass Culture, Postmodernism.* Bloomington and Indianapolis: Indiana University Press.

Jauss, Hans Robert (1982). *Toward an Aesthetic of Reception*, trans. Timothy Bahti, introduced by Paul de Man. Minneapolis: University of Minnesota Press.

Jones, Amelia (1994). *Postmodernism and the En-gendering of Marcel Duchamp*. Cambridge: Cambridge University Press.

Jones, Caroline A. (1993). "La politique de Greenberg et le discours postmoderniste." *Les Cahiers du Musée national d'art moderne*, nos. 45–6, Fall/Winter:105–37. A version of this article will appear in Caroline A. Jones "Greenberg's Postmodernism," in *Eyesight Alone: Clement Greenberg's Modernism and the Bureaucratization of the Senses*. Chicago: Chicago University Press, 2006.

Krauss, Rosalind E. (1977). "Notes on the Index." *October*, no. 3, Spring:66–81.

—— (1986). "The Originality of The Avant-Garde." In *The Originality of the Avant-Garde and Other Modernist Myths*. Cambridge, MA and London: MIT Press. 151–70. Originally published in *October*, no. 18, Fall 1981:47–66.

Laplanche, Jean (1989). *New Foundations of Psychoanalysis*, trans. David Macey. Oxford: Blackwell.

Lyotard, Jean-François (1984). *The Postmodern Condition: A Report on Knowledge*, trans. Geoff Bennington and Brian Massumi, introduced by Fredric Jameson. Minneapolis: University of Minnesota Press.

McWilliam, Neil (1993). *Dreams of Happiness. Social Art and the French Left 1830–1850*. Princeton: Princeton University Press.

Mann, Paul (1999). *The Theory-Death of the Avant-garde*. Bloomington and Indianapolis: Indiana University Press.

Meyer, Ralph, ed. (1969). *A Dictionary of Art Terms and Techniques*. New York: Thomas Crowell Company.

Nochlin, Linda (1968). "The Invention of the Avant-garde: France, 1830–1880." In *Avant-garde Art*, ed. Thomas B. Hess and John Ashbery. London: Collier Macmillan. 1–24.

—— (1971). "Why Have There Been No Great Women Artists?" In *Women in Sexist Society: Studies in Power and Powerlessness*, ed. Vivian Gornick and Barbara Moran. New York: New American Library.

Piper, David, ed. (1988). *A Dictionary of Art and Artists*. London and Glasgow: Collins.

Poggioli, Renato (1968). *The Theory of the Avant-Garde*, trans. Gerald Fitzgerald. Cambridge, MA and London: Harvard University Press.

Pollock, Griselda (1992). *Avant-Garde Gambits 1888–1893. Gender and the Colour of Art History*. London: Thames and Hudson.

Williams, Raymond (1989). *The Politics of the Avant-Garde. Against the New Conformists*. London and New York: Verso.

Zola, Émile (1970). *Mon Salon*. Paris: Garnier-Flammarion.

11

Facture for Change:
US Activist Art since 1950

Jennifer González and Adrienne Posner

Over the last few decades it has become increasingly common to argue that every art practice has a distinct political character and that all forms of art intersect with unique social and political frameworks of exhibition and public reception. These modes of analysis seek to situate art within its mode of production, deeply imbricating it in funding agencies, questions of financial patronage, the institutions of the gallery and the museum, and ideological structures of cultural patronage. Aesthetics, it is generally agreed, does not exist without politics.[1] This sometimes conscious, but frequently unintentional, political character of aesthetic practice should not, however, be equated with art making that intentionally draws on, or points to, political concerns for the purpose of creating social change. Art practice in the interests of such change, alternatively called "political" art or "activist" art, has its own long tradition. With each successive generation of artists, it can be seen to articulate new forms, discourses, and tactics that run parallel to, and sometimes intersect with, other aesthetic traditions.

Yet the terms "political" and "activist" are not synonymous. Lucy Lippard's distinction between these concepts proves instructive here. She suggests that "political" art is often associated with the liberating achievements of modernists – the radical cultural elite – in their struggle against the repressive impulses of a puritanical bourgeois society.[2] From these traditions emerged a set of art-making practices defined as art that occasionally elaborates upon social issues, is sometimes *concerned* with social issues, and usually reflects these through ironic critique.[3] "Activist" art, on the other hand, is a more instrumental hybrid cultural form that does not formally exist as a coherent and identifiable set of practices until the 1960s. With one foot in the situationists' revolutionary practices and the other in the spirit of "the street"[4] – the politics of participation, inclusiveness, and democratization – activist art employs strategies gleaned from conceptual art and performance art to engage in the "real" world while attempting to blur the boundaries and hierarchies set up by social, political, and economic systems.

In this way, activist art is an interdisciplinary, sometimes transitory or ephemeral practice that can be characterized by a use of public space and a focus on collaboration and coalitional politics. These "socioaesthetic processes of activist art,"[5] take the form of spatial and temporal interventions, designed either to weave themselves into, or to tear apart, the fabric of everyday life. In this way, activist art, as Lippard points out, is not only "oppositional" in terms of its often explicit defiance of social, cultural, and economic hierarchies, but is an attempt clearly and decisively to oppose something while "providing alternative images, metaphors, and information formed with humor, irony, outrage, and compassion."[6] In other words, activist art is community-oriented, visible, and focused on organizational activities; it aims to highlight issues of self-representation, empowerment, and community identity, as well as the process through which artist and participant interact with and influence one another.

One of the virtues of distinguishing between these terms is that "political art" and "activist art" are evidence of more than just divergent methodologies; they also represent *stylistic* rifts, gaps between aesthetic choices and political methods. Extending Lippard's definition, we might say at the outset then that activist art has at least three degrees of political life: it has a political character which produces and is produced by its historical moment and subsequent reception; it has political concerns that motivate its production; and it has unique forms of political engagement with both primary and secondary audiences.

Any serious approach to activist art or to the dilemma of the elucidation of the merging of art and social politics must engage with the historically specific nature of this practice. Here we briefly examine the conditions of activist art's emergence in relation to parallel art practices and social movements over the last 50 years to argue not only for a set of conceptual continuities, but also for a set of distinct and shifting paradigms of practice that emerge over time. Rather than attempting a broad international analysis, we have chosen to focus on the United States. By doing so, we are not making an argument for exceptionalism, for it certainly is the case that activist artists in the United States and elsewhere have been engaged in international struggles and intellectual exchange for decades. Rather, this decision is motivated by a desire to uncover what has worked in US activist art, especially at this time when US national civil liberties and rights are becoming increasingly and overtly threatened. In doing so, we hope to combat the kind of neatly historical framing of racism, sexism, militarism, homophobia, and violence which reads these issues as existing in the past, having been successfully countered by their respective activist responses. Instead, we would like to point out that the issues discussed in the following pages continue to plague our persons and our society, and that some of the methodologies for combating them are still viable; they can still "work," or do certain kinds of work in the national arena. It seems important to consider what one may, practically speaking, draw out from recent political history in the US in order to develop further critiques.

It is probably fair to say that, in the first half of the twentieth century, whether in the name of modernism, socialism or surrealism, art and aesthetic practice was considered central to any social revolution. Much political art of this century has its roots in the defiantly romantic, Marxist formulations of aesthetic practice in the 1920s and 1930s: the struggle against fascism, the perceived creative potential of the "individual" struggling under the oppressive cloak of totalitarianism. Between the late 1930s and the late 1940s, however, there was a major shift in the way that painters in the United States approached the canvas; many artists who had been previously aligned with the political and ideological forces of the left in the 1930s were retreating from realism into abstraction, abandoning social iconography in favor of a more "universal," biomorphic, and mythical aesthetic. In a canonical essay of 1952, the critic Harold Rosenberg stated that "at a certain moment, the canvas began to appear to one American painter after another as an arena in which to act – rather than as a space in which to reproduce, re-design, analyze, or 'express' an object, actual or imagined."[7] This vision of the artist as an avant-garde social actor, in both political and aesthetic arenas, would continue well into the second half of the century. For many European and American artists working after the Second World War, high culture was, in the words of Francis Frascina, "the last defensible enclave of political activity and dissent – revolutionary aspirations having been bracketed by McCarthyism, a consumer boom and cold war imperialism."[8] This desire for a radical political redefinition of Marxism for a totalitarian age emerged from a sense of failure: the failure of socialist and communist opposition, the failure of Trotskyism, the failure of the Popular Front, the end of the New Deal, as well as the rise of extreme conservatism, assimilation, and oppressive cooptation.[9] This movement by leftists to reform Marxism and the politics of dissent located its source of agency in the imaginative and creative potential of individuals: the potential "arena in which to act" was now seen not only as the more properly political realm, but as the canvas itself.

Abstract expressionism, as part of this avant-garde, emerged alongside and in direct dialogue with the left. As Nancy Jachec points out, many painters participated in benefit sales and auctions of their work in support of leftist publications such as *Dissent, Politics, Possibilities,* and *The Tiger's Eye.*[10] Even more directly, some of the abstract expressionists had been explicitly involved in the politics of the left since the 1930s. Pollock, for example, worked as a studio assistant for David Siquerios, who was an active Communist Party member. Mark Rothko was involved in the Artists Union, which was effectively a union for fine artists that focused on the relationship between art and politics.[11] Yet, as Raymond Williams has astutely pointed out, avant-gardes have historically depended on a social, cultural, and economic validation by normative institutions, and therefore their art is easily co-opted and championed by the "culturally transformed but otherwise persistent and recuperated" hegemonic social order.[12] In the late 1940s and early 1950s, abstract expressionism began to take on a new meaning: the defiant rejection of mainstream values, the individualism of these paintings that was their hallmark, was effectively stolen by an expanding capitalist political system in order to promote these painters as "an index of the superiority of American democracy."[13]

Artists like Ben Shahn, Diego Rivera, and David Afaro Siqueiros who specifically questioned this authority were among the few to maintain a political and artistic commitment to the New Deal ethic in a postwar era. While aware of the need for a new aesthetic language to depict the changing political climate, these artists were not interested in abandoning their faith in the basic and fundamental compatibility of art and social change via established political institutions. Their art was based on the idea that political artistic practices were essential to social reform, that social reform was necessary for both political and artistic progressiveness, and that in order to make political art, that art must be ultimately visible and accessible to a large number of people. Their approach was therefore more activist in its philosophy and method, relying to some degree on earlier notions of political revolution and public access.

After WWII, Ben Shahn began working for the CIO Political Action Committee, designing posters intended to highlight the struggle and inequity between labor and big business, and encouraging the public to register to vote.[14] In a poster entitled *We Want Peace* (1946), the figure of an emaciated child looks out at the viewer, obviously recalling the deprivation and suffering brought on by war. Cutting across the child's body is the command "Register to Vote," which was an appeal to returning soldiers and to civilians alike. By choosing the reproducible medium of print and lithography, Shahn recognized the potential of his images to reach a wide, public audience, rather than a small group of art world elites. Among his subjects were the somewhat romanticized portraits of Abraham Lincoln, Frederick Douglass, Ghandi, Martin Luther King, Albert Einstein, and the civil rights workers James Chaney and Arthur Goodman who were murdered by the KKK in Mississippi during "Freedom Summer."[15] Shahn felt that it was possible for artists to revive the human spirit by remaining politically engaged. To be engaged, Shahn stated, implied "the obligation and need of the individual (working in cooperation with others) to do something about the evils of his time."[16]

Shahn's work was a general call to viewers to heighten awareness of inequity and the possibilities of political involvement. It provided a model of art that is both explicitly political *and* accepted by mainstream institutions, is interested in the artist's personal liberation as well as the wide-scale enactment of social change, a general form of liberation that works within hegemonic social models. Shahn's work, therefore, effectively bridges the gap between 1940s- and 1950s-style "political" art and 1960s-style "activist" art.

Overlapping with Shahn's later, more explicitly activist work, are photographic works that shared his humanistic impulse. Although they can neither be considered an artistic movement nor an organized artistic collective, beginning in the mid-1950s, civil rights photographers – namely Ernest C. Withers, Charles Moore, and the amateur and professional photographers working for the Student Non Violent Coordinating Committee (SNVCC) such as Matt Herron and Maria Varela – began to profoundly influence social awareness of racial inequality through the publication of their documentary photographs.

In 1955, Ernest C. Withers self-published a photo essay entitled "Complete Photo Story of Till Murder Case," which outlined in pictures the brutal murder of 14-year-old Emmett Till, who had been kidnapped, beaten, shot, strangled, and thrown in the Tallahatchie River by white racists. Despite the violence done to her son's body and the advanced state of decomposition when his body was found, Till's mother decided to exhibit the body of her son in an open casket service in Chicago. The body was visited by over 100,000 people, many of whom left in tears or fainted at the sight and smell of Till's body.[17] Withers' images of Till in the casket were subsequently published in several high circulation papers, including *Jet* and *The Chicago Defender*.[18] People across the country who might not otherwise have heard of the case were shocked, outraged, sickened, and disgusted by the sheer brutality of the crime. Even though the Supreme Court had just passed the school integration decision in 1954, one year before the murder, these images reminded the entire country of the persistent violence of racism. Three months later, the civil rights movement began a widespread, coordinated, and highly public activist phase, and the Till murder case is often cited as the spark that set the country on fire.

Similarly, Charles Moore's 1963 images of Birmingham protestors huddled against walls as they were battered with high-pressure water from enormous fire hoses or attacked by dogs, constituted one of the most thorough visual examinations of any social struggle in America. It was an essential cold war political strategy to portray the United States as the benevolent provider of democracy to the world. When Moore's photographs appeared on the front pages of newspapers across the nation and abroad, it constituted an "international embarrassment," exposing the hypocrisy and the failure of the national system of "equal" rights.[19] Because the civil rights movement necessitated extraordinary acts of physical courage and composure that were easily filmed and photographed, the movement was probably one of the most media-savvy forms of activism in the US. Protestors and activists moved social radicalism "away from the terrain of industry and mass parties" and into the realm of the personal, "symbolic expression, and spontaneous organization from below."[20] It was the civil rights movement's remarkable use of the street as a theater of action for large, non-violent, and highly visible protests that inspired many subsequent forms of action in the public arena by artists. And it was the frankness of the civil rights protest photographs – their ability to represent extreme violence unsentimentally and effectively, their easy reproducibility, and their effective media impact – that inspired artists and other activists groups to use similar documentary techniques a decade later.

The late 1950s was a period of elastic experimentation in the world of art. The Independent Group in England was celebrating popular culture with bawdy collages cut from the pages of glossy magazines, while pop artists in the US were critically assessing or simply emulating the new world of consumer goods and mass communication. Above all, there was a decisive conceptual shift away from the notion of the artist as an isolated individual who acted only on the canvas, to a conception of the artist as a member of a larger social and economic network. Many artists turned to unconventional forms of art practice, rejecting academic forms of painting and sculpture in favor of neo-Dadaist assemblage, performances, and Happenings that emphasized collaboration. In the fall of 1959 Alan Kaprow staged *18 Happenings in Six Parts*, in which audience members were invited to join in a participatory performance. This was a multi-media event: various sounds, lights, and olfactory components, as well as the choreographed movements of the spectators' bodies, created a collective and temporally unique experience. The intention was expressly to alter the relationship between the viewer and performer, viewer and objects, viewer and mise-en-scène. Alan Kaprow, along with John Cage, Red Grooms, Robert Whitman, Jim Dine, Carolee Schneemann, Merce Cunningham, and others thereby attempted to dispel the myth that art is distinct from life, that art is primarily a visual experience, or that it is something that can only be executed by trained specialists. Their installations and performances were designed to involve the audience, to be relevant to the moment, and to involve the audience in a visceral, literal way.

What becomes evident in the subsequent decade, a decade in which activist art erupts across the United States, is that the respective methodologies of civil rights protests and collective or process-oriented art become merged in a systematic effort by artists to reach a new audience with new expressive means. By the late 1960s, the escalation of aggressive foreign policy in Vietnam in combination with the escalation of tension in the civil rights movement were in direct contrast with the public face of the art world, which, although "political" and "liberal," generally avoided radical politics. Artists working in major metropolises began to draw parallels between the struggles of antiwar and civil rights activists and their own ideological struggles with the world of museum and gallery elites. Key issues were the inherent racism and sexism of these institutions, which seemed to mirror the problems of the nation at large. The Black Emergency Cultural Coalition (BECC), for example, was formed in 1969 as a response to the exhibition "Harlem on My Mind" at the Metropolitan Museum of Art. Frustrated with the sociological approach of the museum, this coalition of black artists voiced their dismay that the MET would claim to present the "cultural" history of Harlem while excluding the work of important black artists. At about the same time in Chicago, the African Commune of Bad Relevant Artists, or AFRI-COBRA, sought to create an expressive art that would foster liberation and solidarity throughout the African Diaspora.[21] Both groups sought to rescue art practice and the art world from the grip of Eurocentric traditions. Similarly, the multiracial Art Workers' Coalition (AWC), a group of more than

60 concerned artist/activists (including some members of the BECC) that met weekly, sought to destroy the political complacency of art museums, the perceived bastions of high culture. They registered their complaints about the lack of representation of black, Puerto-Rican, and female artists with the Whitney Museum and the Museum of Modern art, especially criticizing the trustees of the Modern and the Metropolitan museums for their ties to those who financed the war in Vietnam, thereby drawing a parallel between the two issues. They printed hundreds of lithographic posters taken from a photograph of the My Lai massacre of Vietnamese civilians by the US military in 1968. The words "Q: And babies? A: And babies" frame a sickening pile of dead bodies, among which are the clearly discernible forms of women and infants. The text itself was taken from Mike Wallace's interview of Paul Meadlo, a soldier who personally killed dozens of Vietnamese civilians.[22] These posters were used in political protests in the street, and were also held up beside Picasso's monumental *Guernica* in the lobby of the Museum of Modern Art, New York. Like well-planned Happenings, the AWC actions were always collective, participatory, and were generally staged to attract media attention.

The Artists Protest Committee (APC), based in Los Angeles, also sought to make the connection between racism and war more explicit during a "White Out" event in which several galleries on La Cienega Boulevard covered their paintings with a white strip of paper. As Francis Frascina explains in *Art, Politics, and Dissent*, this action was designed as a two part demonstration: a withdrawal of artists from their role of making art for a society they deemed violent and threatening, and a protest against further escalation.[23] Posters were printed depicting a ladder leading up and off the top frame with the word "STOP" printed at the bottom. Underneath, the words "We Dissent" appeared, followed by a list of six "truths" regarding the dismal state of US foreign and domestic policy and the right of concerned citizen to protest and stage a revolution. Notably, item number five reads "Selma and Santo Domingo are Inseparable," thus articulating a connection between the struggle for freedom "at home" and military intervention abroad.[24]

One year after the APC staged the "white out," the committee rented a vacant lot on the corner of La Cienega and Sunset Boulevard and began construction on the Los Angeles Peace Tower. Standing 60 feet tall, the tower was designed by sculptor Mark DiSuvero and was covered with over 400 war protest panels sent by artists from all over the world.[25] At the same time in New York, the Artists and Writers Protest Committee organized what Lucy Lippard calls the "largest cultural protest since the '40s."[26] Partly drawing on the example of the Peace Tower and the APC's activities in Los Angeles, Angry Arts Week was a large-scale collective event of arts and protest that worked from the examples of Happenings, performance, Brechtian theater, and Dada.[27] In an era when art seemed to be firmly situated within the relatively conservative boundaries of the art world, almost fully and self-reflexively concerned with its own physical properties, these events demonstrated that pop, minimalism, abstract, and conceptual art could be leveraged for political ends. Although the meaning of the Angry Arts Week actions might have been ambiguously received by the unprepared public, they did play an integral role in expressing information and opinions not available in mass media. According to Lippard, such actions, public events, and posters work "like graffiti" in that they "name cultural identities and political positions disbarred elsewhere."[28]

In 1970, the bombing of Cambodia and the murders of student protesters at Kent and Jackson State Universities marked another moment of hybrid political and artistic action. The model of the labor strike came to take on a greater role in political protests around the country. On May 18th, Robert Morris, along with New York University's School of Visual Arts and Poppy Johnson of Guerilla Art Action Group, decided to organize a day of strike and withdrawal. Members of the New York Art Strike Against War, Racism, Fascism, Sexism, and Repression – or the "Art Strike," as it came to be known – sent out letters to major art institutions in New York City requesting that they symbolically close their doors. As a result, on May 22nd the Whitney Museum closed, the Guggenheim Museum remained open but removed all paintings from the walls, the MoMA remained open but charged no admission fee, and Frank Stella closed his one man show.[29] At the same time, hundreds of people converged at the Metropolitan Museum holding signs stating "Artists Strike Against War and Racism." The strike highlighted the power of art as an element of culture that can be used to make a statement both by its presence and by its absence. The performance of the strike as an ideological gesture effectively positioned the visual arts as a social tool and the museum as a social forum to be wielded symbolically on behalf of concerned citizens – both artists and non-artists alike.

The labor strike was also the primary political model used in 1965 by the Chicano civil rights movement, which sought to challenge the unequal treatment of Mexican Americans through direct action, labor unions, and school walk-outs. Artists rallied to the cause, and quickly acquired a central role in the movement's efforts to organize both farm workers and city dwellers in the name of *Chicanismo*. El Theatro Campesino, a traveling theater collective lead by Luis Valdez, supported unionization and strikes with humorous satires that appealed to agricultural communities throughout California. Groups like Mujeres Muralistas in San Francisco and members of SPARC (the Social and Public Art Resource Center) lead by Judy Baca in Los Angeles used their talents to transform the walls of city streets into affirmative visions of Chicano cultural heritage. A number of workshops in Los Angeles, such as Self-Help Graphics, were started in the early 1970s to support artists working in the easily reproducible forms of print and lithography. In a general effort to reclaim a lost or repressed cultural heritage, many Chicano artists turned to traditional Mexican arts for inspiration, while others focused on portraying the struggle of their everyday lives. Increasingly discontent with an ethnically biased curriculum and dilapidated school infrastructures, hundreds of Chicano high school students initiated the East LA "blow outs" in March 1968 by organizing sit-ins, walk-outs, and speeches that

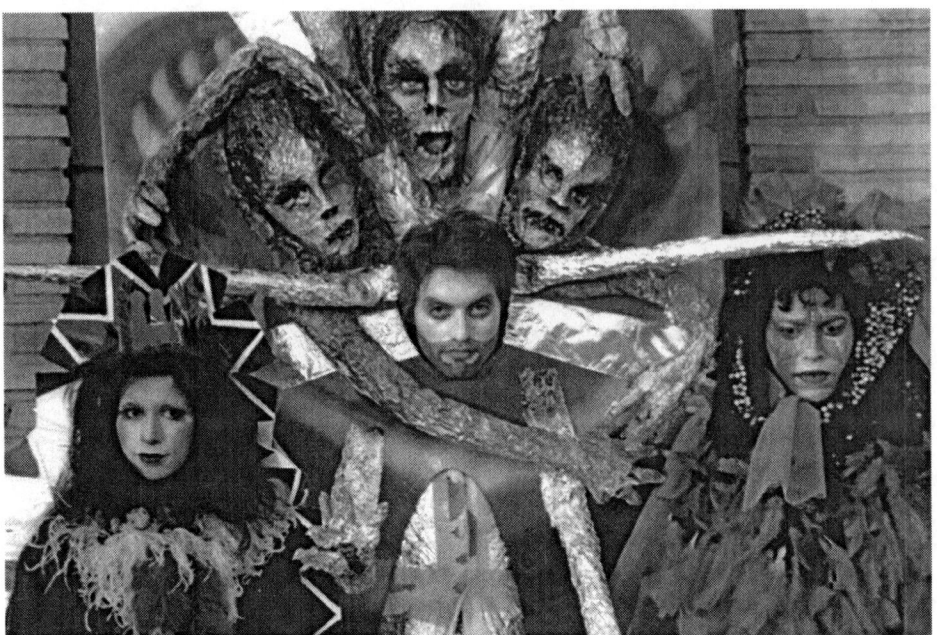

FIGURE 11.1 Asco, *Walking Mural*, 1972. Pictured (l–r): Patssi Valdez, Willie Herrón, and Gronk. © 1972 Harry Gamboa Jr.

lasted for nearly two weeks. Notably, several of their demands were met by the school board, and a new generation of art activists drew inspiration from their success. Harry Gamboa Jr., who was among the student protestors, became a radical artist who, with his collaborators in the Asco group, staged spontaneous agit-prop theater at US draft offices and other public sites, simultaneously criticizing racism and militarism (Figure 11.1). These actions paralleled larger-scale political events, such as the Chicano Moratorium of 1970, which drew several thousand people to the streets of Los Angeles, protesting the fact that Chicanos suffered a disproportionate casualty count in the Vietnam War.

Just as the Vietnam War seemed to bring race-related anxieties to the fore by revealing the inherent connections between various kinds of oppression, it also exposed with a stark clarity the effects of war and violence, both psychological and physical, on women. The legacy of sixties activism resulted at the end of the decade in a wave of co-op galleries, small art presses and exhibitions, street works, independent video, mail art, and countercultural venues in which artists could participate and operate. By the 1970s, feminist art was making use of those countercultural options and strategies and was beginning to broaden the whole notion of political and activist art. Groups like the Women Artists in Revolution (WAR), formed in 1969, and the Ad Hoc Women Artists Committee, formed in 1970, were beginning to draw parallels between global and domestic abuses of power. These groups countered the traditional and formal notions of power

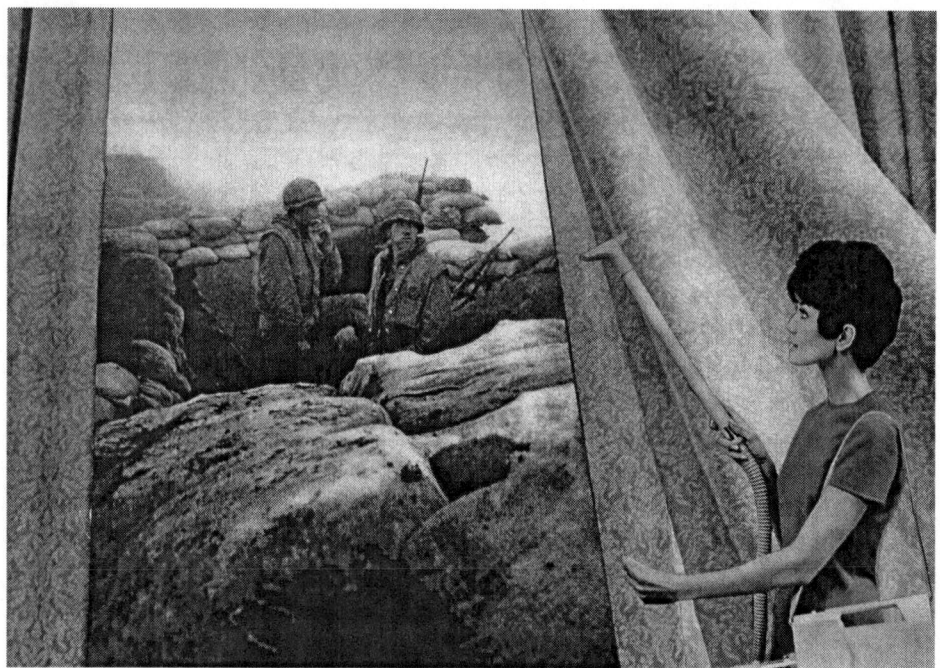

FIGURE 11.2   Martha Rosler, *House Beautiful: Bringing the War Home*, 1967–72.
© Martha Rosler

coming from the top down by drawing connections between the global situation and daily experience, between war, racism, and gendered oppression.

One artist who effectively articulated this connection between racism, sexism, and war was Martha Rosler, who made a series of photomontages in 1967–72 entitled *Bringing the War Home* (Figure 11.2). Rosler designed these photographs to evoke the undeniable connection between domestic politics, economics, and foreign policy. In one photograph, a Vietnamese woman carries a dead and bloodied baby up the stairs of a modern, American home. In another, a middle-class woman vacuums her drapes, and in doing so, reveals soldiers (probably during the siege at Khe Sanh) in a barren sandbag trench, just beyond the frame of her window. The images of violence and destruction are made to fit neatly, even unobtrusively, into their cut-out frames, giving the sense that they belong wholly to the environment in which they are placed. The overall effect literalizes the reciprocal, even symbiotic, relationship between cozy domesticity "at home," and violent oppression "abroad." By surrealistically juxtaposing these images, Rosler exposes their interdependence, explicitly referring to the relationships between race and gender, power and powerlessness, in the first and third worlds.

Like most activist art of the 1970s, much of the feminist art, which took place in the public sphere, also focused on collaboration. In part, this was a conscious assault against the myth of the "individual" artistic genius. It was also an effort to overcome the isolated experiences of many women, particularly professional artists who experienced the art world as a lonely and isolated hostile territory. For these artists, the condition of their labor was a key component in the formulation of their activist approach. Feminist artists working collectively were engaged in "a reaction against an oppressive condition and a progressive critique of it."[30]

Feminist art proved to be among the most innovative art movements of the 1970s, both in terms of its activist strategies and in terms of its material forms. In 1972, Judy Chicago and Miriam Schapiro, working with 21 young women students at the California Institute of the Arts, designed *Womanhouse*, a full-scale installation – a relatively new form of "environment" art at the time – in an abandoned residential building in the middle of Los Angeles. Seventeen rooms were redesigned according to the vision of the artists; kitchen, bathroom, and bedroom were presented as zones of sexual or familial contestation made to reveal the "reality of the woman's condition,"[31] in the confines of the home. Feminist projects of the 1970s frequently represented or engaged in critiques of the home or the bourgeois domestic scene as a site of struggle for middle-class women in a patriarchal society. As a shared location for activist encounter, *Womanhouse* was a site for numerous meetings and performances by feminists, a space of symbolic, social, and political intersection.

Second-wave feminist artists were also innovative in their efforts to encompass domains of life previously unexplored in the more traditional, male-dominated arts. Mierle Laderman Ukeles's *Manifesto for Maintenance Art* was inspired by her own experience of spending each day cooking, cleaning, looking after children, and generally maintaining her household. Between 1973 and 1976, Ukeles offered 17 "maintenance" performances in public places consisting of actions such as scrubbing the streets or museum floors, cooking, and inviting people to eat.[32] Like other "action" artists of the period, Ukeles brought a series of intimate gestures into the public sphere, using her body as a medium of transgression that might incite awareness of generally invisible and abject forms of labor. Her actions were temporary and site-specific, but unlike the planned exhibition of *Womanhouse*, Ukeles performances were meant to catch the viewer off guard with an unexpected, consciousness-raising encounter.

Artists Suzanne Lacy and Leslie Labowitz, along with other activists in the group Ariadne: A Social Network, also worked collaboratively to produce performances exclusively for the public domain. *In Mourning and In Rage* (1977) was one of their first group performances, staged to protest a series of rape-related murders that had been sensationalized by the mainstream press. Part of the goal of the action, which took place on the steps of the Los Angeles City Hall, was to transform the way the mass media portrayed women as powerless victims and to criticize municipal policies regarding police awareness and rape prevention. Wearing black garments that suggested mourning veils and holding red scarves as symbols of violence, the somber group kept a silent vigil, holding banners that read: "In memory of our sisters; Women fight back."[33] As an act of identification that emphasized the shared experience of women as "sisters," the performance appealed to a sense of female solidarity in the face of systematic violence.

If the early years of second-wave feminist art were often directed toward the intimate life of women, the later years focused on the question of the public representation of women as "spectacle" in visual culture. Beyond looking for shared lived experiences – which often mask racial, economic, social, and cultural differences between women – feminist artists working in the late 1970s and early 1980s turned to the social and political forces that shape gendered identities in the mass media and public sphere. Attending to the role of photography, television, fashion magazines, and video in the perpetuation of a sexist and patriarchal image culture, feminists were motivated to produce parodies and critiques of dominant visual culture.

Under the new Reagan administration, the early 1980s was also a time of conservative backlash against feminism and progressive civil rights movements in the US. Because familiar methods of street activism and collective action seemed quaint and ineffectual, perhaps even boring, in the face of a new era of media propaganda and consumer hype, activist artists sought to develop new strategies of representation that could compete with the slick image culture of advertising and the rhetoric of political language. Barbara Kruger found a way to combine archival photographs with graphically striking text to draw attention to the systematic and coercive forms of patriarchy at play in the construction of gender norms. With slogans such as "I shop therefore I am" or "Your body is a battle ground," Kruger drew attention to the way in which women are interpellated as consumers and as embodied subjects whose shopping habits and reproductive rights become the domain of cultural surveillance. While many of Kruger's images were exhibited in galleries, she also placed her work in public, commercial sites such as on walls and billboards (see Figure 10.3). With a similar attention to the critical use of textual forms, artist Jenny Holzer employed the familiar, flashing-red LED displays visible in train stations or the Wall Street stock exchange to install crypto-social aphorisms in public places. Her sound-bite slogans, such as "Abuse of power comes as no surprise" from the *Truisms* series, were presented not only on LED screens but also on public benches and electronic billboards in metropolitan areas such as New York City and Las Vegas. These works changed the way feminist artists engaged with the public sphere, and signaled a larger shift in activist art at the beginning of a new decade.

Most US activist art made before the 1980s, whether in the form of street protests and performances, posters or slogans, was clearly distinguishable from other kinds of art and image culture. Activists found ways to make their works stand out from the environment, and to be recognizable as a form of political communication. In the early 1980s, we see a dramatic transformation of activist art practice which begins to follow the logic of camouflage, appearing in the guise of "real" advertising or masked as a form of popular culture. With wit,

humor, or biting commentary, this new, unsentimental activism sought to leverage the power inherent in mainstream forms of mass communication for itself.
This shift in approach is particularly evident in the art activism accompanying
the first years of the AIDS crisis in the US.

In "The Spectacle of AIDS," Simon Watney argues that the spectacle of AIDS
operates "as a public masque" upon which is projected the punishment of the
homosexual, imagined as the enemy of the family and the purveyor of corruption and depravity, sexual excess, and death.[34] In the dominant representations
of AIDS, the homosexual body becomes a surface upon which the virus itself
makes its mark, enacting the punishment handed down by the dominant instrument of the family, effectively blocking empathetic identification with the body
in extremis by disclosing the mark of guilt. Watney's premise is that "AIDS is
not only a medical crisis on an unparalleled scale, it involves a crisis of representation itself, a crisis over the entire framing of knowledge about the human body
and its capacities for sexual pleasure."[35]

In other words, for AIDS activists, it was simply not enough to produce and
reproduce photographs of ravaged bodies on gurneys, "PWA's [people with
AIDS] close to death, dead IV drug users with needles in their arms."[36] Unlike
during the civil rights and Vietnam era, in the late 1980s "victim photography"
was no longer a feasible option, especially considering the ideological issues of
promiscuity, guilt, and death that swirled around any talk of AIDS or HIV. Rather
than portraying AIDS as a matter of individual misery, abjection, and pathos, it
was necessary to address the social and political context in a more oblique way.
In order to do this, it was necessary to transform the way in which the homosexual body was rendered "radically mute" by the fantasies of dominant representations.[37] At the same time, there was a desire to rely on visual *pleasure* rather
than terror in order to provoke outrage and anger and in order to recuperate a
lost sense of sexual pleasure and a "culture of sexual possibility."[38]

In response to this crisis, AIDS activists formed Gran Fury in 1988, the
propaganda arm of ACT-UP (the AIDS Coalition To Unleash Power), who
produced work for billboards, bus shelters, buses, vending machines, and even
post office boxes. Unlike the deliberately confrontational imagery of 1960s
activism, Gran Fury did not seek to remove itself from the dominant imagery of
consumerism, seeking instead to appropriate the "codes of capitalist pleasure
and visual seduction to capture the viewer's attention and direct it to the AIDS
crisis."[39] For a bus panel entitled *Kissing Doesn't Kill* (1989–90), three interracial couples are pictured. Dressed in bright, fashionable colors, kissing in front
of a white monochrome backdrop, they effectively mimic the appearance of a
"United Colors of Benetton" advertisement. By appropriating the style of popular media, this image functions firstly as a guerilla tactic in an information
environment. Equally important, the poster is accompanied by the text "Kissing
Doesn't Kill: Greed and Indifference Do," thus providing a challenge to governmental and popular misinformation about AIDS, specifically rejecting the widely
held belief that kissing was a "high risk behavior" that might result in HIV

infection. Additionally, Gran Fury was concerned with mobility and visibility. Emblazoned on city buses, their message traveled *on its own* throughout the city, and was probably more effectively received than if it had been carried as a poster by an identifiable group of activists; instead, the poster speaks for itself. Perhaps most importantly, *Kissing Doesn't Kill* affirms the power of queer desire in the face of an ongoing epidemic, deliberately contradicting the image of the pathetic and abject homosexual body by presenting a seductive image of implicit sexual pleasure.[40] By picturing both heterosexual and homosexual couples, the image denies the violent myth that AIDS is a "homosexual disease" or a "gay plague," thereby embracing sexual plurality, exploration, and diversity in the face of a national health crisis.

The seductive imagery and the art of effective sloganeering perfected by AIDS activists created a shock of misrecognition as "an ostensibly familiar form of mass culture gave way to its activist simulation."[41] Gran Fury, as a part of ACT-UP, serves as a suggestive case study for the kinds of new media strategies that emerged at this historical moment. Performing both distinct and inclusive strategies of demonstration, they positioned themselves not against but *inside* of mainstream image culture in order to mobilize public consciousness and to foster social support.

This philosophy has carried forward through the 1990s to the present day, with many contemporary activist artists creating elaborate methods for infiltrating forms of mass communication. This insider activist art is *critically recursive* to the degree that it frequently and self-consciously uses the visual forms and linguistic rhetoric of those it wishes to critique. A work of art that operates recursively can be thought of as dependent, responsive, parasitical, changing, flexible, and mimetic. Rather than abandoning systems of domination in search of new modes, it models itself on these very systems in order to intersect with their easy flow. Recursion shares with the situationist notion of *détournement* a taking and reusing of available signs, but the two terms are not synonymous. To *détourn* is usually to repurpose a sign, perhaps a hegemonic sign from mainstream culture, to give it a new spin, a second life, a new framework. Recursion in art practice is more of a simulation or parody of hegemonic signs that produces new signs to stand in their place and to usurp their position of power. Recursive art works engage the rhetorical heart of systems of representation, borrowing and copying linguistic style and aesthetic techniques in order to blur the boundaries between participation and subterfuge. Recursive forms of critical practice "work" because they are disguised as objects of casual, pleasurable, visual consumption.

At the end of the twentieth century, many activist artists turned to the Internet to address a new mass audience with recursive forms of critical practice. Artist Natalie Bookchin suggests that much of the early art on the Internet had an activist bent, supporting the free distribution of information and software and resisting the drive immediately to commercialize this new form of communication.[42] Others saw the Internet as a site for direct critical response to the military industrial complex, with its intensive reliance on electronic systems of communication. In the late 1990s the artists' collective called the Electronic Disturbance Theater promoted the concept of "electronic civil disobedience" based on the conviction that the streets were no longer the best place for effective social activism. Along with the Critical Art Ensemble, these artists argued that blocking the flow of information in cyberspace should replace traditional civil disobedience, and they presented their culture-jamming practices as a necessary form of contemporary agit-prop and critical art practice. Among EDT's better known projects is *Flood Net Tactical Version 1.0*, which effectively and temporarily disabled then Mexican President Zedillo's website in order to show support of the Zapatista resistance to the Mexican Government and NAFTA.[43]

Other artists have taken a parodic approach to the use of the Internet as a site of activist intervention. In 1999, just before the World Trade Organization protests in Seattle, an art group calling themselves "®™ARK" launched a social-political decoy website at *www.gatt.org*. Natalie Bookchin, one of the members of the group, commented in an interview with Beryl Graham,

> [t]he ®™ARK site appeared, at first glance, to be a mirror of the official World Trade Organization's web page, but upon entering *gatt.org* one discovered critical material about globalization, the WTO, and links or information about the upcoming actions in Seattle. Numerous visitors inadvertently stumbled upon the ®™ARK web page whilst looking for information about the WTO, and thus the site was able to reach not just an audience of anti-globalization activists but WTO supporters and others seeking general data.[44]

In the same year ®™ARK launched a political parody website *gwbush.com*, which provided a humorous critique of the presidential candidate's platform for the 2000 election. The project attracted significant media attention when the Bush campaign complained about the site to the Federal Elections Commission and when George W. Bush was quoted as saying in response to the art work, "[t]here ought to be limits to freedom."[45]

More recently the Institute of Applied Autonomy, another technologically savvy group of artists and engineers, have produced a variety of methods to transform activist practice by leveraging Internet-based mapping techniques and wireless network systems in the public domain. One of their early projects was a critique of the expansion of urban surveillance called *iSee* (Figure 11.3). Using data gathered by the New York Surveillance Camera Project and the American Civil Liberties Union, the artists created a chart of the all the closed-circuit television surveillance cameras on the island of Manhattan. The project allows users to locate paths through the city while avoiding being caught on tape, something the artists call "paths of least surveillance."[46] As an Internet art project, *iSee* simultaneously offers an ominous visual representation of a society of panoptic control while providing a pragmatic solution in the form of dynamic maps. In 2004, the IAA used wireless technology in the project *TXT Mob* to

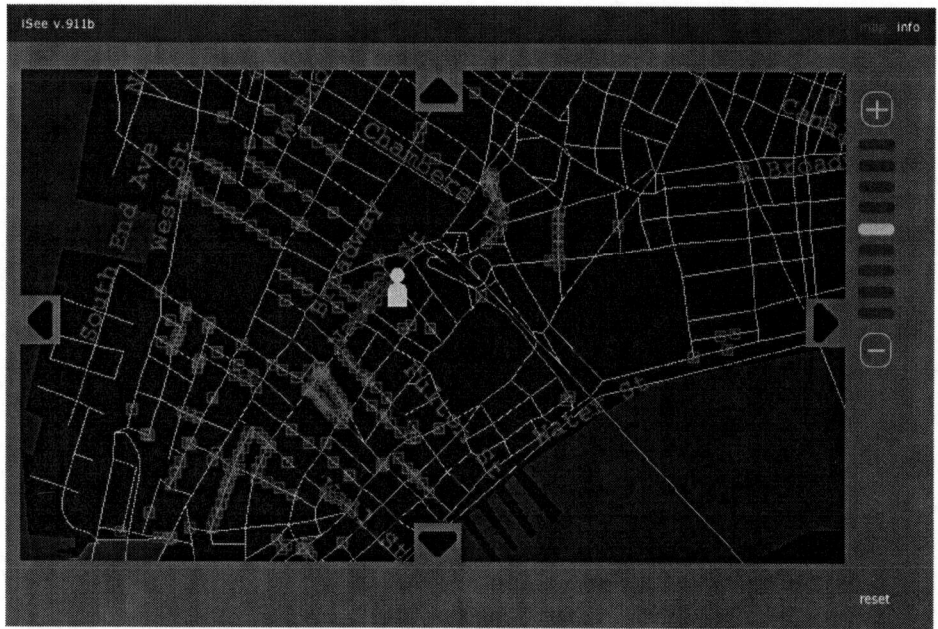

FIGURE 11.3   Institute of Applied Autonomy, *iSee*, 2001–5. © Institute of Applied Autonomy

enhance communication between activists at the Democratic and Republican National Conventions in Boston and New York City. The free service provided a quick and easy broadcast service that allowed person-to-person text messaging, as well as the rapid distribution of tactical information to large groups of protestors. "The text messages have ranged from an offer of a sewing machine for a women's anti-war group called Code Pink, to an alert that protesters in row boats on a lake in Central Park might be arrested, to an update that protesters were allegedly beaten while handcuffed."[47] In the case of the Institute for Applied Autonomy, the activist artist becomes a facilitator of activist practice as much as a producer of critical images.

Activist art, like other kinds of art practice, is formally and conceptually accretive. It is always a kind of hybrid form that creates new tactics while it borrows from its predecessors those techniques and strategies that might best achieve immediate social and political goals. Although supplemented by various forms of performance, design, technology, and a marked sophistication of media, the model of mass social protest that characterized labor movements and civil rights movements of the last century continues to provide an effective source for political expression today. Similarly, newer forms of critical engagement with discourses in the commercial spheres of advertising and broadcast media merge with the painted placards and collective song of earlier decades. Although the issues of civil rights, militarism, war, and racism continue to be the cause of seemingly endless national problems today, the manner in which various problems are manifested *and* the way in which they need to be combated can be radically different. Nina Felshin's edited volume *But Is It Art? The Spirit of Art as Activism* asks whether activist art can be properly understood within the rubric of a fine art tradition.[48] What seems clear is that it is neither the formal characteristics nor the political content of activist art that distinguishes its history or defines its parameters; rather, it is creative flexibility, tactical know-how, and rhetorical sophistication that comprise the consistent traits of effective activist art.

Notes

1 In his introduction to *Art, Activism, and Oppositionality*, Grant Kester cites the work of Kant, Schiller, Hutcheson, and Shaftesbury to argue that the aesthetic is indivisibly wed to political and social realms via its role as an intermediary between subject and object, between affective experience and cognition, between individual subject positions and the world. Kester (1998), 8.
2 Greenberg (1992), 308–14, and Schapiro (1957), 36–42.
3 Lippard (1984), 349.
4 Abbie Hoffman discusses the function of the street in Taylor (1987), 239. On the Situationists see Bowen in this volume.
5 Kelley (1995), 232.
6 Lippard (1984), 342.
7 Rosenberg (1952), 22.
8 Frascina and Harris (1992), 109.
9 There are a number of excellent discussions of this topic. See, for example, Wald (1987), Cockroft (1983), and Schapiro and Schapiro (1983).
10 Jachec (2000), 21.
11 Ibid., 33.
12 Williams (1989), 62.
13 Joselit (2003), 32.
14 Prescott (1982), 8.
15 Pohl (1989).
16 Shahn (1972), 204–5.
17 See Crowe (2002).
18 Kasher (1996), 11.
19 Ibid., 10.
20 Crow (1996), 11.
21 Powell (1991), 101.
22 Ibid., 170–1.
23 Frascina (1999), 30.
24 Ibid., 29.
25 Lippard (1990), 12.
26 Ibid., 13.
27 For a detailed discussion of this event, see Frascina (1999), 108–49.

28 Lippard (1990), 27.
29 Ibid., 33.
30 Parker and Pollock (1987), 3.
31 Reckitt and Phelan (2001), 208.
32 Ibid., 93.
33 Ibid., 126.
34 Watney (1987), 9.
35 Ibid., 9.
36 Grover (1992), 6.
37 Watney (1987), 207.
38 Crimp (1989).
39 Meyer (1995), 52.
40 Ibid.
41 Ibid., 74.
42 Natalie Bookchin (2001).
43 Ibid.
44 Ibid.
45 Cited at http://rtmark.com/gwbush/
46 Institute of Applied Autonomy (2004).
47 Simon (2004), no page numbers.
48 Felshin (1995).

References

Bookchin, Natalie (2001). Interview with Beryl Graham, January. www.newmedia.sunderland.ac.uk/crumb/phase3/pdf/intvw_bookchin_jackson.pdf

Cockroft, Eva (1983). "Abstract Expressionism, Weapon of the Cold War." In *Pollock and After: The Critical Debate*, ed. Francis Frascina. New York and London: Routledge.

Crimp, Douglas (1989). "Mourning and Militancy." In *October*, no. 51:3–18.

Crow, Thomas (1996). "Introduction." In *Rise of the Sixties: American and European Art in the Era of Dissent*. London: Calmann and King.

Crowe, Chris (2002). *Mississippi Trial, 1955*. New York: Phyllis Fogelman Books.

Felshin, Nina (1995). *But is it Art: The Spirit of Art as Activism*. Seattle: Bay Press.

Frascina, Francis (1999). *Art, Politics and Dissent: Aspects of the Art Left in Sixties America*. Manchester and New York: Manchester University Press.

Frascina, Francis, and Jonathan Harris, eds. (1992). *Art in Modern Culture: An Anthology of Critical Texts*. New York: HarperCollins.

Greenberg, Clement (1992). "Modernist Painting." In *Art in Modern Culture: An Anthology of Critical Texts*, ed. Francis Frascina and Jonathan Harris. New York: HarperCollins.

Grover, Jan Zita (1992). "AIDS: Public Issues, Public Art." In *Public Art Issues: Taking it to the Street: Public Art and AIDS*, ed. Robert Knafo. New York: Public Art Fund.

Institute of Applied Autonomy (2004). www.appliedautonomy.com

Jachec, Nancy (2000). *The Philosophy and Politics of Abstract Expressionism*. Cambridge: Cambridge University Press.

Joselit, David (2003). "The Private Gesture in Public: Art of the New York School." In *American Art Since 1945.* London: Thames and Hudson.

Kasher, Steven (1996). *The Civil Rights Movement: A Photographic History, 1954–1968.* New York: Abbeville Press.

Kelley, Jeff (1995). "The Body Politics of Suzanne Lacy." In *But Is It Art? The Spirit of Art as Activism*, ed. Nina Felshin. Seattle: Bay Press.

Kester, Grant (1998). "Ongoing Negotiations: Afterimage and the Analysis of Activist Art." In *Art, Activism, and Oppositionality*, ed. Grant Kester. Durham, NC: Duke University Press.

Lippard, Lucy (1984). "Trojan Horses: Activist Art and Power." In *Art After Modernism*, ed. Brian Wallis. New York: The New Museum.

—— (1990). *A Different War: Vietnam in Art.* Seattle: The Real Comet Press.

Meyer, Richard (1995). "This Is to Enrage You: Gran Fury and the Graphics of AIDS Activism." In *But is it Art? The Spirit of Art as Activism*, ed. Nina Felshin. Seattle: Seattle Bay Press.

Parker, Rozsika, and Griselda Pollock (1987). *Framing Feminism: Art and the Women's Movement 1970–1985.* London and New York: Pandora.

Pohl, Frances K. (1989). *Ben Shahn: New Deal Artist in a Cold War Climate, 1947–1954.* Austin: University of Texas Press.

Powell, Richard J. (1991). *Black Art and Culture in the 20th Century.* London: Thames and Hudson.

Prescott, Kenneth W. (1882). *The Prints and Posters of Ben Shahn.* New York: Dover Publications.

Reckitt, Helena, and Peggy Phelan (2001). *Art and Feminism.* London: Phaidon.

Rosenberg, Harold (1952). "American Action Painters." In *Art News*, December, vol. 51:22–3, 48–50.

Schapiro, David, and Cecile Schapiro (1983). "Abstract Expressionism: The Politics of Apolitical Painting." In *Pollock and After: The Critical Debate*, ed. Francis Frascina. New York and London: Routledge.

Schapiro, Meyer (1957). "The Liberating Quality of the Avant-Garde." In *Art News*, vol. 56:36–42.

Shahn, Ben (1972). "Some Questions." In *Ben Shahn*, ed. John D. Morse. New York: Praeger.

Simon, Ellen (2004). "Text Messages Connect Protestors." Associated Press, September 8, 2004. Reprinted in CBSNews.Com, www.cbsnews.com/stories/2004/09/08/tech.

Taylor, Derek (1987). *It Was Twenty Years Ago Today.* London: Bantam Press.

Wald, Alan M. (1987). *The New York Intellectuals: The Rise and Decline of the Anti-Stalinist Left from the 1930s to the 1980s.* Chapel Hill: University of North Carolina Press.

Watney, Simon (1987). "The Spectacle of AIDS." In *Policing Desire: Pornography, AIDS, and the Media.* Minneapolis: University of Minnesota Press.

Williams, Raymond (1989). *The Politics of Modernism: Against the New Conformists.* London and New York: Verso.

12

"The Senators Were Revolted": Homophobia and the Culture Wars

Jonathan D. Katz

At the end of the summer, Andy and I were on the Eastern Shuttle, on our way to the Reagan's state dinner for Ferdinand and Imelda Marcos.
Interview magazine editor Bob Colacello on Andy Warhol[1]

It's sometimes hard to remember that there was a time when avant-garde art and conservative politics were not sworn enemies in the United States, when no less a queer artist than Andy Warhol was invited for dinner at the Reagan White House but a few years after completing a painting series using urine and another of same-sex sex acts and male torsos. This was, of course, before the culture wars had made those two themes in particular – urine and male homosexuality – not only taboo, but, in the eyes of Jesse Helms, the vehicle for a resurgent power to define not just the arts but "morality" itself.

But at one time – December of 1981 to be exact – Nancy Reagan, wife of Republican president Ronald Reagan, was on the cover of Warhol's *Interview* magazine, with the issue itself including the first in-depth print interview granted by the First Lady since occupying the White House (she was interviewed by Warhol, editor Bob Colacello, and his new assistant Doria Reagan, Ron Reagan Jr.'s new wife). The same issue featured photographs of Robert Mapplethorpe out on the town, homoerotic photographs by George Platt Lynes, Herbert List, and even one by Edward Steichen depicting two bare-chested sailors, one intimately examining the other's tattoo. There was also an illustrated interview with Prince, the singer provocatively posed as an upright, full-length odalisque in the shower, dressed only in a low cut thong with his pubic hair curling over, and a crucifix dominating the wall behind him. A nearly naked Prince and a crucifix, Nancy Reagan and Robert Mapplethorpe, all in Andy Warhol's magazine – the battle lines for the coming culture wars had clearly not yet been definitively drawn.[2]

Eight years later, on June 12, 1989, Christina Orr-Cahall, director of the Corcoran Gallery of Art in Washington DC, cancelled the long awaited Mapplethorpe retrospective, *The Perfect Moment*, a few weeks before its opening and a few months after the photographer's death from AIDS, firing off perhaps the single most resounding shot in the culture wars. By this point, conservative politics had become the sworn enemy of progressive art, and the National Endowment for the Arts (NEA) – the only federal-level funding body for the arts in the USA – was fighting for its life. Brilliantly manipulated as a polarizing wedge issue by the Christian right and the Republican-dominated Senate, the question of federal support for an art thematizing sexuality came to dominate a broader debate over whether state funding bodies such as the NEA were indeed the proper business of government at all. The NEA would shortly be forced to implement the so called Helms amendment, which imposed content restrictions on all art supported by the NEA while drastically cutting the agency's budget. These content restrictions overwhelmingly turned on the question of the representation of sexuality, and homosexuality in particular was defined as inherently obscene. While the House would eventually temper some of the virulence of the Helms amendment, by the late 1980s a new era of highly politicized art making and art exhibiting had been launched in the US.

The term avant-garde was derived in the nineteenth century from the French term designating the front lines in a military conflict – and thus served to highlight the modernist ideal of the most innovative artists forging ahead of mainstream culture to shift ways of seeing and thinking.[3] In the late 1980s and early 1990s, the avant-garde in America returned to its etymological roots, becoming a significant player – perhaps even the significant player – in the cultural contestation that became the chief political issue of the twilight of the Reagan administration and that of George Bush Sr., the latter only a slightly modified version of Reaganism in terms of domestic policy. But, as indicated in the example of the 1981 *Interview* issue described above, at the beginning of the Reagan era art and politics were but ships passing in the night, the art world by definition rarely connected to overt political activity. This is not to say that there was no political art – on the contrary; the visual art practices that dominated the US art world in the 1980s were often vociferously opposed to Reagan and the ideologies of the political right his administration represented and put into policy. It is to say that the world of conservative politics as yet saw little instrumentality in the manipulation of that art or its particular circuits of exhibition and dissemination and so ignored it.

This chapter, then, seeks to explore how art and politics leaped from wary cooperation (Colacello tells us that Nancy Reagan agreed to the *Interview* piece because the White House felt it would help her image with younger voters) to a bitter divorce. It asks the questions of why the culture wars came about and why they happened when they did.

National Political Background

I'm not quite sure what it says about America that one of the most intense public controversies in the months between the Tiananmen Square massacre and the breaching of the Berlin Wall had to do with homoerotic photographs and a crucifix suspended in a vat of urine.

Representative Henry Hyde, Republican of Illinois,
"The Culture War," *National Review* April 30, 1990

Hyde's too glib formulation points to knowledge repressed in drawing the reader's attention to the relationship between the fall of the Communist regimes in the East and the onset of the culture wars. For Anthony Lewis of the *New York Times*, however, the relationship between the fall of communism and the American culture wars was far from repressed: "There is a particular irony in the attempt to arouse a repressive American attitude to the arts at this time. We are cheering Eastern Europe's liberation from Communism – a liberation marked by freedom for literature and the arts."[4] The late 1980s were hard times for the Republicans, and the fragility of its governing coalition – so powerfully soldered though the populism of Ronald Reagan in the early and mid 1980s – was increasingly exposed through the less-rousing ministrations of George Bush Sr. (in office from 1988 to 1992). The Christian Right was rocked by the sex scandals of two of its most prominent leaders, Jim Bakker and Jimmy Swaggart, while the memory of the Reagan years as an unblemished time of optimism and "family values" was besmirched by the continuing investigation into the Iran Contra scandals. The economy was shaken by the widespread collapse of the savings and loan industry, including the failure of a savings and loan under the leadership of Neil Bush, the President's son. Budget deficits were high, while a naked skepticism in government for the common good was succinctly captured by the ubiquitous bumper sticker reading: "Whoever dies with the most toys wins." Certainty and constancy seemed in short supply, while economic, political, and religious scandal bloomed amidst the spiraling death toll of the AIDS plague.[5]

Culture wars were, from the perspective of the Right, in part a welcome diversion from the bad news of the day. No wonder Daniel Patrick Moynihan, Democratic Senator from New York, was led to ask in early 1989 what would supplant the Communist East as the embodiment of evil in American eyes.[6] He would have his answer by that summer, as the Mapplethorpe controversy began to boil over. Moynihan's query, born of an historian's interest in American politics, recognized the degree to which the absence of a foreign conflict tended to lead the right toward an increasingly aggressive policing of the domestic sphere in an attempt to solidify its power, for the right's central discourse of defensive containment has long required threatening "others" to define itself against. This was most spectacularly the case following American victory in World War II, with the subsequent rise of McCarthyism during the cold war.[7] Indeed, in an eerie foreshadowing of the late 1980s, the policing of the arts (albeit largely the performing arts and film) through the blacklist and a concomitant federal crackdown on gays and lesbians throughout the so-called Lavender scare had been central tenants of cold war-era McCarthyism.

Though the fall of Communist regimes may have in part ignited a search for new enemies against whom a mythic American consensus could be constructed and antagonized, the culture wars were by no means exclusively a cynical attempt to shore up a crumbling Republican coalition. And they didn't work as such either, as sociologist Steven Dubin notes: "From mid August to early October 1990 – a period when the debate over government sponsorship of the arts was especially heated – Mr. Bush's approval ratings fell fourteen percentage points."[8] If the goal was exclusively political popularity or the consolidation of political power, art bashing was lousy strategy.

In fact, it wasn't really art in itself that the conservative wing of the Republican party and its Christian fellow travelers were after, but rather that which the art came to denote or stand in for. The culture wars were thus in large part a direct response to a new player on the political scene, one that had come to signify as Moynihan's embodiment of evil – a newly militant gay and lesbian community. The same year in which Moynihan wondered about the new evil, Representative William Dannemeyer of California, a leading right-wing ideologue, published a book called *Shadow in the Land: Homosexuals in America*, which included this striking claim: "Currently we are a divided nation. Such a division has not existed in America since the Civil War." For Dannemeyer, the division was between an upstanding, moral citizenry living by Christian values and "the homosexuals," who increasingly endangered family values by seeking to overturn the rule of Christian morality. He argued that the only way to heal this painful divide was to "[r]einstate traditional prohibitions against homosexuality in order to establish a sense of order and decency in our society, to reconnect us with our normative past."[9]

On June 23rd of this same year, Senator Jesse Helms of North Carolina said on the Senate floor, "Mr. President, some days I decide that things cannot get any worse, but then they do. The U.S. Postal Service took a big step this week to accommodate the perversion. Tomorrow and Sunday, June 24 and 25, several post offices in New York City will issue a postmark to 'honor' Gay and Lesbian Pride Week. . . . The homosexuals are in a battle against American values."[10] While in fact all the Postal Service proposed to do was set up a six-foot table to issue commemorative cancellations at a temporary "Stonewall Station" near the site of the Stonewall Riots (the 1969 bar riots that launched the modern gay liberation movement) on their twentieth anniversary, the intent of the martial language is clear. Helms, like Dannemeyer, had himself declared war against the Lesbian/Gay/Bi/Trans (LGBT) community.[11]

Since the late 1980s, then, the phrase *the culture wars* has become a kind of shorthand for describing that particular constellation of forces introduced here: the Christian right political agenda, more moderate Republican appeasement, the National Endowment for the Arts, the cultural avant-garde, the gay and lesbian rights movement, and AIDS activism – which resulted in a policing of the visual arts not dissimilar from the policing of the popular arts under McCarthyism. In assessing as accurately as possible the exact alchemy of this particularly volatile mix, it is important not to lose sight of its newness. The political and discursive force of the culture wars is such that it seems impossible in retrospect to imagine how it came to pass that Robert Mapplethorpe secured an NEA grant under the Reagan White House in 1984, a mere five years before the controversy erupted.[12]

But in the 1970s and early 1980s support for expressly homoerotic photography was hardly unusual, as the NEA had previously supported edgy, distinctly homoerotic work by photographers as diverse as Arthur Tress, Joel-Peter Witkin, and Larry Clark without complaint. Indeed, in 1978 an NEA-funded gallery in San Francisco, 80 Langton Street, rescued Mapplethorpe by agreeing to show the very S/M pictures that a commercial San Francisco gallery had recently rejected, and which would figure as among the most objectionable during the *Perfect Moment* scandal. Years later, Mapplethorpe remarked in terms now thick with irony, "I got the Curator at Berkeley interested in my sex pictures and he helped me to find one of these free spaces, Langdon [sic] Street, which exist through the National Endowment of the Arts, they don't have restrictions."[13]

The mid to late 1980s saw a new kind of homophobia, more active and virulent than the casual homophobia of an earlier era. Indeed, in certain urban circles, a mere five years before, homophobia had seemed increasingly a thing of the past, as gay and straight artistic and popular cultures found greater and greater commonality. Studio 54, the epicenter of Manhattan's druggy nightlife scene in the 1970s, had been in part premised on a refusal of such categorical divisions. "[E]veryone wanted to go to Studio 54 not because it was gay, but because it broke down all the old-fashioned barriers between gay and straight, young and old, rich and poor . . . 'A tossed salad' is what Steve [Rubell – a co-owner], always said he wanted it to be, and that's what it was."[14] It was entirely possible to find Margaret Trudeau, estranged wife of the Canadian Prime minister, dancing on the ground floor while groups of gay men enjoyed public sex on the balcony above. Indeed, the general rapprochement between straight and gay cultures was widely evidenced in disco, and, as with Studio 54, groups as diverse as the Village People and Two Tons of Fun played with gay stereotypes to mainstream success. Sylvester, a flamboyantly gay cross-dressing disco singer, dominated the disco charts and Bette Midler once proudly proclaimed her origins as a gay bathhouse chanteuse. When an old gay bathhouse in New York, the Continental Baths, became Plato's Retreat, a giant sex club for straights, it simply underscored the new mingling of gay and straight sexual culture – and Warhol, especially through his *Interview* magazine, became its Boswell.[15]

Thus the 1970s' increasingly open, legible culture of unapologetic same-sex sexuality in fact catalyzed not stringent policing but precisely its opposite, a general loosening of proscriptions – cultural and legal. Bathhouses and sex clubs flourished openly, queer sexually-explicit films dominated the underground film world, and not least, gay ghettos and their attendant cultural reorientations and revisions – sartorial and political – began to be felt in major urban population centers. The more the gay community insisted on its own dissident cultural visions and beliefs, the more they were simply picked up and commodified as lifestyle indicators by a common cultural machinery invested in the next trend. As a result, gayness became cool in a way it hadn't been before. Another way of putting this is to say that an increasingly essentialized notion of gay communal identity, instead of politicizing the broader public's conception of sexual identity, was producing its converse, a de-essentialized vision of gayness as a matter of cultural exchange, of style – sexual, sartorial, and otherwise. Despite setbacks such as Anita Bryant's highly publicized roll-back on gay civil rights in Florida, the decade that ended with the election of Ronald Reagan overall saw an enormous increase in visible gay culture, with comparatively little backlash.

What, then, revitalized this rapidly dissipating homophobia in the early 1980s, and once again put Nancy Reagan and Robert Mapplethorpe at odds? In a word, AIDS. The very discourse of a divided nation that Dannemeyer employed at the end of the decade was embraced to horrific effect almost as soon as AIDS, tellingly first named GRID or Gay Related Immune Deficiency Syndrome, first presented in the gay communities of New York and San Francisco. The division, embraced both actively and passively, was between those who were deemed "at risk" for AIDS, and those who falsely assumed the plague would never touch them, or more hideously still, who welcomed it as the "natural" consequence of gay men's and/or drug users' lives. As Gary Bauer, Reagan's assistant, told the television show "Face the Nation" in 1987, the reason the president had not even uttered the word AIDS publicly until late in 1985 was due to the fact that "[i]t hadn't spread into the general population yet." Here "general population" is more than a marker for heterosexual non-IV drug users; it is a quite specific indicator of the politics of inclusion and exclusion animating the right's response to AIDS.

For a not insignificant part of Bauer's "general population," AIDS hideously concretized still circulating stereotypes of homosexuals, linking them to contagion, the seduction and corruption of youth, sexual excess, pathos, and early death. Now it was claimed that homosexuality, once merely repugnant, was in fact lethal, and the repression of GLBT civil rights was recast as a public health issue. Jesse Helms repeatedly and aggressively sought to twin homosexuality with AIDS – from his 1987 call for the federal quarantine of the HIV positive, to his 1989 amending of a federal AIDS bill that outlawed any educational materials which could be taken to "promote, encourage, or condone homo-sexual sexual activities." In an exceptionally clear instance of his regular confla-tion of homosexuality with AIDS, Helms said on the Senate floor on June 23, 1989, "Mr. President, instead of denouncing the homosexual 'lifestyle,' count-less politicians, some in this Chamber, fall in line with a repugnant organized political movement – and that is what it is – attempting to persuade the Ameri-can people that this is a desirable way to conduct their lives. . . . In the mean-time, thousands more in this country will continue to die from AIDS while the homosexuals continue to proclaim the virtues of their perverse practices."[16] Conflating the blood-borne transmission of AIDS with vastly more contagious infections, he remarked defensively, "We used to quarantine for typhoid fever and scarlet fever, and it did not ruin the civil liberties of anybody to do that."[17]

Culture wars

The active, hot phase of the culture wars began in April 1989 when Donald Wildmon, founder and director of the American Family Association and a long time advocate for conservative Christian censorship in mass media, circulated what he claims were a million copies of a letter denouncing Andres Serrano's 1987 *Piss Christ* as anti-Christian bigotry. The Christian right itself was a fairly new phenomenon at this moment, and Wildmon's activities originated barely a decade earlier, when, offended at what he took to be excessive sex and vio-lence on TV, he began a successful strategy of pressuring sponsors to withdraw from programs he deemed offensive. He founded the National Federation for Decency in 1977, later changing the name to the far more strategic (and less censorious sounding) American Family Association once he hit on his hard-to-impeach tactic of protest in the name of "family values" and defenseless chil-dren. Seeking to control public discourse through appeal to governing authorities on such "moral" grounds proved to be a brilliant way of transforming a numer-ically small demographic into an overwhelming pressure group – and it was precisely this tactic that Helms borrowed and introduced into the culture wars. By 1981, Wildmon had teamed up with Jerry Falwell of the far larger Christian-Right political lobby called the Moral Majority in a short-lived alliance, and by mid decade he had hundreds of local affiliates and had raised millions of dollars. Indeed, in 1989, the year he secured the ear of the Senate and thus the nation, *AdWeek Magazine* named him "Marketer of the Year."[18] Clearly the emergence of the Christian right as a political force, and the idea that a narrowly interpreted vision of Christian ethics should be the sole arbiter of legislative merit, was born of the same forces that gave rise to the culture wars.

In Wildmon's hands *Piss Christ* was anti-Christian, a sentiment echoed by Republican Senator Alfonse D'Amato of New York. D'Amato then carried the controversy to public attention by tearing up a catalog featuring *Piss Christ* on the Senate floor. But Helms took D'Amato's issue and married it to his own, more winnable strain of homophobic obsession, transforming *Piss Christ* into a visual exemplar of post-AIDS fears about "bodily fluids" and the attendant orifices of their emergence. D'Amato, in short, handed Jesse Helms an issue he could make his own, and the latter's already ignominious record of anti-gay attacks assured a ready audience for the fireworks. *Piss Christ* was the perfect object for Helms' attacks, visualizing as it does the unholy alliance of (homo)sexuality and religion that Helms could productively wield as needed in advancing the avalanche of events that came to include the cancellation of Mapplethorpe's ironically entitled retrospective, *The Perfect Moment*. Exemplifying the pervasiveness and influence of Helms' rhetoric, in 1990, the president of the Massachusetts chapter of Morality in Media observed upon the opening of *The Perfect Moment* in Boston, "[p]eople looking at these kinds of pictures become addicts and spread AIDS."[19] Here, succinctly realized, was the crux of the issue, a stunning series of elisions now yielding the horrifying equation art=gay=AIDS.

No surprise, then, that the day *The Perfect Moment* opened in Cincinnati, the museum and its director were charged under pornography and child pornography statutes, all for exhibiting coolly formal and classicizing male nudes and a portrait of an eight-year-old that had been taken on the explicit request of his mother.[20] While artists who are not gay or lesbian were certainly caught up in the culture wars – Karen Finley and Andres Serrano most prominently – the legislative and legal consequences of the new restrictions on the arts turned on homophobia, and even these artists were made "queer." In his book on the culture wars, Dubin notes, "[m]any artists confirm that they knew the original targets were all gay and lesbian, and that Finley was moved into the condemned category only belatedly as a result of [a] negative newspaper column."[21] Indeed, this conflation of the avant-garde with homosexualities is one of the most salient aspects of the late 1980s culture wars, a clue toward what was at stake. Nor should this ascription of a generalized queerness in the homophobic attacks on the arts surprise us for displacement, at least in its original, Freudian formulation, was a central aspect of all phobias.[22]

The debate on NEA funding in the Senate helped cement the conceptual slippage between art, homosexuality, and AIDS, the terms "infecting" one another with unchecked discursive promiscuity. When the AIDS activist coalition Gran Fury sought permission to put up posters on Chicago's buses, a city alderman tried to block the move, saying it was "directed at children for the purposes of recruitment."[23] As a result of this AIDS awareness campaign, the Illinois State Senate passed a sweepingly homophobic bill prohibiting "physical contact, within a carnal, erotic, or sexual context, by members of the same sex in advertising on vehicles that carry individuals under 21."[24]

Again and again Helms hammered away at the essential equivalency of art, homosexuality, and AIDS, reanimating, zombie-like, the corpse of Robert Mapplethorpe to bear his message. How else can we explain the *Washington Times* journalist Richard Grenier's fantasy of dousing Mapplethorpe's corpse in kerosene and setting it alight?[25] The melding of art, homosexuality, and AIDS into that singular homophobic node which derailed *The Perfect Moment* is perhaps most succinctly captured by this typically un-nuanced Helmsian Senate floor oratory: "It is an issue of soaking the taxpayer to fund the homosexual pornography of Robert Mapplethorpe, who died of AIDS while spending the last years of his life promoting homosexuality."[26] In a catechism eerily reminiscent of the "commie, pinko fag" terminology of the 1950s, here we can once again glimpse the ideological work the homosexual has long been called upon to do for the right in constituting a pervasive domestic threat just as foreign threats recede.

Despite the explicit and repeated homophobic dimension to this controversy, the arts establishment was at pains to recast and contain the Mapplethorpe debate from a dangerous public referendum on homosexuality into a less off-putting narrative of a group of country bumpkins presuming to talk about art, all the while in service to naked political haymaking. Even as they attacked the Corcoran's cancellation of the exhibit, for example, the *Washington Post*'s editorial board denied that homophobia was a significant factor. And the National Gallery's celebrated director J. Carter Brown furthered the ideological isolation of Mapplethorpe in advocating a politically astute division between the gay subject matter of the photographer's work and the civil rights implications of its censorship: "We have to keep the first amendment rights apart from the controversy."[27]

Tellingly, Helm's grandstanding about the NEA was almost identical to his successful theatrics a year before, which resulted in the amending of a huge AIDS research and education bill to "[p]rohibit the use of funds provided under this Act to the Centers for Disease Control from being used to provide AIDS education information, or prevention materials and activities that promote, encourage or condone homosexual activities or the intravenous use of illegal drugs."[28] Despite the fact that the amendment thus explicitly prohibited addressing risk reduction for the two populations most affected in their own terms, the amendment passed 94 in favor and but two – Senators Weicker of Connecticut and Moynihan of New York – against. In securing that lopsided victory, Helms pioneered the instrumentalization of the "homo-visual" – the mobilization of representations of same-sex sexuality which assumed spectatorial disgust, and which he would exploit to even greater effect a year later. According to his own report in the Congressional record, Helms "received a copy of some AIDS comic books that are being distributed by the Gay Men's Health Crisis, Inc. of New York City, an organization which has received $674,679 in Federal dollars for so-called AIDS education and information. These comic books told the story, in graphic detail, of the sexual encounter of two homosexual men."[29] He then goes on to report that having obtained a copy of the book, he made additional copies for 15 or 20 Senators. "I sent each of the Senators a copy – if you will forgive the expression – in a brown envelope marked 'Personal and Confidential, for Senator's Eyes Only.' Without exception, the Senators were revolted . . ."[30]

He repeated this "brown envelope" stratagem a year later during the Mapplethorpe debates, but when the House/Senate Compromise Committee showed signs of weakening resolve in supporting Helm's amendment to the NEA appropriation, he felt sure that simply showing them Mapplethorpe's work would carry the day and – ordering the pages and "ladies" out of the chamber – proceeded to do so. Once again, the mere sight of same-sex sexuality was assumed to be sufficiently repugnant to catalyze opposition without need for rational argumentation.

Art=Gay=AIDS

Some 13 years after the culture wars, Richard Woodward of the *New York Times* could write in a review, "[i]t would be salutary to determine in what ways, if any, Mapplethorpe . . . should be considered [a] political artist . . ."[31] A sanguine index of how far we've come since the late 1980s, this query is also an index of what we've lost, not least the inherently political dimension of an unapologetically gay art. From the start of his career, Mapplethorpe deliberately sought to frame his own sexuality, to put on a pedestal (sometimes literally) images that refused legibility outside of the context of an explicit gay male subculture. In deliberately foreclosing other interpretive matrices, Mapplethorpe was opposing the "gay" art of his day, which instead tended to work toward a multivalence that allowed it to accrue signification far outside the gay cultural nexus of its origins.

For example, an artist like Warhol may have secured gay men from Studio 54 to urinate on his canvases in the "oxidation paintings" of 1977, but, despite the resulting images' sardonic commentary on Protean Pollock myths, these "piss" paintings bear few traces on their elegantly abstracted surfaces of the damp truth of their facture. And Keith Haring's trademark cartoonish elegance was almost definitionally anti-narrative despite its easy legibility. Indeed, a serious student of gay postmodernist approaches to meaning like the cut-up techniques of William S. Burroughs, Haring deliberately sought to camouflage his authorial voice, even if the homoeroticism of the imagery is unmistakable. He reports that in the early 1980s, when he was doing his infamous subway drawings, people would constantly ask him what they meant, what he was trying to say. Seeking to avoid the question, but not wanting to appear rude, Haring devised the strategy of smilingly handing out a button with his signature radiant baby image, but saying not a word.[32]

My point is that the gay art of Mapplethorpe and the subsequent artists caught up in the culture wars was of a profoundly different sort than the gay art of Warhol or early Haring (late Haring grew more and more explicitly political), or their spiritual forbearers Robert Rauschenberg, Cy Twombly, and Jasper Johns. Broadly postmodernist, this latter, closeted generation, coming of age amidst the virulent homophobia of McCarthyism, produced an art that was made (imperfectly) discontinuous with their authorial identity in a heads down, duck and cover genuflection toward the viewer as the sole repository of meaning. Perhaps the ur "anti-Picasso," Warhol's famed wan, laconic style was in part a means of making himself obscure and unknowable, thus preventing his work from being mediated through an image of the artist and his personal obsessions. From his very first meeting with potential collectors, when he put on a blaring rock album, covered his face in a mask, and gave the collectors masks as well, the troubling of normative communicational processes has been a central Warhol tenet. Indeed, he compared himself to a mirror, visualizing his authorial persona as but a reflection of readerly investments.[33] In a similar vein, Johns, for example, could say, "I have attempted to develop my thinking in such a way that the work I've done is not me – not to confuse my feelings with what I produce. I didn't want my work to be an exposure of my feelings."[34] In a manner deeply intertwined with the tried and true self-camouflaging techniques of the closet, these gay artists' strategies refused to specify and name an authorial voice, much less locate that voice within a socio-historical context – even if, as with Warhol, they occasionally figured an explicit homoeroticism.[35] Rather, when gayness could be read off of these works – and in some instances, with effort, it could – such a reading was, like Warhol's mirror, deliberately more an index of readerly investments than anything that could be left at the authorial doorstep.

By contrast, the new gay art not only worked very hard to fuse the authorial voice with the autobiographical, but furthermore embedded that voice within an explicit socio-cultural demographic under siege. Borrowing strategies from feminist art of the 1960s and 1970s, these gay male artists no longer embraced open-ended postmodernist meaning making; rather they had something to say, and each term in that equation for authorial meaning was made stable and explicit. Theirs was a performative self-identification in and through the work – Mapplethorpe telling us that the black men in his photos were former lovers, for example, or that he photographed only those S/M scenes in which he had taken part – yielding a statement of affiliation, a speaking-as-a-gay-man.[36] By locating the artist within a specific locale and locution, this art therefore made a statement about both the artist's identity and about the place of that identity within the art world and beyond. And as we've seen, prodded by the renascent homophobia following in the wake of AIDS throughout the 1980s, the terrain of gay identity they sought to navigate was growing more and more tendentious and politicized, and thus the call to arms the work represented grew increasingly explicit.

From the beginning of his career, Mapplethorpe sought to frame, in some cases literally, aspects of gay culture a straight world worked hard not to notice. From his early reworking of gay male pornographic imagery to emphasize a same-sex kiss or male genitals – both strikingly absent from the art world of the their historical moment – to his subsequent evocation of a highly phallic man in a position of implicit penetrability, Mapplethorpe worked from what could be called a gay identitarian political perspective, one which had little use for audience-centered meaning making. His was a self-conscious and deliberately oppositional aesthetic which, like nineteenth- and early twentieth-century bohemianism, cast the artist as guide to a world the presumptive viewer knew little about. In place of the more mainstream postwar gay avant-garde's attempts to erase the distinction between artist and viewer – as in for example Rauschenberg's infamous early 1950s *White Paintings* – Mapplethorpe's work instead presumed a gulf between them, othering the viewer and placing her squarely on the side of the socio-cultural norms this work sought to interrogate and even erase. Mapplethorpe, in seeking to frame that which he wanted us to notice, thus reanimated that old avant-garde schism between audience and viewer.

The point is that Helms and company read Mapplethorpe and his cohorts perfectly accurately – that the new queer art that was the object of senatorial scorn was in fact nakedly political, fully in step with a renascent and distinctly oppositional gay politics engendered by the AIDS-driven homophobia of the moment. In response to the cynical exploitation of their lives by the likes of Helms, artists like Mapplethorpe and David Wojnarowicz – a slightly younger but equally politicized queer artist – adumbrated an authorial voice not only contiguous with their imagery, but with an entire demographic, a newly vocal queer community in the US.

But in the art world of the early 1980s, making art work into a mouthpiece was a tired strategy, redolent of hippie era political naiveté and self-delusion. Theorists of postmodernism argued that meanings were always readerly (that is, determined as much through the act of reading as through the act of writing or making), and that identity in art was itself but the citation of a widely circulated code for identity. The early years of the Reagan administration favored seemingly more sophisticated strategies that turned on the appropriation and reworking of a common visual vocabulary, such as Warhol's repetitive use of Da Vinci's *Last Supper* (itself known from prints), or Sherrie Levine's re-photographings of famous photographs. Now distanced from their origins, these historical images were indissolubly saturated both with their own original historical moment and their utility to the present, and thus made over into commentary on the process of meaning circulation. Cast thus in the role of the always already mediated, they were an implicit critique of more normative forms of aesthetic originality, which sought instead to produce itself – falsely – as self-generated.

To ventriloquize through these historical forms was to throw one's own voice, to evacuate the category of the original, self-identical statement. Using the conventions of representation to cast doubt on what they represented, they put particular pressure on the notion of the authentic, the real, and especially the sincere. In the early 1980s, earnestness in art was out and a winking acknowledgment of complicity in the "always already" (the postmodern sense of everything existing as a simulation or as a reproduction of something else equally non-original) took its place, recast as a more foursquare, more realistic, and certainly more intellectually nimble understanding of the conditions of meaning making. At its best, this admission of an inescapable imbrication became a critique of easy identity politics; at its worst, it could slip into the aesthetic equivalent of "whoever dies with the most toys wins," its cynical tone in sync with the Reagan administration's trickle-down economics.

Indeed, the articulation of identity, of the idea of the self as anchored by an authentic, self-identical authorial voice, was deemed so suspect, so suffused with false consciousness, that a even a queer critic like Douglas Crimp in a 1983 article took no note of Mapplethorpe's sexuality – which is to say his subject matter – finding the photographer to be just another old-time modernist, all slick surfaces and formal delectation.[37] Unfavorably comparing Mapplethorpe's work to Sherrie Levine's appropriations of Edward Weston photographs, Crimp championed Levine's work as critiquing "that discourse . . . in which Mapple-thorpe's photographs naively participate."[38] But by 1990, that comparison was haunting him and his subsequent commentary, "The Boys in My Bedroom," has the feel of a confession. Like the critic Craig Owen, who also came to distance himself from his own earlier postmodernist celebration of the death of the author, and concomitant inattention to identity, by the late 1980s these gay critics rediscovered the import of identity under the dual pressures of homophobia and plague, rediscovering the self at the precise moment at which their selves were under siege – when the death of the author ceased as metaphor.[39]

Ending the Silence

The culture wars, in sum, were about the end of the regime of silence that had for generations governed gay and lesbian art, not to mention lives. Alternatively understood as the closet, as maintaining aspects of oppression, or as a postmodernist decentering of the authorial voice and carrying the promise of liberation, the valence of the voice was perhaps the central issue in queer art in the eighties. As long as gayness remained in the realm of the readerly, aided and abetted by both gay artists and gay critics who could – and did – self-camouflage as intellectually and ideologically more pure and sophisticated than crude self disclosure, gay art could flourish unmolested in the US. Even Steve Rubell, the owner of Studio 54, the most famous gay bar in America, was in the closet. But post AIDS, post Helms, newly queer politics insisted on claiming agency and a key aspect of that was naming – naming both oneself and one's enemies. Whereas Cage's 1956 4'33" of silence – a piano composition in which every note, though written, was to be "played" silently – was once defining of a dominant vein of queer postmodernist, and hence readerly, art, in the 1980s universe, as ACT UP famously claimed, silence equals death.[40]

The imperative became to speak. Seeking to render the chasm of unconcern between the oppressed and the oppressor, the I and the you, ACT UP and queer rights organizations like Queer Nation engaged in campaigns of public disruption – blocking San Francisco's Bay Bridge during rush hour, interrupting mass at New York's St. Patrick's Cathedral, crashing rowdy straight bars to engage in mass same-sex kissing. The idea was to disturb daily life as we had

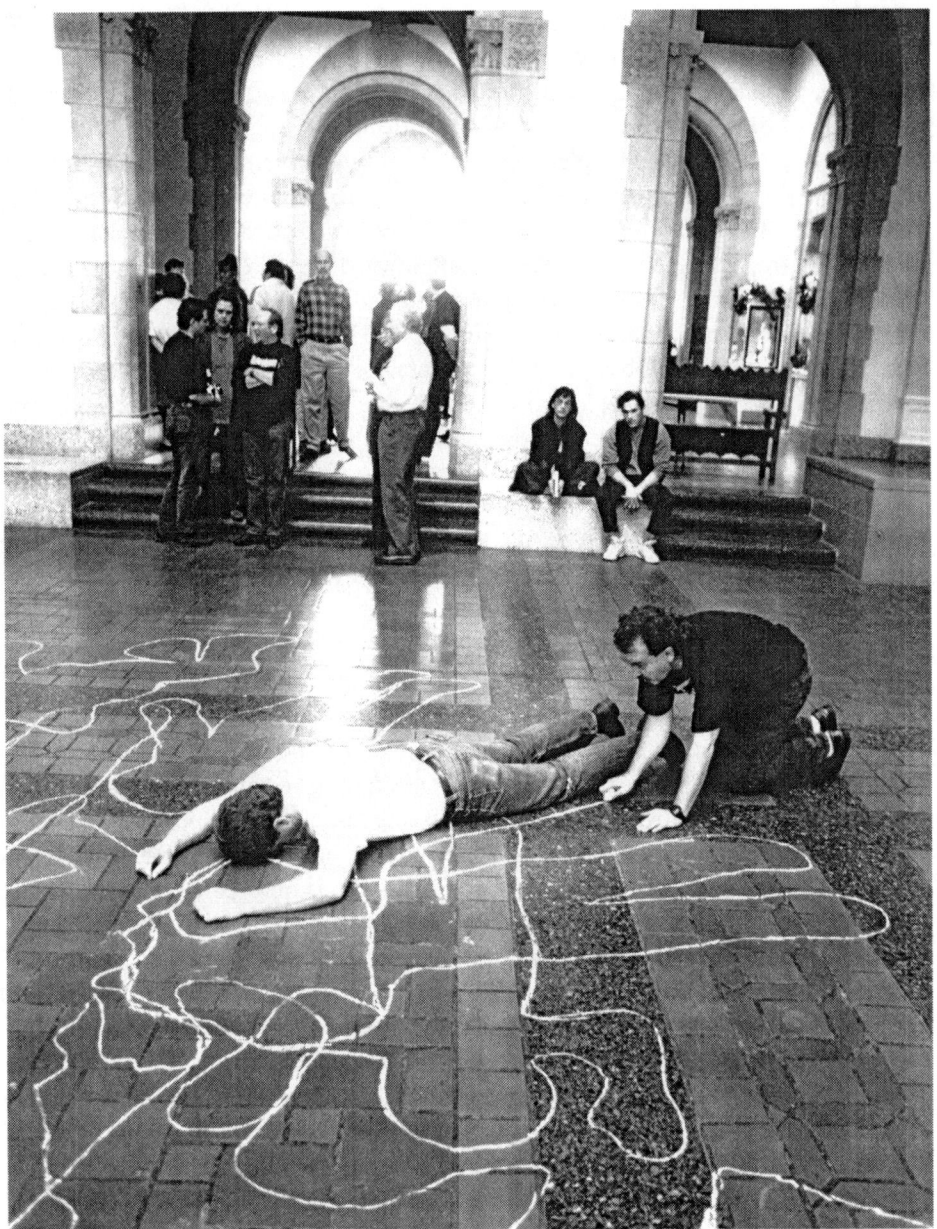

FIGURE 12.1　Rudy Lemcke, Installation at the De Young Museum, San Francisco for *World AIDS DAY/Day Without Art*, 1992. Courtesy of the artist

been disturbed, to halt business as usual, in a pale evocation of what it felt like to live as a queer under the twin plagues of AIDS and homophobia. As David Wojnarowicz wrote in one of his more famous rants: "I'm a sixteen-foot tall five hundred and forty-eight pound man inside the six-foot body and all I can feel is the pressure, all I can feel is the pressure and the need for release."[41]

In the wake of the Helms amendment (and tellingly, rarely before) many museums and galleries opened their doors to artist/activists. For World AIDS Day/Day Without Art in 1992 the De Young Museum in San Francisco invited local queer artist Rudy Lemcke to stage a die-in in the museum's neoclassical court, complete with the chalk outline of bodies inscribed on the museum's polished floor (Figure 12.1). In the highly contested 1989 exhibition *AIDS: The Artists Response*, the catalog opens to a centerfold reading in bold face: "WITH 47,524 DEAD, ART IS NOT ENOUGH. OUR CULTURE GIVES ARTISTS PERMISSION TO NAME OPPRESSION, A PERMISSION DENIED THOSE OPPRESSED/OUTSIDE THE PAGES OF THIS CATALOG, PERMISSION IS BEING SIEZED BY MANY COMMUNITIES TO SAVE THEIR OWN LIVES."[42] In a classic counter discourse, if, as Helms repeatedly claimed, art was equated with gayness and gayness with AIDS, then the art world and queers would join together to battle their common enemies.

Throughout the 1990s, as AIDS was increasingly in evidence outside of the gay community, the art/gay/AIDS catechism itself lost much of its coherence, and thus its currency. Art bashing did little useful work, for now AIDS was of little use in securing and confirming the inherent pathology of queerness. New fronts of the culture war opened with little connection to art, and by and large the issue of censorship receded. Tellingly, though, these new fronts in the culture wars were, and are still, centrally and obsessively concerned with the central term in the catechism, gay – although issues like gays in the military and same-sex marriage have assumed the place "queer" art once occupied. In the 2004 presidential election, an election that featured a national debate and 11 state referenda on same-sex marriage, 21 percent of the electorate claimed "values" as the key determinant of their vote. The fact that the culture wars remain with us, and that they remain centrally focused on same-sex sexuality, bespeaks the degree to which art censorship in the late 1980s was merely instrumental, a kind of placeholder for the real issue, homosexuality.

Notes

My thanks to undergraduate scholars Jennifer Row and Brian Hughes for their extraordinarily able research assistance. This chapter is dependent on their labors and should be acknowledged as such.

1 Colacello (1991), 461.
2 *Interview*, vol. 11, no. 12 (December 1981).
3 The use of the term avant-garde for art is a coinage of Claude Henri de Rouvroy, Comte de Saint-Simon (1760–1825), from his 1825 *De l'Organisation Sociale*. See Lamoureux in this volume.
4 Lewis (June 8, 1990), 31.
5 See Dubin (1992).
6 Moynihan (January 23, 1989).
7 This logic pointed out by Moynihan has been evidenced again in George Bush Jr.'s articulation early in his administration, following Reaganite logic, of an "axis of

evil" including North Korea and Iraq, which had to be suppressed or eradicated by American democracy. The destruction of the World Trade Towers and part of the Pentagon on September 11, 2001 served to justify Bush's construction of the world into "good" (US and allies) versus "evil" nations.

8   Dubin (1992), 16.
9   Dannemeyer (1989), 227 and 221.
10   Helms (June 23, 1989).
11   The expansion from lesbian and gay to separately articulated bisexual and transgender identities was a product of roughly this same moment in the late 1980s, as the commonality of their oppression by heteronormative forces, including Helms, became manifest.
12   According to the list of awardees requested from the NEA itself, Robert Mapplethorpe received a $15,000 individual artist grant in 1984. Curiously, at the time of the attack on the Mapplethorpe exhibition at the Corcoran, this fact was not noted. The grant is also listed in the NEA's publication *Legacy of Leadership* (2000), a booklet celebrating the thirty-fifth anniversary of the NEA with a look back at its grants and activities. It was also, nervously, confirmed by the NEA archivist's office (telephone call by the author, January 11, 2005).
13   Meyer (2002), 200.
14   Colacello (1991), 354.
15   James Boswell (1740–95), a Scottish writer whose journals are perhaps the most famous eye-witness chronicle of their time.
16   Helms (June 23, 1989).
17   Helms as cited by Crimp (1987), 262.
18   Dubin (1992), 230.
19   Butterfield (July 31, 1990), A8.
20   In 1990, after the controversy broke out, an 18-year-old McBride replicated the now infamous photo, again in the nude, for an article entitled "The War on Art," published in the *Village Voice*. The idea for the restaging was McBride's and in the article he dispelled any rumors that his posing had been anything other than voluntary and joyful. See Meyer (2003), 132–4.
21   Dubin (1992), 150.
22   Hart (1992), 1–15.
23   Pearson and Wagner (June 23, 1990), C.1.
24   Ibid.
25   Grenier (June 28, 1989), in Dubin (1992), 175.
26   Helms (September 28, 1989).
27   Kastor and Hall (September 22, 1989), 127; Brown (June 29, 1989), A24.
28   Helms in Crimp (1989), 259.
29   Ibid., 260.
30   Ibid.
31   Woodward (September 5, 2004), 24.
32   See Gruen (1991), 72–3.
33   Warhol (1975), 7. On the closeting of Rauschenberg et al. see Katz (1992).
34   Cited in Raynor (1973), 20–2.
35   See Doyle, this volume.
36   See Mapplethorpe interviewed in the 1988 documentary film *Robert Mapplethorpe*, London, Arena Films. As Mapplethorpe claimed in the film, "I was part of it,

yeah, . . . some of those experiences I later recorded I had experienced first hand, without a camera."

37 Crimp (1983), 30.

38 Ibid.

39 Crimp (1990). See Christopher Reed's brilliant account of the politics of post-modernism within the gay male art critical universe, and the impact of AIDS on their thinking (Reed 1994).

40 For more on Cage's use of silence, see Katz (2001).

41 Wojnarowicz (1991), 162.

42 Grover (1989).

References and further reading

Atkins, Robert (June 26, 1990). "Scene and Heard." *Village Voice*, p. 92.

Brown, J. Carter (June 29, 1989). "And the Corcoran Mess." *Washington Post*, p. A24.

Butterfield, Fox (July 31, 1990). "In Furor Over Photos, an Echo of the City's Past." *New York Times*, A8.

Colacello, Bob (1991). *Holy Terror: Andy Warhol Close Up*. New York: Harper Perennial.

Crimp, Douglas (1983). "Appropriating Appropriation." In *Photography: Image Scavengers*. Boston: Institute of Contemporary Art.

—— (1987). "How to Have Promiscuity in an Epidemic." In *AIDS: Cultural Analysis, Cultural Activism*, ed. Douglas Crimp. Boston: MIT Press.

—— (1990). "The Boys in My Bedroom." *Art in America*, vol. 78 (February).

Dannemeyer, William (1989). *Shadow in the Land: Homosexuality in America*. San Francisco: St. Ignatius Press.

Dubin, Stephen (1992). *Arresting Images*. New York: Routledge.

Grenier, Richard (June 28, 1989). "A Burning Issue Lights Artistic Ire." *The Washington Times*.

Grover, Jan Zita, ed. (1989). *AIDS: The Artist's Response*. Exhibition catalog, University Gallery, Ohio State University.

Gruen, John (1991). *Keith Haring: The Authorized Biography*. New York: Prentice Hall.

Hart, Lynda (1992). "Karen Finley's Dirty Work: Censorship, Homophobia and the NEA." *Genders*, no. 14 (Fall):1–15.

Helms, Jesse (June 23, 1989). *Congressional Record*, vol. 135, no. 86.

—— (September 28, 1989). *Congressional Record*, vol. 135, no. 127.

Kastor, Elizabeth, and Carla Hall (September 22, 1989). "Mapplethorpe's Aftermath." *Washington Post*, p. 127.

Katz, Jonathan (1992). *Andy Warhol*. New York: Rizzoli.

—— (1996). "Passive Resistance: On the Critical and Commercial Success of Queer Artists in Cold War American Art." *L'image*, no. 3 (Winter).

—— (2001). "John Cage's Queer Silence; or, How to Avoid Making Matters Worse." In *Writings Through John Cage's Music, Poetry, and Art*, ed. David Bernstein and Christopher Hatch. Chicago: University of Chicago Press.

Legacy of Leadership: Investing in America's Living Cultural Heritage Since 1965 (2000). National Endowment for the Arts. Washington DC (NF 2.1:L 46 GOVDOC-STK).

Lewis, Anthony (June 8, 1990). "Abroad at Home: Fight the Philistines." *New York Times*, A 31.

Meyer, Richard (2002). *Outlaw Representation: Censorship and Homosexuality in American Art*. New York: Oxford University Press.

—— (2003). "The Jesse Helms Theory of Art." *October*, no. 104 (Spring):131–49.

Moynihan, Daniel Patrick (January 23, 1989). *End of the Marxist Epoch. The New Leader*, vol. 72:9–11.

Pearson, Rick, and Paul Wagner (June 23, 1990). "Senate Votes to Ban AIDS Posters From CTA." *Chicago Tribune*, C1.

Raynor, Vivian (1973). "Jasper Johns: 'I Have Attempted to Develop My Thinking in Such a Way that the Work I've Done is Not Me.'" *Artnews*, no. 72 (March):20–2.

Reed, Christopher (1994). "Post-Modernism and the Art of Identity." In *Concepts of Modern Art*, 3rd edn., ed. Nicos Stangos. London: Thames and Hudson.

Robert Mapplethorpe (1988). London: Arena Films.

Warhol, Andy (1975). *The Philosophy of Andy Warhol: From A to B and Back Again*. New York: Harcourt Brace Jovanovich.

Wojnarowicz, David (1991). *Close to the Knives: A Memoir of Disintegration*. New York: Vintage Books.

Woodward, Richard B. (September 5, 2004). "Battleground Art: Revisiting the Culture Wars in Cincinnati." *New York Times*, p. 24.

13

Crowds and Connoisseurs: Art and the Public Sphere in America

Grant Kester

At first glance the concept of a "public art" would seem tautological. At what point in human history was art *not* a part of public discourse? In what way could the cathedrals of medieval Europe, the frescoes of the Italian renaissance, or the salons of eighteenth-century Paris not be understood as making some claim to a "public" relevance and authority? In fact, it is only possible to define a form of art that appeals to a public audience as somehow distinct during the modern period, when art as such is seen to be increasingly detached from the praxis of daily life: a self-referential and even elitist activity of concern primarily to the collector and the cognoscenti. Even then, this movement toward a privatized or insular art practice is consistently counterbalanced by a desire to connect with viewers outside the specialist precincts of the art world. How else are we to understand Courbet's use of vernacular imagery, Monet's fascination with the quotidian spaces of bourgeois life, Kandinsky's interest in folk art, the murals of Siqueiros, or the graphics of El Lissitzky? The by now routine cycle of scandal surrounding "shocking" art works, evident in the controversy provoked when Chris Ofili's cow dung painting *Holy Virgin Mary* (1996) was exhibited at the Brooklyn Museum in 2000, reminds us that even relatively esoteric forms of contemporary art can become matters of significant, if fleeting, public concern. An analysis of public art must, then, be based on a consideration of the particular conditions of modern art – from the influence of the art market, to competing forms of mass or consumer culture, to the emergence of the concept of the public itself in the early modern era.

  These historical and semantic qualifications notwithstanding, the term "public art" carries with it an obvious connotation. It refers to the creation of sculpture and murals for parks, plazas, airports, and other nominally public spaces, and funded through municipal, state, federal (and occasionally private) arts patronage. These works – the 1969 Picasso sculpture in Chicago's Daley Square or Calder's 1967 *La Grande Vitesse* in Grand Rapids, Michigan, for example – are often integrated with larger urban planning schemes.

Public art is thus linked to the history of architecture as well as a tradition of commemorative sculpture and mural painting that extends back to antiquity. The term "public art" first emerged in the United States during the late 1960s in conjunction with National Endowment for the Arts and General Services Administration initiatives such as the "Art in Public Places," "Art in Architecture," and "Percent for Art" programs. It is associated with an expansive, philanthropic view of government characteristic of the Great Society era. Early public art programs sought to ensure that the cultural good of art was equitably distributed, and not solely dependent on the (implicitly elitist) delivery mechanisms of the private art market.

Over the past three decades the field of public art has expanded dramatically to encompass an international network of artists, commissioning agencies, publications, and funding protocols. While the core belief system of public art (the idea that art should be accessible to people in their daily lives) remains intact, the movement has lost much of its ideological coherence. There are a number of reasons for this. First, in the US, the ameliorative concept of the state dominant during the late 1960s and early 1970s has been severely eroded by over two decades of concerted attack by right-wing politicians, foundations, and activists eager to demonize the state and redeem the market system as the primary mechanism of social cohesion. Art funding agencies at the federal, state, and local level have seen their budgets slashed. While innovative projects continue to be produced, public art is increasingly dependent on "partnership" arrangements with private sector entities (redevelopment agencies, tourism boards, corporations, etc.) whose definition of the public good is often politically ambivalent. Public art has become a standard urban amenity, recognizable in a now routinized landscape of neon enhanced people-movers, fiber art curtains, and generic sculpture trails. At the same time, the last 20 years have witnessed a proliferation of art projects that address audiences outside galleries and museums, with little or no reference to the conventions of traditional public art. Today we find artists working in areas as diverse as digital media, performance, and community-based practice claiming some investment in the public sphere.

The following chapter is not intended as a synoptic overview of conventional public art practice. While I examine the emergence of an institutionalized public art field during the 1960s and early 1970s I also explore the broader philosophical and political issues raised by the conjunction of "public" and "art" within the history of modernism, and the ramifications of these concerns on contemporary art. Further, in order more fully to convey the complex and contextually-specific issues raised by public art I will concentrate on developments in the United States.

The Invention of the Public

The modern concept of the public is associated with the rise of a mercantile middle class struggling for political representation against the absolutist rulers of seventeenth- and eighteenth-century Europe. It is first articulated in the work of Enlightenment thinkers such as Thomas Hobbes, John Locke, and Jean-Jacques Rousseau. In his first *Treatise of Government* (1690), Locke argues that political authority must be based on the consent of "free men," and anchored in a justification subject to reasoned consent and debate.[1] Governmental power, according to Locke, should depend not on the arbitrary will of a monarch, but on the will of the people themselves ("a collective body of men"), expressed in the form of a legislature and united by a "social contract."[2] The social contract rests on two key assumptions: the existence of a public sphere or civil society within which debate may take place among equals, and the possibility that this debate can result in the formation of a common social will. However, this scenario immediately raises questions of origin; did the "will" pre-exist civil society, or is it created (or imposed) by civil society? Is civil society the space within which this public will can be produced – an incubator, so to speak, of social consensus? Or is it the natural and organic outgrowth of an *a priori* common humanity? And if this common humanity doesn't exist how can we assume that any amount of dialogue and debate will result in a consensus?

These ontological uncertainties are complicated by a series of epistemological questions. Liberal democracy is based on a mimetic circuit that begins with an original social will that is represented by the consensus reached by civil society in the process of public deliberation. This consensus is in turn represented by the state, which engages in political decision making that is the unmediated expression of the needs and interests of civil society. In conventional (liberal) political theory it is presumed that the institutions of representative democracy constitute the self-identical voice of "the people."[3] However, in eighteenth-century Europe these institutions (civil society, the state, and the public sphere) tend to be biased toward the specific interests of the bourgeoisie (the "public" at this point consisted, of course, of property-owning white men).

The privileging of property as a precondition for public agency introduces a central tension into liberal discourse. The concept of the public challenges the stasis of social roles prescribed by divine right. The public isn't a fixed entity, but rather, a process or mode of interaction that is available to all. But this openness can be sustained only so long as it is never fully tested – so long as the public sphere is limited to like-minded members of the same, property-owning class. The public thus retains a metaphysical dimension. On the one hand it refers to a physically proximate, empirically verifiable process of social exchange and deliberation, and on the other it is an as-yet unrealized ideal, limited for now to a select few (propertied men). Property introduces a second point of tension as well. The public actor enters into political exchange with a commitment to

252 ■ ■ ■ GRANT KESTER

acknowledge and respect the differences represented by other actors, and with an implicit willingness to revise his beliefs in response to these others and on behalf of a collective good. But the possession of property is premised on an unyielding self-interest and individualism. The boundaries between the motivations of the private self of the market, and the public self of civil society are notoriously difficult to maintain.

It is precisely this tension in the relationship between self-interest and altruism, and between self and other, that leads to the emergence of the aesthetic as a central category of Enlightenment thought. In the writings of Hume, Kant, Schiller, and Shaftesbury the aesthetic comes to embody a cosmopolitan openness to difference: a willingness to set aside our normal acquisitive self-interest when confronting objects in the world and to proceed instead from the point of view of an enlightened disinterest. Under the tutelage of an aesthetic encounter we become radically open to otherness. Rather than subjecting the object to a rigorous conceptual classification we simply let it work on us in all its uncategorizable alterity. Through our interactions with works of art we learn to approach the world as such from a less instrumentalizing and self-interested perspective. We are thus prepared to participate more effectively in the public realm of democratic will-formation, which requires us to see the other's point of view, and to treat our fellow subjects not as "means to an end" but as equal interlocutors. Through aesthetic experience we intuit the existence of a common cognitive capacity and a potentially universal ground for human social exchange. This *sensus communis* is not conveyed to us from above like a divine diktat, but rather, is something we experience on the most intimate and subjective level. We *feel* the potential reconciliation of our singular selves (and the unrelenting individualism demanded by the market) and a common humanity.

The concept of the public challenges the metaphysical certainty of absolutist rule. It is precisely a non-metaphysical mode of authority that depends on the experientially specific interaction of bodies in space and the contingency of human deliberation. This somatic dimension binds the public and the aesthetic in the early modern period. This linkage is evident in the emergence of the salon, or public art exhibition, in eighteenth-century France. By the early 1700s factions within the nobility, along with rising bourgeois financial elites, were pressuring Louis XV to open the bureaucratic and institutional channels of state power to new actors and, by implication, to acknowledge the possibility that the identity of the French people might be formed independently of monarchical will. The public, as such, was not a stable, singular entity but a space of conflict and contestation, based around competing claims of political representation, self-interest, and inclusion. With the consolidation of the salon in the 1730s the commissioning and exhibiting of art became a key site in the struggle to define this nascent French public. Works of art that had previously been sequestered in palaces or churches were presented for the first time in a free and open public forum. The response to this work was no longer assumed to be simple veneration, but rather, the kind of autonomous judgment that had previously been the prerogative of royal and aristocratic authority. The collective space of the salon, as art historian Thomas Crow has demonstrated, was unique in pre-Revolutionary France, as visitors from across the range of social orders jostled for space in the grand galleries of the Louvre; not as artisan and aristocrat, but as citizen-viewers, each bearing a singular, and equally valid, opinion. "Long before liberalism could be tried out in the larger arena of political life," Crow writes, "the exhibition space provided a kind of temporary model in microcosm."[4]

The Privatization of Art

The freedom of judgment tolerated in the salon was due in part to the distance separating the objects on display (paintings of historical and mythological subjects, portraits, etc.) from the realities of daily political and social life in France. While salon works could be proximate to current social concerns, through allegorical and historical references or genre scenes for example, they were sufficiently separate to insulate the salon from the kind of policing that would have accompanied the free expression of opinions in other, more formally political, contexts. In fact it was this very distance that allowed the salon to function as a training ground for liberalism, facilitating a deliberative exchange that mirrored the process of "real" political discourse without the concrete risks and consequences. This distance reflects a crucial stage in the transition to modern art. As the work of art becomes less directly accountable to a specific patron it achieves a quasi-autonomy under the protection of the salon, which is obligated to preserve a degree of openness with regard to the specific content of work commensurate with the ideals of a liberal public sphere.

Despite their centrality during the early- to mid-nineteenth century the salon and academy were clearly intermediary institutions, marking the gradual transition from direct religious and courtly patronage to the rise of the modern art market. By the late nineteenth century the salon would become synonymous with mediocrity and a range of new movements would emerge that would view the "public" demands and standards of the academy as an intolerable constraint on individual creativity and innovation. Impressionism, with its strong links to a nascent international network of dealers and collectors, was symptomatic of this shift. The academic system, which preserved at least a notional commitment to art as a form of public culture, entitled to state patronage and subject to public adjudication, is replaced by a system of private dealers and collectors which bears a more complex, and ambiguous, relationship to the public. On one hand the market provides artists with an unprecedented level of freedom. They are no longer forced to regurgitate the hidebound conventions of past artistic practice or submit themselves to the conformist demands of academic elders jealous of their talents. On the other, it involves a process of re-privatization as the work of art is channeled through a closed network of spaces and personalities: the artist's studio, the dealer's gallery, and the collector's living room. This hardly means that Paul Durand-Ruel or Duncan Philips were latter-day Medicis, dictating color and composition to Picasso and Matisse. The modern collector was no longer buying slavish veneration, but rather the radical individuality of the artistic personality itself. The liberal cosmopolitanism of the aesthetic is projected onto the artist, who emerges as a paradigm of modern subjectivity: a creative, entrepreneurial spirit, unbound by social or artistic convention.

The prototypical work of modernist art is equally non-conformist, seeking to destabilize familiar representational modes and challenge the viewer's reliance on habitual forms of perception. As a result artists began to abandon the common formal and symbolic vocabulary that allowed salon paintings to become catalysts for collective exchange among a diverse public. This process of semantic privatization coincides with, and is complicated by, the rising power of consumer culture and mass media. During the late nineteenth and early twentieth centuries advertising, cinema, and print media began to take over many of the mythopoeic functions previously performed by high art. In fact, these two events are linked. Art discovers a new social relevance as a condition of its growing marginalization by taking on the role of *agent provocateur* hovering subversively on the periphery of mainstream culture. This is an oversimplification, of course, as even the most committed advocates of formal purity in the modernist tradition often believed that they were achieving a form of art that was more rather than less accessible. Nevertheless, there is a growing divide during the twentieth century between the work of art (understood as formally complex, unfamiliar, and even threatening) and the quotidian world of public culture. Along with it came a condescending, and at times aggressive, attitude toward the average viewer, seduced by the Platonic shadow play of realist painting or *Joe Millionaire* re-runs.

The centrality of the market to the circulation of modern art produces a kind of cognitive dissonance in which artists are compelled to demonstrate the radical difference between their creations and mere commodities. But in the very act of resisting commodification the work of art becomes subordinate to its values, only able to define itself through a process of cultural negation. If consumer culture is simplistic and ingratiating, art will be complex, critical, and aloof; if mass media is committed to a naive verisimilitude then art will be abstract and obsessively self-reflexive. The ethical pathos of modern art derives from the tension between what it promises (an aesthetic community which transcends the relentless self-interest of the capitalist system), and the fact that its continued existence as a cultural form depends on precisely this system. In a corollary manner, the modern concept of the "public" seeks to challenge aristocratic social hierarchies on behalf of a common good, even as it introduces a whole new system of social and economic hierarchies based on class. The utopian openness of the public and of art is compromised by persistent, but unacknowledged, social divisions imbedded in each concept at an *a priori* level. The dynamic relationship between utopian postulate and practical realization is a central feature of the modern avant-garde tradition. The concept of "public art" introduced during the 1960s will both perpetuate and challenge this dynamic.

The Public Re-Discovered

The gradual privatization of art during the modern period set the stage for the emergence of public art as an innovative or novel category in the late-1960s US. Public art was, of course, only one of a number of new movements that began to erode the boundaries between high art and popular culture or to move outside the gallery space. This gesture was not always populist in orientation. Earth artists such as Michael Heizer and Robert Smithson, for example, simply exchanged the cultural isolation of the museum for the physical isolation of nearly inaccessible sites in the deserts of California and Nevada. Public art, for its part, tended to be committed to making itself more, rather than less, accessible. The discourse of public art operates in three, related, registers of meaning. The first is spatial. Public art was understood as art located outside the physical precincts of sanctioned art institutions. There was a recognition here that the gallery and museum often enforce obeisance rather than open-ended inquiry. The second register of meaning concerns the viewer or audience. Rather than the self-selecting gallery-going elite, public art engages the pluralistic multitudes of the street corner, the office building, and the subway station. The third register of meaning concerns the effect of public patronage on art production. Where gallery-based art was legitimated through its appeal to the tastes of wealthy collectors or the idiosyncratic concerns of the individual artist, there was an assumption that federal or state arts funding carried with it some obligation to a broader constituency.

Although it would be left to the administration of Lyndon Johnson in the mid-1960s to organize a formal program of funding for public art, the philosophical framework was established under John F. Kennedy. In a lecture at Amherst College in 1963 Kennedy celebrated the artist as "the last champion of the individual mind and sensibility against an intrusive society and an officious state." Rather than the state dictating to the artist, the artist would educate the state, by acting as an independent, willfully individual voice of conscience ("If sometimes our great artists have been the most critical of our society, it is because their sensitivity and their concern for justice . . . makes [the artist] aware that our Nation falls short of its highest potential").[5] For Kennedy, and advocates such as his cultural advisor August Hecksher, the experience of art was understood to have a therapeutic effect on the American body politic. The artist represented the creative and intellectual freedom of the United States against the stale conformity of the Soviet Union. The critical discourse of art demonstrated the inherent superiority of American culture, while also providing a kind of inoculation against the anti-capitalist appeal of communism at the height of the cold war. This curious combination of political pragmatism and artistic romanticism led to the paradoxical concept of state-sponsored art that, at the same time, embodied a symbolic resistance to state authority.

This approach was effective in overcoming resistance to federal arts funding among members of congress who feared, precisely, the artistic meddling of an

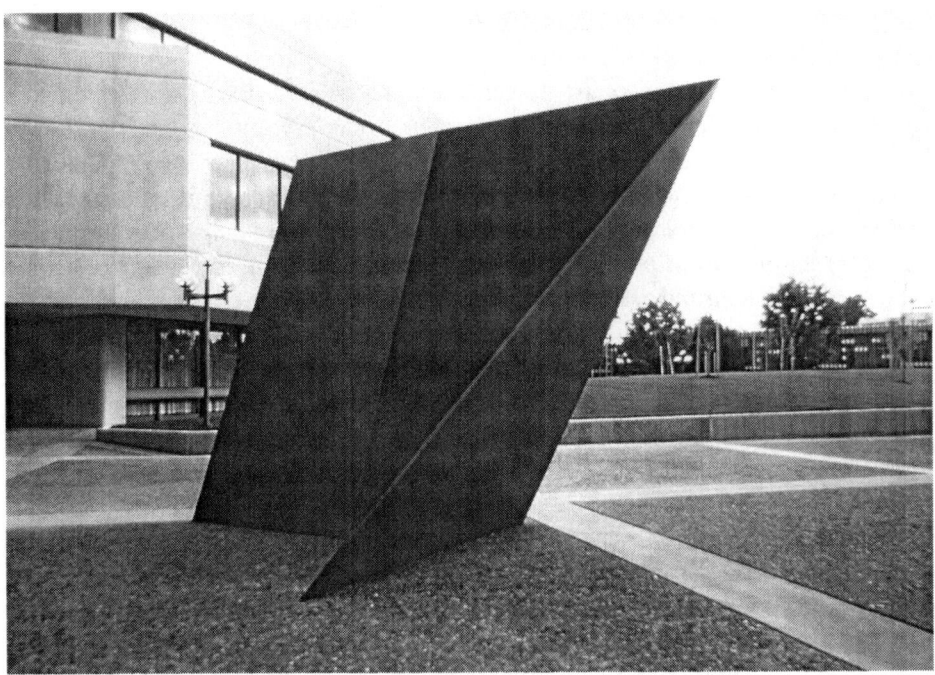

FIGURE 13.1 Robert Maki, *Trapezoid E*, 1975, Eugene, Oregon. Photograph courtesy of the artist

"officious state." However, when it came to actually funding public art under the early GSA and NEA programs, quasi-metaphysical concepts of "artistic spirit" and "personal vision" were of limited value. What, specifically, were the truths against which the artist would measure the state? What expertise justified the elevation of the artist to the post of ethical exemplar for the nation? And in what language would the "great artist" tutor American society? The answer to this final question is evident from even a cursory review of projects funded by the Art in Architecture and Art in Public Places programs during the late 1960s and 1970s. Guide books published at the time present an uninterrupted vista of stone obelisks, biomorphic blobs, jutting metal girders and angular neon; a veritable bone yard of abstraction drawn from the formal traditions of modernist sculpture. In fact, the public art programs of the 1960s were distinguished from earlier traditions of mural painting or memorial sculpture by their overt commitment to the challenging, formally complex language of avant-garde art. If artists were to be the new moral compass of the nation, they would speak to us in a vocabulary of rough-hewn granite, painted steel and poured concrete (Figure 13.1).

The predilection for abstraction has much to do with the spirit of the times. By the late 1960s abstraction had become safely canonical (via a formalist version of modern art history codified by Herbert Read, Irving Sandler, Clement

Greenberg, and others), while still retaining an aura of radical experimentation. Historian Erika Lee Doss associates the rise of abstraction with the outlook of a "well-educated, liberal cadre of arts professionals" that came to dominate early public art policy and funding.[6] This nascent subculture of artists, arts administrators, and consultants reflected the technocratic optimism of the New Frontier, as the "best and the brightest" struggled to solve recalcitrant social problems with the most up-to-date analytic tools. Doss's cadres would take the open-ended justifications for federal arts funding adumbrated by Hecksher and others and mold them into a coherent public art policy, centered around the commissioning of large sculptures and murals in plazas, federal office buildings, airports, and other public spaces. The largesse of the Art in Public Places and Art in Architecture programs soon gave rise to a new profession: the "public artist," who survives through an ongoing series of commissions, or the gallery-based artist, who is able to open up a lucrative sub-specialty in public projects. The dominant figures during the first decade of the public art movement were, with a few exceptions, uniformly committed to abstraction (e.g., Louise Nevelson, Alexander Calder, Peter Voulkos, George Rickey, Athena Tacha, Mark Di Suvero, Stephen Antonakos, Tony Smith, etc.).

Doss traces the bias toward abstraction to a complex cultural and political dynamic. Public art advocates shared the conventional modernist antipathy to realist or representational art, which was compromised by its association with the artistic traditions of fascism and Stalinism on the one hand and vulgar consumer culture on the other. Abstract art, and the very complexity of abstraction as a process, fit quite naturally with the self-image of public art professionals as an intellectual elite in command of a specialized technical language that allowed them to see the world in new ways. It represented a self-contained, ostensibly value-free system of meaning with which to improve and civilize viewers unaccustomed to the white cube of the gallery. As Doss writes:

> Modern abstract art, was seen as a great unifying force because it was seemingly apolitical and rational. Because it was non-figurative . . . abstract art could not be used to prop up any deviant political ideology. Because it concentrated on itself – on the physical properties of paint, for instance, or steel – abstract art suppressed any romantic or subjective overtones and was thus inherently reasonable. . . . The postwar elite saw abstraction as the ideal form to "cultivate" the masses.[7]

Early public art professionals sought to confront the viewer with mysterious, un-categorizable totems, set down in the midst of the banal, commercialized, urban landscape like alien spacecraft. Freed from the deadening cultural force field of the museum, Louise Nevelson's cryptic black pillars or Tony Smith's geometric steel modules would challenge the viewer's preconceptions, producing liberal, self-reflexive citizens rather than mindless drones. We encounter again here the promise of the Enlightenment aesthetic, encouraging a cosmopolitan openness to new experience. We encounter as well the belief, outlined in

Crow's analysis of the eighteenth-century salon, that the experience of art could prepare the viewer to be a more effective participant in public, political discourse. Despite these historical parallels there is a crucial difference between the galleries of the Louvre and the streets of New York, Chicago, or Seattle. The artists of the 1960s and 1970s could no longer speak to their public in the lingua franca of biblical narrative, national history, and virtuoso realism. They relied instead on the esoteric formal language of abstraction. But without the ritualized sanctity of the museum to buffer and contextualize the epistemological shock of this unfamiliar tongue, abstract works were often experienced as alienating and unintelligible.

The spatial and epistemological shift from the museum to the street revealed an underlying tension in abstraction as a public discourse during the 1960s and 1970s. On the one hand abstract public art would unite viewers into a civilizing *sensus communis* through its ecumenical formal language. On the other, abstraction was positioned as a destabilizing interruption in the semantic field of urban space, challenging the viewer's preconceptions. The latter perspective, epitomized by figures like Richard Serra, acknowledges the mythic nature of the public embraced by Doss's cadres, but can offer as an alternative only a "community" of the alienated, united by their collective inability to speak a common language. The conflict between public space as a site of coherence and unification and a site at which existing unities and identifications are called into question, is reflected in the genealogy of the public itself. It was necessary for the nascent bourgeois state to speak on behalf of all of its citizens in order to challenge aristocratic elites who sought to cloak naked self-interest in the guise of national patrimony. At the same time, this global concept of the public implied that it was possible to identify a single set of interests representing all of society, and required the imposition of a false unity on a population that was, in fact, disparate and fractious. The public, as a political construct, is defined by this Janus-faced condition.

The Boulevards of the Inner City

As suggested above, abstract public art was not always experienced as an incitement to civic dialogue. The history of the field is replete with stories of well-intentioned projects greeted with indifference, scorn and/or outright hostility (Stephen Antonakos's *Neons for the Tacoma Dome* in 1984, for example, or Serra's *Tilted Arc* in 1981).[8] By the late 1980s these controversies would catalyze a broad interrogation of the methods and imperatives of public art, and art's function in public, especially urban, space. This critique concentrated on two aspects of the established public art tradition. First, artists and historians such as Rosalyn Deutsch, Suzanne Lacy, Patricia Phillips, Arlene Raven, Martha Rosler, and Krzysztof Wodiczko questioned the ways in which the public itself was defined within this tradition. During the 1970s public art practice coalesced into a set of standardized commissioning protocols and funding bureaucracies.[9] Within this system projects were often planned by teams of artists, designers, and administrators and imposed on a given site with little reference to the specific concerns of the people who actually lived and worked there. While the artist was privileged in all of his or her exemplary individuality, the public was treated as an undifferentiated and essentially passive mass on whom a work of art would be benevolently conferred. Consultation, when it did occur, typically involved forums in which completed proposals were presented for "feedback." The only agency left to the public was the simple act of registering its approval or disapproval.

The second area of critique concerned the reliance of first-generation public artists on abstraction. It soon became evident that the vaunted complexity of abstraction as a formal language did little to prevent abstract works from functioning at the same level of kitsch-like simplicity as the most conventional hero-on-a-horse monument. In fact, the process of formal reduction and the lack of a specific referent typical of abstract sculpture made it relatively easy for works to be transformed into municipal logos or banal advertisements for a city's commitment to high culture.

The relationship between art and public space in the 1980s was complicated by significant changes in the political economy of urban America. As capital began to flow back into cities for the first time since the 1960s, vast swathes of land-banked property in Baltimore, Chicago, Cleveland, New York, San Francisco, and other cities became available for investment and redevelopment. The vacuum into which this capital flowed had been created 30 years before, as the white middle class began to abandon America's urban centers in a rush precipitated by black migration, subsidized by federal highway construction and mortgage programs, and accelerated by a series of destructive urban rebellions during the 1960s. As a result, property values and tax revenues plummeted and America's inner cities were faced with deteriorating housing stock, a disappearing job base, and a crumbling public service infrastructure. The results were entirely predictable: rising crime rates, unemployment, drug economies, and violence. Although many communities managed to thrive despite these challenges, the image of the American inner city, relentlessly portrayed in the news and entertainment media of the 1970s, was uniformly bleak, even apocalyptic.

This process of cultural abjection was a necessary precondition for the reinvestment strategies of the 1980s, which were built on a funding paradigm established during the Nixon administration. Decrying the perceived excesses of Great Society-era state intervention, Nixon sought to return decision-making (and money-spending) power to elites at the state and local level. Federal housing and urban infrastructure funds were bundled into "block grants" which required matching support from the local private sector. Inevitably, this meant involving real estate developers, bankers, corporate investors, and large property owners, who soon grasped the potential benefits of block grants in facilitating large-scale gentrification schemes.

Since block grants utilized public monies it was necessary to maintain at least the pretense that they would assist the urban poor, rather than simply provide taxpayer subsidies to already affluent corporate investors and real estate interests. In this view the state represents, and mediates among, the interests of *all* of its citizens, not just the rich and powerful. Further, the state, as the embodiment of a general public will, is obligated to challenge certain structural forces (e.g., racism, class-based access to capital, education, and business networks, etc.) that predetermine to some extent one's ability to succeed. This ameliorative view of the state was, and is, intolerable to conservatives, who argue that, far from helping to buffer its citizens from the dysfunctional effects of capitalism (cyclical unemployment and depression, downward pressure on wages and benefits, lack of corporate accountability, etc.), the state should seek every possible way to reinforce the discipline of the marketplace and to reward, rather than penalize, the wealthy.

This returns us to an underlying contradiction in the modern concept of the state or, more accurately, its bifurcation into two conflicting models. As I suggested above, the generosity of the early public sphere stood in latent conflict with the economic hierarchies of capital (imbedded in concepts of the state through the stipulation of property ownership as a precondition for citizenship). This contradiction placed ongoing pressure on the coherence of liberalism as a political ideology. In order to resolve this contradiction it was necessary to construct a political narrative in which the ownership of property, rather than being a product of contingent social and historical conditions, was instead a reflection of the individual's innate capacities. The ability to accumulate property becomes a test of one's fitness as a subject, based not on the arbitrary legacies of birth or blood, but on one's ability to extract value from nature. If some members of society are poor, homeless, or unemployed it is the result of personal failure, not an indication of a more systematic set of forces that require the adjudication of the state.

The 1980s was a period of political realignment, as the ameliorative state that came to influence during the 1960s was displaced by a conservative model of the state, embodied in the rise of Reaganism. This transition was, however, gradual and not absolute. Block grant funding made it possible to sustain the still necessary fiction of an ameliorative state while effectively turning federal funding decisions over to municipal governments that were far more responsive, and vulnerable, to entrenched economic interests. Once the linkage between the economic process of urban redevelopment and the compensatory benevolence of the liberal state was established it was possible to jettison even the nominal demand for consultation with the poor required by early block grant guidelines. This occurred through a discursive shift in which "the city" (seen as diseased or damaged) was disassociated from its actual residents. The city became an abstraction: to be reborn aesthetically, in the form of new office towers, pedestrian malls, and shopping arcades, even as its residents were being expelled by the development process.

This process explains why art, with its redemptive, quasi-spiritual associations, played such a crucial role in urban gentrification in the US during the 1980s. It provided a ready-made set of metaphors and images ("urban renaissance," and even the city itself as a "work of art") that transformed the crass, bottom-line calculations of the real-estate speculator into the ennobling cultural aspirations of a Florentine prince. The linkage between culture and commercial property investment was pioneered by real estate firms like the Rouse Company, whose festival marketplace concept was franchised in New York's Seaport Village, Boston's Faneuil Hall and, most famously, Baltimore's Harborplace. By the early 1990s the NEA, under John Frohnmayer, was giving funding for "public" art programs directly to developers such as Rouse through an Art in the Marketplace program.[10]

The basic methodology of urban redevelopment was well established by the mid-1980s. Initial experiments in Baltimore, New York, Los Angeles, and elsewhere provided a template that has been applied nationally and internationally since, and which continues to pattern uses and perceptions of urban space in the US. Public art was, from its inception, linked with real-estate development (Calder's *La Grande Vitesse*, for example, was part of an urban renewal project in downtown Grand Rapids), but it was during the 1980s that the public art genre itself was uncoupled from public funding and incorporated into the process of speculative real-estate development. A guide to commercial real estate in Washington DC, produced during the late 1980s notes that: "When shopping for space, discerning tenants of course, consider economics, location, parking, and transportation . . . But the sculptures and paintings on display can be an added enticement . . . These properties have a competitive edge, and their higher occupancy rates reflect it."[11]

It is, of course, not technically accurate to refer to art in this context as "public art," since the spaces in question were privately controlled. However, these works made use of the conventions of the public art genre (and the ameliorative associations of public space itself). The granite clad corporate atria, shopping arcades, and urban parks of America's gentrifying downtowns were filled with large paintings and sculptures, bringing the calming salve of art to people in the midst of their work-day routines. Developers were often able to trade the provision of publicly accessible amenities, such as art, for increases in the commercial footage allowed in a given building. Precisely because it was perceived as a general public good, art could be exchanged for permission to violate zoning regulations intended to place some limits on the private monopolization of space. This perception is rooted, however tenuously, in the historical function of art as an open field of cultural inquiry, free from the demands of both the market and the state, and able to provide a critical perspective on the operations of each. In the corporate public art of the 1980s this political function was decanted into a set of aesthetic protocols intended to enhance rather than question these operations.

The privatization of public art was symptomatic of a broader erosion of the institutional and spatial boundaries between the public sphere and the private sector that began under Ronald Reagan, and which continues to this day. It was Reagan who initiated the relentless drive to remove all cultural and political barriers to the imperatives of the market system (aside from an ideologically compliant faction of evangelical Christianity). The state was to abandon any critical or adjudicatory relationship to the private sector, reducing corporate oversight, eliminating all forms of public assistance that might offer a nominal alternative to low-wage labor, and privatizing its most basic functions (education, social security, and, more recently, defense). While this perspective is widely accepted in today's political culture, during the 1980s there was a stark recognition of just how damaging these changes could be.

The sense of crisis surrounding the contraction of public space precipitated by Reaganism transformed the field of public art while simultaneously inspiring a new generation of artists and collectives to locate their practice outside the gallery and the museum. We find a parallel response among artists in the United Kingdom during the 1980s, in response to Prime Minister Thatcher's attack on the public programs of the Greater London Council. The artists who emerged at this time shared a particular sensitivity to the politics of public space and a conviction that the established tradition of abstract sculpture was incapable of grasping the complex matrix of economic, political, and cultural forces at work in the post-industrial city.

Post-Public Public Art

Public art practice began to fragment during the 1980s as artists experimented with a range of new formal strategies and methodologies. Many artists sought to challenge the limitations of the dominant "plop art" paradigm (a single, sculptural object dropped into a existing plaza or other location) by demanding greater professional autonomy. By the mid-1980s artists were developing ambitious proposals for large-scale developments ranging from marine terminals and municipal waste facilities to recreational sites. In projects such as Michael Heizer's *Effigy Tumuli* in Ottawa, Illinois (1985), Scott Burton's work at the Sheepshead Bay Fishing Piers in Brooklyn (1987), and the design of the Phoenix Solid Waste Facility by Linnea Glatt and Michael Singer (1993), artists worked with teams that included engineers, architects, and designers. While this growing professionalization reflected a robust sense of ambition within the field, it also raised certain questions about public art's disciplinary boundaries, especially as artists with little or no relevant training began to encroach on the domain of the architect, the landscape architect, the planner, and the civil engineer. While these disciplines had well-established methodologies and evaluative criteria, it was not always evident what kind of expertise or technical skill justified the artist's involvement with the complexities of land-use, restoration ecology, and regional planning. Further, the default response, which was to identify the artist with the possession of a kind of globalizing, but inchoate, sense of "creativity"

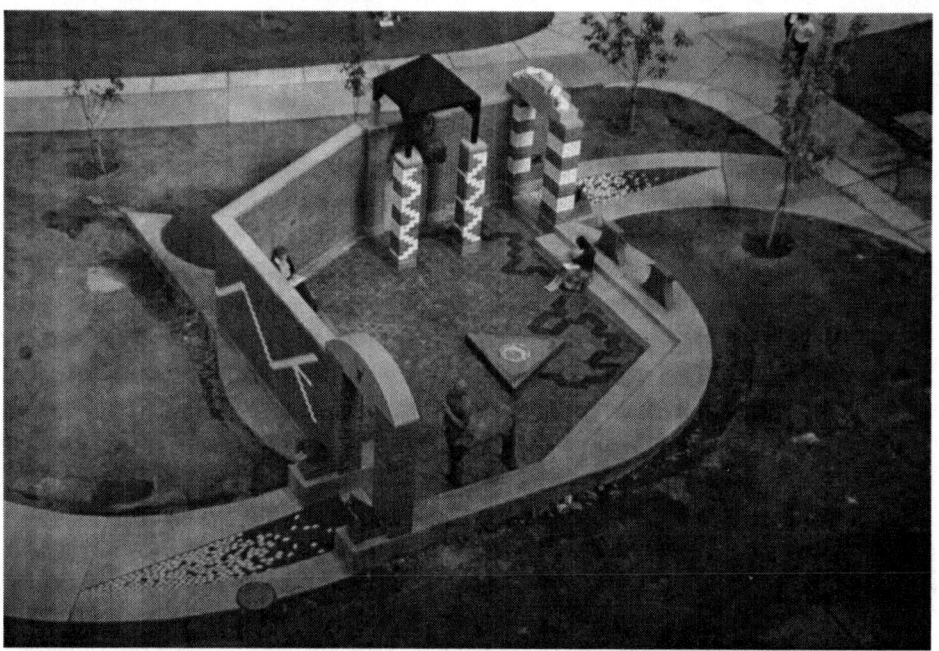

FIGURE 13.2   Andrew Leicester, *COBUMORA*, 1984. Veterinary College,
Washington State University, Pullman, Washington. Photograph courtesy of the artist

or "vision," antagonized professionals in other fields who were reluctant to
consign their own insights to the realm of banal utilitarianism.

As I noted above, abstract works sited in public space tended to devolve into
either a kitsch-like graphic simplicity or alienating opacity. The perceived failure
of abstraction led second-generation practitioners to reconsider the formal and
conceptual vocabulary appropriate to public art. Two main tendencies have
emerged since the mid-1980s, both of which attempt to reproduce the epistemological rupture characteristic of avant-garde art, without recourse to abstraction. First, we find artists synthesizing the formal experimentation of gallery-based
art with a recognizable symbolic vocabulary (often drawn from historical and
cultural references). The resulting hybrid genre is epitomized by Andrew Leicester's large-scale projects for Frostburg, Maryland (*Prospect V–III*, 1982) and
Cincinnati, Ohio (*Cincinnati Gateway*, 1988), which address local traditions
(mining, meat-packing) through quasi-architectural outdoor installations. The
intended effect is a spatial and visual history of a given locale that challenges the
reductive simplicity of conventional touristic narratives (Figure 13.2).

A second approach involves the display of text and photographic imagery via
billboards, outdoor projections, wall posters, and other two-dimensional media.
Artists such as Dennis Adams, Jenny Holzer, Barbara Kruger, and Krzysztof
Wodiczko, and collectives such as Gran Fury, Group Material, REPO History,

and David Avalos, Louis Hock, and Elizabeth Sisco sought to contest the re-privatization of public, and especially urban, space (see Figure 10.3). Influenced by the montage and agit-prop traditions of constructivism, they challenged conventional public art on a number of levels. Wodiczko's nocturnal projections, Adams' bus shelter light boxes, and Gran Fury's AIDS activism graphics circumvented the cumbersome, bureaucratized commissioning process necessary for permanent works (along with the political compromises confronting projects created in conjunction with urban renewal schemes).

As a result of these strategies these artists were able to create timely, strategic interventions in response to specific events and sites (political conventions, public policy debates, embassies, etc.). They reclaimed the urban public sphere as a space in which differences of privilege and political power could be revealed and questioned rather than suppressed. Wodiczko described this as a form of "critical" public art, designed to challenge "the city structures and mediums that mediate our everyday perception of the world." Critical public art would produce "aesthetic-critical interruptions, infiltrations and appropriations that question the symbolic, psycho-political and economic operations of the city."[12] Wodiczko operates through a process of juxtaposition. A swastika projected on the pediment of the apartheid-era South African Embassy or a padlock on a gentrified building in lower Manhattan achieve their effect through the montage of image and symbolic architecture (Figure 13.3). A similar process of appropriation occurs in Sisco, Hock, and Avalos's *America's Finest Tourist Plantation* bus posters, timed to coincide with the 1988 Super Bowl held in San Diego. The posters played on the city's smug self-appellation ("America's Finest City"), with photographic montages featuring the immigrant workers whose often invisible labor sustained its tourism-based economy.

The relationship between critical and traditional public art is more complex, and contradictory, than this outline would suggest. A fuller understanding requires us to return again to the question of abstraction as it relates to the constitution of the public. There were, as I noted above, two discursive models of abstract public art. The first relies on a universalizing notion of abstraction, able to unify a diverse public through the mythic language of ur-form. The second model identifies abstraction with the subversive rupturing of shared norms or conventions, producing a public of epistemologically enlightened, but isolated, monads. The critical public art of the 1980s and 1990s repudiates the universalizing model of abstraction, while reiterating many of the central features of disruptive abstraction. The critical public artist will expose the hidden (political and social) meaning lurking behind the kitsch-like "ideological theater" of commercialized urban space, even as the abstract sculptor will reveal the complex reality underlying the ideological simplification of realist art and consumer culture. While this is a useful and durable paradigm for art practice it also has its limits. There is no way here to imagine a shared or collective public experience that is neither naive or politically abject. And yet, embedded in the early modern concept of the aesthetic, and in the very cosmopolitanism of urban

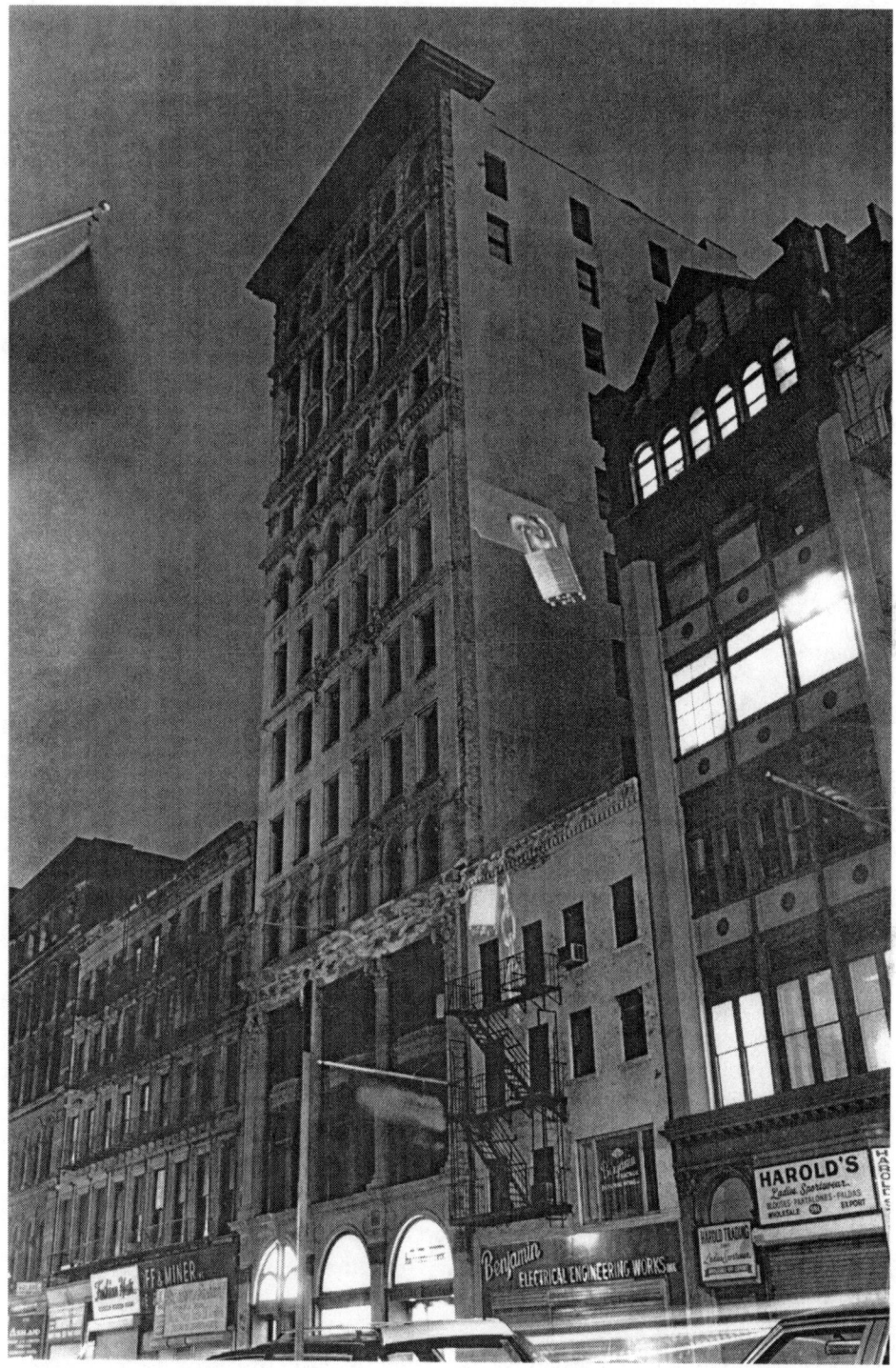

FIGURE 13.3   Krzysztof Wodiczko, *Astor Building*, 1984. Public projection held at the Astor Building of the New Museum of Contemporary Art, New York. Photograph © Krzysztof Wodiczko. Courtesy of the Galerie Lelong, New York

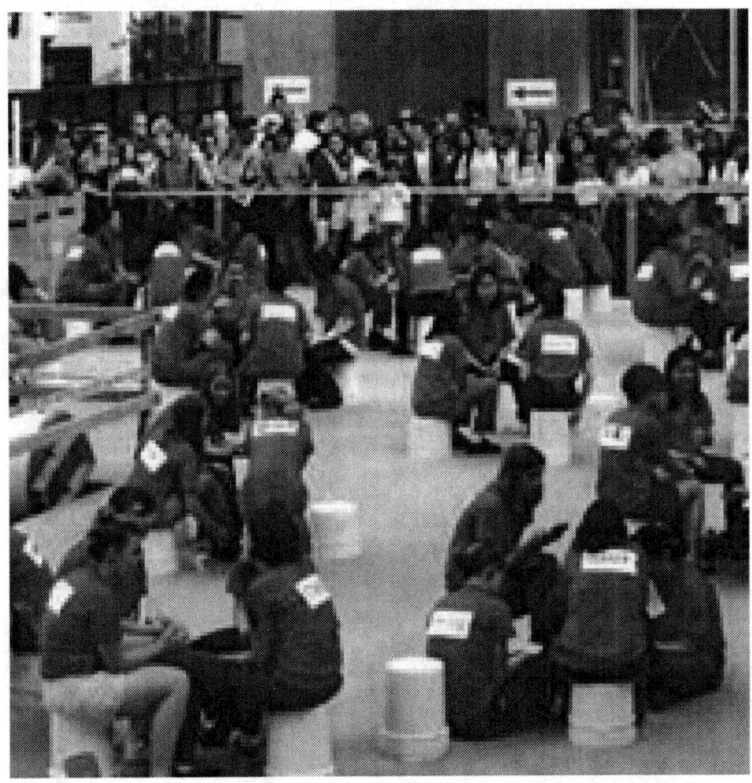

FIGURE 13.4 Suzanne Lacy with Barbara Clausen and 30 young women from Vancouver High Schools, *Turning Point: Under Construction*, 1997–8. Vancouver, Canada. Photograph courtesy of the artist

space, is the promise that we can experience our selves as part of a public or collective body while remaining open to the radical difference represented by its other constituents; that the very act of forming a public identity allows us to reflect critically on our own singularity.

The relationship between aesthetic and collective experience is central to the third area of public art practice to emerge during the 1980s. Projects by Judy Baca, Helen and Newton Harrison, Suzanne Lacy, Mierle Laderman Ukeles, and others sought to re-frame public art around forms of collaborative and participatory interaction (Figure 13.4). This "new genre" public art, to use Lacy's term, was influenced by activist and performance art traditions associated with Alan Kaprow and Joseph Beuys, as well as a history of collaborative mural painting extending back to David Alfaro Siqueiros.[13] In these projects the insights generated by the experience of collaborative interaction, often documented in a final performance or display, are an integral part of the work of art itself. Thus *Lagoon Cycle* (1974–84) and *Atempause für den Sava Fluss* (1989) by the Harrisons, were built up through a series of extended conversations with individuals involved with a given eco-system, leading to public installations that distilled those exchanges into concrete proposals for environmental remediation. Ukeles's *Touch Sanitation* (1977–80), in which she personally thanked, and shook hands with, 8,500 New York City sanitation workers, returns us to the somatic dimension of the salon described by Thomas Crow. Where both critical and traditional public art construct the viewer as the passive recipient of an aesthetic experience prepared in advance by the artist, new genre public art implicates the viewer directly in the production of the work, and in the process proposes a new model of collective interaction. At the same time, the very intimacy of this interaction exposes new genre public art to unique forms of political compromise and co-option, especially in those projects involving less privileged collaborators.[14]

By the late 1990s the proliferation of qualifiers ("critical," "new genre," etc.) necessary to contain such a diverse range of work within the umbrella of public art suggests that the term had begun to lose its heuristic value. Today a well-established practice, centered around the fabrication of large, permanent sculptures and murals (abstract and otherwise) continues to thrive, but it appears no more or less "public" than any number of other contemporary practices. Over the past decade the desire to make art relevant to people in their daily lives, or to bring the materiality of those lives into the gallery or museum, has become nearly ubiquitous. The relentless push by artists to escape the very institutions and discourses that have, for so long, allowed art to retain some autonomy in the blizzard of modern mass culture may only be a passing fad, or it may be that the condition of insular privatization against which public art first emerged some forty years ago has outlived its usefulness, and art in the twenty-first century is destined to assume a new identity. If this is the case, then the designation "public art" may one day be viewed as a historical curiosity, briefly glimpsed against the fading corona of high modernism.

Notes

1 Locke (1690/1969), 10.
2 Ibid., 168.
3 Barker (1948), 260.
4 Crow (1985), 18.
5 John F. Kennedy, cited in Wetenhall (1992), 152.
6 Doss (1995), 43.
7 Ibid., 46.
8 See Senie (2001), and Weyergraf-Serra and Buskirk (1990).
9 See, for example Phillips (1988), 92–6, and Deutsch (1996).
10 Doss (1995), 89.
11 See Kester (1989), 21.
12 Wodiczko (1987), 42.
13 See Lacy (1995).

14   See, for example, the controversy surrounding John Ahearn's "Bronx Bronzes" in 1991. Finkelpearl (2000), 81–100.

References and further reading

Barker, Sir Ernest (1948). "Introduction." *Social Contract: Essays by Locke, Hume, and Rousseau*. London: Oxford University Press.

Crow, Thomas E. (1985). *Painters and Public Life in Eighteenth-Century Paris*. New Haven: Yale University Press.

Deutsch, Rosalyn (1996). *Evictions: Art and Spatial Politics*. Cambridge, MA: MIT Press.

Doss, Erika Lee (1995). *Spirit Poles and Flying Pigs: Public Art and Cultural Democracy in American Communities*. Washington: Smithsonian Institution Press.

Finkelpearl, Tom, ed. (2000). "John Ahearn on the Bronx Bronzes and Happier Tales." *Dialogues in Public Art*. Cambridge, MA: MIT Press.

Kester, Grant (1989). "The Ruins that Profit Wrought: DC's Devastating Developments." *New Art Examiner* (June).

Lacy, Suzanne, ed. (1995). *Mapping the Terrain: New Genre Public Art*. Seattle: Bay Press.

Locke, John (1690/1969). *Two Treatises of Government*, ed. Thomas I. Cook. New York: Hafner Publishing Company.

Matzner, Florian, ed. (2004). *Public Art: A Reader*. Ostfildern-Ruit, Germany: Hatje Cantz.

Miles, Malcolm (1997). *Art, Space and the City: Public Art and Urban Futures*. New York: Routledge.

Mitchel, W. J. T., ed. (1992). *Art and the Public Sphere*. Chicago: University of Chicago Press.

Phillips, Patricia C. (1988). "Out of Order: The Public Art Machine." *Artforum* (December).

Senie, Harriet (2001). *The* Tilted Arc *Controversy: Dangerous Precedent?* Minneapolis: University of Minnesota Press.

Wetenhall, John (1992). "Camelot's Legacy to Public Art: Aesthetic Ideology in the New Frontier." In *Critical Issues in Public Art: Content, Context and Controversy*, ed. Harriet Senie and Sally Webster. Washington: Smithsonian Institution Press.

Weyergraf-Serra, Clara, and Martha Buskirk, ed. (1990). *The Destruction of* Tilted Arc: *Documents*. Cambridge, MA: MIT Press.

Wodiczko, Krzysztof (1987). "Strategies of Public Address: Which Media, Which Publics?" In *Discussions in Contemporary Culture*, no. 1, ed. Hal Foster. Seattle: Bay Press.

PART V

Identity/Subjectivity

14

The *Writerly* Artist: Beautiful, Boring, and Blue

Carol Mavor

There was a man who stood on high,
Upon a lofty wall;
And every one who passed him by,
Called out "I fear you'll fall."

Lewis Carroll, "The Headstrong Man" [1]

In 1968, the French Philosopher, Roland Barthes, wrote his short, but famed "Death of the Author." [2] Although Barthes' essay is not necessarily linked to the French student revolts (in fact Barthes felt left out of the student uprisings that almost overthrew the French government in May 1968), it nevertheless was a time of change and Barthes was a part of it. [3] The critic, the author and, in turn, the artist was "teetering on the brink," of becoming something else, of teetering off the wall, like Humpty Dumpty himself.

Critical to Anglo-American artists, art historians, and critics, "Death of the Author" marks a key turn toward the postmodern practice of "making the reader no longer a consumer but a producer of texts." [4] For Barthes, all utterances are texts (whether they exist in the form of a novel, a painting, a Citroën, a film, the face of Greta Garbo, a photograph); and he wants us to take notice of how such texts are filled with symbolic energy, which relentlessly defers a final, singular meaning. For Barthes, this free play of the signifier is not a site of frustration, but rather a space of pleasure.

As readers, we collaborate with texts and give them, not necessarily, or not only, the meaning that the author may or may not have intended, but rather those meanings that are also in tune with our individual, cultural, and historical specificities. Our role in reading, Barthes teaches us, is to be *writerly (scriptible)* rather than *readerly (lisible)*: we must write along with the author. Embracing what he understands as the inherent "performativity" of writing (resulting in a subject–subject status as opposed to the traditional subject–object status), Barthes makes good language's natural inadequacies. Reader and author both *play* as subjects, rather than the reader being *subjected to* the authorial reign of the Great Author, Author as God.[5] Barthes refuses to privilege Author over reader.

Barthes envisions writerly readers through what he famously calls the *writerly text*:

> The writerly text is. . . . *ourselves writing* before the infinite play of the world (the world as function) is traversed, intersected, stopped, plasticized by some singular system (Ideology, Genus, Criticism) which reduces the plurality of entrances, the opening of networks, the infinity of languages.[6]

As the American literary critic Jonathan Culler explains: "against a literary criticism focused on authors – interested in recovering what authors thought or meant – Barthes champions the reader and promotes literature that gives the reader an active, creative role."[7]

It is in this vein that we might consider the open lacework abstractions of Jackson Pollock, as in his beautiful *Autumn Rhythm* (1950) or *Number 1* (1948), as more writerly than readerly. The meanings of these paintings are necessarily dependent upon, and as varied as, our own individual subjectivities. Consider the critical texts that Pollock's work has given rise to. Modernist critic Clement Greenberg understands Pollock's famed splattered canvases as "advanced . . . [as the pinnacle of] painting's evolution as a modernist art . . . [as] a process of self-purification . . . [as] the unrealized Picasso."[8] In contrast to Greenberg's Pollock, Jean Baudrillard's involves rescuing the splatters as hot expressionist gestures at play with the *intangible* cold war, "a desperate, nervous, pathetic and explosive abstraction . . . the last moment of illuminated painting in the context of historical darkness."[9] In turn, John Berger turns poetic and inward to reveal the splatters as "pictures painted on the inside walls of his [Pollock's] mind."[10]

Yet, despite such writerly interpretations of writerly work/art, Pollock's cultural reign as Author, obviously, continued to ride high even after his death in 1956, as is evident in Andy Warhol's 1962 quip to art dealer Ivan Karp: "You mean I don't have to drip?"[11] Likewise, and in a continuum of Authorial reign, Andy Warhol's silk-screened portraits of famous pop icons, whether they be Elizabeth Taylor, Elvis Presley, or a can of Campbell's tomato soup, shout "Warhol," despite his gesture at celebrating an Authorless approach. After all, he took his subjects from pop culture; he used a commercial art process and he made multiples of the same image. Warhol traded the once-coveted indexical "touch" of the artist for a slick surface without depth. Yet, as everyone knows, along with the stars and the soup, Warhol, too, became an instantly recognizable celebrity. Now, as a household name, "Warhol" is a kind of "Pollock" in his own mass-produced fashion.

In sum, the arguments that proved to be so deeply influential from "Death of the Author" inherently produce endless *contradictions* that themselves must be embraced by the writerly reader: they are part of the *play*.

Must a Name Mean Something?

The French philosopher Michel Foucault jumped to the task of, perhaps, being a *writerly reader* in 1969 when he wrote a response to Barthes' "Death of the Author": the very influential essay entitled "What is an Author?"[12] In this essay, Foucault emphasizes the historical changes that have taken place over the centuries between author and the text: from the earliest authorless sacred texts to the rise of authorship in the eighteenth century, the period which secured literature as *authored* and science as the product of *anonymous objectivity*. This entrenching of authorship with writing was the corollary, according to Foucault, of punishing authors for their transgressive thinking. As a result, critical theory was developed, so as to snatch up and cinch what was understood as *simply* the missing links between text and life.

This psychobiographical approach necessarily focused on the highly problematic notion of intentionality and the overwhelming, if inaccurate, desire to read the artist in relation to his madness, his depression, his "perverse" sexuality, etc. Such stories are familiar in academic talk and popular mythologies, and to this day they remain unquestioned as the basis for the cultural discourse of Authorship. One need only to think of how many critical interpretations turn on, for example, the mother problem. Destructive mothers (whether she be cruel or too dangerously close) are behind the *myths* of the geniuses of our time: from Charles Baudelaire (too-close, then remarried and left her adolescent son rejected and angry) to Jackson Pollock (cruel), Andy Warhol (meddling, embellishing her son's art with her whimsical penmanship and drawings, even signing his commercial illustrations into the 1960s), and, certainly, Barthes (tied him to her apron strings, verged on mother-lover). Mothers aside (at least for now), Barthes writes:

> The image of literature to be found in ordinary culture is tyrannically centered on the author, his person, his life, his tastes, his passions, while criticism still consists for the most part in saying that Baudelaire's work is the failure of Baudelaire the man, Van Gogh's his madness, Tchaikovsky's his vice. The *explanation* of a work is always sought in the man or woman who produced it, as if it were always in the end, through more or less transparent allegory of the fiction, the voice of a single person, the *author* "confiding" in us.[13]

The last fragment of Barthes' "Death of the Author," reads like this: "the birth of the reader must be at the cost of the Author." Yet many readers (blind to Barthes' subtle turns) overlook the capital "A" of Barthes' text. This is a Big mistake. When Barthes makes the Author with a capital "A" pay, its deadly taxation does not kill off the authors and artists we love (for Barthes this would be the French novelist Marcel Proust and painters like Cy Towmbly and Jackson Pollock,[14] to name just three), but rather it erases the authority that the "A" of Authorship claims. Metaphorically the Author is stripped of his policeman's badge and hat; he is no longer a member of the force, but rather one of many actors in a theater group. In this theatrical space roles are constantly on the move, characters can be changed, readers become writers: we lose track of who is speaking behind the masquerade; we are caught in a great carnival, "where masks are constantly reappearing."[15] Foucault, on stage with Barthes, imagines a utopian time when we just might shockingly ask: "What difference does it make who is speaking?"[16]

Killing or death as a necessary act to give way to performance is a recurring Barthesian theme, as in the entirety of his *Camera Lucida*, in which every picture is the death of a moment offered up to the viewer for a writerly photographic performance. (Not coincidentally, Barthes wrote *Camera Lucida*, his final book, after his mother's death and shortly before his own.[17]) As the American art historian Henry Sayre has brilliantly pointed out in his book *The Object of Performance*, performative art is linked with the kind of performative criticism that we associate with Barthes.[18] In fact, we might go so far as to say that the very story of the *supposed* shift from modernism to postmodernism that replaces Authorship/Artist with something loosely held by the word "performance" is a tale of death turned to performance. (But let us not bury the question that American Marxist literary and cultural critic Fredric Jameson asks in his pivotal book *Postmodernism, or, The Cultural Logic of Late Capitalism*: Is postmodernism nothing more than a continuum of high modernism?[19])

Many of the postmodern artist/authors – if we choose to locate this shift somewhere in the late sixties or early seventies (Sayre suggests a loose and flexible 1970[20]) – make use of photography because it is inherently authorless and infinitely reproducible. If we understand "photographicness" as dismantling the Author, and in turn dismantling the singular Great Object, the medium of photography is particularly ripe for enacting the "Death of the Author" – as is evident in the privileged use of photography by such as artists Andy Warhol, Robert Rauschenberg, Sherrie Levine, Cindy Sherman, et al. Furthermore, as Amelia Jones has so artfully described in her groundbreaking "'Presence' in Absentia: Experiencing Performance through Documentation" (1997) – all we have left of the once-present performance or body work of the 1960s and 1970s is its photographic documentation. Too young to have seen the critical performances of Carolee Schneemann, Vito Acconci, Yoko Ono, or Adrian Piper, Jones has had no choice but to write of this "explosive and important period"[21] through the Author dismantled, at least thrice: first through the work's anti-object, anti-heroic artist content, second through its anti-object, anti-heroic artist form, the ethereal medium of performance itself, and third through the performance's authorless documentation by way of photography, video, and other ephemera.

In sum, Barthes' "Death of the Author" was certainly part of the force propelling the change toward what we call postmodernism, but his text was only one card in a deck that performs the period's peculiar domino effect: cards falling and rising on both ends at once, as the movement (if it is indeed one) purposely evades beginnings, endings, and even in-betweens. Nevertheless, it is useful to turn to Allan Kaprow, one of the first performance artists of the postwar period and the inventor of Happenings, looking closely and his comment on the destruction (death?) of painting. In 1958, Kaprow wrote his famous article "The Legacy of Jackson Pollock," in which he claimed that Pollock "created some magnificent paintings. But he also *destroyed painting*."[22] It was as if painting had become so flat (Mark Rothko, Barnett Newman), so black (Ad Reinhardt), so all-over (Pollock) that the Object/Art/Painting (all in capital letters) was destroyed: performance was the inevitable outcome. Authors became little "a" authors, if only because they left no objects behind.

Given the conflicting and multiple interpretations that are often given to Pollock – as both male Artist with a capital "A," as a stepping stone to Happenings, even as an actual performance artist, producing works in which the canvas became, as Harold Rosenberg so famously wrote, "an arena in which to act"[23] – we can see the possibilities of always being a writerly reader, even when the Artist/Author does shout out with a masterly voice. Barthes seeks to keep the "a" of author (artist), written in pencil, not as a proper name, but as a subjectivity that we all already necessarily embody every time we pick up a book, every time we look at a painting.

Barthes' "author" is akin to the French psychoanalyst Jacques Lacan's notion of desire as encapsulated *not* by the unreachable Other (*Autre*), but rather by the little things that the other (*autre*) cleaves to and releases: a host of things which fall under the illusively described *objet petit a*. The writings of both Barthes and of Lacan stress that not only is the subjectivity of the author/artist always in question, but so is the subjectivity of the reader/viewer: no one escapes the fact that he/she is always decentered, like language itself. Our gaze, our subjectivity, is always made crooked and is fractured by the fact that we too are *part* of the picture, looked at from all directions. Fragmentation is inevitable.

Lacan made much of the relationship between the misrecognized image of self as whole, as if our reflection in the mirror were telling the Truth. While we might see ourselves as whole – what is in the mirror is, *in fact*, a story of misrecognition (albeit that such ego-illusion armor is necessary for survival). Birth guarantees that we are always already fragmented.

According to Lacan, then, our selves, and even our unconscious, are structured like a language: and language is as fictional as our image in the mirror. In "The Mirror Stage as Formative of the Function of the I as Revealed in Psychoanalytic Experience,"[24] amidst his famously difficult theory, Lacan makes this straightforward point: the pronoun "I" is simply an empty receptacle, which only happens to reflect whoever happens to be using it at a given time. Your "I" is also my "I": no one holds Authorship of this inadequate personal pronoun (or any pronoun for that matter); we can only haunt its parameters, just as our image haunts the mirror. It is in this way that Barthes' "Death of the Author," and even Lacan's theories of the self, become not so much radical as an abstruse form of common sense.

In 1973, the French Feminist Monique Wittig wrote her beautiful and disturbing book-length theory-poem *The Lesbian Body*, which is a revolutionary enactment of the problem of pronouns. In the body of the text, Wittig performs her "I" as always split, as holding no True place for her (as not only woman, but particularly as a lesbian woman), thereby when she writes "I"/*Je*, it is always split as J/e, as are all the pronouns throughout the book – el/les, t/u, etc. In translation, however, the *I* for J/e is italicized because the single-letter English pronoun for self cannot be split. The brutality of *The Lesbian Body* comes through not only via the tearing of the pronouns, but also the ways in which the characters, J/e and t/u, violently break each other apart with Sapphic and Dionysiac pleasure. As a result, *The Lesbian Body* is *performative* in at least two ways: one, for the ways in which the two lovers switch back and forth their dominant and submissive roles, so much so that it is impossible to trace who is eating, tearing, filling, and cutting who; and two, for its writerly form that encourages the subject–subject relationship that the lovers themselves embody, if with violence. *The Lesbian Body* performs the necessary violence in order for women to enter language: "M/y most delectable one *I* set about eating you. . . . Having absorbed the external part of your ear *I* burst the tympanum, *I* feel the rounded hammerbone rolling between m/y lips, m/y teeth crush it, *I* find the anvil and the stirrup bone, *I* crunch them, *I* forage . . ."[25] As is emphasized in all of Wittig's books, just as women are marked by gender in language (particularly in French), so are they marked in the social world, always particular, never universal as is "man."

In the 1970s, many feminists (whether they be artists, writers, or filmmakers) re-found the female body, like Hope under the lid of Pandora's jar. Sphinxes, mothers, novelists, poets, madwomen, painters, artists, artists' models, mothers, laughing Medusas – all were reborn as alive and well. The result was a big jump in the birth of writerly readers and writerly authors (who may or may not have read Barthes), who produced a feminine language as an intervention against traditional masculinist discourse. The French feminist Hélène Cixous wrote it in white ink, and showed us that the Medusa was in fact beautiful and laughing. The French feminist Luce Irigaray created her *parler femme*. Barthes' highly acclaimed student-turned-star-philosopher, Julia Kristeva, usurped the term "semiotic" from Saussurian linguistics and redefined it as a pre-Oedipal form of non-traditional language shared between mother and child, which exists before, and beyond speech. Such work struggled to articulate a new kind of authorship varied in style, subject matter, and approach, causing the German feminist Sylvia Bovenschen, in 1976, to ponder the question: "Is there a feminine aesthetic?" To this question, Bovenschen answers "yes and no," because to claim *a definable* aesthetic for the feminine might be as limiting as the singular, traditional, masculine notion of the aesthetic that her feminist vision sought to undo.[26]

In response to Bovenschen's inquiry, the Italian-American feminist Teresa de Lauretis offers the, perhaps more solid, category of a "feminist *deaesthetic*." But that was just a start too. For, in the interest of promoting further rethinking, de Lauretis ends her essay with nothing more, nothing less than an ellipse: three dots toward a writerly move, three dots that call for writerly reading. De Lauretis concludes and restarts her essay at once with these words and three dots: "and if the word [*deaesthetic*] sounds awkward or inelegant to you . . ."[27]

It is important to emphasize that these authors of feminine, or even feminist aesthetics or even feminist *deaesthetics*, found allies in texts and images that were not necessarily female and were not necessarily contemporary. For example, Irigaray, Cixous, de Lauretis, and Kristeva all have celebrated the writerly voice of Lewis Carroll: decidedly non-linear, filled with puns, puzzles, and portmanteau words. Recall Alice herself, an amazing multiple heroine who shrinks and grows her way through Wonderland as she exposes Authorial bodies as nonsense makers. Likewise, Kristeva can find the "semiotic" in early Renaissance works such as Bellini's Madonna paintings and the blue of Giotto's *Scrovegni* in the Arena Chapel in Padua.

For some artists and filmmakers, who rose as authors in the mid-1970s – like installation-artist Mary Kelly (who produced the controversial installation *Post-Partum Document*, 1973–79), critic and filmmaker Laura Mulvey (critical writer on visual culture and "the male gaze," but also producer, with Peter Wollen, of the film *Riddles of the Sphinx*, 1977), and filmmaker Chantal Akerman (who, among other films, made *Jeanne Dielman, 23 Quai du Commerce, 1080 Bruxelles* in 1975) – the work that they produced centered on the shared beauty, tedium, and clutter of domestically-centered female life – a kind of "female writing" of its own.

For example, *Post-Partum Document* documents the first seven years of Kelly's son's life from a mother's point of view. In response to Freud's prohibition of female fetishism, it exemplifies maternal fetishism. According to Freud, the fetish is solely the prerogative of men; women are often hysterics, but they are almost never festishists.[28] Kelly's work allows women the possibility of being perverts in their own right. *Post-Partum Document* is a kind of baby book gone mad with the sensibility of the archaeologist turned minimalist artist: the child's infant shirts are coupled with Lacanian diagrams on the topic of subjectivity; framed, stained paper diaper ("nappy") liners are presented with a medicalized record of every bit of food that her son had eaten that particular day; first words and writings are presented on Rosetta-like stones (Figure 14.1).

Kelly made work out of the clutter of maternal life. The American literary critic Susan Rubin Suleiman has gone so far as to suggest a linkage between the multiple, not-Authorial, feminine writerly voice of such texts with the two-fold experience of a maternally-split female body, a body that ensures life amidst disorder and clutter.[29] As is suggested by Suleiman, there is a worthy linkage between the maternal content and the maternal form that we find in the art of Kelly (as well as that of others like Mulvey and Wollen, and Akerman), and while the alarm bells of dangerous essentialism and biologism must necessarily

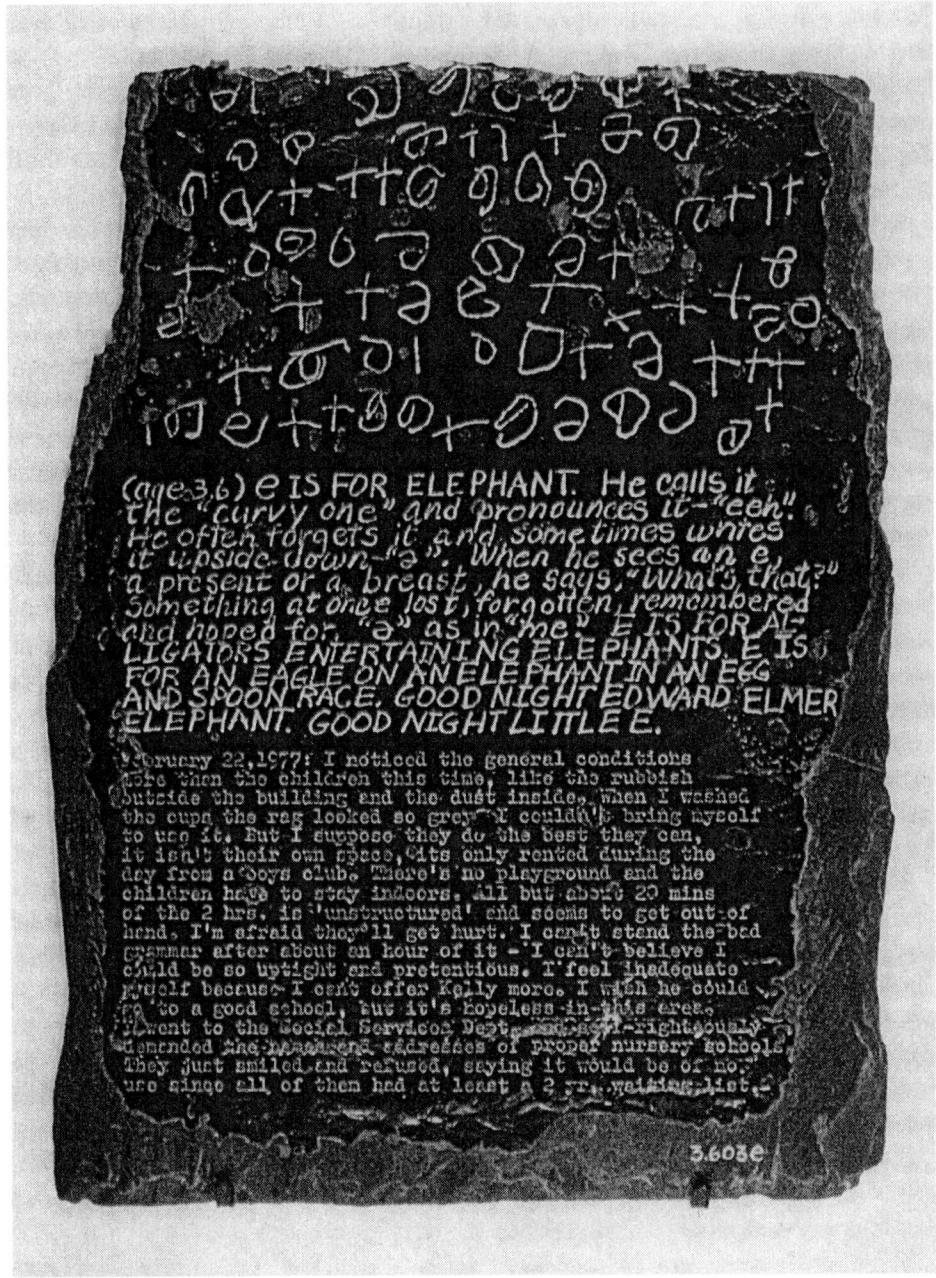

FIGURE 14.1 Mary Kelly, *Post-Partum Document*, 1973–9. Document VI, Pre-writing alphabet, exergue, and diary 1978. Detail (3.603e): One of 15 units, "E is for Elephant," 11 × 14 in. Collection, Arts Council of Great Britain

send out their warning here, let us at least remember and entertain Irigaray's useful words: "We also need to discover and declare that we are always mothers, just by being women. We bring many things into the world apart from children: love, desire, language, art, social things, political things, religious things, but this kind of creativity has been forbidden to us for centuries. We must take back this maternal creative dimension that is our birthright as women. . . ."[30]

Unlike many of the male artists who sought, Oedipally, to kill off the father figures who came before them (from Pollock's "killing" of painting to Warhol's flattened portraits of the famous and the great, including Goethe, Herman Hesse, Alexander the Great, Leonardo's *Mona Lisa*, Mickey Mouse, and Mao, pulled through the silk-screen with all the emotion and reverence given to his cans of tomato soup), select women artists of the 1970s (like Kelly, Mulvey, and Akerman) sought to keep the mother alive, while still creating their own independent works/words. How could they kill off the mother, when she had not even been given a voice in the first place?

Expanding on this trajectory of thought from Barthes through feminists such as Irigaray and Kelly, I conclude this chapter with my own performance of a writerly approach to Belgian filmmaker Chantal Akerman's important 1975 film *Jeanne Dielman, 23 Quai du Commerce, 1080 Bruxelles*. Akerman, the film itself, the character of Jeanne Dielman, the Proustian influence that feeds the film – all could not be more writerly, more beautiful, more blue. I offer this text as a *blue*print for understanding the ways in which meaning is produced as *not* coming from a centered author, whose intentions are directly embedded/reflected in the labor, but as *coming* from a complex circuit of desire circulating around texts: like the famed circular camerawork of *Riddles of the Sphinx*, like a wheel of smiles, a turn of winks, a cycle of blood, a tummy of round flesh pushed out, a dance of umbilical ribbons. Hope is out. Her spirit spawns a miniature funnel cloud of petite poetics. Spun with the desires of Akerman (and her domestic mother-housewife character Jeanne), Proust (and his domestic cook-and-sometimes-nanny-character Françoise), myself and, quite naturally, you: I, hopefully we, make a storm, but not a Storm.

Beautiful, Boring, and Blue

Each time I read A la recherche du temps perdu *right through . . . I always felt such an intimate connection with Marcel, I would speak to him in a familiar way, I'd call him "Marcel dear", the way I would a younger brother, he was almost like one of my own family with his obsessions, his secret places, the same themes he kept returning to and developing so often and so well.*

Chantal Akerman[31]

I have seen the long, slow moving *Jeanne Dielman* (clocking in at 198 minutes) over and over. I have seen this beautiful, but undeniably boring film more

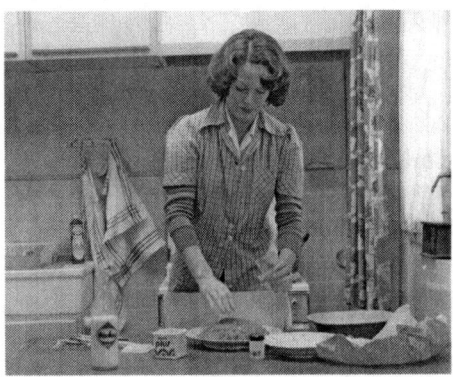

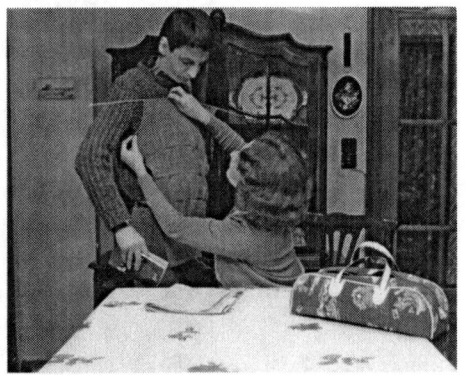

FIGURE 14.2   Chantal Akerman, still from *Jeanne Dielman, 23 Quai du Commerce, 1080 Bruxelles*, 1975. *"Slowness is the essence of tenderness."* (Cixous)

FIGURE 14.3   Chantal Akerman, still from *Jeanne Dielman, 23 Quai du Commerce, 1080 Bruxelles*, 1975. *Akerman does not sabotage our boredom by distraction*

than any other film. It changed my life; it affected me deeply. I made a habit of showing it in my courses. It affects my students deeply. With *Jeanne Dielman* before us, slowness becomes a gift. In *Vivre l'orange*, Cixous dedicates the gift of "slowness" to her "amies [friends] for whom loving the moment is a necessity." "Slowness," claims Cixous, "is the essence of tenderness"[32] (Figure 14.2). For "saving the moment is such a difficult thing, and we never have the necessary time, the slow, sanguineous time . . . that has the courage to let last."[33] Akerman has the courage to "let last." Perhaps the seed of that courage grew from reading Marcel Proust's 4,300 page labyrinth *In Search of Lost Time*. As Akerman said in a recent BBC interview: "I grew up reading Proust all my life and he is very dear to me."[34] Akerman (b. 1950) has had a prolonged relationship with Proust (1871–1922). His labor is very dear to her.

Jeanne Dielman labors, affectively, as does Proust's *Search*.[35] Both film and book share much: a passion for tedium; the comfort and horror of habit; an ability to turn boredom into pleasure; a prideful precision of exquisite detail; narrative without its classical narrative structure; an insistence on women's labor as art; an anxious regard for holding time; a talent for using color as a feminine language.

Jeanne Dielman takes place over a drawn-out period of three days. Jeanne is not only a housewife and a widowed mother of an adolescent son, she is also a part-time prostitute. Her professions are all professions that are not quite professions. As prostitute, she is affectless, robotic, and bored in *the* labor of intimacy taken to exchange. An exception to her affectlessness in bed comes at the end of this film: Jeanne, quite surprisingly, has an orgasm with one of her johns. Her pleasure, as revealed in the distress of her face, gives her great pain. So much pain, that she is driven to murdering her sleeping post-coitus john with a pair of scissors. She metaphorically kills off time-honored masculinist discourse with a tool both feminine and feminist: dressmaking scissors, with the potential of "castration."

The violence and gender trouble of Akerman's castrating Jeanne (a snip away from John, a john) hails Barthes' "Death of the Author." While *Jeanne Dielman* ends with the metaphors of castration, the "Death of the Author" begins with a castrato disguised as a woman from Balzac's *Sarrasine*. The first two lines are as follows: "In his story *Sarrasine*, Balzac, describing a castrato [a male soprano who has been castrated before puberty] disguised as a woman, writes the following sentence: '*This was woman herself, with sudden fears, her irrational whims, her instinctive worries, her impetuous boldness, her fussings, and her delicious sensibilities.*'"[36] In turn, the reader must ask: What is woman herself? And who is speaking? Woman? Man? Queer? We, as Barthes testifies "shall never know."[37] Nevertheless, Barthes (through Balzac) is consciously playing with Authorship, authorship, and gender. With the first words of his "Death of the Author," Barthes unmasks the reality that it takes violence (if metaphorical) to hear the women's voice. The birth of the writerly reader (feminine, though not necessarily female) comes as the cost of the death of the Author (masculine, though not necessarily male). So, in the high-pitched song of Barthes'/Balzac's castrato, as in the extreme language of Wittig's *Lesbian Body* and the masochistic drone of Akerman's *Jeanne Dielman*, the utterance of the other (whether she be reader, song maker, lover, mother) turns to violence to form her language/ subjectivity.

Yet, in *Jeanne Dielman*, despite sex and murder, seemingly "nothing happens"[38] – paradoxically, because nothing is left out. For example, as if Akerman were Proust masquerading as a 1970s feminist, we do not witness just the eating of the meal, we witness the meal in its entirety: its purchase, preparation, consumption, the cleaning up of the table, and the washing of *every* dish. We learn, at what cost, what it means to labor (to sing) as woman.

The tedium and the pleasure of Akerman's art (both the filming of it and the watching of it) as well as the tedium and the pleasure of Proust's art (both the writing of it and the reading of it) are mirrored in the tedium and the pleasure of domestic labor as represented in both *Dielman* and *Search*. Just as the narrator's cook, the famed Françoise, is particular about choosing the best pieces of meat and enriching it with the perfect juices when she is slowly and carefully making her exquisite *boeuf à la gelée*, so do we learn how Jeanne Dielman shops at the butcher, how she dips her veal cutlets in egg and just how she kneads (painfully massages) her ground beef into a meat loaf. Whereas I have no desire to eat a bite of any of the food made at 23 Quai du Commerce, 1080 Bruxelles (Dielman's cooking is weighed down by the heft of her gendered, lonely, middle-class life), there is much that appeals to me on Françoise's menu in the country home in Combray. The table alight with the delights of asparagus, brioche, chocolate crème, chicken, creamed potatoes, gives the lengthy meal a heavenly air suspended by the winds of winged bourgeois life, the pleasures of the Belle Epoque.

But what both Akerman and Proust portray in their texts is not so much the details of food, but rather a special love for portraying the tiny habits and gestures that make a woman's work a piece of art in long, women's time. (Kelly spent seven years at it with her *Post-Partum Document.*) As if reenacting a scene from the *Search* (but with a stark modernist approach, not so far from Kelly's *Post-Partum* minimalism), we follow Jeanne's search from store to store for the exact button to replace the one missing from her son's jacket. Just as Proust and Akerman search for just the right gesture, moment, detail to frame in their fictions, Jeanne, too, will settle at nothing less than perfection. The precision of the detail given by each artist to their loved characters of hyper-domesticity (Françoise and Jeanne) becomes a model for their own art. As Proust writes in the final volume of the *Search (Time Regained)*:

> And – for at every moment the metaphor uppermost in my mind changed as I began to represent myself [as a writer] more clearly and in a more material shape the task upon which I was about to embark – I thought that . . . under the eyes of Françoise, who like all unpretentious people who live at close quarters with us would have a certain insight into the nature of my labours . . . I should work beside her and in a way almost as she worked herself . . . and, pinning here and there an extra page, I should construct my book, I dare not say ambitiously like a cathedral, but quite simply like a dress. Whenever I had not all my "paperies" near me, as Françoise called them, and just the one that I need was missing, Françoise would understand how this upset me, she who always said that she could not sew if she had not the right size of thread and the proper buttons. And then through sharing my life with me had she not acquired a sort of instinctive comprehension of literary work . . . ?[39]

Akerman and Proust brilliantly keep the viewer/reader fascinated by everything "normally left out" of movies, novels, while using the precision of mundane domesticity as a model for their approach.[40] They bring beauty to boredom.

Just as Proust *holds* time still and at a distance with his labyrinthine sentences, *Jeanne Dielman* achieves its incredible boredom through its *held* still "shallow-boxed framing,"[41] with no reverse shots, as if life took place in a diorama or a Joseph Cornell box. The always-frontal camera angle defies the classic cinematic pattern of shot reverse shot.[42] Furthermore, the camera always stays at the same, "respectful" distance.[43] In Akerman's own words: "I didn't get too close, but I didn't get too far away." She avoids "cutting the woman in a hundred pieces . . . cutting the action in a hundred places."[44] We watch Jeanne making filtered coffee in a thermos – dutifully having a snack – repeating the customary question of her son before a meal, "Did you wash your hands?" – polishing her son's shoes – knitting – smoothing down the white towel on the bed before she gives sex to the afternoon john – lifting the lid of the clean, white soup tureen, placing the cash made from her sex work inside the bowl, placing the lid back on top – all done with the same tidiness and precision that marks her every gesture, her every move, her every habit. She is "a human metronome." Like Jeanne's thorough cleaning, there are no short cuts in Akerman's filmmaking. With "perfect mathematical inhale-exhale clarity. . . . we are made to feel the length of time . . . the number of spoonfuls it takes to eat soup."[45]

Habit, as is the case for Proust in his *In Search of Lost Time*, is both Jeanne's pleasure and the bane of her existence. As Proust informs us, "the heavy curtain of habit . . . conceals from us almost the whole universe" – or "As a rule it is with our being reduced to a minimum that we live; most of our faculties lie dormant because they can rely upon Habit" – yet, it is also the narrator's habit of turning away from reading his book, toward daydreaming "about something quite different for page after page"[46] that enables him to invest his imagination, to become a writerly reader, to become a writer.

Akerman does not sabotage our boredom by distraction (Figure 14.3); she makes it an intellectual achievement, our intellectual achievement. *Jeanne Dielman*, like the *Search*, is a writerly text, making a place for the reader/viewer, a place that de Lauretis simply calls "me."[47] By both engaging and disengaging the viewer, these works present us with a kind of pleasure that allows us to think, remember, participate in the making of the meaning of the film, the novel. As Cixous puts in her *Three Steps on the Ladder of Writing*: "A real reader is a writer. A real reader is already on the way to writing."[48]

Although Proust and Akerman cannot choose what will *not* be read, what will *not* be seen, what will be overlooked, it is this *absence* marked into the text by the reader/viewer which will send the receiver dreaming (into writing) and will enable the pleasure of the text: in Barthes' own words, "it is the very rhythm of what is read and what is not read that creates the pleasures of great narratives." Barthes reassures us that our bad reading habits are okay: "Proust's good fortune: from one reading to the next, we never skip the same passages."[49] Likewise, in seeing *Jeanne Dielman* over and over, I never see the same thing from one viewing to the next.

Jeanne Dielman is a peculiar political production, wearing its twofold desire on its French-Belgium cuff and workman's sleeve: a desire to valorize the beauty of women's labor *and* a desire to pinpoint how tedious it is. Jeanne's labor is difficult to swallow – not only because it is *not* the production of goods (for it is always the production of more work, as is in the tired cliché "a woman's work is never done") – but also because it is so relentless. It is an affective labor: its product, whether it be the care for her son, the care of the house, even the sex work for the johns who appear on her afternoon schedule, is intangible. Rather than material goods, Jeanne produces some *thing* "corporeal and affective," what Michael Hardt and Antonio Negri describe as "a feeling of ease, well-being, satisfaction, excitement, or passion."[50]

It is in this way that Jeanne's affective labor hails that of Françoise's, as well as that of Proust's *real-life* devoted, personal servant, Céleste Albaret, who provided her employer with all of the ease and well-being that she could muster during the writing of most of the *Search*.[51] Since we now live (and even more so than when *Dielman* was produced) in an age "of the informatization of produc-tion and the emergence of immaterial labor,"[52] an age where labor has been continually abstracting itself since the rise of industrialization and mechanization – so that we find the weaver's hand loom moving to the power loom and now finally to the computerization of production – immaterial labor has reached new heights. It is not just women's work that is immaterial, but almost all work. As Hardt and Negri *almost* gesture toward (mentioning, but failing to account fully for the advances of feminism): both forms of immaterial labor (the global infor-mational economy *and* what Jeanne Dielman does – what feminists have called "women's work" a labor "in the bodily mode"[53]) come at the cost of the loss of self. A fact heightened by the film's full title, addressing Jeanne Dielman as commerce itself: specifically *23 Quai du Commerce*.

While Jeanne's labor is affective, because it is bodily and immaterial, it is also "aneconomic," because it is a "gift," a problematic gift in the Derridian sense.[54] As Derrida tells us in *Given Time: I. Counterfeit Money*, economy, like time itself, is circular in nature; but the gift (though related to economy) disrupts the circle. The gift, argues Derrida, is a demand; the gift gives power to the giver and is not, despite all who claim differently, a gesture based on mutual reciprocity. When the mother gives her gift, even if with love and self-sacrifice, even if seemingly without the ego, it is nevertheless a demand. (Proust, a mother to his servants in his own inverted right, especially to Céleste, seemed to understand this well: "he gave sumptuous presents, but he would never accept them from others:"[55] this was key to his character.) Turning around the loving photograph of the boy-Barthes being held by his mother, a picture that Barthes captions as *The demand for love* – the image becomes the mother's demand for love, per-haps picturing a dangerous "maternal appetite"[56] (Figure 14.4).

In the *mise en scène* of Dielman's world, we painfully see her gift as a form of entrapment for her son *and* her self. The maternal appetite eats away at thin Sylvain and at Jeanne too, who, midway in the film, begins to find herself slipping out of her ritualistic domestic habits, tasks usually completed like clock-work. (She makes a cup of coffee and does not drink it. She kneads the meat loaf for far too long. She forgets to turn a light off. She burns the potatoes.) The maternal appetite also eats away at *Jeanne*'s viewers. Affected, we feel the prod-ucts of her labor: boredom, pleasure, perhaps even bliss (*jouissance*), frustration, terror, care.

Blue

The most striking thing in the room, apart from the cork, was the color blue – the blue of the curtains.

Céleste Albaret, Monsieur Proust[57]

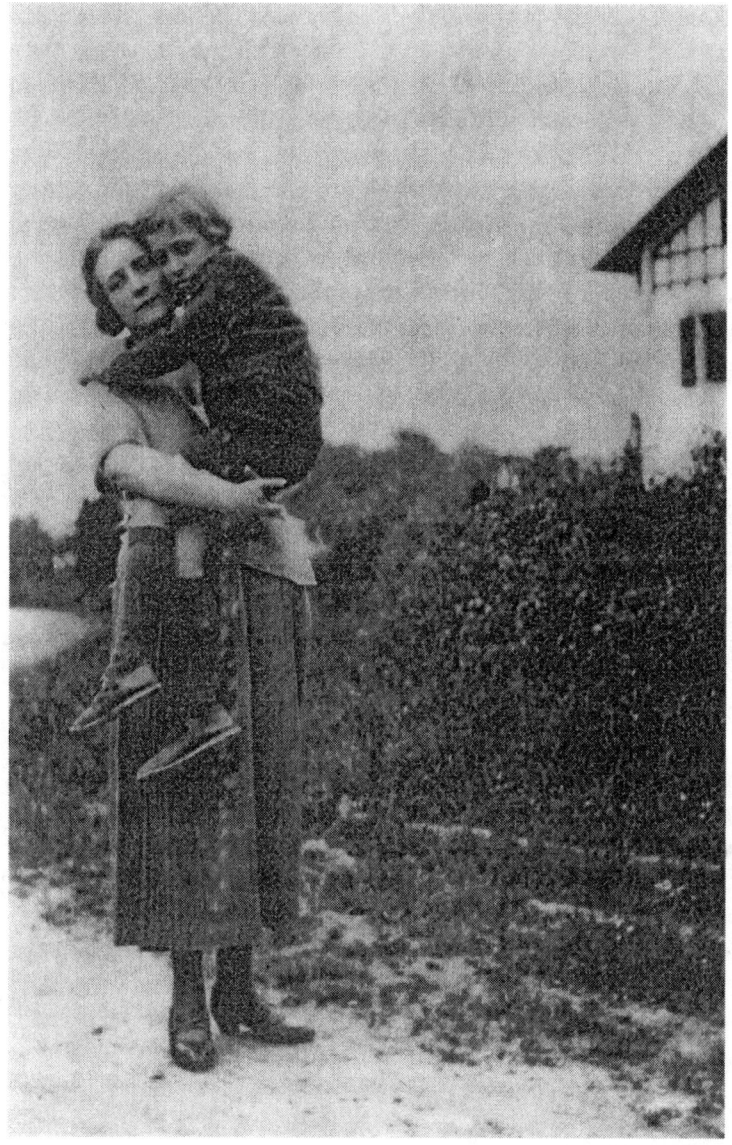

FIGURE 14.4   Family snapshot of Roland Barthes with his mother, as reproduced in
Barthes' *Roland Barthes;* . . . *the image becomes the mother's demand for love*

Throughout the film, Jeanne's mostly silent son is *colored* by the claustrophobic
interior of 23 Quai du Commerce, 1080 Bruxelles. Resonating with Roger
Caillois' 1930s discussions of animal mimicry that appeared in the surrealist
journal *Minotaure*, the son takes on the colors of *Jeanne Dielman*. Although the
film appears naturalistic, the choices of objects shot and worn participate in

a carefully controlled and limited color schema that hails the 1950s color-field work of Rothko, or the blue walls of Giotto's early Renaissance Arena Chapel frescos. Jeanne's housecoat, her sweater, the marble tiles on the bathtub wall, her radiator, her wallpaper, her robe, her bedroom wall, etc. are all in a range of toothpaste blues, which soak up the screen and are punctuated by tastes of mahogany reds and even spots of pure red that build as Jeanne begins to fall apart, culminating in the appearance of blood in the final murder scene.

I love this beautiful resonating bottom of the swimming pool color, this *hygienic* blue-green that can be found in the hospital: I call it Jeanne-Dielman blue. I understand color in Kristeva's sense as a feminine language (as in the case of Bellini's Renaissance Madonnas and Giotto's blue walls, where color sings its own song beyond figuration and narrative). Color, when handled with the shocking sensibility of Bellini, Kristeva tells us, operates "beyond and despite corporeal representation."[58] So, when seeing the overgrown boy Sylvain going to bed in Jeanne-Dielman blue pajamas, there is a kind of violence that occurs. Boredom is disrupted; we are struck by the color. Whether Sylvain has been eaten by Jeanne's maternal appetite or whether he is camouflaging himself from his mother by *giving in*, by taking on the colors of her and her home, the effect/affect is costly. "Mimicry," Caillois argues, "is the loss of. . .[self-possession], because the animal that merges with its setting becomes dispossessed, derealized, as though yielding to a temptation exercised on it by the vast outsideness of space itself, a temptation to fusion."[59]

When talking to the shoe repairman, during one of her precious excursions out, Jeanne confesses: "I don't know what I'd do without him." Yet, from all appearances, Sylvain seems to be in a constant state of imagining life without her. After Jeanne ties a wool scarf around the neck of her overgrown child (a man-boy, a Mama's boy, a feminized male adolescent) before he departs for school, we see in his eyes the look of an animal before it is let out of its cage: desire and fear. The domesticated animal (the de-clawed housecat) desires to be out, yet has little chance of survival. Latched, locked, and secured by Jeanne, who is herself caged in the role of "smother mother." Jeanne's affective labor, then, is an immaterial gift. As a result, Jeanne's gift comes, not only at the cost of self (in both a Marxist and a feminist sense), but also at the cost of profoundly alienating her son (in the aneconomic Derridian market of the gift).

Overly attached to the mother, the son hails the stereotype of the gay man in the hands of a lesbian filmmaker, who caresses the mother by giving space to her gestures. When Jeanne matter-of-factly scrubs her entire body, which leaps out from the background of turquoise blue tiles in the opening bathing scene, only to conclude by scrubbing out the bathtub with the same anarchistic intensity, turning her hand around the corner tiles with the same attention that she gave to her own breasts, I fall in love with the orderliness of Jeanne and Akerman too. As Akerman said in an interview on the making of *Jeanne Dielman:* "I give space to things which were never, almost never, shown in that way, like the daily gestures of a woman. They are the lowest in the hierarchy of film images . . . If you choose to show a woman's gestures so precisely, it's because you love them."[60] Akerman not only loves women's gestures, she loves women. "Because *Jeanne Dielman* is devoted to observing a mother in what Akerman has described as loving detail," we can understand it as "a love letter to the mother."[61]

The precision and the duration of the film's focus on Jeanne's gestures enable her habits to disable our own. After leaving the film, we return home to a sudden (almost shocking) disruptive awareness of how and when we turn the light switches on when entering and leaving a room . . . how we make a cup of coffee and whether or not we remember to drink it . . . how our shoes sound on the floor . . .how we wash our body . . . how we say goodnight to our loved one. Just as a crumb of tea-soaked madeleine, given to the grown-up Marcel by his mother, suddenly prompts forgotten memories of childhood (the first of a series of involuntary memories), so after watching *Jeanne Dielman* Jeanne becomes us. Proust writes: "This new sensation having had the effect, which love has, of filling me with a precious essence; or rather this essence was not in me, it *was* me."[62]

Boredom becomes the gift of pleasures that my long novel and my long film afford, and that is the focus of this chapter. But what makes *Jeanne Dielman* and the *Search* especially memorable? Along with a love and respect for the mother, along with incredible attention to detail through a heightened realist use of imaging within space that threatens to become real time, along with a profound sense of loss (whether it be Jeanne's identity of affected labor, or Marcel's never again attainable madeleine cake), the spot of glue that holds these excessive texts together (the *Search* and *Jeanne Dielman*) is the Jeanne-Dielman blue. Akerman's controlled use of this color makes *Jeanne Dielman* as memorable to the viewer as the *remembered* color of the enticing Gilberte's eyes become to Marcel. Yet, Gilberte's eyes are not really blue at all: they are black. But, because Gilberte had such an affect on young Marcel, they shine as memorably "too blue." Memory and affect had exaggerated their true, objective color. In the words of Proust: "whenever I thought of her, the memory of those bright eyes would at once present itself to me as a vivid azure, since her complexion was fair; so much so that, perhaps if her eyes had not been quite so black – which was what struck one most forcibly on first seeing her – I should not have been, as I was so especially enamoured of their imagined blue."[63]

Blue, I would argue, is the ultimate color of "given time": it is the color of pleasure (blue skies forever more), and the color of cost (too blue to go on). What could be more pleasurable and more full of loss than the color blue? Barthes must have realized this when he decided to begin *Camera Lucida*, not with text, but with a blue photograph: Daniel Boudinet's *Polaroïd* (1979). Womblike: a bed with a turquoise-grey pillow is nearly lost in the blue-black shadows; the light from the window is diffused by the gauzy curtains. Soaked in precious robin's egg blue, *Polaroïd* is the only color photograph among a total of 25; the others are in black and white. As Diana Knight has observed, the radiance of *Polaroïd* recalls the *remembered* color of Barthes' mother's eyes.[64]

When searching through old photographs, Barthes reminisces on the luminosity of his mother's eyes: "For the moment it was quite a physical luminosity, the photographic trace of a color, the blue-green of her pupils."[65] Blue, in the *Search*, in *Camera Lucida*, and in *Jeanne Dielman*, is the color of *affect*.

As Brian Massumi writes in his chapter "Too Blue," when the German researcher David Katz was working in the first decade of the twentieth century, he discovered that when his subjects were asked to match a color of an intimate everyday object that was out of sight the subjects inevitably "selected a color that was 'too bright to match a bright object,' 'too dark to match a dark object,' and 'too saturated to match an object which is known to have a distinct hue'." Massumi concludes: the cofunctioning of language, memory, and affect 'exaggerates' color."[66]

Derek Jarman knew all about blue as an affective color when he produced his famous film *Blue* (1993): seventy-two minutes of a beautiful, monochrome blue, inspired by the work of Yves Klein, with a moving voiceover of his farewell to the cinema. Dying of AIDs, Jarman produced this final work, in which (like Proust and like Akerman, though in a much different fashion) he will take pleasure in the little everyday things in this obsession with temporality, with death at his doorstep. As when Proust tries to remember and make use of everything in his great novel so as to hold onto time by killing it and overstuffing it like the taxidermist, by freezing it like a series of stop-time photographs taken by Muybridge, as when Jeanne tries to kill time (Figure 14.5) by murdering a john at the end of Akerman's real-time film, Jarman's blue screen (where nothing happens) is an effort to kill time with the "given time" of the color that hails it.

> I step into a blue funk . . .
> Blue flashes in my eyes . . .
> The sky blue butterfly . . .
> Sways on the cornflower . . .
> Lost in the warmth
> Of the blue heat haze
> Singing the blues . . .
> Slow blue love
> Of delphinium days . . .
> Blue stretches, yawns and is awake . . .
> Blue protects white from innocence
> Blue drags black with it . . .
> (Derek Jarman, from the script
> for his film *Blue*)[67]

The drawing of boredom as a good thing, or even a blissful thing, takes me toward the beauty of time wasted in the *Search* and *Jeanne Dielman*.[68] As Gilles Deleuze has taught me, "what constitutes the unity of . . . [the] *Search* . . ." is "not simply an exploration of memory . . . Lost Time is not simply 'time past'; it is also time wasted."[69] And this necessary wasting of time (taking us all of the

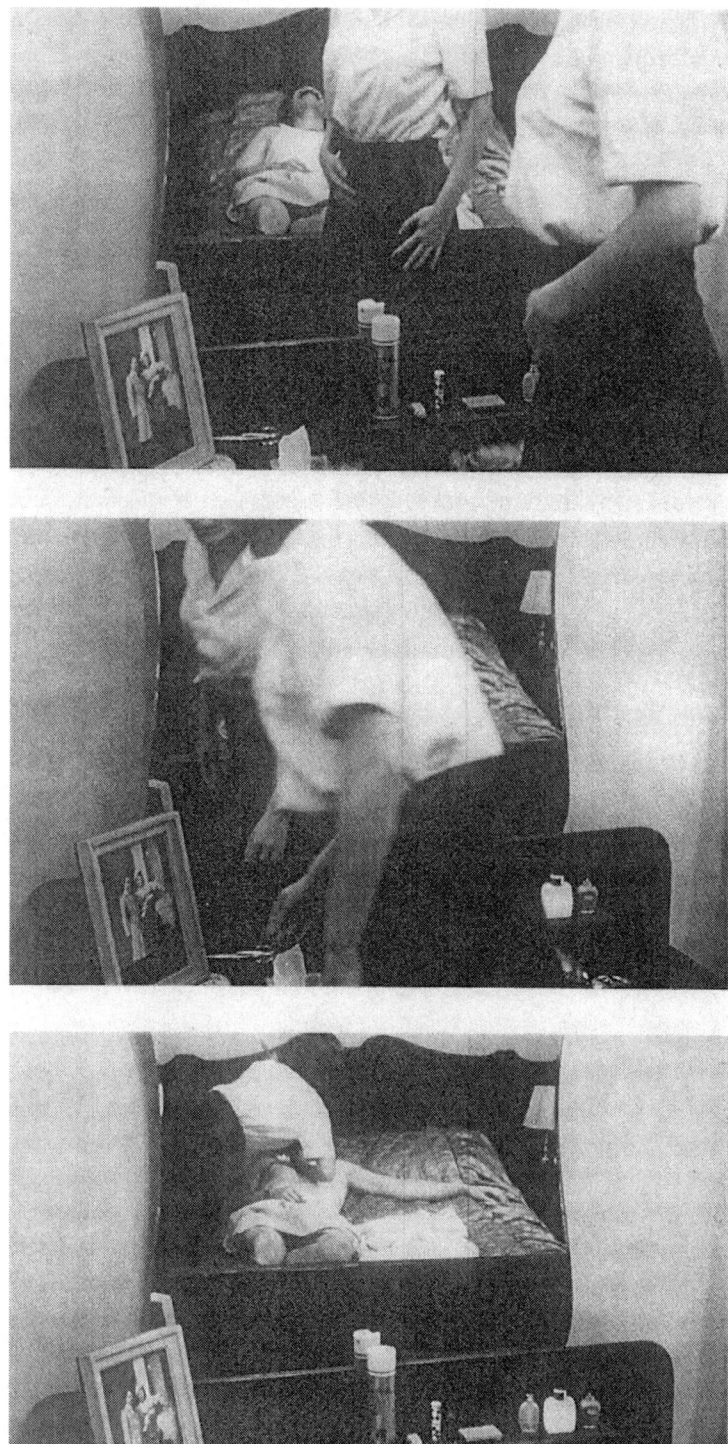

FIGURE 14.5 Chantal Akerman, stills from *Jeanne Dielman, 23 Quai du Commerce, 1080 Bruxelles*, 1975. . . . *to kill time* . . .

way to boredom), enables us without us knowing what we are doing to "pursue an obscure apprenticeship until the final revelation of 'lost time'" comes, breaks through.[70] In other words, until knowledge is enabled and allowed to intervene, bringing forth the interpretation of the sign. But this interpretation comes *long* after, not before, the experience. Interpretation postponed is repeatedly acknowledged in the *Search*: "I had recognised the taste of the piece of madeleine soaked in her decoction of lime-blossom which my aunt used to give me (although *I* did not yet know and *must long postpone the discovery* of why this memory made me so happy)."[71]

Similarly, when I was a much, much younger woman watching the tedium of Akerman's *Jeanne Dielman* for the very first time, I did not yet know and would have to long postpone the discovery the significance, the signified, of *Jeanne Dielman*. I was left with its memory, a blue souvenir that until now remained in my pocket: unsignified.

Blue Souvenir: In Lieu of an Ending

Marcel tells of the pleasure of a blue souvenir, bought for him by Gilberte, while the two were playing at the Champs-Elysées:

> I gazed at the agate marbles, luminous and imprisoned in a bowl apart. . . . Gilberte, who was given a great deal more pocket money than I ever had, asked me which I thought was the prettiest. . . . I pointed out one that had the same colour as her eyes. Gilberte took it, turned it round until it shone with a ray of gold, fondled it, paid its ransom, but at once handed me her captive, saying: "Here, it's for you. Keep it as a souvenir."[72]

In the spirit of Gilberte, I leave you with two, too-blue souvenirs. The first is the marble that Marcel believes is the same color as Gilberte's eyes: it is an affected object. The second is the affected labor of Jeanne Dielman: objectless, but also blue. But not blue like a sky or even blue in mournful song, but turquoise-blue: like hospital green, like toothpaste blue, like blue Comet for cleaning. Jeanne Dielman's beautiful blue labor scrubs away at our comfort. As Cixous writes: "the gift of pleasure brings in a return, loss . . . Really there is no 'free gift.'"[73] Marcel knew that, even when Gilberte handed him the blue agate marble and he understood himself as her "captive." Likewise, long after the last reel, long after the final one hundred and ninety-eighth minute of Akerman's too-blue film, she (a quintessence of Jeanne and Chantal) is "not in me," she is "me."

> And afterward?
> – What to write now? Can you still write anything?
> – One writes with one's desire, and I am not through desiring.
> Roland Barthes[74]

Notes

1   From Carroll's 14-stanza poem, written when he was 13, which, as Martin Gardner writes, "anticipates Humpty might fall." Gardner (2000), 220.
2   Barthes (1968/1977), 142–8.
3   Calvet (1990/1995), 163–86.
4   Barthes (1970/1974), 4.
5   Barthes (1968/1977), 147.
6   Barthes (1970/1974), 5.
7   Culler (1983), 10.
8   Greenberg (1961), 208, 212.
9   Baudrillard (1992), 23, 26.
10 Berger (2001), 16.
11 Andy Warhol to Ivan Karp as quoted in Harrison (2000), 162.
12 Foucault (1969/1979).
13 Barthes (1968/1977), 143.
14 See Barthes (1975/1994), 116.
15 Foucault (1977), 161.
16 Foucault (1969/1979), 160.
17 Barthes (1981).
18 Sayre (1989).
19 Jameson (1991), 1–2.
20 Sayre (1989), xiv.
21 Jones (1997), 11.
22 Kaprow (1958/1999), 85.
23 Rosenberg (1952/1959), 25.
24 Lacan (1966/1977), 1–7.
25 Witting (1973/1975).
26 Bovenschen (1977), 111–37.
27 de Lauretis (1987), 175.
28 Emily Apter discusses an exception to this in Freud's theory; see Apter (1991), 102.
29 Suleiman (1990), xvii.
30 Irigaray (1987/1993), 18.
31 Akerman (2000).
32 Cixous (1979/1989), 18.
33 Ibid.
34 Akerman (2001).
35 Akerman has since made a film that directly embraces Proust's novel, *La Captive* (2000), which is very loosely based on the fifth volume of the *Search* (*La Prisonnière*).
36 Barthes (1968/1977), quoting Balzac, 142. Italics in original.
37 Barthes (1968/1977), 142.
38 See Margulies (1986).
39 Proust, vol. 6 (1927/1993), 509.
40 See Indiana (1983), 56.
41 Patterson and Farber (1977), 48.
42 Margulies (1986), 68.
43 Akerman (1977), 119.

44 Ibid.
45 Patterson and Farber (1977), 49.
46 Proust (1925/1993), 732; Proust (1919/1992), 319; Proust (1913/1992), 56.
47 de Lauretis (1987), 142. For de Lauretis, films like Jeanne Dielman make "a place for what I will call me, knowing that I don't know it, and give 'me' a space to try to know, to see, to understand," 142.
48 Cixous (1993), 21.
49 Barthes (1973/1975), 11.
50 Hardt and Negri (2000), 293.
51 Albaret (2003).
52 Hardt and Negri (2000), 292.
53 Ibid., 293, noting the 1987 work of Dorothy Smith, *The Everyday World as Problematic: A Feminist Sociology.*
54 Derrida (1992), 7.
55 Tadié (2000), 407.
56 Barthes (1973/1975), 26. The photograph is reproduced and captioned as the unpaginated preface of Barthes (1975/1994).
57 Albaret (2003), 54.
58 Kristeva (1980), 243.
59 Callois, cited in Krauss (1985), 74.
60 Akerman (1977), 118–19.
61 Bergstrom (1999), 102; she is quoting Brenda Longfellow with the latter phrase.
62 Proust (1913/1992), 60.
63 Ibid., 198.
64 Knight (1997), 138.
65 Barthes (1981), 66.
66 Massumi (2002), 210.
67 Jarman (1994), 3–15.
68 For more on the possible value of boredom, see Barthes (1973/1975) as well as Phillips (1993).
69 Deleuze (1964/1972), 3.
70 Ibid., 22.
71 Proust (1913/1992), 64.
72 Ibid., 572.
73 Cixous (1975/1986), 87.
74 Barthes (1975/1994), last page (unpaginated).

References

Akerman, Chantal (1977). "Chantal Akerman on *Jeanne Dielman*: Excerpts from an Interview with *Camera Obscura*, November 1976." *Camera Obscura*, no. 2 (Fall).
—— (2000). "Interview with Director Chantal Akerman (text)." In *The Captive*. DVD, Artificial Eye.
—— (2001). Interview with David Wood. http://www.bbc.co.uk/films/2001/04/26/chantal_ackerman_the_captive_interview.shtml London: British Broadcasting Corporation, 26 April.

Albaret, Céleste (2003). *Monsieur Proust*, trans. Barbara Bray. New York: New York Review of Books.

Apter, Emily (1991). "Splitting Hairs." *Feminizing the Fetish*. Ithaca: Cornell University Press.

Barthes, Roland (1968/1977). "Death of the Author." In *Image Music Text*, trans. Stephen Heath. New York: Hill and Wang.

—— (1970/1974). *S/Z*, trans. Richard Miller. New York: Hill and Wang.

—— (1973/1975). *The Pleasure of the Text*, trans. Richard Miller. New York: Hill and Wang.

—— (1975/1994). *Roland Barthes by Roland Barthes*, trans. Richard Howard. Berkeley: University of California Press.

—— (1981). *Camera Lucida*, trans. Richard Howard. New York: Hill and Wang.

Baudrillard, Jean (1992). "Hot Painting: The Inevitable Fate of the Image," trans. Richard Miller. In *Reconstructing Modernism: Art in New York, Paris, and Montreal 1945–1964*, ed. Serge Guilbaut. Cambridge, MA and London: MIT Press.

Berger, John (2001). "Jackson Pollock." In *John Berger: Selected Essays*, ed. Geoff Dyer. New York: Pantheon Books.

Bergstrom, Janet (1999). "Invented Memories." In *Identity and Memory: The Films of Chantal Akerman*, ed. Gwendolyn Audrey Foster. Trowbridge, England: Flicks Books.

Bovenschen, Sylvia (1977). "Is There a Feminine Aesthetic?" *New German Critique*, no. 10 (Winter).

Calvet, Jean-Louis (1990/1995). *Roland Barthes: A Biography*, trans. Sarah Wykes. Bloomington and Indianapolis: Indiana University Press.

Cixous, Hélène (1975/1986). "Sorties: Out and Out: Attacks/Ways Out/Forays." In *The Newly Born Woman*, trans. Betsy Wing. Minneapolis: University of Minnesota Press.

—— (1979/1989). *Vivre l'orange* in idem, *L'Heure de Clarice Lispector* (in French and English), trans. Ann Liddle and Sarah Cornell. Paris: Éditions des Femmes.

—— (1993). *Three Steps on the Ladder of Writing*, ed. Sarah Cornell and Susan Sellers. New York: Columbia University Press.

Culler, Jonathan (1983). *Roland Barthes*. New York: Oxford University Press.

Deleuze, Gilles (1964/1972). *Proust and Signs*, trans. Richard Howard. New York: G. Braziller.

Derrida, Jacques (1992). *Given Time. I, Counterfeit Money*, trans. Peggy Kamuf. Chicago: University of Chicago Press.

Foucault, Michel (1969/1979). "What is an Author." In *Textual Strategies*, ed. J. Harari. Ithaca: Cornell University Press.

—— (1977). *Language/Counter-Memory/Practice*, ed. D. F. Bouchard, trans. D. F. Couchard and S. Simon. Ithaca: Cornell University Press.

Gardner, Martin (2000). "Introduction" and "Notes." In *The Annotated Alice: The Definitive Edition* by Lewis Carroll. Introduction and notes by Martin Gardner. New York and London: W. W. Norton and Company.

Greenberg, Clement (1961). "American-Type Painting." In *Art and Culture*. Boston: Beacon Press.

Hardt, Michael, and Antonio Negri (2000). *Empire*. Cambridge, MA: Harvard University Press.

Harrison, Helen A., ed. (2000). *Such Desperate Joy*. New York: Thunder's Mouth Press.

Indiana, Gary (1983). "Getting Ready for the Golden Eighties: A Conversation with Chantal Akerman." *ArtForum*, no. 21 (Summer).

Irigaray, Luce (1987/1993). "Body Against Body: In Relation to the Mother." In *Sexes and Genealogies*, trans. Gillian C. Gill. New York: Columbia University Press.

Jameson, Fredric (1991). *Postmodernism or, The Cultural Logic of Late Capitalism*. Durham, NC: Duke University Press.

Jarman, Derek (1994). *Blue: Text of a Film by Derek Jarman*. Woodstock, NY: The Overlook Press.

Jones, Amelia (1997). "'Presence' in Absentia: Experiencing Performance through Documentation." *Art Journal*, vol. 56, no. 4 (Winter).

Kaprow, Allan (1958/1999). "The Legacy of Jackson Pollock." Reprinted in *Jackson Pollock: Interviews, Articles and Reviews*, ed. Pepe Karmel. New York: Museum of Modern Art and Harry N. Abrams.

Knight, Diana (1997). "The Woman Without a Shadow." In *Writing the Image After Roland Barthes*, ed. Jean-Michel Rabaté. Philadelphia: University of Pennsylvania Press.

Krauss, Rosalind (1985). "Corpus Delicti." In *L'amour fou: Photography and Surrealism*. New York: Abbeville Press.

Kristeva, Julia (1980). "Motherhood According to Bellini." In *Desire in Language: A Semiotic Approach to Literature and Art*, ed. Leon S. Roudiez, trans. Thomas Gora, Alice Jardine, and Leon S. Roudiez. New York: Columbia University Press.

Lacan, Jacques (1966/1977). "The Mirror Stage as Formative of the Function of the I as Revealed in Psychoanalytic Experience." In *Ecrits: A Selection*, trans. Alan Sheridan. New York: Norton.

de Lauretis, Teresa (1987). *Technologies of Gender: Essays on Theory, Film, and Fiction*. Bloomington: Indiana University Press.

Margulies, Ivone (1986). *Nothing Happens: Chantal Akerman's Hyperrealist Everyday*. Durham, NC: Duke University Press.

Massumi, Brian (2002). "Too Blue." In *Parables for the Virtual: Movement, Affect, Sensation (Post-Contemporary Interventions)*. Durham, NC: Duke University Press.

Patterson, Patricia, and Manny Farber (1977). "Kitchen Without Kitsch." *Film Comment* (November–December).

Phillips, Adam (1993). *On Kissing, Tickling and Being Bored: Psychoanalytic Essays on the Unexamined Life*. Cambridge, MA: Harvard University Press.

Proust, Marcel (1913/1992). *In Search of Lost Time*, vol. 1, *Swann's Way*, trans. C. K. Scott Moncrieff and Terence Kilmartin, rev. D. J. Enright. New York: Modern Library.

—— (1919/1992). *In Search of Lost Time*, vol. 2, *Within a Budding Grove*, trans. C. K. Scott Moncrieff and Terence Kilmartin, rev. D. J. Enright. New York: Modern Library.

—— (1925/1993). *In Search of Lost Time*, vol. 5, *The Fugitive*, trans. C. K. Scott Moncrieff and Terence Kilmartin, rev. D. J. Enright. New York: Modern Library.

—— (1927/1993). *In Search of Lost Time*, vol. 6, *Time Regained*, trans. Andreas Mayor and Terence Kilmartin, rev. D. J. Enright. New York: Modern Library.

Rosenberg, Harold (1952/1959). "The American Action Painters." Reprinted in *The Tradition of the New*. New York: Horizon Press.

Sayre, Henry (1989). *The Object of Performance: The American Avant-Garde Since 1970*. Chicago: University of Chicago Press.

Suleiman, Susan Rubin (1990). *Subversive Intent: Gender, Politics, and the Avant-Garde*. Cambridge MA: Harvard University Press.

Tadié, Jean-Yves (2000). *Marcel Proust: A Biography*. London and New York: Viking.

Wittig, Monique (1973/1975). *The Lesbian Body*. Trans. David La Vay. Boston: Beacon Press.

15

Diaspora: Multiple Practices, Multiple Worldviews

Steven Nelson

As British painter R. B. Kitaj once insisted, diaspora, from the Greek verb *diaspeirein* (to scatter), "is as old as the hills (or caves) but new enough to react to today's newspaper or last week's aesthetic musing or tomorrow's terror."[1] The first explicit use of the term exists in *Septuagint*, the third-century BC Alexandrian translation of the Hebrew Scriptures. Aimed at the Hellenistic Jewish communities of Alexandria, the text employed diaspora as a means to describe Jews living in exile from Palestine. Even in this ancient text, diaspora suggests dislocation from a place of origin and relocation in a new setting, underscoring diaspora as not only the scattering of peoples but also an indication of their relationship to the new places they inhabit. From Los Angeles to London, Seoul to San Juan, Jerusalem to Johannesburg, Munich to Madrid, Nairobi to New York, Caracas to Calcutta, diasporas are everywhere, creating transnational communities that overlap and link with one another, changing the complexions – literally and figuratively – of their hosts.

In a world that is increasingly interdependent, and increasingly structured by international flows of capital, technology, information, and media, diaspora has taken on changed and increasingly complex significations. Diasporas not only are comprised by peoples who have been "dislocated" for centuries or millennia, but they also are constructed by newer migrants, refugees, exiles, and travelers. Today, not all diasporic peoples live in exile or dispossession. In fact, some travel quite freely between their places of origin and their new locales. Diaspora communities have also been restructured by the telephone, television, and the Internet. Instead of being fixed in a neighborhood, or *shtetl*, diasporic communities are continuously constructed though flows that keep them not only in close contact with one another, but also with their "homes."

Defining Diaspora

Diasporas are multivalent, diasporas are centers of hybridity (although not all hybrid formations are diasporic), and diasporas are spaces that, in the words of Arjun Appadurai, "[run] with, and not against, the grain of identity, movement, and reproduction."[2] W. E. B. Du Bois' 1903 exegesis on double consciousness has become a tour de force in thinking about diaspora. Du Bois also articulated in 1903 what would become a critical part of a contemporary politics of diaspora:

> The history of the American Negro is the history of this . . . longing to attain self-conscious manhood, to merge his double self into a better and truer self. In this merging he wishes neither of the older selves to be lost. He would not Africanize America, for America has too much to teach the world and Africa. He would not beach his Negro soul in a flood of white Americanism, for he knows that Negro blood has a message for the world. He simply wishes to make it possible for a man to be both a Negro and an American, without being cursed and spit upon by his fellows, without having the doors of opportunity closed roughly in his face.[3]

Such a position, such desire, such a discursive reading of identity, and, moreover, the view of subjectivity as constructed out of a number of constituent parts would be echoed in related contexts throughout the twentieth century.

These terms of Du Bois' formulation energize much of the critical work on diaspora and the kind of ongoing, even deferred subjectivity he describes has become part of the basis for thinking of diaspora vis-à-vis the nation-state. What is vital to recognize in this context is not so much Du Bois as the primordial father of diasporic identity and politics, particularly with respect to studies of the Jewish Diaspora, which, as Gilroy reminds us, constituted a blueprint for thinking through the Afro-Atlantic Diaspora.[4] Rather, the crucial point is to note the persistence of the necessity of articulating a politics in and against hegemonic structures that invoke racialized and racist discourses as a means to maintain their control over the public sphere and the lives of those living in it. These interventions strike at the heart of hegemonic discourses, at times questioning them, at times de-centering them, and always deconstructing notions of national cultures that rest upon the conflation of race, gender, sexuality, class, and belonging (such a move is readily visible in the construction of Americanness or Englishness as white, male, heterosexual, and middle class).

James Clifford characterizes qualities of diaspora quite succinctly: "history of dispersal, myths/memories of the homeland, alienation in the host (bad host?) country, desire for eventual return, ongoing support of the homeland, and a collective identity importantly defined by this relationship."[5] Diaspora as such not only encompasses movements of people, it also includes their experiences. In this way, to think about diaspora also is to think about histories of assimilation, acculturation, and hybridity. It also involves considering the existence of links that transverse national boundaries, either by the invocation of memories (real or imagined) of places of origin (i.e. "Mother Africa") and/or political, cultural, and intellectual links among members of diasporic groups (i.e. Pan-Africanism, a term for various movements that have as their goal the unity of Africans throughout the world to fight and overcome colonization and white oppression; Negritude, an affirmation of African cultural heritage that resists the domination of the west; Pan-Arabism, a movement for unification among Arab nations and peoples, etc.).

Diasporas have always been transnational in nature. Nicholas Mirzoeff suggests, "[i]n the nineteenth century, diaspora peoples were seen as a disruption to the natural economy of the nation state . . . an excess to the national need . . ." As such, diasporas were things that could not be assimilated into the body politic; they were something to "be disposed of by migration, colonial resettlement, or ultimately by extermination."[6] In contemporary terms, diasporas are still often understood as being outside of the function of the nation-state, and thus as unassimilable. In historical or contemporary terms, however, the inability to digest the diaspora within the economy of the nation-state underscores the place of diaspora as a counterpoint to the nation. In the words of Clifford, diaspora has become part of "an unruly crowd of descriptive/interpretive terms [that] now jostle and converse in an effort to characterize the contact zones of nations, cultures, and regions: terms such as 'border,' 'travel,' 'creolization,' 'transculturation,' 'hybridity'."[7] While invocations of diaspora can accommodate nationalist fictions (invocations of Africanisms in Brazil's national fictions are a good example of such a move), diaspora within the family of these terms has been invoked in order to complicate and challenge nationalist fictions of homogeneity in terms of both the formation of modern nation-states and national identities. Jana Evans Braziel and Anita Mannur note, "[a] glance through recent academic journals reveals an increasing preoccupation with theorizations and problematizations of diaspora and nation."[8] In a similar context, artist Allan deSouza insists, "[c]rossing a frontier, any frontier, makes vision more complex, as one retains the memory of the vision from the other side."[9] DeSouza's own visual practices, which explore nationalist mythologies that simultaneously suppress and highlight colonial and racist hegemony in the Irish and American landscapes, emphasize the complex and hybrid worldview of diasporic artists, and participate in the deconstruction and disruption of historical narratives of race and nation.

Diaspora as a Mode of Reception

My concern here is not an overview or genealogy of the term diaspora, but rather an exploration of how diaspora has functioned within contemporary art practices, and how, within such a framework, diasporic art has challenged homogeneous fictions of nation, nationality, and citizenship. How have diasporic discourses affected art practices, particularly with the advent of increased globalization and migration worldwide? How have diasporic artists used and changed the visual languages of modernism and postmodernism? If diasporas indeed counter hegemonic narratives of nation and national culture, do they not also question the universalist claims made by modernist art? How does a consciousness of diaspora complicate the history of postwar visual practices? The assumption that lay behind such questions is that diasporic artists have not worked completely outside of the mainstream worlds of visual cultures, but rather, they have worked alongside, inside and around them, taking their languages, twisting them to suit their own agendas.

However, in many accounts of twentieth- and twenty-first-century art, the production of diasporic artists is still seen as somehow separate from the world-at-large. And such a move is not only the failure of mainstream critical apparatuses. All too often diasporic critics view diasporic art in a vacuum, which belies the very fact that artists in diaspora – as do people in diaspora more generally – have multiple worldviews, worldviews made up of the experience, memory, or mythologization of at least two different cultures. Moreover, as Jean Fisher has noted, works by non-European artists are often viewed in terms of universalizing western aesthetics, which they almost always fail to uphold; they are often understood and admired only for their "otherness"; and/or they are addressed only with their respect to socio-political context.[10] The latter is particularly troublesome in an art world in part made up of both conservative and sympathetic liberal art critics who routinely see the political work of non-European artists as only exotic (Congolese artist Cheri Samba's paintings from the late 1980s and early 1990s are particularly relevant here), whining (look at almost any review of "multicultural" or "global" art exhibitions such as the 1993 Whitney Biennial in New York City or the Documenta XI exhibition of 2001–2 in Kassel, Germany), aesthetically boring (ditto), and/or just bad art (ditto). In other accounts of contemporary practices, critics in the late twentieth century acknowledged the dire social conditions – the pressures of racism, sexism, AIDS, political conservatism, the culture wars in the US – that constituted the backdrop for art practices centering on identity politics, but failed to give any reading of the work that would allow for a full understanding of the motives behind as well as the political and cultural stakes in these particular practices.

Along similar lines, some artists strongly identify as diasporic subjects: African American artist Lyle Ashton Harris is a case in point. Other artists become identified as such by their inclusion in shows focused on diaspora. Moshekwa Langa, a South African artist who lives in Amsterdam, was included in New York's Museum for African Art's 2003 exhibition *Looking Both Ways: Art of the Contemporary African Diaspora*. When Kobena Mercer asked him, "[w]hat does 'diaspora' mean to you?" Langa replied, "... I didn't know I was in the Diaspora ... I suppose 'diaspora' would mean having a community that you're part of, but I live in a Dutch neighborhood, not a separate community. My situation is unfixed, so 'traveler' is much more resounding for me."[11]

African American artist William Pope.L responded to the connection of his work by Cair Crawford to West African Fon *bocio* figures in the following fashion: "Let me say loud and clear: I bear no malice towards Ms. Crawford ... when I say: How come all these white people know more about African culture than I do? In fact, how come one of them knows more about *me* than I do?"[12] However, Pope.L also acknowledges his own complicity in the equation, noting that he wants people to pay attention to his work:

> ... so I go along with the fact that there is, in fact, a link between my work and that of *bo* artist activators. But in the same breath I also say to myself: Why is it not enough that I am a black American artist? Apparently I need to get blacker. More authentic. I must become the black American artist with dark, mysterious, atavistic roots in some primitive Otherness. ...
>
> Eccentric black other. Perverted black other. Spiritual black other. Each representation requires a purity of being which denies for black folk the kind of psychological complexity typically assigned to white mental worlds. ...
>
> The only *bo* I can make is *bo* that does not know itself.[13]

If "diaspora" or "diasporic" is a name we give to ourselves, it is also an avenue of reception, and as such, it is also a name others give to us (and whether the work of artists of color is diasporic or not is not entirely up to the artist, but rather determined as well by the critic, scholar, or curator, or even the author of this very chapter). Whether in a neo-colonial, conservative environment that dilutes the creative energies of diasporic artists or in a dialogue that ties art practices *solely* to the alterity of the artist, the critical apparatus generally manages to keep the work of the diasporic artist at arm's length.

Hence the paradox: diasporas are everywhere, but they are always *over there*.

Becoming "British"

Postwar Britain saw a marked increase in the numbers of immigrants from its former colonies. Peoples from Africa, the Afro-Caribbean, and South Asia streamed into the center of the former empire, resulting in diasporic communities of millions of people. During the 1980s a generation of descendents of these immigrants came of age, and their cultural and critical activities changed in fundamental ways our understanding of diaspora. The cultural and political activities of this new generation of African, Afro-Caribbean, and Asian artists, activists, and critics (termed "Black" in Britain) challenged post-imperial British racism both on the streets and in institutions, and in the process, they waged a war that understood representation as one of its primary battlefields. In the course of these battles, subjectivity and identity were understood as neither natural nor complete, but rather as fluid and discursive constructions that came out of the intersection of race, gender, sexuality, and class. All of these issues coming to the fore in the social and political context of postwar Britain were grounds upon which a new understanding and a new politics of diaspora were created.

The racist and racialized discourses and institutions of postwar Britain provided the motivation for the development of these diasporic politics. The diasporic communities of Africans, Afro-Caribbeans, and South Asians which emerged in British cities as a result of the great migration of the subjects of former British colonies to Britain, as Paul Gilroy has noted, were perceived by many in the white majority as a threat to British life itself, prompting acts of racist persecution against these communities and, in response, anti-racist protests.[14] During the 1950s and 1960s, anxieties surrounding race were thus most often coded in terms of the large volume of black settlement in Britain, and housing issues ignited much of the racist agitation of the period. By the 1970s, however, images relating to Black Britain had become synonymous with criminality, and black culture was often pointed to by both the right and the left as *the* visible sign of British decay.

This ideological connection of blackness and criminality in part allowed for the ascendance of the Police Federation's "Law and Order" campaign in 1975. Courting both public opinion and the media, this campaign relied on the new hypervisibility of black crime for its evocative force. The coding of blackness as crime thus allowed for the consolidation of white political power at a time when that very power was threatened. In practice, the "Law and Order" campaign aimed at repressing and prosecuting not only black crime, but also black political protest – thus restricting the movement and freedom of black British subjects. In addition, attacks on blacks were commonly ignored by the police. For example, after 13 black teenagers were killed in a firebomb attack in southeast London in 1981 and the British media and government remained silent and inactive, the Race Today Collective organized a national protest.[15] The protest moved from black neighborhoods in southeast London to the centers of British media and jurisprudence, where the police intervened in what had been a peaceful demonstration.

The police responded to these skirmishes, which were constructed by the British press as further evidence of Britain's decay at the hands of lawless blacks, by instituting a massive stop and search policy in the London neighborhood of Brixton, prompting an explosive uprising of protest in Brixton. While the Brixton events were met by shock in Britain-at-large, black communities were not surprised, and located it, in Kobena Mercer's words, "in a prior history of the racist character of policing practices in the social history of black postwar settlement."[16] However, the Brixton uprisings also spoke to the place of black people in Britain. Mercer writes:

> . . . that if we were invisible, marginal and silenced by subjection to a racism by which we failed to enjoy equal protection under the law as common citizens, this was because we were all too visible, all too vocal and all too central, in Britain's postimperial body politic, as a reminder and remainder of its historical past, and of the paradoxical disadvantage of an early start of one of the key factors of its present day, post-Empire decline: *we are here because you were there.*[17]

Beyond the increasingly militaristic force used against black British subjects on the streets and exclusion from the British establishment, black British cultures of resistance also came of age in a vacuum created by the breakdown of the British left and the ascendance of Thatcherism and the New Right after 1980. Despite their different points of origins and specific cultural practices, artists, critics, and cultural workers from overlapping diasporic communities – African, Afro-Caribbean, and South Asian – shared the burden of British structural racism and thus formed a coalition of cultural resistance. This cutting across diasporas, while reminiscent of Pan-Africanism and Negritude, did not essentialize differences, but formed alliances accounting for the interrelatedness of race, class, gender, and sexuality.[18] Adding to such activity was the attention paid to the work of black feminists on both sides of the Atlantic as well as, in the visual arts, to the American Black Arts Movement of the 1960s. Mercer notes, "[w]hat was being crystallized was a set of critical positions, sharpening differences while seeking to make the arena of cultural struggle more inclusive."[19]

The activities of black British cultural producers in the 1980s had concrete local effects. The art world became somewhat more inclusive, and black artists started to receive funding and national recognition. Such cultural activities also had global implications. Alongside visual production, a critical apparatus challenging ingrained ideas that cast postwar Britishness as white, was developed. The work of writers such as Hazel Carby, Paul Gilroy, Stuart Hall, Kobena Mercer, and Pratibha Parmer among others provided conceptual tools for artists and other activists, and they articulated with force the incredibly complex terrain informing British politics and society. In their work, a ruthless examination of "race" as a predominant symbol of differentiation struck at the core of British ethnocentrism, and provided a basis for the work of cultural producers and social scientists throughout the world. Building on the important work of these critics, the journal *Third Text* appeared in 1987. Always at the center of discourse of global art and the first journal to take it seriously, it remains today as one of the preeminent sites for thinking through global contemporary art practices. The understanding of identity on the part of artists, writers, and activists as contingent and messy opened up new zones for activity, new oppositional spaces. In the hands of these cultural workers, diaspora was opened up as subject position and as tool. Also, in their exploration and recreation of subjectivities, what they sought were ways to be both black and British, a stance echoing Du Bois' ideas at the beginning of the twentieth century.

Conceptualizing Diasporic Consciousness

Mercer's, Hall's, Gilroy's, and, more recently, Irit Rogoff's work have become paradigms for thinking about the relationship of diaspora and cultural politics. For all of them, most important is the casting of subjectivities that look not to the past, but rather to the present and the future. Hall, discussing the emergence of Caribbean film in 1980s Britain, sees diaspora and cultural identity working in two directions. On the one hand, Hall describes the concept of diasporic identity as defined by notions of a singular common culture, which reflects common historical experiences (i.e. the Middle Passage), and essential cultural traits (i.e. "Africanness"). For Hall, this concept, while it played a crucial role in movements such as Negritude and Pan-Africanism, is limited in that it insists on identity as static and unchanging.[20] On the other, Hall points to a more fluid notion of identity developed by black cultural workers in Britain in the 1970s and 1980s. Unlike the first conception, this view recognizes similarities while also making space for the enunciation of significant differences between and among groups and individuals, understanding identity as a "becoming," as contingent upon histories, experiences, and shifting positions within and around narratives of the past. In this sense, the Hall's latter notion of identity embeds itself not in the past, but rather in the present and future.[21]

Zarina Bhimji, Isaac Julien, and Keith Piper are only three of the many artists who emerged from the political turmoil and oppositional activity of 1980s Britain. Their work, global in outlook, is engaged in an ongoing dialogue of belonging, of dispossession, repossession, and re-creation that follow Hall's call for negotiation and "becoming."

Bhimji's photographs take notions of migration, of racial otherness as well as the interrogation of history and colonial experience as a means to question power and to transgress boundaries constructed between Africa and the west as well as self and other. Bhimji's 1995 photograph *We are cut from the same cloth*, produced during a residency in the pathology laboratory of London's Charing Cross Hospital, is a Foucaultian intervention into the terrains of knowledge, power, and representation informed by the artist's multicultural, transnational lens. The photograph, which shows a human eye with its brow floating in a glass container of formaldehyde, at once undermines the imagined objectivity of science and positivism, and situates itself as an interrogation of the body's vulnerability. The body-in-decay signals the body's own impending absence and its limits as a representation through the aegis of western epistemology. In her own experience of diasporic exile, and in her understanding of Georges Bataille's 1957 text *Erotism* as producing the very dissolution of the bodies of African women, the dissected eye then becomes a signpost not only for the artist's locational and psychological exile, but also for the possibility of her own dissolution under the production of western knowledge.

Piper's work also focuses on the intersection of colonial experience, the production of knowledge and the black body. In his multimedia works from the 1980s and 1990s, Piper explores the over-determined heterosexual black male body in ways that articulate the parasitic nature of the colonial enterprise and render problematic the connections made in British culture between the black male body and criminal violence. In his 1996 conceptual interactive installation *Fictions of Science*, for example, the black male body is substituted for the perfect white male of Leonardo da Vinci's 1498 *Vitruvian Man* (Figure 15.1). In

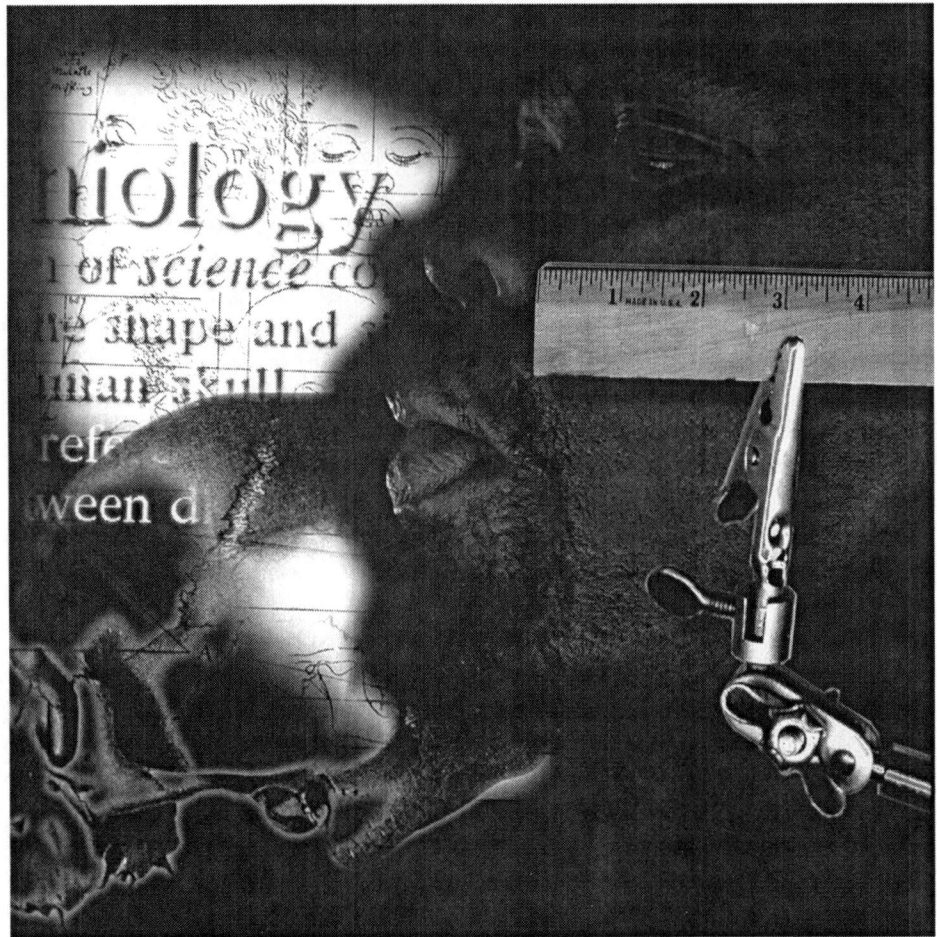

FIGURE 15.1　Keith Piper, *The Fictions of Science*, 1996. Interactive installation using computer and video projection. Courtesy of the artist

different electronic tableaux, dictionary definitions of terms such as "anthropology," "craniology," "ethnography," and "sociology," are superimposed on photomontages of the British Empire's colonized Africans and Asians. Beneath the definition of craniology (the scientific study of the human skull) sits an image of Piper's own profile, which is being measured by a wooden ruler. Piper's installation excavates hidden histories, exploring what could be called colonialism's racialized subconscious.

Julien's work addresses the discursive construction of black gay subjectivity. In his 1989 film *Looking for Langston*, Julien reconstitutes the sexual ambiguity of the Harlem Renaissance in a postmodern, diasporic British framework. Merging a meditation on the Harlem Renaissance with the 1980s poetry of the late

African American gay writer Essex Hemphill, Julien connects transatlantic black gay subjectivities with the Harlem Renaissance in a fashion that explores the intersection of race and same-sex desire. The black and white film's editing and its mixture of historic and contemporary images constitutes a dreamscape that does not offer a concrete view of subjectivity, but rather one that is suggestive. While the film serves as a space for Julien to explore and recast his own subjectivity, the artist's insistence on the centrality of homosexuality in the making of black culture registers as a challenge to the homophobia of black nationalism and black historical narratives that silence sexual difference.

All of these artists share the use of fragmentation, of *bricolage*, of montage as a means to bend formal languages to serve their political goals. Although Piper insisted that he was looking for a black visual aesthetic that was exclusively his, he still took elements from previous conceptual practices in order to develop his own visual idioms.[22] But Piper's insistence on a new visual language, and, in general, the very objects that diasporic artists create, call for an inquiry into their relationship to the dominant western forms of modernist and postmodernist art.

Diasporic Consciousness and Abstract Form

Certain artists such as Yoko Ono were at the center of the Euro-American art worlds from the early 1960s, and the importance of her varied practices, straddling conceptual art, minimalism, performance, film, and music, are a function of her dislocations (she was exiled from Tokyo during World War II and lived in the United States both as a child and adult), of her interest in Zen Buddhism and existentialism, and of her association with figures such as John Cage and George Maciunas. Her instruction paintings, compiled in her 1964 anthology *Grapefruit*, are hybrid forms (Ono as a child imagined the grapefruit as a cross between an orange and a lemon) that bring together Ono's psychological sense of her in-betweeness between east and west and her position, in her words, "as a spiritual hybrid."[23] Although Ono was largely ignored and/or marginalized in critical accounts of the time due in part to art world racism and in part to her relationship with John Lennon, her practices are becoming more central in the narratives about art since the 1960s.[24] Ono's practice, however, is important not only for its contribution to the development of contemporary art. Ono's diasporic viewpoint does not emphasize subjectivity or identity politics in ways that we commonly associate with diasporic visual practices; her instruction paintings focus instead on the dematerialization of form as a means of mental liberation, and on a connection with the world through the privileging of experience.

Korean American artist Byron Kim's abstract painting takes its cues from the formalism of the New York School abstractionists such as Ad Reinhardt, Marc Rothko, and Brice Marsden. Many of Kim's monochrome paintings, like their predecessors, explore opticality and the materiality of paint and canvas. Unlike their predecessors, some of Kim's abstract paintings refer to the skin tones of himself and his friends, whose names become those of the canvases. In that sense, Kim has robbed abstraction of its supposed autonomy, infusing it instead with references to specific individual bodies identified simply by dint of their skin tone, and interrogating the obsession with skin tone as *the* marker of subjectivity. Along with such monochrome works, which are at times arranged in serial formats, Kim has also explored similar issues using the grid as his organizing principle.

Rosalind Krauss has maintained a formalist model of European modernism, arguing that the grid has succeeded in dominating modernist art on three levels: "a sheerly quantitative success, involving the numbers of artists in [the twentieth century] who have used grids; a qualitative success through which the grid has become the medium for some of the greatest works of modernism; and an ideological success, in that the grid is able – in a work of whatever quality – to emblematize the Modern."[25] Understanding the history of modern art and the grid as emblem of that history, Yinka Shonibare, an artist of Nigerian descent born in London, uses that format to explore the relation between modernism and colonialism. Shonibare's works, such as *Feather Pink* (1997), are grids of solid background upon which the artist places squares of Dutch wax prints and amorphous acrylic paintings that reference the textiles (Figure 15.2).

The Dutch print, while signifier of "Africanness" for both Africans and non-Africans, was manufactured in England and sold to colonized peoples on the African continent. Along the lines of what Krauss calls the centrifugal grid, one that "posits the theoretical continuity of the work of art with the world,"[26] Shonibare's works rob the modernist grid of its self-proclaimed autonomy, polluting it through the conceptual use of fabrics that, linked to the domain of popular culture and markers of an (in)authentic ethnicity, evoke racial and cultural difference and the histories of colonialism. Shonibare's grids are paradoxical. As the artist insists, such works negate modernism while exhibiting his attraction to art's formal qualities. However, one could also argue the opposite: that Shonibare's grids enact a form that, while still modern, in its move away from abstraction, could continue to signify, to borrow Krauss's words, "a statement of man-made systems in the world."[27]

The same back and forth between the negation and confirmation of modernism is relevant to Kim and Japanese American artist Lynne Yamamoto. Kim disputes the autonomy of the grid by making reference to the assignment of identity based upon the color of this sitters' skin, while Yamamoto disrupts it through the introduction of her own hair and notations relating to the history of her grandmother, inserting her history as a poor immigrant woman.[28] Shonibare, Kim, and Yamamoto point explicitly not only to the play of form that is paramount in visual production, but also to the ways in which form becomes a site for the construction of experiences and the resurrection of histories.

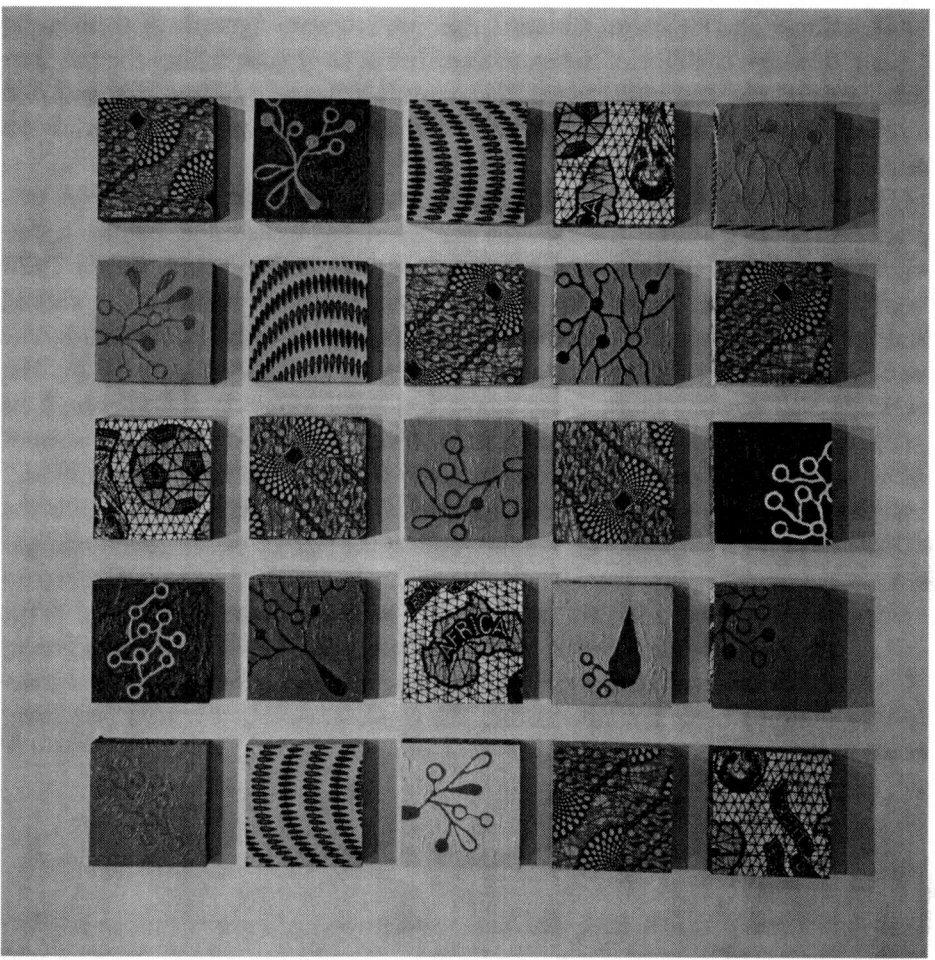

FIGURE 15.2 Yinka Shonibare, *Feather Pink*, 1997. Acrylic on stretched African textile. 30.5 × 30.5 cm. The Art Institute of Chicago. Gift of the Peter Norton Family Foundation, 1998.352. Photograph by Robert Lifson

Reading Diaspora

However, the play of form is not always about the relationship of diasporic artists to western art practices. In the work of Wenda Gu, who now works in the United States, calligraphy forms the formal foundation of a practice that negotiates his sense of his own Chineseness and his sense of being a citizen of the world. Calligraphy, which Gu came to through his reading of Ludwig Wittgenstein and Bertrand Russell's philosophies of language, straddles the boundary between the real and artifice. His writing is taken from Chinese seal script, yet it does not say anything. As such, the calligraphy registers to readers differently.

For those with a knowledge of Chinese, the text is an unreadable language; for those without knowledge of Chinese, the text becomes figuratively readable as "Asian" through the dint of the exoticism that in large part defines the relationship between the west and China. The result is a fantastic misreading, and that misreading constitutes, in Gu's words, "the essence of our knowledge of the material world."[29]

The written word and misunderstanding also informs part of Shirin Neshat's practices. Residing in the gap between exoticism and knowledge, Neshat's photographic self-portraits play with Orientalism *à la* Edward Said, in his 1978 book by that name. Neshat, an Iranian-born artist who works in the United States, makes photographs that sometimes feature her own body, covered by the black *chador*, or her face or feet, covered with Arabic script (Figure 15.3). The portraits also contain guns: some point up, some point at the viewer. Like calligraphy in Gu's practice, Neshat's script functions as readable to her western audience only as a marker of Islam, but also of a more general "foreignness," and rests inside the exoticism through which the west defines and contains the Middle East. Most importantly, Neshat renders the stereotypes of Islam ambiguous in her practice; however, while she occupies the stereotype – a powerful exegesis on her own position as a Muslim woman in the west – she never explodes it. Adding even more to the images' ambiguity, Neshat confuses two of the west's predominant stereotypes of Islam: the submissive veiled Islamic woman and the radical Islamic fundamentalist. The result is work that cannot be pinned down.

They Dreamed of Africa

Diasporic visual practices have also been understood and articulated in relation to the survival of cultural forms in diaspora, despite the Middle Passage and European imperialism: examples of this dynamic include Africanisms in the material arts of the New World; the arts of Haitian Vodun, Cuban Santerià, and Brazilian Candomble; Jewishness in modern American, European, and Jewish Israeli art. Robert Farris Thompson's influential 1983 *Flash of the Spirit* thus painstakingly chronicles the migration, persistence, and continuity of African forms, sounds, and worldviews in the arts and architecture of peoples of African descent in the western hemisphere. Thompson's text, aside from offering a new means to think about the manifestations of Africanisms in the black visual cultures of the New World, also opened a space for artists of African descent to imagine and create links to the African continent.

Writers on the work of African American artists have rightly explored the ways in which ideas of diaspora have informed the artists' visual choices, motivated by the desire to convey notions of "home" and the possibility of recuperating a lost "African" past. Within this arguably romantic paradigm, African American artists use "Africa" – often in a utopian gesture – as a means metaphorically to

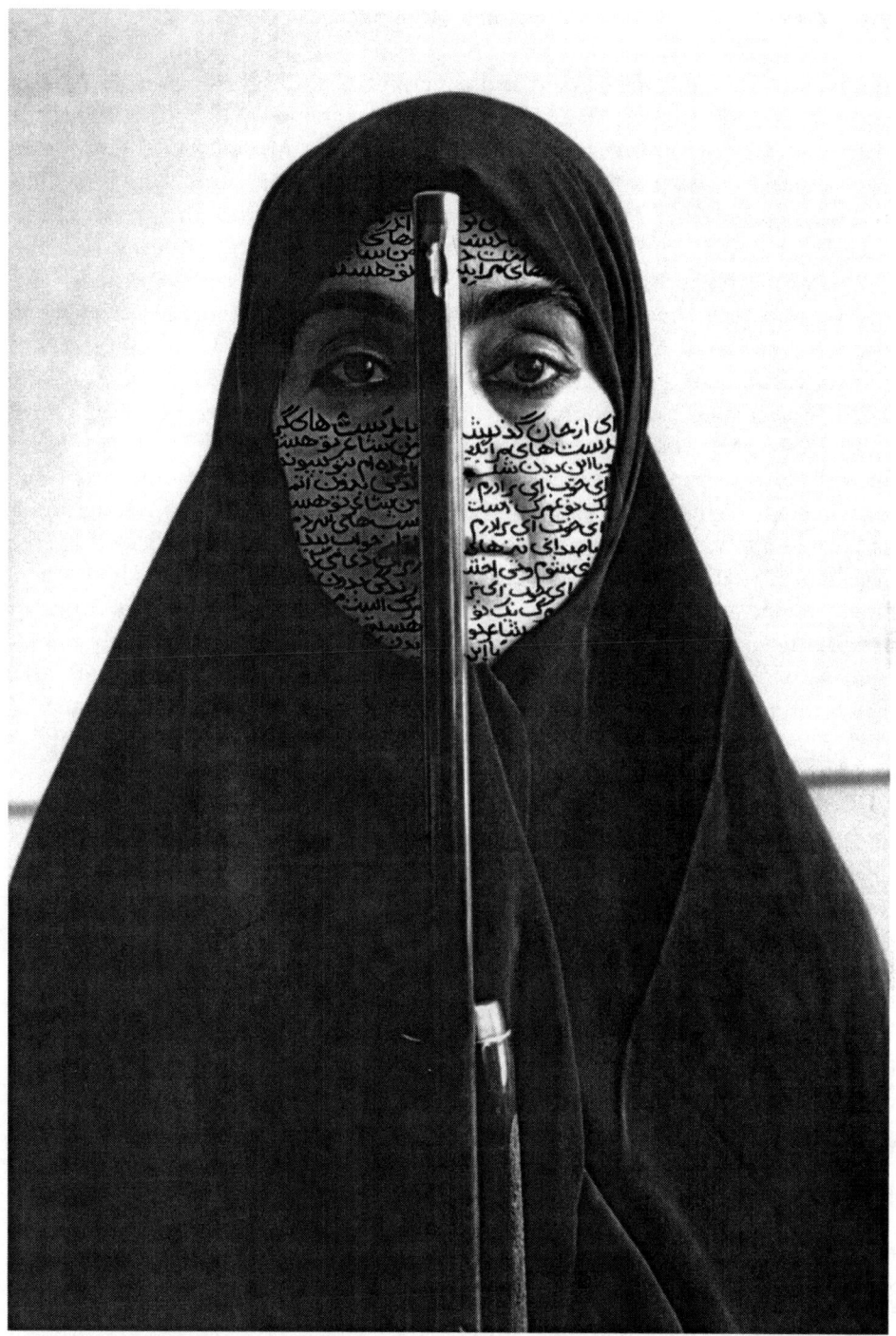

FIGURE 15.3 Shirin Neshat, *Rebellious Silence*, 1994. Black and white RC print and ink. 11 × 14 in. Copyright © Shirin Neshat 1994. Courtesy of the Gladstone Gallery, New York

recuperate and mediate the pain and suffering of the both the Middle Passage and racism in the United States. Such a move is paramount in the public murals that have filled American cities since the Black Arts Movement of the 1960s. Such a move is also a staple of what Thelma Golden has called "Black Romantic" painting.[30] These practices, reminiscent of Hall's conception of an essentialized diasporic cultural identity, insist on a static, primordial myth of Africa for their evocative power.

Not all African American diasporic work is static, however. Also engaged in the recuperation of Africa as lost origin, but with a nod toward the present and future, Renée Cox produced a series of self-portraits in 1997–8 that calls up "Africa" as a source of power. Superimposing her body, dressed in a superhero outfit and neatly coiffed dreadlocks, onto small-scale surroundings, Cox gives herself the appearance of having superhuman powers. In one image, she overcomes cross burnings; in another, her massive form threatens in King Kong fashion to grab a speeding taxi in Times Square. Dramatically inflected by her southern African American roots and brought to consciousness by Thompson's book, Renée Stout produced her 1988 *Fetish #2*, a work that invokes Africa to reverse the fragmentation and forced dispersal of peoples so commonly associated with diaspora and its communities (Figure 15.4). Stout's encounter with Kongo practices, while provocative and better informed than the fantasies of Africa perpetrated on many urban murals, still positions Africa romantically as mother, using Africa to assist in the completion of a fragmented African American identity. A remade Kongo *N'kisi*, Stout's solid body defuses the notion of the fetish, while simultaneously highlighting and empowering her own subjectivity. Hers is a body that is concrete, one that attempts to reconcile the present with lost origins.

Lifestyles of the Diasporic Artist

While the relationship to Africa for artists born in Africa but currently living in the west is undeniably different from what it is for African American artists who experience the place from a distance as a primordial homeland, there is one thing that ties these groups of cultural producers together: the structural racism in their host countries. On that level, while an artist such as Iké Udé, who was born in Nigeria and lives in New York, indeed has a vastly different relationship to Africa than do Cox or Stout, once in the United States, Udé experiences more or less the same forms of racialization as do the others. However, while Udé, like these African American artists, is deeply informed – and indeed othered – by Euro-American culture, Udé's practice does not reconstruct blackness out of its fragments but instead rearranges its shards. His own body is the centerpiece of both his 1990s "Cover Girl" and "Celluloid Frames" series, which use race and gender critically as a means to underscore the racialized nature of Euro-American concepts of beauty. His 1994 *Nigerian Vogue*, for example, takes the magazine and places Nigeria and the Afro-Atlantic Diaspora into what is

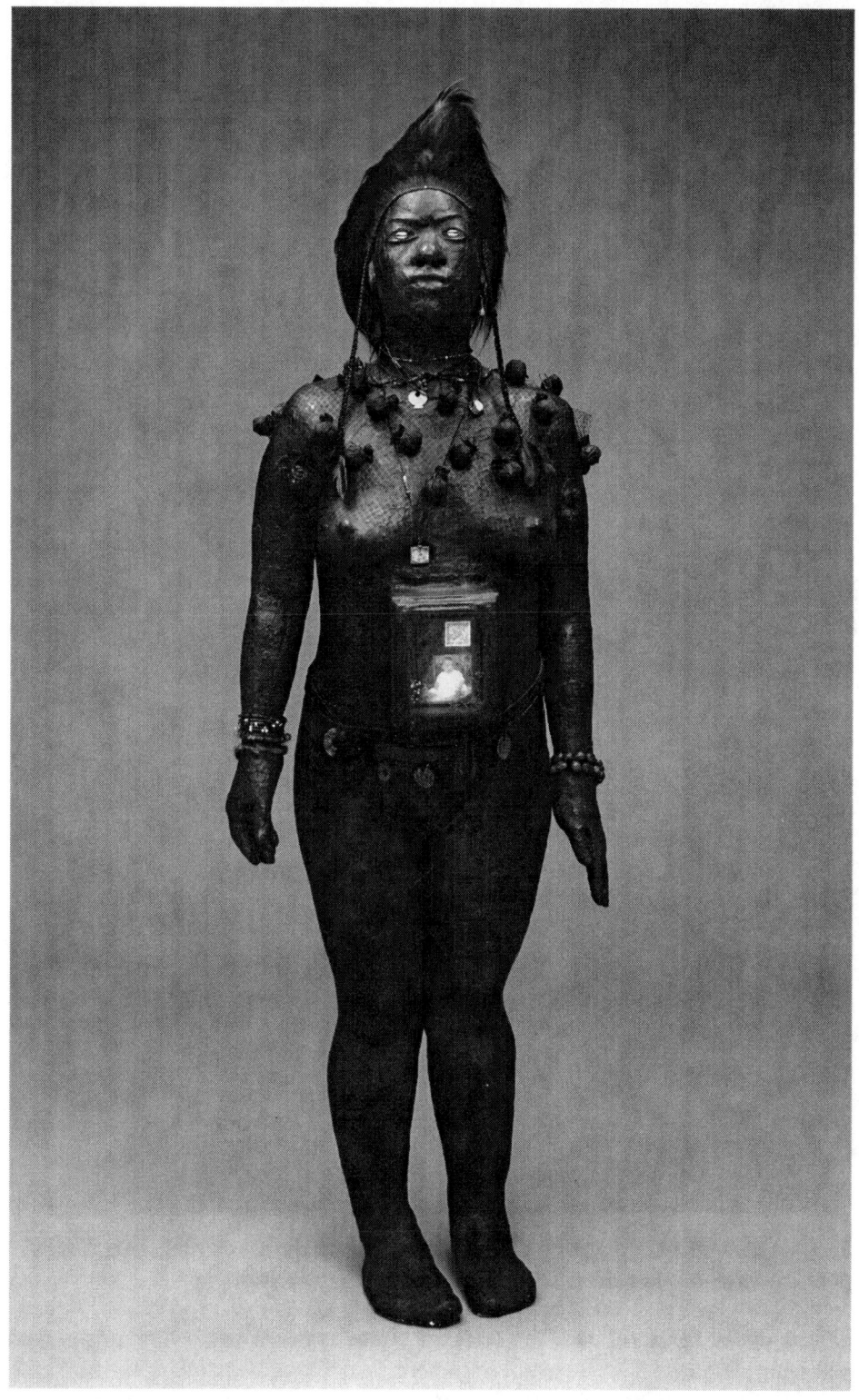

FIGURE 15.4   Renée Stout, *Fetish #2*, 1988. Mixed media (plaster body cast). Height 64 in. (1 m 62.56 cm). Dallas Museum of Art, Metropolitan Life Foundation Purchase Grant

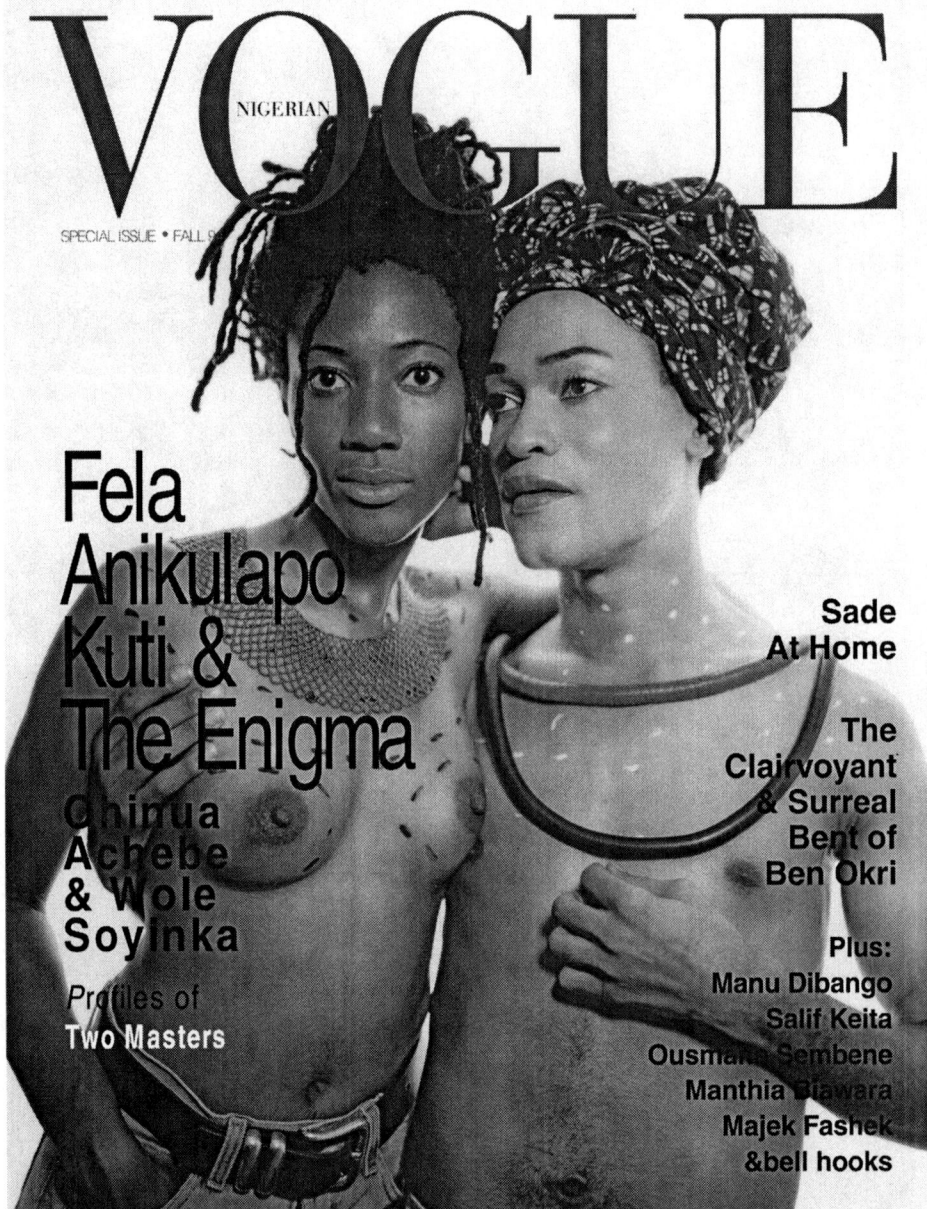

FIGURE 15.5 Iké Udé, *Nigerian Vogue*, 1994. Part of the *Cover Girl* Series. Type-C print mounted on aluminum. 11 × 8.5 in. Courtesy of the artist

commonly understood as a hallmark of haute couture and white upper-class privilege (Figure 15.5). Instead of supermodel Claudia Schiffer, we see Udé himself embracing a gorgeous woman of African descent. Instead of articles about and by Euro-American luminaries, we see an array of intellectuals and cultural producers of African descent: Sade, Wole Soyinka, and bell hooks.

Udé has referred to these performances as masks. In terms of androgyny, they revel in *Adanma*, an Igbo practice, which reads like drag in the west, where men masquerade as women. In Udé's own words, "[t]here is no true accountable self. The self is a negotiable entity . . . Like the *Adanma* masquerade, my work addresses itself to issues such as propaganda, ambivalence, vanity, denial, glamour: all the contradictions of our society – the mere artificial constructs of our everyday consumerist culture in which anything can be bought and everything is for sale."[31] By his own admission, Udé traffics in the familiar, and trades in both narcissism and popular culture as a means to denaturalize familiar codes. Circulating in the artificial worlds of capital and "lifestyle" so characteristic of the recent *fin de siècle*, Udé has articulated a diasporic blackness, one that is well-heeled, androgynous, and quite fabulous. Moreover, it is a diasporic blackness that disrupts a normative whiteness.

The Unbearable Whiteness of Being

In a sense, much of the activity of diasporic artists is not just about the otherness of diaspora, it is also about whiteness and the ways in which whiteness, in colonial and racist terms, has been parasitic of other cultures both at home and away. Mercer suggests that, in the case of Britain, "[b]y forging diasporic dialogues beyond the boundaries of nation, black initiatives were effectively "successful" in moving the legacy of the Left forward into a new era of globalization by creolizing or hybridizing it in relation to the legacy of other memories, knowledges and traditions from elsewhere."[32] And it is in that creolization/hybridization of national culture that diasporic artists challenge a sometimes blinding whiteness.

That said, Cuban-born, New York-based artist Ernesto Pujol, reminds us, ". . . when whiteness is the unspoken standard of quality for visual art, whether hidden within modernism, as in the New York School of painting, or behind the aesthetics of Minimalism, Conceptual art, or the 1990s international style, addressing it is perceived as distasteful, if not anti-intellectual. And yet, whiteness remains the high aesthetic fascism into which everything, regardless of its origin, must be translated within the new globalism in order to be exhibited and sold."[33] Pujol's words stand as a reminder that diaspora is not only that which communities name themselves, but that it is also a term of reception, a niche that is still dominated by mainstream taste and desires. Moreover, in an atmosphere where racism has ideologically shifted from practices of exclusion to those of inclusion without the privilege of full participation, the attempt on the part of diasporic artists to effectively shift their ways of working to meet these new challenges is of the utmost importance.

Clifford insists, "[d]iaspora consciousness is produced positively through identification with world historical/cultural forces like 'Africa' or 'China.' The process may not be as much about being African or Chinese, as about being American or British, or wherever one has settled, differently. It is also about feeling global."[34] This is an important distinction, for instead of merely representing the past, diaspora consciousness points to present (and future) myths and realities. In the hands of diasporic artists, diaspora is a subject position, and it is also a tool, a means to an end. As the work of these and many other artists shows, diaspora is not only a condition of multiple worldviews, but also a cacophony of visual practices that speak to recreation, re-presentation, and reinvention.

Notes

1   Kitaj (1989), 19.
2   Appadurai (1996), 171.
3   Du Bois (1903/1989), 3.
4   Gilroy (1993), 205–12.
5   Clifford (1997), 247.
6   Mirzoeff, "Introduction: The Multiple Viewpoint: Diasporic Visual Cultures," in Mirzoeff (2000), 2.
7   Clifford (1997), 245.
8   Braziel and Mannur (2003), 3.
9   deSouza (1994), 50.
10 Fisher (1996), 33–4.
11 Mercer (2003), 106.
12 Pope.L (2002), 70; italics in original.
13 Ibid., 71–3.
14 Gilroy (1987), 86. This text informs much of the following summary; see, especially, pages 72–111.
15 On the protest, see ibid., 103.
16 Mercer (1994), 7.
17 Ibid.; italics in original.
18 See ibid., 11.
19 Ibid., 13.
20 Hall (1990), 223–5.
21 Ibid., 223.
22 Piper, as cited by Mercer (1994), 5.
23 Ono quoted in Munroe with Hendricks (2000), 83. My description of *Grapefruit* is based on and indebted to Bruce Altshuler's description of *Grapefruit* and his correspondence with Ono, in Altshuler (2000), 83. Altshuler also notes that the symbolic nature of the grapefruit is evident in the title of Ono's 1961 performance piece *Of a Grapefruit in the World of Park*.
24 See Ross (2000), 56.
25 Krauss (1985), 12.
26 Ibid., 21.
27 Ibid.
28 Higa (1996), 6–7.
29 Gu, cited in Leung and Kaplan (1999), 88.
30 See Golden (2002).
31 Udé (1999), 71.

32 Mercer (1994), 22.
33 Pujol (2000), 100.
34 Clifford (1997), 206.

References and further reading

Altshuler, Bruce (2000). "Instructions for a World of Stickiness: The Early Conceptual Art of Yoko Ono." In Munroe with Hendricks (2000), 55–7.

Appadurai, Arjun (1996). *Modernity at Large: Cultural Dimensions of Globalization.* Minneapolis: University of Minnesota Press.

Araeen, Rasheed (2002). "The Other Immigrant: The Experiences and Achievements of Afro-Asian Artists in the Metropolis." In *Race-ing Art History: Critical Readings in Race and Art History*, ed. Kymberly N. Pinder. New York: Routledge. 359–70.

Araeen, Rasheed, Sean Cubitt, and Ziauddin Sardar, eds. (2002). *The Third Text Reader on Art, Culture and Theory.* New York: Continuum.

Baigell, Matthew, and Milly Heyd, eds. (2001). *Complex Identities: Jewish Consciousness and Modern Art.* New Brunswick, NJ: Rutgers University Press.

Bhabha, Homi (1994). *The Location of Culture.* New York: Routledge.

Braziel, Jana Evans, and Anita Mannur, eds. (2003). *Theorizing Diaspora.* Oxford: Blackwell.

Clifford, James (1997). *Routes: Travel and Translation in the Late Twentieth Century.* Cambridge, MA: Harvard University Press.

deSouza, Allan (1994). "Re-Placing Angels: Extracts and Extractions." In *Tracing Cultures: Art History, Criticism, Critical Fiction*, ed. Miwon Kwon. New York: Whitney Museum of American Art. 29–52.

Du Bois, W. E. B. (1903/1989). *The Souls of Black Folk.* New York: Bantam Books.

duCille, Ann (1996). *Skin Trade.* Cambridge, MA: Harvard University Press.

Edwards, Brent Hayes (2003). *The Practice of Diaspora: Literature, Translation and the Rise of Black Internationalism.* Cambridge, MA: Harvard University Press.

Farrell, Laurie Ann, ed. (2003). *Looking Both Ways: Art of the Contemporary African Diaspora.* New York: Museum for African Art.

Fisher, Jean (1996). "The Syncretic Turn: Cross-Cultural Practices in the Age of Multiculturalism." In Gangitano and Nelson, eds. (1996), 32–8.

Foster, Hal (1996). *The Return of the Real: The Avant-Garde at the End of the Century.* Cambridge, MA: MIT Press.

Gangitano, Lia, and Steven Nelson, eds. (1996). *New Histories.* Exhibition catalog. Boston: The Institute of Contemporary Art.

Gilroy, Paul (1987). *There Ain't no Black in the Union Jack: The Cultural Politics of Race and Nation.* Chicago: University of Chicago Press.

—— (1993). *The Black Atlantic: Modernity and Double Consciousness.* Cambridge, MA: Harvard University Press.

Golden, Thelma (2002). *Black Romantic: The Figurative Impulse in African-American Art.* New York: Studio Museum in Harlem.

Hall, Stuart (1990). "Cultural Identity and Diaspora." In *Identity, Community, Culture, Difference*, ed. Jonathan Rutherford. London: Lawrence and Wishart. 222–37. Also reprinted in Mirzoeff (2000), 21–33.

Higa, Karin (1996). "Some Thoughts on National and Cultural Identity: Art by Contemporary Japanese and Japanese American Artists." *Art Journal*, vol. 55, no. 3:6–13.

Joselit, David (2003). *American Art Since 1945*. London: Thames and Hudson.

Kitaj, R. B. (1989). *First Diasporist Manifesto*. London: Thames and Hudson.

Krauss, Rosalind (1985). *The Originality of the Avant-Garde and other Modernist Myths*. Cambridge, MA: MIT Press.

Leung, Simon, and Janet A. Kaplan (1999). "Pseudo-Languages: A Conversation with Wenda Gu, Xu Bing, and Jonathan Hay." *Art Journal*, vol. 58, no. 3:86–99.

Mercer, Kobena (1994). *Welcome to the Jungle: New Positions in Black Cultural Studies*. New York: Routledge.

—— (2003). "Moshekwa Langa: In Conversation." In Farrell, ed. (2003), 99–113.

Mirzoeff, Nicholas, ed. (2000). *Diaspora and Visual Culture: Representing Africans and Jews*. New York: Routledge.

Munroe, Alexandra, with Jon Hendricks (2000). *Yes: Yoko Ono*. New York: Japan Society.

Pope. L, William (2002). "Bocio." In *William Pope. L: The Friendliest Black Artist in America ©*, ed. Mark H. C. Bessire. Cambridge, MA: MIT Press. 70–3.

Pujol, Ernesto (2000). "Notes on Obsessive Whiteness." *Art Journal*, vol. 59, no. 1:98–100.

Radhakrishnan, R. (2003). *Theory in an Uneven World*. Oxford: Blackwell.

Read, Alan, ed. (1996). *The Fact of Blackness: Frantz Fanon and Visual Representation*. Seattle: Bay Press.

Rogoff, Irit (2000). *Terra Infirma: Geography's Visual Culture*. New York: Routledge.

Ross, David (2000). "Not Here." In Munroe and Hendricks (2000), 55–7.

Said, Edward (1978). *Orientalism*. New York: Vintage.

—— (1993). *Culture and Imperialism*. New York: Knopf.

Shonibare, Yinka (2003). "Of Hedonism, Masquerade, Carnivalesque, and Power: A Conversation with Okwui Enwezor." In Farrell, ed. (2003), 163–77.

Sussman, Elisabeth, Thelma Golden, John G. Hanhardt, and Lisa Phillips (1993). *1993 Biennial Exhibition*. New York: Whitney Museum of American Art.

Thompson, Robert Farris (1983). *Flash of the Spirit: African and Afro-American Art & Philosophy*. New York: Vintage.

Udé, Iké (1999). "Between Mask and Fantasy: A Conversation with Iké Udé and Okwui Enwezor." In *Beyond Decorum: The Photography of Iké Udé*, ed. Mark H. C. Bessire and Lauri Firstenberg. Cambridge, MA: MIT Press. 70–3.

16

Power and Pleasure: Feminist Art Practice and Theory in the United States and Britain

Laura Meyer

Feminist thought, activism, and art making have had a profound (if sometimes unacknowledged) impact on contemporary art. Since its inception in Britain and the United States in the 1970s, the feminist art movement has been fraught with controversy; many of its most publicly visible and seemingly successful strategies have drawn fire, not only from conservative critics, but also from within the ranks of women and avowed feminists. The very richness and diversity of art work produced by women over the past 35 years demonstrates a lack of consensus among artists and theorists about how best to achieve, or even define, feminist goals. Roughly speaking, however, it is possible to divide feminist art and art theory into two main approaches or schools of thought. The first approach might be classified as the "woman power" branch of feminism. The second approach, which arose almost immediately in response to the first, might be characterized as feminist "deconstruction."

The first phase of the feminist art movement began around 1970, buoyed by the civil rights movement, the rise of the New Left, and the nascent women's movement of the 1960s. Feminist activism at this time was characterized by an idealistic commitment to bettering the position of women both inside and outside the art world. Between 1969 and 1972 activist groups mounted public demonstrations and drafted petitions demanding increased representation of women artists in major museums including the Museum of Modern Art and the Whitney Museum of American Art in New York City, the Los Angeles County Museum of Art, and the Corcoran Gallery of Art in Washington DC. Statistics compiled by these groups revealed a shocking gender disparity in the exhibition practices of major art institutions and, in many cases, resulted in substantial improvements. For example, the Ad Hoc Committee of Women Artists revealed that women made up fewer than five percent of the artists represented in the 1970 Whitney Annual (now Biennial), an exhibition focused on the latest developments in contemporary American art; their complaint prompted the museum to increase that figure to 21 percent in 1971. Women art historians also organized several important historical exhibitions during the 1970s, including the major revisionist survey, *Women Artists: 1550–1950* (organized by Linda Nochlin and Ann Sutherland Harris for the Los Angeles County Museum of Art), which provided striking evidence of the large number of gifted women artists throughout European and American history.

Complementing efforts to raise the visibility of women artists in public exhibition venues, women writers began to formulate a body of feminist art history and art theory, ranging from Linda Nochlin's groundbreaking analysis of the historical impediments to women artists' achievement, "Why Have There Been No Great Women Artists?" (1970), to Lucy Lippard's 1976 volume of contemporary art criticism, *From the Center: Feminist Essays on Women's Art*, and Miriam Schapiro and Judy Chicago's controversial article, "Female Imagery" (1973), which theorized the possibility that, even across divergent media and historical circumstances, women artists might make images characterized by some type of specifically feminine "sensibility" or aesthetic.

The most controversial aspects of the feminist art movement in the 1970s centered around the celebration of women's art and, more broadly still, women themselves, as a distinct category united by a common sexual identity and shared social experiences. Three main strategies for celebrating and empowering women can be identified. First, large numbers of women artists, determined to wrest control of their body image from male artists and to counteract the limited and demeaning stereotypes of women dominating the mass media, set out to create new, more "positive" images of women. The logic behind this move to promote the strength and dignity of the female body and female sexuality paralleled that motivating the celebratory slogan of African American activists in the 1960s – "Black is Beautiful." Second, many women used their art work to address distinctively "female" cultural experiences, and a related feminine aesthetic. Artists working in this vein often explored personal, autobiographical subject matter through the use of fabric, decorative crafts, and other media associated with women's handwork and traditionally excluded from the realm of high art. Finally, early feminists' belief in the power of art to improve women's lot was underwritten by their strong faith in the effectiveness of collaboration and solidarity among women. In many cases, this involved developing separate institutions for educating women artists and exhibiting and critiquing women's art.

The second phase of the feminist art movement, which developed in the 1970s but only came to dominate feminist art production and theory in the 1980s, arose in response to the perceived shortcomings and misconceptions of the first. Soon after the founding principles of feminist art were formulated – including the promotion of positive images of women, "female imagery," and collaboration among women – these principles were called into question. Not surprisingly, some conservative critics objected to feminist artists' emphasis on autobiographical and ideological content to the supposed detriment of aesthetic values.[1] The most vehement protests, however, were raised by other women artists and self-identified feminists who contended that early feminist art promoted a stereotyped or "essentialist" view of female identity.

So-called anti-essentialist feminism, closely allied with poststructuralist linguistic theory and the philosophical critical strategy of deconstruction, reformulated the goals of feminist art point by point. In response to early feminists' efforts to create positive images – or representations – of women, poststructuralist feminists such as Griselda Pollock and Lisa Tickner (both based in Britain) emphasized the problems of representation itself. According to this line of thinking, visual images constitute a symbol system analogous to that of language. Thus images, like words, have no inherent meaning, but assume meaning through habitual use. Furthermore, these meanings are structured according to a system of binary oppositions in which "woman," for example, functions as the negative and opposite of "man." If "woman" is customarily used to denote meanings like "passivity" and "weakness," in contrast to masculine "activity" and "strength," then it may not be possible to simply create an image denoting female strength. What is needed, instead, is a systematic analysis of the ways in which meaning is produced, or constructed, within the larger cultural context.[2] Only through such rigorous analysis can apparent "truths" about so-called femininity, masculinity, and so forth be deconstructed and thus deprived of their persistent power.

Pollock and others also rejected early feminists' focus on personal, autobiographical subject matter and the use of media and techniques historically connected to "feminine" craft. As Pollock, one of the most prominent voices of anti-essentialist feminism argued in 1988, "[s]o long as we discuss women, the family, crafts, or whatever else we have done as feminists we endorse the social giveness of woman, the family, the separate sphere."[3]

The early feminist art movement's idealistic faith in women's solidarity came under fire from more than one source in the 1980s and after. Feminist artists and writers intent on deconstructing the notion of "woman" as a category questioned the wisdom of lumping women together as a unified field or coalition. They stressed the importance of conceptualizing "woman," by contrast, as "an unfixed category, constantly in process, examined through her representations and ideological constructions within a male system."[4] Women of color, lesbian women, working-class women, and others who felt marginalized by the predominantly white, middle-class, and heterosexual feminist groups that presumed to speak for *all* women's interests in the early days of the movement likewise emphasized diversity among women. Such criticisms emphasized that, while middle-class Euro-American women might feel relatively voiceless in relation to white men, they also assumed certain privileges denied non-white, less economically advantaged, and/or non-heterosexually identified women.

Crucially, these criticisms also opened up the question of how power relations come into play *among* women. Did the goals of middle-class white feminists have anything to do with the needs of Asian, Hispanic, or Black women? Middle-class women's demand for the right to work outside the home, for example, might have little meaning for poor women who had never known anything else. White women's complaints about the sexualization of female models by the mass media seldom, if ever, addressed the sexual "options" proffered to (or forced on) black women, described by Lorraine O'Grady as a choice between identifying as "castrata" or "whore."[5] And what about the relationship between gay women and straight or bisexual women? Too often feminist organizations repressed or ignored the voices of lesbians for fear of damaging their "public relations" image in mainstream society, while at other times heterosexual women felt their families and male lovers were unwelcome in feminist organizations oriented toward creating an all-female environment.

Debates about how best to promote the interests of women in the art world, and even more fundamentally, about what it means to be a *woman* as well as an *artist* have broadened and deepened the scope of feminist thinking and art making in Euro-American society.

Celebrating Women

In spite of – or perhaps because of – its relatively undeveloped art world infrastructure, Southern California was an especially vibrant nexus of experimental activity in the early years of the feminist art movement. Rather than focusing on gaining equal status in already-existing male-governed institutions, feminist artists in and around Los Angeles concentrated their efforts on establishing alternative, female-governed institutions for educating women artists and for producing, displaying, and critiquing women's art. Probably the single most important figure in the early years of the movement was Judy Chicago, who in 1970 developed the first feminist art education program designed exclusively for women (the Feminist Art Program, founded at Fresno State College, now California State University, Fresno, and later relocated, in collaboration with Miriam Schapiro, to the California Institute of the Arts). Chicago subsequently co-founded the Los Angeles Woman's Building, the longest-lived feminist art center in the United States (1973–1991), and masterminded *The Dinner Party* (1979), a monumental, collaborative art installation that has toured to record-breaking audiences around the world.

The Feminist Art Program was conceived as an "antidote" to the alienation Chicago felt as a young woman artist in Los Angeles in the 1960s, when the vast majority of critically and commercially successful artists were men and the polished, industrial look of Los Angeles minimalism (the "finish fetish" movement that included artists such as Craig Kauffman and Larry Bell) dominated the local gallery scene. After earning a master's degree in sculpture from the University of California at Los Angeles in 1964, Chicago achieved national recognition exhibiting minimalist geometrical sculpture made with industrial materials. In retrospect, however, Chicago concluded that her modest success had been won only at the cost of abandoning her genuine artistic interests and suppressing her sense of gender identity. As she later analyzed her defensive response to the male-dominated art world of the sixties:

> In an attempt to compensate for the often uncomprehending responses [of men], the woman artist tries to prove that she's as good as a man. She gains attention by creating work that is extreme in scale, ambition, or scope. . . . She resists being identified with woman because to be female is to be an object of contempt. And the brutal fact is that in the process of fighting for her life, she loses herself.[6]

Chicago's principal aim for the Feminist Art Programs at Fresno and CalArts was to help women art students develop a positive sense of identity, both by encouraging them to expand their ambitions and to free themselves from traditional conceptions of what Chicago called the "female role," and by affirming "female experience" as a valid subject of art. In Fresno, the program's first project was to remodel an off-campus studio space where Chicago and her 15 female students "could evaluate themselves and their experiences without defensiveness and male interference."[7] Rejecting the formalist orientation that prevailed at most art schools, Chicago encouraged her students to conceptualize their art work in terms of personally meaningful content, rather than generating assignments based on formal or medium-specific problems. In consciousness-raising sessions, she and her students tackled emotionally charged issues ranging from money and ambition to personal relationships and sexuality, "going around the room" so that each woman had the opportunity to share her experiences and feelings. Consciousness-raising was a way of brainstorming ideas for art work; it also encouraged the young women students to confront their personal circumstances as part of a larger cultural pattern that could be analyzed and changed. Program participant Faith Wilding later recalled the process:

> As each woman spoke it became apparent that what had seemed to be purely "personal" experiences were actually shared by all the other women: we were discovering a common oppressions based on our gender, which was defining our roles and identities as women. In subsequent group discussions, we analyzed the social and political mechanisms of this oppression, thus placing our personal histories into a larger cultural perspective. This was a direct application of the slogan of 1970s feminism: the personal is political.[8]

One theme that emerged with disturbing frequency in group discussions was the prevalence of violence and sexual exploitation in women's lives. The young artists confronted and responded to sexual violence in their art work. In an early student performance described in Chicago's autobiography, for example, a "male" character extracts "service" from a woman with a milking machine and then drenches her body with the bloody contents of his bucket.[9] Faith Wilding confronted the social shame of menstruation in *Sacrifice*, a tableau in which a wax effigy of the artist, heaped with decaying animal intestines, lay before an altar of feminine hygiene products. One of the first public performances to address the topic of rape, *Ablutions*, was staged in Los Angeles in 1972 by Chicago and program participants Suzanne Lacy, Sandra Orgel, and Aviva Rahmani, based on discussions that had begun in Fresno.

Chicago, Schapiro, and their students used art to foster an empowered sense of sexual identity. To counteract dominant cultural traditions that define female sexuality as either passive (in "nice" women) or, alternatively, as dangerous and shameful (in sexually assertive women), they invented myriad "cunt" art works, "vy[ing] with each other to come up with images of female sexual organs by making paintings, drawings, and constructions of bleeding slits, holes and gashes, boxes, caves, or exquisite vulval jewel pillows," and thus reframing a derogatory sexual epithet as a symbol of pride.[10] From Chicago's abstract acrylic-on-Plexiglas "donuts, stars, and revolving mounds" (*Pasadena Lifesavers*, 1969–70), to Karen Le Cocq's anatomically-detailed plush velvet *Feather Cunt* (1971), cunt art focused on female sexuality as a vital and multivalent aspect of female experience.[11] In their 1973 "Female Imagery" essay, Chicago and Schapiro proposed, furthermore, that women artists have often organized their compositions around a "central core" image that functions as a metaphor for the female body, thus providing a "symbolic arena where [the woman artist] establishes her sense of personal, sexual identity."[12] Drawing on numerous historical examples (including Georgia O'Keeffe's sexually-evocative 1926 *Black Iris* and Barbara Hepworth's hollowed-out *Nesting Stones* (1937), this controversial essay generated vehement responses, both positive and negative, from women across the art world.

Women artists throughout North America and Britain attempted to reclaim and reframe the female body as a locus of strength and integrity in the early years of the feminist art movement; one of the boldest and most popular means to this end was goddess imagery. Linking the female body with the ancient practice of goddess worship, women artists created paintings, sculptures, altars, installations, performances, and photographs evoking historical and contemporary goddess figures and celebrating the female body more generally as a marker of spirituality. Goddess imagery often exploited traditional associations between femininity and the generative power of nature.

Cuban-born, New York based artist Ana Mendieta, for example, used her own body as well as fire, flowers, earth, and other natural materials to evoke a feminine cosmic force in her "Silhueta" series (1973–80), several hundred color photographs documenting site-specific events staged across the United States and Mexico. In *Arbol de la Vida* (Old Man's Creek, Iowa, 1977), Mendieta is bodily present – coated with mud and twigs and standing with upraised arms against an enormous tree – but also strangely transformed into something more than herself. Other works in the series picture the female body as a fleeting presence, an avatar of the cosmic cycles of creation, destruction, and transformation. In *Silueta en Fuego* (Miami, USA, 1975), for example, flames shooting from the bare earth emblazon a female silhouette in the blackness of an autumn night (Figure 16.1). In *Silueta No. 259* (Oaxaca, Mexico, 1976), a female form erupts from the earth in a mass of red flowers, inspired by the local tradition of marking holy sites with colourful petals.

Mendieta's work stands as an extended meditation on the artist's experience of living as a woman in a woman's body, addressing feelings of loss, vulnerability, and alienation, as well as a drive for empowerment and connection. It also points to the way in which one's identity as a woman is always experienced and articulated in relation to other aspects of one's identity, including, but not limited to, nationality, race, ethnicity, and class. Mendieta had first incorporated her own body in a performance piece staged in response to a series of brutal campus rapes at the University of Iowa in 1973, in which invited viewers were shocked to find the artist lying bloody and half-undressed across a low table in her student apartment. Subsequently, in the Siluetas, Mendieta acknowledged and attempted to repair the dislocations of her childhood, and to express a femininity conditioned by specific national and ethnic cultural experiences. As a young girl, she had been sent away by her family after the communist takeover of Cuba, and grew up in US orphanages and foster homes, separated from her parents, her homeland, and her first language. In adulthood, she developed an interest in Cuban Santería – a blend of Catholicism and African Yoruba spirituality predicated on a belief in powerful spirits at work in the earth – as a means of re-connecting with her lost childhood home. She called her earth-body sculptures a symbolic "return to the maternal source" and a means of reestablishing "the bonds that united me to the universe."[13]

As Mendieta's work demonstrates, goddess imagery provided scope for artists of diverse ethnic and cultural backgrounds to foreground a variety of cultural traditions. Yolanda López and Ester Hernández, for example, have incorporated attributes of the dark-skinned Mexican Virgin of Guadalupe in portraits of female family members and friends, while Amalia Mesa-Bains has fashioned elegant altars to personal and cultural role models including Mexican surrealist painter Frida Kahlo and Hollywood film actress Dolores del Rio. Betye Saar's mixed-media collages, constructions, and environments refer to black female spiritual traditions from Africa and Haiti. Mary Beth Edelson and Betsy Damon have staged performances inspired by goddess cult rituals practiced in ancient Europe. Something of the depth and breadth of interest in spiritual practices centered on female deities can be appreciated from the broad influence of Marija Gimbutas' 1974 archaeological study, *The Gods and Goddesses of Old Europe: Myths, Legends, and Cult Images*, as well as the popularity of the bestselling 1978 "Great Goddess" issue of the feminist art journal *Heresies*.[14]

Women's handwork traditions, including sewing, needlework, and interior decorating, provided an avenue for women artists in the 1970s to address women's

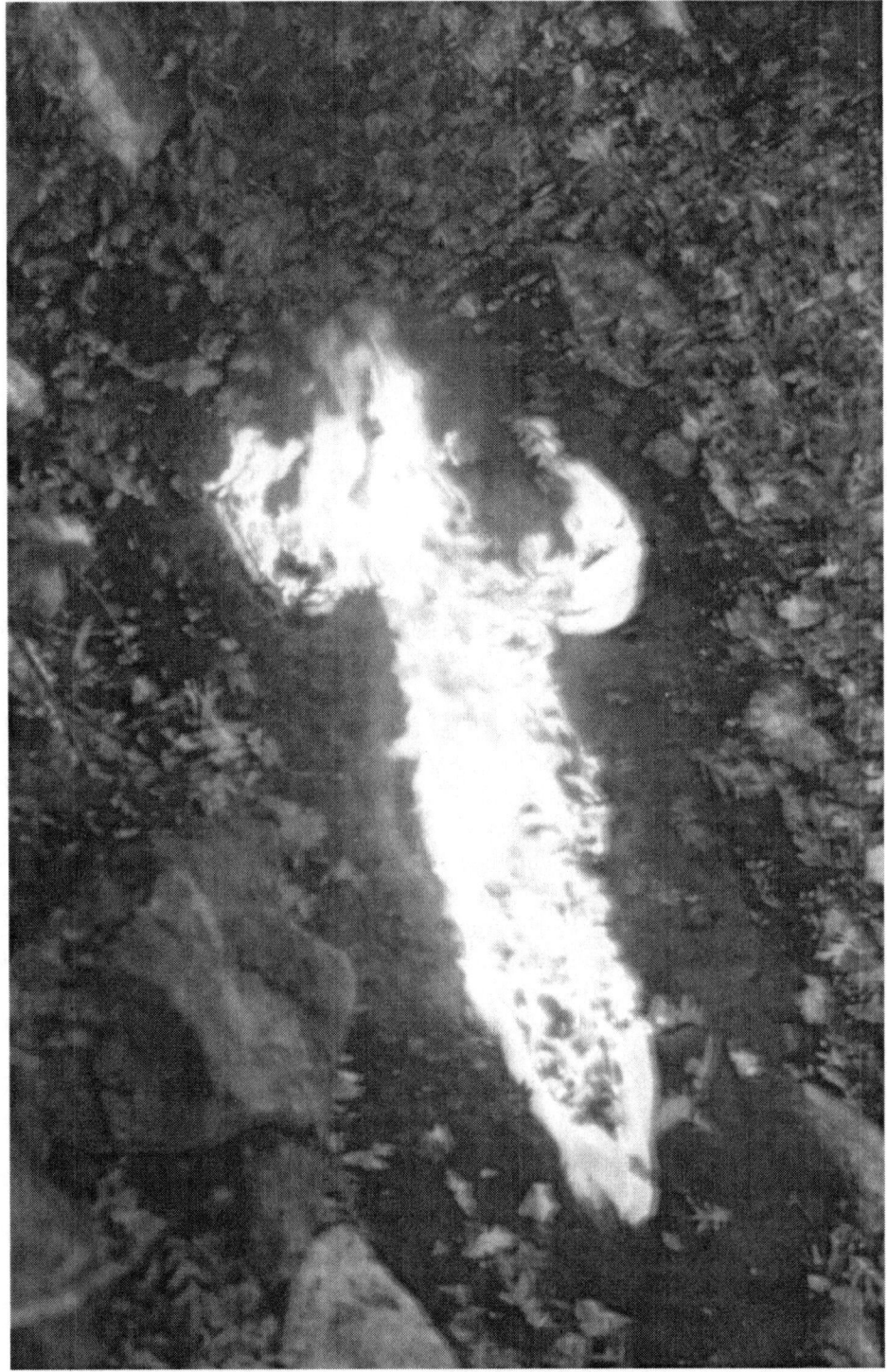

FIGURE 16.1 Ana Mendieta, *Alma Silueta en Fuego* [Soul Silhouette on Fire], 1975. Documentation of performance with fire, cloth, and earth, in Miami. Lifetime color photograph from 35 mm slide, 10 × 8 in. Courtesy of the Gallery Lelong, New York. Copyright © estate of Ana Mendieta

traditional domestic involvements and simultaneously challenge the distinction between "crafts" and "fine art." Among the most inventive artists working in this vein is Faith Ringgold, who first joined art to politics in the early 1960s with her "American People Series" (1963–70), depicting scenes of interracial hostility, violence, and tentative attempts at reconciliation. In 1972, Ringgold abandoned oil painting in favor of African women's handwork techniques – tie-dye, beading, mask-making, and so forth – which she had been teaching to others in crafts classes but had not initially considered appropriate to her professional art practice. Ringgold described her change of medium as a deliberate survival strategy for black women like herself, who often experienced black men's accusations of disloyalty, as well as white racism, because of their participation in the white-dominated feminist movement: "I saw that large groups of black women were not moving out together. I began to see that I would have to do my working-out on my own. And that it would be a very lonely life."[15]

Drawing on memories of the supportive community of women who populated her Harlem childhood, Ringgold created a series of life size soft-sculpture portraits. *Mrs. Brown and Catherine* (1973), for example, represents a smiling black woman with cornrows, holding a big-eyed baby on her lap (Figure 16.2). For Ringgold, creating this double portrait was a way of summoning up memories of love and sharing them with others:

> As I set to work, I began to remember how, back in the 1930s when I was a child, people were close to other people. How Harlem then was a friendly beautiful place. I remember there was a Mrs. Brown, who was like another mother to me. So I did Mrs. Brown in cloth, and sat her in a chair. Then I did Catherine, her child, and put her in her arms.[16]

One of Ringgold's most ambitious art works of the seventies is *The Wake and Resurrection of the Bicentennial Negro* (1976), an installation and performance piece that confronts the institutionalized social ills of racism, black self-hatred, and drug abuse, while simultaneously offering hope for a better future. As the performance begins, the bodies of "Buba" and "Bena" lie side by side, the husband dead of a heroin overdose and the wife of a broken heart. The audience is invited to participate in a vocal mourning ritual led by the dead couple's mothers, "Nana" and "Moma," and accompanied by black voices ranging from Aretha Franklin and Billie Holiday to the choir of Harlem's Abbyssinian Baptist Church. Ultimately, the combined strength of the mourners and the cathartic power of the group ritual bring about the young couple's symbolic resurrection.

Ringgold's art work is collaborative at many levels, from the process of its creation to its completion through audience participation. The initial impetus to make African textile arts the foundation of her art work arose partly at the urging of her craft students, who wanted to see their instructor put her teachings into practice. At first, most of Ringgold's figures' body parts were indicated summarily, with only ropes for legs, for instance. Over time, however, viewers convinced Ringgold that it was important to complete the bodies, and so she

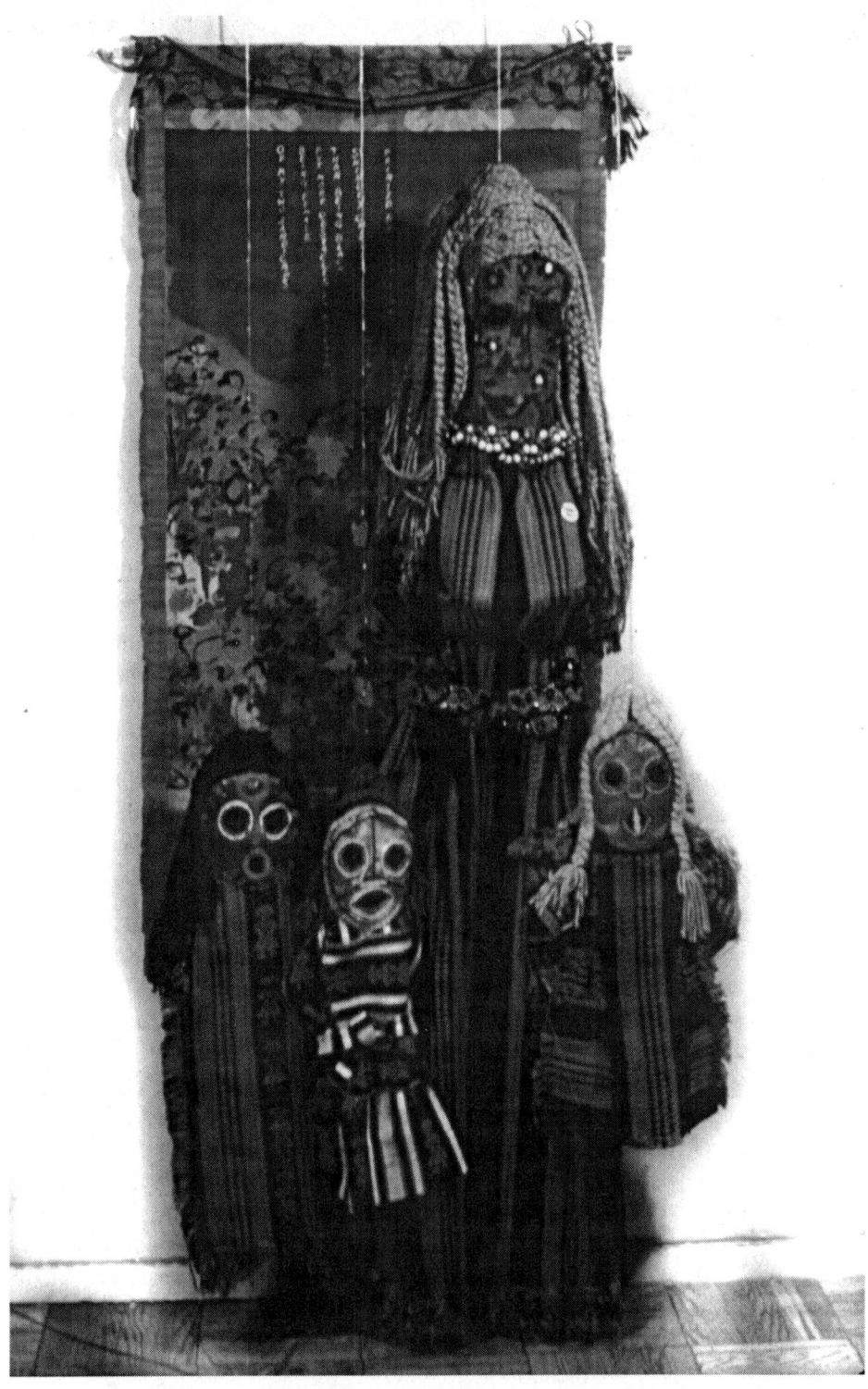

FIGURE 16.2   Faith Ringgold, *Mrs. Brown and Catherine*, 1973. Cloth, beads, thread, and ribbon. Life-size. Courtesy of ACA Gallery

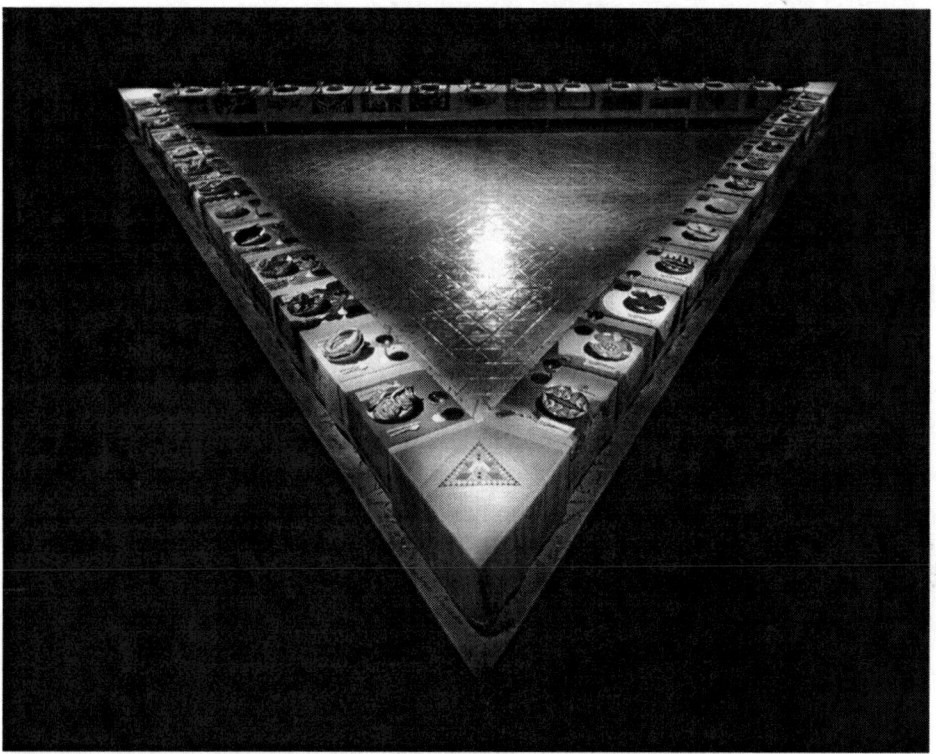

FIGURE 16.3   Judy Chicago, *The Dinner Party*, 1979. Mixed media. 48 × 42 × 3 ft.
Collection of The Brooklyn Museum of Art, gift of The Elizabeth A. Sackler
Foundation. © Judy Chicago 1979. Photograph © Donald Woodman

turned to her fashion-designer mother, Willi Posey, for help creating foam-filled,
painted bodies for them, even including "their sexual parts, the women and
the men."[17] In performance, works such as *The Wake and Resurrection of the
Bicentennial Negro* are activated by audience participation, developing in different ways each time they are enacted. "I tell the story to the [audience],"
explains Ringgold, "and then they perform it. I don't tell them what to do. I
just let them experience it."[18]

Faith in the transformative power of collaboration among women was one
of the principal philosophical underpinnings of the feminist art movement in
the 1970s. Judy Chicago's best-known art work, *The Dinner Party* (1979), is a
paean to female solidarity, from its subject matter, to its collaborative process
of manufacture, to its intended audience (Figure 16.3). *The Dinner Party* takes
the form of a monumental, triangular table with symbolic place settings for
39 mythological and historical women in western civilization. The sexual identity of each figure represented at the table is celebrated with a different vaginal
design, each "central core" image worked into a unique, hand-moulded, and

hand-painted porcelain "plate." A little-known history of powerful female deities and cultural luminaries, beginning with the ancient "Primordial Goddess" and ending with the twentieth-century artist Georgia O'Keeffe, is thus evoked through the more familiar traditions of anonymous women's domestic handicrafts.

More than 400 professional and non-professional artists collaborated on the production of *The Dinner Party* over a five-year period from 1975 to 1979. Paid workers and volunteers together researched women's history, helped produce the plates, and stitched elaborate hand-embroidered silk runners for each place setting and the three corners of the table. The efforts of key collaborators are described in exhibition materials designed to accompany the piece, as well as in the book by Chicago, *The Dinner Party: A Symbol of Our Heritage*. One of the key controversies surrounding the piece, however, was the nature of this collaboration – with feminist art historians particularly harsh critics of the way in which Chicago supposedly exploited the women contributing to the piece, subordinating them to her creative moniker (the piece is exhibited as a "Judy Chicago" even as the women are identified in the exhibition and book).[19]

Chicago also aimed to reach out to a broad audience of viewers, choosing china painting and needlework as her principal media partly for the pragmatic reason that more women would be able to identify with these crafts than with abstract painting. After opening at the San Francisco Museum of Modern Art in 1979 to record-breaking crowds, *The Dinner Party* traveled to dozens of venues across North America, Europe, and Australia, often appearing in alternative spaces arranged by women's community groups when traditional art institutions declined to exhibit it.[20]

Deconstructing "Woman"

Nearly as soon as the principal strategies of the early feminist art movement were formulated, these principles – including positive images of women, female imagery, and collaboration among women – drew fire from feminists and conservative critics alike. Some traditional art critics, not surprisingly, objected to feminist artists' emphasis on autobiographical and ideological content to the supposed detriment of aesthetic values. The movement's most vehement critics, however, were other women artists and self-identified feminists who argued that the use of female body imagery, female handcrafts, and the like effectively betrayed feminist goals by reinforcing a stereotyped or "essentialist" view of feminine identity. Ensuing debates over how best to promote the interests of women in the art world and, even more fundamentally, about what it means to be a woman or even whether it is advantageous to claim "woman" as a coalitional site from which to generate an effective political practice, have broadened and deepened the scope of feminist thinking and art making.

In response to a special issue of *Everywoman* magazine publicizing the activities of the Fresno Feminist Art Program, New York-based art critic Cindy

Nemser countered with an argument against "central core" imagery in the *Feminist Art Journal*. According to Nemser, Judy Chicago's celebration of "female imagery" had touched off a "counterwave of anti 'Cunt Art' protest from New York feminists who objected furiously to [Chicago's] efforts to categorize women's art within the bounds of such outworn, male invented stereotypes."[21] Nemser's close identification of female sexual imagery with California is not entirely accurate; to name only one prominent counter-example, New York artist Hannah Wilke had been making delicate, vulviform terracotta sculptures since the early 1960s, and continued to expand on this theme in the seventies with a tremendously inventive body of work, ranging from tiny (chewed!) vulvar chewing-gum pieces to large, quivering and fleshy, poured-latex wall sculptures.[22]

Attributions (and recriminations) aside, however, the larger question of whether "positive" images of the female body constitute an appropriate feminist strategy is an important one. The issue is bound to be controversial for a number of reasons. Naturally, there will always be critics who deem such imagery vulgar or even obscene. The line between art and pornography is continuously contested both in public opinion and the courts (witness the debate over public funding for the *Dinner Party* in the US Congress in 1991, wherein California Representative Robert Dornan described the piece as "ceramic 3-D pornography.")[23] It is important to keep in mind, however, that there is a long, venerable history of art with sexual themes, much of it canonized in museums and art history surveys and most of it created by male artists with male viewers in mind. The more important question in these debates is whether images of the female body, regardless of their subtlety or explicitness, can effectively function in *opposition* to the limiting and depersonalizing notion of "woman" as sex object. Despite the fact that Chicago, Schapiro, and Wilke described their sexual imagery as a means of offering a new, more complex, and more humane perspective on female sexuality, Nemser and others have interpreted their art as confirmation of male-invented stereotypes. Do artistic representations of women's bodies, and especially women's sex organs, reinforce the notion, drawn from Freudian psychology, that anatomy is destiny?

Perhaps the most powerful argument against "female imagery" has been articulated by British feminist art historian Griselda Pollock. In a 1977 essay provocatively titled "What's Wrong With Images of Women?" Pollock emphasized that visual images, like words, acquire meaning over a long period of time by being *used* in a particular way in a given culture. The female body, she argued, cannot effectively represent female self-determination in a culture where it has traditionally stood for male control (just as the color green cannot effectively signify "Stop" in a culture where it has always meant "Go"). As representations – or signs – operating within the larger symbol system of contemporary western society, so-called images of women actually, she argues, have little to do with women at all. Rather, "woman" functions as the opposing (and negative) cipher that defines "man" as the positive term within "a total discourse whereby the meanings carried by male and female are predicated on difference and asymmetry."[24] Operating within the larger symbol system of contemporary western society, a system based on patriarchal and capitalist principles, images of women inevitably function as signifiers of male ownership, no matter who deploys them or how.

In Britain, the feminist art movement initially centered around socialist politics and a Marxist-informed analysis of the sexual division of labor. Margaret Harrison, Kay Hunt, and Mary Kelly, for example, three artists interested in Britain's workers' rights and trade unions, staged a 1975 documentary exhibition about the Southwork Metal Box Company factory called *Women and Work*. Combining film footage with large charts and tables comparing women and men at work, the installation analyzed how traditional sex roles and ideals of femininity have had material consequences – such as unequal wages – for women working in industrial settings. Psychoanalytic theory and poststructuralist theory also had a major impact on British feminist artists and writers from the early 1970s. Paradigmatically, Laura Mulvey's widely influential 1975 essay "Visual Pleasure and Narrative Cinema," published in *Screen* (a key site for the development of British poststructuralist feminist discourse), adopted psychoanalytic theory (specifically Freud's theory of fetishism, as glossed by French analyst Jacques Lacan), to argue that Hollywood cinema like modern patriarchal visual culture, more generally is structured in accord with a mastering male gaze, a gaze that asserts its power by claiming the spectacle as its feminine target and other.[25]

Exemplifying this turn to psychoanalytic and Marxist theory is Mary Kelly's *Post-Partum Document* (1973–9), which examines the artist's relationship to her son during early childhood. *Post-Partum Document* draws in part on Jacques Lacan's theories about children's early psychological formation, beginning with the child's self-identification in relation to the caretaker in the "mirror stage" and ending with its initiation into the "symbolic order" (using spoken and written language).[26] (See Figure 14.1.)

Post-Partum Document, which consists of six parts or "Documentations," tracks and analyzes mother–child interactions in much the same way that *Women and Work* documented women's activities in the metal box factory, juxtaposing childhood artifacts with Lacanian diagrams, transcripts of recorded conversations, and analytical commentary. In *Documentation II: Analysed Utterances and Related Speech Events*, for example, numbered and dated entries track the development of speech during the child's seventeenth and eighteenth months. A typical entry juxtaposes a typewritten transcript of the child's utterance, "/ah/ be-be dere/be-be/be-be/be-be/(excitedly)/siyeh bebe dere/" with the artist's gloss of the utterance's literal meaning, "see baby there," and her determination of its symbolic function, "existence." Any sentimental response such childish speech might ordinarily arouse is summarily cut short. By interrupting viewers' potential emotional responses with analytical discourse, Kelly challenges the traditional view of women as "instinctive" nurturers, creating a visual analogue to her well-known statement: there is "no preexisting sexuality, no essential femininity . . . to look at the processes of their construction is also to see the possibility of deconstructing the dominant forms of representing difference and justifying subordination in our social order."[27]

The "anti-essentialist" argument formulated by feminists like Mulvey, Pollock, and Kelly holds that feminist art must disrupt dominant visual codes by introducing analytical distance between viewers and their customary visual pleasures. By refusing to provide pleasing visual images, *Post-Partum Document* therefore defies traditional expectations of womanhood (and/as motherhood), as well as traditional expectations of art. Neither mother nor child is pictured anywhere in the art work. Instead, the piece emphasizes the power of representations to influence people's beliefs and perceptions. Each individual element of *Documentation II*, for example, consists of two parts: a typewritten sheet of "raw data" recording the context and content of the child's speech, and a section of a typesetting tray, in which blocks of type (with reversed characters) appear above the imprint of the text they spell out. The materiality of these blocks of type, which literally "imprint" the child's speech on the page, function as a metaphor for the material power of (verbal or visual) language to mould the human psyche.

Driven by the insights of these anti-essentialist theories and practices, feminist art and theory in the 1980s focused on analyzing and deconstructing the representational codes that produce, or "construct," sexual difference. An important 1984 exhibition of US and British feminist art entitled *Difference: On Representation and Sexuality* defined this theoretically-informed approach in opposition to earlier feminists' supposedly essentialist vision of sexual identity. In the exhibition catalogue New York-based writer Kate Linker stated:

> Over the past ten years, a significant body of work has explored the complex terrain triangulated by the terms of sexuality, meaning and language. In literature, the visual arts, criticism, and ideological analysis, attention has focused on sexuality as a cultural construction, opposing a perspective based on a natural or biological truth. This exhibition charts this territory in the visual arts. . . . Its thesis – the continuous production of sexual difference – offers possibilities for change, for it suggests that this need not entail reproduction, but rather a revision of our conventional categories of opposition.[28]

Many of the art works in the exhibition juxtaposed appropriated and deliberately low quality black and white imagery with text, thus eschewing visual pleasure and emphasizing the parallels between visual and verbal representations. Barbara Kruger, one of the artists whose work was featured in the show and is paradigmatic of the dominant "text–image" type feminist art from this period, has described her art work as "a series of attempts to *ruin* certain representations."[29]

Kruger's image-and-text compositions mimic the language of advertising in order to illuminate, and thus undermine, the ideological impact of visual images in the public sphere. Kruger's *Untitled (You Thrive on Mistaken Identity)* (1981), for example, deploys its caption in bold graphics across a black and white photograph of a woman's face, which is blurry and dimpled as if seen through textured glass (Figure 16.4). The distorted image, with the word "mistaken"

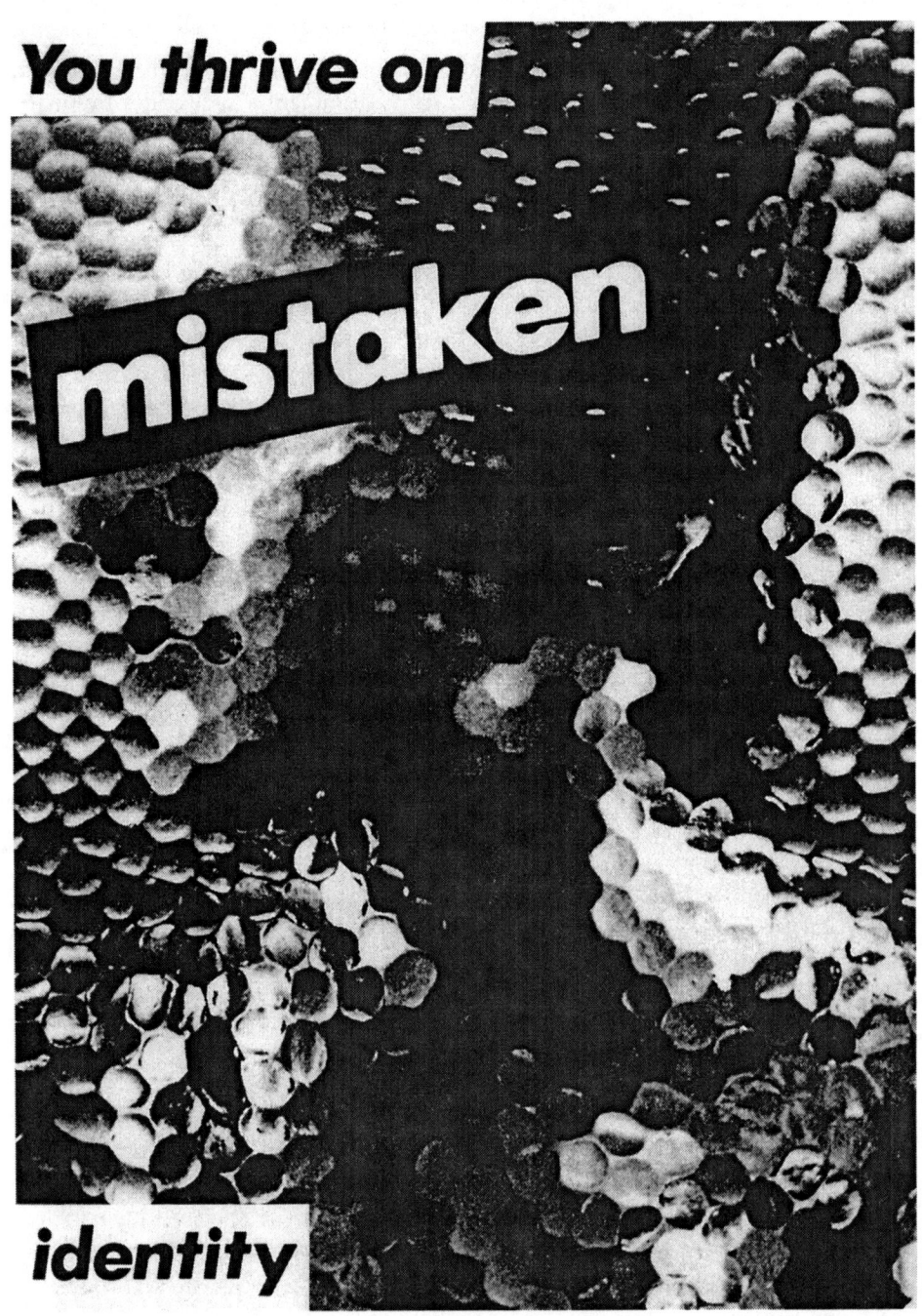

FIGURE 16.4   Barbara Kruger, *Untitled (You Thrive on Mistaken Identity)*, 1981.
Photograph. 60 × 40 in. Courtesy of the Mary Boone Gallery, New York

slapped across the woman's eyes like a crime photograph hiding the suspect's identity, suggests that words and pictures lie. Identity is, in effect, mistaken. But whose mistake is it? Kruger's "You" may function as an accusation of male sexism, challenging men who benefit from their mistaken assumptions about, and objectification of, women. But "You" might also refer to the female subject who internalizes female stereotypes. Begging the question of address, Kruger's art work illuminates the complex relationship between language and identity, suggesting that each informs the other.

Lorna Simpson likewise combines images with words to show how both can be used to objectify women, and especially women of color, by forcing individuals into predetermined categories for the purpose of identification. In Simpson's *ID* (1990), for example, two black-and-white photographs hang side by side, each captioned with a single word. The photograph on the left, which reads "identify," presents an oval of dark curly hair, barely legible against a black background. In the image on the right, captioned "identity," we see the back of an African American woman, her head occupying roughly the same position as the disembodied hair in the corresponding photo. If the first photo-caption evokes a guessing game, prompting us to "identify" the subject of the photograph, then the second stresses the violence done to individuals when identity is imposed by others on the basis of superficial and incomplete information, as in the case of an African American woman identified by her hair. Undermining the notion of identity as the "natural" possession of the self, Simpson suggests that identification is a social process that may in part, at least, be imposed from outside both on the body and within the psyche of the individual.[30]

Women and Difference

The feminist art movement faced growing criticism in the 1980s and 1990s from women who felt marginalized by its predominantly white, middle-class, and heterosexual leadership. Although early feminist organizations included many lesbian participants, lesbian issues did not develop into a central focus of discussion until the late 1970s. One of the first attempts to address lesbian art practice and theory was the Natalie Barney Collective, founded by art historian Arlene Raven at the Los Angeles Woman's Building in 1977 to "discover, explore, [and] create lesbian culture, art, and sensibility; make visible the contributions of lesbians to human culture; [and] create a context for that work to be understood."[31]

After the Natalie Barney Collective disbanded, Terry Wolverton organized a long-term performance project at the Woman's Building titled *An Oral Herstory of Lesbianism*. The Oral Herstory project began as a series of discussion sessions structured around consciousness raising and journal writing. It culminated in a performance featuring more than a dozen vignettes addressing the tremendous diversity of lesbian experience as well as the shared struggles faced by lesbian women.[32] In 1980 the Woman's Building sponsored a series of exhibitions in collaboration with the Gay and Lesbian Community Services Center under the umbrella title The Great American Lesbian Art Show (GALAS). The series had a tripartite structure that included an invitational exhibition in Los Angeles featuring ten well-known lesbian artists, a national network that facilitated local lesbian art shows across the nation, and a slide registry to document art work exhibition in the national GALAS network, as well as performances, film screenings, poetry readings, and other events. The whole project was oriented toward helping lesbians, and especially lesbian artists, forge a sense of connection with a larger creative community.

For her performance in An Oral Herstory of Lesbianism, artist Cheri Gaulke described the conflicting emotions she felt on her first visit to the Woman's Building in the summer of 1977. At that time, she still identified herself as a heterosexual. She had cut her hair very short, she explained, as

> part of my sort of radical identity. And I remember I walked into the Woman's Building and there were all these women with . . . very, very short hair, like shaved heads like me. . . . And I freaked out because . . . I recognized something that was very scary, that I'd sort of been flirting with but hadn't realized in a conscious way.[33]

Because she did not identify herself as a lesbian at the time, when Gaulke initially decided to participate in workshops for An Oral History of Lesbianism at least one woman threatened to boycott the play if Gaulke was in it. Midway through the project, however, she decided she was a lesbian, and one conflict was averted, even as her coming out signaled new conflicts with her family and religious background (Gaulke's father was a Lutheran minister).

Gaulke addressed the complicated bonds that pulled her between old identifications and new ones in a 1982 performance entitled This Is My Body, echoing the words traditionally used to invite Christians to partake in Communion (Figure 16.5). In a photograph documenting the performance, Gaulke stands before the projected image of a Renaissance painting of Adam and Eve, her own naked body replacing that of Eve. Mimicking Eve's gesture in the painting, Gaulke reaches with one hand to grasp an apple from the Tree of Knowledge. With her other hand, however, instead of giving the fruit to Adam, she brings it to her own mouth.

Despite the participation of substantial numbers of Black, Hispanic, and Asian women in the early years of the feminist art movement, racism in many forms hampered recognition of the needs, and the contributions, of women of color. In its most obvious forms, racism often resulted in indifference and neglect on the part of white feminists. For example, when Betye Saar curated Black Mirror, an exhibition and workshop series around black women artists in the newly-founded Womanspace Gallery in Los Angeles, she recalls that it was mainly black women and men who turned out for the events: "It was as if we were invisible

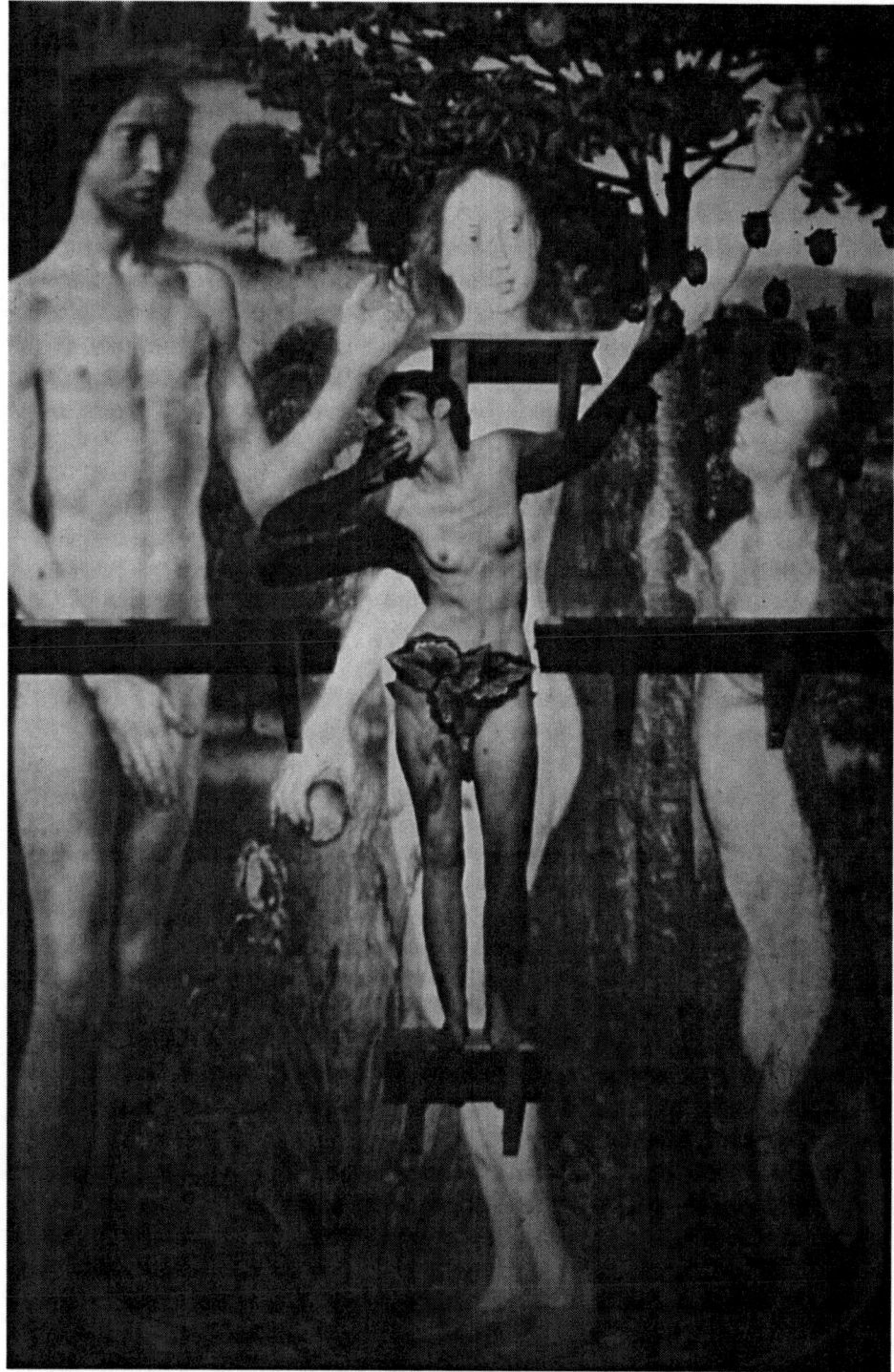

FIGURE 16.5 Cheri Gaulke, *This Is My Body*, 1982. Photograph documenting a performance at Espace DbD, Los Angeles. 20 × 24 in. Framed. Collection of the artist. Photograph: Sheila Ruth

again. The white women did not support it. I felt the separatism, even within the context of being in Womanspace."[34]

In more subtle but equally damaging ways white women's unexamined assumptions about the appropriate goals and strategies of feminist activism often silenced discussion of important cultural differences among women. A special issue of the Los Angeles Woman's Building newsletter *Spinning Off* was addressed to "Racism in the (White) Women's Movement"; here, writers articulated common frustrations experienced by women of color in the feminist art movement. Giving voice to the frustration of many Asian women at the Woman's Building, for example, an article by Ariene Inouye-Matsuo pointed out that European American feminists' ignorance of cultural differences often fosters a false sense of superiority:

Asian women [working with white feminists] have expressed feelings about being perceived as young, naïve little sisters who lack maturity and sophistication and therefore do not have to be taken seriously. Although Asian women are generally less verbal and tend to avoid conflict, these racist attitudes are not justified.[35]

The Comision Feminil Mexicana, a Mexican American feminist group that submitted a statement to the newsletter, likewise stressed the barriers imposed by insensitivity to differences in race, class, and religious background:

One of the problems about the term feminism is that it's been so associated with the Anglo community that anyone that doesn't meet their criteria, whatever it is, gets left out. If you look at the early woman's movement, Anglo women were demanding . . . to get out of the house . . . or equal pay and access to executive positions. Most of our women are heads of households [with] demanding jobs, period. . . . When we talk about abortion or sterilization, our perspective is again different, this time because of our religious upbringing. Because people don't look at that, we get told we are not feminist. We get neglected.[36]

Summing up the position of many, Betty Gilmore expressed a desire "to see Third World women at the Building . . . in important roles . . . treated with the respect they do not often receive."[37]

Artist and writer Margo Machida has emphasized the close intergenerational ties between Asian immigrants and their family members, emphasizing values that sometimes have put women of color at odds with white feminists' focus on personal independence. In an article written in conjunction with a 1991 symposium she organized in New York, "(re)ORIENTING: Self Representations of Asian American Women Through the Visual Arts," Machida pointed to Tomie Arai's serigraph *Laundryman's Daughter* (1988), drawn from an archival photograph of a seated mother and her standing daughter, as emblematic of "the immigrant legacy of all Asian women" because it "emphasizes the close intergenerational ties between them."[38] In oil paintings like *Mu Nu (Mother and Daughter)* (1997), based on a photograph of rural laborers in Maoist China,

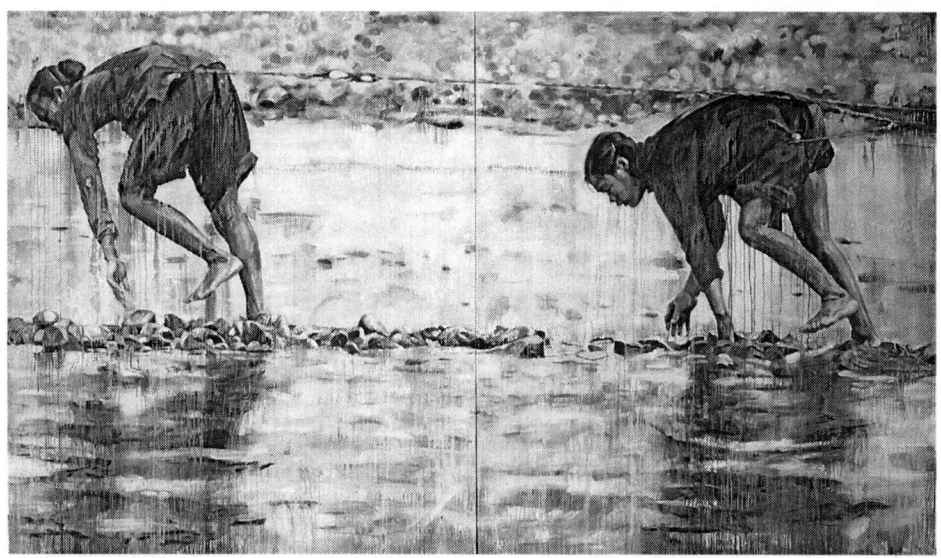

FIGURE 16.6 Hung Liu, *Mu Nu (Mother and Daughter)*, 1997. Oil paint on canvas, diptych. 80 × 140 in. Courtesy of the Kemper Museum of Contemporary Art

Chinese American artist Hung Liu likewise illuminates a powerful immigrant legacy of family unity and family hardship (Figure 16.6).

Amalia Mesa-Bains, whose altars to personal and cultural icons combine spirituality with politics, explicitly addresses the experience of immigration in a 1990 installation entitled *Borders*. Staged as a domestic tableau, the installation invokes painful private memories, as well as collective hopes and dreams. A small private altar is erected atop a large chest of drawers, beside which lies a suitcase packed with letters. Like inescapable memories of the homeland left behind, a fountain of earth floods the dresser drawers, overflowing onto the floor around its base. As Jennifer González notes, "[t]he unlikely presence of earth folded into the crevices of domestic furniture invokes both a burial and remembrance of land and life left behind."[39] For many who attempt the border crossing lose their lives. The dangers and losses faced by countless immigrants are captured in the individual memory of a young boy, inscribed on the wall: "The coyote [the hired guide who helps others across the border] put me in a sack in the back of a truck with potatoes and told me to be totally quiet until he came. It was so hot I couldn't breathe. I cried with no sounds. After hours he came to get me. We had gotten across, but where was my mother?" A poignant reminder of the threat to family stability posed by economic and political hardship, *Borders* is also a testament to the fundamental power of family bonds.

Women of color have made crucial contributions to feminist art, investing its forms with complexity and flexibility that belie the charges of essentialism so often leveled at feminist art that is not explicitly critical or deconstructive. In

Shopping (1996), a large acrylic painting set in a mythic clothing boutique, for example, Judith Lowry invokes classical feminist motifs – including vaginal imagery, goddess worship, and domestic themes – and weaves them into a cautionary tale about representation and power. The daughter of an Australian mother and a Native American father (of Mountain Maidu/Hamawi Pit River descent), a lieutenant colonel in the US Army who led the family in a peripatetic life around the globe, Lowry's paintings depict intimate family stories set in mythic worlds. The female protagonists of *Shopping* (mother and daughter perhaps?), dressed and coiffed in the style of pre-Columbian Mayan goddesses, examine a garment offered for their inspection by a smiling blond saleswoman. We recognize the robe, which the women finger critically, as the starry cape of the Mexican Catholic saint, the Virgin of Guadalupe. This charged encounter between pre-Columbian deities and the Mother of Christ raises complex questions about culture, representation, and power.[40] Is the Virgin of Guadalupe an appropriate indigenous goddess, or an assimilated European substitute? And what is the implied relationship between women, spirituality, and sexuality? The robe itself takes center stage, a rich red fall of velvet that, even as it represents the virginal saint, slyly evokes the vaginal associations of feminist "central core" imagery. Confronted with such important choices, viewers are encouraged, like the protagonists of *Shopping*, to think before buying.

The diverse strategies encompassed by feminist art practice and theory over the past 40 years have had a profound impact on contemporary art, expanding its media, deepening its human impact, and shaping the questions with which it confronts artists and viewers. Rather than marking simplistic divisions between early feminists' "positive images of women" and anti-essentialist feminists' "critiques of representation," or between a commitment to collective, coalitional action versus awareness of the differences among women, the many sides of feminist art, theory, and activism illuminate the multifaceted relationships among art, power, and personal identity.

Inspired, in part, by the civil rights movement of the 1950s and 1960s, feminist art in turn laid the groundwork for the identity politics central to art making of the 1980s and 1990s and beyond. The feminist validation of women's traditional handwork and decorative crafts has produced repercussions across the international art world, from the rarified spaces of elite galleries and museums to the gritty ones of impoverished South African neighborhoods. At one end of this spectrum (to cite just one example), Philip Taaffe's ornately decorative abstract oil paintings are arguably feminist-inspired. At the other, in poor townships and rural areas of South Africa, the Voices of Women project (Amazwi Abesifazane) sponsors the production and display of embroidered "memory cloths," created by indigenous women to commemorate unspeakable losses, from the murder of family and friends under apartheid to the deaths of entire extended families from AIDS.[41] Feminists' insistence on the ideological implications of representation has changed the way we interpret even abstract forms, from modernist grids to Rachel Whiteread's cube-shaped 1993 *House*, formed by spray-casting in steel-reinforced concrete the interior of a condemned rowhouse on London's working-class East End. Like all good art, the best feminist art eschews static visions and simple answers. In this age of contested bodies/spaces, globalization, and renewed imperialism, the need for feminist politics is as urgent as it ever has been.

Notes

1   See Jones (1996) for a discussion of Hilton Kramer's 1980 *New York Times* article, "Does Feminism Conflict with Artistic Standards?"
2   For example see Pollock (1977), 25–32.
3   Pollock (1988/2003), 12.
4   Gouma-Peterson and Mathews (1987), 346.
5   O'Grady (1992/2003), 175.
6   Chicago (1971), 25.
7   Wilding (1977), 11.
8   Faith Wilding (1994), "The Feminist Art Programs at Fresno and CalArts, 1970–75," in Broude and Garrard, ed. (1994), 35.
9   Chicago (1975), 89–90.
10 Wilding (1994), 35.
11 Chicago (1975), 55. Chicago describes these shapes as centers of movement and sensation: "I made shapes where the central holes contracted and expanded, clicked around in a circle, twisted, turned, dissolved, thrust forward, and became soft, both consecutively and simultaneously. I repeated the forms in an effort to establish a continuum of sensation," 55. The Le Cocq is reproduced in Jones (1996), 91.
12 Chicago and Schapiro (1973/2003), 40.
13 Ana Mendieta, statement in Perrault (1987), 10.
14 Gloria Feman Orenstein discusses the importance of feminist "goddess" imagery in "Recovering Her Story: Feminist Artists Reclaim the Great Goddess," in Broude and Garrard, ed. (1994), 174–89.
15 Faith Ringgold, quoted in Munro (1982), 414.
16 Ibid.
17 Ibid.
18 Ibid., 416.
19 Amelia Jones discusses this and other criticisms that have circulated around *The Dinner Party* in Jones (1996).
20 The piece was finally purchased by feminist collector Elizabeth Sackler and donated to the Brooklyn Museum of Art in 2002. It will be put on permanent display in the Sackler Center for Feminist Art at the BMA in 2006.
21 Nemser (1973–4), 9.
22 Wilke noted that "nobody noticed [the early terracotta pieces]. If you do little things and you're a woman, you're doomed to craft world obscurity." Later, however, after interest in her work increased during the 1970s, she explained that she had been trying to create "a positive image to wipe out the prejudices, aggression and fear" associated with women's genitalia, a statement that was made intelligible, even possible, by Chicago's and Schapiro's writings. Wilke's statement, made in

conjunction with her 1977 Ontario performance, *Intercourse With* . . . , is quoted in Sims (1984), 45.

23 See Jones (1996), 92–3. For an extended discussion of the Congressional debates and the pressure applied to the University of the District of Columbia to discourage it from accepting donation of Chicago's piece, see Lucy R. Lippard, "Uninvited Guests: How Washington Lost The Dinner Party," *Art in America* 79 (December 1991):39–49.

24 Pollock (1977), 32.

25 Mulvey's "Visual Pleasure and Narrative Cinema" article was initially written in early 1970s, but first published in *Screen* in 1975.

26 See "The Mirror Phase as Formative of the Function of the I" (1936, 1949) and "The Function and Field of Speech in Psychoanalysis" (1953) in Lacan (1989), 1–7; 30–113.

27 Kelly (1982), 35.

28 Linker (1985), 5.

29 Barbara Kruger, in Squiers (1987), 79, my emphasis.

30 My discussion of Barbara Kruger and Lorna Simpson's work is indebted to Joselit (2003), 221–2.

31 Lesbian Art Project manuscript, May 24, 1978, cited in Moravec (1998), 132. Natalie Barney was an American lesbian expatriate who hosted a famous literary and artistic salon in Paris in the 1920s.

32 For photographic documentation of *An Oral Herstory of Lesbianism* and other events at the Woman's Building between 1973 and 1991 see the Woman's Building Digital Image Archive at <http://www.womansbuilding.org/wb/>. See also Wolverton (2002) and Meyer (2003).

33 Cheri Gaulke (1992).

34 Betye Saar, cited in Yolanda M. López and Moira Roth, "Social Protest: Racism and Sexism," in Broude and Garrard, ed. (1994), 152.

35 Inouye-Matsuo (1980), 3.

36 Comision Feminil Mexicana (1980), 12.

37 Gilmore (1980), 6.

38 Margo Machida, quoted in Lopez and Roth, "Social Protest: Racism and Sexism," in Broude and Garrard, ed. (1994), 156.

39 González, "Landing in California," in Fuller and Salvioni, eds. (2002), 222.

40 See Theresa Harlan, "Indigenous Visionaries: Native Women Artists in California," in Fuller and Salvioni, eds. (2002), 196.

41 The Voices of Women project was initiated by sculptor Andries Botha. Botha hoped to bring into focus the often-undocumented lives of indigenous women, whose voices were not widely represented in the testimony gathered by the Truth and Reconciliation Commission (established by the African National Congress in 1996 under the leadership of Bishop Desmond Tutu with a mandate to reconstruct the history of life under apartheid). See Becker (2004).

References

Becker, Carol (2004). "Amazwi Abesifazane (Voices of Women)." *Art Journal*, vol. 63, no. 4 (Winter):116–34.

Broude, Norma, and Mary D. Garrard, ed. (1994). *The Power of Feminist Art: The American Movement of the 1970s, History and Impact*. New York: Harry N. Abrams.

Chicago, Judy (1971). "Woman as Artist." *Everywoman*, no. 2 (May 7):24–5.

—— (1975). *Through the Flower: My Struggle as a Woman Artist*. New York: Penguin Books.

—— (1979). *The Dinner Party: A Symbol of Our Heritage*. Garden City, NY: Anchor Books/Doubleday.

Chicago, Judy, and Miriam Schapiro (1973/2003). "Female Imagery." *Womanspace Journal*, no. 3 (Summer); reprinted in Jones (2003), 40–3.

Comision Feminil Mexicana (1980). "Creating a Vehicle for Change." *Spinning Off* (May):12.

Fuller, Diana Burgess, and Daniela Salvioni, ed. (2002). *Art/Women/California: Parallels and Intersections, 1950–2000*. Berkeley: University of California Press.

Gaulke, Cheri (1992). Interview by Michelle Moravec, August 6. Woman's Building Oral History Project. Available by permission of the Woman's Building Board of Directors, Los Angeles, California.

Gilmore, Betty (1980). "Racial Prejudice is a Serious Social Disease." *Spinning Off* (May):6.

Gouma-Peterson, Thelma, and Patricia Mathews (1987). "The Feminist Critique of Art History." *Art Bulletin*, vol. 69, no. 3 (September):326–57.

Heresies (1978). "The Great Goddess" issue, no. 5 (Spring).

Inouye-Matsuo, Arlene (1980). "Confront White Feminists." *Spinning Off* (May):3.

Jones, Amelia (1996). "The 'Sexual Politics' of *The Dinner Party*: A Critical Context." In *Sexual Politics: Judy Chicago's* Dinner Party *in Feminist Art History*. Berkeley and Los Angeles: University of California Press. 84–118.

—— ed. (2003). *Feminism and Visual Culture Reader*. New York and London: Routledge.

Joselit, David (2003). *American Art Since 1945*. London: Thames and Hudson.

Kelly, Mary (1982). "No Essential Femininity: A Conversation Between Mary Kelly and Paul Smith." *Parachute*, vol. 37, no. 26 (Spring):31–5.

—— (1983). *Post-Partum Document*. London: Routledge and Kegan Paul.

Lacan, Jacques (1989). *Ecrits*. Trans. from the French by Alan Sheridan. London: Routledge.

Linker, Kate (1985). "Foreword." *Difference – On Representation and Sexuality*. New York: New Museum of Contemporary Art. 5.

Lippard, Lucy (1976). *From the Center: Feminist Essays on Women's Art*. New York: E. P. Dutton.

Meyer, Laura (2003). "The Los Angeles Woman's Building and the Feminist Art Community, 1973–1991." In *The Sons and Daughters of Los: Culture and Community in L.A.*, ed. David James. Philadelphia: Temple University.

Moravec, Michelle (1998). "Building Women's Culture." Unpublished doctoral dissertation. University of California at Los Angeles.

Mulvey, Laura (1975/2003). "Visual Pleasure and Narrative Cinema." Reprinted in Jones (2003), 44–53.

Munro, Eleanor (1982). *Originals: American Women Artists*. New York: Simon and Schuster.

Nemser, Cindy (1973–4). "The Women Artists' Movement." *Feminist Art Journal*, no. 2 (Winter):8–10.

Nochlin, Linda (1971/1988). "Why Have There Been No Great Women Artists?" Reprinted in *Women, Art, and Power and Other Essays* (1988). New York: Harper and Row. 145–78.

Nochlin, Linda, and Ann Sutherland Harris (1976). *Women Artists: 1550–1950.* Los Angeles: Los Angeles County Museum of Art.

O'Grady, Lorraine (1992/2003). "Olympia's Maid: Reclaiming Black Female Subjectivity." Reprinted in Jones (2003), 174–87.

Perrault, John (1987). "Earth and Fire: Ana Mendieta's Body of Work." *Ana Mendieta: A Retrospective.* New York: New Museum of Contemporary Art. 10–27.

Pollock, Griselda (1977). "What's Wrong With Images of Women." *Screen Education,* no. 24 (Autumn):25–33.

—— (1988/2003). "Feminist Interventions in the Histories of Art: An Introduction." In *Vision and Difference.* London: Routledge Classics.

Sims, Lowery (1984). "Body Politics: Hannah Wilke and Kaylynn Sullivan." *Art and Ideology.* New York: New Museum of Contemporary Art. 45–56; 69–71.

Squiers, Carol (1987). "Diversionary (Syn)tactics." *Artnews,* vol. 86, no. 2 (February):76–85.

Tickner, Lisa (1988). "Feminism, Art History, and Sexual Difference." *Genders* no. 3 (November): 92–129.

Wilding, Faith (1977). *By Our Own Hands: The Women Artists' Movement, Southern California, 1970–1976.* Santa Monica, CA.: Double X.

Wolverton, Terry (2002). *Insurgent Muse: Life and Art at the Woman's Building.* San Francisco: City Lights.

17

Queer Wallpaper

Jennifer Doyle

The nearest Warhol print to which I have regular, free access is from his 1978 *Sex Parts* series of silk-screens. The image is a print of a pornographic photograph, a close-up of anal sex between men. Normally, this is a very difficult image to gain access to – recent large scale retrospectives of Warhol's paintings and prints have excluded any example of this series. Very few Warhol catalogues include this work – as a result, very few people even know that Warhol made work like this. I came across it by accident.

This particular print hangs on the back wall of M.J.'s, a local gay bar in my neighborhood in Los Angeles. Because most of my friends are queer, and many of them are gay men, I sometimes go to M.J.'s for an evening cocktail (Figure 17.1). The print hangs on the wall with other "gay art" – art by gay men, depicting gay sexual life (far less graphically) – and with oversized posters for gladiator movies. There is no wall text explaining what you are looking at – it's there as decoration, as the background for cruising, drinking, dancing, and more. As queer wallpaper.

The function of the word "queer" in writing about art is hard to pin down. But I am sure that the fact that a Warhol hangs in my local gay bar (not a *hip* gay bar, but an old neighborhood gay bar where it probably goes unrecognized by most of the bar's patrons) is a queer thing.

When we use the word "queer" to describe art or criticism, we are certainly saying something about the importance of sexuality to art – but we are not always "outing" the work of an artist or writer as "gay." That Warhol's image depicts sex between men may make it gay, but this doesn't necessarily make it queer. We often use the word "queer" to signal the things that can come with being gay and lesbian, with being a member of a lesbian and gay community, but which are not exactly reducible to sexual identity. Thinking about queer visual culture, in other words, is more than thinking about art by gay men and lesbians. To pursue this line of inquiry is to ask questions about where and how

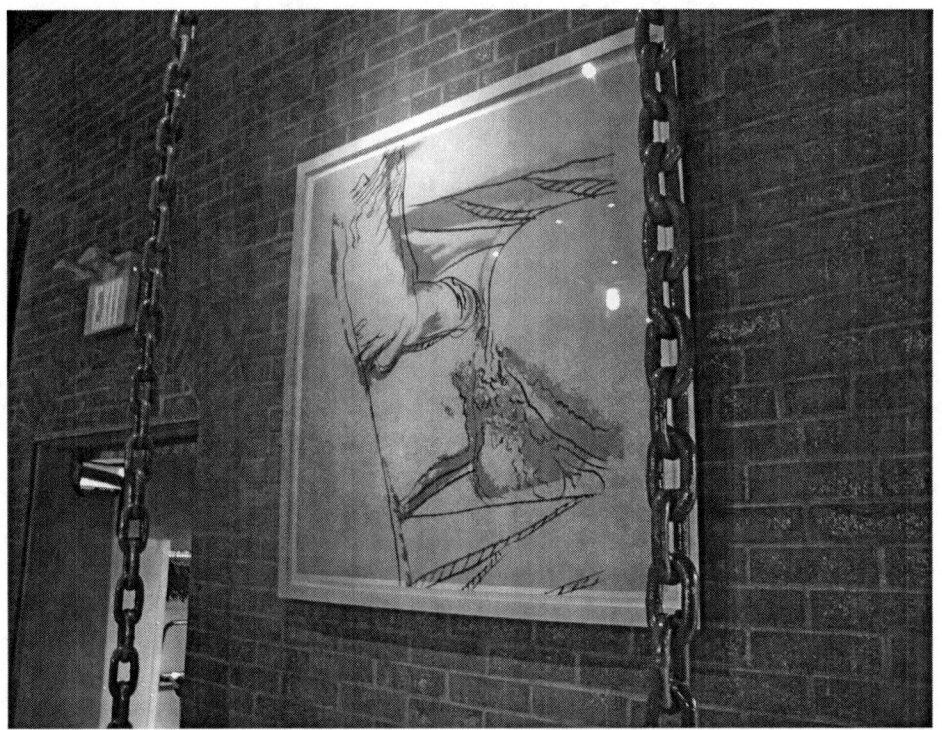

FIGURE 17.1   Andy Warhol, *Sex Parts*, 1978. © 2005 Andy Warhol Foundation for the Visual Arts/ARS, New York. "At home on the back wall of a gay bar"

that art happens, about who that art addresses, how that art is visible in some contexts and invisible in others, about what kinds of things art makes possible. It is also to look differently at art in general – at the sexual politics of all art, at what art can tell us about the world, and at how the lines around the category "Art" are drawn. For me, counter-intuitively, what's queer about that Warhol image is not exactly what it depicts, but where hangs – and what its location makes visible.

M.J.'s *Sex Parts* print is arguably one of the more accessible "real Warhols" in Southern California, requiring neither an entrance fee nor an invitation into a private mansion to see it. During business hours, anyone can walk into M.J.'s and check out the Warhol on the back wall, as long as he or she is willing to walk into a gay bar.

A straight person who crosses M.J.'s threshold but is not used to gay spaces might find himself wondering "Am I welcome here?" or thinking "I don't belong here." This is perhaps not entirely unlike the feeling that a lot of people have about museums. The grand institutions of art have a way of making many feel like outsiders. The unease of feeling unwelcome in such spaces is not entirely unlike how many queer scholars feel about the discipline of art history.

You can take a class on the history of art since 1945 and never hear a word about sexuality. You can attend a major museum exhibition on Andy Warhol and never learn that he was gay – never mind that homoerotic and explicitly sexual images animate the entire range of his artistic production.[1] In fact, the particular de-gaying effect of "official" disciplinary rhetoric is perhaps most obvious in the history of critical writing about Warhol, who is also, paradoxically, in Richard Dyer's words, "the most famous gay man who ever lived."[2] Mandy Merck writes, "as out as Warhol may have been, gay as [Warhol's films] *My Hustler, Lonesome Cowboys, Blow Job* may seem, his assumption to the postmodern pantheon has been a surprisingly straight ascent, if only in its stern detachment from any form of commentary that could be construed as remotely sexy."[3] The full discussion of sexuality and art is a very recent development in art history – as central to art history as queer people are (as, for example, artists, critics, collectors, and curators), the subject of sexuality still remains outside the official boundaries of the field. Those writers (such as Jonathan Weinberg, Harmony Hammond, Gavin Butt, and Richard Meyer) who do take up sexuality in their work are, in essence, carving out a new field of scholarship.[4] The long-standing hostility of art history to the subject of identity is the reason why so much of the most influential queer writing about art and visual culture comes from outside the discipline. Queer scholars in more politicized fields such as film (e.g. Richard Dyer), performance studies (Sue-Ellen Case, José Muñoz), visual/cultural studies (Douglas Crimp, Judith Halberstam), and critical theory (Judith Butler, Teresa de Lauretis, Michel Foucault, Eve Kosofsky Sedgwick) have provoked dramatic shifts in how we understand some of the most significant artists of this period.[5]

For those of us attached to queer subjects – such as Andy Warhol's fascination with gay porn; the sexual radicalism of films by Jack Smith, Carolee Schneemann, and Cheryl Dunye; the coded queer subtexts embedded in the work of Robert Rauschenberg, Larry Rivers, and Jasper Johns; or the utopian drive of lesbian feminist artists like Harmony Hammond – the systematic negation of queer sexualities from art history's official record can leave us feeling, well, as though we've walked into the wrong bar.

Queering Criticism

Writing about sexuality and art after 1945 differs from similar scholarship about other periods because unlike art preceding this era, many of its most famous figures (like Andy Warhol, David Hockney, Isaac Julien, Harmony Hammond, Catherine Opie) were and are openly and recognizably gay and lesbian. Toward the end of the 1960s, in the US and Western Europe gay men and lesbians formed new social and political movements around sexual identity, and began en masse to fight homophobia – in the US this movement was famously sparked by the Stonewall uprising, a protest led largely by Latina drag queens in response to a

1969 police raid on a gay bar in New York City.[6] In late twentieth-century art we see artists and audiences publicly identifying themselves as gay and lesbian, and we see curators organizing exhibitions that explore the idea of gay and lesbian identity and what it means to be a gay artist, as well as the history of representations of homoerotic bonds and identities.[7] The word "queer" emerges as a key term in conversations about sexuality against this backdrop – in which, on the one hand, we see the proliferation of representations of queer communities in all their varieties and on a range of fronts (in film, performance, painting, photography, etc.) and, on the other, we nevertheless find the systematic exclusion of art and writing by gay and lesbian artists from art historical scholarship.

In the 1980s, the AIDS crisis added a new level of urgency to the battle against homophobia – and it is at this moment that we begin to see the word "queer" circulating in academic writing, and in and around contemporary art. "Queer" was recuperated in the late 1980s from its more everyday use (often as a homophobic insult) by gay and lesbian activists working especially with ACT UP (AIDS Coalition to Unleash Power) – as in the rallying chant, "We're Here, We're Queer, Get Used to It!"[8] A number of the intellectuals now associated with queer scholarship in art criticism and visual culture (such as Douglas Crimp and Simon Watney) have been deeply involved with AIDS activism, AIDS organizations, and ACT UP itself.[9] The particular impact of AIDS on artists, on the art community, and on contemporary intellectual life cannot be understated, and the energy and political commitment that animates much writing about sexuality, art, and politics in the late 1980s and early 1990s should be understood in that context. The role of homophobia in state and public indifference to the AIDS epidemic made the project of anti-homophobic inquiry feel not just important, but a matter of life and death. Some of the most influential writings on sexuality and visual culture (such as Watney's 1987 *Policing Desire: Pornography, AIDS, and the Media*) grew directly from the need to intervene against homophobic systems of representation. Artists, activists, and scholars found themselves asking questions such as: "How do we mourn the loss of people whose lives have already been ignored, erased, or stigmatized as degenerate?" and "How do we assert the importance of gay underground sexual culture in a society that associates same-sex and non-monogamous sexual practices with disease and death?" On the intellectual movement that formed in response to the AIDS crisis, Lauren Berlant and Michael Warner write,

> AIDS activism forced the issue of translating queerness into the national scene. AIDS made those of us who confronted it realize the deadly stakes of discourse; it made us realize the public and private unvoiceability of so much that mattered, about anger, mourning, and desire. . . . AIDS also showed that rhetorics of expertise limit the circulation of knowledge, ultimately authorizing the technocratic administration of peoples' lives. Finally, in a way that directly affects critics of polite letters, AIDS taught us the need to be disconcertingly explicit about things such as money and sexual practices, for as long as euphemism and indirection produce harm and privilege.[10]

In their emphasis on the challenge the AIDS crisis posed to intellectuals, making their writing carry the urgency of the moment, Berlant and Warner gesture toward queer criticism's double edge: for not only does queer criticism bring sexuality and desire to the center of our attention; it sometimes also experiments with (and therefore "queers") the practice of criticism itself – often by injecting a personal or anecdotal voice into scholarly writing.[11]

In "Getting the Warhol We Deserve," Douglas Crimp gestures toward the relationship between the personal and the political in queer criticism when he writes,

> That is one reason why an art such as [underground film-maker Jack] Smith's – and Warhol's – matters, why I want to make of it the art I need and the art I deserve – not because it reflects or refers to a historical gay identity and thus serves to confirm my own now, but because it disdains and defies the coherence and stability of all sexual identity. That to me is the meaning of *queer*, and it is a meaning we need now, in all its historical richness, to counter both the normalization of sexuality and the historical reification of avant-garde genealogy.[12]

Crimp re-asserts one of the principle themes of queer criticism – its investment not in the articulation and production of concrete categories of sexuality and gender, but in the very real ways that queer art (be it a novel, a photograph, a film, a performance) can cut across and dismantle the attempt to produce sexual subjects as inevitable members of a "type," and, at the same time, call into question the disciplinary narratives that have formed around queer art that has been absorbed into the canonical record (such as work by Robert Rauschenberg, Jasper Johns, or Andy Warhol), or that stubbornly remains "underground" (such the films of Jack Smith, the performances of lesbian punk bands such as Tribe 8 or The Butchies, or the performances of the Los Angeles-based artist Ron Athey).

To approach the subject of sexuality and art from questions like these is to re-imagine the subject/object relation that structures much art historical scholarship. It is to push art historical writing beyond the rhetoric of connoisseurship and expertise. It is to place special emphasis on the character of the relationship between ourselves and our objects, photographs, paintings, and films – to ask what it is that we get out of our love for art. In paying attention to these artists we discover that their "queerness" resides not only in the domain of the sexual, but in how they make art, in the kinds of relationships between people and art they foster. Eve Kosofsky Sedgwick's 1993 essay "Queer and Now" thus speaks to how we become attached to certain works of art because they seem to speak to us, to speak about us – and because they seem, in particular, to speak to the experience of living at odd angles to dominant culture:

> I think that for many of us in childhood the ability to attach intently to a few cultural objects, objects of high culture or popular culture or both, objects whose meaning seemed mysterious, excessive, or oblique in relation to the codes most

readily available to us, became a prime resource for survival. We needed for there to be sites where the meanings didn't line up tidily with each other, and we learned to invest those sites with fascination and love.[13]

We feel recognized in those sites where meanings don't "line up tidily with each other," in part because they mirror our struggles with those moments when, Sedgwick writes, "all institutions are speaking with one voice," when "religion, state, capital, ideology, domesticity, the discourses of power and legitimacy" unite as a monolith around one word, such as "family" or "nation."[14] For those of us (which is probably most of us) who find ourselves living at odd angles with these monolithic structures (because we are, for example, gay, black, working-class, an immigrant, etc.), art is not a luxury, but a necessity – queer readings of books, novels, films, paintings, and performances give us our maps, our user's manuals for finding pleasure in a world more often than not organized around that pleasure's annihilation. Robert Reid-Pharr thus writes that queer political work "must necessarily be the politics of the moment, the politics of action, the politics of bombast, the politics of innovation, and most especially the politics of joy."[15] Queer artists share this suspicion of the rhetoric of connoisseurship that defines art history, and have furthermore shaped their practices not around developing a presence in the gallery system, but around the cultivation of an alternative community. The London-based body artist Franko B, for example, describes his political commitment in the following words:

> I try to work against the imposition of moral codes that dictate what is right or wrong. I started using my body as a "fuck you" to Section 28, to the age of consent, to the Spanner trial [three British legal sites that specifically criminalize gay and lesbian sex]. I said "fuck you" to the ignorance and bigotry around issues of desire, sexuality and race that thrive in institutions from the so-called liberal environment of the art academies and galleries to the tabloids and the right-wing rags. . . . My work is . . . rooted in the problems of protection, love, and freedom.[16]

At its best, queer art and queer art history is animated by exactly this blend of passion and commitment.

Imaginative Genealogies: Visualizing Queer Art Histories

Although queer criticism and theory coalesces as such in the late 1980s and early 1990s around the intense activist, intellectual, and creative energy of AIDS activism, it also has an immediate relationship to the identity-based movements of the 1970s and 1980s – to, for example, radical feminism, to the Stonewall uprising and gay liberation, to the civil rights movement – as well as to a range of critical schools of thought. This is to say that one might imagine multiple genealogies for queer scholarship and art. Given the importance of the inter-section of different aspects of identity (like race and gender) to queer criticism one might, for example, ground its intellectual history in the writings of lesbian feminists of color (such as Cherríe Moraga and Gloria Anzaldúa) and the groundbreaking anthology *This Bridge Called My Back* (1981), or in the black feminist radicalism of lesbian poet Audre Lorde.[17] Much queer theory – such as Judith Butler's seminal work on the nature of gender and sexual identity in *Gender Trouble* (1990) – is anchored in feminist theory, in the writings of Simone de Beauvoir (who famously declared "One is not born a woman" in *The Second Sex*), the philosophy of Monique Wittig (who declared in *The Straight Mind* that "Lesbians are not women"), and in the work of psychoanalytic theorists like Joan Riviere (whose 1929 essay "Womanliness as Masquerade" is crucial to psychoanalytic readings of the constructedness of gender difference).[18] One of the foundational texts in queer theory, *Between Men* (1985), Eve Sedgwick's analysis of the dynamics of homophobia and the social regulation of relations between men, begins with an assertion of the importance of materialist and radical feminism to the book's project.

Many of the artists and intellectual leaders of gay, lesbian, and queer feminist communities have furthermore been Marxists – their political radicalism is not only about re-imagining family and forms of intimacy, but also about generating a critique of capitalism's investment in hetero-patriarchy. For some of the artists most profoundly identified with queer art making the "queerness" of their ethos is directly linked to their antipathy toward consumer culture and the careerism of the art world. Jack Smith not only filmed the camp classic *Flaming Creatures* (1963, arguably queer visual culture's filmic ur-text), but penned inspired rants against "landlordism."[19] We can also look to the DIY (Do-It-Yourself) aesthetic of video artist George Kuchar (who has made hundreds of videotapes about everything from tornadoes to cats), queer 'zine culture (e.g. Tammy Rae Carland's *I "heart" Amy Carter* (c.1992–4), Vaginal Davis's *Fertile Latoya Jackson* (1982– 91), and the collectively produced *LTTR* (2002–present) – "Lesbians to the Rescue" – as modes of art making that resist the market-driven ethics of official museum and gallery culture.

David Wojnarowicz explored the relationship between corporate greed, homophobia, and the AIDS crisis in his writings and in his art. *Untitled (Hujar Dead)* (1988–9), for example, memorializes his friend (an artist who had died of AIDS) and considers "the deadly economics of the AIDS crisis."[20] *Untitled* consists of a collaged series of photographs of Hujar's corpse (images of his face, hands, and feet) underneath a layer of text. Nearly the entire surface is covered with a 46-line long paragraph, a single sentence which moves back and forth between despair and outrage – at the narrator's own decline, at this high cost of healthcare, and, more pointedly, at the smug and murderous attitudes of public officials and corporate executives. The artist writes, "there's a thin line a very thin line and as each T-cell disappears from my body it's replaced by ten thousand pounds of rage . . . it's been murder on a daily basis for eight count them eight long years and we're expected to pay taxes to support this public and social murder and we're expected to quietly and politely make house in this windstorm of murder. . . ." Hujar is buried beneath this breathless and moving single sentence and framing both the rant and the images of Hujar are dollar bills. Like Hujar, a number of the names we associate most often with queer art making (from Jack Smith to Andy Warhol to the Italian artist, film-maker, and poet Pier Paolo Passolini) often made capitalism and consumer culture as the subject of their work (as in Warhol's silk-screens of Campbell's soup cans and of celebrity icons like Marilyn Monroe).

We can construct other contexts and histories for contemporary queer art, or, better yet, we can look at the work of contemporary artists to see how they imagine alternative historical contexts for themselves. In part because so much of the history of gay and lesbian life is a history of exclusion and erasure, much queer art takes history (and even "Art History") as its subject. The Japanese artist Yasumasa Morimura, for example, performs a series of cross-racial, cross-cultural, and cross-historical identifications when he photographs himself in drag as Marilyn Monroe, as the Mexican artist Frida Kahlo, or as the white prostitute in Manet's 1863 painting *Olympia*. The Black British artist Yinka Shonibare imagines himself in a series of photographs as a Victorian dandy – surrounded by dissipated bohemians in a bedroom orgy, or by dignified intellectuals in a masculine salon. As these artists identify with and re-work the past, they practice what Elizabeth Freeman has called "temporal drag." The term "temporal drag" exploits the associations that the word "drag" has with cross-gender performance and also "with all of the associations that the word drag has with retrogression, delay, and the pull of the past on the present." Temporal drag, Freeman continues, is the "stubborn identification with a set of social coordinates that exceed[s our] own historical moment."[21] Freeman develops this term in her analysis of *Shulie* (1997), Elizabeth Subrin's shot-by-shot recreation of a 1967 film of the same title about Shulamith Firestone. In 1967, Firestone was then a student at the Art Institute of Chicago, but later, in 1970, she would write *The Dialectic of Sex*, one of radical feminism's most important manifestos. In recreating this film (which was suppressed by Firestone), Subrin asks "what Second Wave feminism might mean to those who did not live through it except possibly as children."[22] We see a similar deployment of temporal drag in David Wojnarowicz's photographic series "Arthur Rimbaud in New York" (1978–9), in which the artist photographs a young man in a range of urban bohemian underground settings (on the subway, cruising for sex, shooting heroin, masturbating), all with a mask of the French poet covering his face.

Closely related to queer projects that imagine temporal slips and hauntings, that fill the present with the past (and vice versa), is work that explores the often overwhelming sense of loss that marks especially artists who were making work throughout the 1980s and 1990s, and were therefore grappling with the impact of AIDS on the artistic community. Wojnarowicz photographed himself almost completely buried in sand, produced images of Buffalo tumbling off a bluff, and, as noted, superimposed a rant against corporate greed and indifference over a photo collage of the corpse of his friend the photographer Peter Hujar, who had died of AIDS. Felix Gonzalez-Torres covered billboards with an enormous and profoundly melancholic image of an empty bed (1991). Video artist Ming Yuen S. Ma's *Sniff* (1997) shows the artist naked, crawling in a bed searching for the scent of an absent lover as the video image itself appears to disintegrate. One of the most influential works in this vein is Isaac Julien's film *Looking for Langston* (1998), which at once articulates the importance of the Harlem Renaissance poet Langston Hughes as a black gay artist, mourns the erasure of homosexuality from representations of the Harlem Renaissance, and connects these subjects to the fragility of queer black queer bohemian communities today.

Wall Text

Several years ago (in 2002) a friend of mine got me into the press preview for the self-declared definitive retrospective of the work of Andy Warhol at the Museum of Contemporary Art in Los Angeles. I was already familiar with critiques of the show from my colleagues in London, who had seen it at the Tate, and were floored, as I would be, by the particularly cynical framing of the exhibition, which excluded huge sections of Warhol's oeuvre – namely, anything visibly sexual — from its "survey" of his career. I walked through the exhibit, tried to keep an open mind, and then settled into the crowd gathered to hear the men responsible for the exhibition – the mayor, the curator, and the director of the museum – speak.

The mayor's remarks at the press conference stayed well inside the museum's official line on Warhol and Los Angeles – "Andy always did love Hollywood."

It took a while for the shock of the spectacle to settle in: the mayor of Los Angeles delivered his rambling speech, most of which was about money – money donated, money the city hoped to squeeze out of art patrons visiting downtown Los Angeles for a glimpse of superstardom – all this was spoken at the foot of a giant Warhol portrait of Chairman Mao. The devastating political irony of the Mao portrait, which renders the face of Communist China into a "brand" (*à la* Campbell's Soup or Coca-Cola), was, one suspected, lost on the museum and city officials behind this media event. For some, however, the image of Mao can never be fully emptied out of its historical force. If the museum had imagined its constituency as comprising, in part, the range of Asian communities that make up Los Angeles, it might not have been so casual in visually pairing the mayor and museum director with Chairman Mao, the iconic image of the Cultural Revolution, as they announced their desire to bring more money to the city.

The thoughtlessness of the pairing was a reflection of the exhibit's perspective on Warhol's work as an existential exercise in nothingness – which is, as it happens, one of the ways through which Warhol is "de-gayed" by museums. The "de-gaying" effect was reinforced by the fact that the exhibit had no wall text: the museum wanted to let the works "speak for themselves."

Once the speeches were over, the museum director offered to take questions. Since I am a Warhol scholar who has written about the active refusal of museums to acknowledge the importance of Warhol's sexuality to his work, I felt it was up to me to be the loose canon and ask the "sex question." Reluctantly, I stepped up to the mike and asked how it was possible that one could curate a survey of the career of one of the most famously gay men ever (an artist who, for instance, premiered his films in gay porn houses) and elide the subject of sexuality from all discussion of the importance and meaning of the work.

My voice seemed to disappear into the space of the gallery. I felt like I was talking in a room full of pillows. The mike wasn't on (in fact, I'm not even sure it was even plugged in) and the room emptied out as I posed my awkward, and oddly academic, question. I forced myself to get to the end of my sentence, even though I felt with each word the increasing pointlessness of my intervention.

I heard myself: shrill, nervous, slightly hysterical. I saw myself, in that context, as small, and – most painfully – low-class. (To ask a question like that!) In my battered leather coat, jeans, and ponytail, I felt like an ANGRY WOMAN, and thought about Valerie Solanas, a radical lesbian who shot Warhol in 1968 and nearly killed the artist. I pictured her in her long leather coat, carrying a wrinkled paper bag hiding a gun and a sanitary napkin. A manifesto in one hand, a gun in the other, she was destined to an obscure form of infamy. A flash-image that expressed a fantasy about my own importance to this scene.

What response could he give? the museum director explained, slightly annoyed. Since I'd seen "it" (meaning the gay stuff) – "it" was in the work itself, and didn't need any explanation. Which was as much as saying that if one doesn't see "it," "it" isn't there either. And which, for me, felt about as good as hearing that I wasn't there at all. And, on some level, I felt my critical love affair with Warhol come to an end. Why bother? "Why bother explaining what 'it' is, and what's missing from the show to people who could care less?" I thought. And I let it go.

I am not sharing this anecdote because I think it represents a good example of a critical intervention. Quite the opposite. As much as I wanted to intervene in the rinsing out of Warhol, I knew in my heart I wasn't in any position to pull off that intervention. My attempt to speak out in that context was ridiculous. It was not only ridiculous of me to think I might be heard, it was ridiculous even to think that the microphones were plugged in. A huge institution like MOCA, dependent on the good will of its most conservative constituents, is expert at avoiding the mess of subjects like Warhol's queerness, and the long history of homophobic responses to that topic on the part of critics, historians, and museums. And, it is expert at managing our feelings – on making us think, "Why bother?"

We cannot underestimate the impact of this problem not only on critics, but on artists themselves. The economic pressures, the political forces that determine what goes in museums and galleries and gets printed in art journals, magazines, and newspapers are, for some, not just overwhelming, but annihilating – for some, figuring out how to make work in this environment isn't a career problem, it's a matter of survival.

And then one night, looking for a good place to have a cocktail with an old friend of mine who is a gay man, I wandered into M.J.'s, and saw the Warhol on the back wall – exactly the kind of work that you never see in museums. And in M.J.'s, Warhol's *Sex Parts* doesn't need wall text explaining to bar patrons its art historical significance. No one is there looking for a lesson in art history.

And I remembered: *that* – the integration of art into life – is just the sort of thing that queer art is all about.

Notes

1 See Doyle et al. (1996).
2 Dyer (1990), 149.
3 Merck (1996), 225.
4 Some of the best examples of gay and lesbian studies in art history and visual studies include: Hammond (2000); Weinberg (1995); Meyer (2002); Butt (2005).
5 Some examples of influential scholarship on sexuality and visual culture produced by scholars trained and/or working outside of art history: Bad Object Choices (1991); Butler (1989); Case (1988–9); Cvetkovich (2003); Doan (1994); Dyer (1990); Foucault (1978); Halberstam (1998); de Lauritis (1994); Mercer (1994); Merck (1993); Muñoz (1999); Newton (1979); Waugh (1996). The disciplinary locations of these works include art criticism, film studies, cultural studies, and performance studies.
6 For more on Stonewall and its relationship to the gay and lesbian rights movement, see McGarry et al. (1998) and Duberman (1993).
7 To name a few: Harmony Hammond's 1978 *A Lesbian Show* at Greene Street Workshop in New York; *The Great American Lesbian Art Show* (at the Women's Building in Los Angeles and cooperating galleries and spaces in the 1980s); 1982s *Extended Sensibilities: Homosexual Presence in Contemporary Art* at The New Museum in New York (organized by Dan Cameron); *All But the Obvious: A Program in Lesbian Art* at Los Angeles Contemporary Exhibitions (LACE). Catherine Lord and Harmony Hammond organized *Gender, Fucked* in 1996 for The Center for Contemporary Art in Seattle. Major museum exhibits which are not organized explicitly around gay and lesbian identity, but which are centered on queerness include Jennifer Blessing's 1997 *"Rrose is Rrose is Rrose": Gender and Performance in Photography* at The Guggenheim Museum; Russell Ferguson's 1999 exhibition for the Museum of Contemporary Art in Los Angeles, *'In Memory of My Feelings': The Art of Frank O'Hara and His Circle.*
8 See Crimp and Rolston (1990) for a history and overview of ACT-UP initiatives and demonstrations; and Berlant and Freeman (1993) for a definitive statement on queer activism and politics in the early 1990s. See also Katz in this volume.
9 See Crimp (2002) or Watney (2000).
10 Berlant and Warner (1995), 345.
11 See, for example, de Lauretis (1991); and Sedgwick (1993).
12 Crimp (1999), 12.
13 Sedgwick (1993), 3.
14 Ibid., 6.
15 Reid-Pharr (1986), 38; cited in Cooper (1996), 26.
16 Franko B (2004), 218.

17 José Muñoz, for example, grounds his work in *Disidentifications: Queers of Color and the Politics of Performance* (1999) in the work of radical women of color such as Moraga and Anzaldúa. See Lorde (1984).
18 de Beauvoir (1949/1952); Wittig (1992); Riviere (1929/1986).
19 See Leffingwell (1997) and Hoberman (2001).
20 Rizk (1998), 58.
21 Freeman (2000), 728.
22 Ibid., 731. For more on camp, drag queens, and performance, see Newton (1979).

References and further reading

Bad Object Choices (1991). *How Do I Look?: Queer Film and Video*. Seattle: Bay Press.
de Beauvoir, Simone (1949/1952). *The Second Sex*, trans. H. M. Parshley. New York: Knopf.
Berlant, Lauren, and Freeman, Elizabeth (1993). "Queer Nationality." In *Fear of a Queer Planet*, ed. Michael Warner. Minneapolis and London: University of Minnesota Press. 193–229.
Berlant, Lauren, and Warner, Michael (1995). "What Does Queer Theory Teach Us About X?" *PMLA*, vol. 110, no. 3:343–9.
Butler, Judith (1989). *Gender Trouble: Feminism and the Subversion of Identity*. New York: Routledge.
Butt, Gavin (2005). *Between Me and You: Queer Disclosures in the New York Art World 1948–1963*. Durham, NC: Duke University Press.
Case, Sue-Ellen (1988–9). "Towards a Butch-Femme Aesthetic." *Discourse*, no. 11:55–73.
Cooper, Emanuel (1996). "Queer Spectacles." In *Outlooks: Lesbian and Gay Sexualities and Visual Cultures*, ed. Peter Horne and Reina Lewis. London and New York: Routledge. 13–27.
Crimp, Douglas (1999). "Getting the Warhol We Deserve." *Social Text*, no. 59:49–65.
—— (2002). *Melancholia and Moralism: Essays on AIDS and Queer Politics*. Cambridge, MA and London: MIT Press.
Crimp, Douglas, and Adam Rolston (1990). *AIDS Demographics*. Seattle: Bay Press.
Cvetkovich, Ann (2003). *An Archive of Feelings: Trauma, Sexuality, and Lesbian Public Cultures*. Durham, NC: Duke University Press.
Doan, Laura, ed. (1994). *The Lesbian Postmodern*. New York: Columbia University Press.
Doyle, Jennifer, Jonathan Flatley, and José Muñoz (1996). "Introduction." In *Pop Out: Queer Warhol*. Durham, NC: Duke University Press. 1–19.
Duberman, Martin (1993). *Stonewall*. New York: Penguin.
Dyer, Richard (1990). *Now You See It: Studies on Lesbian and Gay Film*. London and New York: Routledge.
Foucault, Michel (1978). *The History of Sexuality*, vol. 1, trans. Robert Hurley. New York: Vintage.
Franko B. (2004). "I Feel Empty." In *Live: Art and Performance*, ed. Adrian Heathfield. New York: Routledge.
Freeman, Elizabeth (2000). "Packing History: Count(er)ing Generations." *New Literary History*, no. 31:727–44.
Halberstam, Judith (1998). *Female Masculinity*. Durham NC: Duke University Press.

Hammond, Harmony (2000). *Lesbian Art in America*. New York: Rizzoli.

Hoberman, J. (2001). *On Jack Smith's* Flaming Creatures *and Other Secret-Flix of Cinemaroc*. New York: Granary Books.

de Lauretis, Teresa (1991). "Queer Theory: Lesbian and Gay Sexualities." *differences: A Journal of Feminist Cultural Studies*, vol. 3, no. 2:iii–xviii.

—— (1994). *The Practice of Love: Lesbian Sexuality and Perverse Desire*. Bloomington: Indiana University Press.

Leffingwell, Edward, ed. (1997). *Flaming Creatures: The Life and Time of Jack Smith*. London: Serpent's Tale Press.

Lorde, Audre (1984). *Sister Outsider: Essays and Speeches*. New York: Crossing Press.

McGarry, Molly, Fred Wasserman, and Mimi Bowling (1998). *Becoming Visible: An Illustrated History of Gay and Lesbian Life in Twentieth-Century America*. New York: Studio.

Mercer, Kobena (1994). "Reading Racial Fetishism: The Photographs of Robert Mapplethorpe." In *Welcome to the Jungle: New Positions in Black Cultural Studies*. New York and London: Routledge. 171–220.

Merck, Mandy (1993). *Perversions: Deviant Readings*. New York: Routledge.

—— (1996). "Figuring Out Warhol." In *Pop Out: Queer Warhol*, ed. Jennifer Doyle, Jonathan Flatley, and José Muñoz. Durham, NC: Duke University Press. 224–37.

Meyer, Richard (2002). *Outlaw Representation: Censorship and Homosexuality in Twentieth-Century American Art*. Oxford: Oxford University Press.

Moraga, Cherrie, and Gloria Anzaldúa, eds. (1981). *This Bridge Called My Back: Writings by Radical Women of Color*. New York: Kitchen Table/Woman of Color Press.

Muñoz, José (1999). *Disidentifications: Queers of Color and the Performance of Politics*. Minneapolis: University of Minnesota.

Newton, Esther (1979). *Mother Camp: Female Impersonators in America*. Chicago: University of Chicago Press.

Reid-Pharr, Robert (1986). "Queer Art at the Whitney." *Fuse Magazine*, vol. XVI, no. 4 (May/June):38.

Riviere, Joan (1929/1986). "Womanliness as Masquerade." Repr. in *Formations of Fantasy*, ed. Victor Burgin, James Donald, and Cora Kaplan. New York: Routledge, Chapman and Hall. 35–44.

Rizk, Mysoon (1998). "Reinventing the Pre-invented World." In *Fever: The Art of David Wojnarowicz*, ed. Amy Scholder. New York: Rizzoli. 45–67.

Sedgwick, Eve Kosofsky (1985). *Between Men: English Literature and Male Homosocial Desire*. New York: Columbia University Press.

—— (1993). "Queer and Now." In *Tendencies*. Durham, NC: Duke University Press. 1–20.

Watney, Simon (1987). *Policing Desire: Pornography, AIDS, and the Media*. London: Methuen.

—— (2000). *Imagine Hope: Gay Identity and AIDS*. London and New York: Routledge.

Waugh, Thomas (1996). *Hard to Imagine: Gay Male Eroticism in Photography and Film from the Beginning to Stonewall*. New York: Columbia University Press.

Weinberg, Jonathan (1995). *Speaking For Vice: Homosexuality in the Art of Charles Demuth, Marsden Hartley, and the First American Avant-Garde*. New Haven: Yale University Press.

Wittig, Monique (1992). *The Straight Mind and Other Essays*. Trans. Louise Turcott. Boston: Beacon Press.

18

Implications of Blackness in Contemporary Art

Pauline de Souza

[handwritten annotations: rela. btw. identity ? contemporary art / pol. of representation ? race]

Exploring the relationship between identity (including identifications of class, race/ethnicity, gender, sexuality, nationality, etc.) and contemporary visual practice is a challenge. There is now a vast body of work on the politics of representation and race in cultural studies, art history, and visual culture studies (including the history and theory of photography), and feminist and queer theory. Beyond these areas, recent debates around digital technology and new art forms have also explored the complex relationships among visual images and social or individual identities.

In this chapter I will focus on aspects of race and ethnicity as these have played out in the visual arts and culture of Britain and the United States, and on blackness as a signifier of racial difference (leaving aside for now the open-ended complexities of other aspects of racial and ethnic difference in these two cultures). It is important to note that blackness reads differently in the US versus Britain. Although "black" had a more permeable meaning in the US before the twentieth century (being applied, for example, to the Irish immigrant population), at this point it largely refers to African Americans (per the notorious "one drop" rule, this includes people who have any amount of African blood, most likely having descended from slaves). During the civil rights movement in the US in the 1950s and 1960s, of course, the term "black" was adopted and given a positive slant – coming to refer to aspects of black pride and, later in the 1960s, to the Black Power movement itself. In Britain during the 1980s it applied broadly to designate practically any group that is not northern European in origin, but now Asian artists tend to define themselves more explicitly as Asian, Pakistani, or Indian artists. Recently the term "black" has also been used in relation to the different diasporic experiences among eastern European immigrants entering Britain.

[handwritten margin annotations: race ethnicity; G.B. / U.S.; Blackness; reads diff. in US / G.B.; US / G.B.]

Here, as the context demands, I will move back and forth between the two meanings of blackness. I will *not* capitalize the adjectival "black" unless it was capitalized by the original group I am discussing (the very capitalization of the word was often a strategic move to revalue black culture). I will pivot my discussion around the work of artists such as Kara Walker and Roshini Kempadoo who explore the complexity of racial and ethnic identity through strategic visual practices.

Frantz Fanon and the (Post)Colonial Gaze

Roshini Kempadoo, a British artist of Indian and Caribbean descent, produced a 1996 series entitled *Sweetness and Light,* the title of which refers to the notion of innocence as understood within Caribbean cultures (an innocence that can disrupt the effects of Western colonialism). The digital photographs also refer to fifteenth-century sugar plantations in the Caribbean. They consist of scanned images made from photographs that were originally taken in the nineteenth and twentieth centuries and then superimposed on representations of monumental buildings and landscapes. Kempadoo describes these photo-constructions as documentary images of Western colonialism, and as such her work opens up an

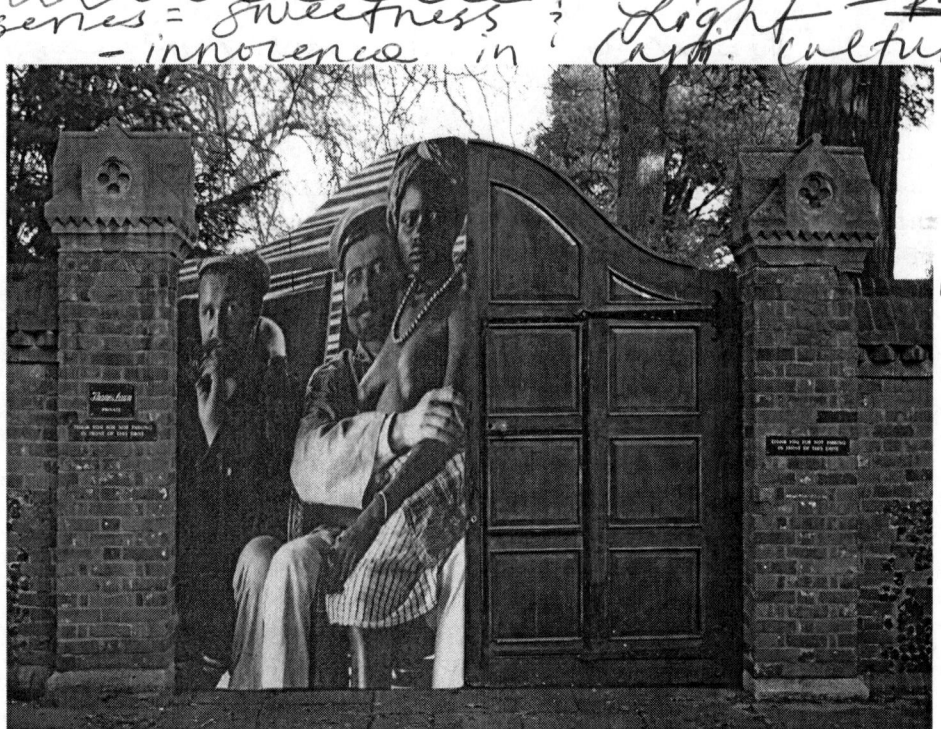

FIGURE 18.1   Roshini Kempadoo, *The Great House People*, part of *Sweetness and Light* series, 1996. Courtesy of the artist

investigation into the representation of racial and ethnic difference under colonial regimes.

The development in eighteenth- and nineteenth-century Western cultures of the natural sciences, ethnology, and anthropology provided methods for the documentation of the cultures of non-Western peoples. Many nineteenth-century institutions, from universities to natural history museums, developed programs, methods, and concrete architectural structures to assist in the project of collecting, organizing, and displaying the cultural artifacts of the countries invaded by the West. The aim of such institutions was to quantify and thus control the people they governed by systematically and unfavorably comparing their cultures and ways of life to the cultural achievements of the West. Under the guise of furthering knowledge, cultures outside the Western European traditions were classified as primitive, degenerate, and stagnant, thus reinforcing the fantasized superiority of European culture.

In the image *The Great House People* from the *Sweetness and Light* series (Figure 18.1), a black female slave sits on a white man's lap; another seated white man is beside them smoking. The image is accompanied by the quotation, "whichever way the eye is turned it is regaled with an endless variety of pleasing prospects." Through this juxtaposition of figures and text, Kempadoo looks at the relationship between the West and its "others," pointing to the parallel between the white man's ownership of the land and his possession of the black female body.

Making use of the kind of photographic snapshots that were widely disseminated in the high colonial period, Kempadoo directs our attention to the way in which the photographic image-as-spectacle tends to exploit human difference to produce a frisson of erotic and commercial desirability. She also points to the way in which such images, while ostensibly documenting other cultures in a purely "scientific" manner, as rationalized through the academic and museological discourses of ethnography and anthropology, served to justify the commercial dissemination of a plethora of images of naked and semi-naked black women. Kempadoo's images also signal the way in which the difference between the colonial master and the semi-naked female figure reinforces her otherness (her role as an object, a signifier representing the submission of the "inferior" culture), and confirms the confluence between racial and sexual identity (the black woman is inferior both *as woman* and *as black*). These images of the subordinated black woman, represented implicitly as promiscuous and desirable but also as anonymous body (itself reduced to one particular erogenous zone: the breast), confirm that stereotypical codes and conventions regarding race and gender are culturally constructed in visual images via complex dialectics of power.

Frantz Fanon addressed the dilemma of the black female in the chapter entitled "The Woman of Colour and the White Man" in his epochal 1952 book *Black Skin, White Masks*. Whether she is a Negress or mulatto, the black woman, Fanon argues, comes to represent the disreputable side of colonialism. For other cultural theorists engaged with postcolonial theory the black female body tends to play the same role. The dynamic through which the "superior" European must construct the body of the colonized *as* other, projecting his insecurities outward, is founded in the psychological uncertainty of the colonial self – what French philosopher Jean-Paul Sartre explored as the fundamental alienation of the subject. Within this logic, the black *female* is doubly (racially and sexually) othered.

As Fanon argued, it is via the gaze (motivated by this psychological uncertainty) that the colonizer assigns the colonized other particular attributes, projecting his distorted fears outward. Fanon's emphasis on the gaze puts the visual regime at the forefront of how the mechanism of racial and sexual differencing takes place and how it is understood in Western postcolonial theory. Through this model, it is argued that the black woman is accused of desiring the white male body (thus exonerating the white male for "taking" her), while the black male body is subjected to a violent dynamic of fragmentation that destroys his self-esteem and threatens his masculinity. The only escape for the black woman is to strive to erase her blackness. Fanon argues, "[f]irst of all, there are two such women: the negress and the mulatto. The first has only one possibility and one concern: to turn white. The second wants not only to turn white but also to avoid slipping back."[1]

The cultural error of racism is caused by the exploitation of the "negro," who is despised by a colonialist capitalist society that is inherently white. Black women living under colonialism were forced to be made aware of their exchange value while the black man, in his desire to communicate with whiteness, was forced to plead for active understanding in order to be viewed as "whole". These relations, of course, continue into the present. Drawing on Fanon's theories, the art historian Kobena Mercer has explored the continued fragmentation of the black male body within postcolonialism and postmodernism. Under late (or global) capitalism, the economic system of postcolonialism, black men "have become the bearers – the signifiers – of the hopelessness and despair of our so called postmodern condition . . . black masculinity is not merely a social identity in crisis. It is also a key site of ideological representation, a site upon which the nation's crisis comes to be dramatized."[2]

While the black man is thus a locus for the dramatization of national and individual anxieties, in Fanon's model the body of the black woman functions to highlight the desirability of the white female body, which is ideologically invested with the attributes of purity and self control (in contrast to the "promiscuous" black woman). In *Black Skin, White Masks*, he argues that the white woman actively desires sexual intercourse with the black man but is afraid of what she perceives to be his animal instincts; she is frightened of being raped but simultaneously wants to be raped: "If we go farther into the labyrinth, we discover that when a woman lives the fantasy of rape by a Negro, it is in some way the fulfillment of a private dream, of an inner wish. Accomplishing the phenomenon of turning against self, it is the woman who rapes herself."[3] For

Fanon, the black woman is conscious of the black man's inferiority and recognizes his need to possess her violently through rape.

The limits of Fanon's model in exploring the confluence of racial and sexual difference are clear. Implying that all black women are the same, Fanon follows this by essentially arguing that all women are the same [all women want to be raped by the black man]. While brilliantly arguing the limits of the colonial gaze in racial terms, Fanon himself did not acknowledge the different position different women could hold within this dynamic. Clearly, the black woman poses a profound challenge to many of the dominant models for conceptualizing racial difference in Euro-American culture – Kempadoo's work suggests as much. Before exploring the way in which black women have addressed this challenge by developing a black feminist model of cultural critique and artistic practice, a brief history of the black arts movement will be useful in clarifying some of the other limits of racial discourse and critique as these have inflected the practices and institutions of the visual arts.

The Black Arts Movement and the Problem of Ethnicity

In the 1970s and 1980s, racial riots and increased racism in Britain and the US led artists from non-Western backgrounds to think deeply about their cultural identity. Because of this interest in identity, ethnicity emerged as a dominant cultural term, based on important studies such as Naseem Khan's 1976 report entitled *The Arts Britain Ignores*, which used the term to define black arts as something different from British culture, and thus to make it more visible and to emphasize the contribution that ethnic arts could make to British culture. Based on this argument, in the early 1980s the Greater London Council set up the first Ethnic Arts Sub-Committee, which organized the 1982 "Ethnic Arts Conference," where participants discussed terminologies to signify the cultural differences in Britain. In 1984, the group Indian Artists: United Kingdom organized the *Into the Open* exhibition in Sheffield, the first national show of the work of Indian artists living in Britain, and in 1985 the "Vision and Voice" conference deployed the term "black art." By the mid-1980s the terms "black art" and "Black British" were commonly deployed in describing the alternative art scene in Britain.[4]

Other artists living in Britain whose families came from non-European backgrounds became aware of inequalities they experienced as representatives of "ethnic" cultures. The Young Black Art Group, founded in 1980 by Eddie Chambers in Wolverhampton, set out to give voice to the radical political and social concerns of black art students. The group changed its name to the Black Art Group in 1981, expanding its membership. In its critique of Western art practice and definitions of history, identity, and culture the Black Art Group was influenced by the political art works of Eric Pemberton and the ideas of US-based Harlem Renaissance leaders such as Marcus Garvey, civil rights leader

Martin Luther King, and Black Power advocate Malcolm X. Black British cultural theorist Paul Gilroy mirrored the coalitional interests of the Black Art Group (and the tendency to suppress or ignore aspects of identity other than race), in his 1987 book *There Ain't No Black in the Union Jack*, in which he argued that the legitimacy of black culture lies in the political and social unity amongst black people, a unity destroyed by the articulation of separate interest groups within black identity.

The sense of belonging, identity, and community important to the Black Art Group and to Gilroy – leading to the development of an idea of visual arts practice based on a coalitional politics of cohering black British identity – is to some extent put in question by black British cultural theorist Stuart Hall's arguments in his 1990 essay "Cultural Identity and Diaspora." Here, interrogating the tendency of coalitional politics to assume an inherent or essential group identity, Hall argues that "cultural identities are . . . the unstable points of identification or suture, which are made, within the discourses of history and culture. Not an essence but a positioning. Hence, there is always a politics of identity, a politics of position, which has no absolute guarantee in an unproblematic transcendent 'law of origin'."[5] Hall's formulation has been extremely influential in complicating the notion of race and ethnicity within black British art practice and discourse.

Hall's argument signaled a shift in the late 1980s in the theorization of racial identity and culture in Britain and the US. Around this time black British artists influenced by the black arts movement began to change direction. Postcolonial theorists such as the US-based Homi Bhabha began to present more nuanced models of identity that moved away from structuralist models systematizing difference in binary terms; these more nuanced models, some have argued, diffuse the polemical force of models based on clear categories of cultural difference based on race alone. In this way, in his 1994 book *The Location of Culture*, Bhabha, arguing that there is no clear opposition between sameness and separateness, established a more amorphous, non-dichotomous ideological space that to some extent neutralized the antagonism between the colonizer and colonized. Bhabha's work typifies the move toward a complex notion of racism as culturally and socially constructed, as deeply implicated in other aspects of identity, and as impossible to pin down in relation to binary models of self and other, and toward a questioning of ethnicity altogether as a means for understanding culture.

The notion of ethnicity was also called into question because of its institutional ties. In his 1987 essay "From Primitivism to Ethnic Arts," Rasheed Araeen describes how the cultural artifacts of non-European ("ethnic") artists have traditionally been classified as primitive (the products of stagnant or "timeless" cultures), in comparison with the rapid cultural developments of Western modernism.[6] Araeen argues that the same attitude can be found within Britain, noting that non-Western artists living in Britain are expected to produce art objects that reflect their particular cultural heritage (while white artists presumably

[margin notes: no clear opposition btw sameness & separateness ↓ not black & white ↓ focus on grey in btw.]

[margin notes: self vs. other]

[margin notes: rela. btw. ethnicity & culture]

[bottom notes: expectations of today's non western British artists — reflect own cultural heritage compared to white artists → mod.]

make ethnically "neutral" modernist or postmodernist works). Araeen further notes that the term "ethnic" is suspect in that it began to be widely deployed in the arts by British cultural institutions in the 1980s looking to categorize artists from immigrant communities in Britain. Pointing out that all black and Asian people were placed under the umbrella of ethnicity, he argues convincingly that these institutions showed no interest in considering the differences in the cultural backgrounds of these artists.

Diaspora and Racial Identity

The history of black slavery, the forced immigration of Africans to slave-holding nations and colonies, remains an undercurrent in discourses of black identity and visual culture. In the late 1980s and early 1990s debates about British black art and identity frequently referred to a diaspora population, a community that had been dispersed and relocated elsewhere. The concept of diaspora, which in Britain has come to refer primarily to the cultural status of the immigrants from the Caribbean, was initially borrowed from the Jewish experience of displacement and persecution. (See Nelson in this volume.) Caribbean-British peoples had thus brought their own cultural traditions, linked to Africa, to Britain and had to cope with the racial antagon-ism they encountered because of these "alien" traditions and the pressure of historical colonial beliefs about race.

These cultural traditions began to be openly acknowledged and celebrated by the second generation who were born in Britain. As Eddie Chambers argued,

> We of a younger generation find ourselves to be no less "immigrants" than our fathers and mothers. And our feelings of alienation are often no less complete than those of our parents. Indeed, I ought really to say that in the case of Black people the term "immigrant" is really one which transcends strict definitions of where one was born, and the country to which one relocates. Instead the term "immigrant" can reasonably be used to describe the position and status of Black people in England. Both those born here and those born elsewhere.

At the same time, in Britain, the term "immigrant" was problematic for the first and second generations. The members of the first generation did not see them-selves as immigrants per se, but felt driven to try to belong to the colonial motherland – Britain. Specific diasporic discourses used by the members of the second generation absorbed both their parents' cultural traditions and the cultural forms of Britain. Diasporic discourses reveal the tensions between indigenous and immigrant cultures, the politics of the nation-state, and problems of assimilation. Thus younger generation black artists continue to stress their connection to the homeland of their ancestors, often surrounding this imagined "native" culture with mythological symbolic references.

These issues are taken further by Edward Said, who argued throughout his career that the transgressive insight borne of the experience of displacement

[handwritten top margin: Brit. black art movement mapped out global interconnections]

enables a diasporic person to position him/herself critically in the world. Diasporic discourses, for example, have encouraged black artists in Britain to develop a global consciousness of other postcolonial experiences. This consciousness has been encouraged over recent decades for two reasons: firstly the experience of economic interdependence between North America and Europe caused changes in world power and cultural consumption; secondly, with the shifts of late capitalism and global communications networks national or state boundaries no longer act as economic and cultural barriers as they did in the past. Freedom of movement and interaction has created a new symbolic order of time and space that has provided a new framework for joint cultural experiences, redefining cultural relations of power. *[handwritten: — new framework for joint cul experience redefining cultural relations of power]*

Thus, the British black art movement has mapped out global interconnec- tions, linking up to African American and Caribbean cultures. Paul Gilroy used the term "the black Atlantic" to describe this particular network.[8] This sense of global interconnections is expanding as other black artists become involved in the visual arts, and as artists and critics become increasingly aware of the pressures and effects of globalization, as well as the crucial insights of ethno- *[handwritten: pressures & effects of globalizatio]* graphy and other related disciplines. In her 1992 essay "Pan-American Post- nationalism: Another World Order," Coco Fusco privileges global connections, attacking previous, essentialist African American views, and welcoming the dia- logue between African American and British black cultural critics and artists: "it's a cause for joy, because among other things it signals the waning of the isolationist view of culture characteristic of postwar American thought."[9]

This awareness of globalization in the art world is also exemplified by the 1997 *Documenta X* exhibition, curated by Catherine David, which took place in Kassel, Germany. *Documenta X* explored globalization through the issues of violence and social, economic, and cultural transformations, pulling together an international group of works that questioned assumptions about representations and reality. Along with other major exhibitions putting identity at the forefront, such as the 1993 Whitney Biennial, *Documenta X* emphasized the inescapability of addressing racial and ethnic – as well as sexual, gender, national, and class – identity in understanding the cultural significance of visual art works.

Black Feminism

Inspired by the civil rights and Black Power movements in Britain and the US (in particular sparked by the influential early 1970s article by Angela Davis, "Women and Capitalism: Dialectics of Oppression and Liberation," and the work of Olive Morris and the Organisation of Women of African and Asian Descent founded in 1978 in Britain), black feminists have been motivated to redress both the blindness to gender within postcolonial theory and the blind- ness to racial and ethnic difference within mainstream feminism. To this end, black feminism has placed history within a political and social framework in

[handwritten bottom margin: addressing blindness to gender/racial & ethnic diff.]

order to attack the tendency within mainstream feminism to pose a "universal sisterhood" while implicitly ignoring issues of race and class. In the mid-1980s British Black feminism, developing out of the Black British art movement as an independent, politically conscious group in its own right, set out to rearticulate a black woman's point of view and to make it possible to represent black and women's history.

Lubina Himid has argued it is essential for black female artists to position themselves in relation to black cultural identity but also to ensure that their identity as artists is not restricted by the terminology: "Positive conceptions of ethnicity at the margins [lead to] a recognition that we all speak from a particular place, out of a particular history, out of a particular experience, a particular culture, without being contained by that position."[10] Black feminists have thus been driven by the imperative of attempting to transcend self-negating identification with whiteness (as promoted in mainstream feminism) and self-affirming identification with blackness (as promoted in postcolonial theory).

Returning to Kempadoo's *Sweetness and Light*, *The Great House People* image, it is notable that the text accompanying the image – "whichever way the eye is turned it is regaled with an endless variety of pleasing prospects" – positions both the female and, potentially, the male bodies in the field of the desiring gaze (see Figure 18.1). The black woman offers pleasing prospects to her owner; as a trophy of colonialist power, she endorses his status and racial supremacy. And yet the black man, also a slave, is posed also as a "pleasing prospect," albeit of a different variety in this presumptively heterosexual racial matrix.

Kempadoo relates contemporary structures of oppression to those from the past, and implicates gender and sexuality in the structures of racial oppression. In contrast to Fanon's attitude toward women (his tendency to imply that all women are the same), Kempadoo's images also make the point that the history of the black subject, as understood from slavery to postcolonial theory, still places the Western black body within the context of first world intellectual practices. From this perspective black women placed outside the West are studied as "third world women" whose experiences are deeply rooted in the experience of developing countries. Such categorizations are profoundly limiting. As Elizabeth Sussman argues in her essay for the 1993 Whitney Biennial, cultural positions are not unchanging and it is time to move beyond monolithic concepts of identity groups.[11] Gayatri Chakravorty Spivak situates herself within the same debate, arguing in a published interview with Walter Adamson that it is impossible for one group to speak for everyone.[12] As Kempadoo's complex works make clear, race, gender, and sexuality are inextricably connected, and never in a stable way, in the positioning of the subject in the modern and contemporary worlds.

Black feminist artists and art theorists have also explored aspects of the history of colonialism and its impact on identity. Like Kempadoo, African American artist Kara Walker makes reference to the past (primarily the history of American

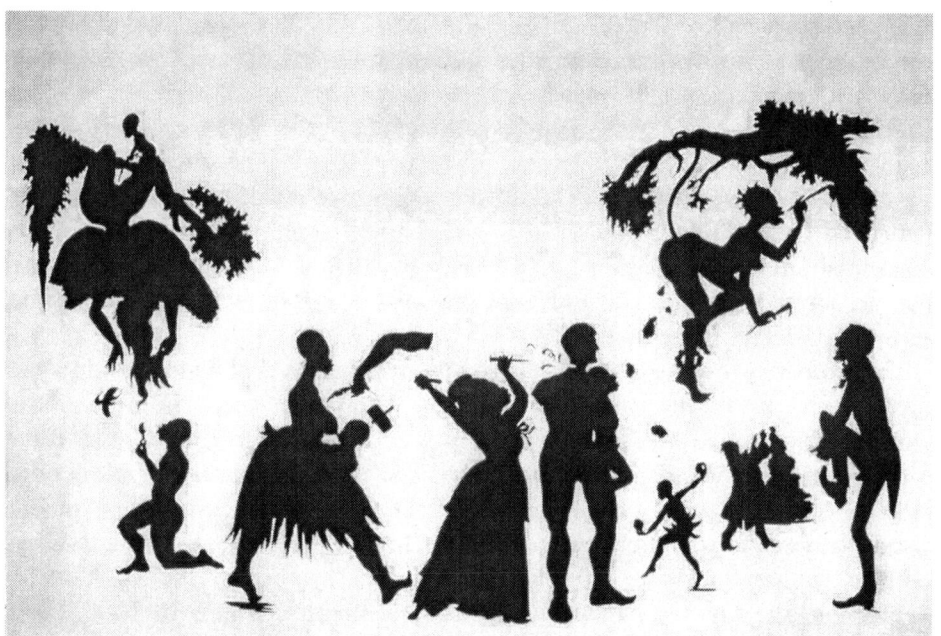

FIGURE 18.2 Kara Walker, *World's Exposition*, 1997. Room-sized mural of cut-outs. Courtesy Jeanne Greenberg Rohatyn Gallery

K.W. – makes references to the past in order to highlight racism/sexism in the present

slavery) in order to point to the continuation of the intertwined forces of racism and sexism in contemporary culture. Walker's 1997 *World's Exposition* (Figure 18.2), one of her silhouette cut-out pieces, depicts a woman in a grass skirt breastfeeding a child, a woman with a monkey tail painting and shitting as she hangs from a tree, and Josephine Baker, the famous black dancer of the Harlem Renaissance movement, in her banana skirt (a costume she wore on stage when performing titillating "indigenous" African dances). The work represents the black female repeatedly as sexually promiscuous – as in the fourth woman who hangs upside down on a tree, her legs are apart next to a small boy holding a stick who appears as if he is going to penetrate her.

black female body ↓ sexually promiscuous

   In the 1960s and 1970s the American media tended to represent the African American woman as a black matriarch who metaphorically castrated the African American male, therefore making it impossible for him to embrace his masculinity. The African American matriarch also became a threat to American society, as epitomized in the famous 1965 Moynihan Report ("The Negro Family: The Case for National Action") in the US, in which it was stated: "In essence the Negro community has been forced into a matriarchal structure which, because it is so out of line with the rest of American society, seriously retards the progress of the group as a whole, and imposes a crushing burden on the Negro male."[13]

60's 70's v.s w.s ↓ black matriarch

In her 1979 book *Black Macho and the Myth of the Super Woman*, Michele Wallace argues that the myth of the matriarchal African American woman was constructed by mainstream American institutions to shift the blame of poverty onto the African American population. Wallace notes that this view was emphasized in 1970 at the First Modern Pan-African Congress held in Atlanta, where Akiba Ya Eliman claimed in her speech that "[b]lack men and women were separated, given conflicting roles, and the reaction of various myths assured our nation to be disunified. One of the most harmful myths was the idea of the black matriarch. The black woman's role was defined in such an intentional manner so as to emasculate our men and give them limited responsibility to guarantee broken black homes."[14]

Unfortunately it was not only mainstream institutions that contributed to this myth in the 1970s. Built on long-standing fantasies of the African American woman from earlier in the century as power homemaker and primary wage earner during the Harlem Renaissance, as the primitive sexually promiscuous jazz dancer or singer (embodied in Josephine Baker), as a strong but uneducated matriarch in the Great Depression, or, in the 1960s speeches and writings of black activists such as Eldridge Cleaver, as a symbol of the black man's oppression, the myth expanded in the late twentieth century. In 1995 Louis Farrakhan, leader of the Nation of Islam (an offshoot of the Black Power movement of the 1960s), organized the Million Man March in Washington DC, a march to celebrate black male pride which effectively reinforced a notion of black masculinity predicated on traditional models of gender difference subordinating women to men (men were celebrated as engaging with the financial decision-making of the family and black community as a whole while women were encouraged to remain in the home).

Wallace's *Myth of the Super Woman* argues that there was a silent agreement between the African American male and female, resulting in the idea that she would not question African American patriarchal forms of culture and instead would prioritize the struggle against racism. But, Wallace notes, "the black man has not really kept his part of the bargain they made when [the black woman] agreed to keep her mouth shut in the sixties. When she stood by silently as he became a 'man' she assumed that he would subsequently grant her long overdue 'womanhood' but he did not."[15] The African American male has tended to assign the African American female a simplistic and often sexualized role – a role that has permeated hip hop culture through the labeling of her as a "bitch" or "hoe."

Despite these antagonisms between African American men and women, African American women simultaneously were motivated by their own sense of cultural community and family to emphasize some form of unity with African American men. Inez S. Reid in 1972 realized that African American women had a different attitude to the women's movement in the US, where mainstream feminism failed to address the concerns of African American women: "Black women have a movement going on that I couldn't very well call liberation because the average Black woman is trying to get back to her "rightful position" with her man."[16] Black women struggled both within and beyond their communities to articulate a position from which they could speak and be heard.

The black liberation struggles in the US during the 1960s and 1970s centered on the economic crisis. Wallace accuses the Black Power movement of defusing its revolutionary thrust by subjecting itself in the 1970s to the whims of the white American power structure in order to subsidize its poverty and scholarship programs. Even though social and economic concerns were a priority there was a shift toward funding cultural programs as well. This led to a "culture of poverty" framework where members of the dominant power structure took it upon themselves to teach African Americans their own history, in turn leading to the widespread development of state-funded black cultural programming, and to the growth of interest in African American art by white art critics and art historians in the late 1960s and early 1970s. The National Endowment of the Arts and other liberal-minded private foundations provided money. Exhibitions of African American art were held regularly, black museums and groups soon appeared across America – including the Studio Museum and Wesui, an African American art center, in Harlem, the Black Emergence Cultural Coalition, the Museum of the National Center of Afro-American artists in Boston, and the conference of Southern California Artists.

Black Power's revolutionary attitude had a major impact on debates about black identity and the visual arts. In his article "Black Nationalism" Ron Karenga argues, "Black art, like every thing else in the Black community, must respond positively to the reality of revolution. It must become and remain a part of the revolutionary machinery that moves us to change quickly and creatively. We have always said, and continue to say, the battle we are waging now is the battle for the minds of Black people. . . . It becomes very important then, that art plays the role it should play in Black survival."[17] This call for the central role of black art was echoed 18 years later across the Atlantic in Britain. In the late 1980s, Eddie Chambers in a discussion with Rasheed Araeen argued:

I would define Black art as art produced by black people largely and especially for the black audience, and which, in terms of its content, addresses black experiences. It deals with in its totality the history of slavery, imperialism and racism, which affects the position of black people here in the West as well as other parts of the world – in the Americas, and in Africa itself. The function of Black art, as I saw it a few years ago was to confront the white establishment for its racism, as much as address the black community in its struggle for human equality. I think Black art has still that role to play.[18]

In contrast to Araeen's call for black people to make art largely about black experience, many African American artists and critics have rejected black cultural nationalism. Raymond Saunders thus argued in 1990 that, "art projects beyond race and color, beyond America. Counter-racism, hyper awareness of difference or separateness arising in the black artist himself is destructive."[19] The mass media have often taken a negative view of British black art, as reflected in a 1989 *Sunday Telegraph* article stating:

> A few weeks ago, the national newspaper editors got together and agreed . . . never to mention an individual's colour, except where this was deemed to be relevant. Those of a progressive disposition thought this to be a "good thing". But only last week considerable publicity was given to an exhibition called "The Other Story". . . [which] is the first exhibition of contemporary British art held at a major public institution of which the criteria for inclusion are explicitly and exclusively racial. How can this be a good thing?[20]

Ultimately, this confluence of beliefs between Saunders and the writers of the *Sunday Telegraph*, presumably motivated by entirely different exigencies, points to the dangers for anti-racists of taking a position that entirely abandons the connection between race and cultural expression. Nonetheless, the need to complicate the more simplistic assertions of Black nationalism was clearly established by the 1990s.

Race and Queer Identity

Black nationalism derives its power from black heterosexual masculinity and, specifically, the frustrations black men have experienced living in white-dominated cultures. In Kara Walker's *World's Exposition* (Figure 18.2) a statuesque white man sodomizes a black boy while a black woman cuts off a statue's head. Menacing references to pedophilia, homosexual rape, and even the Pygmalion fantasy (a classical myth in which a male artist creates a "real" woman – which the Walker piece reverses) are mitigated by the melodramatic excess of the work. *World's Exposition* nonetheless explicitly narrates forbidden sexual fantasies – both of the heterosexual and homosexual variety – exposing to view the *sexual logic of racial oppression.*

Gay and lesbian discourses burgeoned in the late 1970s, developing in tandem with the politicization of sexual and gender identities in the feminist movement. Too, these discourses owed much to the energies of the civil rights and Black Pride movements. In his 1994 book *Welcome to the Jungle: New Positions in Black Cultural Studies*, Kobena Mercer claims that Gay Pride adopted the term pride from Black Pride but, dominated by white men, the movement failed to acknowledge the debt. Equally it must be stressed that homophobia remains rife in the various black civil rights movements, Eldridge Cleaver's 1968 book *Soul on Ice*, for example, criticized black homosexuality as being driven by a racial death wish, writing, "it seems that many Negro homosexuals, acquiescing in this racial death wish, are outraged and frustrated because in their sickness they are unable to have a baby by a white man."[21]

The topic of non-normative black sexuality drew interest in the early 1980s when sexuality became a topic of academic study and began to gain mainstream visibility; sexuality and sexual identity were increasingly viewed in relation to the homo- vs. heterosexual matrix and, in the late 1980s, the term "queer" was adopted to describe lesbian and gay sexuality and culture. From the mid 1980s onward black lesbians and gay men in Britain and America began to assert their voices and visibility in order to challenge the racial stereotyping of black people in the lesbian and gay communities, which had to that point been dominated largely by whites. In 1982 the Gay Black Group in Britain published an article questioning ethnocentric assumptions. The debates between socialist-separatist lesbians and heterosexual feminists caused deep, painful divisions in the women's movement; these debates failed to engage with the experience of black lesbians.

The critiques leveled by the women's and gay and lesbian rights movements paralleled – and some would say partially *caused* – the development of divisions within the black rights movement. Until the 1980s, black gays and lesbians had largely kept silent about their sexuality in order to consolidate the black rights movement and to benefit from the black community support against racism. In *Home Girls* Barbara Smith argues that in Britain "the anti-family rhetoric did not suit black lesbians and gays. The black family and community offered essential support against racism. [Black gays and lesbians] have to live two lives; they have to hide their sexuality from their family and friends while maintaining a relationship with the community."[22] Regardless of these caveats and critiques, by the 1980s black gays and lesbians were no longer willing to keep quiet. For example, Maud Sulter organized the Elbow Room gallery for black heterosexual and lesbian women artists in the early 1990s.

Regardless of these caveats and critiques, by the 1980s black gays and lesbians were no longer willing to keep quiet. They wanted to assert publicly a strong sense of self, and to challenge the general belief in black culture that homosexuality is a white man's disease and thus is a foreign epidemic affecting the black community (even Fanon had perpetrated this attitude, stating, "[t]here are . . . men who go to 'houses' in order to be beaten by Negroes [as well as] passive homosexuals who insist upon black partners").[23]

Kobena Mercer could be argued to be extending this attitude further in his 1994 article "Fear of a Black Penis," where he claims that the white homosexual, with his stereotypical view of black masculinity, has a sexual desire for the unknown. Mercer argues that the gaze of the white male takes place within the political arena of Western civilization, enabling the white homosexual to maintain control and have power over the black body on display. The black heterosexual male is concerned that the macho image he constructs to overcome the position of powerlessness from racism is threatened by the black lesbian and homosexual. Lloyd Jordan in his 1990 article "Black Gay v Gay Black" argues that it is the sense of self loathing among black homosexuals that causes them to attempt to redeem themselves by taking white lovers. If they sleep with black homosexuals they treat them as sexual objects in the same way they are treated by their white lovers. In contrast, Derrick Scott argues that homosexual relationships between black men can be revolutionary if they prompt a recognition of differences within the black community.[24]

Black Class Consciousness

Along with gender and sexuality, class consciousness is another concern that conditions, limits, and sometimes undermines the concept of a unified black identity. In his 1988 article "New Times," British black cultural theorist Stuart Hall argues that the shift to new information technologies and more decentralized forms of labor has produced a shift in discourses of class, subjectivity, and community. Hall notes that class is no longer controlled solely by labor relations and capitalism. Instead all social and political forms of society are ideologically defined by culture and the new economic forms of late capitalism, allowing for the organization of new forms of antagonism and of new social movements of resistance. The movement from class to culture at the intersection of social and political power traced in Hall's work is an essential feature of the postcolonial paradigm. In the United States, Cedric Robinson's 1983 *Black Marxism* assessed the class and cultural relationships between African Americans and white America.[25] According to Robinson (in contrast to Hall), members of the ruling classes do continue to make history, but not under conditions of their own choosing. For Robinson, the processes of class rule are subordinate to Western racial cultural constructions, whose primary characteristic is a kind of fundamental violence.

Black class consciousness is defined by economic and cultural forces. These forces shape the sub-communities of educated, upwardly-mobile black business people and educators who comprise the black middle classes and, as such, are frequently accused of losing touch with their roots and denying their culture. Economic and cultural forces also shape the conditions of the black underclass in British and American cities. State policies in both Britain and the US contribute to the public image of a black underclass living in the ghetto by a creed of violence; this violence is closely linked to black popular culture, which is seen as both defining and contributing to it.

Responding to these conceptions, the confrontational images of the British black art movement and images made by African American artists since the 1980s often adopt popular cultural references. Referencing the tendency to connect African American black urban culture with basketball, David Hammons' 2001 *Basketball Drawing* is a ten-foot-long sheet of paper covered with marks from a bouncing basketball. Hammons began making art on the basketball theme in the early 1980s and is interested in interrogating the stereotypes that stem from such connections – which reduce the black urban poor to stock images of basketball-playing male teenagers.

Multiculturalism, Hybridity, and a Global Black Community in the Visual Arts

Despite all this fragmentation and the disagreements within the global black community, many have continued to attempt to create a sense of belonging – if not, as previously, to construct a fully coherent black identity – through the concepts of multiculturalism and hybridity, both of which came to the fore in 1980s Britain and North America, driven by the effects of globalization. Globalization prompted a move from an understanding of identity as forged through local common connections to a conception of identity as stemming from a more global recognition of group experience.

Recently black British discourses about diaspora have begun to acknowledge the cultural concerns of first- and second-generation Chinese immigrant populations. In 1991 the British Chinese Artists Association was formed in London to support British Chinese artists who explore aspects of ethnicity and cultural identity in their art. Exhibitions such as *Far from the Shore*, and *Another Province: New Art from the Chinese Diaspora* (both in London in 1997), and the establishment of the Chinese Arts Centre in Manchester in 1986 pointed to the richness and diversity of the visual cultures of British diasporic communities.

American conceptions of racial identity, as noted, have differed radically from those articulated in the British context. Since the 1980s, discourses of multiculturalism in the US, linked to the rise in academia of postcolonial theory, have offered a way of acknowledging the emergence of plural ethnic cultures coexisting within dominant cultures such as the Euro-American art world. The rise of multiculturalism afforded artists from non-European backgrounds living in the US an opportunity to explore new forms and practices and to emphasize ethnic difference as a component of their work. Museums and art galleries began to show the work of artists of color from a range of non-European backgrounds; African American artists thus began exhibiting their work in group shows including work by Asian American and Latino artists.

The American art world in the 1980s and 1990s was dominated by "multicultural" exhibitions and events, including the 1987 Dia Art Foundation symposium "Of Other Peoples: Beyond the 'Salvage' Paradigm," the 1990 exhibition *The Decade Show*, hosted by the New Museum in New York City, which highlighted issues of identity, and the notorious 1993 Whitney Biennial. It was the latter show that marked a watershed in the influence of discourses of multiculturalism on American art, sparking huge controversy in both the art and popular press. Ironically, this "multicultural" Whitney Biennial also pointed toward the end of this influence, as the art world began to retreat from the challenges posed by multiculturalism in the mid-1990s, embracing a return to more "autonomous" aesthetic concerns with the rising dominance of art critics such as Dave Hickey and Peter Schjeldahl, both of whom argued for a return to concerns of "beauty" and a rejection of the political concerns that had dominated the production and interpretation of visual art works since the 1970s.

In the US context, however, multiculturalism had not by any means been uncritically embraced by non-white practitioners and theorists. As the Vietnamese American filmmaker and theorist Trinh T. Minh-ha noted, such discourses "work toward your erasure while urging you to keep your way of life and ethnic values within the border of your homelands. This is called the policy of 'separate development' in apartheid language."[26] And, as Elizabeth Sussman and Abigail Solomon-Godeau argued in the catalogue for the 1993 Whitney Biennial, discourses of multiculturalism needed to address globalization and to move beyond specifically *American* conceptions of identity. Solomon-Godeau argues here that multiculturalism is a response to the pressures exerted by postcolonial political and social relations – including global migrations – demanding an acknowledgment of the diverse cultural histories that coexist in contemporary urban communities. In her essay, Sussman states that the art world needs to be understood not as a seamless united entity but as a cultural collective that involves exchange and the conflicts arising from cultural difference.[27]

Also linked to globalization, the term "hybridity" is meant to construct an alternative space where cultural differences can operate. In his work, as noted, Homi Bhabha defines postcolonialism as moving beyond the dichotomous forms of colonial and anti-colonial identity, creating a third space for the articulation of differences. What this means is that art work can no longer be discussed just within the boundaries of cultural difference as defined in a static or fixed way; other forms of dialogue must take place.

For example, one of the segments of the 2002 Documenta 11 exhibition that took place in St. Lucia in the West Indies – Platform 3 – explored the meaning of "creole." In the catalogue to the show, Stuart Hall and François Verges argue that the term "creole" relates strongly to the contrasting institutions of slavery and colonialism under British and French Imperialism, but is also a site where modern subjectivity and history emerge from the aftermath of that imperialism.[28] (In the French Caribbean, the French language and notions of negritude dominated, whereas in the English Caribbean, the experience of slavery and the combination of African languages created a different environment.) Irit Rogoff described creole in another way, claiming that it can be extrapolated to contemporary art practices that mesh different cultural images, symbols, and languages.[29] Creolization, then, can incorporate everything and everyone; it functions as a combination of hybridity and multiculturalism.

The Creole language described the multiple uses of words and sounds that came from the array of different cultures defining Caribbean culture. Now creolization looks at how fragmented histories no longer need to create a coherent narrative but can position themselves multiply; within this concept, the notion of time is no longer conceived as a linear process but, rather, is fragmented, enabling the confluence of multiple dialogues and positions. Rather than being viewed as "illustrating" or "defining" identity in their work (as with the conception of, say, black art resting on models of coalitionally-based identity), creolization is understood as a complex texture of identity stemming from the interpretation and cultural positioning of the work.

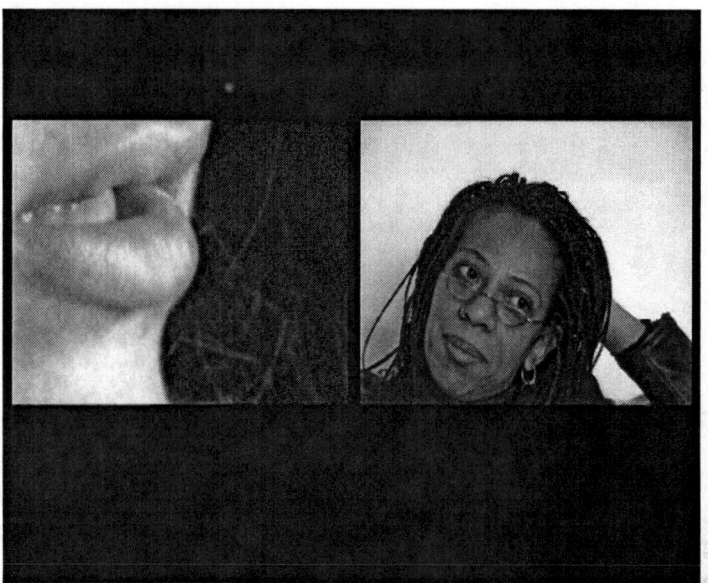

FIGURE 18.3   Rachel Garfield, *So You Think You Can Tell*, 2001. Still from video installation. Courtesy of the artist

Creolization and hybridity are useful terms in understanding the complexities of race and ethnicity in Jewish diasporic art as well, and in teasing out the conflicts between Jewish and black cultures in Britain and the US. Rachel Garfield's 2001 video work *So You Think You Can Tell* tells the story of two women. One looks obviously black and the other obviously white (Figure 18.3). The narrative is divided into five chapters: 1) background; 2) stepping in/ stepping out; 3) men; 4) children; 5) the final word. As the women talk it is never clear who is Jewish and whose children are white; the information is censored by the people talking – they reveal what they want you to know, and the rest depends on the listener. Garfield argues, "[m]aybe through acceptance of the incoherent subject one can recoup what Paul Gilroy calls a 'liberating ordinariness' which lies between multiculturalism and a liberalism that blames [racism for the creation of minorities]."[30] Garfield is interested in exploring the slippages of blackness, challenging the essentialist view that blackness is visible or genetically determined. If we take Garfield's point, Jewish and Black identity are contingent and played out through performative, lived experience. Both are diasporic interlopers who have disallowed the easy delineation of concepts of national identity in Europe and the US.

Digital culture has played a crucial role in the expansion and complexification of conceptions of racial and ethnic identity in the contemporary visual arts. Kempadoo's images, for example, are often described as incorporating the past and present – the black bodies in her photo-constructions are not bound into any one temporal context. In *The Field Gang* the notion of the self as a free

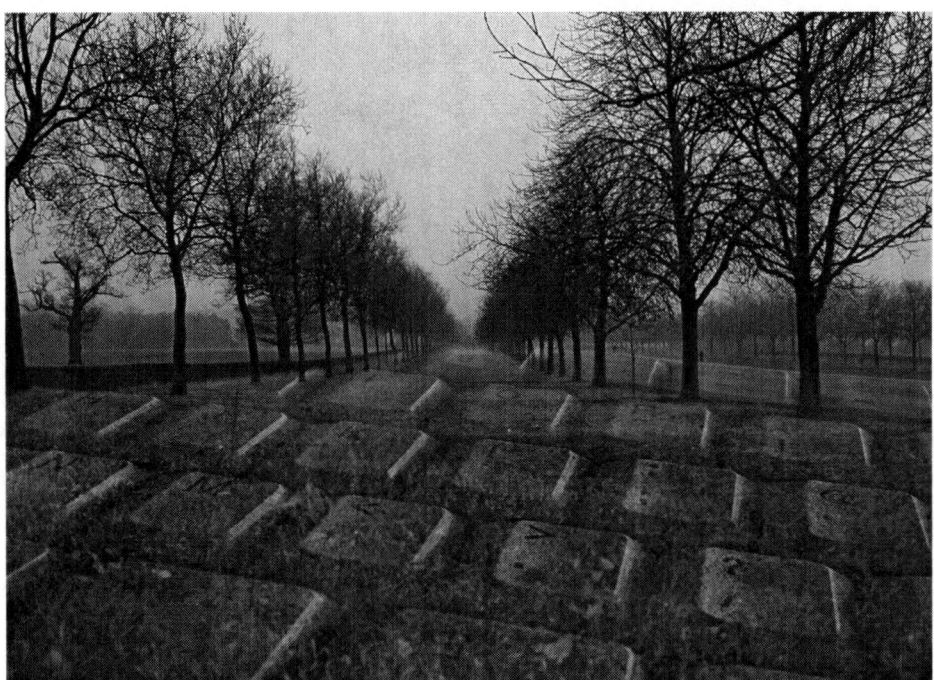

FIGURE 18.4 Roshini Kempadoo, *The Field Gang*, part of *Sweetness and Light* series, 1996. Courtesy of the artist

individual in a global context is the main issue (Figure 18.4). Landscape and computer keyboards are juxtaposed with an image of the slave owner's Great House, pointing to complex interconnections. The title of the work and the reference to the Great House point to the hierarchical status privileging the domestic servant over the field slaves (a hierarchy often based on, or confirmed by, skin color since the domestics often had lighter skin). The literal interface of the computer is symbolized by the keyboard, and the metaphoric interfaces of cyberspace and digital technologies, which interpellate individuals as global cyborg subjects, are also indicated. In the world of global capitalism the search for identity (whether ascribed or constructed) becomes the fundamental source of social meaning, and digital cultures are often viewed in a celebratory way as offering unmediated access to an array of chosen identities.

Kempadoo challenges this false utopianism, referring to the interactive process but also focusing attention on the parameters of and constraints on interaction. As she has noted, "[a]s my inevitable exploration of media, cyberspace, information networks and the use of new technology take hold I began to look at analogies and comparisons. My thoughts and experiences take me to colonialism and the European expansionist past. More specifically I begin to look at the continuous replication of structures, hierarchies and power bases."[31] For Kempadoo, who links the digital interface to the history of colonialism (the keyboard to the Great House), computer culture is compromised through this connection.

Other artists and theorists internationally have also interrogated utopian myths about the freeing potential of digital culture. In 1998 the International Symposium of Electronic Arts arranged an event in Liverpool called "Mediated Nations," including an invited panel on the impact of technology on cultural identity, with participants Gilane Tawardos, Director of the Institute of International Visual Arts, Mustafa Rasid, a specialist in Kurdish folklore, and Simon Tegala, an artist who works with computer engines. The panelists questioned the assumption that computer technologies engage with all audiences and could be seen as a tool for abolishing cultural differences – for example, by offering the possibility of constructing imaginary selves through bodily assemblages. Per the latter, in Russia a group of scholars and artists called United Digital Nations have designed an interactive program in which body parts can be submitted by users and are built into bodies by the artists. Similarly, the British group Mongrel chooses all the body parts based on images of the artists, who are black, Asian, white, and mixed race. In United Digital Nations users can mix sex, age, and race; in Mongrel's program they can mix only racial features. The Mediated Nations panel pointed out that, while such programs can perpetuate racial stereotypes by fixing them onto body parts, the morphed mixture of racial features can also serve to question racial stereotypes – just as, in Kempadoo's *The Field Gang*, race, gender, and ethnicity continue to remain forces of discrimination and oppression to be interrogated.

The work of artists such as Garfield and Kempadoo points to a complex and nuanced understanding of race and ethnicity in our globalized, networked culture. Through this extended analysis of such work, as well as of the interconnections between British and American black arts discourses and practices, and between notions of multiculturalism and globalization, I hope to have provided a useful framework for understanding the ways in which these particular terms of identity and identification have functioned in art practices and discourses over the past decades. Clearly, at the very least, I hope to have demonstrated the centrality of race and ethnicity in the visual arts – the way in which no image or exhibition can be properly understood without a deep consideration of how conceptions of racial and ethnic identity conditioned their terms of articulation.

Notes

1 Fanon (1952/1967), 54–5.
2 Mercer (1992), 23.
3 Fanon (1952/1967), 178.
4 Stuart Hall's essay "Cultural Identity and Diaspora" discusses how the term "black" became a plural signifying category of black identity around this time.

5   Hall (1990), 223.
6   See Araeen (1987). Araeen's career began with his involvement with the Artists for Democracy from 1974–7. At its inception, this group focused on particular cultural and political tasks. Later it broadened to become an avant-garde group that dealt with issues of identity in relation to visual practice. Araeen has been a founding publisher of two critical journals: *Black Phoenix* and *Third Text*.
7   Chambers (1991), 93.
8   Gilroy (1993), 3.
9   Fusco (1992), 45.
10 Himid (1985), 26.
11 Sussman "Coming Together in Panto," in Sussman et al. (1993), 12.
12 Spivak (1990), 57.
13 Moynihan (1965), 12.
14 Eliman, cited in Wallace (1979), 64.
15 Ibid., 122.
16 Reid (1972), 23.
17 Karenga (1971), 32.
18 Araeen and Chambers (1988/9), 51.
19 Saunders (1968), 2.
20 Fuller (1989), 10.
21 Cleaver (1968), 27.
22 Smith, *Home Girls: A Black Feminist Anthology* (1983), cited by Conerly (2001), 13.
23 Fanon (1952/1967), 177.
24 Scott (1996), 12.
25 Robinson (1983).
26 Trinh (1987), 138.
27 Solomon-Godeau "Mistaken Identities," and Sussman "Coming Together in Panto", in Sussman et al. (1993), 10.
28 In Enwezor et al. (2002), 51.
29 Irit Rogoff was in the audience at the discussions about creolization in the West Indies at Platform 3 of Documenta 11.
30 Garfield (2004).
31 Cited in Willis (1997), 12.

References

Araeen, Rasheed (1987). "From Primitivism to Ethnic Arts." In *The Myth of Primitivism*, ed. Susan Hiller. London: Routledge.

Araeen, Rasheed, and Eddie Chambers (1988/9). "Black Art: A Discussion." *Third Text*, no. 5 (Winter):51–78.

Chambers, Eddie (1991). "Black Art Now." *Third Text*, no. 15 (Summer).

Cleaver, Eldrige (1968). *Soul On Ice*. New York: McGraw Hill.

Conerly, Gregory (2001). "Are You Black First Or Are You Queer?" In *The Greatest Taboo: Homosexuality in Black Communities*, ed. Delroy Constantine-Simms. Los Angeles: Alyson Publications.

Enwezor, Okwui, Carlos Basualdo, and Uta Meta Bauer, ed. (2002). *Documenta 11*. Ostfildern, Germany: Hatje Cantz Publishers.

Fanon, Frantz (1952/1967). *Black Skin, White Masks*, trans. Charles Markmann. New York: Grove Press.

Fuller, Peter (1989). "Black Artists: Don't Forget Europe." *Sunday Telegraph* (December 10).

Fusco, Coco (1992). "Pan-American Post-Nationalism: Another World Order." In *Black Popular Culture*, ed. Michele Wallace. Seattle: Bay Press.

Garfield, Rachel, (2004). "Some Thoughts: Visibility and Invisibility or Why I Make Videos." Unpublished paper given at "Unframed: The Practices and Politics of Women Painting," conference at Camberwell School of Art, The London Institute (May 7).

Gilroy, Paul (1993). *The Black Atlantic: Modernity and Double Consciousness.* London: Verso.

Hall, Stuart (1988). "New Times." In *The Hard Road to Renewal.* London: Verso.

—— (1990). "Cultural Identity and Diaspora." In *Identity*, ed. Jonathan Rutherford. London: Wishart and Lawrence.

Hiller, Susan (1991). *The Myth of Primitivism.* London and New York: Routledge.

Himid, Lubina (1985). "New Ethnicities." *ICA Documents 7.*

Karenga, Ron (1971). "Black Nationalism." In *Black Aesthetic*, ed. Addison Gayle. New York: Doubleday.

Mercer, Kobena (1992). "Engendered Species: Danny Tisdale and Keith Piper." *Artforum*, no. 30 (Summer).

—— (1994). *Welcome to the Jungle: New Positions in Black Cultural Studies.* London: Routledge.

—— (1994). "Fear of a Black Penis." *Artforum* vol. 32 (April):81, 122.

Moynihan, Daniel (1965). *The Negro Family: The Case for National Action.* Washington, DC: Department of Labor.

Reid, Inez (1972). *Together Black Woman.* New York: Emerson Hall.

Robinson, Cedric (1983). *Black Marxism: The Making of the Black Radical Tradition.* London: Zed.

Saunders, Raymond (1968). "Black is a Colour." A small pamphlet self-published through Oakland Press.

Scott, Derrick (1996). "Jungle Fever? Black Gay Identity Politics, White Dick and the Utopian Bedroom." In *Queer Theory Sociology*, ed. Steven Seidman. Oxford: Blackwell.

Spivak, Gayatri (1990). "The Problem of Cultural Self-Representation." In *The Postcolonial Critic: Interviews, Strategies, Dialogue*, ed. Elizabeth Sussman. London: Routledge.

Sussman, Elizabeth, Thelma Golden, John Hanhardt, and Lisa Phillips (1993). *1993 Biennial Exhibition.* New York: Whitney Museum of American Art.

Trinh, T. Minh-ha (1987). "Of Other Peoples: Beyond the 'Salvage' Paradigm." In *Discussions in Contemporary Culture*, ed. Hal Foster. Seattle: Bay Press.

Wallace, Michele (1979). *Black Macho and The Myth of the Superwoman.* New York: Dial Press.

Willis, Deborah (1997). *Roshini Kempadoo.* London: Autograph.

19

The Paradoxical Bodies of Contemporary Art

Christine Ross

"In writing this study of the body I have become increasingly less sure of what the body is."[1] This comment by Bryan Turner, published in the introduction of *The Body and Society*, is highly relevant for any art historian attempting today to give a sense of how corporeality has been one of the main motors of art, theory, and criticism since the 1950s. There is no contemporary art without a fundamental concern for the body. Yet, while the body is everywhere in its various enactments as *bodies*, and while it has become a subject of great debate in art discourse, it easily evaporates despite its solidity and mass. Bodiliness is evoked but disclaimed, denied or put into brackets; it is desired but refused, and is still thus very much a *terra incognita*. For sure, contemporary art has been highly critical of the mind/body dualism of Cartesian philosophy but, in its manifold attempts to displace what Elizabeth Grosz has called "the centrality of mind, the psyche, interior, or consciousness . . . in conceptions of the subject through reconfigurations of the body" this project has not gone without doubts, contradictions, and resistance, as though the immediacy of new bodily investigations had to be buffered by a constant recourse to textuality.[2]

Carolee Schneemann's radical sexualization of body art, Bridget Riley's pictorial eye/body, seeing/feeling "op art" interpellations, Richard Serra's use of precariously tilting massive steel walls whose weight brings the spectator back to his or her vulnerability, and Judy Chicago's empowering investigations of womanhood *as* body: from 1960 onward these aesthetic embodiments were initially reproved, only to be accepted in time and sometimes even embraced as radical practices that have pushed the boundaries of modernism. In light of this delayed appreciation, one wonders if the Cartesian perception of the body, as an unruly and uncontrollable physicality (to be transcended for the sake of the mind), is not still more of a structuring belief than many postmodern theorists have

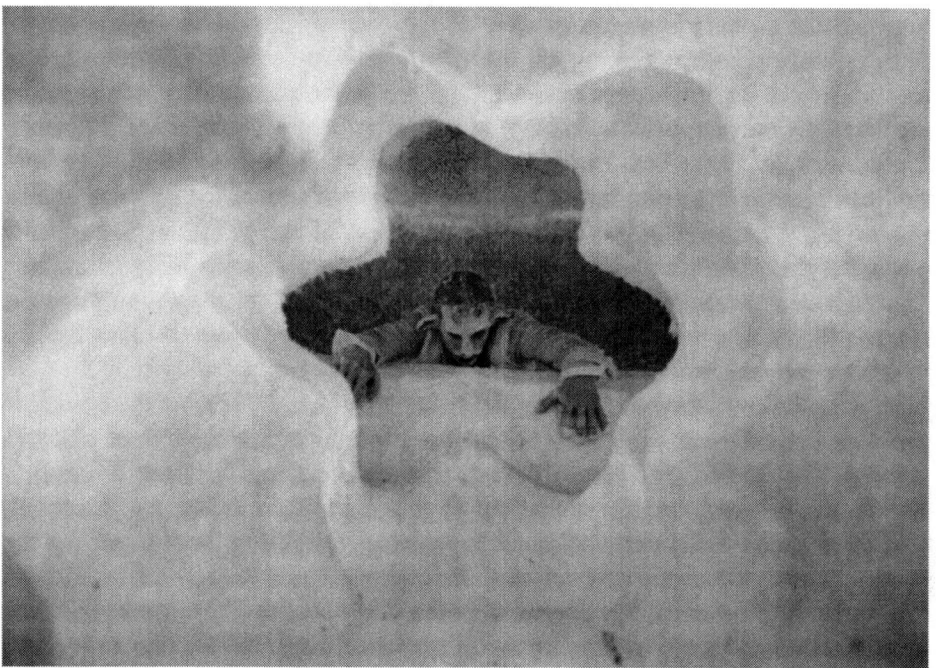

FIGURE 19.1   Matthew Barney, *Cremaster 4*, 1994. Production still. © 1994
Matthew Barney. Photograph: Michael James O'Brien. Courtesy of the Gladstone
Gallery

claimed. To come to accept art of the past might be just another way to compensate for our inability to address the body here and now; it is surely a safer
process than to try to cope with, let's say, Matthew Barney's disturbing fleshy
Cremaster (1994–2002) environments inhabited by bi-? a-? post-? sexual, semi-
animal semi-human beings, in which form – in its intertwined psychological,
biological, and geological states – unfolds according to varying laws of transformability (Figure 19.1).

Arthur Frank observed that sociology's renewed interest in the body during
the late 1980s and early 1990s (one, I would note, paralleled in the art world)
has been shaped by "the contradictory impulses of modernity" – between the
positivist spirit that posits the body as a solid and separate object, linked to
the Enlightenment belief in a transcendental reason beyond the body, and
the poststructuralist and postmodernist sense of constant flux in which the body
gains in impermanence and fragmentation.[3] This dichotomy between a founda-
tionalist objectivism and a nihilistic relativism spells out quite well the body/
anti-body debates I am trying to describe here, which have deeply informed the
production and interpretation of contemporary art: a dichotomy or tension
between the concomitant desire to produce the body as a tangible physicality
leading to some truth about the subject *and yet*, the need to counter, deconstruct,

or historicize this desire. This has much too often led to an artificial split between the so-called essentialist view of the body as a tangible reality located outside history (untouched by culture or inversely universally oppressed), *and* the constructivist, anti-essentialist view of the body as an effect of discursive practices, whose supposed essence is but itself a historical construct. Although essentialism, as Diana Fuss has argued in her astute description of the essentialist/constructionist debate, is condemned by constructionists for its naïve understanding of the natural as providing "the raw material and determinative starting point for the practices and laws of the social," and for its inability to address "the historical production of these categories," it is hard to imagine – given the material bases of art making – how any constructivist theorist or artist can do "without recourse to irreducibilities."[4]

In what follows, I would like to delineate what I believe are the key trajectories of embodiment in contemporary art, those that have triggered its main debates. They are the following: 1) performance art; 2) minimalism; 3) aesthetics; 4) the poststructuralist rendering of the disciplined body; 5) abject art; 6) the aesthetic enactment of the disappearing, vanishing body; and 7) the cyborg. These trajectories are set out chronologically, although some of them do overlap in time and cover several decades. They also overlap in some of their investigations and many of the art works examined here may be said to encompass more than one orientation. Moreover, while I do not have the space to explore feminism, queer performativity, and postcolonialism as specific trajectories, they are guiding perspectives that inform all of these moments except, arguably, minimalism, of which they are partially a critique. There is no body in contemporary art that is not sexed, gendered, raced, or oriented relative to class, nationality, and health. Finally, although I see performance art and minimalism as the two key practices to have initiated the major change of paradigm toward corporeality in art, it is mostly through the development of the other – and chronologically later – art trajectories, in their indebtedness to but also critique of these two practices, that the far-reaching significance of performance art and minimalism can be truly recognized and assessed.

Performance Art

The reemergence in the 1960s of body, action, and performance art (which could be said to have their roots not only in Dada poetry actions of the late 1910s but also, for some artists, in non-Western tribal rituals) was a crucial moment in the embodiment of aesthetics, introducing a form of artistic practice in which the artist's body could be used both as material and expressive language. Since 1950, performance art (to use the more general term) has taken different configurations and denominations: from Jackson Pollock's action paintings and John Cage's explorations of sound, silence, and music, to Allan Kaprow's Happenings and Fluxus events, to Annie Sprinkle's intersubjective explorations of the desiring subject, to Hannah Wilke and Jo Spence's autobiographical deployments of illness, to the enactments of identity by Adrian Piper, Sadie Benning, and Ma Liuming. All these bodily manifestations stage a body in time and space (often in front of an audience but not necessarily), a body that discloses itself not so much as matter than as a materialization necessarily mediated by the contexts in which it is lived, located, perceived, acted out, and acted upon.

The notion of *presence*, in its theorization and deconstruction by French philosopher Jacques Derrida, has been crucial to the assessment of performance. Body art has often been accused of falling into the metaphysics of presence – the desire for a transcendental signified, for a meaning that transcends all signifiers and all signs – in which presence through the body is perceived as providing unmediated access to the essence of things. Derrida himself reproved Antonin Artaud's 1938 *The Theatre and Its Double* (an influential text for the group of performance artists associated with Viennese actionism), in which the artist advocated a cathartic theater to reverse the privilege of the intellectual over the sensory through rituals of gestural and vocal exaltation brought to the limit, as manifesting a nostalgia for presence.[5] It is also on the basis of its supposed reliance on an essentializing notion of presence (to be secured by the body) that feminist artist Mary Kelly condemned performance art in her 1981 essay "Re-Viewing Modernist Criticism": "In performance work it is no longer a question of investing the object with an artistic presence: the artist is present and creative subjectivity is given as the effect of an essential self-possession."[6] This critique was not isolated but was common to the feminist anti-essentialist discourse that emerged in the United States and in the United Kingdom in the 1980s. In line with feminist filmmaker and theorist Laura Mulvey's psychoanalytically informed "Visual Pleasure and Narrative Cinema," the anti-essentialist feminist argument was preoccupied by the gendered structuring of the gaze in modern and contemporary visual culture, whereby women systematically occupy the position of to-be-looked-at-ness in relation to the masculine viewer's position as bearer of the look.[7] Following Mulvey, constructionist feminists informed by psychoanalysis and poststructuralist theory became highly suspicious of any representation of the female body and favored avant-gardist distancing strategies to counter visual pleasure and the seductive powers of the image.

But, despite this critique and because performance is usually known through photographic or filmic documentation, art historian Henry Sayre has posited that performance art has always taken its power from the tension it sets up between presence and absence, playing on the temporal dislocation of the document to secure its lasting effects.[8] This is even true for body works dealing with more direct bodily experiences, such as pain, masochism, and suffering. Hence, while the Viennese actionist Rudolph Schwarzkogler used photography to represent himself bandaged as though in the aftermath of a self-castration, he in fact abused the documentary function of photography by using another's body as his stand-in in what was a *faked* rather than actual castration. Dennis Oppenheim's *Reading: Position for Second Degree Burn* (1970) – two assembled photographs recording the before and after of the artist lying in the sun with a book on his chest until the skin not covered by the book was badly sunburned – only exists through the mediation of photography. As David Hopkins has argued, "photographic documentation, precisely by being 'after the fact,' dramatized the insufficiency of the sense of 'presence' that performance was able to summon up both for artists and their audiences. As a genre, performance oscillated between being experientially 'available' and poignantly 'lacking'."[9]

Amelia Jones's study of body art has articulated the most important critique of the anti-essentialist condemnation of performance and its "turn away from the corporeal." Exploring a phenomenological (Merleau-Pontyan) approach, she has shown how body art "opens art-making and viewing processes to intersubjective desires and identifications."[10] For Jones, performance is much more about representation than presentation; it articulates a presence which is always about a certain form of absence because of its intersubjective structure, whereby the self is systematically deployed both as object and subject, as dependent and contingent on the other for its formation and actualization. This deployment is crucial for the understanding of Jackson Pollock's redefinition of painting as a performance "contingent on the act of reception."[11] In his abstract paintings of the 1950s, the drips function indexically to embody the act of painting – contra the canonical reading of Pollock's work by Clement Greenberg, which makes the artist's body invisible by naturalizing it, thus securing the equation of artist and maleness. This embodiment, which functioned as a kind of feminization, was explored by many subsequent body artists such as Shigeko Kubota, who, in her 1965 *Vagina Painting*, squatted over a piece of paper on the floor and covered it with red paint from a brush attached to her crotch.

Much effort, then, has been put into demonstrating that performance is about immediate presence or, inversely, about the discursiveness of presence, its intersubjective reliance on otherness and indubitable relation to absence. Looking back at these essentialist/constructionist/phenomenological struggles, one cannot but conclude that they manifest the persistent (Cartesian) uneasiness toward the unruly and often unpredictable dimensions of corporeality. Most performances, however, are not reducible to these debates. When Carolee Schneemann staged the multi-body *Meat Joy* in 1964, for example, hers was not just a critique of the modernist tradition of painting or a mere unmasking of the politics of the female body, but also a celebration of the flesh in which bodies and meat (raw fish, plucked chickens, uncooked sausages) were explored to produce an orgasmic sexuality, an ecstasy of excess (influenced by Artaud's excremental philosophy) (Figure 19.2). The performance not only brought vision, smell, taste, and touch to play interactively, but also potentially affected the psychic dimension of sexual experience. The limits of constructivism are exposed by such visceral works. Even Judith Butler's critique of constructivism and theorization of the body as a performative materialization whereby the body exists not as a constructed matter but as a "reenactment and reexperiencing of a set of meanings already socially established"[12] are exposed as leaving unimagined the how and why of *re*-enactment, of nature–culture difference, of corporeal transformations and bodily extensions into the world. Schneemann's work, like that of many performance artists, is still under-theorized, and interpretive

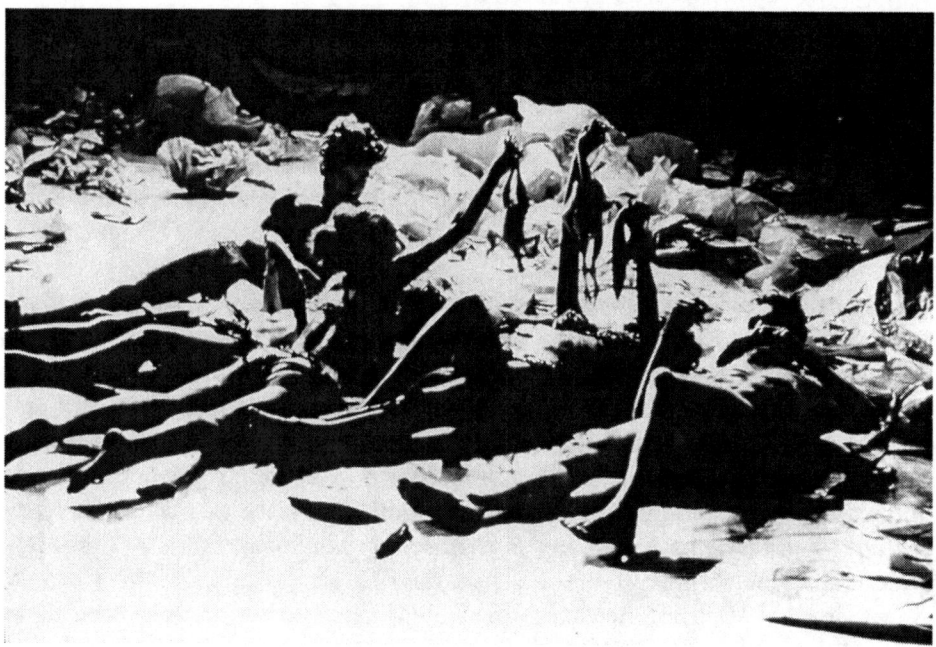

FIGURE 19.2   Carolee Schneemann, *Meat Joy*, 1964. Performance: raw fish, chickens, sausages, wet paint, plastic, rope, paper scrap. Photograph: Al Giese. Courtesy of the artist

models based on the essentialist–constructionist opposition remain insufficient in addressing it.

To move beyond this dichotomy and provide ways of revisiting earlier body art, attention might be paid to Isaac Julien's, Richard Fung's, and Jerry Tartaglia's cross-racial (for the first two) and queer video/filmic explorations of sexual pleasure and to the recent sexualized performances of Marisa Carnesky, Kira O'Reilly, Claire Shillito, Lisa Wesley, Helen Paris, and Katherine Adamenko. In these more direct non-theatrical actions, the body is conveyed not as being before or beyond language but as articulating meaning in a way distinct from the codes and structures of language; the body is explored precisely for the contradictions it puts into play, for the moments when, as Lisa Wesley describes, "the live element breaks free" from the text governing the structure, "becoming ritualistic, improvised, chaotic."[13]

The Phenomenology of Minimalism

The development of minimalism in the mid 1960s brought with it a new sensibility of beholding, opening out the ways in which the viewer perceptually brings meaning to the objects s/he experiences. In this, it is deeply informed by phenomenology, an approach dedicated to delineating the structures of experience as they present themselves to consciousness, and more specifically to Maurice Merleau-Ponty's existential phenomenology which emphasizes the role of the involved body in human knowledge. Art historian Rosalind Krauss was a key figure in the understanding of minimalism in relation to phenomenology and the awareness that Merleau-Ponty's theorization of the body – as an "I" engaged in action with things the "I" perceives – articulates a major questioning of the Cartesian mind/body dualism, presupposing the relatedness of the mind and the body in the subject's experience of world and literally binding them together.[14]

Minimalism puts emphasis on the material objects (a cube, a square, a triangular prism, a prop, a column, a serial arrangement of volumes) of aesthetic contemplation as they appear to us in our experience of them as well as on the meanings they acquire in our experience. Its "specific objects" – artist and theorist Donald Judd's term for the single, large scale, indivisible, non-illusionist, non-anthropomorphic, and non-relational volumes presented by the minimalists – were contingent on the temporal experience of the viewer; they did not (could not) have meaning *in* themselves. Minimalists such as Judd thus undermined the modernist neo-Kantian view of art (as adopted by Clement Greenberg and Michael Fried) according to which meaning presents itself in an unmediated way to the disinterested viewing subject.

Providing one of the most precise readings of minimalism but dismissing it because of its theatricality, Fried contended in his 1967 article "Art and Objecthood" that Judd's and Robert Morris's large-scale galvanized steel, mirrored, or fiberglass forms presented in isolation or repeated throughout the exhibition space were a "negation of art" in their non-illusionism and non-relational nature which prevented the unfolding of meaning *from within* the artwork.[15] Meaning now relied on the embodied and durational viewing activity of the beholder, that is on a beholder who was asked to perceive the object from different viewpoints, in diverse spatial contexts and in relation to the *outside*. For Fried, the problematic theatricality of minimalism, an art "concerned with the actual circumstances in which the beholder encounters" the art work as an object "*in a situation* – one that, virtually by definition, *includes the beholder*," lay precisely in these qualities.[16]

As Hal Foster, Douglas Crimp, and others contended a decade or more after Fried's article appeared, it is in its theatricality, in its emphasis on the temporality of perception in the apprehension of art, that minimalism radically questions and breaks with modernism as an aesthetics without duration, one in which "at every moment," explains Fried, "the work itself is wholly manifest."[17] The embodiment of perception meant that what lies beyond the frame of the art work could be acknowledged as an integral part of art. While, as Foster has also pointed out, the "I perceive therefore I am" of phenomenological minimalism was surely a limited break because it was still "lodged" in an unsexed subject who remained "somehow before or outside history, language, sexuality, and power," its analysis of perception was nevertheless crucial as it "prepared a further analysis of the

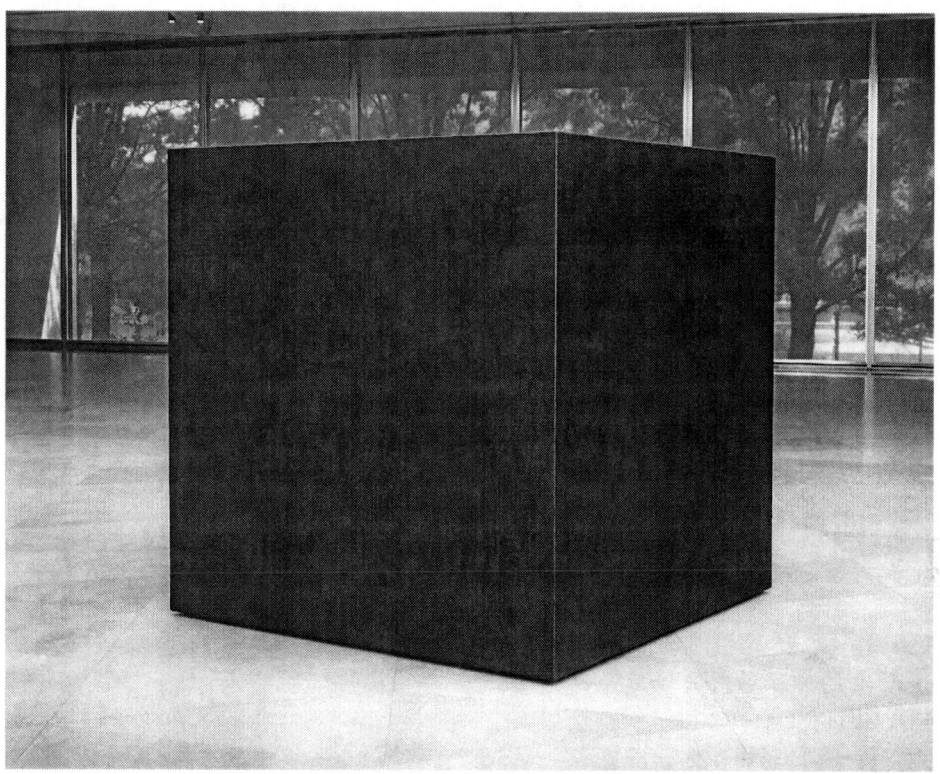

FIGURE 19.3   Tony Smith, *Die* (model 1962, fabricated 1968). Steel with oiled finish. 72 × 72 × 72 in. Gift of the Collectors Committee, 2003.77.1. Image © Board of Trustees, National Gallery of Art, Washington. © Estate of Tony Smith/SODRAC (Montreal) 2004

conditions of perception," leading for instance "to the critique of the institution of art" in the works of Michael Asher, Daniel Buren, and Hans Haacke.[18]

Of significance here is how much the minimalist body – like that of performance – could be said to activate a form of contradictory presence. In minimalism, the unitary and symmetrical object functions as a body or, at least, as an "other" in relation to which the viewer is asked to define him/herself. Moreover, while minimalism attempted to suppress anthropomorphism through the use of industrial materials and serial repetition, it was never able to simply eliminate it, a "failure" that has in fact enriched the corporeal presence of the minimalist object and dramatized the experience of the viewer. Georges Didi-Huberman has shown that the minimalist object is even more radical than the statements of the artists suggested, arguing that the works often entailed a critical de-centering of the viewer precisely because of its anthropomorphism. With Tony Smith's *Die* of 1962, for instance, the evidence of the black volume (its singleness and wholeness) rapidly recedes into a hollowness, an inside invisibility (Figure 19.3).

The large scale of the cube creates a dialectic of distance and immersion, fullness and emptiness – a mass and a tomb. In these dialectical moments, it is the sovereignty of the viewer's gaze that is disrupted: I am perhaps looking at the cube but the cube, in turn, also looks at me, disrupting my centrality and bringing me to my own mortality.[19]

The Aesthetization of Aesthetics

Much in the same way as minimalism was excoriated by Fried, Bridget Riley's black and white abstract "op" paintings done during the same period were often depreciated for their phenomenological sensibility. Rosalind Krauss, for example, while supporting minimalism's phenomenology, reproached op art (including Riley's work) for its "duplicity" – the deceptive ways in which the paintings tricked the eye of the observer through their transitory post-effects[20] (Figure 19.4). In contrast, Anton Ehrenzweig supported Riley's aesthetics because of its acute tension between control and chaos, aggressiveness and reassurance, whereby assaulting visual information transforms itself into a voluptuous sensation in the body.[21] The point of contention was thus not their lack but their excess of illusionism, their uncontainable stripe irradiations, line undulations, and blur-to-clear fluctuations. As recent research by art historian Pamela Lee has shown, while Riley (an intensive reader of Merleau-Ponty) was thought of as producing an op art of pure visuality, her work addresses the very "*blind spot* to Op's obsession with the technological": the haptic experience of the viewer, the manifold ways in which seeing is intertwined with feeling, together with the temporality of vision, its transformability, and fallibility.[22]

The aesthetic investigation of feeling and affect is another crucial trajectory by which the Cartesian mind/body dualism has been problematized in contemporary art, but as the Riley case superbly demonstrates, it is only recently (with hindsight) that the corporeal nature of that investigation has started to be reckoned with. This reappraisal has been supported, even made possible, by at least three decisive areas of research: neuroscience, aesthetics, and recent affect-oriented art. Neuroscientific studies on emotion have burgeoned in the last two decades. Of relevance here are the studies by neuroscientist Antonio Damasio, notably his *Descartes' Error* published in 1994. Summarizing Damasio's work, Ian Hacking writes that "Descartes' error . . . was to separate thinking, rationality, the capacity for language, and so on from the body . . . [T]he deep error, the separation of reason from emotion, prevented Descartes from conceiving the entire organism as a thinking, feeling being."[23] Science is thus starting to understand how reason and emotion, thinking and feeling interrelate through bodily processes and to stipulate that it is imperative to examine these interconnections.

In parallel, Richard Shusterman's philosophical studies on aesthetics have brought to the fore the necessity of re-embodying aesthetics. In his *Performing Live*, he persuasively argues that, in light of Anglo-American philosophy's dis-

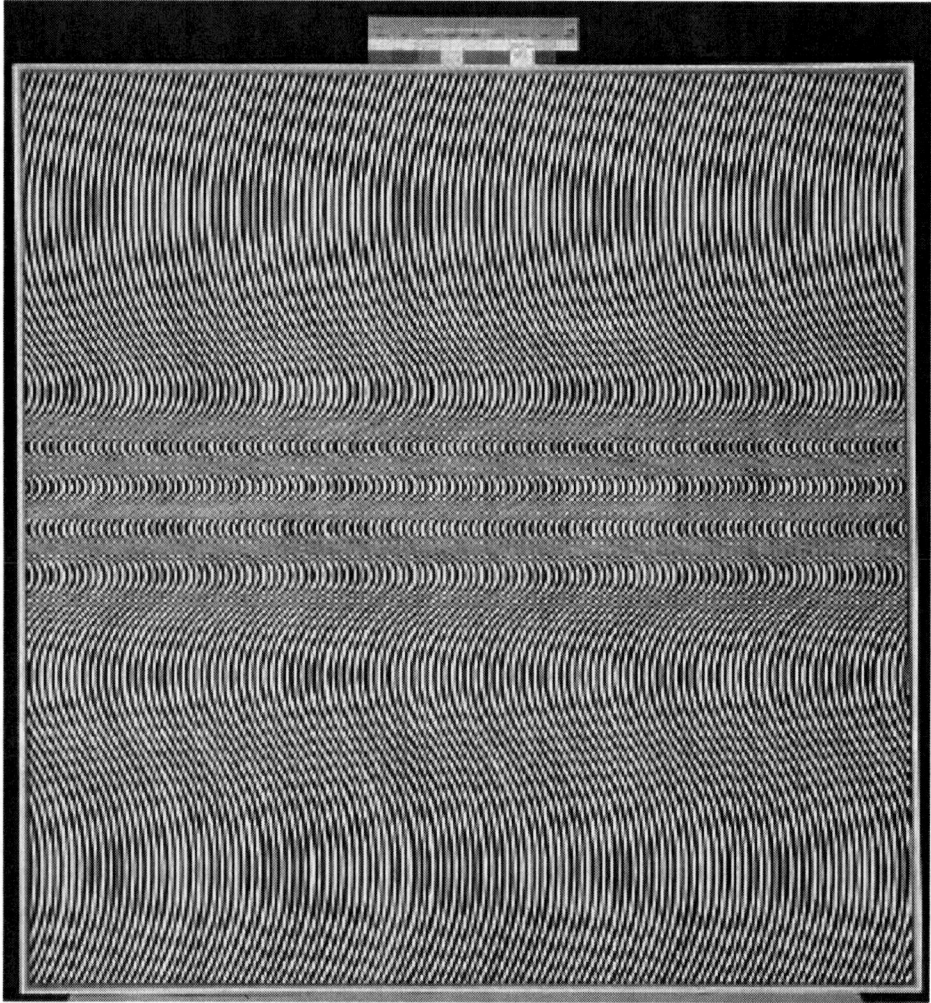

FIGURE 19.4 Bridget Riley, *Current*, 1964. Synthetic polymer paint on composition board. 58⅜ in × 58⅜ in Philip Johnson Fund. (576.1964) The Museum of Modern Art, New York. Digital Image © The Museum of Modern Art/Licensed by SCALA/ Art Resource, New York. © 2005 Bridget Riley, all rights reserved

missal of the aesthetic experience (as articulated mainly in the work of John Dewey, Monroe Beardsley, Hans-Georg Gadamer, Nelson Goodman, and Arthur Danto on the grounds that it falsely assumes that the art work can be immediately experienced and that interpretation is required to shape experience), the task of revaluing the sensory and affective dimensions of aesthetics has become pressing. Experience is never solely linguistic.[24]

As suggested above, a third factor has played a chief role in the reappraisal of feeling in aesthetics: recent affect-oriented art revolving around experiences

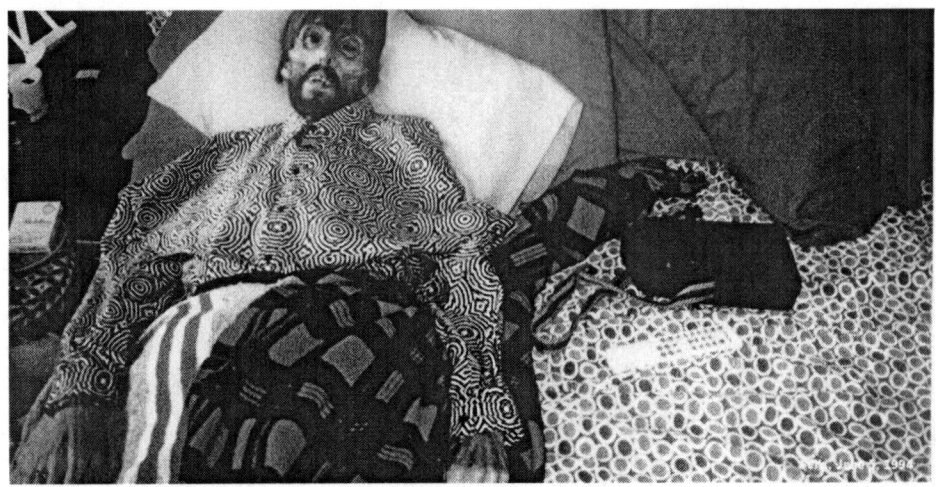

FIGURE 19.5 AA Bronson, *Felix, June 5, 1994* (printed 1999). Lacquer on vinyl. 213.1 × 426.5 × 4 cm. Purchased 2001. National Gallery of Canada, Ottawa. Courtesy of the artist

of illness, loss and mourning, aging, trauma, depression, shame, diaspora, exile, and immigration. During the 1980s and 1990s, the AIDS crisis led many gay artists to investigate the troubling intersections of desire, sexuality, and mourning while also forcing the examination of the cleavage between public perceptions and private experiences of AIDS, together with the politics of visibility/ invisibility whereby some subjects – those that disturb predominant representations of healthy, heterosexual, and white subjects – are erased from representation. For example, after the death of Jorge Zontal and Felix Partz, two members of the collective General Idea, the sole surviving member of the group, AA Bronson, made a series of large-scale photographic representations of his dying and dead friends, some of them displayed on city billboards to function as memorials (Figure 19.5); David Wojnarowicz created his *Sex Series* (1988–9), a group of black and white text-image works in which negative prints of American landscape scenes are punctuated with small circles of forbidden, sexually explicit, images, affirming the homosexual's right to pleasure; Robert Gober made wax sculptures of male body parts with phallic votive candles sprouting from them; and Gregg Bordowitz's video and film work of the late 1990s reflected on the conflicts between the subjective and objective, personal and political experiences of the disease.[25] All of these works explored the affect of loss in its relation to love, sexuality, pleasure, illness, and mourning.

But the exploration of loss expanded beyond the AIDS crisis. It became in fact part of a dominant sensibility in the 1990s. Relevant here are the autobiographical photographs of Jo Spence, Hannah Wilke, and Matuschka of the 1980s and 1990s, representing their struggles against cancer by evoking their shattered bodies and breaking with the idealizing tradition of the female nude.[26] British artist Sam Taylor-Wood's large-screen video projection, *Pietà* (2001), also represents the artist's struggle against cancer: here, she holds on her thighs the limp body of Robert Downey Jr., the film celebrity who was treated for drug and alcohol addiction, depicting an intersubjective fight against death. Canadian artist Rebecca Belmore's *Vigil* (2002) performance brings together anger, shame, and sadness to constitute a live memorial to the 65 predominantly aboriginal female sex workers who have disappeared from Vancouver since the 1980s.[27]

These are but a few examples of what could be called the aesthetization of aesthetics through the representation or enactment of emotions that address the viewer affectively – works in which feeling cannot be merely subsumed by reason or dismissed as being located in a mindless body. Many of these aesthetic explorations have this productive effect of stressing the fact that some of the chief human emotions, such as shame (to borrow here from Eve Kosofsky Sedgwick's study on queer performativity), may intensify or alter "the meaning of – of almost anything: a zone of the body, a sensory system, a prohibited or indeed a permitted behavior, another affect such as anger or arousal, a named identity."[28] This trajectory sets into play an important problematization of the essentialist/constructionist divide as it addresses concerns about identity, while acknowledging that identity never truly stands as an essence (subject as it is to misinterpretation and misrecognition).

In light of these developments, many aesthetic movements and art productions of the 1960s through the 1990s can and must be re-examined so as to see how they have indeed addressed what Damasio has called the Cartesian error (the splitting of reason and emotion). I mention here a few: the Italian movement Arte Povera, which employed non-industrial, ephemeral materials such as horses, lettuce, sawdust, and coal as a structuring principle and privileged process, action, and energy over the finished object; the sculptural work of Eva Hesse, which turns the distancing effect of the minimalist "specific object" into an effect of touch, feeling, and rapprochement; the mythic performance works of Joseph Beuys, which employed animals as well as materials argued to have healing powers (felt, fat, gold, and honey); the relational objects of Brazilian artist Lygia Clark; the chocolate or wax perishable cubes of American artist Janine Antoni; and the pictorial works of Anselm Kiefer, Jenny Saville, and Cecilia Brown. These productions share a concern for the sensory, sensual, and feeling effects of the material, some of them invested in the emotional healing powers of materiality.

The Disciplined Body

It is important to note, however, that the constructionist, anti-aesthetic investigation of corporeality dominated the 1980s and is still a vibrant stream of art today. Underlying this crucial trajectory, we find Michel Foucault's disciplined body, which he describes in relation to his genealogical approach to history:

> The body is the inscribed surface of events (traced by language and dissolved by ideas), the locus of a dissociated self (adopting the illusion of a substantial unity), and a volume in perpetual disintegration. Genealogy, as an analysis of descent, is thus situated within the articulation of the body and history. Its task is to expose a body totally imprinted by history and the process of history's destruction of the body.[29]

Foucault's model breaks with the quest for the origin and the linear laws of historical change partly by situating the body as *the* central element of study; it shows how what was traditionally thought to escape the laws of history (by its exclusive obedience to the laws of physiology) is in fact "molded" and "broken down" by a variety of regimes.[30] A privileged site of control and power, Foucault's poststructuralist body exists as acted upon, "a featureless *tabula rasa*," in the words of Terence Turner, "awaiting the animating disciplines of discourse," while sometimes (rarely) able to resist through deviant erotic practices.[31] In the more conceptual art works dealing with the ways in which the body is shaped by social rules prescribing normative gender, sexuality, race, and nationhood, the tendency has been to develop visual strategies that disclose these hidden mechanisms of power. Disclosure becomes here a form of agency – a mode by which the viewer is made conscious of the forces that turn the subject into a docile body.

The feminist, postcolonialist, and conceptualist work discussed in detail elsewhere in the book testifies to the importance of this discursive stream. I will not add to these much more focused studies, except to discuss a single-channel video-tape by Martha Rosler, *Semiotics of the Kitchen* (1975), which exemplifies the Foucauldian approach to contemporary embodiment. *Semiotics of the Kitchen* parodies a cooking demonstration, with Rosler in a kitchen picking up, naming, and demonstrating a variety of utensils, but through excessive, slashing gestures that transform passive domesticity into a scene of frustration and anger. As the semiotics of kitchen is being displayed, the increasing aggressiveness of the gestures discloses how the undisciplined (perhaps uncontrollable) body emerges from within the disciplining structures of domesticity. As in Foucault's work, the body is not approached in phenomenological terms but as a conceptual category. Rosler's piece thus stresses history's imprint on the body to the detriment of the active body, downplaying its dimension as material activity.

The Abject

The end of the 1980s is often characterized as the period in which contemporary (especially American) art and theory turned to the body, moving away from and reacting against the prohibition against the body evident in the work

of artists and theorists such as Mary Kelly, cited above. While this characterization is highly problematic, since it denies the manifold ways in which art of
previous decades leading up to the 1980s had fundamentally questioned the
mind–body dualism, it does usefully single out the period as a pivotal moment
in which corporeality came to the fore in a new way. The turn (or *re*-turn) to
the body was quite specific in its preoccupation with fragmented, hysterical,
vulnerable, grotesque, de-sublimated, and non-idealized bodies. This aesthetics
rapidly took the shape of a polemic between two concepts – the abject and the
informe (unformed or formless) – representing two very different takes on the
turn to the body. While both concepts had initially been theorized by French
philosopher Georges Bataille, they came to designate an oppositional model of a
referential (content oriented) versus a structural (form oriented) understanding
of art.

In *Powers of Horror: An Essay on Abjection*, Julia Kristeva uses the notion of
abjection to describe the revulsion and the horror experienced by the child as it
attempts to separate itself from the pre-Oedipal mother in the passage to the
symbolic (paternal, social) order.[32] Abjection, in its most archaic form, is an oral
disgust, a refusal of the mother who is experienced as abject so that the child
might expel itself from the mother–child dyad and become a subject. But for
Kristeva, the experience of the abject doesn't stop there, for the abject never
ceases to haunt the borders of identity; it constantly threatens to dissolve the
unity of the subject. The abject belongs to the category of "corporeal rubbish,"
of the incorporated-that-must-be-evacuated, indicating the incapacity of Western modern cultures to accept not only the mother but also, as Elizabeth Gross
underlines, the materiality of the body, its limits and cycles, mortality, disease,
corporal fluids, excrement, and menstrual blood.[33] Explored as an aesthetic
strategy, the abject may thus become (as Kristeva contends) a critical practice
that puts subjectivity into crisis; it is a work by which categories of identity are
abruptly questioned and disrupted.

The 1990s was a forceful moment in its production of art works dealing with
processes of abjection in which "corporeal rubbish" was brought to the fore and
bodily boundaries (whose function is to separate the inside from the outside)
were critically eroded. The Whitney's 1993 *Abject Art: Repulsion and Desire in
American Art* was one of the key exhibitions responsible for the terminology
and the relatively loose (often contradictory) use of the term to qualify the work
of a diverse range of artists, from Robert Rauschenberg, Robert Mapplethorpe,
and Yayoi Kusama, to Mike Kelley and David Wojnarowicz. Cindy Sherman's
photographs of fragmented dolls suggesting horrific scenes of rape, death, and
hysteria, Andres Serrano's *The Morgue* series (1992) of pristine formalist photographs of actual dead bodies, and Kiki Smith's bronze, latex, resin, or papier-
mâché skinned or leaking bodies and body parts, exteriorized body fluids and
organs, were exhibited as works that exemplify the abject, acting, in the words
of co-curator Simon Taylor, as an "assault on the totalizing and homogenizing
notions of identity, system and order," while also reenacting "psychic traumas,

personal obsessions, and phobias" and "challenging the stability of our bodily gestalts."[34] Beyond the Whitney show, since 1990 the Young British Artists (YBAs) have also explored bodily debris or dysfunctionality: Damien Hirst's notorious formaldehyde-filled, glass containers enclosing animal carcasses; Jake and Dinos Chapman's life-sized sculptures of children with displaced genitals, bad wigs, and running shoes joined up in hellish Siamese-twin-like configurations; Ron Mueck's silicone half life-size naked *Dead Dad* (1996–7), whose exposed deflated penis de-phallicizes the figure of the patriarch; Tracey Emin's *My Bed* (1998), complete with dirty sheets, vodka bottles, used condoms, and a bloody tampon; and Chris Ofili's paintings with clumps of elephant dung incorporated.

In an article titled "*Informe* without Conclusion," however, Rosalind Krauss criticizes the focus on abjection as unfolding exclusively as "a thematics of essences and substances"; to the abject she opposes the notion of the *informe*, which takes its transgressiveness from the fact that it is more of an operation than an expressive mode, a process of alteration "in which there are no essentialized or fixed terms, but only energies within a force field."[35] Hal Foster has also questioned the effectiveness of the abject: if indeed it is an unconscious force "opposed *to* culture," how can it be transgressive once it is "exposed *in* culture"?[36] Attempting to move beyond the essentialist/constructivist, content/form divide structuring the abject/*informe* polarity, he saw the 1990s turn to the body as a crucial, "perhaps irreversible shift" in contemporary art and theory, whereby the postmodern conception of "*reality as an effect of representation*" is replaced by a conception of "*the real as a thing of trauma.*"[37] In these works, argues Foster, the screen function of the image, which used to protect the viewer from the Real (the realm of the unrepresentable, of what lies outside the symbolic process) by only letting it obliquely emerge as a traumatic point (Jacques Lacan's *tuché*; Roland Barthes' *punctum*), has dissolved itself to reveal the real as traumatic and repulsive, truthful in its abjection. The problem with this aesthetics, maintains Foster, is that the damaged or diseased body becomes "the evidentiary basis of important witnessings to truth, of necessary testimonials against power," with all the dangers such a siting of truth entails, including "the restriction of our political imaginary to two camps, the abjectors and the abjected, and the assumption that in order not to be counted among sexists and racists one must become the phobic object of such subjects."[38]

Although Foster is right in identifying the problems of affirming the body as truth (Foucault has indeed shown how the modern body, at least since the nineteenth century, has been constructed as a truth – a secret – to be confessed and thus better disciplined), he leaves open and unresolved the body's uncontrollability and its role in intersubjectivity. British Palestinian artist Mona Hatoum's *Corps étranger* (1994) is a pivotal work in this regard. The video installation is delimited by two semicircular partitions around a floor-displayed video projection of endoscopic images of various internal and external features of Hatoum's body and accompanied by an ultrasound recording of heartbeats, punctuated at regular intervals by breathing sounds. As the viewer follows the camera moving in the visceral body, s/he continuously needs to negotiate between feelings of dominating over another's body and being absorbed by that very body. A similar sense of ambiguity is at play in Canadian artist Jana Sterback's dress made of raw flank steak, *Vanitas: Flesh Dress for an Albino Anorectic* (1987), where the container function of the skin is presented as dysfunctional yet potentially renewable, the body uncontrollable and so capable of permeating the spectator's own bodily and psychic space.

The Disappearing, Vanishing Body

In the early 1970s, New York-based artist Adrian Piper used the visibility of her body, the fact that she is a light-skinned black woman who can pass as white, to question the power of racial categorization and the role of the visual "as a criterion for categorizing others"[39] (Figure 19.6). Defining racism as "an anxiety response to the perceived difference of a visually unfamiliar 'other',"[40] she produced work that would feed that anxiety so as to raise awareness of racism. In her unannounced public performances of the 1970–1 *Catalysis* series, for instance, she dressed and behaved in ways that confused categories of gender and race, in order to confront people with cognitively dissonant situations and thus potentially "catalyze" white viewers out of their limited perceptions.[41] A few years earlier, Austrian artist Valie Export had performed *Action Pants: Genital Panic* (1968), in which she walked unannounced into an art film theater in Munich wearing pants with her crotch exposed, challenging people to look at the "real thing" instead of passively consuming pictures of women.[42] Again, the body was explored as a strategy of visibility to question the politics of the gaze.

But these works beg the question: is there a way of thinking about the body through its invisibility? For surely, if the body – as most of the art works discussed thus far indicate – is a visibility, then perhaps its vanishing from sight and site is also a form of embodiment that can and has been explored in art to pose questions of memory and place, non-recognition, and absence. Ana Mendieta, a Cuban immigrant living in the US, for example, produced a series of earthworks entitled *Siluetas* in the 1970s – imprints of her body in the landscape outlined by various symbolic materials such as gunpowder, fire, stones, and flowers – to reflect on questions of exile. Photographs and films documented these transient works, but only as an indication of what was once there and had eventually been absorbed by nature (see Figure 16.1). These ritual communions with nature, in which embodiment entails both a form of bonding and disappearance, transmitted the transitional difficulties of exile: "The making of my silueta in nature," Mendieta stated, "keeps the transition between my homeland and my new home. It is a way of reclaiming my roots and becoming one with nature."[43] Yet, her images have the paradoxical function of a memento mori – both a memory of life and an acknowledgment of its ultimate dissolution. They are body works, but only through the absenting of the body and as a means to activate remembering.

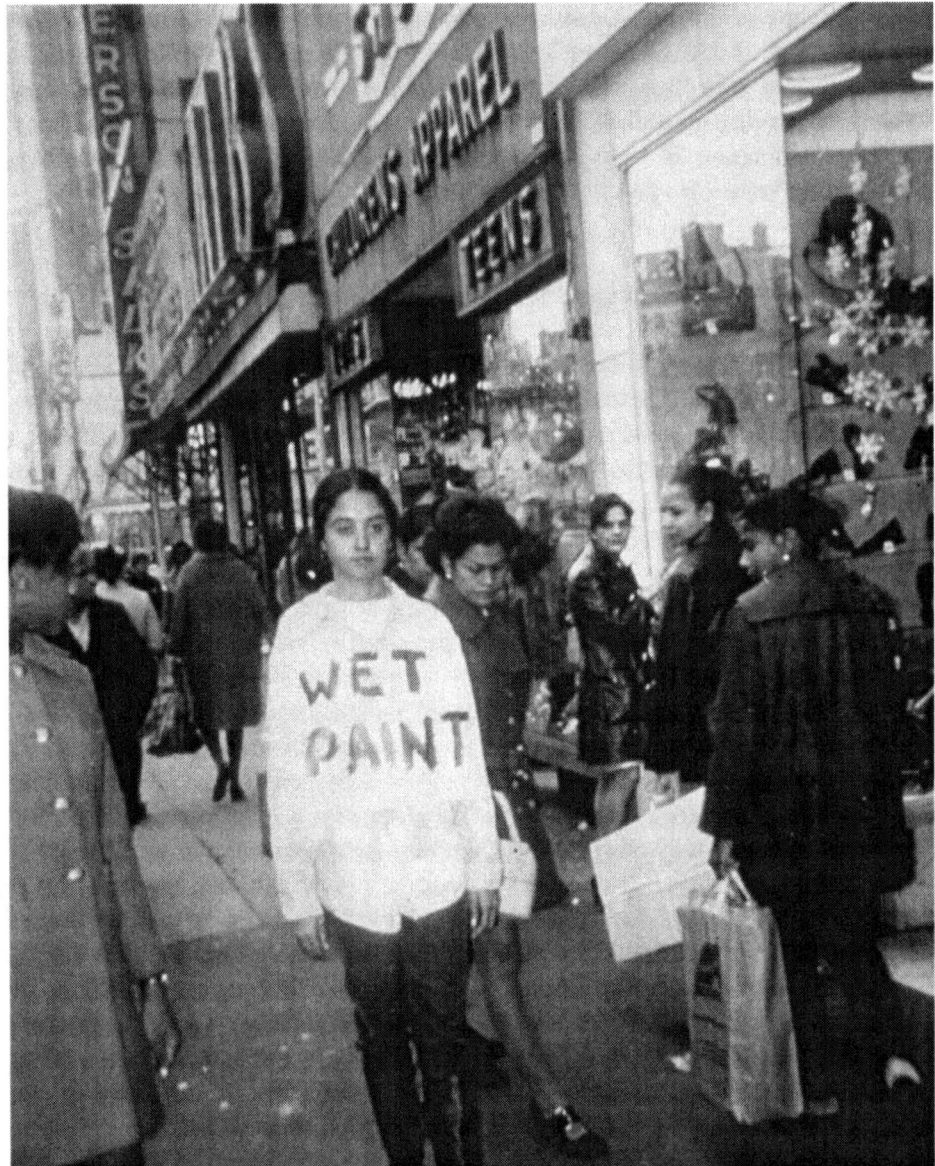

FIGURE 19.6 Adrian Piper, *Catalysis III*, 1970. Photograph: Rosemary Mayer. Collection of the Generali Foundation. Courtesy of the artist

Blue (1993), the last film completed by British filmmaker Derek Jarman before his death from AIDS complications, also activates memory through bodily absence. A one hour and seventeen minute long projection of unchanging yet luminous blue, the film is a screen that makes the body present through its soundtrack of sounds, music, and Jarman's meditations on his encroaching blindness and approaching death. It is paradoxically only by making the body unseen that a form of identification takes place, for as Jarman speaks about his attempt to come to grips with the fading of all images from his field of vision, of his own self-image into the blue of death, the spectators of the piece are confronted by their own blindness to their own inevitable dissolution. Invisibility thus becomes a means by which mourning can start to unfold. (See Mavor in this volume.)

Such is also the case with Felix Gonzalez-Torres's candy works – cellophane-wrapped licorice, Baci chocolates, or Bazooka bubble gum piled up in corners, squared-off on the floor, or spilled in arcs – and their aesthetics of infinite cyclical appearance-and-disappearance. The candies are body surrogates offered to and eventually eaten by spectators. In *Untitled (Placebo)*, for example, an installation presented at Hirshhorn Museum in Washington DC, Gonzalez-Torres displayed on the ground (in a carpet-shaped rectangle of approximately 6 × 12 ft) hundreds silver-foil-wrapped candies representing the combined weight of the artist and his lover, who died of complications from AIDS. The body here is again invisible but made present (through the candies); when totally depleted, it will be fully reconstituted as bodily waste, only to undergo again the same inexorable vanishing act.[44] These works reflect on the unfulfillable desire to preserve the loved one, the melancholic act of trying to keep the loved one inside – identifying with him or her to the point of ingestion – and the related impossibility of letting go.

Rachel Whiteread's 1993 *House* also deploys itself as a memento mori through its activation of absented bodies. The house (demolished, as planned, three months after its construction) was a cast of the interior of a condemned house initially located in the East End of London. Made by filling the house with concrete and then by stripping the mould (that is, the exterior of the house itself – roof tiles, bricks, mortar, doors, and windows), Whiteread's *House* required the destruction of the initial house to exist. As Doreen Massey has argued, *House* entailed three main operations: it made present an absent object through its casting; it turned the space inside out (opening the private to public view); and it solidified what had been the living space of the house – muting and deadening the social time-space made of movement, noise, and interchange.[45] Hence, although *House* (a body turned inside out, preventing any other body from coming in) was thus a monument drawing attention to houses lived and left, it had to mute life to become a memory of it. All these bodily explorations, as those elaborated by Christian Boltansky, Gerard Richter, and Luc Tuymans among others, activate in the viewer a form of post-memory, what Marita Sturken has described as "the continuation of memory and its regeneration in those for whom memories are experiences once or twice removed."[46]

Concluding (with the Cyborg)

In her *How We Became Posthuman*, Katherine Hayles observes that the related fields of computer technology, information theory, virtual reality, and cybernetics rest on the assumption that "information can circulate unchanged among different material substrates."[47] In other words, information is assumed as not needing a body or a medium to be instantiated, a belief which has its roots in Claude Shannon's theory of information, according to which information is a probability function with no dimensions, no materiality, no necessary connection with meaning and context. When information is conceived as such, not as a presence but as a pattern, the body risks becoming, and this is Hayles' warning, "a mere supplement to be discarded."[48] In an era in which the union of human and artificial intelligent machines has already occurred, Hayles convincingly advocates for a "posthuman" or a cyborg "that embraces the possibilities of information technologies without being seduced by fantasies of unlimited power and disembodied immortality, that celebrates and recognizes finitude as a condition of human being that understands human life is embedded in a material world of great complexity, on which we depend for our survival."[49]

Although I do not have the space here adequately to examine the work of artists working on the posthuman, Hayles' remarks reveal how much the mind/body dualism is still with us in unsuspected ways. Many cyborg artistic investigations point to this persistency. In *Play with Me* (1994), Japanese artist Mariko Mori poses as a cyber cover-girl against the background of a Tokyo techno district, yet this posed embodiment discloses how much her body image is a reflection of male (often Western) fantasies.[50] Since 1990, French artist Orlan has gone through nine plastic surgeries to prove how bio-technology can shape the body to fit the person's fantasy of how they want to appear, but through this gesture, she has problematically reproduced the costly and often dangerous procedures of cosmetic surgery while also underestimating the limits of the body in relation to such procedures. In his prosthetic and robotic experiments, Australian artist Stelarc constantly searches for ways to use technology to improve the human body, but he considers the latter to be completely obsolete. By producing a live green fluorescent rabbit (*GFB Bunny*, 2000) through DNA transfer technologies, US-based Brazilian artist Eduardo Kac not only discloses the state of affairs in genetic engineering, he also participates problematically in the embrace of technology at the cost of ethical concerns.

These works beg the following question: has contemporary art displaced the Western mind/body split? As I hope to have shown, it has in many ways. But corporeality still remains little understood in its complex effects. While (post)humans would surely lose by reducing *the* body to truth (whose body would that be? whose body would that exclude?), this cannot foreclose the need to reflect on the passages between reason and emotion, between senses, between mind, body, and environment. Recent art productions dealing with the performativity of affect are crucial in this regard, as are recent works exploring space and place. These works replace the fixation on the body per se by enlarging – de-individualizing – it in relation to its environment and complexifying the view of the body as bounded individualistic unit. As Jean-Luc Nancy has insightfully observed, the body should be envisaged both as a relation and "a thinking of the gap whereby we touch."[51]

Notes

1 Turner (1984), 7.
2 Grosz (1994), vii.
3 Frank (1990), 133, 160.
4 Fuss (1989), 3–20.
5 Derrida (1978), 232–50.
6 Kelly (1981), 95.
7 Mulvey (1975), 6–18.
8 Sayre (1989), 1–34.
9 Hopkins (2000), 188.
10 Jones (1998), 26.
11 Ibid., 53–5.
12 Butler (1990), 140.
13 Wesley cited in Ayers (2000), 27.
14 Krauss (2000), 126–35; Merleau-Ponty (1945/1962), 408.
15 Fried (1968), 125.
16 Ibid., 124.
17 Ibid., 145.
18 Foster (1996), 59, 43.
19 Didi-Huberman (1991), 33–59.
20 Krauss (1965), 75.
21 Ehrenzweig (1965), 20–4.
22 Lee (2004), 157.
23 Hacking (2004), 33–4.
24 Shusterman (2000), 20.
25 See Bordowitz (2004).
26 See Dykstra (1995), 18.
27 See Lauzon (2004).
28 Sedgwick (2003), 62.
29 Foucault (1984), 83.
30 Ibid., 87.
31 Turner (1994), 36.
32 Kristeva (1982).
33 Gross (1990), 80–103.
34 Taylor (1993), 60.
35 Krauss (1996), 98.
36 Foster (1996), 156.
37 Ibid., 146. Italics in original.
38 Ibid., 166.
39 Heartney (2001), 136–8.
40 Piper (1999), 94.
41 Johnson (1997), 29–31.
42 Rush (2000), 135–9.
43 Mendieta (n.d.), n.p.
44 Storr (1996), 75.

45 Massey (1995), 34–49.
46 Sturken (1999), 10.
47 Hayles (1999), 1.
48 Ibid., 11–12.
49 Ibid., 5.
50 Hara (2001), 241–2.
51 Nancy (2000), 23. I thank Tamar Tembeck for pointing out this passage to me.

References and further reading

Ayers, Robert (2000). "Body Language." *contemporary visual arts*, no. 27:24–31.
Bordowitz, Gregg (2004). *The AIDS Crisis is Ridiculous and Other Writings 1986–2003.* Ed. James Meyer. Cambridge, MA: MIT Press.
Butler, Judith (1990). *Gender Trouble: Feminism and the Subversion of Identity.* New York: Routledge.
Derrida, Jacques (1978). *Writing and Difference*, trans. Alan Bass. Chicago: University of Chicago Press.
Didi-Huberman, Georges (1991). "Ce que nous voyons, ce qui nous regarde." *Les Cahiers du musée national d'art moderne*, no. 3:33–59.
Dykstra, Jean (1995). "Putting Herself in the Picture: Autobiographical Images of Illness and the Body." *Afterimage*, vol. 23, no. 2:16–20.
Ehrenzweig, Anton (1965). "The Pictorial Space of Bridget Riley." *Art International*, vol. 9, no. 1:20–4.
Foster, Hal (1996). *The Return of the Real: The Avant-Garde at the End of the Century.* Cambridge, MA: MIT Press.
Foucault, Michel (1984). "Nietzsche, Genealogy, History." In *The Foucault Reader*, ed. P. Rabinow. New York: Pantheon Books. 76–100.
Frank, Arthur W. (1990). "Bringing Bodies Back in: A Decade Review." *Theory, Culture & Society*, vol. 7, no. 1:131–62.
Fried, Michael (1968). "Art and Objecthood." In *Minimal Art: A Critical Anthology*, ed. G. Battcock. New York: E. P. Dutton and Co. 116–47.
Fuss, Diana (1989). *Essentially Speaking: Feminism, Nature & Difference.* New York: Routledge.
Gross, Elizabeth (1990). "The Body of Signification." In *Abjection, Melancholia and Love: The Work of Julia Kristeva*, ed. John Fletcher and Andrew Benjamin. New York: Routledge. 80–103.
Grosz, Elizabeth (1994). *Volatile Bodies: Toward a Corporeal Feminism.* Bloomington: Indiana University Press.
Hacking, Ian (2004). "Minding the Brain." *The New York Review of Books*, LI, no. 11:32–6.
Hara, Makiko (2001). "Others in the Third Millennium." In *The Uncanny: Experiments in Cyborg Culture*, ed. Bruce Grenville. Vancouver: Vancouver Art Gallery. 237–47.
Hayles, Katherine N. (1999). *How We Became Posthuman: Virtual Bodies in Cybernetic, Literature, and Information.* Chicago: University of Chicago Press.
Heartney, Eleanor (2001). "Blacks, Whites and Other Mythic Beings." *Art in America*, no. 11:136–40.

Hopkins, David (2000). *After Modern Art 1945–2000.* Oxford: Oxford University Press.

Johnson, Ken (1997). "The Artist as Intellectual Warrior." *Art in America*, vol. 85, no. 1:29–31.

Jones, Amelia (1998). *Body Art/Performing the Subject.* Minneapolis: University of Minnesota Press.

Kelly, Mary (1981). "Re-Viewing Modernist Criticism." Originally published in *Screen* and reprinted in *Art after Modernism: Rethinking Representation*, ed. Brian Wallis. New York: New Museum of Contemporary Art and David R. Godine Publishers, 1984. 87–102.

Krauss, Rosalind (1965). "Afterthoughts on Op." *Art International*, vol. 9, no. 5:75–6.

—— (1996). "*Informe* without Conclusion." *October*, no. 98:89–105.

—— (2000). "Richard Serra: Sculpture." In *Richard Serra*, ed. Hal Foster and Gordon Hughes. Cambridge, MA: MIT Press. 99–145.

Kristeva, Julia (1982). *Powers of Horror: An Essay on Abjection*, trans. Leon S. Roudiez. New York: Columbia University Press.

Lauzon, Claudette (2004). "What the Body Remembers: Rebecca Belmore's Memorial to Missing." Unpublished paper. Montreal: McGill University.

Lee, Pamela M. (2004). *Chronophobia: On Time in the Art of the 1960s.* Cambridge, MA: MIT Press.

Massey, Doreen (1995). "Space-time and the Politics of Location." In *House/Rachel Whiteread*, ed. James Lingwood. London: Phaidon Press/Artangel. 34–49.

Mendieta, Ana (n.d.). In http://www.guggenheim.org/artscurriculum/lessons/movpics_mendieta.php.

Merleau-Ponty, Maurice (1945/1962). *Phenomenology of Perception*, trans. Colin Smith. London: Routledge Kegan and Paul.

Mulvey, Laura (1975). "Visual Pleasure and Narrative Cinema." *Screen*, no. 6:6–18.

Nancy, Jean-Luc (2000). "Nancy/Pontbriand: An Exchange." *Parachute*, no. 100:14–31.

Piper, Adrian (1999). *Adrian Piper: A Retrospective.* Baltimore County: Fine Arts Gallery, University of Maryland.

Ross, Christine (1997). "Redefinitions of Abjection in Contemporary Performances of the Female Body." *RES, Journal of Anthropology and Aesthetics*, no. 31:149–56.

Rush, Michael (2000). "Body Image." *Art in America*, vol. 88, no. 4:135–9.

Sayre, Henry M. (1989). *The Object of Performance: The American Avant-Garde since 1970.* Chicago: University of Chicago Press.

Sedgwick, Eve Kosofsky (2003). *Touching Feeling: Affect, Pedagogy, Performativity.* Durham, NC: Duke University Press.

Shusterman, Richard (2000). *Performing Live: Aesthetic Alternatives for the Ends of Art.* Ithaca: Cornell University Press.

Storr, Robert (1996). "Setting Traps for the Mind and the Heart." *Art in America*, vol. 84, no. 1:70–6, 125.

Sturken, Marita (1999). "Imaging Postmemory/Renegotiating History." *Afterimage*, vol. 26, no. 6:10–12.

Taylor, Simon (1993). "The Phobic Object: Abjection in Contemporary Art." In *Abject Art: Repulsion and Desire in American Art*, by Jack Ben-Levi, Craig Houser, Lesley C. Jones, and Simon Taylor. New York: Whitney Museum of American Art. 59–83.

Turner, Bryan S. (1984). *The Body and Society: Explorations in Social Theory.* Oxford: Blackwell.

Turner, Terence (1994). "Bodies and Anti-bodies: Flesh and Fetish in Contemporary Social Theory." In *Embodiment and Experience: The Existential Ground of Culture and Self,* ed. Thomas J. Csordas. Cambridge: Cambridge University Press. 27–47.

PART VI

Methods/Theories

20

A Shadow of Marx

Neil Cummings and
Marysia Lewandowska

It's June 16, 2001, and I'm [Cummings] standing behind a rope barrier with a crowd of people in a sloping field, on the edge of a village in Orgreave, South Yorkshire, England. On the other side of the rope are hundreds of people practicing how to perform a running battle. They shout at each other; one side charges and the other retreats, and then vice versa. Some are dressed as police officers – I can see riot gear, shields, snarling dogs, and even horses – the others, the civilians, are all men dressed in slightly out of date clothing, from around the 1980s. A voice comes over a loudspeaker system and a number of small two-person film crews with digital cameras mingle with the participants.

And then it starts – shouting, charges, chanting, the throwing of surrogate stones and other objects, skirmishes; dogs are used and people are apparently arrested. The confrontation gets very violent and everyone surges into the far bottom corner of the field, and then the action stops. The participants move to another location obscured from my view, although I can see thick black smoke and smell burning rubber. Eventually a loudspeaker crackles into life and we are asked to move down onto a nearby road, where a terrifying battle is raging. Cars are overturned and on fire; there is blood. Mounted police gallop down the road followed by a hail of thrown rocks and debris, confrontations flare up; beautifully choreographed violence leaves bloodied and injured men scattered along the road. A claxon sounds and the violence subsides. People stop skir-mishing, help each other up, start smiling and hugging, and begin clearing things away.

This is all taking place at the spot where, 20 years ago, 4,000 striking miners from across the UK tried to stop coal moving into a coke works and were confronted by a force of 3,000 police officers brought by the government to ensure the coal was delivered. The pitched battle that ensued was one of the

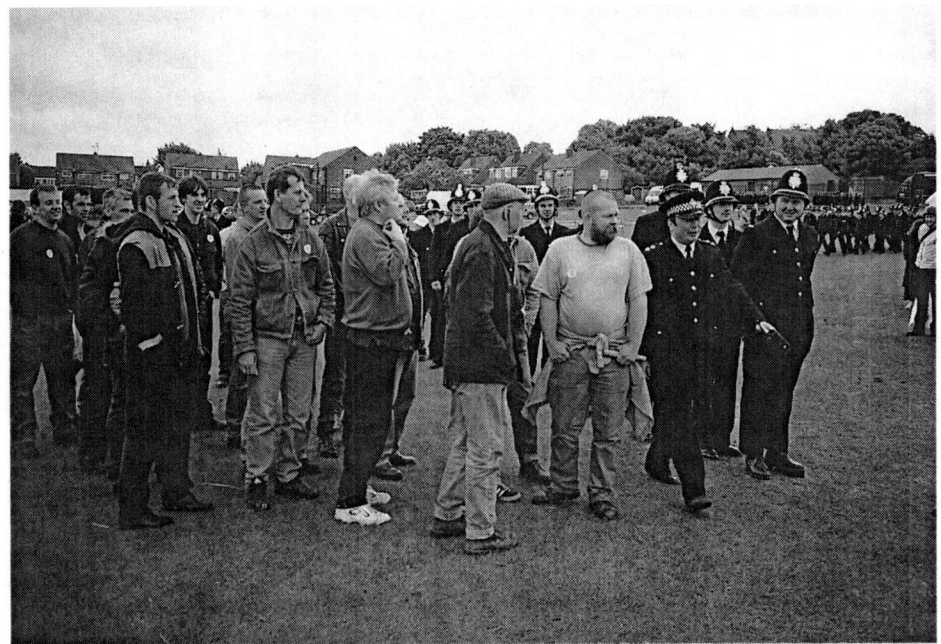

FIGURE 20.1   Jeremy Deller, *English Civil War, Part II* (*The Battle of Orgreave*). Document of event in Orgreave, South Yorkshire, June 2001. Photograph © Neil Cummings and Marysia Lewandowska. Courtesy of *chanceprojects.com*

most bitter of an already desperate struggle between the remnants of unionized labor and a government determined to introduce deregulated markets as a disciplinary force. For many, this event was a defining moment for contemporary Britain.

The 2001 restaging of the event is one of the most powerful art works made in England for as long as I can remember – Jeremy Deller's *The English Civil War Part II*, colloquially known as the *Battle of Orgreave*. This amazing event was conceived by Deller and organized through Artangel, an independent commissioning agency that works with artists to realize site-specific projects.

For the previous 18 months Deller had been researching in and around Orgreave, talking with residents, ex-miners, local historians, and the police. For *The English Civil War*, Deller meticulously reconstructed the battle, choreographing 800 people (including 300 ex-miners and police officers, some of whom had taken part in the original confrontation), in collaboration with amateur re-enactment groups, whose members are known for dressing-up as soldiers and replaying battles belonging to deep historical time. On this occasion the historical battle was within living memory. The audience consisted of local people and a smattering of art-world types who had been persuaded to leave London for the day.

The event was, and is, difficult to describe because it occupied many different cultural categories at once: it was a work of art, a re-enacted battle, an extraordinary celebration, a struggle to represent history and part film set – the film director Mike Figgis had been commissioned by Channel Four television to make a film of the strike using the reconstruction as source material, and this partly paid for the art work. Overall, it was very difficult to pinpoint the experience in relation to a particular object or "site" *as* a work of art, or even to acknowledge where the various components of the "art" project began or ended. But over time, it became clear that Jeremy Deller had produced an extraordinary art work, the effects of which are still reverberating.[1]

Marxism and Ideology

We are, all of us, enacting a text written elsewhere. And this text, whether we like it or not and whether we can name it or not, is called ideology. Jeremy Deller's *The English Civil War* is a rich, profound, and provocative contemporary art work that uses the legacy of Marxist cultural critique to bring one strand of this ideological text explosively into the present. The "battle" memorialized a profound historical moment, denying us the luxury of forgetting its effects, and simultaneously challenged contemporary art to engage with important issues of social representation. At the same time, it avoided reducing those formative events and complex social processes to illustration, entertainment, or empty spectacle.

Deller deployed one of the most powerful tools in contemporary art, which is the use of "research" or "fieldwork" in the making of the work within a specific location. Because the "work" of a contemporary work of art increasingly takes place through distributive, communicative, or social networks, research is beginning to replace "site specificity" as a means of engagement between an artist and a location. And it is now understood that the "site," like the art work itself, doesn't simply preexist its display and interpretation; both the work and its site are made simultaneously through the act of engagement.

In the case of *The English Civil War*, it is clear that an art work as complex as this cannot be bound by the physical exhibition space of a gallery or museum. Its site – which is one among many – is the social imagination. *The English Civil War* exists differently for each of its different participants and audience members: from those participants who fought in the initial confrontation and collaborated with the restaging, to those who have read the countless accounts of it in magazines, websites, and journals the world over. And now, even those of you reading this text.

As huge areas of social life are spiraling into abstraction largely as a result of the complexity of our globally networked economies, the most basic functions of our daily life, such as the simplest purchase of a pair of shoes, involve lines of debt and credit, chains of labor relationships, and complex supply routes of materials, images, and information which circle the globe. If art has traditionally been able to make visible and thus give form to the most subtle yet powerful of beliefs, it is not surprising that the most ambitious contemporary art would seek to engage with these forces.

In our networked economies the exchange of accumulated value as capital has become slippery and complex. It is no longer clear where the creation of value, the foundation of political economy, fits into our accelerated exchange of signs, services, and information. The theory of value based on the accumulated profit extracted from labor, which emerged in industrial-age economic models and is principally identified with the work of Karl Marx, has little or no purchase on the possibilities introduced by immaterial labor. The kinds of ephemeral "products" manufactured by contemporary cultural, entertainment, and creative industries like museums and galleries, or in public relations departments and advertising companies, are difficult to represent. But what *is* clear is that art is no longer a luxury by-product of financial capital that can transcend political and economic structures; it must be seen as central to these "new" economies.

Art's dissolution into the space of the commodity was critically deployed by a group of American artists during the 1980s. Jeff Koons, Sherrie Levine, and Heim Steinbach, for example, utilized the material vocabulary and syntax of "goods," to intensify the lack of art's representational authority.

At the same time, other artists have critiqued the commodification of art, opening out its structures of reproduction. Daniel Buren traces the intersection between the work of art and "everyday" aesthetic exchanges; Hans Haacke investigates the corporate, state, and private investments inherent in the circulation of art through cultural institutions; and Michael Asher explores the misrecognized obligations – such as the commercial imperative behind art's exhibition and display – that produce the *work* of the work of art. Collectively, their practice of interrogating the institutions of art since the 1970s has laid the ground for the 1980s–1990s work of Group Material, Fred Wilson and Andrea Fraser, defined by its strategic "institutional critique."

Jeremy Deller is one of a range of contemporary artists – including Mathieu Laurette, Thomas Hirschhorn, and the members of collaborative groups such as Inventory, The Free Copenhagen University, or Superflex – who are building on this legacy of institutional critique. Artists such as Deller have turned their attention away from the institutions of art themselves to concentrate on the network of economic, political, and social structures of which art is increasingly an integral part. Rather than merely illustrating these structures through art works and exhibitions, they attempt vividly to re-animate the world as experience through critical reception. The encounter with art, the art work, or the event is no longer a passive encounter through the medium of display, but is articulated as a place of engagement and production. Art works are no longer viewed as points of origin, imagined to be founded on the artist's creativity, or of termination, housed in museums and galleries or their stores, but as nodes in networks of exchange. Such art works and practices are only possible because of a wide and deep-rooted engagement with cultural criticism, the legacy of which owes an enormous debt to a Marxist-inspired engagement with culture.

Classic Marxism

Marxism is the political practice and/or social theory based on the works of Karl Marx (1818–83), a German philosopher, economist, and revolutionary. Marx borrowed a core philosophical model from Friedrich Hegel, a political economy derived from Adam Smith, and aspects of nineteenth-century French socialism to develop a critique of European society. This critique achieved its most systematic expression in his major unfinished three-volume work, *Capital: A Critique of Political Economy.*

Marx used Hegel's model of historical progress, in which ideology and knowledge gradually develop toward their intended conclusion, but inverted its cause and effect, proposing that material circumstances shape ideas, instead of – as in Hegel's model – the other way around. Marx's material theory of history, otherwise known as historical materialism, is beautifully summarized in his *A Contribution to the Critique of Political Economy,* where he notes, "[t]he mode of production of material life conditions the general process of social, political and intellectual life. It is not the consciousness of men that determines their existence, but their social existence that determines their consciousness."[2]

Marx could see that the means of controlling the material reproduction of life had divided society into two broad social classes:

(1) The *working class* or *proletariat*: Marx characterized this class as individuals who sell their labor but do not own the means of production, and argued that, through their labor and the profit extracted from it, the members of the industrial working class are responsible for creating all the given wealth in a society.

(2) The *middle class* or *bourgeoisie*: those who own the means of production and extract the profit from the labor of the proletariat.

A traditional Marxist view of capitalist society is seen through this prism of class antagonism, played out through the means of production. However, since 1945 – sometimes referred to as the period of "late" capitalism[3] – there has been a relentless drive to overlay the ideologically determinative spaces of production with the equally disciplinary spaces of mass or popular consumption. The development of a vast, interlinked media system of radio, television, film, magazines, advertising, and retail culture could be seen as an extension of the ideological arena of bourgeois culture through which various class, ideological, aesthetic, and/or political interests are reproduced. And art works, which were once seen as resistant to, or outside of, ideological influence, must now be seen as having become (if not always having been) absorbed into the very symbolic terrain through which ideology is contested and capital reproduced.

Frankfurt School Marxism

What has become known as the "Frankfurt School" inaugurated a Marxist-inspired critical study of the ideological effects of the burgeoning mass culture of fascism in Germany. The Institute of Social Research, which opened in 1924, was inspired by Marx's "classical" method of historical materialism; the original staff members of the Institute, including Theodor Adorno and Max Horkheimer, were intent on trying to combine theory and empirical research.

In January 1933, the Institute was raided by Nazi storm troopers. Many, including Adorno (who was part Jewish), managed to escape. After their arrival in the USA, Adorno and Horkheimer began to realize that they were living under a new and an even intensified system of capitalist social relations in which a popular mass-media culture, including radio, Hollywood movies, and the record-player, was extending relations of production out into apparent leisure time. For Adorno, who worked on a social research project funded by the Rockefeller Foundation in 1937 studying the effects of new forms of communication on society, the space remaindered by labor – that of culture – was beginning to obey the rules of mechanical production just like any other industry.

In *The Dialectic of Enlightenment* (1947), Adorno and Horkheimer developed the first critical theory which addressed the crucial roles of mass culture and communication in contemporary society, and coined the paradoxical but hugely influential phrase "the Culture Industry." Here, the authors argue that "[c]ulture now impresses the same stamp on everything. Films, radio and magazines make up a system which is uniform as a whole and in every part" (120).

Adorno and Horkheimer identified a fatal flaw in classic Marxism. Marx, via Hegel, predicted that the inevitable historical development of the working class would drive its members to seize control of their own means of production, which suggested that capitalism contains the revolutionary potential to generate a genuinely free society. In a society driven by productive relations, which extends into commodification and communication, mass culture becomes a logical extension – a superstructure – to Marx's primary economic base. But for Adorno and Horkheimer the products of a "culture industry" held no such promise of emancipation, because mass culture forsakes real freedom in the pursuit of endless novelty and entertainment. Through this logic, whereby Adorno and Horkheimer begin to identify the structures of what would later be called "late capitalism," the evolution of capitalism through culture is not toward freedom but toward even tighter discipline and domination.

So Adorno and Horkheimer look for the sources of revolution elsewhere. And they identify in the supposed autonomy of the most demanding, difficult, avant-garde art works of their time the radical emancipatory potential envisaged by Marx's political economy. In this potential they locate a "pure purposelessness," which offers a means of contesting, denying even, the utility and instrumentality that reigns in mass cultural production and entertainment.[4] Of course Adorno and Horkheimer recognize that works of art are commodities, and therefore subject to the logics of exchange, but as *pure* commodities, they never have any recourse to utility and therefore fall outside of Marx's ethical distinction between objects.[5]

The autonomous work of art offers an *unconscious* promise of freedom, because its autonomy, its purity, can never be instrumentalized. But Adorno and Horkheimer's position is further complicated because avant-garde art is to be appreciated, but only by the exclusion of the working class: it is the latter's freedom and emancipation with which "art keeps faith precisely by its freedom from the ends of the false universality."[6] Now, there is clearly a contradiction in critical theory claiming that autonomous bourgeois art is what sustains the promise of freedom for the members of the working class in the moment of their exclusion. Adorno and Horkheimer thus deploy an infuriating, paradoxical, and contradictory Marxist-inspired critique, but use it to productive effect. They simultaneously engage with and disengage from coherent criticism, opening a sort of non-place of criticism as a negative dialectic that mirrors the ideal position of the art work they champion.

Adorno and Horkheimer were working at the pinnacle of industrial or managerial capitalism, which disciplined workers through relations of production, and they could glimpse a homogenous mass media through film, radio, and soon television, which would extend those productive relations into the spaces of leisure. And yet the culture industry was never as coherent or homogeneous as Adorno and Horkheimer proposed. Although there was and continues to be a corporate and monopolistic drive, its products are more varied, dynamic, and conflictual than they credit. Also, the audience of the culture industry are not necessarily the passive dupes of a cynical mass deception. In popular music for example, which Adorno in particular famously detested, there is the potential for building communities of ideological resistance – as in the case of jazz, which has been intimately linked to the development of a radical black urban culture in Europe and the USA. Essentially, Adorno and Horkheimer forgot the sociology of Marx, failing to produce any empirical analysis of the political economy of the culture industry or of the actual processes involved in the *uses* of mass culture by its audience.

Adorno and Horkheimer's model of culture, which only ascribes critical and emancipatory potential to privileged autonomous art, is thus highly problematic. Avant-garde art of the 1950s such as American abstract expressionism – which art critic Clement Greenberg claimed to be autonomous from the social – would lose any critical purchase when the mass culture against which it was so negatively opposed fragmented and ceased to exist. At the same time, as the work of Mark Rothko illustrates, art's very negativity (the potential of color-field painting to "critique" bourgeois aesthetic values) would be absorbed by sections of the culture industry – like corporate lobbies – and redeployed as a marketing device. The legacy of Marxism needed a more sensitive model of art and culture to account for new developments in the modes and methods of cultural production, dissemination, and reception at all levels.

A Practice of Everyday Life

A flea market is where objects fall from their position within the circuits of mass consumption imagined by the retail industry and enter their rich and varied lives. A logic of *use* is at work in the flea market: it re-imagines retail culture's intentions by diverting commodities from their expected pathways; objects switch contexts and gain new potential based not on their image, but on their utility. For example, the novelty mug, designed to remind you of a past visit to a tourist attraction – to remind you in fact of a moment of consumption – can be remaindered and purchased at the flea market; the new owner can put it to use perhaps to store pens and pencils, or to catch the drips from a leaking radiator. The original "intention" inscribed on the novelty mug by its producers and promoters – the refreshment of capital through a commodity economy – is subverted through its secondary purchase at the flea market and re-imagined

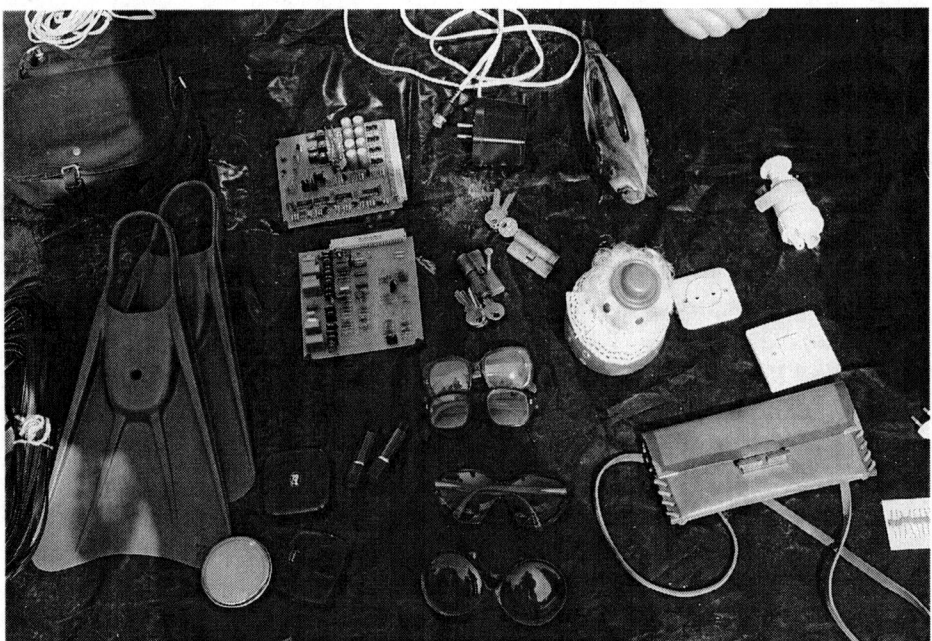

FIGURE 20.2   Flea market in Warsaw, Poland, 1997. Photograph © Neil Cummings and Marysia Lewandowska. Courtesy of *chanceprojects.com*

uses, which, through diversion and deviation, offer a means of producing different kinds of value.

The Situationist International (SI) was a primarily French group of artists, intellectuals, and activists who, from 1957 into the 1960s, proposed a revolutionary reinvention of life through the enactment of situations that disrupt the habitual order of things that jolt people out of their customary ways of thinking and behaving. In place of petrified labor and commodified life, they proposed the *dérive* – a wandering, improvisery flow of acts, encounters, and images – and the *détournement* – a rerouting of existing events, actions, and images toward unintended consequences. A perfect *dérive* is wandering through a flea market, driven by an aimless need rather than the imperatives of instrumental exchange.

The situationists dedicated themselves to such hybrid *maneuvers* simultaneously through art and politics, through public institutions and the street; they produced a staggering quantity of journals, paintings, pamphlets, scrapbooks, tape-recorded presentations and lectures, conferences, exhibitions, events, performances, and architectural models. They made films, organized boycotts, and initiated disruptions of "spectacular" official cultural events. What united these activities, these moments, these situations, was the situationists' collective desire to resist producing objects that could be commodified as "official" art, or texts that could be reified as "political theory."[7] Through diverse practices, and by all means necessary, they hoped to act as catalysts within Marx's revolutionary process, encouraging vandalism, strikes, and sabotage as a way of disrupting the forces of production, and the commodity realm of "spectacle."

Guy Debord was the most prolific and influential theoretician of the SI. The group emerged from previous formations influenced by Dada and surrealist actions, specifically the COBRA group based in Copenhagen, Brussels, and Amsterdam, and the Letterist International movement based in France. The SI was an intentionally small group, free of national allegiances, designed to be mobile, militant and extreme; as such, they were to mirror the evolution of global capital itself. They were dissatisfied with politics as represented by the pro-capitalist political parties of the "west" and the socialist (read Stalinist) alternatives in the "east." They also had no faith in the existing forms or institutions of contemporary art. In complete contrast to Adorno and Horkheimer the SI saw that for contemporary art and political action to have any creative potential they would have to reconnect with and not retreat from the lives of the majority.

Debord's important and influential 1967 book, *The Society of the Spectacle*, is a tirade against the ways in which corporate life and impersonal bureaucracies were increasingly dominating, controlling, and exploiting the lives of individuals. Capitalism had turned virtually all relationships into commodity exchange and, having treated workers with the utmost contempt as producers, now lavishly seduced them as consumers. The images and information that constitute and regulate a public sphere had been appropriated by advertising. Society had been reduced to "spectacular" commodity consumption, and divided into professional media agents and spectators. The SI advocated taking to the street, the factory, the home, and the flea market, places where the creativity of most people still flourished outside of the spaces of commodification.

Debord's book, and Raoul Vaneigem's 1967 *The Revolution of Everyday Life*, served as virtual manifestos of the situationist moment. In opposition to the society of spectacle the situationists proposed a society that abolished money, commodity production, wage labor, classes, private property, and the control of the state. Pleasure would replace profit, and the historic antagonism between labor and leisure would dissolve. Above all, they insisted that every individual should actively participate in the construction of everyday life through the creative enactment of "situations" that would enable all individuals to release their own potential and obtain their own freedoms.

Extraordinarily, these ideas had widespread political influence during the May 1968 student rebellion and the wildcat strikes that followed, which paralyzed France for over two weeks. The SI had been predicting the spontaneous potential of the "situation" for almost a decade; they quickly grasped the importance of events, were able to mobilize quickly, act with confidence, and contribute effectively during what they called the May "festival." Consequently, the uprising could not fail to have certain distinctly situationist flavor – images appropriated from, altered, and then used critically against popular culture deployed the tactic of *détournement*; demands for the revolutionary alteration of everyday life exemplified the radical *dérive*; and much of the graffiti daubed on buildings, and banners used in demonstrations – such as "Free the passions, never work, live without dead time" – quoted freely from Debord's book.

Despite the prescience of their critique, and the fact that much of their work predicted the strikes and confrontations that engulfed France in spring 1968, politically the SI seem wildly optimistic, contradictory, even naïve. But once again, as with Adorno and Horkheimer, this critical ambiguity becomes a creative device. If the situationists strove against an alienated consumer lifestyle, they also offered – through interventions and situations – alternatives to art simply becoming a commodified extension of the society of spectacle. It has now become commonplace for contemporary artists to re-inscribe the products of culture with different intentions and potentials, but these are all too easily absorbed as marketable differences by the collectors, dealers, and institutions that make up the "market" for art. The situationists' project was much more radical in that it attempted to interfere with the value system of the market itself.

Toward a Theory for the Practice of Everyday Life

Intellectually, the situationists were more indebted to Henri Lefebvre, who taught in the sociology department at the University of Nanterre where Debord and Vaneigem attended his classes, than anyone else.[8] Lefebvre was central in reintroducing the writings of Marx into academic and popular discourse in

France, translating key early texts of Marx into French in 1933 and instigating a peculiarly French interpretation of Marxism that was tinged with humanism.

Lefebvre's influential 1939 book *Dialectical Materialism* emphasized Hegel's dialectic model of historical progress as a key methodological and theoretical concept for Marx. Lefebvre recognized in the dialectical model of thesis, antithesis, and synthesis the potential to transcend both ideological theory and social practice, hinting at a resolution of these habitual oppositions through praxis. For Marx praxis is the process by which a theory becomes part of lived experience, where an idea ceases to be an abstract concept and becomes an everyday reality. With the publication of Lefebvre's *Critique of Everyday Life* in 1947 praxis was put to work. Unlike Adorno, who scorned the lived or popular practices of the majority, Lefebvre reanimated Marxism as a critical philosophy of social action. It was not enough for critique to engage with conditions of production and culture at the level of theory – Lefebvre admonishes theorists who witness and judge life from *the outside*, arguing that critique through praxis had to produce the means to transform lived experience.

Lefebvre developed the theme of alienation from Marx into a key theoretical concept. Alienation, a deep historical process viciously accelerated by industrial production, describes the process through which the surplus derived from workers' labor, transformed into sparkling commodities, or "free" time, returns in a form unrecognizable to them, as dispossessions. And for Lefebvre this disembodied return of labor value causes an impoverishment of everyday lived experience. Alienation turns all of life into an abstraction (such as the division of life into the brutal opposites of work and leisure). Workers no longer produce their own lived experience, they produce financial, material, and cultural capital; the time, space, and materiality of the modern world becomes alien to the very people who are reproducing it.

"Man must *be* everyday, or he will not be at all" leaps from the first few pages of Lefebvre's *Critique*, introducing the radical theme of a revolutionary attention to the practices of everyday life. In the foreword to the book he also sets forth a new method for analyzing the culture of the everyday:

> Thus the simplest event – a woman buying a pound of sugar, for example – must be analysed. Knowledge will grasp whatever is hidden within it. To understand this event it is not enough to describe it; research will disclose a tangle of reasons and causes, of essence and "spheres": the woman's life, her biography, her job, her family, her class, her budget, her eating habits, how she uses her money, her opinions and her ideas, the state of the markets, etc. Finally I would have grasped the sum total of capitalist society, the nation and its history (57).

Here, Lefebvre is groping toward a kind of ethnographic method, where the empirical study of Marx is wedded with a new kind of philosophical and political sociology. Lefebvre advocates the study of trivia and the overlooked, of the products of everyday social exchanges and not the products of an already prescribed "culture." In the book's foreword, Lefebvre expressly pays homage to Marx for uniting economic and political theory with its living formation in ordinary social relations, in everyday experience.

As some critics have pointed out, however, Lefebvre shows a troubling lack of criticality in his romantic embrace of French peasant culture, especially in the chapter "Notes Written One Sunday in the French Countryside" from the *Critique*. Here he suggests that in rural France there is no differentiation between work and leisure and thereby that people live without alienation. Although he did turn to study urban life in 1968 with his book *Everyday Life in the Modern World*, Lefebvre tended to downplay the urban present as insignificant in contrast with the profound certainty of a rural past.

Critical attention to the everyday was taken up by the Jesuit historian Michel de Certeau, who burst into cultural consciousness with a series of dazzling articles that analyzed the political and cultural fallout from the strikes and demonstrations of May 1968 in France. The articles built upon the work of Lefebvre, although they opened a new critical potential latent in urban cultural production. By attending to "anonymous" or "everyday" creativity through the unconventional and inventive ways people use "things" de Certeau challenged the perception, all too common in mid-twentieth-century Marxism, that the popular masses engage in passive consumption. De Certeau proposed to attend to the practices and habits of the users of culture who in countless ways appropriate the property, intentions, and values of more powerful economic and cultural forces, arguing that, through tactical mobility, technical invention, and moral resistance they operate between the institutions of social and cultural regulation.[9]

In the work of Lefebvre, Debord, and the SI there is a tacit assumption that social life is inevitably atomizing toward the alienated individual. But de Certeau spectacularly reversed this logic, suggesting that, rather than being assumed as a coherent "self" preexisting the social, an individual could only be understood as a nexus of complex social relations, as a subject constructed from a network of shared beliefs, habits, and practices. De Certeau set out to trace these networks, mapping fields of everyday practice that have no institutions, official or otherwise, that leave no record in "official" culture; that cannot be easily capitalized by the media class, have no coherent ideologies or manifestos and yet are not indeterminate because there is a logic at work in their enactment and deployment.

De Certeau's *The Practice of Everyday Life*, first published in French in 1980, articulates terms to clarify these ideas – in particular, "strategy" and "tactic." A strategy assumes a place that can be circumscribed, a proper place. Strategy, he suggests, is a mode of operation through which legitimate power operates from within a designated field; for example, through language, political structures, retail culture, the law, discourses of the body, and so on. In short, strategy is the place of official power. A tactic, in contrast, cannot count on a proper place or field of action. The place of tactics is the place of the "other" and the tactical is a mode of operation used by all those unrecognized producers of culture whose lives are constrained by the impositions of others. A system of production and its ancillary forces of promotion and consumption are imposed upon us; tactics are the means for taking back that which belongs to us from production.

In the chapter "Uses of Language" de Certeau considers reading as an example of a tactic used against the strategic field of the published text – as a kind of "poaching." A book is the result of strategy, the proper record of a text produced by the power of finance, including structures of commissioning, editing, printing, distributing, advertising, and selling, all of which are protected by the force of the law. The writer through the field of publishing assembles words into social authority. From the editor's and writer's point of view, the reader is imagined to be following the logic of the book from the beginning to the end, reading each text thoroughly to retrace their intended meanings. Copyright protects the text as the author's or publisher's property.

And yet, even as you read this text here, I suspect – no I know – that your attention is wandering, you are skipping sentences, paragraphs, and even cutting to the end; you may be listening to music or reading with half an eye on the television. And if you want to, you will take the words ordered by me, and pass them off as your own. You will use the book for your own devices, which will be many and varied. Perhaps you will use it as a doorstop for propping the door open. All of this is to recall the words of literary theorist Roland Barthes, who famously argued that reading is the origin of writing and not its destination.[10] Or, as de Certeau might say, the tactical reader slips effortlessly into the author's place.[11]

Critical Consumption

Since the 1970s, Belgian artist Guillaume Bijl has been investigating the endless equivalence between objects as commodities in situations of social exchange, installing facsimiles relating to or approximations of different social contexts in galleries and museums. In 1979, for example, he installed *Driving School Z*, and a voting booth in Galerij Ruimte, Antwerp. These installations consisted of meticulously recreated tableaux with the appropriate architectural features, including furniture, décor, plants, and relevant technologies. There quickly followed, amongst other things, a fitness center (1983), a used car salesroom (1984), a conference and waiting room (1988), and a wax museum displaying artist, curator, and collector at Documenta IX at Kassel (1992) (Figure 20.3). Over almost 30 years Bijl has displayed many of the spaces through which individuals are inducted into the appropriate behavior for social life. He arranges these threshold spaces between the individual and the social around the various points of exchange between work and leisure. The playful consistency of the installations could be seen as tracing a trajectory for contemporary capital – a trajectory wherein leisure itself, traditionally outside of productive labor, is fully absorbed into retail culture and turned into a site of production.

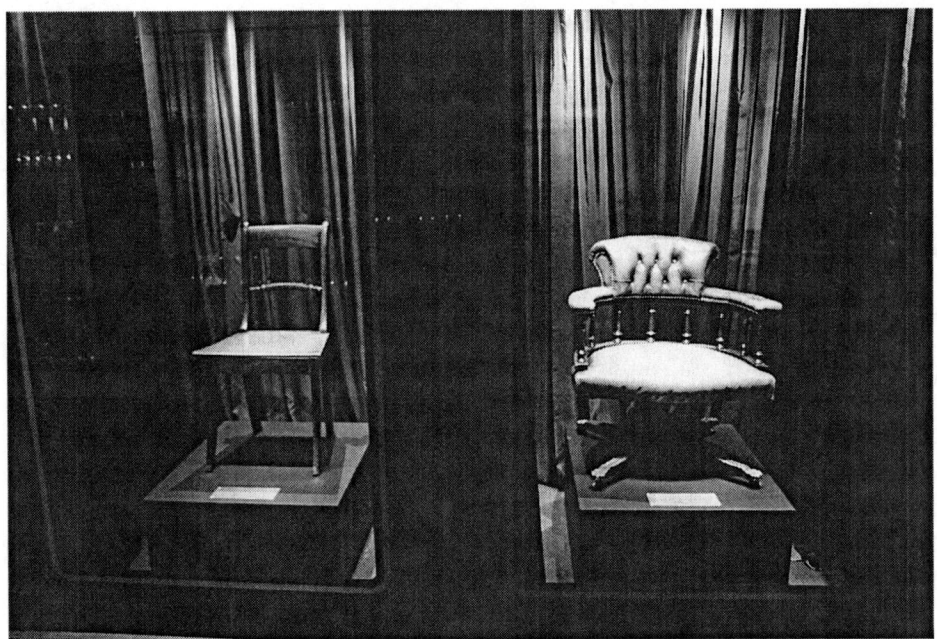

FIGURE 20.3   Guillaume Bijl, *Famous Furniture*, 1997. Museum-style installation at Habitat furniture store, part of *Collected*, a multi-site exhibition coordinated by the Photographer's Gallery, London. Photograph © Neil Cummings and Marysia Lewandowska. Courtesy of *chanceprojects.com*

Following the logic of capital's trajectory, during the 1990s the museum and gallery entered the lexicon of Bijl's social spaces. A suite of installations including a Wunderkammer, an auction house, a museum of transport, a collector's apartment, and a gallery exhibition were all displayed rhetorically within various actual, functioning museums and galleries. Bijl was inviting visitors to link the represented "cultural" spaces to his previous installations of more familiar spaces of commercial exchange. At the 1994 Basel Art Fair, Bijl installed a trade stand promoting and selling crystal chandeliers. With a simple gesture Bijl deprived the art fair of its principle alibi – the notion that commerce is a disinterested consequence of cultured aesthetic engagement – and exposed the operational logic (the exchange of money) which is at work underneath all aesthetic exchange.

In all of this work Bijl reveals that he shares with American artists of the early 1980s and the 1990s a fascination with commodification and the endless potential – as theorist Jean Baudrillard so perceptively noted – "of playing with the code."[12] If Marcel Duchamp, with his purchase of the bottle rack in 1914, signaled the creative potential in consumption, he also moved the locus of the creative act from a struggle to produce to a struggle to choose – the ultimate shopper's dilemma. And so the endless manipulation of marginal difference that defers monotony for the shopper transfers to the gallery visitor, as one object or one artist replaces another in the circuitous play of similarity and difference. Consumption becomes the creative motor and destructive motive in any exchange, and this is what gives artists who work with its forces a critical and corrosive nature.

Bijl literally exhibits the common processes of manipulation through which we structure the value between things in any commodity exchange. And these processes are indeed common to all objects, even the art works themselves; objects are sourced for the installations, bought from shops or markets, classified, arranged, and displayed for exhibition. After the duration of the exhibition he either sells the objects as art works – to be frozen in galleries or museums as "art" – or dismantles the installations, dissolving the objects again into the secondhand commodity circuits of flea markets, thrift stores, and car-boot sales. The temporary suspension of exchange through gallery exhibition enables consumer desire itself reflexively to *become* the object of the work. We only desire what others like us also desire. And so this interrupted exchange is a way of gaining a critical purchase on processes that are otherwise so habituated as to be below our level of everyday comprehension. With Bijl's work we are offered not the goods themselves, nor the glories of "disinterested" aesthetic contemplation, but the endless process of "becoming-ourselves" through shopping. Bijl thus points to the fact that consumption is no longer limited to the appropriation of goods but has become the very means by which we are socialized.

Much was and continues to be made of the irony of art works that engage with commodification only to become commodified themselves. What once was a critical intent (such as the impulse initiated by Duchamp's readymades, picked up by Andy Warhol's practice, and reworked by Jeff Koons and Haim Steinbach) quickly becomes absorbed as *knowing* consumerism. But unlike these more celebrated American artists, Bijl does not rely on irony. His project is a visual and critical archaeology of a particular moment in which the scene of capital's reproduction shifted from the spaces of material production, the factory, to the spaces of consumption and culture – where the spaces of art are seen as a continuum with those of the shop, solarium, hairdresser, and fitness center.

Toward a Theory of Critical Consumption

While the influence of Marxism in France took the form of tactical resistance that fractured into studies of everyday life, in Britain a different genealogy developed, dominated by what is now called cultural studies. A mode of intellectual inquiry, cultural studies has generally been concerned with the very materials that Adorno despised – popular and mass mediated cultural forms such as magazines, radio, film, broadcast television, advertising, shopping, and so on. In Britain we could start this genealogy with the work of Richard Hoggart's 1957 book *The Uses of Literacy*, a nostalgic anthropological account of his own working-class environment in relation to an emerging popular culture, and Raymond Williams's two early books *Culture and Society: 1780–1950* (1958) and *The Long Revolution* (1961).

Williams, the most influential figure in British cultural studies, proposed that a proper study of society cannot just be concerned with only some of its products – such as the fine art, literature, furniture, and architecture of a particular class – but should attend to the whole of material production. He argued that distinctions made between types of cultural production – avant-garde art and popular music for instance – are ideologically invested. While Adorno and Horkheimer imagined passive consumers, fooled by a culture industry beyond their control, and Lefebvre and de Certeau sought for sites of resistance outside of the commodity system in the forms and processes of everyday life, Williams suggested the possibility of active and critical consumers who endlessly contest the ideological forces of capitalism. Williams does not – as some critics would contend – reduce culture (including art) to ideology, but rather insists on recognizing the often hidden forces at work in structuring cultural forms, and their modes of dissemination and participation. Williams insists that the struggles within our political economy are played out through representation; they do not merely exist elsewhere in abstracted relations of labor and capital and thus they can no longer be excluded on the basis of the projected, or desired "autonomy" of art.

In his book *Communications* (1962) Williams turns his attention directly to the relationship between political economy and the new communication industries. This book marks an important step on the part of Marxist theorists toward understanding rather than (per Adorno and Horkheimer) simply dismissing the products and structures of the culture industry. Williams recognizes that through the development of manufacturing technologies, industrial labor was beginning to lose its centrality as a source for capital; correlatively, the agent of historical transformation, the working class, had begun to disappear as an easily defined "mass." Williams argues that the communications, information, and service economies introduce new modes of exchange that are less amenable to the kinds of crude Marxist analysis that had dominated cultural theory in the mid twentieth century.

To replace this crude determinist model, wherein culture was placed as a "superstructure" subordinate to the economic and ideological "base" of society, Williams suggested that culture is simultaneously composed of dominant, residual and emergent forces and thus no longer simply reflects the "base." Culture is thus defined by Williams as a potential site of contestation, where different groups or communities can struggle over their relationship to dominant capitalist forces, both those emerging from below (the popular) and those imposed from above ("high" culture and the mass media).[13] The study of culture in Williams' terms –which became the designation "cultural studies" – subverts academic boundaries because the tools needed to grasp its movements combine social theory, cultural analysis, history, visual culture studies, aesthetics, art history, and political theory.

Williams' colleague Stuart Hall has been the most powerful figure in the institutionalization of cultural studies in Britain through his directorship of the Birmingham Centre for Contemporary Cultural Studies (founded in 1964), and his later tenure at the Open University.[14] Hall and his colleagues were among the first *actually* to study the effects of newspapers, radio, television, film, and other broadcast cultural forms on audiences. They also focused on how differently constituted audiences interpreted and used broadcast culture in varied and often contradictory ways; in so doing they developed methodological models for *doing* cultural studies. Hall's particular influence has been a sustained engagement with writing on culture, race, class, and identity – what we might now refer to as postcolonial studies. It was Hall who began the ongoing dialogue of what multi-ethnic British identity might consist of, questioning what it means to be black and British. British cultural studies, which started by focusing on the potentials for resistance and contestation in working-class cultures, had begun to look for new agents of social change as, in the 1980s, sectors of the working class were being seamlessly integrated into Margaret Thatcher's radical conservative ideology. Cultural studies turned its attention to researching broader-based and yet less homogenous oppositional subcultures.

In the work of Hall and others, British cultural studies went on to appropriate successive waves of race, feminist, film, psychoanalytic, gay, and lesbian theory, and began to cross fertilize with art history and literary studies as well as with the social sciences. Journals such as *Screen* and *Block*, the latter published by the art history department at Middlesex Polytechnic from 1979 to 1989, meshed aspects of cultural studies with art history, helping to inaugurate the cross-disciplinary field that we now recognize as called "Visual Culture."[15] And in works such as *Subculture: The Meaning of Style*, (1980) and *Hiding the Light* (1988), cultural theorist Dick Hebdige, who studied under Hall, began to look at the potential of youth or ethnic subcultures to resist dominant forms of culture and identity.

And yet the deficit of a critique built around resistance and subversion is obvious: its focus on subcultures, on the shared meanings and values of a group within a dominant ideology, tends to ignore the fact that capitalism is replicating itself and expanding into a globally exploitative system. Within this drive toward "globalization" we crudely feel the effect of capital's force as it roams the world looking for advantage, but the mechanisms directing these forces are abstract, complex, and slipping beyond our control, even comprehension. Cultural studies, with its enormous overemphasis on local resistances, fails to acknowledge and come to terms with the actual political economy of capital; something of Adorno and Horkheimer's ambition is missing.

A Shadow Recast

There is a general consensus within theories of contemporary culture, economics, and politics that under our contemporary networked and electronically facilitated forces of globalization, economic relations of exchange have become divorced from previous political controls. Some people celebrate this unleashing of the "market" from political restraint and state interference, while others mourn the demise of systems through which we can contest the remorseless logic of capital – its inexorable tendency to extend its influence and continually maximize profit. If this contestation has any future, we will need to inhabit the same structures and spaces as global capital itself – which is to say everywhere, in everything, and all the time.

In our global economies of trade, the traditional source of wealth – productive factory labor – is certainly being augmented, and perhaps even being superseded, by "creative" economies founded upon communication, aesthetics, and service. And in these communicative and information-based "industries," the production of profit is founded on immaterial labor – labor that produces "commodities" like knowledge, images, cultural experiences, brand loyalty, and informational databases. Within these economies the exchange of capitals – whether economic, ideological, emotional, or symbolic – becomes slippery and complex.

At the moment, perhaps the most accurate portrait of this immaterial realm is drawn by the idea of value as represented by money. Money swirls in markets and flows between them; it gathers in pools and congeals as capital. And yet money in the form of material currency represents only 3 percent of value currently in circulation; the remaining 97 percent of value has little or no material presence – it exists as networks of obligation etched in computer hard drives in financial centers the world over. The fashion of the moment is to keep congealed capital in the smallest amounts possible; value is more productive when in motion, being absorbed and refreshed by exploiting the tiny differences in each and every market. Money is both a force wielding extraordinary power and a communicative medium, and nothing moves outside of its sphere of influence. Everything is permeated by money.

So, the financial expert can no longer ignore the force of what Adorno might call "aesthetic experience" or disregard the effects of culture – its passions, complexities, and negations – as "un-economic" or as merely superstructural to a more primary economic base. And likewise, the artist cannot be ignorant of the forces of capital, as they increasingly merge with, dissolve and influence the very symbolic terrain on which artists are encouraged to work. This is not merely to acknowledge that art is bought and sold, or that artists should be conscious of a market, but to recognize that exchange is a powerful aesthetic object in and of itself.

Clearly capital, as an index of creativity, is peerless. The formal structures that frame different economies, their rules, restrictions, and subsidies, give form to exchange, and by extension to the social and creative relations they facilitate. Exchange, per Marx's model, is first and foremost a social transaction, destined to produce relationships. For contemporary artists such as Deller, Thomas Hirschhorn, and others who engage with the power to define, produce, present, and disseminate the work of the work of art, a move out from the comfort of

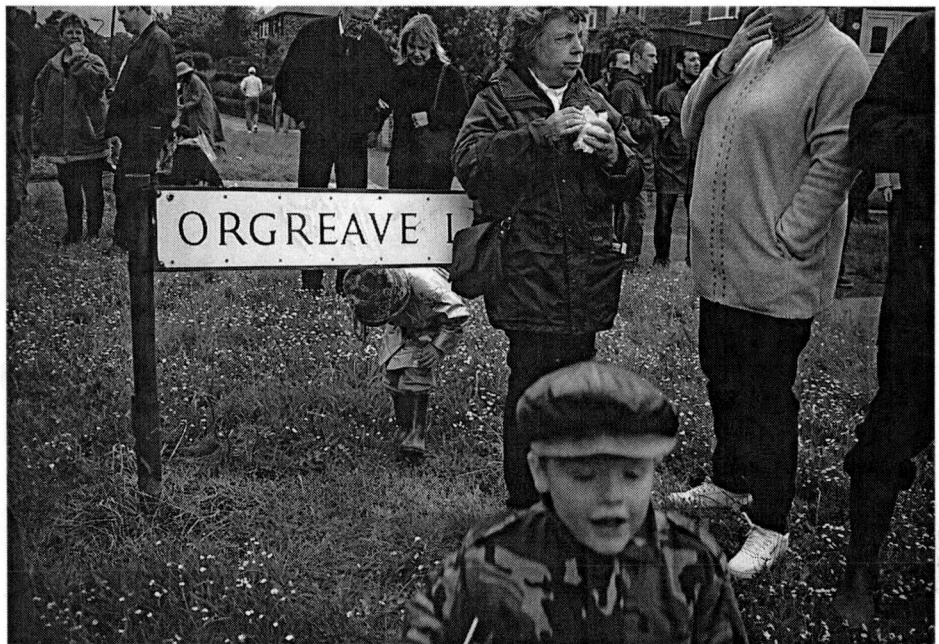

FIGURE 20.4 Jeremy Deller, *English Civil War, Part II* (*The Battle of Orgreave*).
Document of event in Orgreave, South Yorkshire, June 2001. Photograph © Neil
Cummings and Marysia Lewandowska. Courtesy of *chanceprojects.com*

the institutions of art and into interlocking fields of social practice, economy,
and knowledge has become necessary. Art has to stop pretending to sublimate
consumer desire, and, like Jeremy Deller's *English Civil War*, reengage with the
social imagination.

Notes

1 As I'm writing this, Jeremy Deller has been nominated for the 2004 Turner Prize
   [Editor's note: Deller received the prize in December 2004].

2 Marx, Karl, the famous preface from *A Contribution to the Critique of Political
   Economy* (1859), trans. S. W. Ryazanskaya. Progress Publishers: Moscow, 1977.
   Available at http://www.marxists.org/archive/marx/works/1859/critique-pol-
   economy/preface.htm.

3 "Late Capitalism" is a term defined by Frederic Jameson (1991), where it designates a new cultural situation driven by post-industrial financial, entertainment, and
   service-driven economies.

4 See especially Adorno's essay "Culture and Administration" in Adorno and
   Horkheimer (1991), 107.

5 In Marx's political economy *use value* is virtuous and accrues to tools that maximize
   the bounty of nature, producing essential things like food, shelter, and warmth.

Exchange value is bad, adhering to commodity objects made for exchange that leverage labor through profit.

6 Adorno and Horkheimer (1973), 135.

7 Of course later, these activities are recouped by the market through collectors trading in the detritus of "documents," and museums desperately gather relics to authorize events, but in both cases the evidence points to the fact that things happened, but does not deliver the substance and experience of those events.

8 Daniel Cohn-Bendit, who was to become a major figure in the May 1968 uprising, also studied in the sociology department with Lefebvre. And Jean Baudrillard's doctoral thesis, "Le système des objets," was also completed in 1968 under the supervision of Lefebvre and published in English as *The System of Objects*.

9 See "General Introduction," De Certeau (1980/1984), xi–xxiv.

10 Barthes (1977), 148. See Mavor in this volume.

11 David Garcia and Geert Lovink's 1997 online manifesto, "The ABC of Tactical Media," repositions De Certeau at the heart of the struggle over access to digital media. Tactical Media is what happens when the cheap "do it yourself" access, made possible by the revolution in networked desktop computers comes into conflict with established media conglomerates who are trying to maintain control of the mediums of distribution.

12 See Baudrillard (1988).

13 Williams found the term "mass culture" unacceptable because of the implication that its products are somehow produced by the masses – which patently they are not.

14 The Birmingham department was closed in 2002.

15 Page one of the inaugural issue noted that *Block* intended "to stimulate debate around specific issues including Art and Design; Historiography and Education; Visual Propaganda; Women and Art; Film and Television." *Block* published writings by artists, art and design historians, and cultural theorists including Jon Bird, Dick Hebdidge, Lucy Lippard, Griselda Pollock, Lisa Tickner, and Judith Williamson. See also Smith in this volume.

References and further reading

Adorno, Theodor, and Max Horkheimer (1947/1973). *Dialectic of Enlightenment*. London: Allen Lane.

—— (1991). *The Culture Industry*. London: Routledge.

Barthes, Roland (1968/1977). "Death of the Author." In *Image Music Text*, trans. Stephen Heath. London: Fontana.

Baudrillard, Jean (1988). *The Ecstasy of Communication*, trans. Bernard and Caroline Schutz. New York: Semiotext(e).

—— (1968/1996). *The System of Objects*, trans. James Benedict. London: Verso.

Bijl, Guillaume (1998). *Guillaume Bijl*. Antwerp: MUHKA.

Debord, Guy (1977). *Society of the Spectacle* (1967). Detroit: Black and Red.

De Certeau, Michel (1980/1984). *The Practice of Everyday Life*, trans. Steven F. Rendail. Berkeley: University of California Press.

Deller, Jeremy (2001). *English Civil War Part II: Personal Accounts of the 1984–85 Miners' Strike*. London: Artangel.

Garcia, David, and Geert Lovink (1997). *The ABC of Tactical Media.* http://www.waag.org/tmn.

Hall, Stuart (1988). *The Hard Road to Renewal.* London: Verso.

Hebdige, Dick (1980). *Subcultures: The Meaning of Style.* London: Methuen and Co.

—— (1988). *Hiding the Light.* London: Comedia.

Hoggart, Richard (1957). *The Uses of Literacy.* London: Chatto and Windus.

Jameson, Fredric (1991). *Postmodernism, or the Logic of Late Capitalism.* Verso: London.

Lefebvre, Henri (1939/1968). *Dialectical Materialism,* trans. John Sturrock. London: Cape.

—— (1947/1991a). *Critique of Everyday Life,* trans. John Moore. London: Verso.

—— (1974/1991b). *The Production of Space,* trans. Donald Nicholson-Smith. Oxford: Blackwell.

Marx, Karl (1971). *A Contribution to the Critique of Political Economy* (1843–44), trans. S. W. Ryazanskaya. London: Lawrence and Whishart.

—— (1976). *Capital: A Critique of Political Economy,* vol. 1 (1867), trans. Ben Fowkes. London: Penguin.

—— (1977). *A Contribution to the Critique of Political Economy* (1859), trans. S. W. Ryazanskaya. Moscow: Progress Publishers.

Vaneigem, Raoul (1983). *The Revolution of Everyday Life* (1967), trans. D. N. Smith. London: Left Bank Books.

Williams, Raymond (1958). *Culture and Society.* London: Chatto and Windus.

—— (1961). *The Long Revolution.* London: Chatto and Windus.

—— (1962). *Communications.* London: Penguin.

21

Poststructuralism and Contemporary Art, Past, Present, Future . . .

Sarah Wilson

In the celebrated opening chapter to his 1966 book *The Order of Things*, a key text in the development of what is now called poststructuralism, Michel Foucault examines Diego Velasquez's 1656 *Las Meninas*. The painting provokes reflections on knowledge-systems, the writing of history, the author-function, and self-reflexivity, serving to introduce nothing less than "an archeology of the human sciences."[1] In *24 Hour Foucault*, Thomas Hirschhorn's all-night installation at the Palais de Tokyo, Paris, in October 2004, the artist transformed the 1930s museum spaces with his parcel tape and trash aesthetic, honoring Foucault as an object of cult devotion (Figure 21.1). "MF"-emblazoned tee-shirts and ashtrays were part of a "Foucault world" of bad photocopies, where forests of oiled penises from porn magazines obliterated serious critical reviews pasted as "Foucault wallpaper" on the walls, and junk-shop sofas invited conversation in a succession of spaces dominated by images of Foucault in black and white or on color TV. Youthful or middle-aged, his voice was occasionally heard above the background buzz. The aim, 20 years after Foucault's death, was to "derange the codes of official celebration."[2] Hirschhorn declared: "I don't know Foucault's philosophy, but I see his work of art. . . . It permits me an approach, not to understand but to grasp it, to see it, to be active alongside it. . . . There's an affirmation here that the work of art *is* philosophy, that philosophy *is* a work of art!"[3] (See also Figure 21.2.)

Hirschhorn's words mark a crucial confluence in Europe and North America of the visual arts and philosophy, as well as cultural theory – in particular from

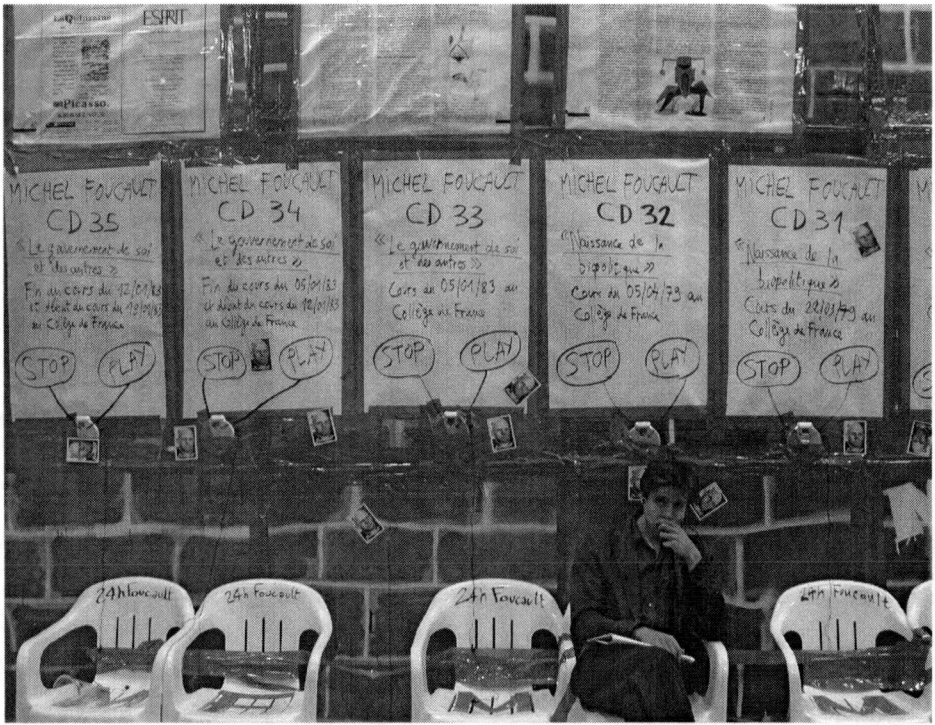

FIGURE 21.1   Thomas Hirschhorn, *24 Hour Foucault*, Paris, 2004. Courtesy of the artist

France. French theory has provided the basis for the loosely defined philosophical movement now called poststructuralism (a term often used interchangeably with "deconstruction"), and François Cusset describes the metamorphoses of postwar French philosophy into poststructuralism on American campuses in his recent *French Theory: Foucault, Derrida, Deleuze et Cie* (2003).

Poststructuralism exists only as an "invention of tradition" that dates to around 1966, when "The Language of Criticism and the Sciences of Man" conference was organized at Johns Hopkins University, Baltimore.[4] Bringing together a number of distinguished French participants freed from their native academic and ideological territories, this event precipitated the first encounters among Jacques Derrida, Jacques Lacan, and Paul de Man. The neutral ground permitted an exchange of ideas constrained in Paris by the very success of structuralism: Hegelians and Marxists became more open to ideas about structure; Barthes and Derrida, associated most closely with structuralism, now for the first time took critical distance from the movement.[5] As a consequence, there followed in Britain and North America the creation of a set of canonical texts that constituted poststructuralism both as a loosely-defined body of potential knowledge linked

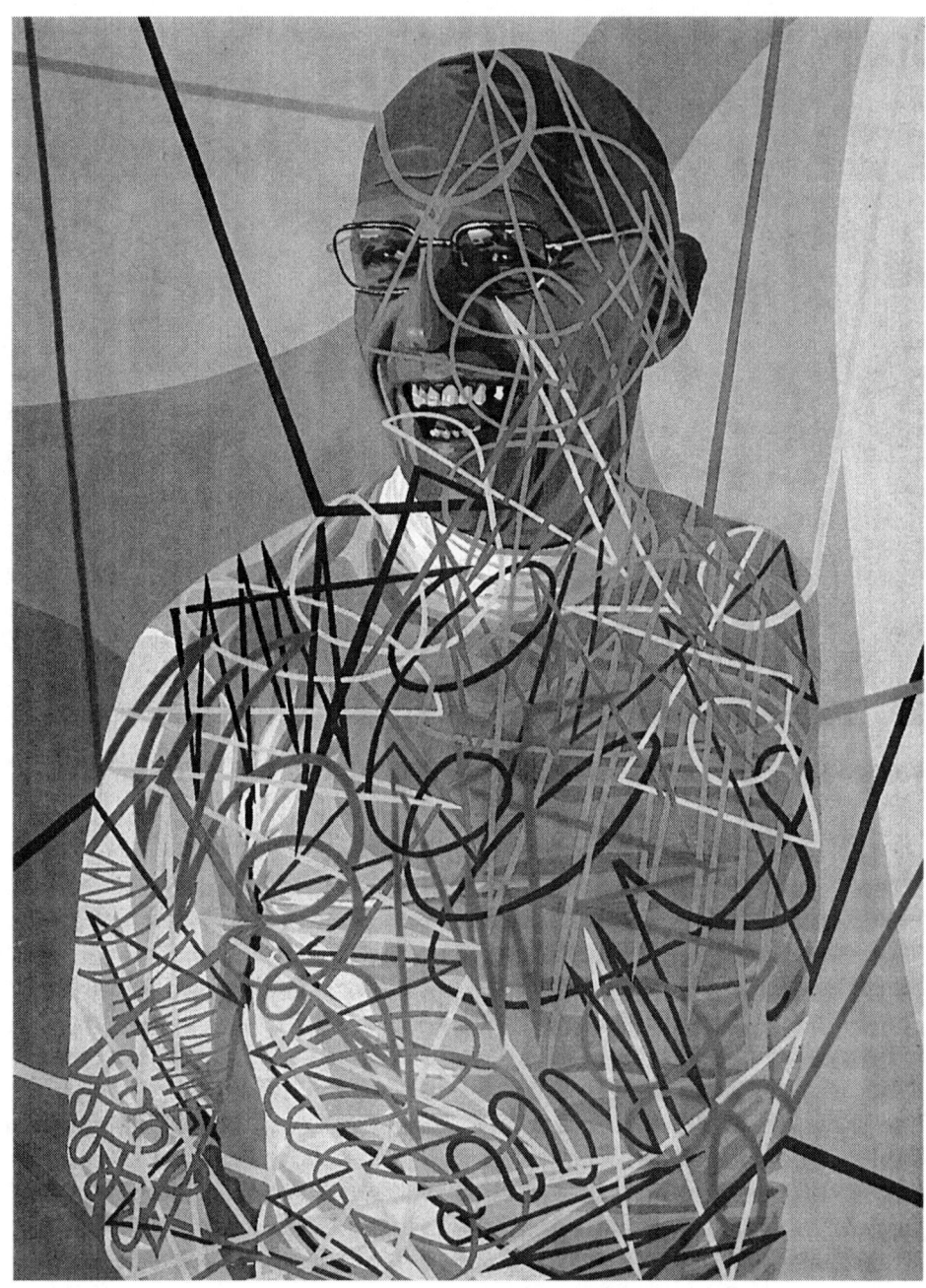

FIGURE 21.2   Gérard Fromanger, *Michel. Portrait de Michel Foucault*, 1976.
130 × 97 cm. Courtesy of the artist

to the broader cultural term postmodernism, and, one could argue today, a term of periodization.

In America today, the great "poststructuralists" such as Foucault, Jacques Lacan, Jacques Derrida, Gilles Deleuze, Jean-François Lyotard, Jean Baudrillard, and Paul Virilio eclipse the French art world in their influence and visibility. The web of influences and interconnecting ideas leading into poststructuralism is complex.[6] Lacan, the psychoanalyst and theorist who began working in the 1930s, reemerged in the 1960s as a new voice of cultural authority, partly thanks to the rise of feminism and other identity movements keen to theorize the psychic construction of sexual and other differences. Jean-Paul Sartre and Maurice Merleau-Ponty, both of whom rose to prominence in the 1950s with their existentialist and phenomenological accounts of self and other, were crucial links in the shift from prewar philosophical models to what would come to be termed poststructuralism, and Frantz Fanon, their contemporary, has come to be seen as a pioneer in postcolonial theory. Emmanuel Levinas and Maurice Blanchot have more recently acquired special status in the expanding field of holocaust studies, while Roland Barthes, whose work has been so important for literary studies, stands out as the "structuralist poststructuralist" (never having fully abandoned semiotic models of meaning formation). Other French theorists – Pierre Bourdieu (on taste), Henri Lefebvre (urban space), and Michel de Certeau (the writing of history) – bring up the rear. Poststructuralism is a man's world: Julia Kristeva, Hélène Cixous, and Luce Irigaray, the "French feminists," offer a feminine "supplement" in the Derridean sense: their contribution is often not viewed as essential, but is missed if absent.

Certainly the story of Parisian intellectual life since the 1970s is too populous, too interdisciplinary, and too political for the French to tell adequately themselves; it is a story complicated by the history and impact of this theoretical work abroad. Of course there is a complex "art story" in France perceived from the inside that is quite distinct from a "poststructuralism story" perceived from the outside.[7] Of the thousands of visual artists and architects based in Paris since the 1960s, only a few – Yves Klein, Christian Boltanski, Annette Messager, Daniel Buren, Orlan, and Sophie Calle – have had an impact in the US, the center of the western art for the second half of the twentieth century. Official French visual arts initiatives abroad have had only moderate effect.[8] The contrast with the international popularity of French postwar literature and film (new wave [nouvelle vague] cinema), which are well catered for by university French departments in English-speaking countries such as the US, is striking.

Moreover, the battles in the Parisian art world, which, for example, pitched the abstract "Supports-Surfaces" group against "Narrative Figuration" artists, each claiming "revolutionary" credentials, do not export well.[9] The complex narratives enlivening the contemporary art scene in France – the impact of Marcel Duchamp; the rediscovery of Kasemir Malevitch; the heritage of situationism; the retreat of artists to the countryside after 1968; the rise of performance;

contemporary art's role in churches; the failure of French feminism to make an impact within the French art world; the failure to provide contemporary art history in the universities; the success story of the Centre Pompidou's historical and contemporary shows; the international career of critic Pierre Restany – these require chronicling outside of France, if we wish to understand the intellectual and historical context of recent art production.

Poststructuralism in the US was always already a hybrid – a *bricolage*, to use a term of French structural anthropologist Claude Lévi-Strauss adopted by contemporary cultural theorists.[10] In the US art world, transformed in the postwar period through the rise of the professionalized art school, with its increased emphasis on reading theory and philosophy, poststructuralism became a guiding force.[11] Theory-driven exhibitions dominated the scene – such as the 1993 Whitney Museum exhibition *Abject Art: Repulsion and Desire in American Art*. Here curators used Julia Kristeva's 1982 *Powers of Horror: An Essay on Abjection* in an oversimplified way as a license to offer an extra aura of "theory" to works as diverse as Eva Hesse's ponderous filigree webs, Kiki Smith's sculptures depicting menstrual fluid, and Mike Kelley's photographs of his body smeared with foodstuffs. All acquired the "abject" label at the expense of Kristeva's complex ideas.[12] As Alison Gingeras has argued, this instrumental use of theory obscures Kristeva's construction of the notion of abjection: "In order to understand the fabrication of her theory the reader must jump to source texts, follow a hyperlink signalled by the proper name, chasing down a bibliographic trail of breadcrumbs. Yet this rarely occurs, because the point of invoking theory is its curatorial application."[13]

As the Whitney show makes clear, the decontextualization may be almost total – poststructuralist "theory" acting as mantra or mood music.[14] Alternatively texts may be explicitly presented as "a 'toolbox' placed before another generation."[15] Either way, the complex intellectual history of debates informing the writing of thinkers such as Kristeva, and the traditions that distinguish "continental philosophy" from pragmatic and positivist Anglo-American tendencies are often lost in translation. Poststructuralist theory "applied" to visual art works may be simplified or misappropriated.

Interdisciplinarity was the hallmark of French thought in the 1970s and was given an institutional face with the Centre Pompidou, inaugurated in 1977; it is in part responsible for the explosion of categories that subsequently created so many new university departments across France. Film was perhaps the first "applied" arena of poststructuralist theory. The pioneering spirit of the *Cahiers du cinéma* of the 1950s and 1960s encouraged the development of film studies departments in France, the US, and Britain as well as the genesis of English-language reviews such as the London-based *Screen*, a crucial site for the exploration of poststructuralist thought in relation to film and the visual arts in the 1970s and beyond. Thus contemporary video- and filmmaker Chantal Ackerman can become the subject in a 2004 issue of *Screen* for an exemplary analysis based on Gilles Deleuze's 1980s theories of time and image.[16] Alternatively, in the recent historical photography show *L'Ombre du Temps (The Shadow of Time)* in Paris, a pioneer experimental film by "Lettrist" poet and theorist Isidore Isou and a recent short by Jean-Luc Godard and Anne-Marie Miéville were featured as plasma-screen exhibits: complex "deconstructions" of the traditional cinematic medium, refigured as art objects.[17]

Architecture and urban theory entered a postmodern phase with the 1966 publication of Robert Venturi's *Complexity and Contradiction in Architecture* and, in 1972, the publication by Venturi, Denise Scott-Brown, and Steven Izenour of the book *Learning from Las Vegas*, and the symbolically resonant dynamiting of the St. Louis, Missouri Pruitt Igoe housing estate (a modernist structure built in 1955). In the 1970s and 1980s architects such as Frank Gehry and others on the west coast of the US began to produce "postmodern" buildings made with inexpensive industrial materials and "deconstructive" – often decorative – quotational forms.[18] The 1988 *Deconstructivist Architecture* show at the Museum of Modern Art, New York, presented a lineage of architectural structures developing from Russian constructivist buildings of the 1920s to the present, showcasing the work of Gehry, Daniel Libeskind, Rem Koolhaas, Peter Eisenman, Zaha Hadid, Coop Himmelbau, and Bernard Tschumi.

The links between postmodern architecture and poststructuralism, wholeheartedly embraced in the English-speaking world by 1990, were sometimes direct. Tschumi's Parc de la Villette project (1982–5) had involved Jacques Derrida's collaboration with Peter Eisenman; Hadid was Tschumi's student in London.[19] Deleuze's 1988 book on the architectural "fold" was published in English in 1993.[20] The performance of Sasha Waltz's 1999 *Dialogue, '99/11* within the unfolding spaces of Libeskind's Jewish Museum, Berlin (architecturally premised upon suprematist diagonals and the void) was surely the ultimate, end-of-century post-Holocaust *Gesamtkunstwerk*.[21]

Political pressures have also had a profound impact on the rise and influence of poststructuralist thought. In Eastern Europe, after the collapse of Soviet-style communism in 1989, scholars and artists are producing new hybrids out of poststructuralist theory: Marta Pszonak's suspended *Paradiso*, 2004, a simu-lacral Madonna – in fact a mirror-studded empty garment, hung like a disco-ball – is produced within the context of a specifically Polish postmodernism[22] (Figure 21.3). France's intellectuals and artists have been intimately involved with communism and with post-communist Marxist or neo-Marxist theory, with the strongest Western European communist party in 1945, the most powerful socialist realist arts movement, and the most explicitly Maoist artistic tendencies in the late 1960s, while political initiatives and cultural diplomacy continue at the state level. After the Year of China in Paris in 2003 came the Year of Paris in China, 2004; a Centre Pompidou branch is planned to open in Hong Kong in 2012.

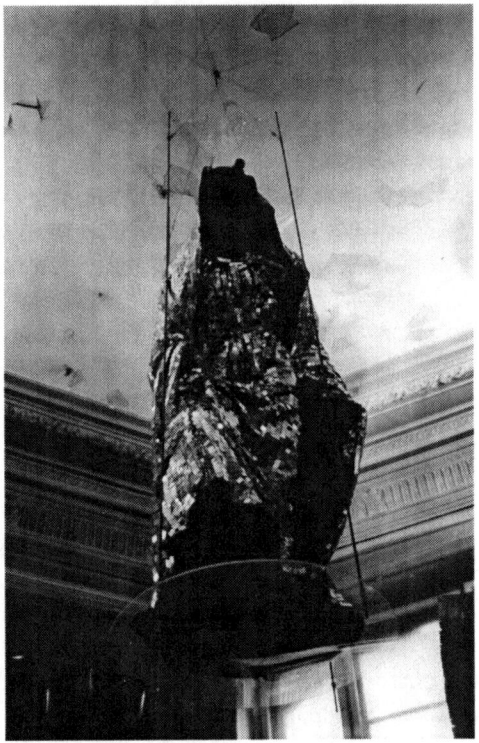

FIGURE 21.3   Maria Pszonak, *Paradiso*, 2004. Courtesy of the artist

Sartre, de Beauvoir, Fanon

"I feel and declare myself to be warmly existentialist."[23] Artist Jean Dubuffet's statement in its relationship to Jean-Paul Sartre's philosophy (dominant on the French scene in the 1950s) parallels Hirschhorn's relation to Foucault; modest as regards intellectual grasp or engaged dialogue, it acknowledges the "spirit of the age." The "spirit of the age," Hegel's *Zeitgeist*, was intimately bound up in his *Aesthetics*, where he theorized art as a progression of styles expressive of respective periods: Egyptian (hieratic), Greek (humanistic), Romantic (revolutionary), etc. Dialectical materialism, inverting Hegel, produced "reflection theory," a matter for endless debate in Sartres' own period. Existential philosophy (which had a profound impact on literature, lifestyle, and fashion in France and beyond) expanded on Marxist ideas to negotiate the dominant French cultural forces of Catholicism and communism.

How might "reflection theory" function, then, trapped between these antagonistic ideological poles? *Terres Cruelles*, the 1950 image of a dead miner by communist party painter André Fougeron, was given Catholic resonances with its Christ-like corpse, but a "nationalist," revolutionary dimension in its quotation of the work of Jacques-Louis David. Its subject, contemporary miners' strikes and police brutality, could be said to "reflect" political realities. A work of socialist realism, it employed the figurative language of "old master" painting to speak to those normally excluded from its circuits.[24] Yet Dubuffet, with his thick impastos, or Wols, the German painter in exile, with his abstract trickles, scratches, bloody colors and evocations of a dissolving Sartrean *nausea*, were equally of their time, while the work of Alberto Giacometti (championed by Sartre) became the sign of an existential humanism rising from the ruins in both Europe and America. Clearly, the "spirit of the age" was polyvocal.

Sartre was a key precursor to poststructuralism both in its philosophical dimensions and as a set of cultural ideas. A major public intellectual detached from the university system, he wrote prolifically, publishing both in his own periodical *Les Temps Modernes* and in newspapers, where he was given front-page space. He participated in political demonstrations internationally, acting as an intellectual ambassador for an economically-shattered but intellectually-prestigious France. Sartre's notorious café lifestyle and open relationship with Simone de Beauvoir exemplified a mode of being that related to his thought; Foucault would follow him in all these areas. Sartre's 1940s had witnessed how the combination of technology with fascist politics had created the Holocaust and destroyed the fabric of European cities. Sartrean existentialism contrasted the problematics of an absurd existence versus "nothingness" with invigorating possibilities of choice and self-invention. The theories of postwar intellectuals in France evolving from existentialism to structuralism, from hard-core communism to neo-Marxisms and to poststructuralism in its different guises, were thus an essential part of the project of European reconstruction and identity formation.

Crucial for contemporary poststructuralist theory – in particular in its postcolonial variants from the work of Homi Bhaba to that of black British artist Yinka Shonibare – is Sartre's concept of the Other, *l'autre*, and its relationship to the "gaze" (*le regard*) of the subject, which first appeared with his reflections on the "Jewish question" in late 1945.[25] The challenge of the Other immediately extended to burning issues of the day. Votes for women were granted to women in France only in 1944–5, and colonial tensions were soon to explode in India, Indochina, Algeria, and Vietnam, contributing to the rise of identity politics and identity-based activist movements (including feminism), with their attention to sexual, gender, ethnic, racial, class, and other differences, in the 1960s and 1970s.

Sartre's formulations provoked instant responses, firstly from de Beauvoir, whose 1949 book *The Second Sex* voiced the obvious: the Other in western society is woman, and day to day cultural formations – such as codes of behavior, clothing, and education – give rise to this construction of woman as Other ("one is not born but one becomes a woman").[26] De Beauvoir became the matriarchal figure for women's writing (*écriture féminine*) in the 1970s: artists such as Gina Pane in France or Cindy Sherman in the US cannot be considered outside the historical trajectory of feminist theories of sexual difference, grounded in de Beauvoir's work.

Secondly, the response to Sartre also came from Frantz Fanon, the Martinique-born psychiatrist and anti-colonialist militant and theorist. Fanon reconfigured the insights of a burgeoning "ethno-psychiatry" by passing its concepts through the discourse of self and other he learned from Sartre, challenging his precursor with the 1952 publication of *Black Skin, White Masks*, which dared to discuss the politics of interracial desire. In the 1990s, when identity politics became increasingly important in the art world, Fanon's *Black Skin, White Masks* inspired many contemporary artists, such as US-based artist Lyle Ashton Harris, who photographs himself in gender and racial masquerade, or British video artist Steve McQueen. The importance of Fanon's work exemplifies the degree to which ethnographic (racial and ethnic) as well as psychoanalytical (primarily gender- and sex-based) concepts of identity became increasingly central to cultural theory and artistic practice, especially from the 1980s onwards, exemplifying third generation permutations of Sartrean theories of self and other. As Fanon becomes the subject for a 1996 conference at London's Institute of Contemporary Art, he becomes "lost in translation," a phantom conditioned by 1990s concepts of sexuality.[27] In Isaac Julien's 1997 biographical film, Fanon the queer poststructuralist icon prevails over the political revolutionary; he becomes an inspiration for the present.

In this way, a crucial transmission of a voice and concepts from the past takes place, at the risk of selectivity and simplification. Of course, as the confluence of concerns dating back to de Beauvoir and Fanon in the postwar period made clear, "masquerade" is not just part of "becoming woman"; it has ritual origins and is a component of African ritual. Anthropologist Jean Rouche's 1954 film *Les Maîtres Fous (The Mad Masters)* shows a frenzied, transsexual parody of colonialist rule in Gold Coast Africa, inspiring Jean Genet to write his 1960s play *Les Nègres (The Blacks)*. The masquerade of the homosexual, parallel to that of woman and to that of the colonized subject, was at the heart of Genet's work, as it is with Isaac Julien's today.

De Beauvoir, Genet, Fanon, Rouch: these sources for a consideration of masquerade, and what is now known as "gender performance," predate the republication in 1966 of Joan Riviere's "Womanliness as a Masquerade" (1929), one of the founding texts for feminist poststructuralism and masquerade theory in Britain and the US. It was in the British periodical *Screen* that writers such as Laura Mulvey and Mary Ann Doane took up aspects of French theory, modifying the Sartrean notion of "the gaze" (previously ascetic and philosophical) via a Lacanian concept of a sexualized – in the first instance masculine and heterosexual – gaze of "visual pleasure."[28] British art historian T. J. Clark's 1980 article in *Screen* on Edouard Manet's 1863 painting, *Olympia*, exemplifies the migration of an empiricist (and/or Marxist) Anglo-American model of art history to this intellectual forum.[29]

As feminism and then queer theory transformed the disciplines associated with film and the visual arts in the 1980s, Lacanian psychoanalysis was mapped explicitly onto masquerade theory in Judith Butler's hugely influential 1990 book *Gender Trouble*.[30] The reception of Butler's *Gender Trouble* exemplifies the tendency to short circuit poststructuralism's intellectual history. The book is often read (in Eastern Europe, for example), as a shortcut, at the expense of the less accessible texts it builds on: ideas pass, already translated, through yet another linguistic and cultural grid before influencing new generations of intellectuals, artists, and critics.

Breton, Bataille, Laure

Other seminal figures for poststructuralism inhabited the postwar universe around surrealism and its dissidents, their ideas serving to challenge the hegemony of dialectical-materialist modes of thought. André Breton, leader of the surrealist movement, has long had an army of exegetes in the worlds of literature and art generating a succession of major exhibitions.[31] Breton's postwar politics were unimpressive, but the surrealist legacy was crucial, informing art practices from those of the Nouveaux Réalistes in the 1960s such as Daniel Spoerri, to that of Jeff Koons in New York in the 1990s. The celebration of the "marvellous" and of the insights sparked by unexpected juxtapositions, the exploration of the city under the aegis of "objective chance" (revised as "psychogeography" by the Situationist International in the 1960s), and above all the principle of rebellion and the belief in the liberating power of the unconscious are still embraced by contemporary artists today. Foucault's posthumous tribute of 1966 readjusts Breton's legacy, posing his work as an antidote to the dominance of Marxist existentialism:

> Breton remoralised writing by demoralising it completely. . . . The deep incompatibility between Marxists and existentialists of the Sartrean type, on the one hand, and Breton on the other, comes no doubt from the fact that for Marx and Sartre writing forms part of the world, whereas for Breton a book, a sentence, a word may by themselves constitute the antimatter of the world and counterbalance the whole universe. . . . What we really owe to him alone is the discovery of a space that is not that of philosophy, nor or literature, nor of art, but that of experience.[32]

Georges Bataille, expelled by Breton from the surrealist group, always had a darker vision, intensified by his experiencing of the occupation of France at first hand (Breton spent the war in the US). Bataille's swerving toward a more tragic analysis of ecstatic limit experiences and his embrace of the relationship between Eros and Thanatos are exemplified in his collaborations with the artist Jean Fautrier: the wound became the sign of the struggles of man in Fautrier's "formless" (*informel*) paintings, which evoke in visual form the darkness of

Bataille's 1943 book *Inner Experience*. Art historians Rosalind Krauss and Yve-Alain Bois, in their 1996 exhibition on the "formless" and accompanying catalogue, *Formless, A User's Guide*, conflate the postwar European *informel* movement with Bataille's 1929 dictionary definition of *informe*. Using Bataille's claim that Manet's *Olympia* has "value as an operation," Bois' essay, "The Use-value of the 'Formless'," is an apotheosis of the "toolbox" approach: he uses Bataille's conceptual terms "base materialism," "horizontality," "pulse," and "entropy" to propose a creative recategorization of a selection of mostly contemporary art works.[33] While reinvigorating the American modernist and postmodernist art history syllabus, this strategy flattens complex and unfixable philosophical arguments circulating in Bataille's work, as well as the historical story of the European *informel* art movement after 1945.

Notably, it was the openness of the American academy to French theory that spurred the immigration to the US of scholars such as Bois, Denis Hollier, the eminent Bataille scholar, and Sylvère Lotringer, who, as editor of *Semiotext(e)* and its "Foreign Agents" series promoted key translations of poststructuralist thought in the US and a way of "doing theory" the way artists "do art."[34] However, many important scholars doing work relating to the visual arts, such as the art historians Hubert Damisch and Georges Didi-Huberman, chose to remain in France. Didi-Huberman's 1995 *La ressemblance informe* offers a close, learned, and never ahistorical reading of Bataille's work: his method provides a powerful contrast to *Formless, A User's Guide*.[35]

Bataille's interaction with Sadean and Nietzschean circles was significant; Sade was important after the war for both surrealists and dissidents such as the performance artist, Jean-Jacques Lebel.[36] The libertine tradition in France, continuing with Gilles Deleuze's 1991 preface to Sacher-Masoch's "Coldness and Cruelty," has been constantly underestimated: in their Anglo-American manifestations, discourses circulating around poststructuralism exhibit a certain puritanism. The libertine Bataille, however, offered an alternative legacy, editing and publishing the posthumous writings of his companion Colette Peignot ("Laure") in 1939. Her writings became crucial for a whole generation of female artists, as well as writers involved with *écriture feminine*. (Hélène Cixous' 1975 essay "Laugh of the Medusa" [*Rire de la Méduse*], with its concept of the power of feminine laughter, is the unofficial manifesto for this movement.[37])

Laure's voice, discovered in conjunction with those of the female mystics, penetrated Bataille's literary space and enabled the development by women writers of a concept of saintly and sexual *jouissance* (previously a Barthesian usage for an essentially masculine textual/fleshly ecstasy). In works such as her 1974 book *Speculum of the Other Woman*, feminist philosopher Luce Irigaray employed the concept of feminine *jouissance* to contest Lacan's definition of woman as a "lack." French-Italian artist Gina Pane performed *Action Laure* at the Galerie Isy Brachot in Brussels in 1977 as an act of commemoration and love; she recommended Laure and Artaud as reading for her students. Yet Pane's work, along with much feminist art in France from the 1970s to the contemporary bodily and facial operations of Orlan, was completely excluded from the large-scale 1995–6 exhibition at the Centre Pompidou, *fémininmasculin, le sexe de l'art* – a tardy attempt to catch up with Anglo-American developments in gender theory and the visual arts. In contrast to Britain and the US, where Lacan has long been mediated by first-generation feminists and where Mary Kelly's explicitly Lacanian *Post-Partum Document* (1973–9) has produced countless poststructuralist exegeses, scholarship on and practices in feminist art in France – the performances of Françoise Jannicot or the work of the collective *Femmes en Lutte*, for example – is just beginning.[38] An "archeological" project to excavate the hidden history of French feminist art, informed by contemporary poststructuralist and feminist theory, is now urgent.

Artaud, Deleuze, Derrida, and Others

Antonin Artaud is arguably one of the most important artistic voices of the later twentieth century, along with Marcel Duchamp, and certainly a most powerful influence on discourses of poststructuralism addressing the visual arts – yet he died in 1948. Artaud's 1947 book *Vincent Van Gogh Suicided by Society* was seminal in its reversal of attention from the notion of the mentally unstable as "victim" to the question of the cultural norms, fears, and practices that traversed Van Gogh the man and his legend. Artaud, released from an insane asylum after receiving painful electroshock treatment, reacted with empathy to Van Gogh's haunting self portraits. Foucault, inspired by Artaud and driven by contemporary debates surrounding what was called *art psychopathologique* (schizophrenic art), worked on *Madness and Civilisation* between 1955 and 1960, offering an analysis of society's institutionalizing of non-conformist individuals.[39] Artist Jean Dubuffet's *art brut* collection, where schizophrenic art rubbed shoulders with naïve art by prisoners and other marginals, displayed moving art works which crossed the boundaries between medical, "criminal" and artistic discourses.[40]

Did Artaud's literary output "reclaim" him from schizophrenia? His work was published in various formats from the 1940s through the 1970s in France; his drawings and film work continue to generate exhibitions today.[41] Foucault notes: "There is no madness except as the final instant of the work of art – the work drives madness to its limits; *where there is a work of art, there is no madness*; and yet madness is contemporary with the work of art, since it inaugurates the time of its truth."[42] Foucault's approach to madness here appears judicious in contrast to that of Gilles Deleuze and Félix Guattari in their 1972 book *Anti-Oedipus, Capitalism and Schizophrenia*, where they develop the notion of "schizoanalysis" and argue that "Artaud is the fulfilment of literature precisely because he is schizophrenic and not because he is not."[43]

In the first pages of the *Anti-Oedipus* we encounter the literary and artistic world of the time: novels by Henry Miller and Samuel Beckett, Dubuffet's journal of schizophrenic art, the *Cahiers de l'art brut*, and Henri Michaux's description of a schizophrenic table (Michaux was a visual artist, writer, filmmaker, and expert on hallucinogenic drugs). A certain delirium in these writings reinforces the authors' aim to abolish the "arborescent" model (the "tree diagrams") of authority, for the "rhizomic" model – an underground, horizontal form of reproduction and proliferation. With such models based on desire and proliferation, Deleuze and Guattari work to counter Freud's Oedipus complex, which is based on the family unit, in turn founded on patriarchal society and thus on a vertical authority structure. Expanding on these ideas, in 1989 Deleuze wrote of the harrowing paintings of Francis Bacon as representing the Artaudian *body without organs*.

The changing art world in the post-1968 context of *Anti-Oedipus*, however, reveals far more exciting developments that were directly contemporary and linked to the rise of an identity politics in France. The Front Homosexuel d'Action Révolutionnaire (FHAR, pronounced *phare* = beacon) was fronted by homosexual activist and gay theorist Guy Hocquenghem, who chose Deleuze to preface his 1974 book *L'Après-mai des faunes*. Here, Deleuze supports "the specificity and irreducibility of homosexual desire, a flux without an aim or origin, an affair of experimentation, not interpretation."[44] The works of the painter, sculptor, performance and video artist, Michel Journiac – such as his 1972 *Homage to Freud: Critical Statement of a Transvestite Mythology* – appear at this moment as an anti-Oedipal apotheosis[45] (Figure 21.4). Travesty, transvestism, and queer masquerade emerge as key artistic strategies in this period – linked to popular cultural figures such as the singer David Bowie.

As opposed to Journiac's "hot" art, the "cold" art of Jean-Pierre Raynaud offered an equally timely response to Foucault and an anticipation of *Anti-Oedipus* and the currents of anti-psychiatry that were shaking both institutional practice and society at large. Traumatized by the Algerian war, Raynaud produced strange "psycho-objects" as early as the mid-1960s. Using white square panels that mimicked the interiors of the hospital, prison, morgue, or museum, he created oppressive environments, often including photographs of asylum inmates to point to the controlling institutions and architectures of society that Foucault had analyzed.

Deleuze and Guattari were not writing in a poststructuralist vacuum: the antipsychiatric publications of R. D. Laing and Donald Cooper in England, rapidly translated into French, and Herbert Marcuse's *Eros and Civilisation* (translated into French in 1968) were also important. Music, fashion, and drug culture moved more rapidly than translations; anti-psychiatric and psychometric experiments appeared in the US long before *Anti-Oedipus* (it appeared in English only in 1983). Moreover Artaud had been absorbed in Paris in the early 1960s by American poets and artists working in the city, such as Nancy Spero and Carolee Schneemann; Schneemann's 1963 performance *Meat Joy* explicitly acknowledges Artaud, while Spero's 1970s *Codex Artaud* uses Artaud as the sign – and voice – of all those "suicided" by contemporary society, particularly women subject to rape and torture. The famous City Lights Artaud anthology, published in 1965,

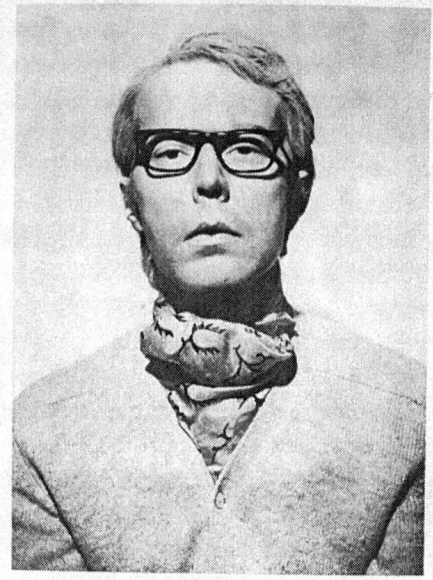

journiac : hommage à freud
constat critique d'une mythologie travestie

PERE : Robert Journiac travesti en Robert Journiac

FILS : Michel Journiac travesti en Robert Journiac

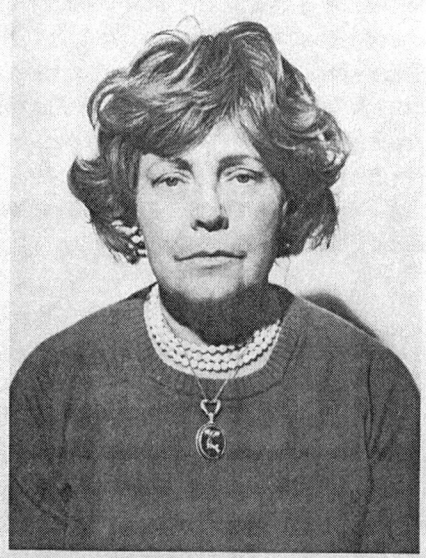

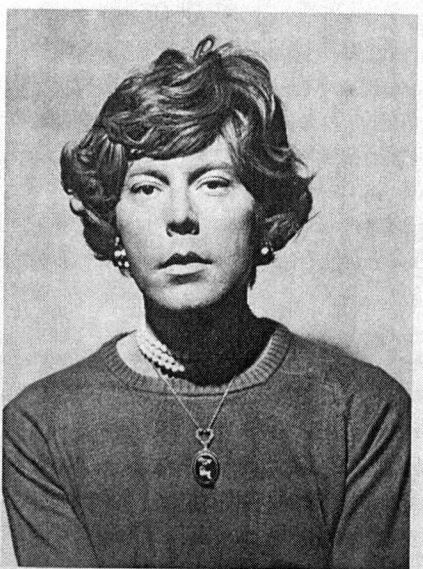

MERE : Renée Journiac travestie en Renée Journiac

FILS : Michel Journiac travesti en Renée Journiac

FIGURE 21.4   Michel Journiac, *Homage to Freud*, 1972–84. Courtesy of Jacques Miège

had an enormous impact on live theater in the US as well as on poets, writers, and artists.

Jacques Derrida's reflections on the work of Artaud extend from 1967 to the year of his death in 2004. His strange text *forcener le subjectile*, ("to unsense the subjectile") literally tries to get "under the skin" of Artaud's powerful and disconcerting drawings. It is also a meditation on the notion of "mother tongue" and translation: it *unsenses* the supports of both paper and text.[46] The collapse of voice, body, writing – of "civilization" itself – with "Artaud" as locus are essential to an understanding of Derrida's project of deconstruction in relation to the visual and literary arts. Artaud transcribed American Indian Tarahumara chants and ecstatic glossolalia; he turned Lewis Carroll's *Jabberwocky* into an insane transliterated screech; he performed in public with screams that refused the possibility of transcription. While Barthes and Foucault, debating the "death of the author," had shifted focus from the "writer" and his authority to the text, Derrida works to bring Artaud's screams back into the body to interrogate the very origins of language, art, and their materializations, arguing elsewhere that "Artaud promises the existence of a speech that is a body, of a body that is a theater, of a theater that is a text because it is no longer enslaved to a writing more ancient than itself, an ur-text or an ur-speech."[47]

Derrida's 1967 *Writing and Difference* has an epigraph from symbolist poet Stéphane Mallarmé's 1897 poem "A Throw of the Dice" (*Un Coup de Dés*), which scatters words on the blank page: "No novelty / but a spacing / of reading." Mallarmé's poetic project in conjunction with Derrida's encounter with Artaud's manuscript fragments and Genet's torn up manuscripts on Rembrandt were all behind Derrida's most impenetrable work, *Glas*, 1974.[48] Two columns of text, on Hegel and Genet, are staged in vibrating juxtaposition, the more historical text deconstructed by the contemporary obscene.[49] As Derrida came to understand the play of textual deconstruction he worked toward the principle of textual "windows" – now so common to us all in the age of the computer – anticipating his pioneering use of a word processor for Jean-François Lyotard's exhibition *Les Immatériaux* at the Centre Pompidou, 1985.

Poststructuralists on Contemporary Art

Culturally, philosophically, and personally Derrida had a deep mistrust of the image. His book *The Truth in Painting*, 1978, is a compilation of essays on visual artists such as Gérard Titus-Carmel and Valerio Adami, "framed" by the title and an introduction entitled "Passe-Partout" (the word for a master key, or for the mount around the work of art – and thus a pun on framing itself). Derrida's essay "Parergon," is a learned, ironically self-reflexive *mise-en-abîme* of Hegelian and Heidegerrian reflections on the aesthetics and the visual arts. With its spatialized "framing" structure and carefully chosen illustrations, the "Parergon" alerts readers to the challenge of framing problems in their own thinking and writing. Departing from the Barthesian emphasis on the death of the author and on the reader as the source of the work's meaning, for Derrida the intersubjectivity of the artist–writer relationship is at stake in any interpretation of the visual arts.

Still, Barthes remains a figure to be reckoned with in understanding the intersection of poststructuralism and the visual arts. Barthes is the structuralist par excellence (he never fully gave up on semiotic models of analysis from structural linguistics even in his more pleasure- and *jouissance*-driven late works) and he remains one of the key mediating figures between Sartre and the poststructuralists. In his 1957 *Mythologies*, a series of essays published originally in *Les Nouvelles Littéraires*, Barthes applies semiotic interpretive strategies to everything from cooking to fashion and electoral posters.

Structuralism had gained momentum in the late 1950s, a period of cultural de-Stalinization. Its synchronic vision of relationships, and therefore formalist emphasis on deciphering signs and codes, was embraced as a welcome alternative to the dialectical materialist world of social realist art which at its most orthodox looked visually back to the past (Fougeron as a new David). Developments in anthropology (Lévi-Strauss's work on binary kinship patterns) and linguistics (drawing on Ferdinand de Saussure's lectures in the early twentieth century) were explored to combat the oppressive weight and cultural grip of Marxist and neo-Marxist thought.

Barthes' attempts to create a structuralist anthropology of everyday life, however, were precisely *not* concerned with the history of French colonialism and the atrocities perpetrated in Algeria, Indochina, Vietnam, or the USSR. Barthes' fascination with the contemporary, whilst maintaining a detachment from politics, involved a certain melancholy, a nausea reflected in his response to Bernard Requichot's sculpture, a homosexual disquiet in his work on Baron van Gloden's photographs of boys in Capri. In his book *Camera Lucida*, memories triggered by his mother's photograph give way to thoughts on photography, death and the past instant of the photographic image: his famous *punctum* – the detail that both reveals and drains away the meaning of the whole – relates to the psychic conjunction which produces a tear and thus to the work of mourning.[50]

While Derrida's importance to the visual arts rests primarily in his philosophical critique of western aesthetics and Barthes' crucial contribution lies in his development of a structuralist model to interpret visual "signs," the question of the role of contemporary art in the broader picture of postmodern culture was opened up by the work of philosopher and cultural theorist Jean-François Lyotard, whose writings on postmodernism became central to debates about postmodern art after 1980. What Lyotard characterized in his important 1979 book *The Postmodern Condition* as incredulity towards "metanarratives" (*grands récits*) applied not only to the "big stories" of Christianity, scientific progress, Marxism, and so on (stories that had structured post-Renaissance Western society), but to the "story" of art itself.[51]

Lyotard frequently wrote about contemporary art. His first text on Daniel Buren, the artist whose uniform stripe paintings were designed to "deconstruct" the premises of their urban or institutional spaces, is nonetheless a structuralist

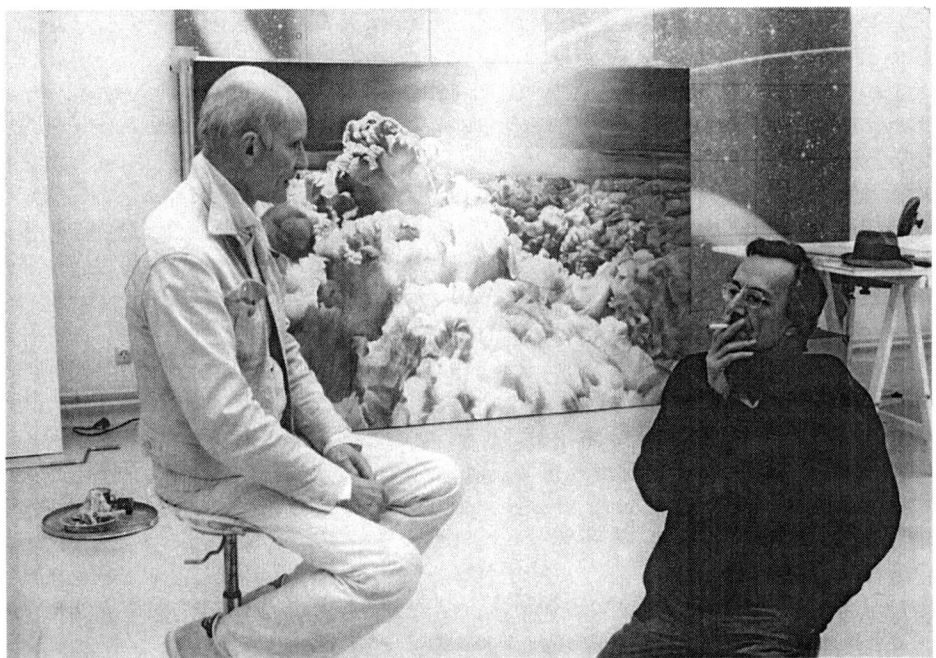

FIGURE 21.5   Jacques Monory and Jean-François Lyotard in Monory's studio, March 1981. Courtesy of the artist

text par excellence, curiously "delayed" to 1981, long after his first texts on art and psychoanalysis, and his engagement with hyperrealism or the "libidinal economy" of Jacques Monory, senior artist of the Narrative Figuration movement[52] (Figure 21.5). His *Story of Ruth*, on the work of Prague-born, Paris-based feminist artist Ruth Francken, broached issues of Jewish wandering and multiple identity long before he addressed these subjects more theoretically in his 1988 treatise *Heidegger and the "Jews."*[53] His 1985 Centre Pompidou exhibition *Les Immatériaux* was a fantastic experimental application of his theses on postmodern, computerized industrial society, in which art, dematerialized, reappears metamorphosed by new technologies.[54] It was the dialectical "Other" of the ambiguous, epoch-making 1989 Centre Pompidou show *Magiciens de la Terre*, which – essentially anti-technological and "earthbound" – was defined by its relativist geographies and uneasy relationship to postcolonial theory.[55]

Baudrillard: Simulacra and Kitsch

Situationist filmmaker and theorist Guy Debord's analyses of the impact of mediatized politics and culture with *The Society of the Spectacle* in 1967, avoided mentioning America: the continent that became the principle ideas- and image-bank for Jean Baudrillard's celebrated theorizations of the "simulacrum" in the 1980s. Baudrillard at first promoted inflatable architecture within the Marxist "Utopie" group (1968–71); he became increasingly pessimistic as the capitalist media explosion, with its mechanism of control and controlled perception, rendered the former theoretical paradigm of the Marxist cultural "superstucture" versus economic "base" increasingly untenable. Baudrillard's move from a relatively Marxist and behaviorist analysis of the "system of objects" in his 1968 book by that title to reflections on art and kitsch in his work of the 1970s and 1980s follows a trajectory mirrored by his Italian counterparts such as Umberto Eco and Gillo Dorfles (who published an influential book on kitsch in 1968); these shifts were taking place in artistic practice, art criticism, and cultural theory. Baudrillard presented American experience as an ahistorical encounter with kitsch in his 1986 book *America* (translated in 1998). The US's quintessential culture of commodification and spectacle related to his buzzword the "simulacrum," a reproduction of something that itself only exists as representation. This has been applied across cultural forms – from the children's TV show *Sesame Street* to academic disciplines. Thus, for art historian Rosalind Krauss, writing in 1986, art history can itself become a simulacrum: "It is only from the vantage of the hyperreal, the simulacrum, that we can really *see* academic practice in the light of its own system."[56]

In a 1990 article with a title deliberately written in German – "Die Mythologie des Kitsches" – Italian artist Enrico Baj writes about the "stylistic emulsion" of a mix of "isms" and styles, and the proliferation of second-rate installation art invading museums. In his discussion of Baj's work, Baudrillard agreed that the great historical and religious allegories of the past had been replaced with an exaltation of everyday banality, represented both by the slickness and lacquered finish of contemporary American art and by "Bad Painting" in an era of art masses, football masses, and mass publicity.[57] However, where Baj saw in the contemporary Andy Warhol retrospective boring and standardized repetition, Baudrillard, drawing on the terms he had established in his influential 1988 book *The Ecstasy of Communication*, saw an ecstatic limit experience.[58] Turning classical Marxist theory on its head, Baudrillard argues that "the mass" is the kitsch product par excellence and yet also a mirror of power – itself so kitsch it can no longer be conceived in terms of political will, but is, rather, "a kind of figuration, a puppet scenario [*fantoche*], precisely because it is reflected by a mass which is itself kitsch."[59] With Warhol at the Pompidou Centre, he proclaimed that kitsch was now "produced by the aesthetic institution itself."[60] In this context of art world "pollution via proliferation" (the Venice Biennale) and "financial kitsch" (Van Goghs sold for millions to the Japanese), Baudrillard used the loaded word "degeneration" (*dégénérescence*).[61] He would be soon be seen to exemplify the right-wing turn in the French art world, as his 1991 book on the first Gulf War, *The Gulf War Did Not Take Place* (translated into English in 1995), claimed that this war "did not take place" precisely because it was experienced on TV sets internationally as "screen warfare": a narrative unfolding of simulacral explosions and destructions mirrored by fake murders on late-night TV.[62]

Poststructuralism Comes Home:
Theory, Archaeology, Memory

In 1994 the American architects artists Elizabeth Diller and Ricardo Scofidio (of Diller + Scofidio) implicitly acknowledged their debt to poststructuralism with respect, specifically, to architect/philosopher Paul Virilio's project of *Bunker Archeology*.[63] Their 1994 book *Back to the Front: Tourisms of War* was initially an investigation in the era of mass tourism of "national narratives," the "aura and authenticity of two kinds of American tourist sites (beds of famous people and battle-fields)."[64] The perfect example of poststructuralism coming home, their project was reinstalled for the Abbaye-aux-Dames, Caen, in 1994, returning – in the fiftieth anniversary year – to the very beaches of the D-Day landings that had inspired Virilio. Virilio's photographic project (1958–65) went beyond the purely morphological, beyond being a "structural" analysis of bunker types: his archae-ological investigations had as their purpose an investigation of the national psyche. He deliberately fixed upon the negative, the unloved, the half-buried bunker – an "anti-object" built with slave-labor as a German defense strategy: "these buildings concentrated the hatred of those who stop and stare as once they concentrated the fear of death for those using them as a protection against the invasion."[65]

In France itself, where Virilio's *Bunker Archeology* project was first exhibited and published in 1975, historian Pierre Nora's influential theorization of sites of memory (*lieux de mémoire*, 1984–93), building on the legacy of a "psychic archeology," has expanded Virilio's discourse. These concepts have influenced, for example, the building of the historical war museum and research center near the WWI battle sites in Northern France. They fed back into Virilio's published response to 9/11 (the destruction of the World Trade Center and part of the Pentagon in the USA on September 11, 2001). This in turn lead to the 2002–3 exhibition project *Unknown Quantity* for the Fondation Cartier in Paris – a post 9/11 spectacle of destruction posited on catastrophe theory.[66] Photography and video revealed the instant memorialization of ruins at the 9/11 site in Manhattan and previous disasters through history.

Evidently poststructuralism "in the world" – rather like the pullulating and promiscuous kitsch of Baj and Baudrillard – now exists in a maelstrom of know-ledge in fragments, often recycled, impure and spectacularized, from which no single strands can be separated out, unless through a genre of commemoration that is kitsch in itself (such as Hirschhorn's *24 Hour Foucault*). A feedback loop exists between televisual technologies, the problem of artistic "authenticity," and a clash of generations and agendas. Each artist, critic, or curator embarking on a scene saturated with images and information must discover or (re)invent

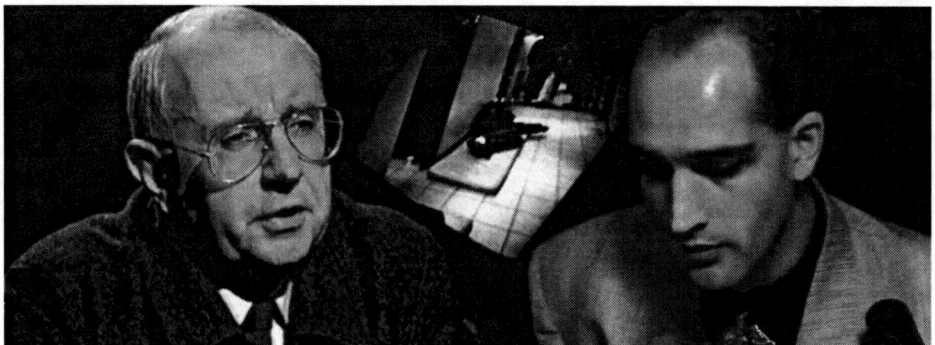

FIGURE 21.6   Paul Virilio with Adrien Sina, *Virtual Urbanity*, 1996. Courtesy of the artist

a position within the current intellectual landscape rather than relating to a consensus-based "heritage."

Virilio's dialogues with younger artists and architects such as Adrien Sina (who theorizes the missing links between cybercities, megacities, and slum cities; Figure 21.6), together with Paris-based German artist Jochen Gerz's involvement of both students and ordinary people in his complex memory-based projects, or Orlan's art-school teaching, all ensure a vital transmission between generations distinct from the discourses of poststructuralism produced in English-speaking art institutions and universities. Yet what Sylvère Lotringer has called "doing theory" is in itself a form of transmission of relatively stable ideas in a world where values continue to destabilize.[67] Similarly, even as the larger world becomes increasingly globalized and decentered, art institutions continue to produce both knowledge and "poststructuralist" spectacle as a way of marketing culture. Compare the simply structured 1986 *Roland Barthes* retrospective at Paris's Pavillon des Arts (a selection of work by the artists he wrote about accompanied by a catalogue reproducing his writings on art), with the 2002–3 Barthes extravaganza at the Centre Pompidou, where labyrinthine installations and easy chairs for listening to tapes and documents on display were juxtaposed with the visual wallpaper of Barthes' personal card index – the latter show curiously suspended between old-style interdisciplinarity and the marketing strategies parodied by Hirschhorn in *24 Hour Foucault*.

American cultural and political dominance over Europe since 1945 has been indisputable, but the body of poststructuralist theory, properly interpreted, sends a powerful message from "old Europe" to the post-WWII superpower. As Derrida asks in *Glas*: "What is left of absolute knowledge? Of history, philosophy, political economy, psychoanalysis, semiotics, sexuality, linguistics, poetics? Of work, of language, of sexuality, of the family, religion, the State . . . ?"[68] In the aftermath of Derrida's death, we hear perhaps the *glas* (a tolling bell) which marks the passing of the heroic era of "French theory" and its American hybrids. But the work must go on. The enterprise was – and remains – no less than to understand the relationships between modernity, philosophy, and contemporary creativity in a time of revolution, a time of kitsch, a time of terror.[69] Derrida's *The Work of Mourning*, 2001, contemplated the deaths of the greatest thinkers of his generation – his friends. *Chaque fois unique la fin du monde* – as its title in French insists: for every individual, the end of the world is unique. . . .

Notes

1　Foucault (1966/1974), introduction, 3–16.
2　Desanges (2004), 5.
3　See Buchloh et al. (2004).
4　Cusset (2003) notes that the "moment of poststructuralism" ironically coincided with the special number of *Yale French Studies* on structuralism and the translation of Lévi-Strauss's *La Pensée Sauvage*; see page 39.
5　Ibid., 38–42.
6　For a discussion of the intellectual trajectory in French theory from the teaching of the Hegelian master/slave dialectic by Alexandre Kojève's seminars in Paris in the early twentieth century through the work of Sartre, de Beauvoir, and Merleau-Ponty, see Jones (1998), 37–46.
7　See Bony (1993) for a brief overview of 1970s French art. Other exhibitions and books have shortcomings: *Les années 70* (2002) lacked women artists and a Paris narrative; *Hors Limites* (1994) foregrounded performance without pioneers Georges Mathieu or Niki de Saint Phalle; *fémininmasculin* (1996) excluded French feminisms.
8　Notably the two official 1998 exhibitions *Rendezvous* and *Premises* in New York involving exchanges between the Solomon R. Guggenheim and Centre Pompidou collections.
9　See Grinfeder (1991) and Chalumeau (2004).
10　See, for example, Sylvère Lotringer's comment: "It was alright that people would tinker with theory – Levi-Strauss's bricolage – and adapt it for various purposes"; Lotringer and Cohen (2001), 127; see www.semiotexte.org.
11　On this shift in art schools see Singerman (1999).
12　See in particular Taylor (1993), 59. And see Ross in this volume.
13　Gingeras (2001), 263.
14　See Todd (1995), n.p.
15　In her introduction to a book by Michel de Certeau (1997), Luce Giard thus notes, "I have tried to assemble this volume of political writings not as a memorial but as a 'toolbox' placed before another generation on whom devolves the responsibility of leading, yes, in its own way, the labor of political clarification," xix.
16　Walsh (2004), 190–205; this essay refers to Kennedy (2000). See also Deleuze's books on cinema (1983/1986 and 1985/1989).
17　See *L'Ombre du Temps* (2004).
18　See Jencks (1996). His architectural genealogy is quite distinct from that of Jean-François Lyotard's in *The Postmodern Condition* (1979/1984).
19　See Derrida on Tschumi (1986); and Kipnis and Leeser (1997).

20 Deleuze (1988/1993). See also Vyzoviti (2003).
21 Dirk Szuszie and Ferdinand Teubner's two-screen installation of *Dialogue 99/11* played at the Barbican Art Gallery, London, as part of the 2004–5 Libeskind retrospective. See *Space of Encounter* (2004).
22 Jaroslaw Lubiak surrounded *Pardiso* with French poststructuralist references in his talk "A Spectrum of Contemporary Polish Art," Paris, Centre Pompidou, November 7, 2004.
23 See "Trente Quatre lettres de Jean Dubuffet à Jean Paulhan," item 114, undated (summer, 1946), in *Jean Paulhan à travers ses peintres* (1974), 98–9.
24 See Stil (n.d.).
25 On Sartre's 1945 essay "Reflections sur la question juive' (*Les Temps Modernes*), see Wilson (1992a), 25–52.
26 See de Beauvoir (2004).
27 See Read (1996). *Lost in Translation* is the title of Sofia Coppola's 2003 film about two Americans who are staying in Tokyo and are unable to connect to Japanese local culture.
28 Riviere's article, first published in *The International Journal of Psychoanalysis* in 1929, was reprinted in Ruitenbeek (1966). See also Mulvey (1975) and Doane (1982).
29 Clark (1980).
30 See in particular in Butler (1990) the chapter "Lacan, Riviere and Strategies of the Masquerade," 43ff, and extended bibliographical note 18, page 159.
31 See *Surrealism, Desire Unbound* (2001); and *La Révolution Surréaliste*. Paris: Centre Pompidou, 2002.
32 Foucault (1966/1998), 172–4.
33 Bois, "The Use-Value of the 'Formless'," in Krauss and Bois (2000).
34 Lotringer, "Doing Theory," in Lotringer and Cohen (2001), 125–62.
35 Didi-Huberman (1995); Didi-Huberman (1982/2003) has also been influential.
36 See Mahon (2005).
37 The writings of Laure are available in Peignot (1971); Cixous (1975).
38 See Quinby (2004); see also Juliet Mitchell and Jacqueline Rose's introduction to Lacan (1982); and Kelly (1999).
39 Foucault (1961/1982), 288–9.
40 See Wilson (1992b), 120–49.
41 Major exhibitions include *Antonin Artaud, Works on Paper*, at the Museum of Modern Art, New York, 1996; *Hommage à Antonin Artaud*, Vienna Museum of Modern Art, 2002, and *Labyrinthe Artaud* at the Kunstpalast in Dusseldorf, 2005.
42 Foucault (1961/1982), 288–9.
43 Deleuze and Guattari (1972/1985), 135.
44 Deleuze (1974), 8–9.
45 See *Michel Journiac* (2003) and www. journiac.com; see also Wilson (2000).
46 See Mary Ann Caws, "Preface: Derrida's Maddening Text: AR-TAU," in Derrida and Thévenin (1998), xii.
47 Derrida (1978), 174–5. On Barthes' text see Mavor in this volume.
48 See Derrida (1974/1986).
49 See Wilson (1997).

50   Barthes (1980/1981).
51   See Lyotard (1979/1984), especially the introduction.
52   On Buren, see Lyotard (1981), 55–64; on Monory, see Lyotard (1998).
53   Lyotard, "The Story of Ruth" (1983) and "Sear of Silence" (1991), in *Ruth Francken, Werke, 1950–1994* (1994); and Wilson (2004).
54   Lyotard and Chaput (1985).
55   Jean-Hubert Martin, curator of *Magiciens de la Terre*, compounded his problematic theoretical stance in the exhibition *Partage d'Exotismes*, Biennale de Lyon, 2000.
56   Krauss (1986), 5.
57   Baudrillard (1990), 9.
58   Ibid., 20.
59   Ibid., 13.
60   Ibid., 11, 17. Baudrillard describes the 300,000 visitors to the Pompidou Warhol retrospective as an "extraordinary cultural cannibalism." Ibid., 21.
61   Ibid. For the right-wing critique that demoralized the French art world, see Michaud (1997).
62   Baudrillard (1995).
63   Virilio built the brutalist "bunker church" of Saint-Bernadette de Banlay, Nevers, 1966, with Claude Parent.
64   See Sylvie Zavatta, "Préface" in *Visite aux armées* (1994); this catalogue was produced for the exhibition *SuitCase Studies: The Production of a National Past/le production d'un passé national*, Diller + Scofidio with Victor Wong, and installed at the Abbaye-aux-Dames in Caen.
65   Virilio (1991), 13. Virilio's photographs from this project were shown in 1975 at the Musée des Arts Décoratifs. Sincere thanks to Adrien Sina for pointing me toward the Caen project.
66   Virilio (2003).
67   Lotringer, "Doing Theory," in Lotringer and Cohen (2001).
68   From the publicity flysheet for the French edition of *Glas* (Jacques Derrida: *Glas*, Paris, Editions Galilée, 1974); my translation.
69   See Borradoni (2003).

References and further reading

Arscott, Caroline, and Katie Scott, eds. (2000). *Manifestations of Venus: Art, Gender, and Sexuality*. Manchester: Manchester University Press.

Barthes, Roland (1957/1993). *Mythologies*. New York: Vintage.

—— (1980/1981). *Camera Lucida*, trans. Richard Howard. New York: Hill and Wang.

Baudrillard, Jean (1990). "Die Mythologie des Kitsches." Baudrillard in conversation with Enrico Baj. *Enrico Baj. Transparence du kitsch*. Paris: Editions de la Différence and Galerie Beaubourg.

—— (1991/1995). *The Gulf War Did Not Take Place*. Bloomington: Indiana University Press.

de Beauvoir, Simone (2004). *The Legacy of Simone de Beauvoir*, ed. Emily R. Grosholz. Oxford: Oxford University Press.

Bony, Anne (1993). *Les Années 70*. Paris: Editions du Regard.

Borradoni, Giovanna (2003). *Philosophy in the Time of Terror. Dialogues with Jürgen Habermas and Jacques Derrida*. Chicago: University of Chicago Press.

Buchloh, Benjamin, Alison Gingeras, and Carlos Basualso (2004). *Thomas Hirschhorn*. London: Phaidon.

Butler, Judith (1990). *Gender Trouble*. New York and London: Routledge.

Chalumeau, Jean-Luc (2004). *La Nouvelle Figurations, une histoire, de 1953 à nos jours*. Paris: Cercle d'Art.

Cixous, Hélène (1975). "Le Rire de la Méduse." *L'Arc*, no. 61:39–54.

Clark, T. J. (1980). "Preliminaries to a Possible Treatment of Olympia in 1865." *Screen*, vol. 21, no. 1 (Spring):18–24.

Cusset, François (2003). *Foucault, Derrida, Deleuze & Cie et les mutations de la vie intellectuelle aux Etats-Unis*. Paris: Editions de la Découverte.

Debord, Guy (1967/1983). *Society of the Spectacle*. Detroit: Black and Red.

Deleuze, Gilles (1974). "Préface." In *L'Après-mai des faunes, Volutions* by Guy Hocquenghem. Paris: Bernard Grasset.

—— (1988/1993). *The Fold. Leibnitz and the Baroque*. London: Athlone Press.

—— (1989/2003). *Francis Bacon, the Logic of Sensation*. Minneapolis: University of Minnesota Press.

—— (1991). "Preface." In *Masochism. Coldness and Cruelty and Venus in Furs*, by Leopold Sacher-Masoch. New York: Zone Books.

Deleuze, Gilles, and Félix Guattari (1972/1983). *Anti-Oedipus, Capitalism and Schizophrenia*. Minneapolis: University of Minnesota Press.

Derrida, Jacques (1974/1986). *Glas*, trans. John Leavey and Richard Rand. Lincoln and London: University of Nebraska Press.

—— (1978). *Writing and Difference*, trans. Alan Bass. Chicago: University of Chicago Press.

—— (1978/1987). *Truth in Painting*, trans. Geoff Bennington. Chicago: University of Chicago Press.

—— (1986). "Point de folie – maintenant l'architecture." *AA Files*, no. 12 (1985):65–75.

—— (2001/2003). *The Work of Mourning*. Chicago: University of Chicago Press; published later in French as *Chaque fois unique la fin du monde*. Paris: Galilee.

Derrida, Jacques, and Paule Thévenin (1998). "Forcerier le subjectile." In *The Secret Art of Antonin Artaud*. Cambridge, MA: MIT Press.

Desanges, Guillaume (2004). "Editorial: Autant qu'une arme, Foucault." In *24H Foucault Journal, 2–3 Octobre 2004*. Paris: Palais de Tokyo. 5.

Didi-Huberman, Georges (1982/2003). *Invention of Hysteria, Charcot and the Photographic Iconographie of the Salpetrière*. Cambridge, MA: MIT Press.

—— (1995). *La resemblance informe, Ou, Le gai savoir visuel selon Georges Bataille*. Paris: Editions Macula.

Doane, Mary Ann (1982). "Film and Masquerade: Theorising the Female Spectator." *Screen*, vol. 23.

fémininmasculin (1996). Paris: Centre Pompidou.

Foucault, Michel (1961/1982). *Madness and Civilisation, A History of Insanity in the Age of Reason*. London: Tavistock Publications.

—— (1966/1974). *The Order of Things: An Archeology of the Human Sciences*. London: Routledge.

—— (1966/1998). "A Swimmer between Two Words." Interview with C. Bonnefoy in *Arts et Loisirs*, 54 (October); reprinted in *Aesthetics, Method, and Epistemology*, ed. James Faubion. London: Penguin Books.

Gingeras, Alison (2001). "Disappearing Acts: the French Theory Effect in the Art World." In Lotringer and Cohen (2001).

Grinfeder, Marie-Hélène (1991). *Les Années Supports-Surfaces*. Paris: Herscher.

Hors Limites (1994). Paris: Centre Pompidou.

Irigaray, Luce (1974/1984). *Speculum of the Other Woman*, trans. Gillian Gill. Ithaca: Cornell University Press.

Jean Paulhan à travers ses peintres (1974). Paris: Grand Palais.

Jencks, Charles (1996). *What is Postmodernism?* London: Academy Editions.

Jones, Amelia (1998). "Subjects in Performance: Postmodernism, Subjectivity, and Body Art." In *Body Art: Performing the Subject*. Minneapolis: University of Minnesota.

Kelly, Mary (1999). *Post-Partum Document*. Berkeley: University of California Press.

Kipnis, Jeffrey, and Thomas Leeser, eds. (1997). *Chora L Works, Jacques Derrida and Peter Eisenman*. New York: Monacelli Press.

Krauss, Rosalind (1986). "The Future of an Illusion." *AA Files*, no. 13 (Autumn): 3–7.

Krauss, Rosalind, and Bois, Yves-Alain (2000). *Formless: A User's Guide*. New York: Zone Books.

Lacan, Jacques (1982). *Jacques Lacan and the Ecole Freudienne: Feminine Sexuality*. London and Basingstoke: Macmillan.

Les années 70 (2002). Bordeaux: CAPC Musée d'Art Contemporaine.

Lotringer, Sylvère, and Sande Cohen, eds. (2001). *French Theory in America*. New York and London: Routledge.

Lyotard, Jean-François (1979/1984). *The Postmodern Condition*. Manchester: Manchester University Press.

—— (1981). "The Work and Writings of Daniel Buren, An Introduction to Philosophy." *Artforum* 19 (February).

—— (1998). *The Assassination of Experience by Painting – Monory*, ed. Sarah Wilson. London: Black Dog Publishing.

Lyotard, Jean-François, and Thierry Chaput, ed. (1985). *Les Immatériaux*. Paris: Centre Georges Pompidou.

Mahon, Alyce (2005). *Surrealism and the Politics of Eros*. London: Thames and Hudson.

Michaud, Yves (1997). *La Crise de l'art contemporain. Utopie, démocratie et comédie*. Paris: Presses Universitaires de France.

Michel Journiac (2003). Strasbourg: Musée des Beaux Arts de Strasbourg.

Mulvey, Laura (1975). "Visual Pleasure and Narrative Cinema." *Screen*, vol. 16, no. 3 (Autumn):6–18.

L'Ombre du Temps (2004). Paris: Galeries Nationales du Jeu de Paume.

Peignot, Jérôme, ed. (1971). *Les Écrits de Laure*. Paris: Jean-Jacques Pauvert.

Quinby, Diana (2004). *La collectif "Femmes-art" à Paris des les années 70*. PhD thesis, Paris-Sorbonne I.

Read, Alan, ed. (1996). *The Fact of Blackness: Frantz Fanon and Visual Representation*. London: Institute of Contemporary Arts.

La Révolution Surréaliste (2002). Paris: Centre Pompidou.

Ruitenbeek, Hendrick, ed. (1966). *Psychoanalysis and Female Sexuality*. New Haven: Yale University Press.

Ruth Francken, Werke, 1950–1994 (1994). Magdeburg: Kloster Unser Lieben Frauen.

Singerman, Howard (1999). *Art Subjects: Making Artists in the American University*. Berkeley: University of California Press.

Space of Encounter: The Architecture of Daniel Libeskind (2004). London: Thames and Hudson.

Stil, André (n.d.). *Les Pays des Mines d'André Fougeron*. Paris: Cercle d'Art.

Surrealism, Desire Unbound (2001). London: Tate Gallery.

Taylor, Simon (1993). "The Phobic Object: Abjection in Contemporary Art." *Abject Art: Repulsion and Desire in American Art*. New York: Whitney Museum of American Art.

Todd, May (1995). *The Moral Theory of Poststructuralism*. College Station, PA: Pennsylvania State University Press.

Virilio, Paul (1991). *Bunker Archéologie*. Paris: Editions du Demi-Cercle.

—— (2003). *Unknown Quantity (Ce qui arrive)*. Paris: Fondation Cartier pour l'art contemporain, and London: Thames and Hudson.

Visite aux armées: Tourismes de guerre/Back to the Front: Tourisms of War (1994; bilingual). Caen: FRAC Basse-Normandie.

Vyzoviti, Sophia (2003). *Folding as a Morphogenetic Process in Architectural Design*. Amsterdam: BIS Publications.

Walsh, Maria (2004). "Intervals of Inner Flight: Chantal Ackerman's *New from Home*." *Screen*, vol. 45, no. 3 (Autumn).

Wilson, Sarah (1992a). "Under the Sign of Sartre." *Paris Post War*. London: Tate Gallery.

—— (1992b). "From the Asylum to the Museum. Marginal Art in Paris and New York, 1938–1968." In *Parallel Visions, Modern Artists and Outsider Art*. Los Angeles: Los Angeles County Museum of Art.

—— (1997). "Genet, Rembrandt, Derrida." In *Portraiture, Facing the Subject*, ed. Joanna Woodall. Manchester: Manchester University Press. 203–16.

—— (2000). "Monsieur Venus. Michel Journiac and Love." In Arscott and Scott (2000). 156–72.

—— (2004). "The Song of Ruth." In *Ruth Francken Michel Butor Dans les Flammes*. Hannover: Sprengel Museum. Unpaginated.

22

"Fragments of Collapsing Space": Postcolonial Theory and Contemporary Art

Mark Crinson

It is widely accepted that postcolonial theory became an important aspect of contemporary art sometime around the mid to late 1980s and, it might be claimed, this relationship reached a certain kind of apotheosis in the exhibition Documenta XI held in Kassel in 2001–2. Associations between postcolonial theory and contemporary art mark out a body of work that is concerned with what has been distorted or excluded by imperialist conceptions of the world – including the representation of cultures or subjects outside the European traditions, forms of Eurocentrism, and the effects of globalizing power on those subordinated to its ends. Because the relationship between the work of leading postcolonial theorists and contemporary art is equivocal, however, a deeper current of engagement between the visual and the history and legacy of colonialism has yet to be fully measured. This chapter explores this shared horizon of understanding through some of the key concepts generated by postcolonial theory and some of the artworks and artistic contexts that have been articulated in relation to these concepts, indeed that have emerged from the same historical nexus.

The complex convergences between postcolonial theory and contemporary art have several temporal markers. The first of these consists of the legacy of colonialism and the post-World War II disintegration of the colonial empires, including especially the breakaway of India from Britain (1947) and of Algeria from France (1962), and the development of a spate of newly independent ex-colonial nations in the 1950s and 1960s. In this context the hopes of truly postcolonial independence, marked often by a sense of renewed interest in pre-colonial cultures as much as a new engagement with modernism, were often cut short or dissipated by a realization that colonial control was often insidiously continued through neo-colonial forms of cultural, economic, and political domination. Related to this was the diaspora of once-colonized peoples to the old colonial powers, particularly Britain and France, where they established a substantial presence in the 1950s and 1960s. (Diaspora in this sense covers not just the relocation of peoples but also the accompanying experiences of immigration and displacement.) It was out of the cultures of resistance to imperialism and then through decolonization and its legacies that the first key thinkers in what we now call postcolonial theory emerged: Amilcar Cabral, Frantz Fanon, C. L. R. James, Kwame Nkrumah, and José Carlos Mariátegui. All of these wrote about how cultural forms could resist the ideologies of colonialism and neo-colonialism, especially the tendency toward essentializing differences between peoples on the grounds of race. Their work also fed into the rise of identity politics, particularly the civil rights movement, in the 1950s onward as well as its accompanying pressure for representation in the artistic fields.

A second, specifically institutional, marker in the convergence of postcolonial theory and contemporary art is that formed by three major exhibitions. The first two of these, *Primitivism in Twentieth-Century Art*, held at the Museum of Modern Art in New York in 1984, and *Magiciens de la Terre*, held at the Georges Pompidou Center in Paris in 1989, both centered on the relation between artists from North America and Europe and those from the less economically privileged southern continents of the world. The Paris exhibition can be seen as expressing a multiculturalist view of art, one in which different cultures represent plural but apparently equally relevant ways of understanding the world. The New York exhibition revisited the older discourse of primitivism, by which certain non-western cultures were deemed to possess qualities of child-like directness or proximity to nature, but added to it the idea of "affinities" between certain modernist artists and this "primitivist" art. Both exhibitions systematically ignored the development of modernism *within* these areas of the world, the New York show in particular generating a storm of critique and much revisionist writing about "primitivism" and its relation to colonialism, while the Paris show staged an imagined relationship between "indigenous art" and Western modernist art across a globalized world. The third important exhibition was the 1989 *The Other Story*, held at the Hayward Gallery in London. This show was crucial in establishing a genealogy for diasporic art in Britain and making the distinctions less rigid between European-style modernist art and this new work informed by postcolonial theory.[1]

A third marker in this convergence is the publication of the first key texts in postcolonial theory by a new generation of theorists associated with postcolonial diaspora. Following on from the crucial 1950s and 1960s work of Franz Fanon, which interrogated the construction of Black identity within French colonialism, Edward Said's paradigm-making book *Orientalism* was published in 1978. The fundamental arguments of Said's model were that the Oriental "other" is a construction on the part of Europeans and that this other is constructed as the negative of the European self. Orientalism, Said argued, was not the objective work of academic scholarship but was intimately connected with the structures of Western economic, political, and military power in the Middle East and beyond. According to Said, Orientalism was thus a way of dominating, restructuring, and having authority over the Orient. It was also a way of representing what was not allowed to speak for itself.

Due to the legacy of identity politics and postcolonial theory as these have pressured art institutions, standard surveys of contemporary art tend, as they address art from the late twentieth and early twenty-first centuries, increasingly often to deploy terms such as "difference" and "identity." The development of this awareness can be seen in the different editions of Charles Harrison and Paul Wood's standard anthology *Art in Theory 1900–1990*. In the first edition (published in 1992), only two texts that dealt with issues of colonialism and postcolonialism were included (Edward Said's essay "Opponents, Audiences, Constituencies, and Community," and Gayatri Chakravorty Spivak's "Who Claims Alterity?"). When the second edition appeared in 2003, texts by Frantz Fanon, Homi Bhabha, Olu Oguibe, and Peter Wollen had been added.

In the most easily available surveys of contemporary art, the rubrics under which the intersecting field of postcolonialism and art is discussed include "Discourses of Race," "Art and Difference," "The Critique of Difference," and "Assimilations."[2] The diverse works of what we might call "postcolonial art" included in such discussions, produced by artists from all over the world, are seen to "renegotiate terms of recognition and legitimation" regarding continuing quasi-colonialist desires, including the consumption of otherness according to those fantasies of racial "authenticity" so common in the colonial imagination.[3] They are seen to be critical of the "suppression of difference" and of "colonialist appropriation,"[4] and to be concerned with the "ambiguities of translation" and with a "more ethically oriented art practice."[5] In a less sympathetic view, it has been argued that, while concerned with moral character, these works may actually act as "unwitting markers of cultural heterodoxy within an overarching status quo."[6] In all these ways postcolonial art is seen to be a subset of postmodernism, which in turn is seen to be a subset of poststructuralist critiques of the universality understood to be at the root of modernism if not of all western philosophy since the Enlightenment. The imaginary causal links in such accounts are a form of shorthand, potentially serving to nullify both more profound differences and more important continuities, such as the contribution of postcolonialism itself to poststructuralist philosophy.[7]

Despite problems with the term, which have been foregrounded by many,[8] "postcolonial" clearly refers to something different from the colonial or even the anti-colonial, although it constantly reconsiders both, attempting to relate their effects to present circumstances. It identifies a culture that is in part a product of a colonialism that is now dead, a culture that is also, importantly, in some ways independent of colonialism. Postcolonialism moves beyond a mid-century cultural movement such as *négritude*, which, in its revaluation and recovering of pre-colonial cultural forms and ideals of Blackness to affect a kind of psychological reconstruction, was not just defensively backward-looking but also bought into the universal subject of humanist essentialism. Postcolonialism's forward-looking aspect can be found in its very name – its "post" is less a description of the present than a kind of promise that, despite the incomplete hopes of de-colonization, a postcolonial future can be imagined beyond the present legacies of colonialism.

This chapter, after an initial discussion of how postcolonial theorists have regarded contemporary art, moves on to examine conceptions of stereotyping, race, and hybridity. From the self and its other the chapter moves to the world, its bounded and contrapuntal dynamics, in order to address the recent claims of a "New Internationalism."

Writing, or not, on Contemporary Art

None of the major postcolonial theorists have addressed visual art, let alone contemporary art, at any length, though the cases where they *have* engaged with it are highly significant. Edward Said, despite the extraordinary cultural reach of his work, has only made the most passing comments on visual art. Ironically, *Orientalism*, which has had a widespread impact on art history, has no references to visual art, whereas his 1994 *Culture and Imperialism*, which has several comments on painters and some extended commentary on architecture, has had only marginal impact on art historical studies. Gayatri Spivak, one of the key theorists of postcolonial culture, has had more extensive but still patchy links with art. Homi Bhabha, another key figure in exploring the uses of postcolonial theory for the study of culture, has written a catalogue essay on Anish Kapoor, and more brief textual mentions on the work of Guillermo Gómez-Peña, Pepon Osorio, and Renée Green.[9] Overall, one has the impression that contemporary art is fairly marginal to these theorists' concerns and that they are more interested in artists' writings than in their art works. When they do engage with contemporary art, they tend to do so in a curiously uncritical fashion that is disturbingly detached from a deeper history of artistic engagement with colonialism.

But although neither Spivak's nor Bhabha's writing about contemporary art is amongst their most influential, there are lessons to be drawn from this aspect of their work. In Bhabha's very beautiful essay on Kapoor, he makes no direct references to the ethics or politics of the postcolonial condition; it is only if we have read Bhabha's other writings that we can we detect that there might be something other than a phenomenological aesthetics behind the tropes he uses to describe Kapoor's work (including interstitial or third space, doubling and displacement, states of transitionality, and disruptive, disjunctive time). The postcolonial might be alluded to in his evocation of Kapoor's prefiguring of a "transitional life, neither secular nor sacred," but that is the limit of Bhabha's historical specificity.[10]

Shorter comments on artists are to be found in the introduction to Bhabha's book *The Location of Culture* (1994). Here he uses Renée Green's writing and art to point to an in-between moment or interstitial space that enables political empowerment beyond fixed notions of community and acts of representation, noting that Green's use of museum spaces exemplifies how an "interstitial passage between fixed identifications" can be imagined (4). Green's work belongs to what Bhabha calls a "'new' internationalism" (I will return to this later), which seeks not to totalize or transcend experience but instead to effect a process of displacement and disjunction, itself evidence of changes in the way international connections and notions of human community can be made in the face of neo-colonialism (5–6). This postcolonial contra-modernity reinscribes or "translates" the way the Western metropolis (as the notional imperial center to which everything else is peripheral) and modernity are imagined. Whether as "baroque allegories of social alienation" or as syncretic and satirical juxtapositions of language, the work of Guillermo Gomez-Peña and Pepon Osorio, in Bhabha's words, "renews the past, refiguring it as a contingent 'in-between' space, that innovates and interrupts the performance of the present" (7). Such comments are brief and certainly Bhabha is not concerned with more in-depth or fine-grained analysis of art works; nevertheless their introductory role in his book is telling. Contemporary art too, it would seem, is a means by which we can come to grips with primary themes that are played out at greater length in the study of history and literature: the concern with cultural displacement as the very condition for a form of empowerment and with cultural interstices as the necessary location for an insurgent, creative invention.

Spivak's most substantial direct engagement with contemporary art came in the form of a collaborative exhibition with the Chilean artist Alfredo Jaar at the Whitechapel Gallery, London, in 1992. The ground floor of the gallery was to be filled with an installation called *Two or Three Things I Imagine About Them*, based on Jaar's color photographs of Asian girls made on visits to local schools and intended to narrate "the social relations of a community – Bangladeshi women living, studying and working in East London."[11] The enlarged photos in light boxes, with superimposed texts derived from a racist statement made by a sweatshop manager, were hung from the ceiling. However, when the girls saw their portraits at the preview they demanded changes to the exhibition and instead the texts were removed and superimposed on Spivak's portrait, which stood by the entrance.[12] Clearly some breach of trust and decorum had been made that might possibly have been bypassed or even become generative of a different approach had the creators engaged more collaboratively with their subjects. The reversal was particularly embarrassing given that one of Spivak's most important theoretical topics is the ability of subaltern subjects to represent themselves.

Clearly, more productive relations between postcolonial theory and art practice must be found elsewhere than the kinds of engagements just described, and the rest of this chapter is devoted to a suggestive adumbration both of where these relations might be found, and also of their conditions and limits.

Looking

The poststructuralist critique of humanism is one of the resources that has distanced postcolonial theory from *négritude* but so too in a related way was the thinking of writers like Fanon who, on the basis of his belief that race was culturally constructed, argued that to emerge from colonialism art needed to aim for a national culture that was engaged with modernity – claiming the latter as something that was not merely Western.[13] Fanon's writings, especially *Black Skins, White Masks* (1952), were taken up by artists in the 1990s because they seemed to offer ways of engaging with the psychological conditions of colonialism and social inequality, the powers involved in everyday exchanges of looks and unconscious mechanisms of encounter, and the cultural and discursive "epidermalization" or "corporal schema" of race and identity.[14]

Amongst the many artists who have explored such formulations of fear and fantasy on the body's surface, including Keith Piper, Lyle Ashton Harris, and Isaac Julien, there are particularly close resonances with the work of Sonia Boyce.[15] Fanon's interest in the relationships between racism and the kind of erotic looking Freud termed scopophilia, between subject-formation and the stereotypes that are both self-alienated and figures of desire, and between that desire and the violence of racism, can be found re-articulated in some of Boyce's work of the mid- to late 1990s. It is particularly interesting here that Boyce moved toward a photographic-based practice at just this time, away from the drawn works that had established her name: it was as if she wanted to move from representation obviously mediated by artistic traditions and into the wider registers of the social body, to effect a "re-epidermalization."[16]

In Boyce's *Head 1* and *Head 2* (1995) (Figure 22.1), the camera takes on the intimacy that a lover, or perhaps a doctor, shows to her/his subjects. The "landscape" of an ear and closely cropped hair and the "portrait" of dreadlocks, reveal almost the same plenitude of visceral details as the body itself, and imply deeper physical processes beyond: tiny fair hairs on the inside lobe of the ear, glistening twists of brown hair that make up the dreadlocks, a spot emerging just beneath the skin. Yet such detail leads to no revelation about the sitters; binary differences of race based on the appearance of skin and hair seem to be established, but they are deliberately cut short of any clear connotative function. As Marcus Verhagen has written, the images point "as clearly as a Benetton advert and in strikingly similar terms, to two urban constituencies. Yet an advert is predicated on the adequacy of stereotypes in a world without history . . . whereas Boyce's paired images are so bluntly reliant on stereotypes that history makes its absence felt."[17] The very glossy sumptuousness of the images, their invitation to an intimacy of touching, and then what we might call a huge gap between this and the simple, phantasmatic icons of the stereotype, all point to the absence of the subject and the scopic thrills of absorption, calling to mind Fanon's description of "an object in the midst of other objects . . . my body suddenly abraded into non-being."[18] In Boyce's work, there is a disturbing fixity on the

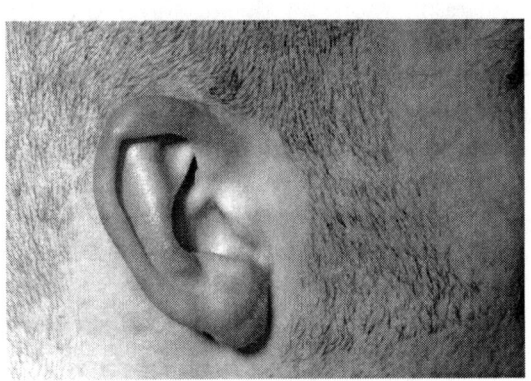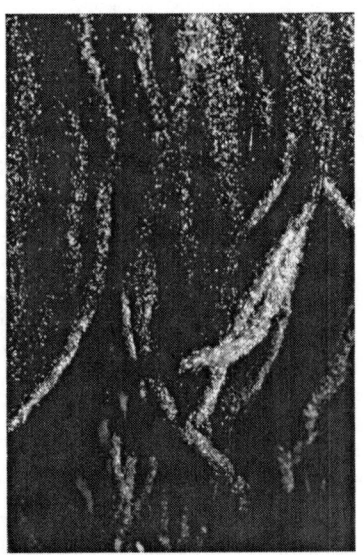

FIGURE 22.1   Sonia Boyce, *Head 1 (Skin)* and *Head 2 (Dread)*, 1995. Photo silk-screen street posters. Courtesy of the artist

fragmented body part and the surface: all is identity, subjectivity is nowhere, yet at the same time the icon becomes mere appearance.

The Hybrid

The stereotype is the antithesis of the concept that has become the master trope of postcolonial theory – hybridity. Although, of course, this term does not originate in postcolonial theory, much of the productive energy that has been generated around hybridity as a conceptual tool derives from the manner in which the understanding of the concept has been reinvigorated within postcolonial debates. Hybridity provided a way of offering a critique of notions of the fixity and purity of subjecthood and identity; having had a history of negative use signifying racial or cultural miscegenation, hybridity could now be used for the positive breaking down of monolithic thinking, of recourses to origins, and of essentialist and utopian notions of identity. Due to the ambivalences of the term itself, the ambivalent position of many of the colonized, caught between the attractions of assimilation and the derogation of pre-colonial cultures that the embrace of the dominant culture through assimilation implied, might itself be taken as having positive political potential.

Hybridity was also a useful term because it was the hybrid – the mimic man, the sly civility of the native, the cross-breed – who evoked the most guilt, anxiety, and revulsion in colonial regimes for the very reason that the existence of these types upset the balance of oppositions on which colonial power was based.[19] But one of the problems with hybridity is the very fact that it bears the unavoidable impress of racial theory. Indeed, in seeking to reverse the terms of approbation, it could be said to remain dependent on them and to reiterate the binary logic of the colonialist mentality: pure is now bad because it betokens racist thinking, the narrowness of an (impossible) insular and isolated racial identity; hybrid is now good both because it stands for intermingling as inherent to cultural identity and because it projects admixtures of disparate elements as essential to creativity.

The most influential writer on hybridity within postcolonial theory is Homi Bhabha, and it is his work that presents hybridity as key to understanding and valuing the giddy prospects of contemporary transnational cultures. As outlined in the essays collected in his book *The Location of Culture*, Bhabha's understanding of it is based on a dual strategy of locating it within the very citadel of its exclusion – colonial discourse itself – and in "strategies of subversion that turn the gaze of the discriminated back upon the eye of power" (112). In the first type of hybridity Bhabha identifies an ambivalence within mimicry which is triggered by what never quite fits and must always therefore have the menacing uncertainty of partial presences (86). His examples of the second type of hybridity are extremely various: they include rap music, Chicano aesthetics, the meaning of *chapatis* in the Indian Mutiny, and, most memorably, an Indianized Bible demanded by Indian catechists outside early nineteenth-century Delhi. All these examples involve "a subversive strategy of subaltern agency that negotiates its own authority through a process of iterative 'unpicking' and incommensurable, insurgent relinking," in Bhabha's words (185).

Hybridity, for Bhabha, is not a neutral third term, merely the product of two dissimilar parents, but a form of heresy that questions authority by failing to observe its rules of recognition. It thereby stirs up deep anxieties of anti-colonial insurrection or psychic breakdown. It also demands the active presence of the colonized or formerly colonized. Bhabha goes on to locate hybridity as an alternative to multiculturalism's view of a world of plural but equal distinctions, the Benetton effect wherein cultural differences are fantasized as being happily integrated like facets of the same prism. Instead hybridity is anti-essentialist, a condition of the contemporary shifting, blending and re-forming of identities, particularly in those migrant minority cultures that he deems interstitial or "third spaces" – neither of the new host culture nor of the homeland.

Hybridity in Bhabha's articulation of it seems to indicate an interactive and bricolage effect where doubled-voiced diasporic discourses are unearthed and revalued as fundamental to cultural innovation. The term has perhaps sometimes been too easily rolled out by some writers as a concept for understanding any kind of mixing of modes, encompassing the work of artists as various as Gordon Bennett, Doris Salcedo, and Rasheed Araeen. In spite of first appearances, then, hybridity might not be a useful term to apply, for example, to the work of Yinka Shonibare, a British Nigerian artist whose work deploys African-patterned fabrics, usually made in England or Holland but based on Indonesian batik, to drape mannequins in eighteenth-century dress. The fabrics clearly have a hybrid genealogy, but Shonibare's work arguably does little more than create a parallel scenography to the repeated revelation of colonial interdependencies. In a sense Shonibare's transitions are too smooth, too comprehensible. At its most useful, Bhabha's hybridity is more intractable, relating to qualities he links to Walter Benjamin's understanding of the impossibility of translation between cultures.[20]

What might this unresolved hybridity born out of translation's failure mean for an artist such as Chris Ofili, also English-born of Nigerian parents, whose work tends to be seen as standing for the metropolitan knowingness associated with "young British art" (yBa)? In Ofili's paintings one form of reference is layered palimpsestically onto another, often using sources that are equally as complex in their cultural make-up as Shonibare's but without simplifying their translational possibilities.[21] Kinky porn-retro, biblical figures, blaxploitation stars – a carnival of stereotypes passes across canvasses which are also layered with richly contrasting skeins of decorative and collaged materials. And it is because of this ironic use of stereotypes, "a joyride in an Afrocentric wonderland,"[22] seemingly borne out of a sense of generational alienation from the debates about multiculturalism and representation in the 1980s, that postcolonial theorists have been skeptical about Ofili's work. For Kobena Mercer, for example, it is as if Ofili's institutional success bears out a suspicion about the depoliticizing effects of his work, its relation to "hyperblackness" in the media and the "global market of multicultural commodity fetishism," and what Mercer calls the "unspoken policy of integrated casting" of the yBa phenomenon.[23]

Yet, I would argue that it is only by ignoring the complexity of Ofili's works that they can be rendered in these terms. Elephant dung might be exemplary here. In Ofili's own account of its presence, it might evoke a consciousness of his roots awakened on a trip to Africa.[24] Dung is never simply abject or ignoble in Ofili's work – it is never smeared and never smelly – though it can, especially in his early sculptures, act as a hyperbolic and ludicrous indicator of racist fantasy, or, in the form of the words "Elephant Shit," as a stand-in for the artist's name.[25] It is a supplement to the work: often decorated with sequins or covered with resin, it is always kept as a separate element, used to prop the works up or manifestly projecting from its surfaces. The shit is not abstractable and it is not assimilable, even if it occasionally has a representational function.

Ofili's work thus renews a playfully disturbing poetics of race in the face of both the history of racism and bureaucratic multiculturalism, re-injecting full intercultural possibilities into hybridity. It bears out an almost Bakhtinian sense of constructing an "intentional semantic hybrid . . . [that is] internally dialogic,"[26] and this, transferred into contexts of racial or colonial authority, is also how Bhabha understands hybridity. The discourses of race and primitivism become precisely the "grounds of intervention" on which an artist like Ofili works,[27] but now they are constituted improvisationally with an ironic recursiveness, indulging the possibilities of a visual heteroglossia.

Worlding

Fanon's and Bhabha's work demonstrates that one of the central elements of postcolonial theory is the critique of colonial and neocolonial forms of essentialism and bipolar modalities of difference. This critique, as has been mentioned, found its most influential statement in Said's *Orientalism* (1978). One of the effects of Said's work was to instigate extraordinarily productive work on the role of the arts within intercultural relations of power and on Western traditions of representing the "other." A vast range of contemporary artists such as Sunil Gupta, Chila Kumari Burman, Mona Hatoum, and Mitra Tabrizian engaged very directly with Said's work on representation, whilst others, like Coco Fusco and Fred Wilson, have provided a parallel critique of the construction of race within the museum and tourism industries. Other offshoots of Said's project are the art theories and practices that construct Europe as itself "other," effectively to create a subversive genealogy by dislodging European thought and art from any notion of inherent centrality and from any exclusive claim upon the category of the modern.[28]

For Orientalism we could also read primitivism, Africanity or aboriginalism, or indeed any of the discursive forms of colonialist knowledge. The elaboration of these terms of recognition and their distortions and ambivalences has been the creative drive behind much of the contemporary postcolonial art that attempts to give voice to subjects previously silenced by the institutions of colonialism itself. This art also seeks to make contradictory and multivalent the cultural identities that Orientalism and other discourses sought to define as culturally uniform. Such work refuses to sit within anthropological or modernist notions defining non-European cultures as residing within a fundamentally different (less advanced) cultural and temporal framework. Instead it cites the constructed forms of essentialism, but within multiple and mutating collage strategies that address the very forms of colonial representation as their mode of political allegory. The work often presents a form of what Said called a "voyage in," a form of hybrid cultural work that sees the metropolitan forms of representation from the margins, playing with and ultimately transforming them.[29]

These strategies are exemplified in the work of Gordon Bennett, an Australian artist whose parents were Aboriginal and English. Rather than embody the notions of place, tradition, and continuity that have mutually constituted "aboriginalism" (and that have given Aboriginal art a certain aura for recent collectors), Bennett's work instead sets up, in Nicholas Thomas's words, "powerful oppositions [between] . . . the universal or pan-human aesthetic statement, and the inescapably local character of history and experience."[30] It thus moves from the personal experience of being formed under racialized regimes of difference,

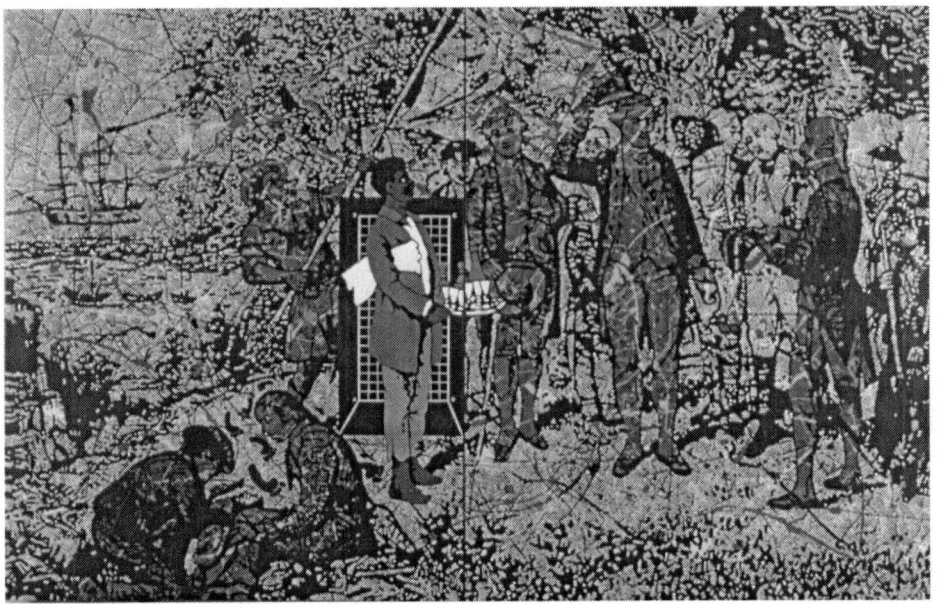

FIGURE 22.2   Gordon Bennett, *Possession Island*, 1991. Oil and acrylic on canvas.
Courtesy of the artist and Sherman Galleries, Sydney

to an interrogation of how one's place in the world and the properties of that
world itself are formed.

Bennett's approach to his subject matter reflects upon similar forces to what
Spivak in other contexts has called the "worlding of a world": "The imperialist
project ... had to assume that the earth that it territorialized was in fact previously uninscribed ... this worlding is actually also a texting, textualising, a
making into art, a making into an object to be understood."[31] In Australia, the
effects of colonial "worlding" continue in the contemporary disputes about the
legitimate ownership of land. Bennett's work might be understood as a matter
of holding this worlding up as the artificial and violently enforced event that it
was, marking intervention and disturbance in the lineaments of the work. *Possession Island* (1991) (Figure 22.2) approaches the scale of a history painting and
is based on an eighteenth-century print of a declaration of ownership crucial in
Australia's history. "Captain Cook Taking Possession of the Australian Continent on Behalf of the British Crown AD 1770," to give the printed source its full
title, commemorates the moment of taking possession of a *terra nullius*: the
Union Jack is flying, a band plays, soldiers mark the moment with a volley,
agriculture begins, and Aborigines either cower in fear or dutifully attend Cook
and his officers who are the embodiment of refined authority.

Bennett's *Possession Island* presents a "reconstitution of national narrative,"[32]
by seeming to overlay the print with marks that "distress" its surface references.
The Aboriginal servant is now picked out in bright red, his figure is backed by a

device which resembles an anthropometrical grid, and he provides the only area of the painting unaffected by a swirl of dots and whip-like drips. The dots make reference to Aboriginal Western Desert painting, while the drips echo Jackson Pollock's famous drip painting technique with its connotations of a reaching beyond psychic frontiers. Each method takes its reference into a new register as a "vehicle for expressing the repressed in the Australian national psyche."[33] These elements form a hybrid approach to painting in that they are not stylistically subsumed or synthesized.

The World, Contrapuntally

There is a fascinating metaphor in Said's *Culture and Imperialism* through which he tries to encapsulate the relays of cause and effect within imperialism. This is the idea of "contrapuntal reading," in which colonial and metropolitan themes play off each other, are mutually constitutive, and create greater meaning through their interplay. As Said puts it, "as we look back at the cultural archive, we begin to reread it not univocally but *contrapuntally*, with a simultaneous awareness both of the metropolitan history that is narrated and of those other histories against which (and together with which) the dominating discourse acts" (59). The suggestiveness of Said's metaphor might be used to unpick Lubaina Himid's *Cotton.Com* (2002) (Figure 22.3). Himid's work was commissioned for the converted nineteenth-century warehouse spaces of Manchester's CUBE gallery.[34] It consists of 100 canvases arranged grid-like in a rectangular formation and faced across the gallery space by a long brass plate with the words "He said I looked like a painting by Murillo as I carried water for the hoe gang, just because I balanced the bucket on my head."

Following Claire Pajaczkowska's argument, the work can be understood as a way of re-situating black female labor within the context of the western industrial city.[35] The paintings effectively excavate this original function of the building as a place to display fabrics, both for the qualities of their material and for their patterns – an intermediary space between the place of labor and the domestic space. In their grid-like formation, Himid's canvases seem to present both a kind of taxonomy of patterns and a modernist grid. With clear borders of unprimed canvas they reveal their own condition as textile. They also evoke Islamic tiles in their squareness and monochrome coloring, but, at the same time, on closer inspection, they are clearly individually painted (or sometimes scratched) objects. The canvases therefore stand for various "feminized" forms of decoration and "Oriental" cultures, which they return to this Victorian commodity display space. But what faces them across the gallery are the words on the brass plate, and it is this confrontation that brings a contrapuntal reading and a mnemonic function to the fore. As Pajaczkowska suggests, the political economy of slave labor is made visible in a place devoted to its invisibility in the form of exchange value.[36]

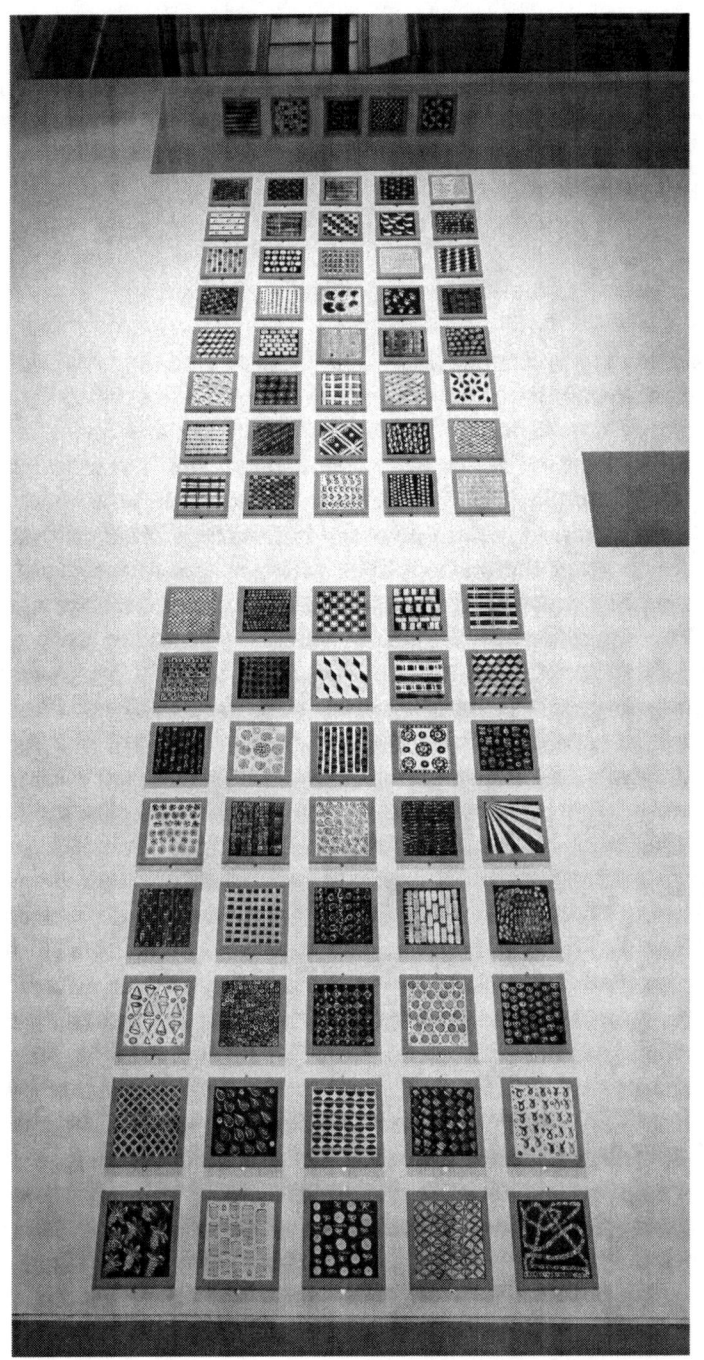

FIGURE 22.3 Lubaina Himid, *Cotton.Com*, 2002 (detail). Acrylic on canvas with brass text panel. Courtesy of the artist

Though imaginary, the inscribed statement identifies a female slave subject whose labor in the cotton plantations of the American South supplied the raw materials for Manchester's wealth. It is this repressed labor that is commemorated in the plaque but, at the same time, it is rescued from oblivion only in the form of the speech of an already objectified other whose (absent) working body has become aestheticized by words given to a male spectator. The dialogue is complex and troubling, partly because Himid avoids the expected relations of the male gaze. It is contrapuntal both in Said's sense of working across space (Manchester and the plantation) and history (from the nineteenth-century dynamics of production and consumption to the practices of the contemporary gallery), and also in that it folds within itself an unequal dynamics of looking and being looked at.

New Internationalism

Earlier I noted Bhabha's comments regarding a "New Internationalism"; an analysis of this term might begin to explain something of the imagined geographies of postcolonial art. The new internationalism has been invoked periodically, particularly in literary studies in preference to the older term "commonwealth literature,"[37] to denote the broadened horizons of art making after modernism. New internationalism attained more-or-less official sanction in visual arts discourse in the early 1990s when it became associated with a number of events and institutions sponsored by the British government-funded Arts Council, such as the Institute of New International Visual Arts (inIVA) in 1993 and the conference on "A New Internationalism" at the Tate Gallery in 1994. New internationalism was thereby ushered in as part of a government-sponsored cultural policy of supporting art outside the white Western mainstream, and its ongoing impact can be seen in the continuing series of exhibitions that seek multicultural inclusion.[38]

New internationalism helps to indicate a certain kind of confidence and potential that is associated with postcolonial independence more generally and with the international or at least border-breaking aspects of postcolonialism. If the old internationalism has associations with, say, the International Style, modernist art, and perhaps even a league of European diasporic nations (that is, those settled generations ago by white British colonizers, such as the US and Australia), then the new internationalism promises a deterritorialized space where the flow of peoples after the dismantling of empires is to be paralleled by an opening up of the border controls of art and its terms and protocols of validation, such that an equality of access to the sites where art is validated will be ensured. Thus the unavoidable internationalism of migration – with its political and social responses in the policing of borders, the burgeoning of xenophobia, and the exploitation of illegal labor – can be seen to have its parallels in contemporary postcolonial art: both result from a situation that is "fluid, constructed and dynamic."[39] New internationalism needs to reflect constantly upon rhetorics of internationalism and globalization: internationalism as competitive and fearful, as forced and bounded community; globalization as free trade for some, as a veil for new imperialisms for others. Translation remains a central concept for new internationalism: the international as a "difference producing space" as much about the untranslatable as about the transparent.[40]

At the same time, as *Documenta XI*, held in Kassel in 2001–2 showed, the tenets of postcolonial theory have perhaps become so widespread that they now pervade most international cultural events. The previous *Documenta* had claimed, amongst other things, to focus its critical attention on decolonization and the "de-Europeanization of the world," although it actually displayed mostly Western-based art works and artists.[41] In *Documenta XI*, the aim was to take this much further: hence, for instance, the organizational structure involved curatorial meetings across four different continents and the selection of a multinational group of curators. *Documenta XI* focused especially on the interface between art and socio-political forces, but to such an extent that the theoretical problematics of this relation were practically overtaken by an apparent collapsing of art into a social documentary mode. Works of art were described in the catalogue by chief curator Okwui Enwezor as bound up in "circuits of knowledge" overriding and beyond both artistic canons and "Westernism" (54).

The exhibition was thoroughly imbued with the tenets of postcolonial theory; Enwezor, for instance, aligned the exhibition with "the site where experimental cultures emerge to articulate modalities that define new meaning and memory-making systems of late modernity," and privileged the idea of "extraterritoriality" and "transculturality" within a context of globalization in justifying its widespread remits (44). Specifically, Enwezor invoked the new subjectivities of decolonization, as identified by Fanon, and the desire to make the "other" visible in the metropolis, an important double move within postcolonial theory (44–5). For Enwezor, postcoloniality offers "counter models through which the displaced . . . fashion new worlds by producing experimental cultures . . . [composing] a collage of reality from the fragments of collapsing space" (45). In spite of these thoughtful theoretical underpinnings, the exhibition has been criticized for setting the seal on already established debates, for institutionalizing them rather than establishing a new paradigm.[42]

If one work from *Documenta XI* can be said to be symptomatic of the difficulties of producing a postcolonial visual practice then it is Steve McQueen's film installation *Western Deep* (2002) (Figure 22.4). The film's subject is the Tautona mine near Johannesburg, the world's deepest gold mine and a place where the wealth, assurance, and glamour normally associated with gold could hardly be further away. Here black South African miners work in the most appallingly claustrophobic, dusty, and noisy of conditions and are treated as chattel by the mine company, brusquely checked for their physical condition and rendered virtually mute, treatment that implies that in South Africa the end of colonialism has not been acknowledged.

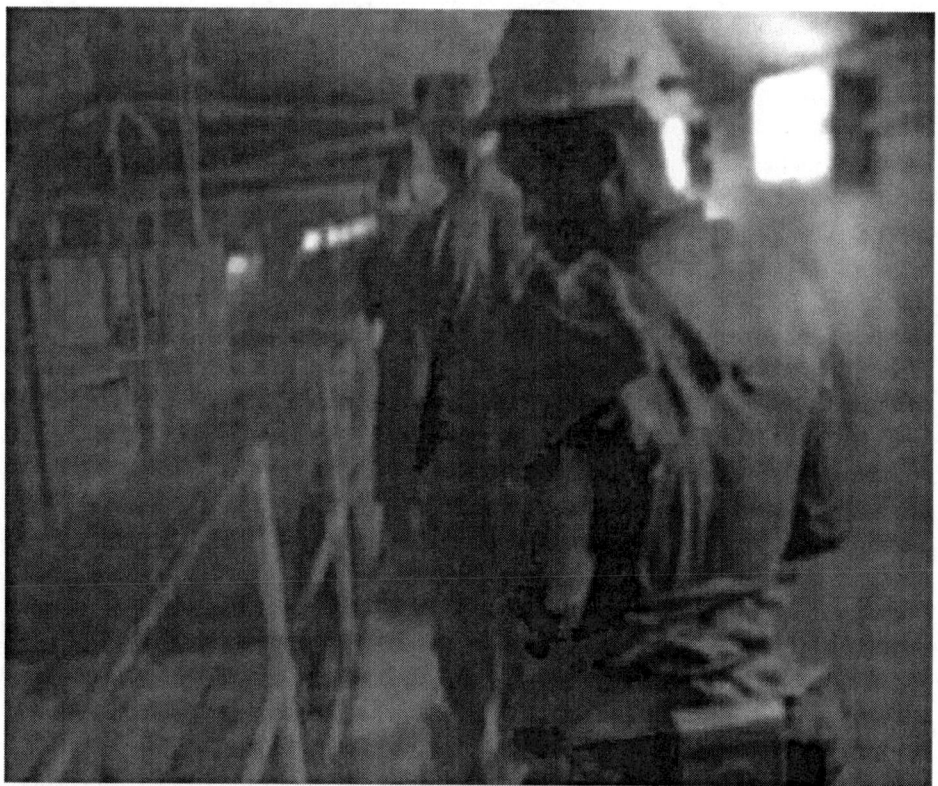

FIGURE 22.4 Steve McQueen, *Western Deep*, 2002. Film installation. Courtesy of Artangel

McQueen represents this firstly through a long, clamorous, and almost totally dark descent two and a half miles down into the bowels of the mine, and then through repetitive images of the men as they wait in changing rooms and as they descend further in cages to the working mineshafts. The depth of darkness in the physical space of the auditorium is used as a kind of echo chamber by McQueen for the claustrophobic obscurity broken by flashing glimpses of rock and bodies in the lifts and shafts. The place is a trap where drills breaking into rock merely seem to scrape at the confines of an unyielding fate. In this "heart of darkness," as its title indicates, the world shown is one that is both figuratively and physically in the deep, below the West's wealth and power – one wants to say it undermines them, but it functions, rather, as an underpinning. McQueen shows all this in a manner that seems to recall some of the great documentary photography of the mid-twentieth century – say, W. Eugene Smith's representations of the Pittsburgh steelyards. The work, like many other examples of work at Documenta XI, aspires to a position in which the testamentary power of representation is allied to an ethical reflexiveness about the transaction of looking.

Conclusion

The continuation of what I have called a shared horizon of understanding between postcolonial theory and contemporary art is bound still to be the subject of debate. It has to remain an open question just how much postcolonial theory played a part in the moves that were made in the 1980s to decentralize curatorial activity, and to open up Western galleries and museums to art practices beyond the West as well as to art produced by minorities in the West itself. Inevitably, because of the frames mentioned earlier, postcolonial art can be identified with artists who were starting their careers in the 1980s, most of whom are now in their late thirties and forties. But the art world, prone to commercially-driven, ever-changing styles and movements, might appear to have left postcolonial art behind. Ultimately the various if not yet concerted efforts to correct the historical record, particularly in terms of the contribution of diasporic artists to art since the war, will provide a more lasting effect. Through this work of recuperation there is the possibility of alternative and multiple histories of modernism and postmodernism. Moving beyond earlier attempts to retrieve and represent "otherness" through positive and perhaps essentializing imagery, the impact of postcolonial theory can also be found in the shift to different ways of art-thinking. It has encouraged what Said called a form of "interference, a crossing of borders and obstacles" and what Spivak described as the modes of "citation, reinscription, recounting the historical," such that diasporic art practices are no longer fixed on an imaginative elsewhere but continue to offer one of the most dynamic and creative areas of contemporary cultural production.[43]

Rather than being played out, postcolonial art might be seen as undergoing transformation as indeed the nature of globalization changes and new imperialisms emerge. There is the kind of demand made by Documenta XI that art deal directly with and somehow be transparent to information flows across the world. On the other end of the scale there is the problem of the subjective voice, however distanced or ironized, and the question of how it might contribute to an atomization that is complementary to globalization. Thus the most important criticism that might be made of some postcolonial theory – important because it starts from a shared political position – concerns its terms of relativism and universalism and the kinds of new subjectivities that it claims to be describing and proposing. As applied to art, this emphasis on subjectivity can lead to the assumption that postcolonial modes of art have a different, even alternative, status because they are wrought in the heat of personal history and cooled in the privileged perspective of memory. Yet the best postcolonial artists, as has been seen here, take these matters as the subject of their work rather than its precondition.

Notes

1 Rasheed Araeen's position, as curator of *The Other Story*, as an artist, and as a founding editor of *Third Text*, is particularly interesting here: see, for instance, Araeen (2000).

2 These section titles are from Taylor (1995), Hopkins (2000), Wood et al. (1993), and Archer (1997).

3 Taylor (1995), 162.

4 Archer (1997), 200, 202.

5 Hopkins (2000), 219, 221.

6 Wood et al. (1993), 240.

7 Particularly noteworthy here, as demonstrated by Robert Young, was the vital contribution that the events in colonial Algeria made to the development of poststructuralist theory; Young (2001), 411–26.

8 See Young (2001), 57–61; and Parry (1994), 7.

9 See Bhabha (1998) and Bhabha (1994). See also Bhabha (1993).

10 Bhabha (1998), 35.

11 See Bird (1994), 37.

12 Araeen (2000), 14.

13 See, for instance, Fanon "On National Culture" (1959), repr. in Harrison and Wood (2000), 711–15.

14 See Hall (1996) and Bailey et al. (1995), which accompanied the *Mirage* exhibition at the ICA, London.

15 Boyce, who had established her name in the 1980s, exhibited several commissioned works in *Mirage*.

16 See Hall (1996), 20.

17 Verhagen (1998), 11–12.

18 Fanon (1952/1968), 109.

19 See Nandy (1983).

20 Bhabha (1994), 224

21 See Corrin et al. (1998), 15.

22 Fusco (2001), 38.

23 Mercer (1999–2000), 56–7.

24 See Ofili's statements in Corrin et al. (1998), 1.

25 See Fusco (2001), 42.

26 Bakhtin as quoted in Young (1995), 21.

27 Bhabha (1994), 112.

28 The most influential text here is Chakrabarty (2000); for related approaches in contemporary art see Hassan and Dadi (2001).

29 One of Said's examples of a "voyage in" is C. L. R. James's *The Black Jacobins* (1938), in which James described how the Haitian insurrectionist, Toussaint L'Ouverture, re-used the very language and values of the French Encyclopaedists: Said (1994), 297ff.

30 Thomas (1999), 199–200. Bennett has himself referred to his work as a "voyage in"; see Bennett (1994), 123, an essay that exhibits Bennett's wide reading in postcolonial theory.

31 Spivak (1990), 1.
32 Thomas (1999), 200.
33 Ibid., 205.
34 See Crinson et al. (2002).
35 See Pajaczkowska (2005).
36 Ibid.
37 That term referred to a particularly British and British imperial situation wherein
    literatures in English within the old empire could be seen to share some common
    ground. The trouble with the use of the word "commonwealth" was that it
    assumed that Britain was still at the center and yet, somehow, the older imperial
    dynamics of power had been shed in favor of a new voluntary combination of ex-
    colonial peoples. The term was particularly unfortunate given the kind of anti-
    colonial literature that was sometimes housed within it, even if it did serve to open
    doors for publication: see King (2004).
38 See Papastergiadis (1993–4) and Mercer (1999–2000), 54.
39 Hassan and Dadi (2001), 15.
40 Maharaj (1994), 28.
41 David (1997), 9.
42 See McEvilley (2002), 81, and Downey (2003), 89.
43 Said (1982/2003), 1058, and Spivak (1993), 217.

References

Araeen, Rasheed (2000). "A New Beginning: Beyond Postcolonial Cultural Theory and
    Identity Politics." *Third Text*, no. 50:3–20.
Archer, Michael (1997). *Art Since 1960*. London: Thames and Hudson.
Bailey, David, Kobena Mercer, and Catherine Ugwu (1995). *Mirage: Enigmas of Race,
    Difference and Desire*. London: Institute of Contemporary Arts.
Bennett, Gordon (1994). "The Non-Sovereign Self (Diaspora Identities)." In Fisher
    (1994).
Bhabha, Homi (1993). "Beyond the Pale: Art in the Age of Multicultural Translation."
    In *1993 Biennial Exhibition*, ed. Elizabeth Sussman. New York: Whitney Museum of
    American Art/Abrams.
—— (1994). *The Location of Culture*. London: Routledge.
—— (1998). "Anish Kapoor: Making Emptiness." In *Anish Kapoor*. London and Los
    Angeles: University of California Press and Hayward Gallery.
Bird, Jon (1994). "Making Visible: Difference and Representation in the Work of Alfredo
    Jaar." *Art & Design*, no. 9:34–9.
Chakrabarty, Dipesh (2000). *Provincializing Europe: Postcolonial Thought and Historical
    Difference*. Princeton: Princeton University Press.
Corrin, Lisa, Stephen Snoddy, and Geoffrey Worsdale, eds. (1998). *Chris Ofili*. London
    and Southampton: Southampton City Art Gallery.
Crinson, Mark, ed. (2005). *Urban Memory: History and Amnesia in the Modern City*.
    London: Routledge.
Crinson, Mark, Helen Hills, and Natalie Rudd, eds. (2002). *Fabrications*. Manchester:
    UMiM.

David, Catherine (1997). *Documenta X: A Short Guide*. Kassel: Cantz Verlag.

Downey, Anthony (2003). "The Spectacular Difference of Documenta XI." *Third Text*, no. 62:89.

Enwezor, Okwui (2002). *Documenta XI, Platform 5: Exhibition*. Kassel: Cantz Verlag.

Fanon, Frantz (1952/1968). *Black Skin, White Masks*. London: MacGibbon and Kee.

Fisher, Jean, ed. (1994). *Global Visions: Towards A New Internationalism*. London: Kala.

Fusco, Coco (2001). "Captain Shit and Other Allegories of Black Stardom: The Work of Chris Ofili." In *The Bodies That Were Not Ours and Other Writings*. London: Routledge.

Hall, Stuart (1996). "The After-life of Frantz Fanon: Why Fanon? Why Now? Why *Black Skin, White Masks?*" In *The Fact of Blackness: Frantz Fanon and Visual Representation*, ed. Alan Read. London and Seattle: ICA, inIVA, and Bay Press.

Harrison, Charles, and Paul Wood, eds. (2000/2003 editions). *Art in Theory 1900–2000*. Oxford: Blackwell.

Hassan, Salah, and Itikhar Dadi, eds. (2001). *Unpacking Europe: Towards a Critical Reading*. Rotterdam: Nai Publishers.

Hopkins, David (2000). *After Modern Art*. Oxford: Oxford University Press.

King, Bruce (2004). *The Oxford English Literary History: Vol. 13 1948–2000. The Internationalization of English Literature*. Oxford: Oxford University Press.

McEvilley, Thomas (2002). "Documenta XI." *Frieze*, no. 69:81.

Maharaj, Sarat (1994). "'Perfidious Fidelity': The Untranslatability of the Other." In Fisher (1994).

Mercer, Kobena (1999–2000). "Ethnicity and Internationality: New British Art and Diaspora-Based Blackness." *Third Text*, no. 49:51–62.

Nandy, Ashis (1983). *The Intimate Enemy*. New Delhi: Oxford University Press.

Pajaczkowska, Claire (2005). "Urban Memory/Suburban Oblivion." In Crinson (2005).

Papastergiadis, Nikos (1993–4). "Disputes at the Boundaries of 'New Internationalism'" *Third Text*, no. 25:95–101.

Parry, Benita (1994). "Signs of Our Times: Discussion of Homi Bhabha's *The Location of Culture*." *Third Text*, nos. 28/29:5–18.

Said, Edward (1979). *Orientalism*. New York: Vintage.

—— (1994). *Culture and Imperialism*. New York: Vintage.

—— (1982/2003). "Opponents, Audiences, Constituencies and Community," in Harrison and Wood (2003).

Spivak, Gayatri C. (1990). *The Postcolonial Critic: Interviews, Strategies, Dialogues*, New York: Routledge.

—— (1993). *Outside in the Teaching Machine*. London: Routledge.

Taylor, Brandon (1995). *The Art of Today*. London: Everyman.

Thomas, Nicholas (1999). *Possessions: Indigenous Art/Colonial Culture*. London: Thames and Hudson.

Verhagen, Marcus (1998). "An Art of the Commonplace." In *Annotations 2 – Sonia Boyce: Performance*, ed. Mark Crinson. London: inIVA.

Wood, Paul, Francis Frascina, Jonathan Harris, and Charles Harrison (1993). *Modernism in Dispute: Art Since the Forties*. London and New Haven: Yale University Press.

Young, Robert J. C. (1995). *Colonial Desire: Hybridity in Theory, Culture and Race*. London: Routledge.

—— (2001). *Postcolonialism: An Introduction*. Oxford: Blackwell.

23

Visual Culture Studies: Questions of History, Theory, and Practice

Marquard Smith

What is visual culture or visual studies? Is it an emergent discipline, a pass-ing moment of interdisciplinary turbulence, a research topic, a field or subfield of cultural studies, media studies, rhetoric and communication, art history, or aesthetics? Does it have a specific object of research, or is it a grab-bag of problems left over from respectable, well-established disciplines? If it is a field, what are its boundaries and limiting definitions? Should it be institutional-ized as an academic structure, made into a department or given program-matic status, with all the appurtenances of syllabi, textbooks, prerequisites, requirements, and degrees? How should it be taught? What would it mean to profess visual culture in a way that is more than improvisatory?

W. J. T. Mitchell[1]

By asking this series of questions at the onset of his article, "Showing Seeing: A Critique of Visual Culture," W. J. T. Mitchell, one of the scholars responsible for the emergence of sustained and critically engaging discussions of visual culture studies in recent years, goes on to encourage his readers to confront some of the field's limitations, pointing to the pervasive myths and fallacies upon which the study of visual culture at present is based.[2] While here is not the place to rehearse his argument, what is of note is that his considerations begin with a series of questions that provoke an engagement, and as such these key questions also need to be foregrounded by us for they are central in any deliberation on the thorny subject of "visual culture studies." This is because his questions are questions of definition, of disciplinarity, and of the "object" of visual culture, as well as questions for the institution and for pedagogy. Mitchell's questions lead us to ask: what do we call this discipline? Is it in fact a discipline, or, perhaps, a sub-discipline, an inter-discipline even, or something else? What objects or artifacts or media or environments are "appropriate" for or particular to this field of inquiry? What does it mean for visual culture or visual studies or visual culture studies to be taught, and how should this teaching take place?

There are many more questions here than there are answers. This is one of the troubles, also one of the pleasures, of visual culture studies – as we shall go on to discover. With this in mind, this chapter will propose complex ways of engaging with these deeply complex questions which have enormous implications for those of us concerned with the study of the past, present, and future of our visual cultures. To this end, the chapter will seek to ask further questions that at first sight appear deceptively straightforward: what is visual culture studies? Why are the bonds between visual culture studies and its intersecting fields of inquiry, the very fields that inform it, so tense? And finally, what is the purview or object domain of visual culture studies, or, rather, what is the "object" of study of visual culture studies? Each of these questions will have one section in this chapter devoted to it. In addition, the final section on the "object" of visual culture studies will conclude by offering a case study, a visual culture study, on the awkward historical, conceptual, and aesthetic question of "place."

The case study is presented as an example of how we might go about "doing" visual culture studies, and the topic of "place" has been chosen for three reasons. Firstly, because it is impossible to consider "place" without being cross- and interdisciplinary from the beginning: in this case study, for instance, we need to take account of debates within and between the disciplines of art, architecture, and urban studies, cultural geography, anthropology, philosophy, and postcolonial studies. Secondly, because the intricate and multifaceted nature of "place" foregrounds our need for lateral thinking, we must explore issues of location, migration, exile, belonging, home, cultural memory, nation, and landscapes, geographies, cartographies, and visual iconographies of travel. Thirdly, because "place" needs to be considered in these ways it comprises an instance of how a visual culture study that begins from the question of "place" itself makes it possible to imagine and engender new subjects and objects of research, of writing, and of practice. The question of "place," then, offers itself up as a perfect instance of all the problems, challenges, and possibilities embodied in the fraught emergence and future development of the field of visual culture studies.

What is Visual Culture Studies?

If we go to our university or college library, to a local bookshop or to any online bookshop, we will encounter numerous books with "visual culture" in the title. When they are not in a section of their own – which rarely happens – visual culture books are shelved throughout the library or bookshop in sections that are in keeping with the categorizing systems of libraries and bookshops and the programmed drifting of the potential purchaser. These books appear in sections as diverse as art history or art theory or aesthetics or critical theory or philosophy or film and media studies or women's studies or black studies or theater and drama or architecture or queer theory or anthropology or sociology. No one quite knows where to put "visual culture" books and no one quite knows where to look for them. Neither authors, publishers, retailers, nor customers are entirely clear as to what a visual culture book should do or where it should be placed.[3]

Why is this? Because books with "visual culture" in the title come in all shapes and sizes, they provide an almost infinite diversity of texts that seem to want to address all historical periods, explore any and every geographical location, conceive of all manner of thematic – and recommend an encyclopaedia of accompanying methodological – tools and practices. So, for example, some books are gathered together diachronically, marking a broad historical timeframe from the Middle Ages to the present, while others amass synchronically across diverse territories from Wales to Latin America. Books that set themselves apart by identifying their frames of reference in these two ways include *Defaced: The Visual Culture of Violence in the Late Middle Ages*; *Reframing the Renaissance: Visual Culture in Europe and Latin America: 1450–1650*; *The Visual Culture of Wales*; and *The Visual Culture of American Religions*. Others cut across a variety of themes or subject matter such as race, class, gender, and sexuality that have been at the heart of debates in the humanities for three decades, and thus are central to the emergence of visual culture studies as a political and ethical field of study. These include *Diaspora and Visual Culture*; *Displacement and Difference: Contemporary Arab Visual Culture in the Diaspora*; *The Feminism and Visual Culture Reader*; and *Outlooks: Lesbian and Gay Sexualities and Visual Culture*.

Ultimately, we find that the majority of books with "visual culture" in their titles are introductions or readers or textbooks, often edited collections, frequently written for pedagogical purposes – for students – and sometimes concerned with pedagogical matters themselves. In the main these books are what we might call methodological inquiries, cabinets of curiosity, since they offer a variety of interpretive ways of engaging with our past and present visual cultures – including semiotics, Marxism, Feminism, historiography, social history, psychoanalysis, queer theory, deconstruction, postcolonial theory, ethnography, and museology. In addition to being concerned with the production, circulation, and consumption of images and the changing nature of subjectivity, they are also preoccupied with what Irit Rogoff has called "viewing apparatuses," which include our ways of seeing and practices of looking, and knowing, and doing, and even sometimes with our misunderstandings and unsettling curiosity in imagining the as-yet un-thought.[4] Examples here include *The Visual Culture Reader*; *The Block Reader in Visual Culture: An Introduction*; and *Practices of Looking: An Introduction to Visual Culture*.

The diversity of books addressing visual culture is certainly testament to the potential historical range and geographical diversity of the study of visual culture, the array of themes visual culture studies is willing to address, that comprise it even, and the multiple methodological practices it is able to put forward in order to engage with the objects and subjects and media and environments included in and thus composing its purview. It is also worth pointing out that these books consider all manner of visual culture – from high culture to popular, mass, and sub culture; from the elite to the everyday; from the marginal to the mainstream; from the ordinary to the extraordinary – and that the objects and subjects and media and environments embraced by visual culture studies can include anything from painting, sculpture, installation, and video art, to photography, film, (terrestrial, cable, satellite) television, the Internet, and mobile screenic devices; fashion; to medical and scientific imaging; to the graphic and print culture of newspapers, magazines, and advertising; to the architectural and social spaces of museums, galleries, exhibitions, and other private and public environments of the everyday.

Interestingly, these books recognize most acutely the points where images and objects and subjects and environments overlap, blur and converge with and mediate one another. They argue for instance, that interacting with newspapers or the Internet always involves a coming together of text and image, of reading and looking simultaneously; that cinema always comprises sight and sound, viewing and hearing at once; that video phones necessitate a confluence of text (texting), image (photographing/videoing), sound (ringtones), and touch (the haptic or tactile bond between the user and his or her unit).[5] These books recognize, then, that every encounter taking place between a viewer, participant, or user *and* her or his visual (and multi- or inter-sensory) culture makes it possible to imagine a distinct new starting point for thinking about or doing visual culture studies, as well as a new "object" of visual culture.

In addition, as I have already mentioned, these books present us with an almost inexhaustible diversity of critical tools, models and methods, and mechanisms and techniques, as well as tropes, figures, modalities, and morphologies. And they do so both to engage with the objects and subjects and media and environments of visual culture themselves *and* to facilitate our doing so by providing us with the meanings by which to grasp, understand, and navigate the numerous historical, conceptual, and contemporary ways of seeing, practices of looking, scopic regimes, and visual metaphors that are crucial to our encounters with visual culture and our studies of it.[6]

At the same time, the huge number of books tells us that the phrase "visual culture" is becoming ubiquitous, omnipresent, that it can and is being used to signify works or artifacts or spaces from *any* historical period, geographical location, thematic concern, or combination of methodological practices.[7] Because of this, the phrase visual culture conveys little that is specific to our past or present visual culture per se. It seems that visual culture is everywhere, and thus nowhere, wholly over-determined and almost meaningless simultaneously.

So where does this leave us with regard to the question with which we began this section: "What is visual culture studies?" As has become obvious in this brief trawl through books with "visual culture" in their titles, the phrase seems to be wholly pervasive, indicating that visual culture studies is fast becoming a prevailing field of inquiry in the humanities and beyond, and yet is also ubiquitous, an unhelpful indicator of both what it is and what it does. What is astonishing about all these books, and somehow not unexpected, is that there is no real common consensus as to what the term "visual culture" actually signifies. The answers to this question very much depend on the specific nature of the inquiry undertaken in each book. Sometimes "visual culture" is employed to characterize an historical period or geographical location such as the visual culture of the Renaissance or Aboriginal visual culture, or as Svetlana Alpers has put it in her discussion of Dutch visual culture, a culture that is bustling with a plethora of "notions about vision (the mechanisms of the eye), on image making devices (the microscope, the camera obscura), and on visual skills (map making, but also experimenting) as cultural resources."[8] Sometimes "visual culture" is used to designate a set of thematic individual or community-based concerns around the ways in which politically motivated images are produced, circulated, and consumed to both construct and reinforce *and* resist and overthrow articulations of sexual or racial ontologies, identities, and subjectivities – such as black visual culture, or feminist visual culture, or lesbian and gay visual culture. Sometimes "visual culture" marks a theoretical or methodological problematic that can be caught up in epistemological debates, or discussions of knowledge, of what determines our looking, seeing, or viewing practices, and how we can articulate this in terms of questions of disciplinarity, pedagogy, and what constitutes an "object" of visual culture.

All in all, then, it's not in fact true, as it often seems, that visual culture studies simply includes anything and everything that is visual – although it's certainly the case that the field of inquiry is preoccupied with the problem of visuality.[9] Rather, the phrase is always used in particular ways for specific ends – and if this doesn't seem to be the case, it may well be that an author is using the phrase in a number of ways simultaneously. So, this is why asking the question "What is visual culture studies?" *in any given instance* is always more valuable than finding an answer to it.

Disciplines, Inter-disciplines, Indisciplines

Later we will go on to consider visual culture as what Douglas Crimp has called an "object of study," what that "object" might be, and how it is established or shaped.[10] In this section, we need to concentrate on the question of the status of visual culture studies as a field of inquiry: is visual culture studies a discipline, in the sense that philosophy or history are disciplines? Is it a sub-discipline, a component, or an off-shoot of a more established discipline such as art history or anthropology – or even of a newer discipline such as film studies or media studies? Is it, like cultural studies, what we might call an inter-discipline – something that exists between disciplines and emerges from within this grey area so that visual culture studies operates between visual cultural practices and ways of thinking? Is it indeed the spark itself created by either the sympathetic or the hostile friction of disciplines rubbing together? Or is it something else altogether? Entertaining these questions of disciplinarity reveals that there are a number of interwoven accounts of the genealogy or the emergence of visual culture studies as a discursive formation.[11]

1.   The search for origins: Some accounts of "visual culture" do their best to locate the origins of the area of study as specifically as possible, trying, for instance, to identify the person who first used the phrase "visual culture," and in so doing identify the founding moment of the discipline. The two often cited winners of this contest are Michael Baxandall for his *Painting and Experience in Fifteenth-Century Italy*, a social history of style and the period eye, and Svetlana Alpers for *The Art of Describing: Dutch Art in the Seventeenth Century*, a study of seventeenth-century Dutch description, representation, images, appearance, cartography, and visuality.[12] I would argue, though, that this quest for beginnings is a red herring – at best it gives us an "official" starting point, although I'm not sure what the purpose of this would be, and at worst it wilfully misleads by intimating that the "naming" of a field of inquiry necessarily pinpoints the first time a certain kind of interrogation has taken place. This is simply not the case: analyses of visual culture were being carried out long before "visual culture" or "visual studies" emerged as academic fields of inquiry, and similarly universities in the UK such as Middlesex and Northumbria have been delivering undergraduate degrees in visual culture studies – without being named as such – for over 25 years in some cases.

2.   The return of the "forefathers": What is more useful to my mind is not to isolate individuals using the phrase "visual culture" reasonably recently, but rather to follow researchers and academics who have begun to excavate the humanities and visual arts for the writings of earlier generations of scholars and practitioners working in and against a variety of disciplines that has led to the emergence of the study of visual culture as a truly interdisciplinary project. Such visual culture studies scholars *avant la lettre* might include Aby Warburg and Erwin Panofsky, Sigfried Kracauer, Walter Benjamin, André Malraux, Roland Barthes, Raymond Williams, John Berger, and Gerhard Richter. Calling these scholars "forefather" is meant to be facetious; they do nonetheless offer earlier prototypical models or visual cultural practices that form part of the genealogy of visual culture studies and a series of methodological techniques that are "proper" to its interdisciplinary nature, its criticality, and its often awkward arrangement of images, objects, and environments of study. See for example Warburg's *Mnemosyne Altas* (c.1925–9), Benjamin's *Passagenwerk* (1927–40), Malraux's *The Voices of Silence* (c.1950), or Richter's *Atlas* (1961–present).

3. The practices of pedagogy: One more useful account of the emergence of visual culture studies as a field of inquiry charts its historical development back to the 1970s and 1980s in the university, former polytechnic, adult education, and art and design school sector of the British education system. Here, art history and design history and studio staff work toward equipping practice-based as well as academic-stream students with the interdisciplinary tools necessary for their craft: to introduce social history, context, and criticality into a considera-tion of art history and fine art practice; to present students with a history of (not just fine art) images; to furnish them with the resource of a diverse visual archive; and to mobilize practice itself. As a history of visual culture studies that emerges specifically from pedagogical and practice-based imperatives, in the main this is a push to encourage students to think outside of or past the tenets of formalism within the discourse of modernism.

4. The limits of disciplinarity: Concomitant with this account, another sug-gests that visual culture studies as a reasonably distinct series of interdisciplinary intellectual practices surfaces around the same time, and that it is brought on by feelings of discontent experienced by academics struggling within art history, design history, comparative literature, and other disciplines in the humanities to become more self-reflexive about their own disciplinary practices. Individuals, clusters of academics, and in some cases whole departments are frustrated by what they feel are the limitations of their own discipline: what subjects and objects can they include in their purview? What range of critical tools do they have at their disposal, and do they have the wherewithal to wield them? How best to motivate their students in a critical analysis of the historical, conceptual, and aesthetic nature of an ever-changing visual culture? Needing to converse with new visual, tactile, sonic objects of convergence, as well as other spaces and environments – how, for instance, would the discipline of art history deal fully with the intricate and inter-sensory multivalences of performance art or video art or installation art or site-specific art? – they were driven by an impulse if not to break down then certainly to *question* established disciplines and to *pressure* existing disciplinary boundaries.[13]

5. Theorizing between disciplines: Allied to this is the impact of "theory." As well as attending to new forms of visual arts practice, along with the emer-gence of the Marxist and feminist "New Art History" in the late 1960s and early 1970s exemplified by the work of T. J. Clark, Linda Nochlin, and Baxandall, scholars began to pay close attention to allied developments in film studies, in particular to semiotics and psychoanalysis. At the same time, they began to integrate the interests of cultural studies – just as cultural studies had drawn on anthropology. For while questions of class and gender and race had already been integral to the development of the new art history, cultural studies offered a means to address analogous concerns focusing more on the ordinary, the every-day, and the popular, and on the politics of representation, difference, and power in ways that reminded us how *cultural practices themselves do make a difference*. Thus emerged what we might call a visual "take" on cultural studies.

Here visual culture studies, like cultural studies before it, begins to function as an inter-discipline, drawing from existing disciplines and ways of thought, and because of it finding techniques to articulate the objects of visual culture differently.

6.   Conferences and programs: Still another flashpoint in the development of visual culture studies is the period 1988–9 during which two events took place. The first was a conference on vision and visuality held in 1988 at the Dia Art Foundation in New York. Participants included Norman Bryson, Jonathan Crary, Hal Foster, Martin Jay, Rosalind Krauss, and Jacqueline Rose. The proceeds of this event went on to appear as the influential collection *Vision and Visuality*, edited by Foster. Of this collection, Martin Jay has recently remarked that its publication "may be seen as the moment when the visual turn . . . really showed signs of turning into the academic juggernaut it was to become in the 1990s [because] a critical mass beg[a]n to come together around the question of the cultural determinants of visual experience in the broadest sense."[14] The second event is the establishment in 1989 of the first US-based graduate program in visual and cultural studies at the University of Rochester, which gave a certain academic and institutional legitimation to visual culture (founding staff in the program included Mieke Bal, Bryson, Lisa Cartwright, and Michael Ann Holly).

Offering this account of the genealogies of visual culture studies is part of the process of legitimizing it as an academic field of inquiry, a discipline in its own right, or at least as a discursive formation, a site of interdisciplinary activity, a "tactic" or a "movement."[15] This is necessary because the question of the disciplinary status of visual culture studies matters, and it matters for two reasons in particular. Firstly, because introducing such accounts of the emergence of visual culture studies as a potentially legitimate discipline, as I have done here, makes us aware of the fact that it *does* have its own distinct, albeit interwoven, histories that need to be acknowledged and articulated. For a field of inquiry that is so often accused of ahistoricism, it is imperative to recognize that visual culture studies did not simply appear from nowhere, as if by magic, at some point in, say, the late 1980s, but does in fact have a series of much longer divergent and interconnecting genealogies. The status of visual culture studies continues to be hotly contested, and everyone has a different story to tell about its origins. Secondly, this question of the disciplinary status of visual culture studies matters because, as I will argue in the final section of this chapter through my case study on "place," it offers new ways of thinking, and of thinking about objects, such that it *is* a distinct field of inquiry.

As Martin Jay points out, visual culture studies *did* become an academic, intellectual, and publishing juggernaut in the 1990s – the number and range of books I listed above testifies to this. With the exception of the "Visual Culture Questionnaire" published by the prominent journal *October* in 1996, on the whole the 1990s and the early years of the first decade of the twenty-first century have seen a multitude of triumphant books and journals, conferences, departments, centers, programs, courses, minors, and modules bearing the name "visual culture" or "visual studies."[16] If visual culture studies was inaugurated out of frustration in relation to the stifling effects of disciplinary policing and border controls, as a call to look self-reflexively both inwardly toward the limitations of one's own discipline and outwardly to the opportunities made available by others, it can safely be said that it continues to do this, and to productive ends. In working with and against other disciplines and between fields of inquiry, following its counter- or anti-disciplinary impetus it has led to disciplines questioning their own foundations and imperatives, even as it has also displayed outward hostility toward the prospect of its own conditions of possibility. Perhaps even more importantly, it has found its own methodologies and its own objects of study. It is a true example of what Barthes, paraphrased by Mieke Bal, says of interdisciplinary study, that it "consists of *creating* a new object *that belongs to no one.*"[17]

Finally, in bringing this section to a close, I would like to offer a word of caution: in its ongoing and ever-more successful search for legitimation, visual culture studies has the potential to become too self-assured, and its devotees too confident. In so doing, it can all too easily lose sight of its drive to worry or problematize other disciplines. It must remember to continue plotting a fractious course between disciplines, learning from them and teaching them lessons in return; and to continue engendering new objects or mobilizing more established things in new ways, by carrying on *doing* the work that it does. Visual culture studies should be careful not to lose, as Mitchell puts it, its "turbulence," its "incoherence," its "chaos," or its "wonder" as an *in*discipline: the "anarchist" moment of "breakage or rupture" when "a way of doing things . . . compulsively performs a revelation of its own inadequacy."[18]

In fact, it is at this point that one comes to realize it is not its disciplinary status that is of interest so much as the prospect that visual culture studies might be a whole new *strategy* for doing research, of seeing and knowing, of outlining our encounters with visual culture, and mining them for meaning, constituting its own objects and subjects and media and environments of study that belong to no one, as Barthes would have it, *and* that can only come into existence, be made, and made sense of as "a way of doing things" that is particular to visual culture studies. It is in this way that the "object" of visual culture, and the question of the "object" in visual culture studies, comes into view.

What is the "Object" of Visual Culture Studies?

This conception of visual culture studies as an *in*discipline is very appealing. Here, the chance to consider attending to the field of inquiry as "a way of doing things" is fascinating, as is gesturing toward the extent to which studies of visual culture have the potential to make evident their own limitations as a necessary part of their capacity and willingness to comprehend and perform these new "way[s] of doing things." So given the work that visual culture studies *does*, with what objects does it engage, and how are they constituted?

Some academics are happy simply for visual culture studies to include an expanded field of vision, an expanded purview, an expanded object domain, to include all things "visual." (Of course some would say that in certain quarters the discipline of art history has already been doing this for years.[19]) Other scholars are more attentive to its particular character. In writing of and on visual culture studies they have returned, explicitly and implicitly, to mull over meticulously the full implications of Roland Barthes' remarks on interdisciplinarity mentioned earlier. Rogoff for instance, has drawn on Barthes' ideas in thinking of visual culture studies, and its interdisciplinarity, as "the constitution of a new object of knowledge."[20] Bal has recently made similar comments, pointing out that "[i]f the tasks of visual culture studies must be derived from its object, then, in a similar way, the methods most suitable for performing these tasks must be derived from those same tasks, and the derivation made explicit." Likewise in suggesting that this field of inquiry has the potential to be an example of interdisciplinarity in an "interesting" sense, James Elkins has suggested that it "does not know its subjects but finds them through its preoccupations."[21] All of this is to say that, whether we are discussing objects or subjects or media or environments or ways of seeing and practices of looking, the visual, or visuality, visual culture studies as an interdisciplinary field of inquiry has the potential *to create new objects of study*, and it does so specifically by *not determining them in advance*.

What does this actually mean? It means that visual culture studies is not simply "theory" or even "visual theory" in any conventional sense, and it does not simply "apply" theory or visual theory to objects of study. Rather, it is the case that between (1) finding ways of attending to the historical, conceptual, and material specificity of things, (2) taking account of "viewing apparatuses," and (3) our critical encounters with them, the "object" of visual culture studies is born, emerges, is discernible, shows itself, becomes visible. In these moments of friction, the "object" of visual culture studies comes into view, engendering its own way of being, of being meaningful, of being understood, and even of not being understood. It is not a matter of *which* "objects" are "appropriate" or "inappropriate" for visual culture studies, but of how beginning from the specifics of our visual culture, our preoccupations and encounters with it, and the acts that take place in and by way of visual culture, *none of which are determined in advance*, make it possible for us to focus, as José Esteban Muñoz has said, "on what acts and objects do . . . rather that [sic] what they might possibly mean."[22]

With this in mind, I would like to turn to a project, a case study, a visual culture study, an instance of how visual culture studies can make such a thing possible.

A Case Study: "The Poetics of Place: Histories, Theories, Practices"

Let me offer an example of how a new object of study, a study of visual culture, might be constituted by such encounters – where what acts and objects *do* is more important than what they might possibly *mean*. The example I offer is of a cross-disciplinary and inter-disciplinary research project I am coordinating on the historical, conceptual, and aesthetic question of "place" in our visual culture.[23] The project itself, entitled "The Poetics of Place: Histories, Theories, Practices," circles around and links together ontological states, states of being and becoming, embodied in the themes of exile, migration, nation, and belonging. In order to confront these challenges, this project cuts across and between fields of inquiry such as art and architectural history, fine art practice, cultural geography, postcolonial studies, critical theory, anthropology, and philosophy.

Based at my host institution, Kingston University, in Kingston-upon-Thames in South West London, the site of the coronation of seven kings of England in the tenth century, the project's objective is to show how the question of "place" in all of its historical, geographical, and aesthetic complexity also needs to be understood in its specificity. That is, when it comes to research projects and in this instance to the question of "place," we have to consider both the general and the particular, the global and the local, the overall story and the details, the wood and the trees.

Because of this dual focus, in putting the project together, it soon became apparent that *no one person* was capable of doing this on her or his own, and that conversation or discourse *between* individuals – whether they agree with one another or not – was the most productive way to proceed. To this end, I decided to assemble a group of individuals who, *together*, could realize such a project: the Italian academic Giuliana Bruno from the Department of Visual and Environmental Studies at Harvard University, whose writings cut across the fields of geography, art, architecture, design, cartography, and film, and whose thought is both materialist in its attention to history and rhythmic in its rhetoric; the American curator Vivian Rehberg from ARC, Musée d'Art Moderne de la Ville de Paris, who has curated international exhibitions and coordinated catalogues on place and globality; and the French artist Jean-Baptiste Decavèle, who works with video/photography responsive to the grain of location, travel, and memory. Each of these individuals was asked to participate in this research project because the character of her or his practice – as writers, curators, and makers – emerges out of a sensitivity to the complex nature of our visual culture. Their starting point is not an abstract idea, or disembodied theory, but, rather each attentive in her or his own way to the particular and peculiar features, contours, disposition of "place" and its way of articulating itself. As such, each of them offers a chance to inscribe the possibility of a nuanced encounter with visual culture itself, and with each other, which is not determined in advance.

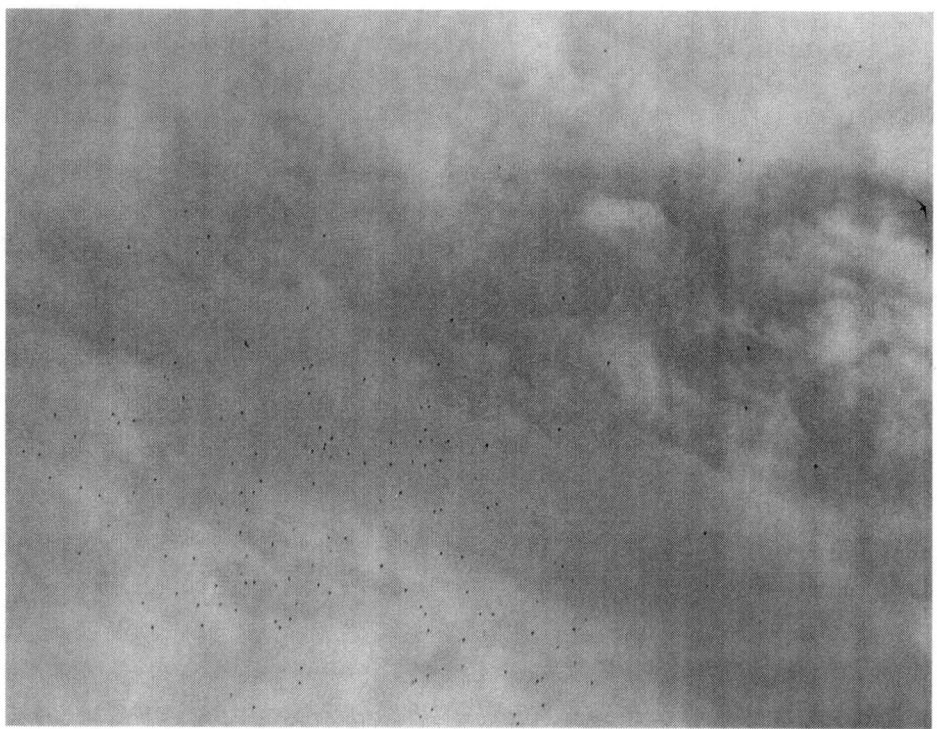

FIGURE 23.1   Jean-Baptiste Decavèle, *Untitled*, 2004. Courtesy of the artist

In order to carry out its task of thinking the general and the particular at the same time, the project has to do two things simultaneously. On the one hand, it should be self-reflexive; on the other hand, it needs to be attentive to detail. That is to say, on the one hand, it should be speculative and curious about its own practices, its own conduct, its own mechanisms. In so doing it can better instigate and take account of the creative links between a group of researchers from distinct environments, with diverse backgrounds and knowledge of the subject at hand, and dissimilar critical tools with which to unearth the problematic disposition of the question of "place." Along with such discrepancies, at the same time members of the research team need to share a cross-disciplinary commitment to establishing collaborative research, writing, informal seminars, public lectures, curating, and making, across and between their respective interdisciplinary areas of expertise into ideas around "place."

On the other hand, the project needs to attend to the historical, phenomenological, and material fact of "place" in its specificity. To this end, it draws on and engages critically with visual and textual archives (engravings, illustrations, paintings, and photographs, postcards, documents, and texts – images, objects, artifacts, and items that are all simultaneously both visual and textual) relating to forced migration to Kingston-upon-Thames and its environs. In so

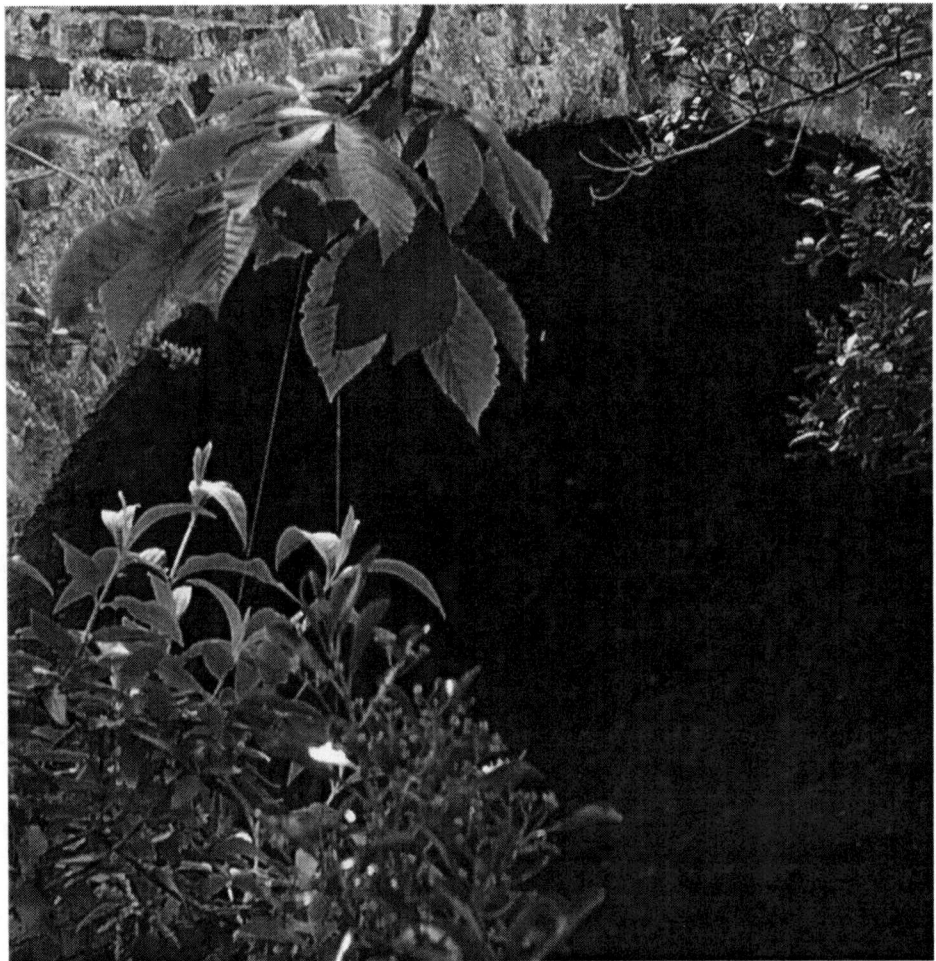

FIGURE 23.2 Jean-Baptiste Decavèle, *Untitled*, 2004. Courtesy of the artist

doing the project will generate debate on the themes of nation, exile, belonging, slavery, cultural memory, and geographies or topographies of travel, making use of various local archives and museums, including the Kingston Museum and the Kingson Local History Centre, and it will interrogate these and other unique archives as well as the local census, parish records, and cemetery records.

The research will begin in the middle of the eighteenth century, the first point at which tangible records are made of a black presence in Kingston and its neighboring districts. These records show the 1761 arrival in Kingston from Senegal of the five-year-old Caesar Picton, who was presented by Captain Parr to St. John Philipps of Norbiton, for whom he began working. Picton was later made a free man and set himself up as a successful coal merchant and gentleman. His former residence, Picton House, where he lived from 1788 until 1807, is a

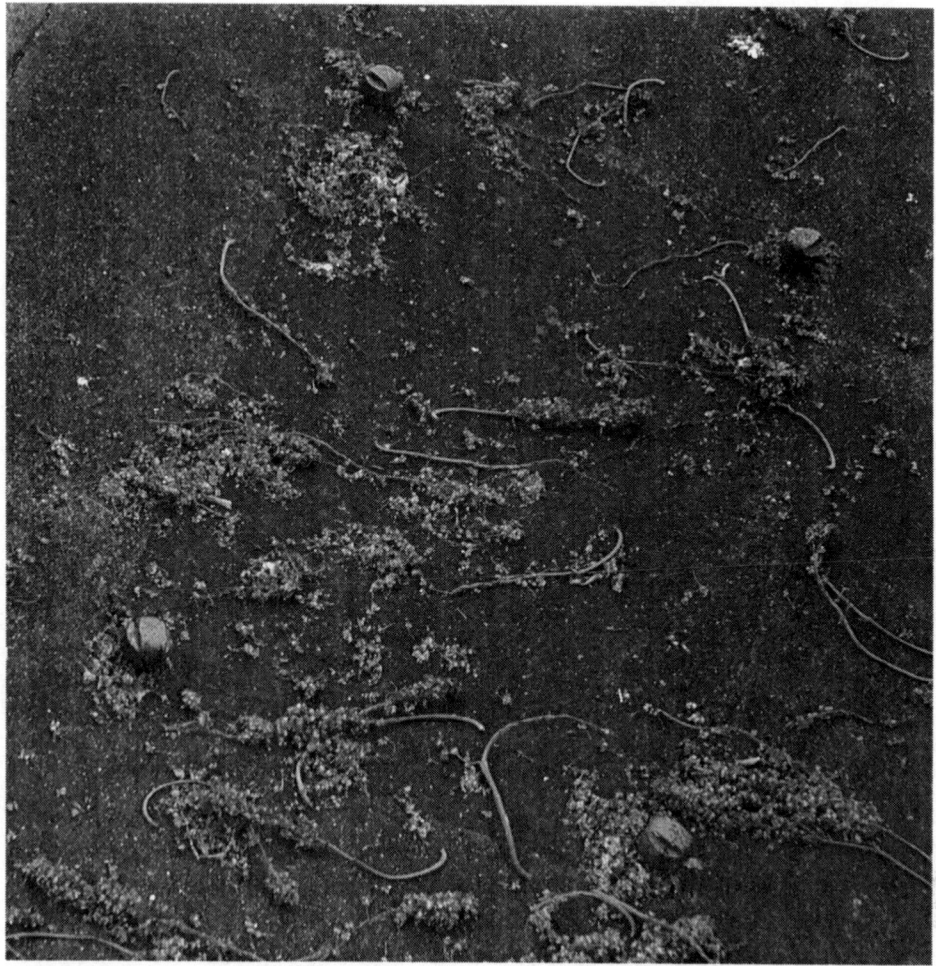

FIGURE 23.3   Jean-Baptiste Decavèle, *Untitled*, 2004. Courtesy of the artist

site of local interest and its former resident has been commemorated with a plaque. This biographical narrative will form a starting point for the research project.

In being self-reflexive and attentive to detail, this collaborative research project will, then, address questions relating to the visual and material culture of "place" that both have wider implications for the study, analysis, and understanding of "place" in our post-colonial and trans-cultural communities but are also specific to the modern, colonial history of Kingston-upon-Thames and its environs. Key research questions to ask are: How do collaborative research practices and the links that individual experts make between one another as a group offer a more complete and detailed understanding of the history of "place" and future discussions of it? In what ways do history, cultural memory, museology, and heritage

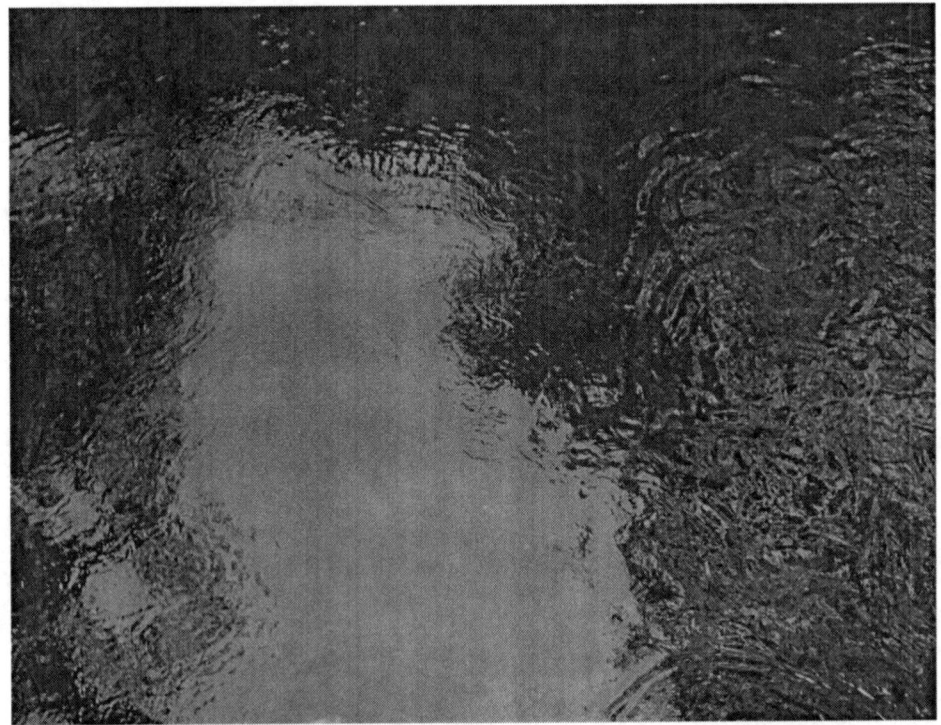

FIGURE 23.4   Jean-Baptiste Decavèle, *Untitled*, 2004. Courtesy of the artist

contribute to the facts and fantasies of nation, landscape, and geographies, cartographies, and visual iconographies of travel? And what can these visual and textual archives, these histories and biographies, tell us about the experience of new ways of living in exile as a member of a migrant population?

As we observed at the beginning of this chapter, there are always more questions than there are answers, and learning how to ask the right questions is key to the study of visual culture, as it is to any critical study. In this instance, asking these kinds of multi-part questions that mingle self-reflexive thought and an attention to historical, material, and aesthetic detail will be particularly pro-ductive. For they will make it possible to enter into dialogue across and between history, theory, curating, and practice in order to both bridge the perceived divide between these areas of concern *and* show that it is only by weaving them together that we can begin to discern a precise sense of "place" and its sensibil-ity in all of its complexity. Starting from the specificity of "place" itself, with all of its intricacies, supports our efforts to ask new questions *of* and thus generate new methodologies *from* it that emerge out of the convergence and interweav-ing taking place in the enactment of the project itself.

Thinking across and between areas of inquiry and across and between visual and textual archives, images, artifacts, and practices, it is the project itself, in fact

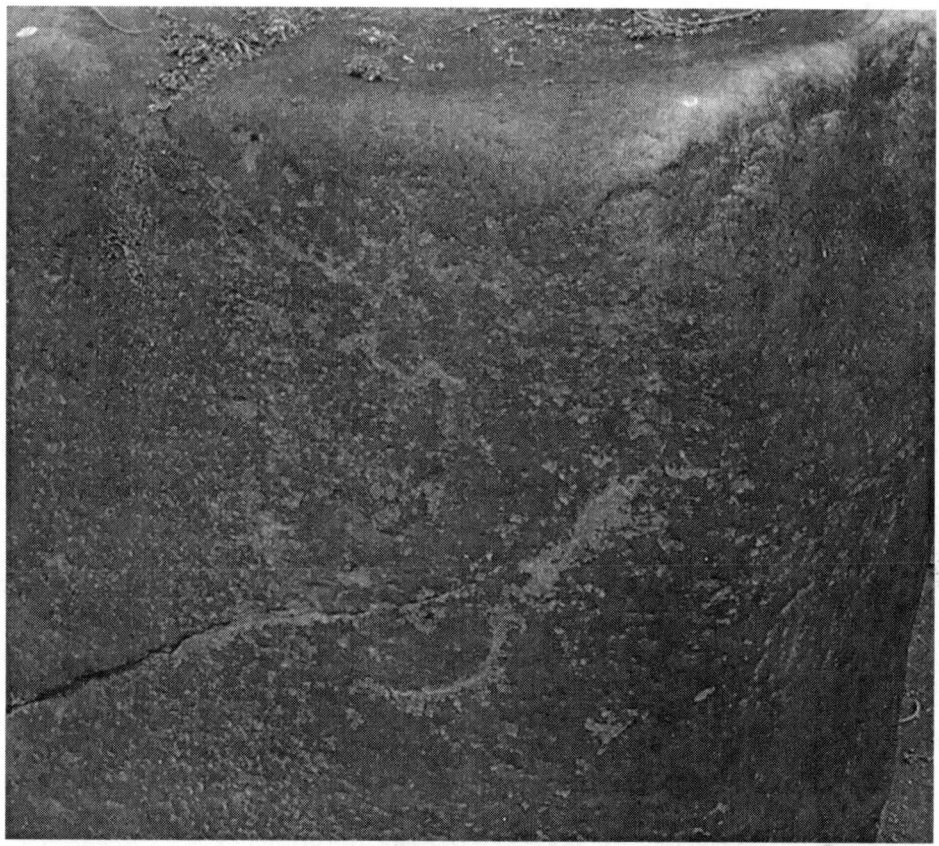

FIGURE 23.5   Jean-Baptiste Decavèle, *Untitled*, 2004. Courtesy of the artist

any given visual culture study, that has the potential to generate new objects of visual culture yet to suggest themselves, that belong to no one, and yet come into being or are materialized in the very "doing" of the project itself. They are made, constituted, by way of the project, by way of the encounters between individuals thinking through a specific topic, and between the historical, conceptual, and material specificity of that topic. Research itself, then, becomes determined by the interdisciplinary nature of the material gathered *for* the project, *in* the project, that comes together *as* the project. It is through debate, collaboration, self-reflexive practices, and convergences between methodologies, archives, encounters, objects, subjects, media, environments, and ways of seeing and doing that a visual culture study takes shape. And it is only *in this taking shape*, through such contingencies, that pressing questions are asked, uncertainties, understanding, and knowledge is generated, unexpected insights come to the fore, and new objects of visual culture become known to us.

Acknowledgments

Thanks to Stuart Daniel, Jean-Baptiste Decavèle, Amelia Jones, Vivian Rehberg, and as always to Joanne Morra.

Notes

1 Mitchell (2002), 165–6.
2 There are extensive ongoing debates concerning the designation of the field of study under consideration here. See for instance *October's* "Visual Culture Questionnaire" (1996), Walker and Chaplin (1997), Sturken and Cartwright (2001), Elkins (2002), Foster (2002), Mitchell (2002), and other texts cited in the references. In this chapter, "visual culture studies" – rather than "visual culture" or "visual studies" – names the field of study while "visual culture" designates the objects, subjects, media, and environments of study. In this I follow Walker and Chaplin (1997) for whom "visual culture studies" does not designate a discipline so much as "a hybrid, an inter- or multi-disciplinary enterprise formed as a consequence of a convergence of, or borrowing from, a variety of disciplines and methodologies" (1), that allows us to consider what Amelia Jones (2003) has called "the formation of new interdisciplinary strategies of interpretation" (2).
3 There are of course many other books on the topic of visual culture that don't include the phrase itself in their title, including books on visual studies (often used interchangeably with visual culture). Some of the most important books and edited collections in the development of the area of inquiry include neither, such as Buck-Morss, *The Dialectics of Seeing*; Jay, *Downcast Eyes*; and Crary, *Techniques of the Observer*. And there are also the accompanying journals, and journal articles, as well as conferences, departments, programs, and courses that have both spawned and been spawned by visual culture. In the English context, it is often said that the first avowedly visual culture journal is *Block*, 15 issues of which were produced by academics based at Middlesex University – then Middlesex Polytechnic – between 1979 and 1989.
4 See Rogoff (1998), 18.
5 On mobile screenic devices see Cooley (2004).
6 On scopic regimes see Jay (1993).
7 There is a concern, of course, within discussions of visual culture studies that the phrase can be applied in such undifferentiated and homogenizing ways.
8 Alpers (1996), 26. See also Alpers (1983) and Jay (1993).
9 Visuality has been defined by Jessica Evans and Stuart Hall (1999) as "the visual register in which the image and visual meaning operate" (41), and more clearly by Amelia Jones (2003) who speaks of visuality as "the condition of how we see and make meaning of what we see" (xx).
10 Crimp (1999), 52.
11 In noting Stuart Hall's insistence that Cultural Studies is a "'discursive formation' rather than a discipline," Amelia Jones makes it possible for us to imagine also characterizing visual culture studies in the same way. See Jones (2003), 2.

12 Evans and Hall (1999) comment that Alpers is the first to use the phrase "visual culture" in her *The Art of Describing* (xxv), but Alpers (1983) herself in that book attributes the phrase to Michael Baxandall (xxv). It is worth noting that those mentioned are firmly established within the discipline of art history. (Incidentally, for all the emphasis that visual culture studies is said by its detractors to place on analyses of the contemporary, it is well worth noting that these so-called earliest instances of visual culture analysis are of fifteenth-century Italian and seventeenth-century Dutch culture.) Walker and Chaplin (1997) say that to the best of their knowledge, the first book to use the term "visual culture" is in fact Caleb Gattegno's 1969 *Towards a Visual Culture: Educating through Television* (6, note 2). To my knowledge, no one writing on the development of visual culture studies from within art history has noticed that in 1964 Marshall McLuhan used the phrase "visual culture" in *Understanding Media*. It needed a scholar with a background in film and media studies, Raiford Guins, to spot this (in conversation).

13 For more on issues raised in points 3 and 4 see Walker and Chaplin (35–50).

14 Martin Jay, "Cultural Relativism and the Visual Turn," *journal of visual culture*, 1:3, December 2002, 267–78, 267, 268.

15 In *The Visual Culture Reader*, Nicholas Mirzoeff (1998) refers to visual culture as a "tactic" (5). Recently Mieke Bal (2003) has referred to it as a "movement" (6).

16 *October*'s "Visual Culture Questionnaire" (1996) continues to be the most engaging critique of visual culture studies. In particular, the questions posed by the editors of the "Questionnaire" rather than the answers to it accuse visual culture studies of *a*historicism (an over-attention to analyses of the contemporary) and of dematerializing the image. On this question of ahistoricism, it's well worth mentioning that art history, along with many other disciplines in the humanities, including visual culture studies, is no stranger to questions of historiography. From their inception, such questions necessarily plague, challenge, and offer ways forward for disciplines themselves. *October* is well aware of this. While the "Questionnaire" has been a huge bone of contention in subsequent discussions of visual culture studies, a clear, extended elaboration of its underlying assertions written by one of its originators can be found in Foster (2002).

17 Roland Barthes, cited in Bal (2003), 7.

18 Mitchell (1995), 541; it is here that Mitchell first uses the wonderfully damning phrase "safe default interdisciplinarity" (541) to characterize a particularly prevalent but ineffectual form of interdisciplinary study. It's a phrase that parallels Stephen Melville's comment in the *October* questionnaire (52–4). Carlo Ginsburg has also reasonably reminded us that "there is nothing intrinsically innovative or subversive in an interdisciplinary approach to knowledge" (51–3).

19 See Donald Preziosi, "Introduction," *The Art of Art History* (1999), where he offers an astute account of art history's efforts to expand its object domain, its willingness and ability to extend its purview.

20 Rogoff (1998), 15.

21 Bal (2003), 23; Elkins (2002), 30.

22 Muñoz (1996), 12.

23 By "place" I refer – following almost verbatim Vivian Rehberg's unpublished proposal for the exhibition entitled "The Poetics of Place" – to the social, cultural, political, and material dimensions and uses of a particular point or position that can

be natural, built, deserted, inhabited, over-crowded, marginal and central, and foreign and familiar at the same time.

References and further reading

Alpers, Svetlana (1983). *The Art of Describing: Dutch Art in the Seventeenth Century.* Chicago: University of Chicago Press.

—— (1996). "Visual Culture Questionnaire." *October*, vol. 77, Summer:25–70.

Bal, Mieke (2003). "Visual Essentialism and the Object of Visual Culture," *journal of visual culture*, vol. 2, no. 1, April:5–32.

Barthes, Roland (1986). *The Rustle of Language.* New York: Hill and Wang.

Baxandall, Michael (1972). *Painting and Experience in Fifteenth-Century Italy.* Oxford: Oxford University Press.

Block Editorial Board, and Sally Stafford, eds. (1996). *The Block Reader in Visual Culture.* London: Routledge.

Brennan, Teresa, and Martin Jay, eds. (1996). *Vision in Context: Historical and Contemporary Perspectives on Sight.* London: Routledge.

Buck-Morss, Susan (1989). *The Dialectics of Seeing: Walter Benjamin and the Arcades Project.* Cambridge, MA: MIT Press.

Cooley, Heidi R. (2004). "It's all about the *Fit*: The Hand, the Mobile Screenic Device and Tactile Vision." *journal of visual culture*, vol. 3, no. 2, August:133–51.

Crary, Jonathan (1990). *Techniques of the Observer: On Vision and Modernity in the Nineteenth Century.* Cambridge, MA: MIT Press.

Crimp, Douglas (1999). "Getting the Warhol we Deserve." *Social Text*, vol. 59, no. 17:49–66.

Doy, Gen (2000). *Black Visual Culture.* London: I. B. Tauris.

Elkins, James (2002). *Visual Studies: A Skeptical Introduction.* London: Routledge.

Evans, James, and Stuart Hall, eds. (1999). *Visual Culture: The Reader.* London: Sage.

Farago, Claire, ed. (1995). *Reframing the Renaissance: Visual Culture in Europe and Latin America: 1450–1650.* New Haven: Yale University Press.

Foster, Hal (2002). *Design and Crime (And Other Diatribes).* London: Verso.

—— ed. (1988). *Vision and Visuality.* Seattle: Bay Press.

Ginsburg, Carlo (1995). "Viteos and Compatibilities. *Art Bulletin*, vol. 77, no. 4, December:51–3.

Horne, Peter, and Lewis, Reina, eds. (1996). *Outlooks: Lesbian and Gay Sexualities and Visual Culture.* London: Routledge.

Jay, Martin (1988). "Scopic Regimes of Modernity." In Foster, ed. (1988).

—— (1993). *Downcast Eyes: The Denigration of Vision in Twentieth-Century French Thought.* Berkeley: University of California Press.

—— (2002). "Cultural Relativism and the Visual Turn." *journal of visual culture*, vol. 1, no. 3, December:267–78.

Jones, Amelia, ed. (2003). *The Feminism and Visual Culture Reader.* London: Routledge.

Levin, David M. (1997). *Sites of Vision: The Discursive Construction of Sight in the History of Philosophy.* Cambridge, MA: The MIT Press.

Lloyd, Fran, ed. (2001). *Displacement and Difference: Contemporary Arab Visual Culture in the Diaspora.* London: Saffron Books.

Lord, Peter (1998–). *The Visual Culture of Wales* (4 vols.). Cardiff: University of Wales Press.

McLuhan, Marshall (1964/1987). *Understanding Media.* London: Routledge.

Melville, Stephen, and Readings, Bill, eds. (1995). *Vision and Textuality.* London: Macmillan Press.

Mirzoeff, Nick, ed. (1998/2002). *Visual Culture Reader.* London: Routledge.

—— (1999). *Diaspora and Visual Culture: Representing Africans and Jews.* London: Routledge.

Mitchell, W. J. T. (1995). "Interdisciplinarity and Visual Culture." *Art Bulletin*, vol. 77, no. 4, December:540–4.

—— (2002). "Showing Seeing; A Critique of Visual Culture." *journal of visual culture*, vol. 1, no. 2 (August):165–81.

Morgan, David, and Sally Promey, eds. (2001). *The Visual Culture of American Religions.* Berkeley: University of California Press.

Muñoz, José Esteban (1996). "Ephemera as Evidence: Introductory Notes to Queer Acts." *Woman & Performance: A Journal of Feminist Theory*, vol. 8, no. 2:5–16.

October (1996). "Visual Culture Questionnaire," 77.

Preziosi, Donald, ed. (1999). *The Art of Art History.* Oxford: Oxford University Press.

Rogoff, Irit (1998). "Studying Visual Culture." In Mirzoeff (1998), 14–26.

Selwyn, Pamela, and Valentine Groebner (2004). *Defaced: The Visual Culture of Violence in the Late Middle Ages.* New York: Zone Books.

Sturken, Marita, and Lisa Cartwright (2001). *Practices of Looking: An Introduction to Visual Culture.* Oxford: Oxford University Press.

Walker, John, and Sarah Chaplin (1997). *Visual Culture: An Introduction.* Manchester: Manchester University Press.

Wollen, Peter, and Lynne Cooke, eds. (1999). *Visual Display: Culture Beyond Appearances.* New York: The New Press.

PART VII

Technology

24

"That's All Folks": Contemporary Art and Popular Culture

Nick Mirzoeff

There is no necessary connection between art and popular culture. But beginning in the nineteenth century, and with ever greater urgency from the 1920s on, critics have insistently connected the two, usually by opposition. Art has come to be defined as that which is not popular culture. Arguably, the very idea of popular culture serves to differentiate "what, at any time, counts as an elite cultural activity or form, and what does not."[1] While it is open to debate when exactly this logic of opposition was initiated, it took on a peculiarly charged importance in discussions about art in twentieth-century Europe and North America. For American critics such as Clement Greenberg, writing in 1939, art was the polar opposite of mass-produced "kitsch," or popular visual culture, the latter exemplified by the covers produced by Norman Rockwell for the *Saturday Evening Post*.[2] By posing this opposition, Greenberg defended avant-garde art as the site of the survival of elite cultural values, threatened on all sides by the forces of capitalism and commodification.

From today's vantage point, however, things look a little different. Rockwell has been the subject of major art museum surveys without art ceasing to exist. Indeed, in many ways one could argue that art is now a type of popular culture, with the ever-expanding global "art world" developing new biennales and periodicals at break-neck speed. The most widely circulated explanation for this state of affairs is that modern art of the kind being promoted by Greenberg failed its mission, leaving way for the incursions of the market to commodify contemporary art.[3] In this chapter, I will suggest instead that this transformation of art into mass culture expresses what was really at stake in the hierarchical tension between art and popular culture – the maintenance of a certain view of history.

In broadening that view to include those formerly excluded from it, the art/popular culture debate comes to seem anachronistic.

In the classic Marxist view, history was a forward-marching dialectical struggle between opposed interests. As Greenberg and others deployed Karl Marx's model of history in exploring artistic developments in the twentieth century, the triumph of popular culture over high art could only be viewed negatively as part of the victory of capitalism over socialism. For all the apparent evidence to support this view, it is based on a set of presumptions about the nature of history, the vital role of America in that history, and the place of culture (popular or otherwise) as its barometer.[4] History was presumed to be a narrative with a beginning, middle, and end like other stories. This particular story, that of capitalism, was presumed to be reaching its end. America was home to the highest form of capitalism and therefore, following Marx, it would be the place where capitalism would be brought down.

According to Greenberg, high culture was the place within the capitalist system where proper values could be safeguarded for the future, while popular culture was the mass-produced, anaesthetized, and debased version of art that constantly threatened to overwhelm it. Such anxieties about popular culture began to wane for artists and critics in the generation following Greenberg's. In the 1960s a diametrically opposed view claimed that popular culture was in fact the place of resistance to capitalism. In this view, now known as cultural studies, the democratic and democratizing forms and practices of popular culture promised to secure a form of socialism. As Stuart Hall famously wrote in 1981: "Popular culture is one of the sites where this struggle for and against a culture of the powerful is engaged . . . It is not a sphere where socialism, a socialist culture – already fully formed – might be constituted. That is why 'popular culture' matters. Otherwise, to tell you the truth, I don't give a damn about it."[5] Whether Hall really subscribed to such Marxist shibboleths or not, his exploration of cultural studies, including a broader understanding of literary and visual culture that embraced texts and images in the mass media and a critical awareness of the legacies of colonialism, led him and others associated with the Centre for Contemporary Cultural Studies at the University of Birmingham to the realization that history did not necessarily march forward and that European "high" culture could no longer be privileged as the endpoint of cultural development.

While cultural studies thus reexamined and reconceived popular culture in terms of its role in constructing racial, gender, and sexual identities, postmodern art discourse (including art making, art criticism, art history, and exhibition practices) began to engage in a new dialogue with popular culture. But for all its claims to radical rethinking, postmodern visual arts discourse all too often replicated the sense that America, and New York City in particular, was the necessary epicenter of art and culture. Paradoxically, then, just as Euro-American culture became increasingly intertwined with global flows and movements, the emergence of an international art world (comprised of all the discourses noted above) emerged to contain those energies.

This chapter will engage with this recent history of art and popular culture, dwelling at a series of key intersections without pretending to present a comprehensive picture of this relationship. Beginning by contrasting Greenberg's negative views about popular culture, as articulated in his 1939 essay, with Walter Benjamin's enthusiasm about the early cartoons of Walt Disney in the 1930s, the chapter goes on to explore the experimental fusion of aspects of modernist style and method with popular imagery in the work of Andy Warhol and other artists of the 1960s, a fusion that at the time seemed to bring this debate to an end. Yet, I will contend, this insular exchange was displaced and transformed under the influence of decolonization to an exploration of ethnicity in and as popular culture. Following Hall's lead, the chapter will thus conclude by exploring the intersection of art and popular culture in African and African American art.

Walter Benjamin, Mickey Mouse, and the Place of Popular Culture

After a 1931 conversation discussing Mickey Mouse with friends, it seemed to Benjamin that "in these films, mankind makes preparations to survive civilization." By this he meant that in his first incarnation as a trickster figure in films like *Steamboat Willie* (1928), Mickey suggested that it is possible to survive, even when the body no longer appears human in any way. In this way, Benjamin argued, "the public recognizes its own life" in cartoons.[6] Benjamin thus had a sense of how representation might move beyond the anthropomorphic and the mimetic, an issue that has all the more powerfully returned in our own era of digital manipulation.

These early animations were not "realistic" but created an image that foregrounded its own artificiality and machine-made quality. These cartoons and the popular comedies of Charlie Chaplin were a key influence on Benjamin's thoughts about art and popular culture, which culminated in his 1936 essay "The Work of Art in the Age of its Technological Reproducibility," written under the threat of Nazism.[7] In this essay, Benjamin developed his ideas as a theory of film. He argued that film sought "to establish equilibrium between human beings and the apparatus." That is to say, in the dehumanizing machine-world created by industrial capitalism, film was both a product of that world and the means by which people could come to terms with it. The closed-in environment of the modern city that Benjamin termed a "prison-world" was opened up by means of cinematic techniques like close-up and slow-motion into a "space for play" [*Spielraum*].[8] Close-up expands space, while slow-motion expands time, in ways that cannot be seen by the naked eye.

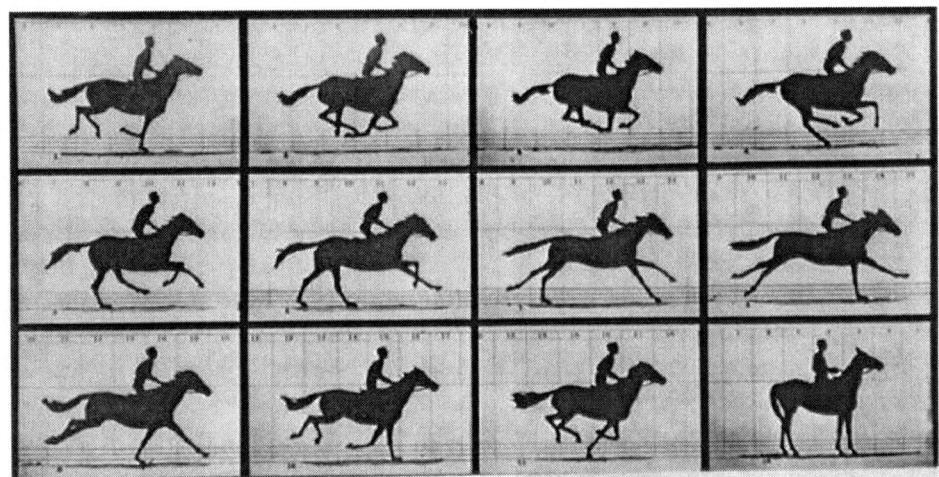

FIGURE 24.1 Eadweard Muybridge, *The Horse in Motion*, 1878. Commissioned by Leland Stanford

For Benjamin, then, the camera reveals what we know must be there but could not otherwise perceive, such as the precise motions used during walking that had been made visible by Eadweard Muybridge's stop motion photographs in the late nineteenth century (Figure 24.1). Benjamin saw this as opening into new modes of visuality, tapping into an "optical unconscious," a counterpart to the "instinctual unconscious" explored in psychoanalysis by means of language (B 117). Moreover, film conveys the very "stereotypes, transformations and catastrophes" that haunt the unconscious mind, leading Benjamin to suggest that the individual imagination had a counterpoint in the collective vision of cinema: "The ancient truth expressed by Heraclitus, that those who are awake have a world in common while each sleeper has a world of his own, has been invalidated by film – and less by depicting the dream world itself than by creating figures of collective dream, such as the globe-encircling Mickey Mouse" (B 118). Benjamin felt that the "collective laughter" produced by such grotesque figures could immunize the audience against the mass psychosis of fascism, even as he recognized that Mickey Mouse himself was quickly being recuperated by capitalism. In short, Benjamin was prepared to allow popular culture of the least cultivated – albeit the most technologically advanced – sort to serve the critical political purpose of his time, the fight against fascism.

Greenberg, in his virtually contemporaneously written "Avant-Garde and Kitsch," took a diametrically opposed view. Both essays were written in the face of the rise of Nazism and of the prospect of a second major world war. Both adopted a position that was Marxist, but not of any orthodox variety. Both started from the presumption that the mass reproduction of images had emerged with the rise of industrialism and thus precisely at the time when Marx was formulating his theory of capitalism. Thus, the new means of capitalist production was also notable for its generation of technologies of reproduction that had far-reaching social and cultural effects.

For Greenberg, the most crucial side effect of the rise of industrial capitalism was the creation of an avant-garde. In order to survive, art had to consider solely its own conditions of (re)production so that artists came to "derive their chief inspiration from the medium they work in" (G 23). Art comes to concentrate on the "imitation of imitat*ing*" (G 24, Greenberg's emphasis), as opposed to mass-reproduced imagery which, for Greenberg, was homogeneous in its low brow appeal and included a wide range of debased forms of kitsch: "popular, commercial art and literature with their chromeotypes, magazine covers, illustrations, ads, slick and pulp fiction, comics, Tin Pan Alley music, tap dancing, Hollywood movies, etc., etc." (G 25). Whereas Benjamin saw film as a revolutionary new medium, Greenberg thus viewed it as yet another manifestation of kitsch, consistent with his belief that "kitsch changes according to style but remains always the same" (G 25).

In a rather convoluted argument, Greenberg claimed that while the "peasant" looking at folk art and the "cultivated spectator" looking at Picasso share the same first impression, a second look gives the cultivated person the advantage of "the recognizable, the miraculous, and the sympathetic," qualities that are in fact "projected" into the painting by the viewer. Thus art represents "cause" while kitsch presents only an "effect" (G 27–8). If the avant-garde imitates the process of imitating, commenting in a critical way on the internal properties of art-making, kitsch "imitates its effects" (G 28). While Greenberg was a partisan of avant-garde art, in accord with Marxist theory he nonetheless saw its separation from what he and Benjamin both called "the masses" as a symptom of the final decline of capitalism.

Benjamin, however, took the argument a step further. Like Greenberg he agreed that the development of technological means of reproduction, namely photography, had instigated the "art for art's sake" philosophy of the nineteenth century. As photography copied what was placed before the camera, art was freed from what Benjamin called "ritual," the cult of either religious or secular beauty so that it could now take on a new social function – that of politics. Benjamin argued that because photography distanced people from nature by substituting a mimetic reproduction for the "real," the popular attitude to art had also shifted: "The extremely backward attitude toward a Picasso painting changes into a highly progressive reaction to a Chaplin film" (B 116). Of course, Greenberg would not allow that the latter was even possible since he argued that kitsch products such as Chaplin's films were diametrically opposed to high art, with its redemptive value.

Benjamin's theory of the optical unconscious expressed by film followed from his sense that "just as the entire mode of existence of human collectives changes over long historical periods, so too does their mode of perception" (B 104). In other words, Benjamin acknowledged something Greenberg did not even address

– what was "progressive" changed in relation to technological shifts, which in turn changed in complex relationship to society as a whole. Film allowed the mass, urban audience created by industrial capitalism to experience a collective response to visual media – a response that could not be evoked by paintings no matter how popular the exhibition in which they were displayed. At the same time, Benjamin still privileged art – particularly Dadaist works – as being the first to express the shock of modernity.

Benjamin and Greenberg were agreed that the primary enemy of all culture was fascism. Greenberg, writing on the brink of war, saw little hope for outright resistance: "Today we no longer look to socialism for a new culture – as inevitably one will appear, once we do have socialism. Today we look to socialism *simply* for the preservation of whatever living culture we have right now" (G 32). In this view, socialism acted as a kind of museum for high culture as it retreated from the mass political movements of the day. He drew only a limited distinction between Nazism, Italian fascism, and Soviet communism, because his version of art could have no application for political propaganda. Again, Benjamin, having been driven out of Germany by the Nazi takeover because of his Jewish background, articulated more subtle distinctions. He argued that fascist spectacle functioned to lure people into feeling they were in charge of their country, even though the ownership of property had not changed at all. The logical goal of such aesthetic spectacles as the Nuremberg rallies or Mussolini's Roman parades was war, following the Italian futurists' vision that "war is beautiful" (B 121). War thus provided the ultimate gratification of the desire for art for art's sake. To this aestheticizing of politics, Benjamin suggested that "Communism replies by politicizing art" (B 122).

Two Marxist art theorists agreed on the necessity of opposing Hitler could agree on nothing else in their groundbreaking analyses of the relationship between art and popular culture. Their fates in relation to the nefarious politics of fascism couldn't have been more different, either. Benjamin was forced to commit suicide in 1940 after Spanish police had refused to admit him to their neutral country from Nazi-occupied France, while Greenberg went on after WWII to become a highly successful art critic in the US, and the key promoter of a depoliticized modernist formalism.

At the end of the Second World War, everything appeared radically different. Even before the war, Benjamin's colleague at the Institute for Social Research, Theodor Adorno, had strongly criticized his endorsement of Disney cartoons. In the 1936 version of his essay on the work of art, Benjamin cut his references to Disney in response to Adorno's insistence that the mass response to these animations was in no way progressive and could even prepare the way for fascism. And, just after Benjamin had lauded Disney, the radical quality of the early cartoons gave way to the lush color and domesticated storylines of the increasingly formulaic animated films put out by the Disney machine, as became clear in the "Magician's Apprentice" section of *Fantasia* (1940), which sees Mickey anticipate the glories of automated household cleaning.

During the war itself Adorno and his colleague Max Horkheimer, stunned by the Holocaust and living in exile in the US, wrote their classic work *Dialectic of Enlightenment* (1944). Here they proposed a theory of the "culture industry," which they saw as dominating and impoverishing modern everyday life in every possible way. In this view, "all mass culture is identical" and serves to deceive the masses.[9] As if to illustrate Adorno and Horkheimer's thesis, Disney became increasingly politicized during the cold war, as numerous commentators have pointed out. By the 1950s and 1960s, Donald Duck cartoons were being used, without any great subtlety, to promote US interests in South-East Asia and Latin America.[10] By the time the skeptical postmodern French philosopher Jean Baudrillard came to assess the United States via Southern California around 1975, he saw Disneyland as the epitome of the "desert of the real" that the superpower had become. The function of Disneyland was simply "to conceal the fact that it is the 'real' country, of all 'real' America, which is Disneyland."[11]

American art critics took a similar but reversed route in hailing, without irony, the "triumph of American painting" in the postwar decades.[12] That is to say, rather than condemning all American culture as kitsch, they praised new American art as the victorious form of high culture, just as the nation had prevailed in war. During the war, American artists expressed a globalized idealism. In a 1943 manifesto that was given wide publicity by the *New York Times* and other media, the artists Adolph Gottlieb, Barnett Newman, and Mark Rothko declared that henceforth American art must work on a "truly global plane." This art was to be both "tragic and timeless. This is why we profess spiritual kinship with both primitives and archaic art."[13] This stance, which detached the avant-garde from contemporary history and asserted the timeless importance of the artist's individual sensibility, did not yet command universal assent. For example, in a 1946 feature in *Fortune* magazine, a photograph of the atomic bomb test at Bikini atoll was paired with an abstract painting by Ralston Crawford. In this light, one can compare Jackson Pollock's postwar works such as *Sounds in the Grass: Shimmering Substance* (1946), a violently rendered, thickly-worked abstract painting that preceded Pollock's drip paintings, to the devastation wrought by the atomic bomb.[14]

Critically, though, the rise of Soviet domination in Eastern Europe produced a rightward drift in many intellectuals, resulting in an increased desire to remove high culture from the incursions of the political. By 1948, in an essay published in the now patriotic *Partisan Review*, Greenberg argued that "the main premises of Western art have at last migrated to the United States, along with the center of gravity of industrial production and political power."[15] The original stance against popular culture was now combined with a sense of American manifest destiny to create a package the US government was happy to support, albeit covertly. As scholars such as Serge Guilbaut have pointed out, while American senators thundered on about abstract art as communism, the CIA and other agencies were quietly supporting exhibitions, magazines, and other outlets for the new American art as evidence of the freedom offered by the United States.

The Factory

The dominance of abstract expressionism for almost two decades after WWII meant that the tensions implicit in the 1930s responses to popular culture were not played out in American art until the 1960s. Although Benjamin had written "any person today can lay claim to being filmed" (B 114) in 1935, it was not until Andy Warhol created his famous Factory in the 1960s that an artist began to explore fully the possibilities inherent in cinematic reproducibility.[16] In his now-clichéd reproductions of commercial art, like the Campbell's Soup Cans and Brillo boxes, or the serial images of stars like Marilyn Monroe and Elvis Presley, Warhol expanded the optical unconscious. Seeing the icons of modern consumerism repeated over and again rendered the constant reproduction of the mechanical era into a visible technique. Consequently, Warhol saw himself as a machine, whose products were to be reproduced as simply as possible: "The reason I'm painting this way is because I want to be a machine, Whatever I do, and do machine-like, is because it is what I want to do."[17] Warhol saw that inherent in the development of consumer culture was a new form of desire that led its subjects, not content with having access to the products of the machine age, to want to *be* a machine. One of the reasons his work seems so elusive and resistant to criticism is the tension that it keeps in play between automatic machine reproduction (mimicked in his work by the rather labor intensive silk-screen method), and the ideologies of modernist art production that extolled the creative individual. This tension frustrates attempts to dismiss the work as nothing but copies.

The silk-screened series, with their grids of almost identical imagery, call to mind the frames of a film and, indeed, Warhol came to work more and more in film as the 1960s progressed. Like Benjamin, he realized that one of the key features of film was the sense that, for the actor, performing for film was always a test before a set of apparatuses rather than a performance for an audience. As Benjamin had argued: "Film makes test performances capable of being exhibited, by turning that ability itself into a test" (B 111). Warhol followed the logic of film as test performance by wanting all his visitors to the Factory to undergo a "screen test." But he refused to fulfill that logic by making "properly" edited films from the footage he shot.

Indeed, Warhol's most striking film work consists precisely of unedited footage, such as *Empire* (1964), his eight-hour film of the Empire State Building in New York City, or *Sleep* (1963), a documentation of a person asleep. As Peter Wollen has noted, "Warhol's reluctance to edit was a constant in all his activities," from his obsessive photography of his everyday life, to his storage of all his personal effects, and the publication of unedited transcripts in his magazine *Interview*.[18] By refusing the edit, or montage, Warhol pushed the element of distraction in contemporary popular culture to its furthest extent. That is to say, by refusing to direct the attention of the viewer through the use of effects, even the most basic effect of editing out unwanted material, Warhol maximized the possibility that the viewer would become distracted. Rather than seeking to absorb the viewer into the work of art, Warhol wanted his work to be absorbed into the audience. In combining the elements of play and ritual, Warhol turned the tension between "art" and "popular culture" into a performance of desire.[19]

Furthermore, the evidently queer nature of that desire set a new set of questions in motion that could not be contained by the Marxist frameworks deployed in debates of the 1930s, nor by the formalist models dominant in art discourse from the 1940s into the 1960s. Warhol's sexuality was well known in the narrow circles of the art world and was celebrated in his semi-private scrapbooks like the "Cock Book." In series like those celebrating Jackie Kennedy-Onassis or Marilyn Monroe, the diva (a camp figure adored within certain gay circles) was celebrated, while other works like *Diamond Dust Shoes* (1980) pushed queerness into public view as camp.[20]

For Fredric Jameson, postmodern works, "which foreground the commodity fetishism of a transition to late capital, ought to be powerful and critical political statements." Because he felt that work like Warhol's failed to provide such a statement, Jameson went on to decry postmodernism as an expression of the cultural logic of late capital rather than a critique of it.[21] Yet there are two assumptions at work here that reduce the force of this charge. First, following Ernest Mandel's supplement to Marx's *Capital*, one could argue that Jameson's presumption that the 1970s marked the transition to "late capital" assumes its imminent decease or decline. Without getting too involved in the complex debates of Marxist economic theory, suffice it to say that it is no longer self-evident that the 1970s were a moment of "late capital"; certainly, capitalism is hardly in retreat today in the early twenty-first century. Rather as Antonio Negri and Michael Hardt have argued, a new "global society of control" has emerged that places capital on a newly secure footing, just as imperialism rescued the contradictions of nineteenth-century industrial capital.[22]

Jameson's second assumption, of normative subjectivity, is based on his inability to register Warhol's queerness. While there is an element of commodity fetishism at work in Warhol's silk-screen, there is also an implication of sexual fetishism that was clear to his subcultural audience. As artist Deborah Kass has pointed out: "He was the first big queer-boy artist and he really made these pictures of the inside of his queer brain, from the women's shoes on."[23] What has often been described coyly as irony in the art historical literature is better seen as a connotation of queer that challenged the then aggressively heteronormative public face of the American art world.

Warhol's meshing of the tropes and methods of high and low culture took another step away from the dialectical dramas of classic Marxist theory in that he made visible the racialization embedded within the logic of high *and* low culture, as well as within the debates distinguishing the two. His series *Race Riot* (1964) depicted police violence against civil rights demonstrators in the South, which can be seen as parodying the then standard description of police-on-black violence as a "race riot." In reproducing the *Electric Chair*, Warhol not only recalled the American predilection for state violence but its disproportionate use against African Americans. In these instances, repetition was necessary to call attention to the commonplace of racialized state violence that was persistently overlooked in the white art world of the period.

This challenge was personified in his collaboration with the graffiti artist Jean-Michel Basquiat. Born in Brooklyn in 1960, the son of Haitian and Puerto Rican parents, Basquiat rose to fame in the 1980s art world, having made a name as a "street" graffiti artist, using the tag SAMO, or Same Old Shit.[24] This reputation led him to work in well-known hip-hop nightclubs of the period and to his adoption by the still largely white art scene. In his work with Warhol, there is a good deal of knowing play on the tension between a white art world, still understanding African culture as the "primitive," and the ironic appropriations practiced by both Warhol and Basquiat. It was in 1984, for example, that the Museum of Modern Art staged its now notorious show *Primitivism and Twentieth-Century Art*, which placed African objects next to modernist art works, ascribing to them no other role than as source material for Western artists.

In their collaboration *Arm and Hammer II* (1985), Basquiat and Warhol restaged such a conjunction to very different effect. On the right-hand side of the canvas, Warhol silk-screened his version of the Arm and Hammer logo from cleaning products and baking soda. On the left, Basquiat painted a revised version from his diasporic perspective, placing a penny at the heart of the logo. Instead of the usual all but anonymous figure of a dead president, Basquiat painted an African or African American with a saxophone coming out of his mouth. The word "commemeritive," spelt as here and struck out, hovers over the coin, as if to suggest that in 1955 (the date on the coin) a commemorative penny for African Americans had been considered and rejected. In Warhol's appropriation of the Arm and Hammer logo, there is apparently less to see. By calling attention to the otherwise overlooked commercial image, Warhol's work highlights the nature of whiteness in American society as "unmarked," always counterposed with the "marked" African American minority.

In the context set out here, *Arm and Hammer* has a further tension within it. The Armand Hammer logo, showing a muscular white male arm in a work shirt clutching a hammer, evokes the heroic workers of socialist realism. In the dominant American critical viewpoint, inspired by Greenberg, such work was not art but kitsch. While Warhol was by this time recognized as a leading artist, his silk-screened contribution to the piece involved less traditional artistic skills than Basquiat's painting. By subverting the conventional alignment of art with "white" and popular culture with "black," Basquiat and Warhol together succeed in showing the extent to which the "art" and "kitsch" opposition contains within it a racialized polarity.

Basquiat liked to claim that he "grew up in an American vacuum," and disavowed all knowledge of his Haitian background. But there is no American vacuum as far as race is concerned, as the response to Basquiat's work from left-wing American critics made clear. At a discussion at the Dia Arts Center in 1986, Thomas Crow claimed that the success of graffiti was "thoroughly reactionary." Going a charged step further in the discussion period, the video artist Martha Rosler concurred: "It is a symbolic representation, on center stage, of the other as tamed entertainer – it's like a minstrel show."[25]

In the American context, no remark could be more intensely charged in terms of racial difference. Contrary to Rosler's suggested alignment of Basquiat with minstrelsy, however, the minstrel performer was typically a white person in "blackface," such as the infamous white actor Al Jolson, who performed in blackface in the first talking picture, *The Jazz Singer* (1927). Examining the function of this mode of performance, Michael Rogin has shown that "racial masquerade . . . moved settlers and ethnics into the melting pot by keeping racial groups out."[26] That is to say, for groups such as Irish, Italian, and Jewish immigrants coming to America minstrelsy could function as a rite of passage in which ethnic minority status could be exchanged for "whiteness" at the expense of subscribing to the foundational American drama of racial distinction between "whites" and "blacks."

Like Greenberg's reference to the "primitive" influence at the heart of avant-garde art in 1939, Rosler's comment thus calls attention to the extent to which the viability of elite art practice was premised on an exchange of energy with a continuingly "authentic" black popular culture. Basquiat's presumed racial cross-dressing was, then, not a pretense of blackness but a pretense of whiteness through his production of gallery-exhibited art. This border crossing was felt to challenge the primary distinction of American art as being not-kitsch. This conjunction of terms suggests that the negative response to graffiti art was not caused in any way by personal racism but by a strong sense that the avant-garde tradition of modernism was collapsing.

Speaking in the same space five years later, Stuart Hall elaborated on the factors that made black popular culture seem so important in the late 1980s. Highlighting the emergence of the United States as the dominant world power following the fall of the Berlin Wall in 1989, Hall saw this moment as marking "both a displacement and a hegemonic shift in the *definition* of culture – a movement from high culture to American mainstream popular culture and its mass-cultural, image-mediated technological forms." The government sponsorship of high culture as an index of political freedom, which had been so significant in the cold war, gave way to the "culture wars" in which the content of art and popular culture was subjected to intense scrutiny by newly assertive religious conservatives. For Hall, these controversies were a consequence of the fact that "American mainstream popular culture has always involved certain traditions that could only be attributed to black cultural vernacular traditions."[27]

Such traditions include icons of American popular culture that had too overt a racialized charge to be included in the work of white artists, such as "Aunt Jemima." Aunt Jemima is a logo representing a middle-aged African American woman of generous proportions wearing a headscarf, which, as Michael Harris has argued, has "become the ultimate symbol and personification of the black cook, servant and mammy."[28] Harris describes how Jemima originated as a character in minstrel shows, derived from an older slave song, calling for a promised but deferred freedom. As performed by the nineteenth-century African American minstrel Billy Kersands, the Jemima character also danced the cakewalk, a parody of white manners. But when Charles L. Rutt, owner of the Pearl Milling Company, saw Kersands' show in 1889, he missed the parody and saw only a suitable emblem of servitude for his pancake mix. Aunt Jemima became the icon of the devoted African American servant, with a fictional biography ascribing to her a happy life on a Southern slave plantation, where she defended her owner against Union troops in the Civil War.

It was in this guise that Aunt Jemima entered American mass culture as "the most famous colored woman in the world," to quote the advertising of the time, and in turn became a key subject for African American artists like Jeff Donaldson, Joe Overstreet, Murray de Pillars, Betye Saar, and Jon Lockard in the pop period. Many of these images showed Jemima giving up her servile ways to join the revolution, as in Overstreet's *New Jemima* (1964), a response to the ongoing violence against civil rights protestors. Here Jemima's trademark smile has become a grin and her pancake iron is transformed into a machine gun, blazing among a shower of pancakes. Perhaps the best known of these works has been Betye Saar's 1972 mixed-media piece, *The Liberation of Aunt Jemima*. Against a Warhol-like repetition of the Aunt Jemima figure, an oversized and intensely-caricatured Jemima figure stands with a broom in one hand and a rifle in the other. This figure frames yet another image, where a notepad might have been placed in one of the many kitsch Jemima figures that were mass produced. This image shows a light-skinned Jemima, holding a still lighter infant, a reminder of the foundational American drama of miscegenation, often forced and even more often denied. Here that scene, so familiar from nineteenth-century photographs, is disrupted by a black power salute, for Saar said that she wanted to take the stereotype "that classifies all black women and make her into one of the leaders of the revolution."[29] Seen against such imagery, Warhol's work looks more intentionally "artistic" and less radical than it is often described in art historical literature.

In 1991, Stuart Hall argued that, despite such tensions, the situation was more optimistic in that a fundamental challenge to the hierarchy of popular and elite cultures had been inaugurated as a consequence of the gains made by the identity-based movements in force since the 1960s. By the later 1990s, black popular culture was in fact enjoying what Herman Gray has called a "hypervisibility," such that it could now be said to have become the dominant vernacular culture of the United States.[30] At the same time, Hall's optimism has to be mitigated by the fact that corporations and other institutions have become remarkably attuned to the language and theory of multiculturalism such that black popular culture is now extensively integrated into the structures of market capitalism. Search on the website of technology-oriented Carnegie Mellon University for multiculturalism, to take a random example, and the Heinz School of Management – rather than intellectual content from the faculties of humanities or social sciences – is the first reference to come up.

In 2003, the exhibition *Only Skin Deep* at New York's International Center for Photography aimed, according to curator Coco Fusco, to investigate "how racial imagery in photography of many kinds has shaped understanding of what Americanness is and who Americans are."[31] The exhibition placed works by pioneers of photography like Thomas Eakins and Eadweard Muybridge alongside popular photographs, postcards, and snapshots, and modern and contemporary art photographs, by artists ranging from Edward Steichen and Man Ray to Cindy Sherman. The curators insisted on the place of race and racialization in photography of all kinds, refusing the choice to create an alternative canon of minority artists or to dismiss race altogether. Far from being seen as radical, the show was supported by both the National Endowment for the Humanities and Altria, an umbrella multinational corporation that includes the tobacco giant Phillip Morris. Does this mean, as some have suggested, that visual culture – including that contextualized in an anti-racist framework – is now simply the tool of global capital? Certainly, at the very least, such a situation points to the fact that the dialectical opposition of art and popular culture has become outdated.

In their wide-ranging theory of globalization as marking a distinctively new phase in human affairs that they call "Empire," Antonio Negri and Michael Hardt have forcefully argued for the latter case. In fact, they go further and suggest that it was the colonial era of the nineteenth century that gave history the appearance of being dialectical (that is to say, as shaped by a clash of opposites that would be resolved into a new synthesis of both). "Reality," they write, "is not dialectical. Colonialism is." By this they mean that it is the goal of colonial practice to turn the encounter between two peoples into a dialectic of the colonizer as the Self and the colonized as the Other. The Other is in every way the opposite to the Self, justifying the power of colonialism as a civilizing mission. But, they continue, "precisely because the difference of the Other is absolute, it can be inverted in a second moment as the foundation of Self. . . . What first appears strange, foreign, and distant thus turns out to be very close and intimate."[32] What is known as identity, whether of the colonizer or colonized, was produced in the dialectical tension between otherness and intimacy.

To the extent that American popular culture was the expression of a black vernacular culture, it existed in tension with both white mass culture and elite culture. The apparent collapse of these distinctions in the past decade is indicative not of the triumph of one side or the other but of the collapse of the framework used to support them. In the new phase of global capitalism, difference can be valorized by multinational corporations in advanced societies even as their wealth is derived from subsistence labor in underdeveloped nations, for, as Hardt and Negri have put it, "the global politics of difference established by the world market is defined not by free play and equality, but by the imposition of new hierarchies."[33] The old play of art and popular culture has been replaced by a new global dynamic of culture, which cannot be traced from the old classics.

Culture and Decolonization

The challenge that now confronts artists, curators, and critics is to make sense of a global history of the modern and modernity without relying on the overlapping binary distinctions between art and popular culture, the modern and the primitive, masculine and feminine, or black and white. One of the most remarkable attempts to engage with this problem has been the curatorial entrepreneurship of Okwui Enwezor. Enwezor was head curator for the traveling exhibition *The Short Century: Independence and Liberation Movements in Africa 1945–1994* (2001–2). Rightly seeing decolonization as one of the primary events of the twentieth century, on a par with the abolition of slavery in the nineteenth century, Enwezor proposed the central importance of "the construction of African modernity in the twentieth century[, which] is inextricably bound to the defense and legitimation of all and every sphere of African thought and life."[34]

Enwezor's exhibition was divided into seven sections – art, photography, film, architecture, graphics, theater, and literature – without overly insisting on the boundaries between categories. For African decolonization movements the exhibition advanced an open theory of culture that was not sub-divided into "art" and "popular culture," as can be seen in the documents collected in the catalog for *The Short Century*. For example, the Guinean Sékou Touré argued in 1959 that "since culture is not an entity or phenomenon separate or separable from a people . . . the culture of a people is of necessity determined by its material and moral conditions. *Man and his milieu make up a whole.*"[35] It might seem to some readers that Touré was arguing for an anthropological view of culture, but Africans, for so long the objects of anthropology, were far from proposing a simple reversal. In a 1965 debate between the French anthropological filmmaker Jean Rouch and the Senegalese director Ousmane Sembène, also collected in *The Short Century*, this topic was central. Sembène refused Rouch's thesis that ethnology depended on the "eye of the stranger," capable of seeing what the insider cannot, arguing that "in the domain of cinema, it is not enough to see, one must analyze. I am interested in what is before and after that which we see." When pushed by Rouch to explain his dislike for ethnography, Sembène explained that "what I hold against you and the Africanists is that you look at us as if we were insects."[36] That is to say, the ethnographic viewpoint is interested in classifying, enumerating and describing, whereas cultural decolonization depended on analytic viewing.

Rather than seeing Africa as being defined by its struggles with the colonizers, one can also see here the emergence of a debate on the passage to global culture. Irit Rogoff has described how visiting *The Short Century* made her aware of the impetus to Western radical movements of the 1960s created by African decolonization, especially the Algerian liberation struggle. In turn, Edward Said has suggested that Western intellectuals were disposed to accept the decentering theses of poststructuralism because of their opposition to the war in Vietnam.[37] Both Rogoff and Said are pointing to the fact that cultural changes thought to be "Western" were actually part of a global network of decolonization. One example could be seen at *The Short Century*. Postmodern irony and photographic appropriation have long been taken as the signature of a New York-based art practice of the late 1970s and 1980s. In 1977, Samuel Fosso began taking stylized self-portraits in Bangui, Central African Republic. In one shot, Fosso stands in front of a curtain that seems to be drawn across a stage (Figure 24.2). Lights are visible, serving both to enhance the air of theatricality and to make the process of staging the photograph transparent. Dressed in high-waisted bell-bottom trousers, a trucker hat perched precariously on top of his "Afro" hairstyle, and extravagant shades, Fosso looks ready to participate in the funk reviews of George Clinton or Funkadelic. But Fosso makes us aware of our inability to analyze the image in terms of Sembène's "before and after," performing the familiar disruption of authority that has come to be associated with the white American artist Cindy Sherman.

Sherman's *Untitled Film Stills* (1977–80) represented the artist in a series of different poses, locations, and costumes, each of which seems to come from a film, but one that can only remain unknown to the viewer. At the heart of this project was, as art critic Craig Owens remarked, "an acting out of the psychoanalytic notion of femininity as masquerade."[38] By the same token, Fosso's work puts into play the complex role of decolonized African masculinity, haunted by the ghosts of sexualized racial domination. Looking back to Sherman to see if we can find an equivalent questioning of race, we would need to turn to her little-known early series *Untitled (Bus Riders)* (1976). Here Sherman posed as black women in a blackface that Lauri Firstenberg has called "flagrantly unconvincing."[39] But if the solution was weak, the question was the right one. Sherman realized that a full exploration of the role of the feminine in popular culture would also have to address its racialized aspects.

For all the power of Fosso and Sherman's work, it must be said that photography in particular and art in general have not been transformed by what was then called "the pictures generation." At a political level, the utopian idealism of pan-African decolonization gave way to the realpolitik of individual nation-states, caught up in the global game of the cold war. With the collapse of the Soviet Union, global capital has been able to reassert itself in very forceful fashion under the political leadership of the United States. In the case of visual culture, the consequence has been the emergence of a globalized "art world." Composed of a series of annual or biennial exhibitions and a number of international art magazines, featuring a broadly similar cast of global artists, the art world has its own vocabulary, structures, and finances. Anchored by such

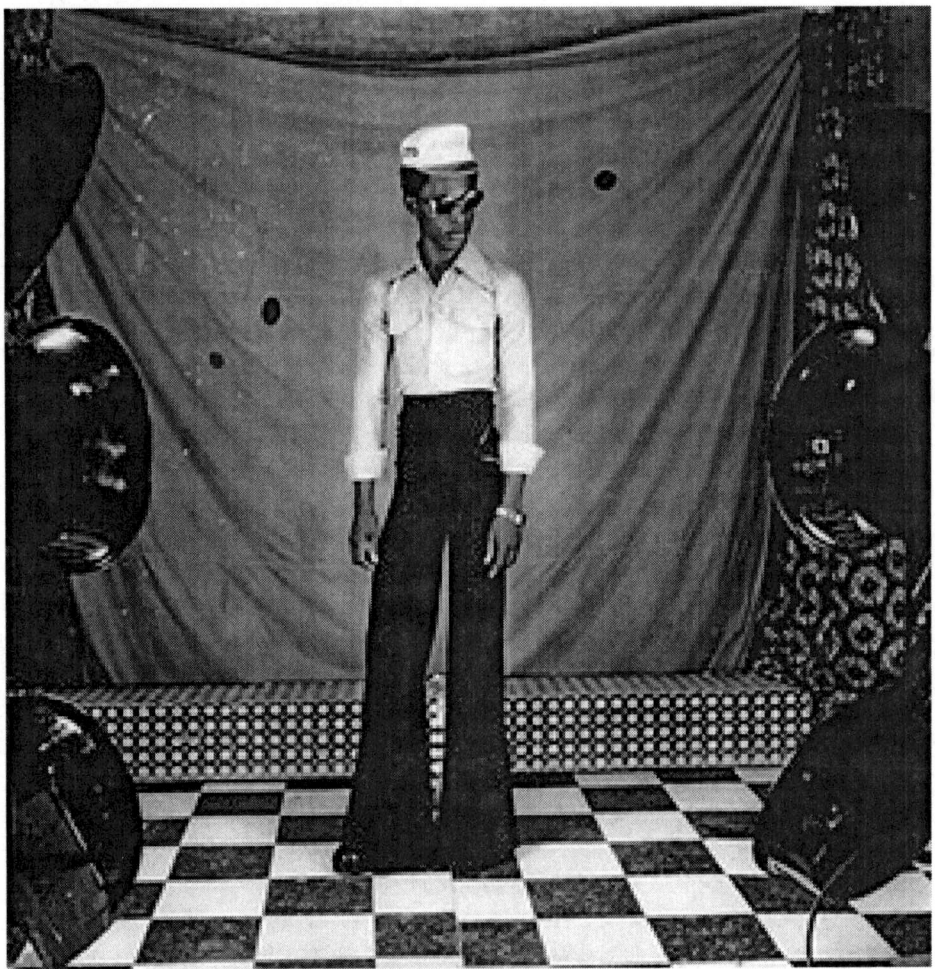

FIGURE 24.2   Samuel Fosso, *Untitled*, 1977. Courtesy of the artist

institutions as the Venice Biennale, Documenta (held every five years in Kassel, Germany), the Whitney Biennial in New York, and magazines such as *Flash Art*, *Artforum*, and *Parkett*, the art world is exhaustive and exhausting. It perceives itself as a space of contestation to global capital, while being almost completely an expression of that capital and its free flow into immaterial labor. For if it was the project of the avant-gardes to find a way of moving from the inside of bourgeois society to an outside vantage point from which a critique against the values of this society could be mounted, there is, in Hardt and Negri's view, no longer such an "outside" view to be had.[40] The aesthetic project of modernism – to act as a moral counterpoint to mass culture – has collapsed, for better or worse, such that art works are now promoted through this globalized niche market as luxury commodities (in this sense, as a kind of specialized mass culture). It is surely the task of those making art, writing about it and going to experience it to come up with a better way to rekindle the emancipatory potential of the work of art.

Notes

1 Hall (1981), 233.
2 Greenberg (1939), 21–33; hereafter cited in the text as G.
3 See Clark (1999).
4 I use the term "America" to refer to the United States.
5 Hall (1981), 240.
6 Benjamin, "Mickey Mouse," (1931) in (1999), 545.
7 This essay is better known under its first translated title "The Work of Art in the Age of Mechanical Reproduction." I am citing here the second version of the essay, before it was revised under the astringent influence of Theodor Adorno. Benjamin, "The Work of Art in the Age of its Technological Reproducibility," in (2002), 101–33. Further citations in the text as B.
8 I prefer to use the literal translation rather than the generic "field of action" offered in the Harvard translations. B 116.
9 Adorno and Horkheimer (1973), 24.
10 Dorfman and Mattelart (1975) and Kunzle (1990).
11 Baudrillard (1984), 262.
12 Sandler (1976).
13 Quoted by Guilbaut (1983), 76.
14 Ibid., 96.
15 Ibid., 172.
16 See Jones (1996).
17 Quoted by Wollen (1993), 165.
18 Ibid., 166.
19 Richard Schechner has suggested that performance is the product of the intersection of ritual and play (2001).
20 See Richard Dellamora, "Absent Bodies/Absent Subjects: The Political Unconscious of Postmodernism," in Horne and Lewis, eds. (1996), 28–47.
21 Jameson (1991).
22 Hardt and Negri (2000), 325–50.
23 Quoted by Wollen (1993), 166.
24 For further details on Basquiat, see Mirzoeff (1995), 162–90, and Muñoz (1999), 37–56.
25 Cited in Mirzoeff (1995), 165–7.
26 Rogin (1996), 12.
27 Hall (1992), 21–2.
28 Harris (2003), 84. See 84–124 for a full account of Aunt Jemima from which the following discussion is derived.
29 Ibid., 117.
30 Gray (1995).

31 Fusco and Wallis (2003), 26.
32 Hardt and Negri (2000), 127, 128.
33 Ibid., 101.
34 Enwezor (2001), 13
35 Sékou Touré, "The Political Leader as Representative of his Culture" (1962), repr. in Enwezor (2001), 369.
36 "A Historic Confrontation Between Jean Rouche and Ousmane Sembène, 'You Look at Us as if We Were Insects'" (1965). Repr. in Enwezor (2001), 440–1.
37 Rogoff (2002), 69 and Said (2004), 12–13.
38 Owens (1992), 183.
39 Firstenberg, "Autonomy and the Archive in America: Reexamining the Intersection of Photography and Stereotype," in Fusco (2003), 327. A full history of female blackface remains to be written but would include Eleanor Antin and Adrian Piper.
40 Hardt and Negri (2000), 128.

References

Adorno, Theodor, and Max Horkheimer (1973). *Dialectic of Enlightenment*, trans. John Cumming. London: Allen Lane

Baudrillard, Jean (1984). *Selected Writings*, ed. Mark Poster. London: Polity Press.

Benjamin, Walter (1999). *Selected Writings, Vol. 2 1927–34*, ed. Michael W. Jennings et al. Cambridge, MA: Harvard University Press.

—— (2002). *Walter Benjamin: Selected Writings Vol. 3 1935–1938*, ed. Howard Eiland and Michael W. Jennings. Cambridge, MA: Harvard University Press.

Clark, T. J. (1999). *Farewell to an Idea*. New Haven: Yale University Press.

Dorfman, Ariel, and Armand Mattelart (1975). *How to Read Donald Duck: Imperialist Ideology in the Disney Comic*. New York: International General.

Enwezor, Okwui, ed. (2001). *The Short Century: Independence and Liberation Movements in Africa 1945–1994*. London: Prestel.

Frascina, Francis (1985). *Pollock and After: The Critical Debate*. London: Harper and Row.

Fusco, Coco, and Brian Wallis, eds. (2003). *Only Skin Deep: Changing Visions of the American Self*. New York: Abrams.

Gray, Herman (1995). *Watching Race: Television and the Struggle for Blackness*. Minneapolis: University of Minnesota Press.

Greenberg, Clement (1939). "Avant-Garde and Kitsch." In Frascina (1985).

Guilbaut, Serge (1983). *How New York Stole the Idea of Modern Art: Abstract Expressionism, Freedom and the Cold War*, trans. Arthur Goldhammer. Chicago: University of Chicago Press.

Hall, Stuart (1981). "Notes on Deconstructing 'the Popular'." In *People's History and Socialist Theory*, ed. Raphael Samuel. London: Routledge and Kegan Paul.

—— (1992). "What is this 'Black' in Black Popular Culture." In *Black Popular Culture*, ed. Gina Dent. Seattle: Bay Press.

Hardt, Michael, and Antonio Negri (2000). *Empire*. Cambridge, MA: Harvard University Press.

Harris, Michael D. (2003). *Colored Pictures: Race and Visual Representation*. Chapel Hill, NC: University of North Carolina Press.

Horne, Peter, and Reina Lewis, eds. (1996). *Outlooks: Lesbian and Gay Sexualities and Visual Culture.* London: Routledge.

Jameson, Fredric (1991). *Postmodernism, Or, The Cultural Logic of Late Capitalism* Durham, NC: Duke University Press.

Jones, Caroline (1996). *Machine in the Studio: Constructing the Postwar American Artist.* Chicago: University of Chicago Press.

Kunzle, David (1990). "Dispossession by Ducks: The Imperialist Treasure Hunt in South-East Asia." *Art Journal,* Summer:159–65.

Mirzoeff, Nicholas (1995). *Bodyscape: Art, Modernity and the Ideal Figure.* London: Routledge.

Muñoz, José Esteban (1999). *Disidentifications: Queers of Color and the Performance of Politics.* Minneapolis: University of Minnesota Press.

Owens, Craig (1992). *Beyond Recognition: Representation, Power and Culture.* Berkeley: University of California Press.

Rogin, Michael (1996). *Blackface, White Noise: Jewish Immigrants in the Hollywood Melting Pot.* Berkeley: University of California Press.

Rogoff, Irit (2002). "Hit and Run – Museums and Cultural Difference." *Art Journal,* vol. 61, no. 3, Fall:63–73.

Said, Edward (2004). *Humanism and Democratic Criticism.* New York: Columbia University Press.

Sandler, Irving (1976). *The Triumph of American Painting.* New York: Harper and Row.

Schechner, Richard (2001). *Performance Studies: An Introduction.* London: Routledge.

Wollen, Peter (1993). *Raiding the Icebox: Reflections on Twentieth-Century Culture.* London: Verso.

25

Image + Text: Reconsidering Photography in Contemporary Art

Liz Kotz

Nothing more than snapshots

In 1969, the artist Douglas Huebler famously asserted: "I use the camera as a 'dumb' copying device that only serves to document whatever phenomena appears before it through the conditions set by a system. No 'aesthetic' choices are possible."[1] Likewise, Ed Ruscha, discussing the images in his 1960s photobooks, disclaimed any relation to art photography, insisting that "they are technical data like industrial photography . . . nothing more than snapshots."[2]

How do we understand the turn to photography and photographic technologies in the art of the 1960s? Viewed from the present-day art world, where monumentally-scaled color photographs seem poised to displace painting as the most visually spectacular and commercially successful artistic medium, it is hard to imagine the radical promise and threat that photography held in the 1960s. Works by artists such as Huebler, Ruscha, Vito Acconci, Victor Burgin, Dan Graham, and Bruce Nauman not only pushed photography to a new centrality in visual art practice, but also adopted its quasi-mechanistic means of image-making in order to disrupt the very position and status of the precious, unique, and hand-crafted art object. Using the camera as a simple tool for accumulating images or documenting actions, 1960s artists generated new models of photography not assimilable to existing traditions of photojournalism or art photography. While photographs were beginning to be used widely to document performances, land art, and site-based projects, it was through what came to be called "conceptual" art that the most systematic work with and on photography occurred, as artists like Huebler and Burgin adopted it as a means to move beyond the object to work directly on representation and cultural sign systems.

Embracing the flat look of amateur, snapshot, and industrial photography, "conceptual" uses of photography implicitly posed themselves against the canon of modernist "art photography" that was being institutionally codified at the same moment. While influential curators such as the Museum of Modern Art's John Szarkowski argued for the technical virtuosity and artistic originality of a select lineage of photographs, understood as the unique expressions of a select group of individual authors, 1960s artists embraced the photographic document as a straightforward, seemingly "neutral" means of presenting information, a "'dumb' copying device" that could presumably be employed by anybody. As critic John Roberts observes, in opposition to "the concurrent development of photographic modernism under the aegis of Szarkowski . . . conceptual art openly embraced photography's functional and anti-aesthetic character, whereas Modernism actively suppressed this through aestheticism"[3] – even if, in most cases, this functional "look" would strategically be severed from any actual social or pedagogical function. With the exception of Dan Graham's magazine works, Roberts notes, "the opening period of conceptual art embraces the culturally disruptive function of photographic reportage only to withdraw it from the social world."[4]

While the self-referential and self-critical aims of much 1960s art would initially preclude direct depiction of political events and issues, photography would nonetheless offer a means to re-engage with the social and cultural upheaval of the 1960s – not only through the referentiality that photographic images inevitably entail, but also through the ways in which photography provided a tool to investigate the worlds of image culture and the mass media. The photographer and critic Victor Burgin recalls his turn to photography as growing directly out of his disenchantment with the perceived isolation of art: "Photography offered a window on the world . . . a window through which you could punch a hole in the gallery wall and bring into the gallery issues that had previously been considered not proper within the gallery. . . . I think it's hard to imagine how shocking it was to see writing and photographs on gallery walls in the late sixties."[5]

Burgin's reference to writing here is not incidental. Indeed, it was this linking of photography to language that marks the crucial innovation of conceptual art. In countless late 1960s and early 1970s "conceptual art" projects, photography appears with language as a kind of dyad: text and image (a perennial pairing that later resurfaced in so much "postmodern" art of the 1980s). This pairing, of course, is by no means new or unprecedented. Since the rise of the illustrated press in the early twentieth century, the fusion of words and photographic images has been among the most basic elements of modern visual culture. In almost all public uses of photography – in printed matter, pages of books or magazines, posters, publicity, even cinema – photographic images appear with language, as caption, headline, surrounding text, intertitle, or spoken voiceover or dialogue. Yet this relation remained repressed in modernist photography (with the exception of photomontage-based work) and ignored in critical and theoretical models that sought to understand the "purely visual" world of images as operating according to fundamentally different laws from those governing linguistic materials.

Against such approaches, Burgin would later argue, "[a]lthough photography is a 'visual medium,' it is not a 'purely visual' medium . . . even the uncaptioned 'art' photograph, framed and isolated on the gallery wall is invaded by language in the very moment it is looked at: in memory, in association, snatches of words and images continually intermingle and exchange one for the other."[6] And during the 1960s, critics such as Roland Barthes and Umberto Eco would propose that photographs be read as discursive and rhetorical, as forms of coded "messages" that could be analyzed according to quasi-linguistic models. In Barthes' analysis, not only does language work to attach cultural "connotations" to "denotational" photographic images, but the repetition, sequencing, and ordering of images creates meaning contextually and contiguously, in ways somewhat analogous to the syntactic arrangements of words.[7]

This inter-relation between language and the photograph is central to 1960s art and to many of the theoretical models that emerged at the time. Yet its complexity remains little explored. One of the paradoxes of this period is that, while in rapidly diffusing semiotic and structural models, photographic images – along with much else – came to be understood as structured "like a language," in visual art, language in many cases would be used "like photography," as if it too could serve as a neutral recording apparatus, documenting the results of a pre-existing system. Part of the enormous productivity of this period comes from artists' efforts to bring together heterogeneous and even incompatible models, translating gestural and pictorial approaches from painting, or performance or process-based approaches from sculpture, to the forms and materials of print culture. The instrumental use of photography and of language as tools for other types of projects helped dislodge them from their conventional functions, and set them into new types of relations with each other.

Perhaps more than any other artists associated with conceptual art, Douglas Huebler and Victor Burgin produced systematic and sustained bodies of work that juxtapose texts and photographic images. Through a comparison of their projects, we can trace a crucial shift from a perceptual and phenomenological analysis (emerging out of minimal sculpture) to an overtly semiotic analysis (engaging with the forms of media culture). This historical trajectory moves from the classic period of New York-based conceptualism to its reception and gradual reformulation in Britain in the 1970s, where Burgin's efforts to go "beyond conceptual art" led him and other artists to participate in more avowedly political projects of feminist critique and media activism, and to embrace the semiotic and psychoanalytic versions of "film theory" that would come to be associated with *Screen* magazine. However, to understand the stakes of this shift – and also to appreciate some of what is lost in this shift from perceptual to semiotic models – I want to set their work in context by outlining some of the conflicting imperatives evident during the formative period of "conceptual" practice.

The "Look" of Information

Around 1966–8, just before the emergence of a consciously-articulated practice of conceptual art, a number of projects implicitly interfaced with pop art by appropriating mass media forms such as advertisements, newspaper photos, and photojournalistic essays, formats which could be either transferred to another medium – as in John Baldessari's paintings[8] – or produced for actual publication, like Dan Graham's celebrated 1966 photo-essay *Homes for America*, or Robert Smithson's mock-travelogue "The Monuments of Passaic," which appeared in *Artforum* in December, 1967 (Figure 25.1).[9] Unlike the subsequent adoption of quasi-scientific formats, the pairings of photo and text in this transitional period were modeled on print media and other mass cultural forms. In contrast to Graham's laconic prose, Smithson's article, with its parody of "grand tour" motifs and ironic references to an American landscape sublime, is

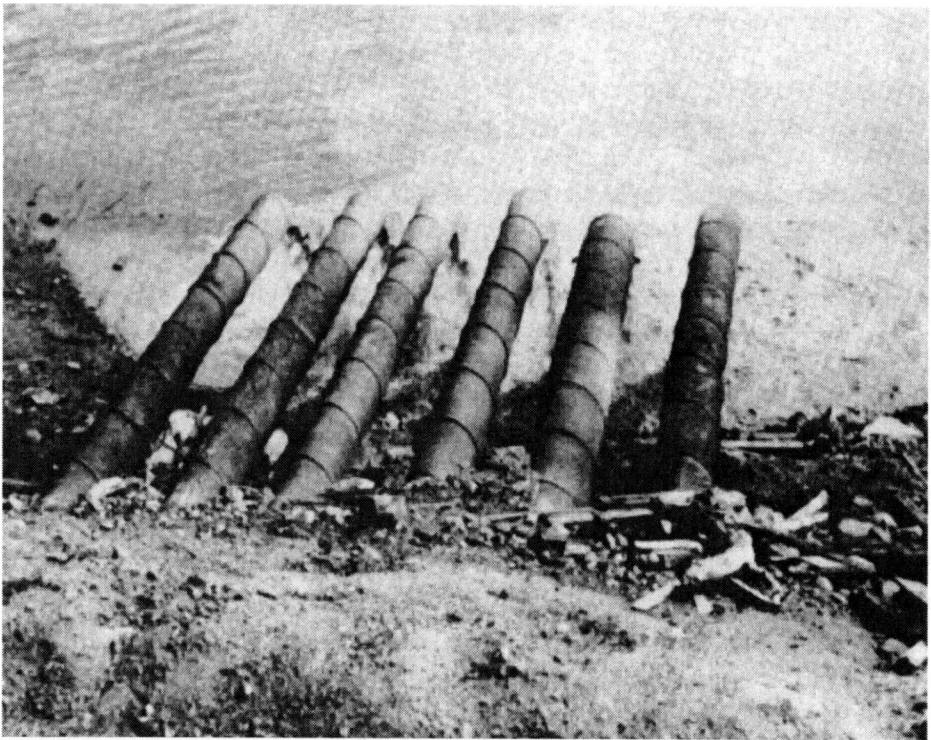

FIGURE 25.1 Robert Smithson, *Monuments of Passaic*, 1967 (detail). Art © Estate of Robert Smithson/Licensed by VAGA, New York

explicitly literary and allegorical. Yet while language tends to appear as a quotation or set of borrowed terms, emphasizing its rhetorical, persuasive, and even visual dimensions, both artists used photographs whose informal "snapshot" aesthetic implies straightforward documentation – although they do so with a tone so ironic that the artist and critic Jeff Wall sees their works as parodying the conventions of photojournalism.[10] The boundary between "pop" and "conceptual" practices is still permeable here: if the seductive visuality of Ruscha's paintings of product logos and commercial signs aligns them with pop, his 1962 book *Twenty-Six Gasoline Stations* is retroactively read as a work of proto-conceptual art, since the simple, serially ordered black and white photographs operate like a neutral presentation of information.

In subsequent, more overtly "conceptual" projects, image–text works often adopt the form of bureaucratic records and scientific documentation: from the maps, diagrams, and instructions of Douglas Huebler's *Location, Duration* and *Variable* "Pieces" and Adrian Piper's assembled documents and notations presented in three-ring binders, to the carefully-typed financial records of Hans Haacke's 1971 *Shapolsky et al. Manhattan Real Estate Holdings, A Real Time Social System* (Figure 25.2). These works suppress an overtly pop engagement with mass culture, and employ language as an apparently transparent vehicle of meaning and historical evidence; yet the very precision with which they mimic and even fetishize the visual and linguistic forms of techno-scientific culture suggests that the "look" of pure information also functions as a style, whether consciously or not – a tendency Benjamin Buchloh identified in his 1990 article by this name as conceptual art's "aesthetic of administration." Smithson's sci-fi tinged photo-essays, particularly his 1966 collaboration with Mel Bochner, *Domain of the Great Bear*, already explored the display systems of outdated science as objects of kitsch attachment, just as Bochner's 1966 *Working Drawings* exhibition presented all manner of diagrams, worksheets, and technical notations as objects of aesthetic fascination – despite the ambivalent subtitle that these were "visible things on paper not necessarily meant to be viewed as art." The striking black and white Photostatted texts of Joseph Kosuth's 1965–67 *Proto-Investigations* and *Titled (Art as Idea as Idea)* series rest uneasily on the boundary between "conceptual" uses of media and the visuality of advertising and corporate insignia – a condition Jeff Wall later critiques as presenting "a condensed image of the instrumentalized 'value free' academic disciplines characteristic of American-type universities (empiricist sociology, information theory, positivist language philosophy) in the form of 1960s high corporate or bureaucratic design."[11]

Despite this repressed entanglement in the visual forms of media culture, the systematic exploitation of both text and photography as documentation in conceptual art paradoxically aspired to the conditions of a "neutral" recording apparatus that would operate with complete "indifference" to aesthetic qualities – as Huebler's remark attests. Paradoxically, both words and images were often understood to function transparently, as if they could provide direct, unmediated access to the things they represent. This focus on the photograph's evidentiary

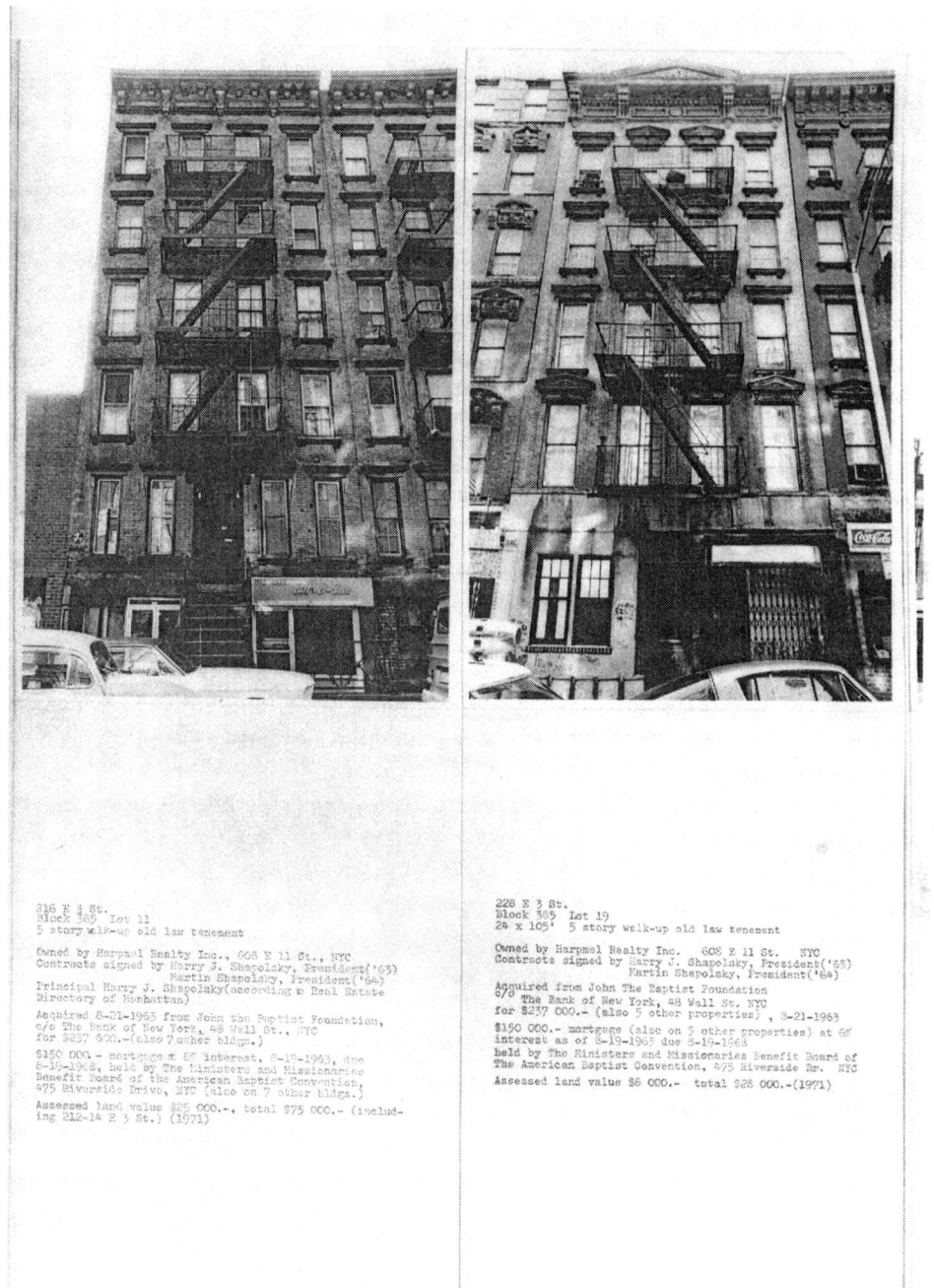

216 E 3 St.
Block 385 Lot 11
5 story walk-up old law tenement

Owned by Harpmal Realty Inc., 608 E 11 St., NYC
Contracts signed by Harry J. Shapolsky, President('63)
                   Martin Shapolsky, President('64)
Principal Harry J. Shapolsky(according to Real Estate
Directory of Manhattan)

Acquired 8-21-1963 from John the Baptist Foundation,
c/o The Bank of New York, 48 Wall St., NYC
for $237 000.-(also 7 other bldgs.)

$150 000.- mortgage at 6% interest, 8-19-1963, due
8-19-1968, held by The Ministers and Missionaries
Benefit Board of the American Baptist Convention,
475 Riverside Drive, NYC (also on 7 other bldgs.)

Assessed land value $25 000.-, total $75 000.- (including 212-14 E 3 St.) (1971)

228 E 3 St.
Block 385 Lot 19
24 x 105' 5 story walk-up old law tenement

Owned by Harpmal Realty Inc. 608 E 11 St. NYC
Contracts signed by Harry J. Shapolsky, President('63)
                   Martin Shapolsky, President('64)

Acquired from John The Baptist Foundation
c/o The Bank of New York, 48 Wall St. NYC
for $237 000.- (also 5 other properties) , 8-21-1963

$150 000.- mortgage (also on 5 other properties) at 6%
interest as of 8-19-1963 due 8-19-1968
held by The Ministers and Missionaries Benefit Board of
The American Baptist Convention, 475 Riverside Dr. NYC

Assessed land value $8 000.- total $28 000.-(1971)

FIGURE 25.2 Hans Haacke, *Shapolsky et al. Manhattan Real Estate Holdings, a Real-Time Social System as of May 1, 1971*, 1971 (detail). © 2005 Artists Rights Society (ARS), New York/VG Bild-Kunst, Bonn

status might seem to emphasize photography's difference from language; as a seemingly raw, purely denotational image, without overt symbolic, ideological, or artistic connotation, the photograph appears as a purely "indexical" sign – an uncoded trace, unlike the inherently arbitrary, figural, coded nature of the linguistic sign. However, repressing these figural dimensions, language was often used quasi-photographically, as a straightforward means of inscription and recording – as seen in the tables and lists that accompany, for instance, Vito Acconci's performance documents of the early 1970s. Yet the extent to which language becomes modeled on photography (as a form of inscription) is perhaps clearest in linguistically-based works without photographic images – Robert Morris's 1962 *Card File*, On Kawara's date paintings and *I am still alive* telegrams, Dan Graham's *Schema (March 1966)*, Hanne Darboven's obsessive journals, or Robert Barry's 1969 *Closed Gallery* piece – whose implicit reference is also to bureaucratic/scientific record-keeping (Figure 25.3). Each employs language as a means of quasi-systematic inscription or documentation, however perverse or apparently non-functional. These "indexical" uses of language structurally link it with photography, as types of signs (indices) that occur through physical trace or imprint, to adopt the terminology of C. S. Peirce's influential writings on semiotics.[12] As Rosalind Krauss argued in her 1977 essay "Notes on the Index," the widespread turn to indexical forms like photography necessitated text, since "the reduction of the conventional sign to a trace . . . then produces the need for a supplemental discourse."[13] Given the uncoded facticity of the photographic image, language *anchors* the sign, renders it readable and intelligible, as Barthes proposes in his classic 1964 analysis "The Rhetoric of Photography."

This semiotic model – the alignment of language with photography in the communicative space of the mass media – aligns these artistic projects with the models of structural analysis emerging at the time. Barthes' early 1960s essays examined photography and language through the medium of the press photograph, understood as a form of mass communications: as a "message . . . formed by a source of emission, a channel of transmission and a point of reception,"[14] produced and interpreted via different types of cultural "codes" which allow both image and text to carry complex social meanings, and be read as "meaningful." While we tend to recognize this approach as characteristic of French structural/semiotic analyses of the 1960s, we perhaps tend to forget the extent to which the underlying model of communicative function derives from American (and British) research conducted during and after the Second World War, in cryptography, cybernetics, "systems theory," "public persuasion" (i.e. propaganda), and mass communications technologies, all of which hinged on processes of "information transmission."[15] For instance, it is in the context of the spatially-distanced dissemination of messages via technologies of radio, telephone, and television, that new analytic models like "information theory" responded to the need to improve transmission of signals over lines subject to electrical interference, or "noise," by finding ways to package data more efficiently. In one sense, phonetic language is both the anchor and model for all the other "coding"

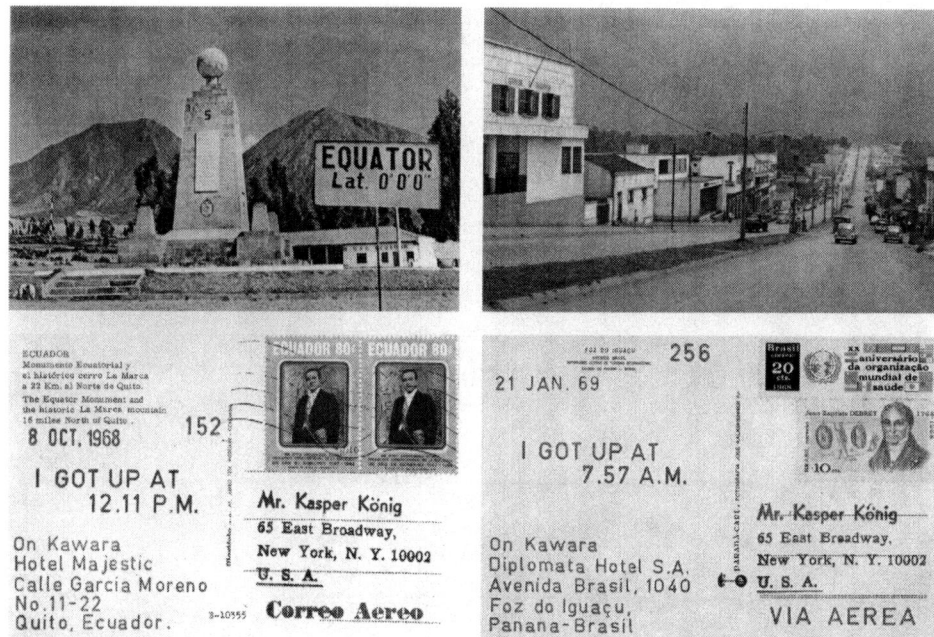

FIGURE 25.3   On Kawara, *I Got Up*, 1968 (details). Courtesy of the artist and David Zwirner Gallery, New York

operations, from television pixels to digitalization, which reduce complex information to articulable series of transmissible units. Yet the communicative capacities of language, structurally dependent on metaphor, connotation, and historical convention, increasing appear deficient in comparison to the apparently more precise, verifiable data of quantified empirical science and mechanical inscription technologies – epistemological pressures already registered in philosophical projects of phenomenology and logical positivism.[16]

As Krauss notes, just as the photograph requires a caption to function effectively as evidence or information, a certain anti-conventional use of objects or materials in art would, since Marcel Duchamp's readymades (mass-produced objects he appropriated and signed as art in the 1910s), require a linguistic supplement to be readable and intelligible.[17] Yet what is so perverse about so much late 1960s art is not the use of text as explanatory discourse, as a kind of caption, but the desire to reduce language itself to something like "the mute presence of an uncoded event"[18] – to the kind of pure facticity and presence of the photograph or indexical mark, whose ultimate message, Krauss asserts, is "I am here." Thus we see in Adrian Piper's *Here and Now* (1968) an effort to reduce the signifying properties of language to a self-enclosed, self-descriptive system: each of 64 square sheets contains a short typed text that describes its place within one of 64 gridded quadrants – e.g. "HERE: the square area in 4th

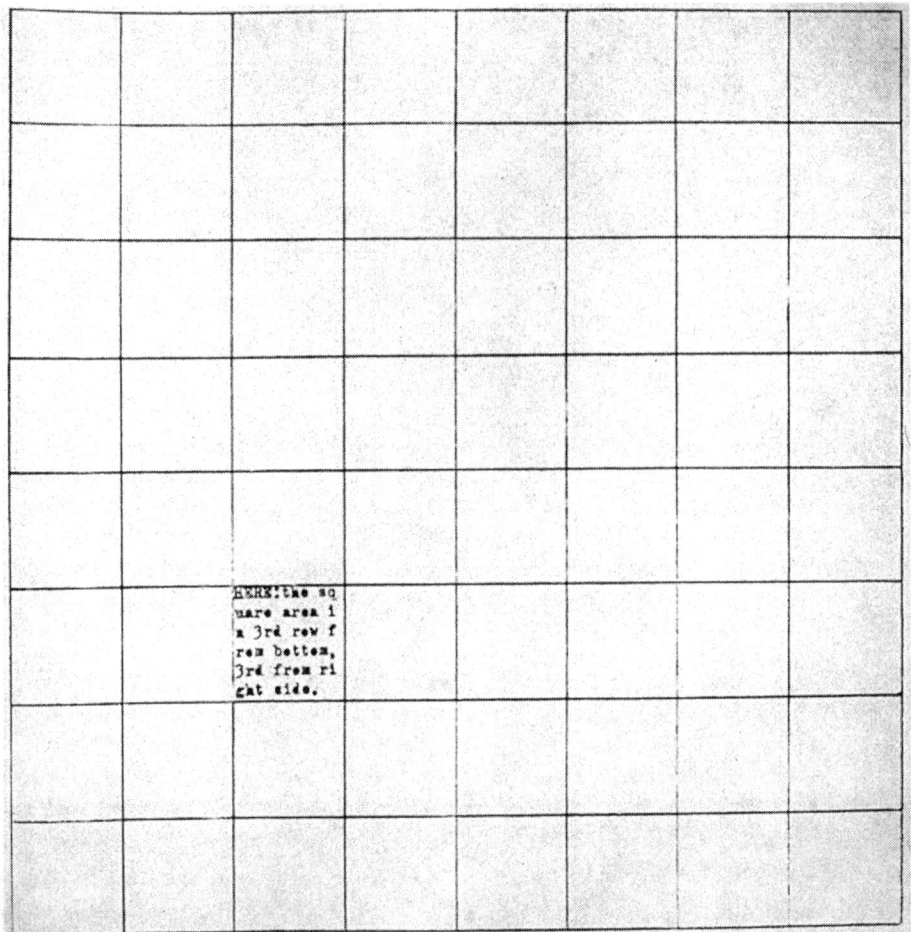

HERE:the sq
uare area i
n 3rd row f
rom bottom,
3rd from ri
ght side.

FIGURE 25.4   Adrian Piper, *Here and Now*, 1968 (detail). Courtesy of the artist

row from top, left side of page" (Figure 25.4). As Ann Goldstein suggests, "[t]he work was constructed to refer continuously to itself, and through the activity of examining the sheets, the self-referential aspect of the work remains indexed to the present as it incorporates the participation of the viewer."[19] A similar principle (without the participatory aspect) animates Kosuth's *Five Words in Blue Neon* (1965) and other tautological projects, in which language "systems" aspire to a degree of precision, certainty, and continual self-presence only possible when any external referent has been abandoned.

Such art works reflect what Stephen Melville has termed "the extraordinary epistemologism of the sixties – the general belief that art was a mode of knowledge and that its particularity as such lay in its self-reference."[20] Yet the contradictory and potentially solipsistic aspects of this self-referential pursuit of analytical rigor were quite evident at the time, as in Sol LeWitt's 1966 statement that "[t]he aim of the artist would not be to instruct the viewer but to give him information. Whether the viewer understands this information is incidental. . . . The serial artist does not attempt to produce a beautiful or mysterious object but functions merely as a clerk cataloguing the results of the premise."[21] Language is reduced to recording the results of a system, even, in works such as Darboven's, to "an arbitrary, abstract principle of pure quantification."[22] Although often couched in a rationalist discourse of communicative function and empirical "facts," these uses of language as inscription device or representational system that claim to operate "like" photography are themselves deeply conflicted and often patently non- or anti-functional, products of a modernist repression of referentiality as much as a fetishized "positivism." That this non-functional condition is not incidental, but somehow a requirement of their being "art," is suggested by the enormous institutional difficulties Haacke's "real time systems" encountered when they sought to present specific information about concrete social situations in an intelligible manner. While black and white photos of tenement apartment buildings may have been a mainstay of street photography since the 1920s, such veiled political critique was no longer acceptable to mainstream art institutions when it was accompanied by prosaic lists documenting exactly who owned the properties and how they came to be in their present condition (as in the *Shapolsky* piece).

Thus it is clear that it is not just the indexical and referential capacities of photography that would make the medium central in these disputes, but the very specific ways in which language attaches to the image to direct and specify its meaning. Yet even in Haacke's *Shapolsky* project, where the use of photography and text arguably resembles more conventional journalistic practices, there is a process-based element, documenting a system over time, that links it to projects like Huebler's. These temporal, procedural dimensions that actively involve the viewer/reader in the construction of the work, will gradually be eliminated from the more politically-oriented and message-driven works undertaken by Haacke, Burgin, and others in the 1970s. In markedly different ways, Burgin and Huebler both sought to integrate aspects of semiotic analysis into their work, using art to play with and disrupt the conventional relations between image and text; yet their efforts to intervene in the wider "image culture" vary enormously.

A Politics of Representation?

Around 1967, both Huebler and Burgin turned to photography as part of a rethinking of the object in the wake of minimal art, adopting practices in which, in Burgin's words, "aesthetic *systems* are designed, capable of generating objects, rather than individual objects themselves."[23] For many artists, photos would be crucial for documenting the results of such systems. For Huebler, this shift occurred in 1968, with his first solo "exhibition" with the dealer Seth Siegelaub – an exhibition that famously appeared only in the form of a catalogue.[24] Abandoning the minimalist-informed sculptures he had made in the mid-1960s, Huebler proclaimed: "I chose not to make objects anymore. Instead I try to create a quality of experience that locates itself 'in the world' . . . I now make work that consists of 'documents' that form the structure of an idea of system whose function is to create a conceptual 'frame' around a space/time content."[25] In effect, we can see how Huebler struggled to transfer the "phenomenological" dimensions of minimal art – focusing on the viewer's encounter with an object in a specific time and space – out of the gallery context and into "the world."

In a 1992 interview, Huebler recalled how, during his preparation for the Siegelaub show, his work was in the process of turning to forms whose vastness and ephemerality required that they could only be presented through documentation:

> When I began work on the catalogue my work was very much in a state of transition, moving back and forth between making specific objects to the fabrication of nothing that qualified as any kind of an object. The catalogue includes examples of both types, for instance, a snow sculpture piece designed to be placed where there would be heating elements installed in the ground which, when heated, would melt snow thereby forming a (minimal) sculptural configuration. That kind of thinking was but a step away from driving long nails into the earth. Or placing self sticking paper "markers" on urban surfaces, etc. Which described geometric (minimal) spaces so vast that there is no way to actually *see* the forms – even from the air.[26]

For Huebler, by expanding the scale of object experience beyond what could be presented in a gallery space, such pieces served strategically to suspend visual experience. Yet unlike the "earth artists" who would construct massive site-based projects in remote, nearly inaccessible rural locations and display photographs and other documents back in the gallery, Huebler's work largely remained located in publicly-accessible urban space, and was constructed in such a way that did not visibly or permanently alter that space, but instead constructed spatial and temporal relations that were made perceptible only through the viewer's encounter with his assembled documentation – thus rendering "vision" and "perception" dependent on the viewer's activity of reading, conceptualizing, and mentally constructing the works.[27]

Since the phenomena he wished to document, such as trips, processes, and geographic borders, could not be represented with visual means alone, Huebler adopted pre-existing sign systems, such as maps and diagrams, which combine visual and textual information:

The pieces I made then could not be seen, but it is possible to *know* the existence of such phenomena by combining language with various kinds of visual signs. Of course, I'm talking about the job maps perform. Not just geographic maps: charts, graphs, architectural drawings, geometric propositions, all represent the kind of conceptual model I mean to employ in the construction of my work.[28]

A collection of such pieces comprised the catalogue, including works such as *Site Sculpture Project, Boston-New York Exchange Shape*, in which a list of six Boston Sites – "'marked' between 12:30–4:48 p.m., August 27, 1968" – are juxtaposed with a list of six comparable New York Sites – "'marked' between 10:30 a.m.–4:10 p.m., September 9, 1968." The work consists of its documentation: twelve photographs and the typewritten page describing the method of making the piece, which notes, "[e]ach site was photographed at the time the marker was placed with no attempt made for a more or less interesting or picturesque representation of the location." The project is typical of many of Huebler's early photo-text pieces, in which the text functions as both description and instruction, outlining the series of procedures undertaken to make the work. In others, such as the untitled drawings made in 1967–8 which were later published in *The Xerox Book*, text would operate somewhat differently, not so much detailing the *making* of the piece as framing it for the viewer – in effect, using language to anchor an otherwise ambiguous visual sign or provide verbal cues for imagining otherwise unrepresentable spatial entities – e.g. "a point located in the exact center of this page"; or a piece consisting of a point situated at the center of the page, to another point, describing "the end of a line located on the picture plane and extending in space toward infinity."[29]

Although better-known for more aggressive text-image works drawing on advertising and mass media, Burgin's earlier more sculptural projects also focused attention on perceptual processes. After finishing his degree at Yale University in 1967, Burgin made a series of works that consisted solely of verbal notations on note cards. The most famous of these, *Photopath* (1967/69), was realized in 1969 (Figure 25.5). In it, Burgin affixed large black and white photographs of wood flooring to the floor itself, so that the images appeared "perfectly congruent with their objects."[30] Presented at the London ICA's version of the landmark exhibit *When Attitudes Become Form* in 1969, the work is an extension of classic minimalist concerns with site and context, foregrounding the viewer's apprehension of the object through a decidedly post-minimal embrace of ephemerality and self-effacement. As Burgin notes, "[i]t was a piece of 'sculpture' in as much as it was material on the floor of the gallery, and had no other function than to be looked at by an art audience. It was very ephemeral at the same time – just paper – photographs that only showed what was already there."[31] The very redundancy of the images – showing what was already there – made the work a pointed reflection about photography and the act of looking.

In a recent interview, Burgin employs terms that recall Huebler's famous pronouncements, to recount how "this method developed in *Photopath* was . . . a

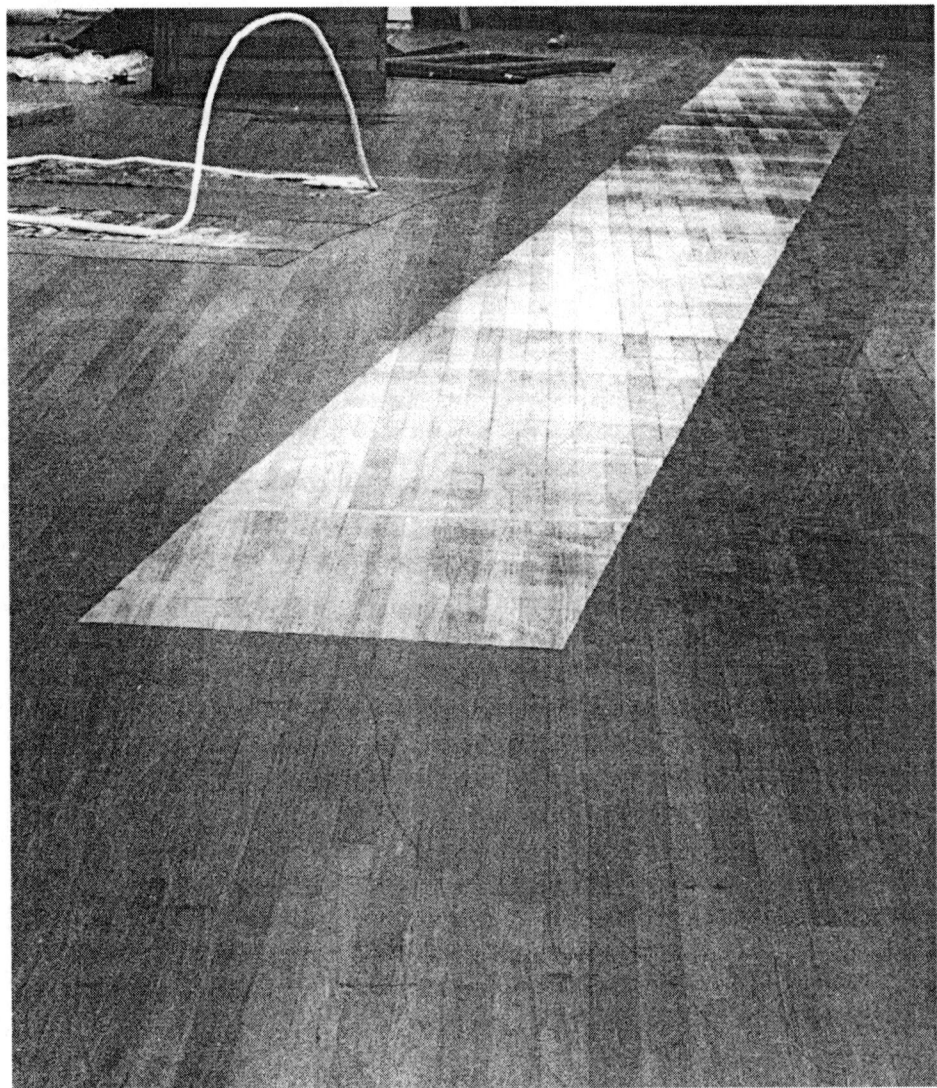

FIGURE 25.5 Victor Burgin, *Photo-path*, 1967–9. Courtesy of the artist

gesture to draw attention to the conditions of perception without actually alter-
ing the environment too much."[32] Yet unlike the other site-based pieces featured in the exhibition, the fact that Burgin's work consisted of *photographs*
completely altered its relation to minimalist sculpture. On the one hand, the
piece is completely reductive and blank, focusing attention on the mute facticity
of the photograph – "what you see is what you see" – and its relation to its
context. Yet, on the other hand, the piece is photographic, and hence inherently
about illusion, representation, and the way that images not only represent reality

but also substitute for and even literally obscure it. Through its uncanny duplication of the flooring on which it lay, *Photopath* played with conditions of perception, forcing viewers to disentangle representation from physical reality. Its implicit interrogation of both site and viewer contains elements that Burgin would later explore in works that went "beyond conceptual art" to incorporate "a systematic attention to the *politics of representation*" including a theory of the subject.[33]

The very doubleness of photography would lead Burgin to consider how "objects" exist not only physically, as objects in the world, but psychologically, as mental and even social constructs. As he proposed in his 1969 essay "Situational Aesthetics," an object such as *Photopath* is "contingent upon the details of the situation for which its is designed." As a consequence of the viewer's apprehension of them, "through attention to time, objects formed are intentionally located partly in real, exterior space and partly in psychological, interior space."[34] This strategy of minimal intervention into the site was employed differently in the text pieces he showed subsequently at Camden Arts Centre in 1970, in which "typewritten sentences . . . focused your attention on the condition of being in the room and adopting a mode of cognition which is traditionally rooted in the spectatorship of art."[35] In these "instruction pieces," which consisted solely of series of statements describing abstract conditions and obscure spatial and temporal relationships, Burgin suggested that "'objects' may be generated through the perceptual behavior" created by verbal instructions; "An immaterial object is created, which is solely a function of perceptual behavior."[36] Yet unlike the more strictly cognitive, descriptive terms of artists such as Robert Barry or Huebler, Burgin's game-like lists have strange narrative and psychological resonances, inviting readers to fill in fragments of a story or imagine a set of complex personal relations underneath the generic language of "events," "acts," and "criteria."

While these process-based concerns were by no means unusual at the time, Burgin was one of the few artists systematically to explore these perceptual and operational investigations as occurring in the medium of *photography*. While many early conceptual artists used photographs quite extensively, they used them as a tool, in seemingly conscious ignorance of, for instance, the critical and historical issues surrounding documentary photography, or the growing use of photography in the mass media. Burgin, however, increasingly oriented his work – as an artist and critic – toward the analysis of the photographic image, helping initiate a type of practice that was also taken up by photo-based artist-critics such as Martha Rosler and Allan Sekula.

For Huebler, photographs retain a nearly neutral status as "document" or transparent recording of "appearance" – a tool that he would strategically employ to strip off the mythic residues that language attaches to an image. In a 1977 interview, he states, "I am interested in freeing nature from the imposition of language, mythology and literature," explaining: "I set the quality of association and then I strip it away. . . . The structure of the work butts a natural event or natural appearance up against a cultural event, the language. . . . The photography is simply a metaphor for nature, a metaphor for appearance."[37] Although Huebler recounts having read Barthes and Alain Robbe-Grillet in the 1960s, his project of semiotic "demythologization" does not yet comprise an articulated analysis of the *rhetoric* of photography. As the artist Mike Kelley, a student of Huebler's at California Institute of the Arts in the late 1970s, notes: "In effect, Doug is telling us that his photographs are transparent. . . . It is possible, because the photos are 'non-aesthetic,' to look through them directly into the system they exemplify. I could never accept this proposition. . . . It is this problem of transparency that I believe primarily separates the first generation of Conceptual artists from the so-called second generation."[38]

Yet Huebler's deceptively "naïve" use of photography belies a deep engagement with the structures of the medium, emphasizing the larger procedural elements created by a work rather than focusing in on the internal structure or analysis of specific individual images. His celebrated work *Variable Piece #70 (1971), Global* pushes photography to the limits of representation. In its laconically-worded statement accompanying the images, Huebler embraces the underlying structure of the photographic archive to absurd extremes: "Throughout the remainder of the artist's lifetime he will photographically document, to the extent of his capacity, the existence of everyone alive in order to produce the most authentic and inclusive representation of the human species that may be assembled in that manner."

The premise to photograph "everyone alive" recalls the curious combination of rigorous completeness and arbitrary sampling characteristic of early conceptual art – evident, for instance, in Ed Ruscha's books documenting *26 Gasoline Stations* (1962) or *Every Building on the Sunset Strip* (1965). Drawing on Cagean principles of random accumulation and non-hierarchical presentation, *Variable Piece #70* enacts the structure of the archive – a collection of equal documents, gathered without regard for quality or aesthetic value. And, like Burgin's *Photopath*, it posits a one-to-one correspondence between object and image, playing on the impossible fantasy of a representation adequate to its object.

Within the rubric of this piece, Huebler then created an ongoing series of works which would combine photographs of people with captions drawn from clichés, proverbs, and other found language – e.g. street scenes of people, accompanied by labels reading: "Represented above is at least one person who would do anything for a laugh," ". . . whose life is an open book," ". . . who has not yet begun to fight." The piece provides no pointers to suggest which figures to attach the captions to, and viewers gradually grasp that the pieces revolve precisely on the *arbitrary* nature of the relation between caption and photo, chance juxtapositions that nonetheless lead us to try to construct a meaningful relation between image and text. Huebler notes: "As in all my work this project is meant to put the question to its audience about how willing it is – and anyone else – to accept arbitrarily constructed relationships between language and appearance."[39]

The desire to invoke and continually undercut the pointing function of language, its capacity to direct our reading of an image, differentiates Huebler's work from artists like Burgin who increasingly sought to use text- and image-based work to construct far more directed meanings, whose veiled allusions and ambiguities resemble the seductions of advertising campaigns. Burgin notes how he eventually became dissatisfied with *Photopath*'s strategy "because it appeared that the spectator wasn't being given enough guidance"; instead, he began using texts that provided something like "a series of prompts where the spectator is urged to look at certain things."[40] Thus in his celebrated poster *Possession* (1976), which mimicked the visual forms of advertising and was installed "on site" in various urban settings, the semantic linkages between the photo and texts, while initially enigmatic, nonetheless generate a set of fairly coherent allusions to the British class system, commodity culture, romantic possession, and the like. Such works presage the strategies of many photo-text works of the 1980s in which the text effectively represses the image, directing our reading, rather than setting off a series of unstable relays between word and picture.

The directive approach, which ultimately closes down meaning around a pre-established if buried "message," is absent from Huebler's more genuinely deconstructive work. In a 1977 project linked with *Variable Piece #70*, Huebler photographed people holding cards with various clichés printed on them – "at least one person who is beautiful but dumb," "one person who is as pretty as a picture," and so forth (Figure 25.7). In this game structure, the cards were distributed completely randomly, thus entailing a risk for those who pose of being associated with a negative or unpleasant description that would then seem attached to them. Huebler recalled the paradoxes of this participatory work, where the random process nonetheless creates quite poignant results: "The desire of people to play this game is extraordinary. They all know it isn't for real, and when it's finished you can look at these associations and say, 'Ah yes, he got one that matches.'"[41]

What makes these images moving? Each cliché, however generic and shopworn, takes on a strange meaning and relevance when attached to the particularity of a face. And of course, the looks of those who pose are, in their own way, generic too – catalogued photographically, faces inevitably fall into types and genres, familiar tropes. By pairing the arbitrary repeated text with the seemingly unique singularity of the face, Huebler's images cross and contaminate their logics. Part of the power of Huebler's work is how it not only exposes the mechanisms of photograph and caption, but, in so doing, also illuminates how our sense of self – and our senses of others – are so often propped on these operations of image and language. It would be tempting to make an argument – in parallel to Benjamin Buchloh's celebrated analysis of conceptual art[42] – tracing conceptual photography's movement from an "aesthetic of administration" to an explicit "politics of representation." Yet while I have traced a rough trajectory from perceptual to semiotic models, the most enduring work bridges these terms,

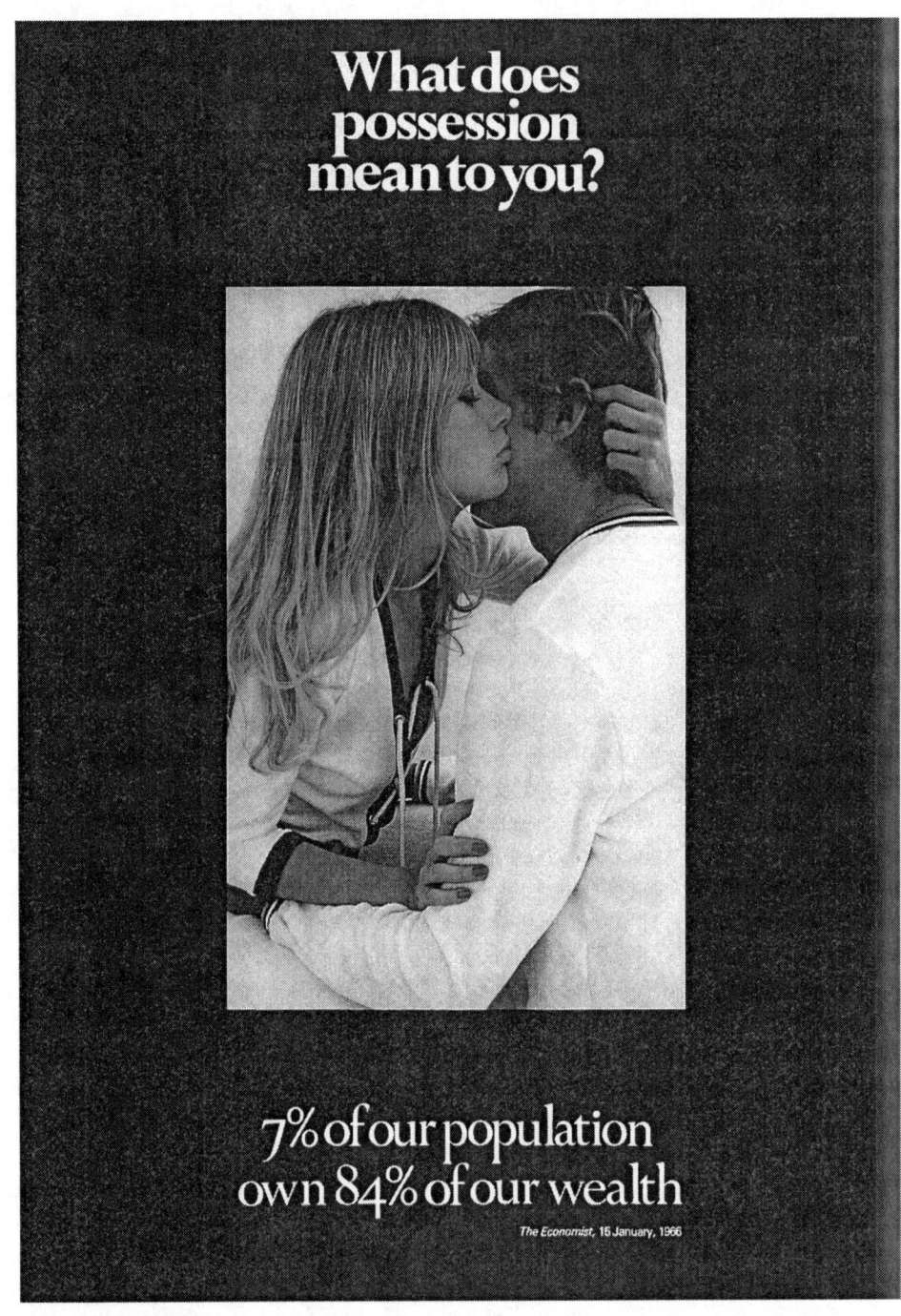

FIGURE 25.6   Victor Burgin, *Possession*, 1976. Courtesy of the artist

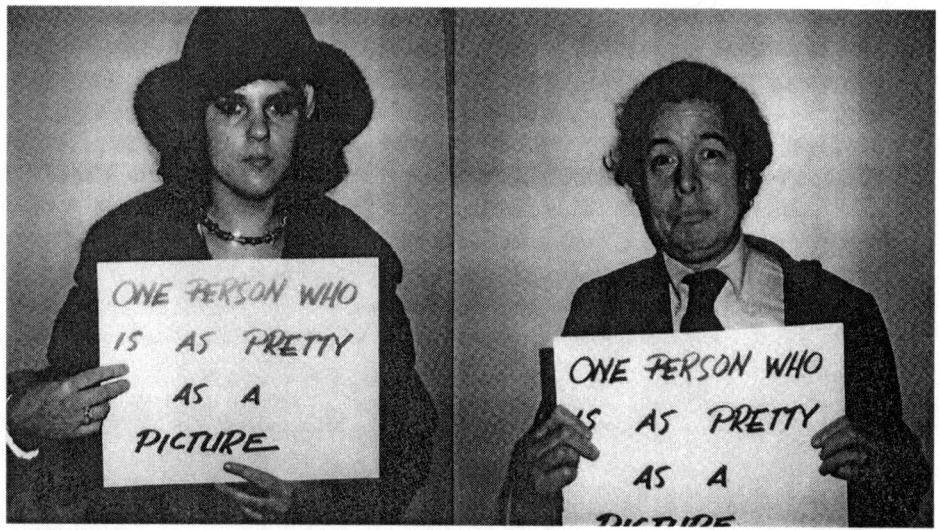

FIGURE 25.7   Douglas Huebler, *100 E/Variable Piece #70: 1971, "One person who is as pretty as a picture,"* 1977 (details). © 2005 estate of Douglas Huebler/Artists Rights Society (ARS), New York

crossing the workings of image culture with a speculative and open-ended address to the viewer.

Notes

1   *Prospect 69* exhibition catalogue statement, October 1969, quoted in Burnham (1970), 41.
2   Ruscha (1965), 25.
3   Roberts (1997), 24–5.
4   Ibid., 26.
5   "Interview with Victor Burgin," in Roberts (1997), 84.
6   Burgin (1980), 64.
7   See for instance the essays collected in Barthes (1977), and Burgin (1982).
8   Despite the apparent resemblance of Baldessari's work to certain conceptual strategies, Joseph Kosuth would dismiss it with the remark that "although the amusingly pop paintings of John Baldessari allude to this sort of work by being 'conceptual' cartoons of actual conceptual art, they are not really relevant to this discussion," in "Art After Philosophy" (1969), reprinted in Kosuth (1991), 29.
9   Alongside the official, self-proclaimed "Conceptual Art" produced by artists like Kosuth, who were affiliated with Seth Siegelaub, a far larger and less strictly-defined set of conceptually-oriented or "conceptualist" practices occurred. Examples of this looser, more international scope of "conceptualism" could be seen, for instance, in the landmark 1970 exhibition Information at New York's Museum of Modern Art.

10   In "'Marks of Indifference': Aspects of Photography on, or as, Conceptual Art," the artist and critic Jeff Wall reads Graham's and Smithson's publication projects as explicit *parodies* of journalism, and specifically as parodies of what he terms "the art-concept of photojournalism" – the historical reliance of modernist photography on instrumental forms of press photography and reportage. Wall concludes that it is paradoxically by the "strictest imitation of the non-autonomous" – by abandonment of the aestheticized "reportage" of modernist photography for a more sustained mimesis of industrial, utilitarian, and amateur modes – that "photoconceptualism led toward the complete acceptance of photography as art." Wall proposes Graham's *Homes for America* as "a canonical instance of the new kind of anti-autonomous yet autonomous work of art. The photographs in it oscillate at the threshold of the autonomous work." In Goldstein and Rorimer (1995), 252, 257.

11   Wall (1991), 13.

12   In Peirce's schema, an "index," or "indexical" sign, "refers to an Object by virtue of being really affected by that Object" – i.e. by physical impact or imprint, including phenomena like footprints, symptoms, or smoke (a sign of a fire); indices are distinguished from "icons" which refer to an object through resemblance or analogy (e.g. images, diagrams), and "symbols" which work by means of law, convention, or historically-forged association (e.g. the cross as symbolic of Christianity). While these functions often overlap within a single sign, in general language is the symbolic, "arbitrary" sign par excellence. See Peirce (1955).

13   Krauss (1986), 211.

14   Barthes, "The Photographic Message" (1961), in Barthes (1977), 15. See also "The Rhetoric of Photography" (1964), also in Barthes (1977), and "Elements of Semiology" (1964), published in Barthes (1968).

15   See Shannon and Weaver (1949).

16   In "Aspects," Stephen Melville discusses the ambivalent attraction to positivist models evident in the 1960s embrace of Wittgenstein. He suggests that, in this context, "Wittgenstein, both early and late, offered ambiguous resources for imagining art's place between the promise and threat of positivism, while the propositional style of the early work and the aphoristic or experimental style of the later seemed to give permission to take one's Wittgenstein as one found (or wanted to find) it, rendering fluid the distinction between the logical concerns of the early work and the grammatical focus of the later. Given these broad readerly permissions and uncertainties, what Wittgenstein seemed to license was a certain practice of self-reference that could nonetheless count as rigorous, as measuring up to a more certain (albeit obscure) standard of objectivity that would let art count as a mode of investigation more or less on a par with . . . modern science." In Goldstein and Rorimer (1995), 234–5.

17   Krauss (1986) draws this point from the immense textual apparatus which accompanies Duchamp's deeply hermetic *Large Glass* (1915–23), but the same analysis can be extended backward to earlier projects like the readymades and *Three Standard Stoppages* (1913), which remain unintelligible without some kind of verbal explanation or textual supplement (even if only a title or signature).

18   Krauss (1986), 212.

19   Ann Goldstein, "Adrian Piper," in Goldstein and Rorimer (1995), 196.

20 Stephen Melville, "Aspects," in Goldstein and Rorimer (1995), 235. As Melville notes, a counter tendency more open to phenomenological and semiotic models also emerged at the time, distinguished by what he terms "its refusal of this fundamentally epistemological orientation (a refusal, then, to identify self-criticism with self-reference) in favor of a different imagination of how language matters for an apprehension of the visual: language is more nearly taken as a condition of a thing or a work's appearing (its being what it is) than as the screen, transparent or opaque, that stands between us and things, ever threatening to supplant them" (236).

21 Sol LeWitt, "Serial Project No. 1 (ABCD)," *Aspen* 5/6 (1966), reprinted in LeWitt (1995), 75.

22 Buchloh (1990), 122.

23 Burgin (1969), 119.

24 See Huebler (1968).

25 Douglas Huebler, Letter to Jack Burham, 1969, reprinted in Huebler (1993), 173.

26 Douglas Huebler, interview by Frédéric Paul, Truro, Massachusetts, 1992, in Huebler (1993), 127.

27 In a 1969 statement, Huebler notes: "My work is concerned with determining the form of art when the role traditionally played by visual experience is mitigated or eliminated. In a number of works I have done so by first bringing 'appearance' into the foreground of the piece and then suspending the visual experience of it by having it actually function as a document that exists to serve as a structural part of a conceptual system." *Artists and Photographs* (NY: Multiple, Inc, 1969), reprinted in Huebler (1993), 173.

28 Huebler, interview by Frédéric Paul, in Huebler (1993), 127. In a 1978 statement, he elaborated: "By late 1967, I was looking for an alternative to object-making and I found it in the idea of the map: the perfect conceptual model, with its reduced visual signs juxtaposed with descriptive language. I created a new body of work which added photographic 'documentation' to the implications of mapping" (175).

29 See Andre et al. (1968), n.p.

30 Burgin, written instruction for *Photopath*, in Burgin (1969), 120.

31 Burgin, in Tony Godfrey, "Interview with Victor Burgin," *Block* 9 (1982), cited in Osborne (2002), 126.

32 "Interview with Victor Burgin," in Roberts (1997), 82.

33 Burgin (1986), 39.

34 Burgin (1969), 119.

35 "Interview with Victor Burgin," in Roberts (1997), 82.

36 Burgin (1969), 119.

37 Huebler, in Auping (1977), 38.

38 Kelley, "Shall We Kill Daddy?" in Van Leeuw and Pontégnie (1997), 163.

39 Huebler, in Van Leeuw and Pontégnie (1997), 134. In an earlier interview, Huebler elaborated that his work is "about the equation between the language you are reading and the image you are seeing. . . . It is an effort to try to make the equation occur in the present moment." An existential concern, also a political concern, "an effort to empty the work of what appears to be the content. It is not to fill the work with content. It is to empty it, to empty it of history, to empty it of mythology, to empty it of literature and to allow it to speak by being empty" (in Auping [1977]

37). He concludes: "there is an enormous amount of irresponsible filling of content into the events of the world and into the appearance of the world . . . in other words, I'm speaking against the irresponsibility of language" (38).

40 "Interview with Victor Burgin," in Roberts (1997), 82–3.
41 Auping (1977), 42.
42 See Buchloh (1990).

References

Andre, Carl, Robert Barry, Douglas Huebler, Joseph Kosuth, Sol LeWitt, Robert Morris, and Lawrence Weiner (1968). *The Xerox Book.* New York: Siegelaub/Wendler.
Auping, Michael (1977). "Talking with Douglas Huebler." *LAICA Journal*, vol. 15 (July–August).
Barthes, Roland (1968). *Elements of Semiology* (1964), trans. Annette Lavers and Colin Smith. New York: Hill and Wang.
—— (1977). "The Photographic Message" (1961), "The Rhetoric of Photography" (1964). In *Image, Music Text*, trans. Stephen Heath. New York: Hill and Wang.
Buchloh, Benjamin (1990). "Conceptual Art 1962–1969: From the Aesthetics of Administration to the Critique of Institutions." *October*, vol. 55 (Winter).
Burgin, Victor (1969). "Situational Aesthetics." *Studio International*, vol. 178, no. 915 (October).
—— (1980). "Seeing Sense." *Artforum* (February).
—— (1986). "The Absence of Presence: Conceptualism and Postmodernisms." In *The End of Art Theory: Criticism and Postmodernity.* Atlantic Highlands, NJ: Humanities Press International.
—— ed. (1982). *Thinking Photography.* London: Macmillan.
Burnham, Jack (1970). "Alice's Head: Reflections on Conceptual Art." *Artforum* (February).
Goldstein, Ann, and Anne Rorimer (1995). *Reconsidering the Object of Art, 1965–1975.* Exhibition catalogue. Los Angeles: Museum of Contemporary Art, and Cambridge, MA: MIT Press.
Huebler, Douglas (1968). *Douglas Huebler.* New York: Seth Siegelaub.
—— (1993). *Douglas Huebler – "Variable," etc.* Limousin: FRAC.
Kosuth, Joseph (1991). *Art After Philosophy and After: Collected Writings, 1966–1990,* ed. Gabriele Guercio. Cambridge, MA: MIT Press.
Krauss, Rosalind (1986). "Notes on the Index, Part II (1977)." In *The Originality of the Avant-Garde and Other Modernist Myths.* Cambridge, MA: MIT Press.
LeWitt, Sol (1995). *Sol LeWitt: Critical Texts,* ed. Adachiara Zevi. Rome: Editrice Inonia.
Osborne, Peter (2002). *Conceptual Art.* London: Phaidon.
Peirce, Charles Sanders (1955). "Logic as Semiotic: The Theory of Signs." In *Philosophical Writings of Peirce.* New York: Dover.
Roberts, John (1997). "Photography, Iconophobia and the Ruins of Conceptual Art." In *The Impossible Document: Photography and Conceptual Art in Britain 1966–1976.* London: Camerawork.
Ruscha, Ed (1965). "Ed Ruscha Discusses His Perplexing Publications." An Interview with John Coplans. *Artforum* (February).

Shannon, Claude E., and William Weaver (1949). *The Mathematical Theory of Communication*. Urbana: University of Illinois Press.

Van Leeuw, Marianne, and Anne Pontégnie, eds. (1997). *Origin and Destination: Alighiero E Boetti and Douglas Huebler*. Brussels: Societé des Expositions du Palais des Beaux-Arts de Bruxelles.

Wall, Jeff (1991). *Dan Graham's Kammerspiel*. Toronto: Art Metropole.

26

Imagine There's No Image (It's Easy If You Try): Appropriation in the Age of Digital Reproduction

Dore Bowen

When art becomes independent, depicts its world in dazzling colors, a moment of life has grown old and it cannot be rejuvenated with dazzling colors. It can be evoked only as a memory.

Guy Debord, *Society of the Spectacle*, 1967, section 188

The Politics of the Artifact

Displayed on two plasma screens approximately 40 inches high by 48 inches wide, American artist Bill Viola's *Silent Mountain* (2001; Figure 26.1) depicts a man and woman whose bodily gestures convey a spectrum of emotion from agony to ecstasy. While the emotional pitch is heightened through theatrical gestures, other factors are contrastingly placid: the actors are clothed in common street wear, placed against a mute background, and the video image is unusually protracted. According to Viola, the stillness of this moving image echoes Renaissance religious painting and yet, as he states: "The old pictures were just a starting point. I was not interested in appropriation or restaging – I wanted to get inside these pictures . . . to embody them, inhabit them, to feel them breathe."[1]

While Viola speaks of this work as a kind of spiritual appropriation that embodies and inhabits Renaissance painting, theorist Mark Hansen calls it a form of "creative embodiment." In *New Philosophy for New Media*, Hansen

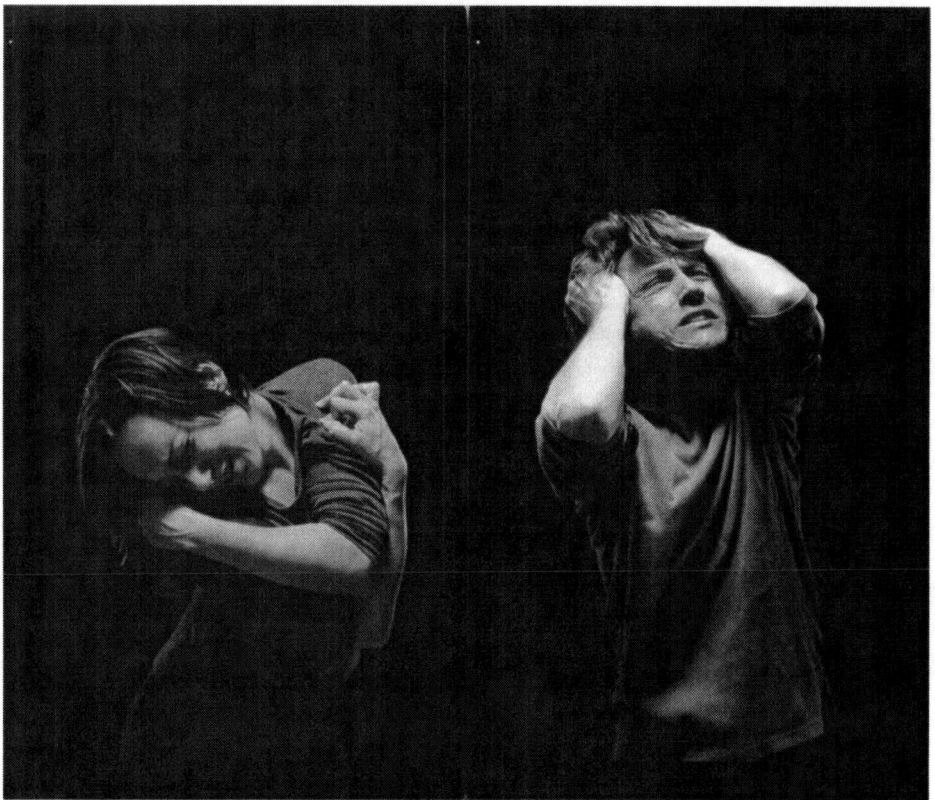

FIGURE 26.1 Bill Viola, *Silent Mountain*, 2001. Still image from video installation, color video diptych on two plasma displays mounted side-by-side on wall. Photograph: Kira Perov. Courtesy of Bill Viola Studio

further asserts that the series *Silent Mountain* is a part of – *The Passions* – exemplifies a "truly creative" engagement with digital technology that reworks perception and ushers in a new age of image-making, thereby reconfiguring the "correlation of the human with the technical" and exploiting "the potential of information to . . . enlarge the scope of the human grasp over the material world."[2]

While both Viola and Hansen emphasize the way that *The Passions* produces an embodied form of perceptual engagement between the image and its viewer, there is an odd discrepancy between Viola's attribution of his work's inspiration to the art historical past while Hansen speaks of its merit in relation to technology's future. I believe that this contradiction arises because neither the work nor Hansen's assessment of it accounts for the relationship between the disclosure that the digital image makes possible and the *current cultural context* in which it arises.[3] Absent from both is a critique of the work as it exists within an already operating economic, historical, and social environment. In fact, Hansen implicitly rejects just such "culturalism." In the preface, for example, he struggles to reclaim Walter Benjamin as a media-ontologist rather than a cultural critic, ignoring Benjamin's overarching interest in the reproducible image's relationship to capitalism and politics in favor his "concretely embodied" engagement with film, thus rescuing the postwar theorist as a "beacon of hope that media can continue to matter in the digital age."[4]

At stake is the role of culture in the interpretation of images. Although Hansen's phenomenology of new media, which insists on bodily relations, comes as a relief after years of poststructuralist analyses that understand the image as if it were solely discursive, and while his discussion unfolds the particularities involved in digital-image practices, he neglects what Don Ihde calls "the politics of the artifact."[5] The politics of the artifact is, for Ihde, what is *missing* from the account of *techne* by philosopher Martin Heidegger. Ihde notes that while Heidegger romanticizes *techne* – particularly as it is exemplified in pre-modern technologies and ancient works of art – he ignores the political, cultural, and environmental horizon that constitutes any form of technology. For instance, while Heidegger champions the Greek temple as a fantastic site that "holds open the Open of the world," this same temple is responsible for the deforestation of its local environment just as surely as a power plant pollutes its environment.[6] For Ihde, what distinguishes the temple from the power plant is not, as one might suspect, what each reveals but, instead, the significant cultural assumptions and details that are left out of Heidegger's description of both.

While Hansen resists such nostalgia, his claims for new media are as romantic as are Heidegger's claims for a Greek temple and an old bridge. Both Hansen and Heidegger hope to reclaim a more intimate relationship between nature, technology, and human beings while ignoring technology's cultural context. Today, the primary factor bearing on image technologies (in production, circulation, storage, and output) is the complex influence of capital. Consequently, before Hansen's argument or the work to which he refers can be more fully evaluated, it is necessary to flesh out the image as it is exists within this context.

The Spectacular Image

Situationist theorist Guy Debord's analysis in his 1967 book *The Society of the Spectacle* is a rich account of the image within a capitalist economy of production and exchange. For Debord the reified image is part of a larger phenomenon – the *spectacle*. The spectacle is, while an image, also a symptom of the alienation that it seeks to conceal. Insisting on the politics of the artifact, Debord repeatedly warns that the spectacle – those images produced by and for capitalist profit – erodes and feeds on authentic experience. To complicate this, he warns the naïve viewer against conceiving of the spectacle as *merely* an image, noting that the spectacle is not an image (or images) but an "*affirmation* of appearance and an affirmation of all human life, namely social life, as mere appearance." Consequently, separation "*has become visible.*"[7] This appearance, this visible form is, however, illusory; it is the separation (negation) of life experience. Ultimately, what the spectacle "achieves is nothing but an official language of universal separation."[8]

Debord employs a dialectical method in order to demonstrate that the spectacle conceals the social relations that comprise it. In doing so, *The Society of the Spectacle* operates as a manual for reading the spectacle against itself. Although the spectacle – in *toto* – cannot be seen, it can be apprehended by attending to the shape it sculpts out. Like the glacier around which a rock bed forms, the spectacle forces space and time to take shape around what it alienates. For instance, Debord notes that "[c]apitalist production has unified space, which is no longer bounded by external societies."[9] For Debord, the unification of space is exemplified by the growing tourism industry, which, while promising to unite territories and cultures, equates diverse geographic sites. The spectacle manifests itself in terms of time as well. As opposed to cyclical-mythical or linear-progressive temporality, time is experienced in the age of the spectacle as historical stasis. The spectacle erases "the historical time involved in traversing cultures" while exhibiting "pseudocyclical time" which, as a form of postmodern ritualism, "is in fact merely a consumable disguise of the commodity-time of production."[10]

Besides his polemical exhortations against the spectacle, Debord advocates an appropriative strategy that seeks to get under its skin, to unearth its possibilities while also accounting for the politics of the artifact. The situationist theory of *détournement* is an appropriate point of departure for considering this approach. *Détournement* is the appropriation of "pre-existing aesthetic elements. The integration of past or present artistic production into a superior construction of a milieu."[11] In "Methods of Détournement" (1956), Debord and Gil Wolman note that the purpose of *détournement* is to prove the "impossibility for power to totally recuperate created meanings, to fix an existing meaning once and for all."[12] In this way, *détournement* aspires to nothing more than to speak its own contingency in order to reveal the contingency of the spectacle as well.

In the *Society of the Spectacle*, Debord describes *détournement* (here translated as "diversion") similarly, as a resistant strategy "that cannot be confirmed by any former or supra-critical reference. . . . Diversion has grounded its cause on nothing external to its own truth as present critique."[13] Yet, here, as opposed to in his earlier text, Debord emphasizes the emancipatory potential of appropriation. While the spectacle's function is "to make history forgotten in culture" and to "congeal time," *détournement* provides a way to rediscover "a common language," thus proving a means to reveal "the community of dialogue and the game with time which have been *represented* by the poetico-artistic works."[14] Elsewhere in this essay, Debord suggests that *détournement* can reintroduce the vital relationship between the image and human experience; it "can confirm the former core of truth which it brings out."[15] Debord's notion of *détournement* parallels Hansen's notion of a creative engagement with media, while also asserting that time and history must be pried from the image (and not merely represented) before an embodied relationship to the image can occur.

Given this possibility, *détournement* is complicated by the fact that, for Debord, the spectacle has no body; it is capital's persona. While the spectacle is both abstract (capitalist alienation) and yet manifests itself concretely (as image), it is neither and both of these; it is a black hole – a zero point of post-capitalist frenzy, *un terrain vague* where what once existed now survives as decay and detritus, feeding on the very capitalist structure it obscures. Following George Orwell's 1948 novel *1984*, and foreshadowing the recent film trilogy *The Matrix*, Debord's "concrete visibility" takes the *commodity-fetish* a step beyond itself. Given this context, how might artists appropriate imagery in order to release time, history, bodily experience? Since capitalism has reached epic proportions, how might artists "take hold" of the spectacle if, as Debord writes, "the society sends back to itself its own historical image as a merely superficial and static history of its rulers"?[16]

Two influential approaches to the commodification of images have developed since Debord's dark predictions emerged in print. The first, known as "postmodern appropriation," was propelled to attention with the 1977 *Pictures* exhibition at Artists Space in New York City. This exhibit featured the work of Sherrie Levine, Louise Lawler, Robert Longo, Troy Brauntuch, Jack Goldstein, and Phillip Smith. Other notables among the postmodern appropriation artists, but not included in the show, are Cindy Sherman, Richard Prince, Jenny Holzer, Barbara Kruger, and Hans Haacke. This work appropriates photographic imagery from commercial culture in order to undercut photography's truth claims, and thereby expose its ideological basis; it involves a critique that, as Debord suggests in his description of *détournement*, reveals the absence at the heart of the spectacle's seeming presence. Like the pop movement before it, yet with critical objectives, this postmodern work delves into the emptiness of the spectacle. As Douglas Crimp, curator of the *Pictures* exhibition, notes in his catalogue essay, "[t]he peculiar presence of this work is effected through absence, through its unbridgeable distance from the original, from even the possibility of an original. Such presence is what I attribute to the kind of photographic activity I call postmodernist."[17]

For example, Cindy Sherman's well known *Untitled Film Stills* series (1977–80) serves as an homage to Hollywood's "B" movies while challenging the separation between self and other, between personal and cultural – distinctions that self-portraiture relies upon. Crimp notes that, "those processes of quotation, excerptation, framing, and staging that constitute the strategies of the work I have been discussing necessitate uncovering strata of representation . . . underneath each picture there is always another picture."[18] Such works puncture the belief in an "original" photographic image via repetition, text, and critical juxtaposition of elements. In refusing the image its authenticity, postmodern appropriation enables a critique of the system of signification that underlies even the most obvious or innocent of images.

A more embodied approach to the spectacle emerged from performance and conceptual art in the 1960s and 1970s. This work explores the relationship between the image and the performer's (or viewer's) body, resulting in novel practices such as performance and installation art. At times this approach borders on ritual; for instance, the Viennese Actionists, Joseph Beuys, and Carolee Schneemann integrate the image in a complex performance that invests photography and film with significance beyond its representational, commodity, or aesthetic value. Still other artists – such as Bruce Nauman, Vito Acconci, and Lynda Benglis – integrate the viewer into a video event. These works – often involving only the artist in his studio, and at times using live video – seduce the viewer into participating within the artist's scenario. For example, Acconci's *Command Performance* (1974) incorporates the viewer into a prearranged confrontation with the artist *via* video. The viewer's image is projected onto a video monitor, thus becoming a part of the image-event and, as Michael Rush writes of this work, "everyone becomes a voyeur in this dance of multiple seduction."[19]

At the same time that such works place the image in relation to the body (of the artist and/or viewer), they also risk neglecting the politics of the artifact, the ideological "load" that postmodernism takes as a given. For this reason, Debord warns against works that purport to introduce "life" and "experience" into the spectacle. He writes that "art in the epoch of its dissolution is simultaneously an art of change and the purest expression of impossible change. The more grandiose its reach, the more its true realization is beyond it."[20]

In his 1963 editorial essay entitled "The Avant-Garde of Presence," Debord criticizes both the pop/postmodern strategy of appropriating images from the mass media and the more performative strategy of integrating the image into a live event. He notes that, while the former approach reveals "the absence at the heart of the spectacle," like its Dada precursor, it will eventually "suppress art without realizing it," or, like surrealism, "realize art without suppressing it." More contempt is heaped on latter approach which, for Debord, is *even worse, [for it attempts] to repair its damage by creating a new viewer, one who is active, participatory, and stimulated.*[21] This stimulated viewer is, in fact, called forth by capitalism and its technological mode of production and, thus, exists within and for the spectacle.

Debord's notion of the "stimulated viewer" provides an important caution to Hansen's eager claim for a "new correlation of the human and the technical." Debord writes: "As for the integration of the viewer into these wonderful things, it is a poor little image of his integration into the new cities, into the banks of television monitors in the office or factory where he works. It pursues the same plan, but with infinitely less force, and even infinitely less guinea pigs."[22] Here, Debord suggests that the image and the stimulated viewer exist both in relation to one another and within a larger phenomenon of tele-visual capitalist development. Thus, the politics of the artifact are within – and not merely outside of – both the spectacle and its viewer. In other words, the spectacle, though defined by separation, is not at odds with politics, experience, or reality. Debord notes that "reality rises up within the spectacle, and the spectacle is real."[23]

Following this, a practice that seeks to transcend the spectacle must also recover those elements seemingly excluded by it; the idea that the spectacle is entirely at odds with life and authentic experience serves only to reify it. Thus, while Debord notes that in spectacular society the viewer is alienated "to the profit of the contemplated object,"[24] Valie Export's *Tap and Touch Cinema* (1968) – in which the she exposed herself to the public bare-chested except for a curtained box attached to her upper body, inviting people on the street to reach into the box and feel her breasts – reveals the viewer to be integral to the spectacle. Rather than showing the image, *Tap and Touch Cinema* exposes the desire of the viewer for the female breast *as* image, perverting and disempowering the spectacle with affect, sensuousness, and chance, while also exposing the viewer's bodily and psychological attachment to the image. Export's performance of this piece thus revealed the spectacle to be inseparable from the fetishistic experience of the viewer, and the material body to be inseparable from the image. On this point, Timothy Bewes suggests that the reified object (in this case, the reified image) "must be reconfigured so as to incorporate the anxiety towards it." Furthermore, Bewes notes that the "thingliness" of objects and the vitality of subjective experience are not at odds with reification, but within it.[25] By extension, there is an interdependent and reversible relationship between the commodity image and the viewer's subjective experience, as well as the "thingliness" of the object.

In "The Intertwining – The Chiasm," Maurice Merleau-Ponty postulates the "flesh" as the perceptual basis that underlies and mediates the reversible relationship between the viewer and the object viewed. He writes:

> The flesh (of the world or my own) is . . . a texture that returns to itself and conforms to itself. I will never see my own retinas, but if one thing is certain for me it is that one would find at the bottom of my eyeballs those dull and secret membranes. And finally, I believe it – I believe that I have a man's senses, a human body – *because the spectacle of the world that is my own* . . . refers with evidence to typical dimensions of visibility.[26]

Following Merleau-Ponty, the "spectacle of the world that is my own" is a fleshy hinge that links the viewer and image. This notion elucidates the potential of an artistic approach that engages with the spectacle, its viewer, and the thingly object by unearthing their common secret – the flesh.

The Reversibility of the Spectacle: Concretism and Durationism

Like Export's *Tap and Touch Cinema*, the work that emerged from Fluxus – a 1960s–1970s conceptual art movement – provides an example of a praxis that incorporates those elements negated by but latent within the spectacle. Dick Higgins notes that fluxworks include both an "underpiece" (a material element; matter) and an "overpiece" (a representational element; form). According to Higgins, the job of the Fluxus artist is to reveal the underpiece of the representational image.[27]

In his 1962 text "Neo-Dada in Music, Theater, Poetry, Art," George Maciunas introduces the term "concretism" to describe the way the fluxwork draws attention to its materiality and, thereby, rejects the notion of pure representation (what he calls "illusionism"). In other words, the fluxwork clings to its specificity. For instance, in Yoko Ono's *Apple* (1966), the artist frames a withering apple. The "content" of the work is organic decay – the action of time upon the object – and not what the apple itself represents. Artists such as Ono, explains Maciunas, "prefer the world of concrete reality rather than the artificial abstraction of illusionism." Thus, a Fluxus artist prefers "the reality of a rotten tomato rather than an illusionistic image or symbol of it."[28]

In a letter to George Brecht written in 1962, Maciunas provides a more nuanced account of concretism, explaining that illusionism and concretism do not stand in opposition but differ by matter of degree. In this letter, Maciunas depicts a cylinder to illustrate his theory. Within the diagram a block of text reads "towards concrete or reality," and is accompanied by an arrow pointing toward the far end of the cylinder while, labeled with the text "towards artificial," another arrow points in the opposite direction. In addition to this, Maciunas marks a point on the mouth of the cylinder "optic" and another, on the opposite end, "acoustic."[29] This chart suggests that the object and its "artificial" representation intersect with the electromagnetic spectrum of light, as well as sound waves, and that these characteristics define the viewer's perception as much as the materiality or immateriality of the object. In this sense, concretism undermines the spectacle's reification of reality by revealing both the concrete object and its representation to be temporary states within a fluid process of transference.

For example, Maciunas's *Kinesthesis Slides* (c.1969) is a work in which "slides" for Fluxus film events consist of nothing more than hollow glass mounts. The mounts are used to frame living matter for projection. Jon Hendricks notes that "one could put any sort of living organism in them to project and watch its movements."[30] Thus, in 1969 Maciunas projected live cockroaches, worms, flies, and caterpillars at a fluxfestival in Stony Brook, New York.[31] It is not clear from textual descriptions whether the *Kinesthesis Slides* operated successfully as "living-transparencies" or annihilated the insects under the hot bulb of the projector. In either case, *Kinesthesis Slides* introduces that which is usually materially abstracted from and by representation into the framed image. Whereas the photograph is an indexical reference to objects and bodies, *Kinesthesis Slides* inserts the referent into the frame itself, pointing to the fact that living matter is not distinct from representation but is constituent with it. *Kinesthesis Slides* reveals the spectacle to be comprised of that which it commonly stands in for, denies, negates, consumes, and transforms into image – the flesh – as well as the worldly and temporal context in which matter persists, decays, and circulates.

The perceptual basis that underlies both the viewer and image operates in time. Fluxworks allow the quality of time absent from the spectacle to creep into the image and challenge what Debord calls "commodity-time" by refusing to be either an "avant-garde of absence" or, conversely, a performative fusion of the body and image.[32] This Fluxus emphasis on time leads naturally to an interest in *duration* – what philosopher Henri Bergson describes as the time experienced while waiting for the sugar cube to dissolve in water "with its own determined rhythm."[33] In its incorporation of unrehearsed and often empty moments, fluxworks concern the time it takes for things to evolve, but also, per Heidegger's existentialist notion of duration, the well-accustomed ways in which human beings experience time based on custom and social convention, the "everyday ways in which we 'make provision.' "[34]

Debord notes that waiting is at odds with "the abstract desire for immediate effectiveness" and "pseudo-revolutionary common actions."[35] In other words, the viewer's uncomfortable experience of waiting attacks the spectacle at its weak point by worrying its stasis. The audience and performer must literally endure time. Fluxus artists who employ this strategy provide a counterpoint to the immediacy of performance as well as an alternative to the more postmodern appropriative works that imitate the commodity-image while proving a critical commentary though text or context. To summarize, "[t]he critique which goes beyond the spectacle," writes Debord, "must know *how to wait*."[36] Following Bewes' theory of reversibility, duration is within the spectacle and not outside of it. Although the commodity-image seems to deny the time of waiting, decay, and growth by absorbing it within pseudocyclical time, it cannot annihilate duration entirely. Consequently, the viewer's unexpected encounter with duration is often experienced as shock or boredom.[37]

For instance, many of the short works included in *Fluxfilms* (1965) – collected and compiled by Maciunas – play the viewer's anticipation of cinematic time against the concrete time taken by the strip of film as it passes through the projector. In Maciunas's *10 Feet* and James Riddle's *9 Minutes*, the film *is* its time and/or length. Maciunas's *10 Feet* measures the film in feet, while Riddle's *9 Minutes* measures the film with a depicted time-piece that tracks its own screening time in minutes and seconds. Other fluxfilms employ high-speed cameras (running at approximately 2,000 frames per second rather than 64), in order to focus on an otherwise momentary and "inconsequential" incident such that the duration of the event is expanded rather than measured in actual time. These include the anonymous *Eyeblink*, Joe Jones's *Smoke*, and Yoko Ono's *Number 1 (Match)*. Another notable among these films is Mieko Shiomi's *Disappearing Music for Face*, an eight-second sequence of time expanded to eleven minutes depicting Ono's lips fading from a smile to a relaxed state. On the other end of the spectrum, Paul Sharits's *Sears Catalogue* bombards the viewer with an array of appropriated images (of, for instance, toasters, televisions, cameras, and models). Here, as opposed to the concretism of *9 Minutes*, or the expansion of *Eyeblink*, the temporality of the film is condensed. Yet, in all the fluxfilms the duration involved in viewing is the subject of the film.

In discussing Viola's *The Passions*, John Walsh notes that certain fluxfilms, such as Shiomi's *Disappearing Music for Face*, "anticipate Viola's interest in shifting states of mind."[38] Certainly, both *Silent Mountain* and Shiomi's piece use slow motion to alter the viewer's relationship to the image. Yet, the very different ends to which these works employ this device must be emphasized as well. In *Disappearing Music for Face*, slow motion introduces the time of waiting and viewing – of perception itself – into the cinematic experience such that the viewer's endurance of the film is integral to the work. In *Silent Mountain*, on the other hand, slow motion is used to draw the viewer into the work or, more precisely, to immerse the viewer within the image. Viola's work creates an illusionist space of reflection; the work and the environment of the installation still the viewer as well, immersing her/him into a state of meditation and communion. In *Disappearing Music for Face*, in contrast, the experience of duration is belabored such that the viewer's experience of the concrete time of viewing is foregrounded rather than transcended.

Digital Liquefaction

The fluxworks discussed above reveal the multiple ways in which those elements abstracted and alienated by the spectacle can be located within it. Do digital media alter or extend this reversibility in a significant way? Do they differ, fundamentally, from prior forms of media? Jonathan Crary ponders these questions when he asks: "Have we entered a non-spectacular global system arranged primarily around the control and flow of information, a system whose management and regulation of attention would demand wholly new forms of resistance and memory?"[39] The difference between Shiomi's *Disappearing Music for Face* and Viola's *Silent Mountain* speaks to the changes that have occurred in relation to the media image from the 1960s to the present. The commodity-image is no longer a part of an alienated yet reversible dialectic; it exists within a larger flow of information. It moves. In the following two sections I explain how digital media enable a new relation between the viewer and the image, yet are also related to prior, analogue practices. Furthermore, I seek to explain why this continuity allows the spectacle to enter into image-making praxis as a malleable form in its own right.

The interactivity afforded by postwar systems of image production takes advantage of the spectacle's reversibility, and, as in the examples discussed above, brings the viewer into its loop. Hansen suggests that digital media involve a new relationship between the image and subject and, ultimately, a new subject, arguing that with digitization, "the image can no longer be restricted to the level of surface appearance, but must be extended to encompass the entire process by which information is made perceivable through embodied experience. This is what I propose to call the *digital image*."[40] Digital technologies enable and reveal this radical integration of body and image to be inherently flexible, thus creating, as Arjun Appadurai notes of late capitalism in general, new forms as well as "new resources and new disciplines for the construction of imagined selves and imagined worlds."[41] For instance, advances in digital projection and image-assembly have altered the status of the image such that it now appears in ways and forms that surpass previous definitions. The image is itself in a state of becoming, existing as only one component within an ever-expanding flow that includes the viewer, but also the gallery and the architectural environment.

In contrast to Hansen's notion of the *digital image*, Philip Rosen argues that the indexicality of photography and film (their capacity to register an imprint of what lay before the camera lens) is not lost but transformed into the digital flow of images; digitization, he argues, "cannot mean the obliteration of referential origins."[42] While Hansen sees the digital image as producing a radically new subject, for Rosen the malleability of the digital image alters the index by placing it in a new context. Bernard Stiegler notes that this hybrid form of the "analogico-digital image-object" (what he also terms the "discrete image") "may contribute to the emergence of new forms of 'objective analysis' and of 'subjective synthesis' of the visible – and to the emergence, by the same token, of another kind of belief and disbelief with respect to what is shown and what happens."[43]

The spectacle has metastasized. No longer defined entirely by the dialectic of alienation/lived experience (as in Debord's description), it is marked by its apparitional flow that operates in and around the index, the local, and the focal, thus producing forms that are an amalgamation of analogue and digital, or that reflect on the analogue through digital means. This characteristic is what I call "digital liquefaction." The relationship between the image and the viewer's subjective experience no longer appears to be oppositional; rather, the mutability struggled for by an earlier generation of artists emerges as the condition of the image. The photo-happenings of French artist Jean-Philippe Baert thus turn the gallery into a projection booth, a theater, and a darkroom. In the process, Baert creates what he calls a "TV imprint" or "image fossil" by passing a monitor in front of photographic paper and developing the image as part of his live performance, resulting in neither an "authentic" experience nor pristine photographs: both are debased through their dependence on each other.[44] In Baert's *Coagulation* (2002; Figure 26.2) – a short video of a well-known French newscaster with a photographic print of this same figure eerily doubled over the screen image – the newscaster's face becomes a hollow shell as the photograph serves to mask the positive video image, thus emphasizing the mute black background rather than the figure's formal coherence. This strategy reveals the

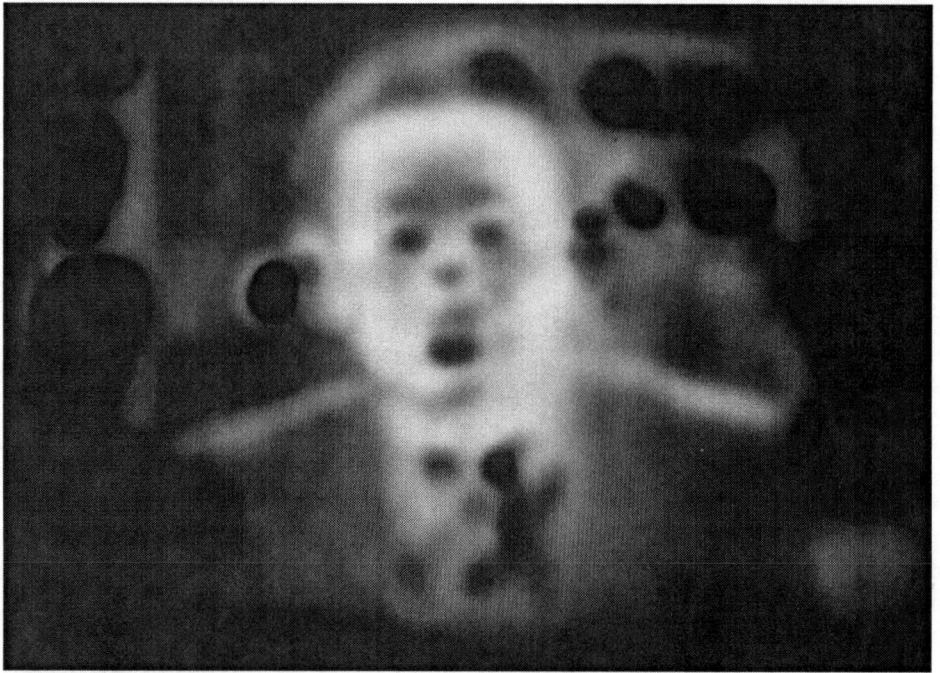

FIGURE 26.2 Jean Philippe-Baert, *Coagulation*, 2002. Still image from video installation, video three minutes and 15 seconds. Courtesy of the artist

ephemeral ground of the image, which nonetheless emerges from a river of information that seems to "coagulate" into a meaningful picture.

Other artists find the organic and the indexical *within* the digital image. For example, Vietnamese American photographer Binh Danh works with both digital files and the photocopy process to create a negative, which he then places on the surface of a leaf for an indefinite amount of time (it may take up to a month for the image to emerge). This process is rooted in Danh's desire to link the scientific quest for knowledge, as well as the political quest for power, to the unhurried and circular tempo of organic processes. In *Mother and Child* (Figure 26.3), from his series "Immortality: The Remnants of the Vietnam and American War" (2001), Danh printed journalistic photographs of Vietnam culled from books and the Internet onto leaves and encased them in resin, merging the documentary, the digital, and the organic into an overarching techno-organic system. Danh writes of this process as a way of revealing "elemental transmigration: the decomposition and composition of matter into other forms."[45] His work speaks to the possibility of linking disparate cultures by way of technology, as well as the effects of war, as part of a cosmic process – liquefaction in the best and worse sense.

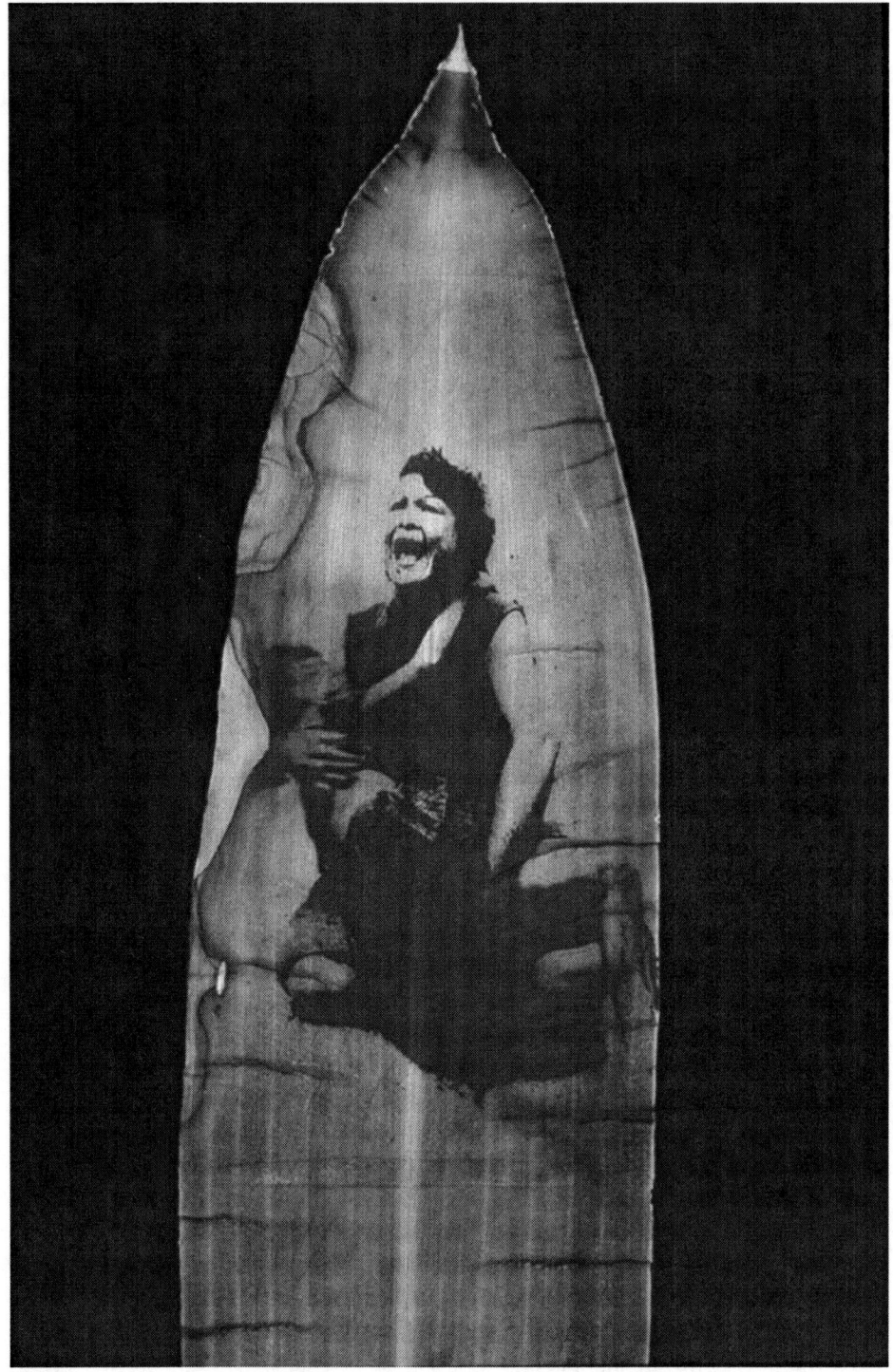

FIGURE 26.3 Binh Danh, *Mother and Child*, from the series "Immortality: The Remnants of the Vietnam and American War," 2001. Chlorophyll print cast in resin. 10 × 8 in. Courtesy of the artist

Appropriating the Spectacle by Working the Screen

Today, artists are able to appropriate and manipulate the flow of memory-images (and the associations that ensue from various combinations of it) rather than *an* image, thereby revealing "another kind of belief and disbelief with respect to what is shown and what happens."[46] As Stiegler notes, digital media's malleability makes a new order of meaning possible. For instance, the fact that analogue films and photographs circulate as digital information in forms unimagined previously means that these cultural artifacts, and the memories that they evoke, coagulate into a new order of memory. This further complicates the dichotomy of spectacle/viewer eroded by the Fluxus artists. Not only is the spectacle reversible, underwritten by the flesh (of the world and my own), it now constitutes, erases, and rewrites cultural narratives as it circulates. Furthermore, the flexibility of the digital image means that the spectacle can bend back to meditate on itself.

According to Stiegler, memories based on fictional or unlived events are advanced by digital technology – particularly with its ability to store and repeat memory-objects.[47] This is what Stiegler terms "tertiary memory." "First memory" is, for phenomenologist Edmund Husserl, consciousness of a present moment that is already past (perception), while "second memory" is the recollection of a past event *as past* (imagination); both are rooted in their relation to a past event. Distinguishing tertiary or third memory from first and second memory, Stiegler notes that although third memory is mediated by technology, it allows previously stabilized memories to be modified. This mnemonic function is linked to the development of time-based storage media beginning in the nineteenth century (e.g., the gramophone, film, and photography). Digitization marks a new stage in this process by allowing former memory-objects to be reformulated into algorithms and circulated in a manner unknown in the analogue age.

In certain contemporary works, the screen is the site where memories converge. For instance, French artist Pierre Huyghe's *The Third Memory* (2000) (Figure 26.4) is an installation that reworks memory as if it were a substance like clay or paint. This installation digitally combines film footage from the 1975 feature film *Dog Day Afternoon* – which tells the story of a bank robbery based on an actual event in which John Wojtowicz organized a heist in order to secure funds to help his lover, Ernest Aaron, secure a sex change operation – with Wojtowicz's restaging of the hold-up for Huyghe's camera. In an adjacent room, these two "memories" of the event are accompanied by newspapers and television accounts from the period, as well as letters by Wojtowicz protesting Warner Bros.' copyright claim on "his" story. The third memory is all of these accounts or, rather, it is the shared yet unlived memory of the event by way of media. Furthermore, as the viewer witnesses Wojtowicz's attempt to wrangle his experience of the event from its media depiction, the spectacle rises like a specter that is challenged and battled on its own ground.

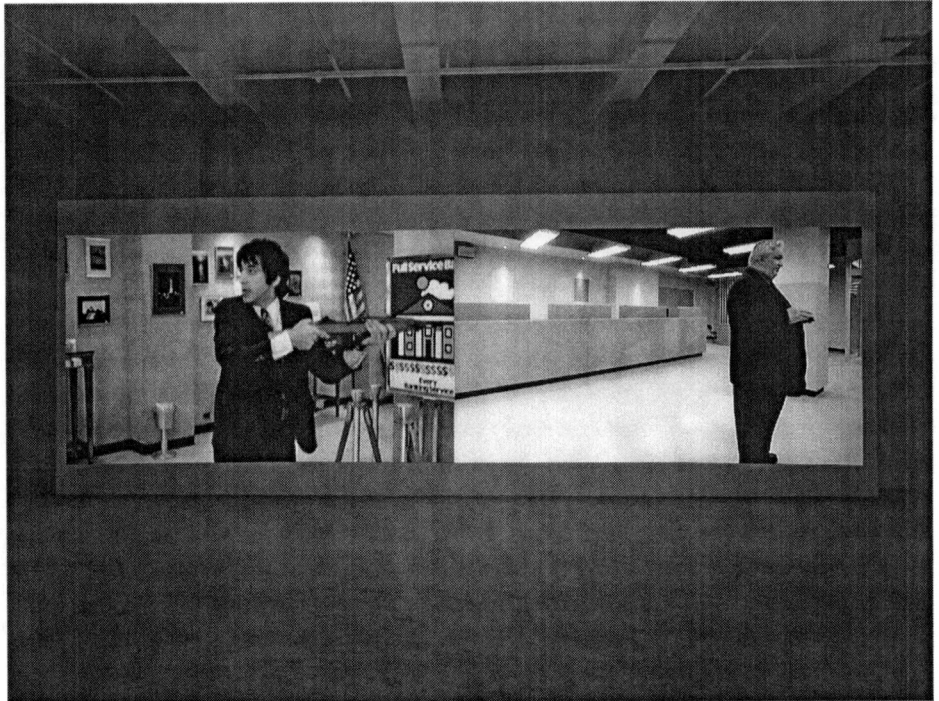

FIGURE 26.4   Pierre Huyghe, *The Third Memory*, 1999. Still image from video installation, double projection, beta digital, video on monitor, nine minutes and 46 seconds. Co-production: Centre Georges Pompidou, Musée National d'art Moderne, Service Nouveaux Medias and the Renaissance Society at the University of Chicago, with the participation of the Marian Goodman Gallery, New York, Myriam and Jacques Salomon, Le Resnoy, Studio national des arts contemporains. Photograph: Jon Abbott. Courtesy of Marion Goodman Gallery

Reading *The Third Memory* through Debord's theory of the spectacle, Jean-Charles Masséra argues that, through his process of reenactment, Wojtowicz lays claim to the consciousness of his life – a consciousness that was lost to Hollywood. According to Masséra, Wojtowicz literally reappropriates his existence. *The Third Memory* thus enables "a form of disalienated self-representation."[48] I find, more importantly, that *The Third Memory* reformulates the viewer's memory of the film narrative by combining Wojtowicz's reenactment of the event with other media accounts. In this way, *The Third Memory* reveals that its *Dog Day Afternoon* narrative is as flexible as the non-linear digital process used to assemble the images. What is also interesting, as Stiegler's theory suggests, is the way in which the Warner Bros. version of the story informs Wojtowicz's memory of the hold-up. On this note, Huyghe notes that "what is interesting today is that, of course, [Wojtowicz's] memory is affected by the fiction itself."[49] Yet *The Third Memory* resists the process of mnemonic accommodation; Wojtowicz's first and second memories are actively reconfigured through his reenactment of the event as event. In the process, the spectacle is taken up as a third memory as well; the dreaded threat of alienation and the attendant longing for authentic experience are staged by Wojtowicz, who struggles to liberate himself from the media depiction of his life.

In Scottish artist Douglas Gordon's *24 Hour Psycho* (1993), the screen is not a battleground but a celebrated site, a public manifestation of third memory. This installation consists of a suspended screen, 20 feet wide, set diagonally in the middle of a gallery. Alfred Hitchcock's film thriller *Psycho* (1960) is digitally projected on the screen at the rate of two frames per second (rather than the cinematic standard 24 frames per second), and thus the film runs for approximately 24 hours. *Twenty-Four Hour Psycho* is about memory and the associations it evokes. Christine Ross notes that the work initiates a struggle with memory; it "activates, in the viewer, perceptual and memory dysfunction." For Ross, this dysfunction is productive: "as the viewer struggles with memory and identity formation, she or he enacts the loss of the paternal [which the film stages] and, with this, a mode of perception more porous to imaginary constructions."[50] The point of *24 Hour Psycho* is, for Ross, the way that it forces the viewer to struggle with the corporeal limits of perception. The viewer's perception becomes the resistant focal point around which the flood of imagery must navigate. That said, *24 Hour Psycho* is about more than the relationship between memory and perception. The work concerns third memory – that is, the way that these infamous images circulate *as* memories and, in doing so, create a collective and shared history. Viewers watch the infamous scene of Marion Crane in the shower as if it were a common language. On this point, Gordon notes:

> I was interested in allowing the micro narrative to become disengaged from the original version, and to let it exist in real time alongside our memories and anticipations of what we think we are about to see. . . . At the same time, we are aware of a new narrative being constructed using the same information as the original.[51]

Jim Campbell's *Illuminated Average #1: Hitchcock's Psycho* (2000; Figure 26.5) is another take on the thriller. Campbell scanned each frame from *Psycho* and, from this information, generated one stunning backlit print that incorporates the entirety of the film. Unlike photographs, which rely upon a spectral chain of luminance in order to link an illuminated moment past to its future moment of viewing, this digital image ghosts by averaging. If the viewer looks closely, each instant in the film is contained within this one image: Marion checks the rear-view mirror as she drives away from her crime; a patrolman raps on the window; a lamp-lit room at the Bates Motel; a room with stuffed birds peering from the wall; seen from a voyeuristic angle, Norman attacks Marion in the shower; blood seeps down the drain; a car is hauled trunk-first from the swamp. Clearly, Hitchcock's *Psycho* is about memory and how film remembers. Campbell's work is about how we remember film.

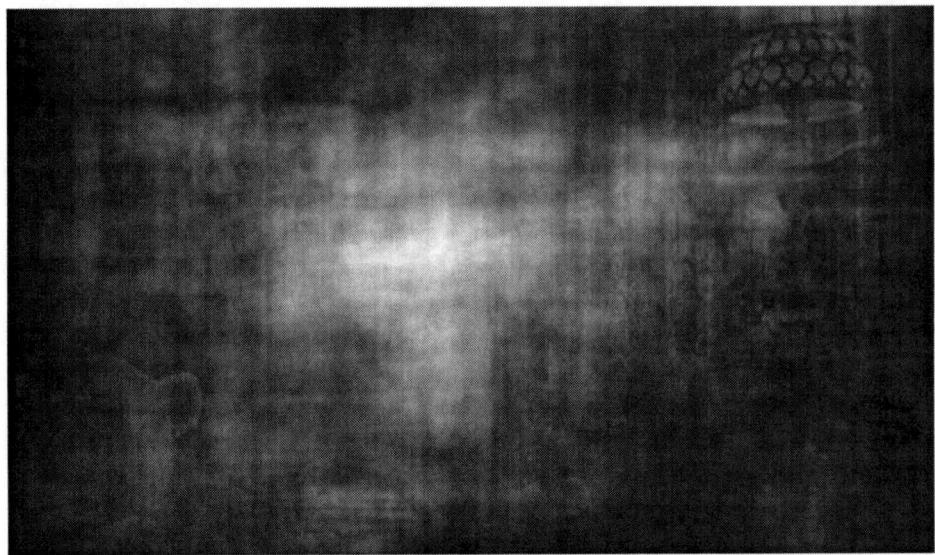

FIGURE 26.5 Jim Campbell, *Illuminated Average #1: Hitchcock's Psycho*, 2000.
Averaged over one hour and 50 minutes (entire film), light box with duratrans print.
30 × 18 in. Courtesy of the artist

Rather than capitalizing on the screen as the site where third memories take shape – as in the examples by Huyghe, Campbell, and Gordon – Swiss artist Pipilotti Rist challenges the screen and the mediating relationship it enables, particularly between the female figure, on one side, and the gaze that seizes, embraces, and gives meaning to the figure on the other. In many of her works, such as *Sip My Ocean* (1996), the camera collides or smashes into the objects before it. When viewed, the effect is like a collision between the screen and the objects depicted.[52] This confrontation is approached allegorically in Rist's *Ever is Over All* (1997), a video installation in which two digital-video images overlap unequally at the gallery's corner accompanied by a sound track with a lilting voice. The right panel is reminiscent of an impressionist landscape while the image on the left depicts a brightly clad woman walking down the street carrying what appears to be a long stemmed flower, joyfully skipping as she smashes the car windows along her path. The car window – a glass screen separating inside and outside – falls to the flower, acting as a metaphor for the screen that mediates gender.

In other works, Rist approaches the screen in a manner that suggests a *temporal* barrier. At moments this temporal barrier is shattered, overleaped, or infiltrated and, consequently, the art work confronts *its own* history. For instance, in her *I'm Not the Girl Who Misses Much* (1986), Rist presents her own hysterical movements – enabled by digital speed and cuts, ultimately losing vertical and horizontal hold – to the camera/gaze, her figure trapped in an eternal present. Concomitantly, the work's sound environment condenses John Lennon's opening lyric to *Happiness is a Warm Gun* (1968) to one line. Peggy Phelan writes of this work: "Thinking of video as a kind of living anthology still pulsing with the history of its earlier forms, Rist encourages her viewers to reconsider the traditional concept of the past and the dead as somehow over, gone, vanished."[53] For Phelan, the memory of the song, but also of Lennon's brutal assassination, resonates for the viewer. Like *The Third Memory*, this work alters the viewer's understanding of an event through the manipulation of mediated, unlived memory-objects that are, in this case, aural. However, while the lyrics evoke a mythical time-past, the figure remains suspended in a technological glitch, unable to transcend the temporal barrier.

In these examples, there is an acknowledgment that appropriation involves staging a confrontation with memory. On this point, Rist writes: "There are different kinds of clouds: those I have seen, and those I imagine. The clouds I imagine (most clouds) I have never seen. The vast majority of clouds are those which others have seen or have imagined or will one day imagine."[54] Here, Rist explains the difference between perception (clouds I have seen) and imagination (clouds I imagine). Yet, her description of clouds resonates with unlived, mediated memories as well. For instance, the sky and clouds are reminiscent of an earlier work, Ono's *Sky TV* (1966), which consists of a television monitor that, through live video, depicts the sky above the gallery. Rist's words also refer to Lennon's *Imagine* album which, released five years after Ono's *Sky TV*, begins with the lyrics: "Imagine there's no Heaven/It's easy if you try/No Hell below us/Above us only sky."

Rist openly acknowledges her debt to Fluxus, particularly Lennon and Ono, and her mediated memories of these previous artists' imaginings.[55] These "tertiary clouds" – clouds seen in a gallery's television, heard on a phonograph, or merely heard *about* – only come to visibility against a screen. The screen is what reveals or, when unaddressed, obscures the relation between memories perceived, those imagined, and third, mediated memories. Complicating this, the screen also represents and is a physical manifestation of the media and its spectacular control of third memory. In her work, Rist stages a confrontation with the screen and, in doing so, the spectacle is summoned and shattered in order that alternative cultural narratives might emerge through its cracks.

Conclusion

The manipulation of digitized analogue material allows a new relation between past and present to emerge. For instance, in *The Third Memory*, Huyghe reveals the economic struggle over the cultural appropriation of Wojtowicz's story and emphasizes the homosexual love story. Rist, in *I'm Not the Girl Who Misses Much*, gestures to the contradictory – feminist, sexual, and political – implications of Lennon's "warm gun." However, Viola's *The Passions* assumes an affiliation with a Renaissance past without fully engaging it and, furthermore, without allowing the present in which the work was created to speak of its own contingency and context. *Silent Mountain*, for instance, leaps over the historical and cultural divide that might allow the present conditions, as well as the particularities of the religious painting to which it refers, to show up. For, although the emotive figures speak to the conflict of religious faith in the political realm today – as witnessed in the current "oil wars," the release of Mel Gibson's 2003 film *The Passion of The Christ*, and the resurgence of Jewish, Christian, Islamic, and Hindu fundamentalism – this "renaissance" is, although imbedded in the work, overpowered by its immersive affect.

Bewes notes that "[t]he concept of globalization represents the 'totality' in a simplified, intellectually graspable but politically immutable form – like the concept of God in an earlier epoch."[56] This statement implies that, today, the notion of globalization stands in for God. At the same time, the popularity of Viola's work (and Gibson's film) suggests that God stands in for globalization. In either case, the longing for totality – be it economic or religious – in the face of modernity's disintegration is satisfied by spectacular immersion, thus offering an antidote to postmodern fragmentation. Technically speaking, *Silent Mountain* gives the viewer this sense of totality through image-immersion. The edges blur; the screen fades. Viola notes that in his earlier work he used scale to create an immersive effect. He writes that upon discovering the liquid-crystal-display (LCD) flat screen (as opposed to the cathode ray tube screen): "I found myself falling into the image, getting lost in its aura. . . . This provided the final link I needed to realize that immersion is not dependant on scale, that it has to do with some other property of the image."[57] The effect sought by Viola in religious painting and found by him in the immersive quality of the screen is, I contend, central to the underlying theme of *The Passions*. Yet, in order for this shared longing for totality to show up as such, the mutable screen upon which the image forms – and, by extension, the boundary that separates and mediates perception, imagination, and third memory – must be recognized.

No longer merely a backdrop, the screen is both a locus and metaphor for artists who manipulate third memories. Of these, the spectacle is the third memory par excellence. It is the narrative of a shared anxiety for and against fragmentation; it is the longing for liberation from economic and experiential image-domination; it is the shadow-story of Disney, Warner Bros., and Nintendo. Engendered by the current stage of capitalism, the digital image allows the spectacle to become an artifact in its own right. The spectacle's threat of domination – as well as its related dialectic of alienation and authentic experience – casts its shadow upon the screen of the present and, as such, is ripe for appropriation.

Acknowledgments

Thanks to those individuals who supported me in this endeavor, particularly Amelia Jones, Lise Creurer, Magdalena Zurawski, and Irina Leimbacher.

Notes

1 Viola (2003), 199.
2 Hansen (2004), 267–8.
3 The fact that the classically expressive figures in Viola's *Silent Mountain* are depicted in street-clothes might be interpreted as an oblique reference to the contemporary context in which the work functions.
4 Hansen (2004), 1.
5 Ihde (1993), 111. Ihde attributes the phrase "politics of the artifact" to Langdon Winner. For more on the relationship between photography and poststructuralism see my essay: Dore Bowen, "Hysteria and the Helio-Trope: On Bodies, Gender, and the Photograph," *Afterimage: The Journal of Media Arts and Cultural Criticism*, vol. 26, no. 4 (January 1999):13–16.
6 Heidegger (1971), 45. See also Heidegger (1977), 32.
7 Debord (1983), section 10.
8 Ibid., section 3.
9 Ibid., section 165.
10 Ibid., section 168:149.
11 Knabb, ed. and trans. (1981), 45.
12 Khayati (1981), 171.
13 Debord (1983), section 208.
14 Ibid., section 187.
15 Ibid., section 208.
16 Debord (1981), 37.
17 Crimp (1993), 111. See also Singerman in this volume.
18 Crimp (1984), 186.
19 Rush (1999), 53.
20 Debord (1983), section 190.
21 Ibid., section 191.
22 Debord (2002), 141.
23 Debord (1983), section 8.
24 Ibid., section 30.
25 Bewes (2002), 110.
26 Merleau-Ponty (1968), 146 (emphasis mine).
27 Higgins (1984), 69–70.
28 Maciunas (1988), 156.
29 This drawing (plus notes) can be found in Conzen-Meairs (1997), n.p.
30 Hendricks, ed. (1988), 362.
31 Ibid.

32 Debord (1983), section 147.
33 Bergson (1991), 205. See also Bergson (1998), 9–10.
34 Heidegger (1962), 140.
35 Debord (1983), section 220.
36 Ibid.
37 Walter Benjamin writes that film initiated a shock effect in its viewers. "The specta-
    tor's process of association in view of these images is indeed interrupted by their
    constant, sudden change. This constitutes the shock effect of the film." Benjamin
    (1968), 238. In this light, it can be argued that fluxfilms contrast the now outdated
    "shock effect of the film" with the pre-mechanical experience of duration.
38 Walsh (2003), 60.
39 Crary (2002), 464.
40 Hansen (2004), 10.
41 Appadurai (1996), 3.
42 Rosen (2001), 307.
43 Stiegler (2002), 152.
44 On this issue, see Auslander (1999), 53.
45 Danh (2003), CD-ROM.
46 Stiegler (2002), 152.
47 This summary of Husserl's arguments is from Stiegler (2001).
48 Masséra (2000), 139.
49 Cited in Huyghe (2004), n.p.
50 Ross (2001): 28–33.
51 Cited in Ibid.
52 Amelia Jones writes of Rist's confrontational relationship with the screen as aiding
    in a "para-feminist" notion of the body and identity that challenges the binary
    structures of sexual difference. See Jones (forthcoming).
53 Phelan (2001), 44–5.
54 Rist (2001b), 130.
55 See Rist (2001a), 8–28.
56 Bewes (2002), 7.
57 Viola (2003), 203.

References

Appadurai, Arjun (1996). *Modernity at Large: Cultural Dimensions of Globalization.*
  Minneapolis: University of Minnesota Press.
Auslander, Philip (1999). *Liveness: Performance in a Mediatized Culture.* London:
  Routledge.
Benjamin, Walter (1968). "The Work of Art in the Age of Mechanical Reproduction."
  In *Illuminations: Essays and Reflections,* ed. Hannah Arendt, trans. Harry Zohn. New
  York: Schocken Books. 217–51.
Bergson, Henri (1991). *Matter and Memory* (1896), trans. Nancy M. Paul and W. Scott
  Palmer. New York: Zone Books/MIT Press.
—— (1998). *Creative Evolution* (1907), trans. Arthur Mitchell. Mineola, NY: Dover
  Publications.

Bewes, Timothy (2002). *Reification, or The Anxiety of Late Capitalism*. London: Verso Press.

Conzen-Meairs, Ina (1997). "Brief von George Maciunas an George Brecht, ca Oktober 1962." In *Art Games die Schachterln der Fluxuskünstler*. Stuttgart: Staatsgalerie Stuttgart.

Crary, Jonathan (2002). "Spectacle, Attention, Counter-Memory." In *Guy Debord and the Situationist International*, ed. Tom McDonough. Cambridge, MA: MIT Press. 455–66.

Crimp, Douglas (1984). "Pictures." In *Art After Modernism: Rethinking Representation*, ed. Brian Wallis. New York: The New Museum of Contemporary Art. 175–87.

—— (1993). "The Photographic Activity of Postmodernism." In *On the Museum's Ruins*. Cambridge, MA: MIT Press. 108–24.

Danh, Binh (2003). "Interview with Binh Danh by David Pace." *Camerawork: A Journal of Photographic Arts* 20 (1): CD-ROM.

Debord, Guy (1981). "Critique of Separation." In *The Situationist International Anthology*. Berkeley: Bureau of Public Secrets. 34–7.

—— (1983). *The Society of the Spectacle* (1967). Detroit: Black and Red.

—— (2002). "The Avant-Garde of Presence." (1963) In *Guy Debord and the Situationist International*, ed. Tom McDonough. Cambridge, MA: MIT Press. 137–51.

Hansen, Mark B. N. (2004). *New Philosophy for New Media*. Cambridge, MA: MIT Press.

Heidegger, Martin (1962). *Being and Time* (1927), trans. John Macquarrie and Edward Robinson. San Francisco: Harper and Row.

—— (1971). "The Origin of the Work of Art" (1935). In *Poetry, Language, Thought*, trans. Albert Hofstadter. New York: Harper and Row. 17–87.

—— (1977). "The Question Concerning Technology" (1953). In *The Question Concerning Technology and Other Essays*, trans. William Lovitt. New York: Harper and Row. 3–35.

Hendricks, Jon, ed. (1988). *Fluxus Codex*. Detroit and New York: The Gilbert and Lila Silverman Fluxus Collection, in association with Harry N. Abrams.

Higgins, Dick (1984). "Underpiece/Overpiece." In *Horizons: The Poetics and Theory of the Intermedia*. Carbondale, IL: Southern Illinois University Press. 64–70.

Huyghe, Pierre (2004). http://www.french culture.org/art/events/huyghes-inter.html.

Ihde, Don (1993). "Deromanticizing Heidegger." In *Postphenomenology: Essays in the Postmodern Context*. Evanston, IL: Northwestern University Press. 103–15.

Jones, Amelia (forthcoming). *Self/Image: The Body and Technologies of Representation*. London: Routledge.

Khayati, Mustapha (1981). "Captive Words: Preface to a Situationist Dictionary." In *The Situationist International Anthology*. Berkeley: Bureau of Public Secrets. 170–75.

Knabb, Ken, ed. and trans. (1981). "Definitions." In *The Situationist International Anthology*. Berkeley: Bureau of Public Secrets. 45–7.

Maciunas, George (1988). "Neo-Dada in Music, Theater, Poetry, Art" (1962). In *Fluxus: Selections from the Gilbert and Lila Silverman Collection*, ed. Clive Phillpot and Jon Hendricks. New York: Museum of Modern Art.

Masséra, Jean-Charles (2000). "The Lesson of Stains." In *The Third Memory*. Paris: Centre Georges Pompidou. 93–139.

Merleau-Ponty, Maurice (1968). "The Intertwining – The Chiasm" (1961). In *The Visible and the Invisible*, ed. Claude Lefort, trans. Alphonso Lingis. Evanston, IL: Northwestern University Press. 130–55.

Phelan, Peggy (2001). "Opening up Spaces Within Spaces: The Expansive Art of Pipilotti Rist." In *Pipilotti Rist*, ed. Peggy Phelan, Hans-Ulrich Obrist, and Elisabeth Bronfen. London: Phaidon Press. 32–77.

Rist, Pipilotti (2001a). "I rist, you rist, she rists, we rist, you rist, they rist, tourist: Hans Ulrich Obrist in Conversation with Pipilotti Rist." In *Pipilotti Rist*, ed. Peggy Phelan, Hans Ulrich Obrist, and Elisabeth Bronfen. London: Phaidon Press. 8–28.

—— (2001b). "Two Untitled Poems." In *Pipilotti Rist*, ed. Peggy Phelan, Hans Ulrich Obrist, and Elisabeth Bronfen. London: Phaidon Press. 130.

Rosen, Philip (2001). *Change Mummified: Cinema, Historicity, Theory.* Minneapolis, MN: University of Minnesota Press.

Ross, Christine (2001). "The Insufficiency of the Performative: Video Art at the Turn of the Millennium." *Art Journal*, vol. 60, no. 1:28–33.

Rush, Michael (1999). *New Media in Late 20th-Century Art.* London: Thames and Hudson.

Stiegler, Bernard (2001). "Derrida and Technology: Fidelity at the Limits of Deconstruction and the Prosthesis of Faith." In *Jacques Derrida and the Humanities: A Critical Reader*, ed. Tom Cohen. Cambridge: Cambridge University. 238–70.

—— (2002). "The Discrete Image." In *Echographies of Television*. Cambridge: Polity Press. 147–63.

Viola, Bill (2003). "A Conversation: Hans Belting and Bill Viola." In *The Passions*, ed. John Walsh. Los Angeles: J. Paul Getty Museum. 189–220.

Walsh, John (2003). "Emotions in Extreme Time: Bill Viola's Passions Project." In *The Passions*, ed. John Walsh. Los Angeles: J. Paul Getty Museum. 25–63.

27

"Life-like": Historicizing Process and Responsiveness in Digital Art

María Fernández

Some currents of contemporary theory expand the notion of life to include the organic, the inorganic, the material, and the virtual. This entails an understanding of nature as constantly unfolding – as linked to a dissolution of boundaries between bodies, objects, and environments. Basing his ideas on the work of the French philosopher Gilles Deleuze, theorist Manuel de Landa explains: "... reality *is a single matter-energy* undergoing phase transitions of various kinds. ... Rocks and winds, germs and words, are all different manifestations of this dynamic reality, or, in other words they all represent the different ways in which this single matter-energy *expresses itself*."[1] This understanding of nature also involves a reconceptualization of space from static to active, a space that, in the words of architect Greg Lynn, has properties of flow, turbulence, viscosity, and drag.[2] Such ideas also call into question the Cartesian division of mind and body, distinctions between the virtual and the material, and the presumed objectivity and reliability of perception.

Following the work of Deleuze and his frequent collaborator Félix Guattari, theorists Brian Massumi and Elizabeth Grosz, among others, have argued that the human body is simultaneously material and virtual. According to Massumi, the relation between the virtual and the corporeal is analogous to the relation of energy to matter: they are mutually convertible dimensions of the same reality. He explains:

This would make the incorporeal something like a phase-shift of the body in the usual sense, but not one that comes after it in time. It would be a conversion or unfolding of the body *contemporary* to its every move. . . . This movement-slip gives new urgency to questions of ontology, ontological difference, inextricably linked to concepts of potential and process and, by extension, event – in a way that bumps "being" straight into becoming.[3]

From these perspectives, works of art should no longer be conceived as static autonomous entities but as *evolving processes* that unfold in relation to both the user and the environment. Massumi and de Landa each call for the development of a process-oriented art where the artist is the initiator of a process but is not in control of its outcome.[4] This entails jettisoning ideas of art as object, as well as of the artist's mastery and control of materials engrained in traditional conceptions of artistic practice.

In the contemporary context, process-oriented art is facilitated by computer technology. The computer enables instantaneous communication, the creation and proliferation of images, creatures and environments, and permits the acceleration of processes such as development, reproduction, and death of synthetic life forms. These procedures are central to artificial life, a field of research concerned with the simulation of living organisms and the generation of lifelike behavior within computers and other synthetic media. According to its founder, scientist Christopher Langton, "there is nothing . . . that restricts biology to carbon-based life; it is simply the only kind of life that has been available to study."[5] Artists have adopted techniques of artificial life – that is, computational processes that emulate or model aspects of biological processes such as evolution and population genetics – to create works that exhibit self-organization, evolution, and various forms of agency and interaction. While the interest in perception, virtuality, embodiment, process, instability, and the relation of various life forms to their environments are central to contemporary digital art, it is important to recognize that these concerns *already* were fundamental to a reconceptualization of artistic practices after WWII.

Pamela Lee has persuasively argued that the 1960s were characterized by an obsession with time. She finds evidence of this preoccupation in Norbert Wiener's theory of cybernetics, art historian George Kubler's influential 1962 book *The Shape of Time*, and the work of multiple artists including Jean Tinguely, Robert Smithson, and On Kawara. Expanding on Lee's excellent exposition, I argue that theorists and artists manifested their concern with time by investigating specific processes and interactions rather than through abstractions. Many artists explored the transformations that objects and materials displayed by interacting with their environment and other entities in it. This led to reflections not only on time but on qualities of liveliness and on the nature of life itself. Some of these early works entailed the construction of "intelligent machines," challenging traditional differentiations between the natural and the artificial, the animate and the inanimate.[6]

In what follows, I will discuss works of kinetic, conceptual, and/or electronic art that involve some of these ideas, as well as their applicability to digital art. My discussion is less a history than a historical exercise. In relating past to present, I intend neither to reduce contemporary work to the art of the past nor to construct a linear history. Rather, my purpose is to discern commonalities while acknowledging differences among diverse works. In order to orient my discussion to digital art, first I must summarize some of the technological and theoretical bases of digital culture.

Contrary to the widespread assumption that the history of digital art is short and simple because it is relatively recent, the history of digital art is vast and multidisciplinary. A cursory examination of this field involves not only the histories of art, science, and technology but also intellectual, social, and military histories. The heterogeneity of this art demands that the history of art expand its frame of reference to include scientific and technical ideas. Without such associations, any discussion of the works would be superficial.

The Foundations of Digital Culture

Scholars trace the beginnings of computer technology to the nineteenth century or even earlier, including among its pioneers the seventeenth-century philosopher Gottfried Wilhelm von Leibniz and the nineteenth-century mathematicians George Boole, Charles Babbage, and Ada Lovelace. The concepts of energy and entropy, central to the science of thermodynamics developed in the second half of the nineteenth century, are also integral to this history. In 1865, Rudolf Clausius coined the word "entropy" to refer to a measure of the energy unavailable for work in a closed physical system. Entropy was thus the negative of energy.[7] In the twentieth century, the concept of entropy would be translated to "information," a move that, as Katherine Hayles, among others, has argued, would link the natural sciences, the humanities, the social sciences, and the arts.[8]

During WWII, the necessity for inscription and decryption of communications exponentially accelerated computer development. Alan Turing's work in crypto analysis and theories of computability led to the invention of the University of Manchester MK1, the first programmable digital computer. Parallel efforts in the USA guided by the Hungarian-born mathematician John von Neumann resulted in the ENIAC (Electronic Numerical Integrator and Computer).[9] After the War, the US Department of Defense continued to fund computer research generously in order to maintain US technological leadership during the cold war.

Artists active in the late 1950s and 1960s inherited the technological advances achieved during the previous decades, as well a variety of newly created disciplines including information theory, cybernetics, general systems theory, and artificial intelligence. These disciplines would exercise a lasting influence on artistic practices, although their impact has gone largely unrecognized in the established histories of modern and contemporary art.

In a book entitled *A Mathematical Theory of Communication* (1949) engineer Claude Shannon, in collaboration with the mathematician Warren Weaver, advanced a mathematical analysis of communication that became known as "information theory." Employed at Bell Labs, Shannon and Weaver were concerned with finding an efficient way to transmit maximum information in telephone networks. In their analysis, this entailed encoding the data into electronic signals by means of an encoding apparatus, transmitting the signals through a specific communication channel with the minimum amount of error, and decoding the message in a receiving apparatus. Shannon and Weaver understood communication exclusively as the replication in the receiver of the data pattern entered by the sender. From this perspective, the semantic content as well as the receiver's interpretation of the message were irrelevant to communication.

Mathematician Norbert Wiener developed cybernetics, a field contemporaneous and related to information theory, which he defined as the science of communication and control between animals and machines as well as between machines and machines.[10] The interaction of a machine with the external world involved the introduction of data (input) to elicit the machine's effect on the world (output). The quality of communication among entities was affected by factors such as feedback, noise, and entropy. For Wiener, feedback was the act of controlling a machine on the basis of its performance. Elements of the machine itself, which he called "sensory members," evaluated the machine's performance.[11] He identified as "noise" elements extraneous to a message which effect its transmission. Like Shannon, Wiener borrowed the term "entropy" from thermodynamics. But while for Shannon entropy was the information measure of a system (he gave entropy the same sign as information), for Wiener it was the degree of disorganization or randomness in a system, the negative of information.[12]

General systems theory, first articulated by the Austrian biologist Ludwig von Bertalanffy, concerned the organization and communication of complex entities both biological and social. Von Bertalanffy's theories merged biology with thermodynamics by proposing that biological organisms were whole systems that interacted with their environments. Just as in Shannon and Weaver's information theory information was independent from the material specificities of the transmitter, for von Bertalanffy, the attributes of systems were independent of their biological and material qualities. Thus he identified the objectives of the biological sciences as the discovery of the principles of organization and behavior. Like contemporary theorists, von Bertalanffy refuted strict differentiation between the organic and the inorganic, biology and physics, the behavioral and the hard sciences.[13]

Artificial Intelligence (AI) originated in the mid 1950s in the work of multiple scientists including mathematician John McCarthy from Dartmouth University, Herbert Simon from the Carnegie Institute in Pittsburgh, and Marvin Minsky from Massachusetts Institute of Technology (MIT). AI had as its goal computer emulation of intelligent behavior and higher intellectual functions such as mathematical problem solving and creativity by the logical manipulation of symbolic systems. In contrast to the more recently established science of artificial life discussed later in this chapter, AI was based on a paradigm of centralized control. The computer was conceived as analogous to the brain in the sense that it governed all functions of the system to be studied. Communications theory, cybernetics, general systems theory, and AI all had in common the study of processes of organization, development, and interaction, concerns shared by various contemporary scientists and philosophers.[14]

Process in Kinetic and Early Cybernetic Art

Visual artists were similarly interested in processes from the early twentieth century on. The properties of light, the impact of movement on vision and the instability of sensory perception can be traced to the 1920s and 1930s in the work of artists such as Marcel Duchamp, László Moholy-Nagy, Man Ray, Len Lye, and Thomas Wilfred. These interests persisted in kinetic art and op art of the 1950s and 1960s. A series of works produced by Israeli artist Yaacov Agam, for example, informed by both the Talmud and scientific literature of his time, depended on the movement of the spectator to unfold. Titled after musical compositional structures (contrapuntal, polyphonic etc), his paintings from the early 1950s revealed various compositions as the spectator walked in front of them. His concern with transience and transformation was evident in his play-objects, where forms and images emphasized transitions from one element to another and vibrations among related elements.[15] Agam's *The Red Touch* (1963) thus consisted of a number of springs mounted on a wooden surface. As the spectator/participant ran her hand across them, the springs moved and visual patterns appeared, transformed, and disappeared. Formally, the work was unstable, for no two spectators achieved the same results. Agam's large-scale games often had *aural* components as the artist amplified the sound from the vibrations of the elements.[16] Agam continued to stress interactions between his works and the user during the rest of his career, involving cybernetics and computers in his later work.[17]

In the late 1940s Nicholas Schöffer, a Hungarian sculptor living in Paris, developed his theory of spatio-dynamism – the dynamic integration of space in a plastic work.[18] He coined the terms "lumino-dynamism" and "chromo-dynamism" to describe the movement of light and color on the surface of a construction according to a pre-determined or random cycle. His *CYSP* sculpture series, combines in its name the first letters of cybernetics and spatio-dynamism. In 1956, choreographer Maurice Béjar commissioned *CYSP I* for the Festival of Avant-Garde Art in Marseille. The work consists of a steel and aluminum frame with 16 movable plates of colored translucent and transparent

Plexiglas set on a base mounted on four rollers. *CYSP I* could travel in all directions at two speeds and rotate, setting in motion the colored plates. Photo-electric cells and a microphone allowed it to react with movement to variations in color, light, and sound intensity in its environment. *CYSP I* exemplified the cybernetic principles of input, output, and feedback. Through simple electric sensors it received messages from its environment and responded by acting on the external world.

Cybernetician Gordon Pask and artist Roy Ascott were key figures in the development of cybernetic art in Britain. Pask, who was a familiar figure in London artistic circles, produced the 1953 project *Musicolour* in collaboration with mathematician, Robin McKinnon Wood. *Musicolour*, a cybernetic system for the theater, projected visual images in response to a musician's performance. The machine reacted to the cues of the music by projecting visual images on to a large screen and the performer could then respond to *Musicolour*, closing the loop.[19] In 1961 Pask published the important book *An Approach to Cybernetics*. Ascott also had an instrumental role in promoting cybernetics in the art world; his work from the 1950s already demonstrated interest in systems and interactivity, and from 1963 to 1970 he wrote influential essays on the applications of cyber-netics to art and introduced cybernetics to art education in Britain.[20]

In these early writings Ascott described an art in which process was more important than results, an art characterized by formal ambiguity and instability as well as by the active participation of artist and spectator in the act of crea-tion.[21] Ascott recognized that modern art was no longer purely visual, thus he proposed the term "behavioral art" to refer to work that employed tactile, postural, aural components.[22] Ascott's propositions were prescient and are still timely, although other artists and theorists have since elaborated sophisticated arguments along similar lines.[23]

Both Pask and Ascott contributed projects to the large-scale 1968 Institute of Contemporary Art exhibition in London, *Cybernetic Serendipity*, which was organized by Jasia Reichardt.[24] Pask's installation, *Colloquy of Mobiles*, included male and female mobiles equipped with a set of programs to determine their possible movements and behavior. Anticipating current artificial-life (a-life) art, Pask provided each mobile with a set of goals and, in order to achieve these objectives, the mobiles had to learn to communicate, cooperate, and compete with one another. The piece also shared the limitation of contemporary a-life narra-tives in its elaboration of a heavily gendered narrative (the males aggressively compete for the attention of the females) to explain the behavior of the agents.[25]

Edward Ihnatowicz, a Polish artist resident in Britain and a pioneer of robotic art, contributed the piece SAM (Sound Activated Mobile) to the Cybernetic Serendipity exhibition. SAM was an interactive electro-hydraulic sculpture con-sisting of a four-petaled, flower-shaped fiberglass "head" mounted on a custom-made, flexible aluminum structure reminiscent of a spinal column. Responding to the voices of gallery visitors, the microphone mounted on each petal activated hydraulic pistons, which caused the column to move.

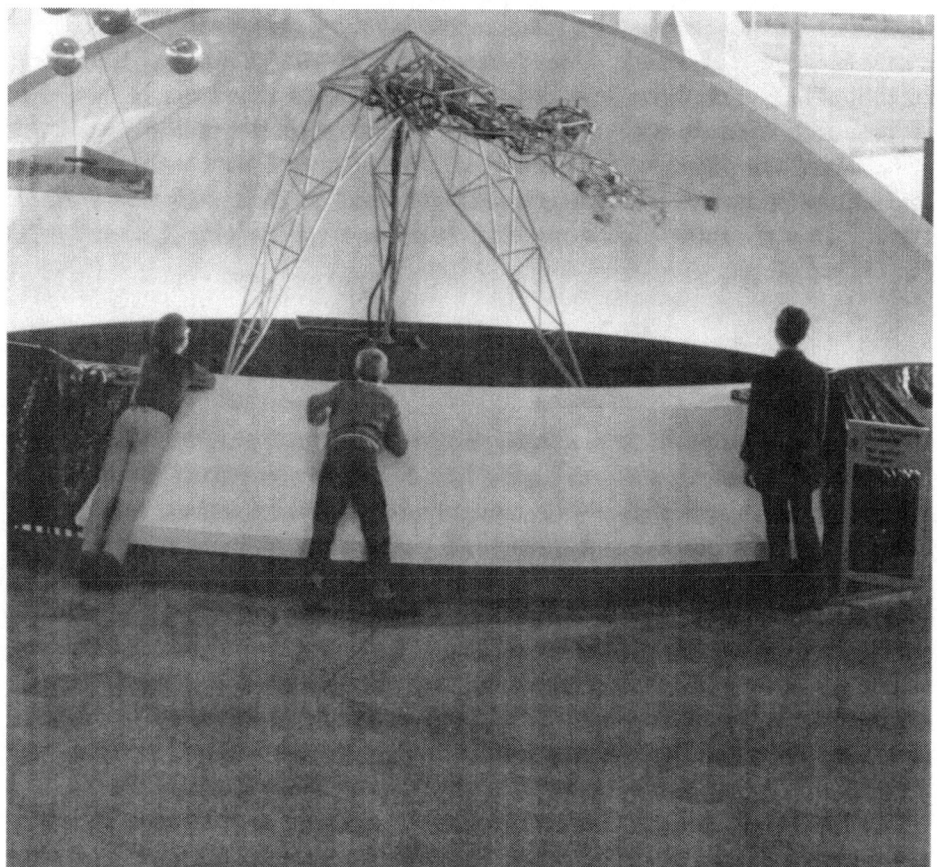

FIGURE 27.1 Edward Ihnatowicz, *Senster*, 1971 (in situ). Photograph courtesy of Mrs Olga Ihnatowicz and the CACHe Project

In 1969, the electronics company Phillips commissioned Ihnatowicz to build a computer-controlled robot, *Senster*, for the Evoluon, the Phillips exhibition hall in Eindhoven, Holland (Figure 27.1). Completed in 1971, *Senster* consisted of six independent electro-hydraulic systems based on the articulation of a lobster's claw. Four microphones placed on its head, along with a close-range radar device, allowed the robot to identify the source of sound and movement and to respond to these stimuli. *Senster* responded to loud sounds and violent gestures by turning away from the participant. It approached only if addressed with a soft voice and gentle movements. *Senster* was a machine that could learn new behaviors according to the sophistication of its programming, thus complicating a clear behavioral differentiation between animals and machines. Although both *SAM* and *Senster* appear as independent entities, the behaviors of each were elicited by the bodily cues of participants. The affective, playful qualities of these works surpassed the instrumentality of Wiener's cybernetic theories.

In 1969 *Cybernetic Serendipity* traveled from London to the Smithsonian Institution in Washington but, due to its technical complexity, the museum finally declined to install it. The Corcoran Gallery of Art agreed to host the exhibition but, in the opinion of artist and critic Douglas Davis, the inexperience of American curators with technological art was apparent in the Corcoran's installation. The pieces were arranged side by side, as if they were traditional painting or sculpture, without consideration paid to their sound and movement.[26] Thus the show contributed little to advance technologically-based art in the United States.

Process, Art, and "The Systems Approach"

In a chapter of his book *Beyond Modern Sculpture* (1968) entitled "Cyborg and Robot Art," American artist and critic Jack Burnham recognized the impact of cybernetics and systems theory on contemporary artistic practices, arguing that "cyborg art" was becoming the next and perhaps the ultimate stage of sculpture.[27] For Burnham, the term "cyborg" referred to both electromechanical systems with lifelike behavior and man-machine systems that, through feedback, paralleled some of the properties of single biological organisms. Anticipating recent claims by a-life artists, he wrote: "For the first time, the word 'organic' ceases to be an unobtainable ideal held out to the artist; following in the wake of cybernetic technology, systems with organic properties will lead to 'sculpture' – if it can be called that – rivaling the attributes of intelligent life."[28]

In a 1968 essay entitled "Systems Esthetics" published in *ArtForum*, Burnham recognized the impact of cybernetics and systems theory on contemporary artistic practices, making clear the need for interdisciplinarity in the education of artists, a need that is only beginning to be recognized in art programs today. Burnham maintained that the de-objectification of art, evident in the art of his day, suggested that contemporary artists were intuitively aware of the importance of the systems approach. De-objectification entailed rejection of the idea of art for art's sake and of craftsmanship, stressing instead the expression of *relations* in the work of art.[29] This required emphasizing connections among the component parts of a work (thus revealing its organizing principles), as well as the interaction of the work with aspects of its environment. In his view, the work of Moholy-Nagy, Robert Smithson, Carl Andre, Hans Haacke, David Medalla, Otto Piene, the French collective GRAV (*Groupe de Recherche d' Art Visuel*), the Japanese group Gutai, and Allan Kaprow (a key figure in the development of Happenings) exemplified the systems approach. Burnham's limited overview of cybernetic art of the 1960s included diasporic artists such as the Argentines Julio Le Parc and Enrique Castro Cid, as well as the Chilean Juan Downing and Korean Nam June Paik. (The scarce number of women and people of color working in this way – the few women working with early "cybernetic art," including Bridget Riley, Martha Botto, and Lilianne Lijn, produced primarily graphics and kinetic light works – might be explained by the poor representation of those groups in both modern art and science).

Hans Haacke, a German artist residing in New York and Medalla, a Filipino living in London, engaged both natural and cybernetic systems in their work. Both artists worked with natural elements such as water and air and explored natural processes, interdependent systems, environmental responses, and instability in material objects. Haacke's *Condensation Cube* (1963) consisted of a Plexiglas box containing air and a little water. Over time, the liquid condensed, changing the appearance of the transparent walls. The form of the work depended on the condensation cycle, stressing the relation of the object with its environment. Because the artist could not determine the final outcome of the process, i.e. the patterns of droplets on the transparent surface, Burnham described Haacke's sculptures as self-organizing and self-stabilizing systems that manifested evidence of natural feedback and equilibrium.[30]

Medalla designed and built machines that transformed natural materials including mud, sand, smoke, coffee beans, salt, and soap through the repetition of simple rhythms. He described himself as both "a poet who celebrates physics" and as "hyzologist," after the ancient Ionian pre-Socratic philosophers who believed all matter to be alive.[31] Medalla's sculpture *Cloud Canyons* (1964) consisted of a set of plywood boxes containing a mixture of soap and water. Air pumps gradually transformed this mixture into foam, which changed form in response to air gravity, atmospheric pressure, and the shape of the boxes. The sculpture thus took form only with interaction with its environment and demonstrated the instability of matter as the elaborate bubble sculptures evaporated. In 1964, Medalla's proposals for future art works included machines for writing instant poetry; "Hydroponic rooms with ceilings planted with a million edible mushrooms"; sculptures incorporating living organisms including shrimps, snails, and ants; transparent sculptures that sweat, perspire, and palpitate; and a flock of "radio controlled flying sculptures."[32] Indicating the continual crosspollinations between artistic ideas and commercial and military technologies, Medalla's proposals were partially possible at the time they were written – in 1965–8, American artist Charles Frazier developed small, radio-controlled, gas-powered flying sculptures capable of flying one mile. Medalla's idea of a flock of robotic birds capable of independent behavior also resembles in an uncanny way the "swarms" of small autonomous flying devices, favored by recent military research.[33]

Although many American artists engaged the systems approach in their work during the mid and late 1960s, cybernetic art in the United States remained marginal. Built in 1966 by Thomas Shannon, *Squat*, a robot electrically connected to an ivy plant placed on a table in the same room, was one of the earliest pieces in the US to explore issues of interspecies communication, feedback, and the interaction of organisms with their environment. Revealing the interdependence of various life forms, in *Squat* the plant responds to the participant's touch with a change in its electrical potential, and this change is amplified and conveyed to the robot, turning its various motors on and off.[34]

Experiments in Art and Technology

The indefatigable efforts of Swiss engineer Billy Kluver to promote collaborations between the sciences and the arts resulted in a brief period of effervescence in the creation of cybernetic art in the United States. A researcher at Bell Laboratories studying the physics of infrared lasers, Kluver continuously offered his expertise to New York artists. He collaborated with Jean Tinguely, Andy Warhol, Merce Cunningham, and Robert Rauschenberg, among others. With Rauschenberg he organized *Nine Evenings: Theater and Engineering* in 1966, which took place at the 69th Regiment Armory on Lexington Avenue in New York City, the location of the famous 1913 Armory Show (the show that introduced Americans to European-style modernism). As a series of collaborations between engineers and artists, including John Cage, Deborah Hay, Yvonne Rainer, Lucinda Childs, Alex Hays, and David Tudor, *Nine Evenings* was a pioneering event, but art critics declared it an artistic flop because of frequent technical breakdowns and unrehearsed performances.

After *Nine Evenings*, Kluver, Rauschenberg, Robert Whitman, and Fred Waldhauer founded Experiments in Art and Technology Inc. (EAT) in 1967. The organization had as its object to facilitate collaborations between engineers and artists. EAT's founders compiled lists of interested parties, organized lectures, published a newsletter, lent out equipment, and sought support from business and industry. In 1968, after receiving more than 100 entries from various parts of the world, they organized the exhibition *Some More Beginnings* at the Brooklyn Museum as an open competition for both artists and engineers.[35] The Pepsi Cola Pavilion at Expo '70 in Osaka, Japan, was EAT's most ambitious project (Figure 27.2). The pavilion was built in the shape of a geodesic dome measuring 50 meters in diameter. Created by the Japanese artist Fujiko Nakaya in collaboration with Tom Mee, a physicist and specialist in cloud formations, a fog "sculpture" sensitive to atmospheric conditions enveloped the building. The form of the sculpture was highly unstable as it depended on light and atmospheric conditions.

The entrance to the pavilion had the form of an inclined tunnel; each visitor received a handset that picked up audio signals from loops embedded on the floor. Listening to the sounds of running and gurgling water, the visitor walked to a dark interior referred to as the clam room, where she or he was showered with colored laser lights. Stairs connected this level with the dome room above, where a hemispherical mirror designed by Robert Whitman and measuring 90 feet in diameter delimited the contours of the space. Here, as is characteristic of spherical mirrors, the mirror produced a three-dimensional inverted image. This inverted image multiplied as the spectator stepped toward the center of the room, producing the impression of multiple holograms shifting in appearance depending on his or her position in the room. The acoustics of the mirror room (with sound system designed by experimental composer David Tudor) were

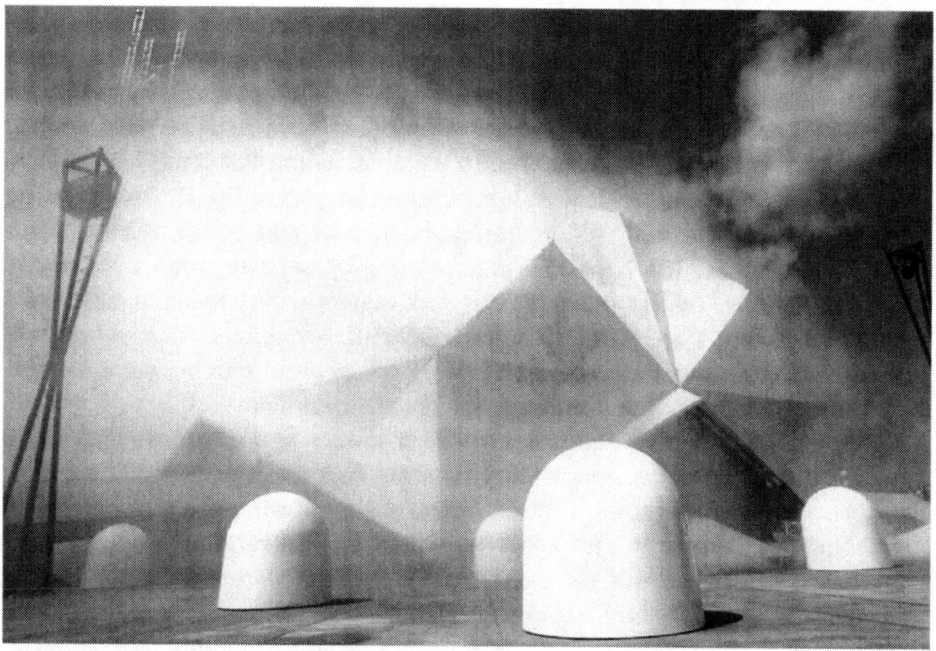

FIGURE 27.2   EAT, *Pepsi Cola Pavilion*, Osaka Japan, 1970. Photograph courtesy of Fujiko Nakaya

as complex as its visual environment. The floor was divided into ten sections of various materials matched with associated sounds (such as, in the "grass" section, the sounds of "ducks, turkey gobbling, birds, aviary, frogs, cicadas, lion roaring").[36]

The Pepsi Pavilion (described by Kluver as a "living responsive environment," and as "total instrument" that could be played by the participants) set an important precedent for future collaborations between artists and scientists and exemplified an environment *responsive* to the behavior of the visitors.[37] As envisioned by EAT, the pavilion functioned only for a limited time; due to an inflated budget and disagreements between the company and the artists, Pepsi Cola withdrew financial support for the operation of the building shortly after the exhibition opened. After dismissing EAT, Pepsi put on its own show, substituting band music for the experimental sound program and a light and color show for the mirror dome.

Liveliness and Responsiveness in Early Video Art

From 1970 to the late 1980s cybernetic art was marginalized in the art world because of its associations with the military, with commerce, and, in the popular imagination, with the on-going Vietnam War. While, until the late 1960s, cybernetic and conceptual artists had been included in the same exhibitions, the exhibition *Conceptual Art,* organized by Kynaston McShine at the Museum of Modern Art, New York, in 1970, marked the break between cybernetic and conceptual art for it included no cybernetic artists.[38] While cybernetic art had thus lost the limelight, numerous practitioners, including Robert Adrian, Lillian Swartz, Harold Cohen, and Roy Ascott, worked on, and in the 1970s a growing number of artists (including Nam June Paik, Woody and Steina Vasulka, Otto Piene, Wolf Vostell, Allan Kaprow, Marta Minunjin, Les Levine, Bruce Naumann, and Keith Sonnier) began to experiment with contemporary media technologies such as television, video, and to a lesser extent, computers. The writings of Marshal McLuhan superimposed on a lingering interest in systems and cybernetics provided the theoretical backbone for these experiments.

Following McLuhan's insights some artists sought to democratize television by offering the viewer the opportunity to contribute to its content. These early attempts at interactivity took various forms: from allowing the participants to alter colors and forms in the television screen, to transmitting to the viewer information excluded from the mass media, such as alternative news. Artists referred to information recorded in the video tape as "software," also the title of an exhibition organized by Jack Burnham at the Jewish Museum in 1970.[39] The utopian expectations that artists and other cultural workers placed on video and television parallel later views of the computer as a liberatory technology and anticipate contemporary notions of life as exemplified in electronic images and artificial creatures.[40] Some artists even argued for the autonomy of the television image – Brice Howard, director at the Center for Experiments in Television at the public television station KQED in San Francisco, for example, argued that the TV picture was a "live" light image creating itself on the inside of the cathode ray before the eyes of the viewer; consequently, as a living thing, it demanded an aesthetic based in movement rather than fixed forms.[41]

In the early 1970s, American computer scientist Myron Krueger was dissatisfied with the limited interaction the keyboard allowed as a computer interface. He designed spaces, which he referred to as "responsive environments," in which the computer perceived the actions of the participants and responded "intelligently" through audio-visual signals.[42] Between 1970 and 1975 Krueger designed a series of works that allowed participants in contiguous or remote locations to interact via video and computer, and he exhibited the first version of his best known work, *Video Place,* at the Milwaukee Museum in 1975. This installation consisted of two or more environments; in each location the participant entered a darkened room where there was a screen on which her or his image along with the images of participants in the other space(s) were projected. The participants could interact on the screen through movement. Because the images were projected on a neutral background they could be easily digitized and manipulated by the artist. *Video Place* had strong sensorial and affective impact as the participant interprets the changes made to his image as actions upon his person.

Telematics

The term "telematics," coined by French Government officials Simon Nora and Alain Minc in 1980, refers to the convergence of computers and communication systems.[43] Although artists such as Roy Ascott had long envisioned the artistic possibilities of this unification, access to computer systems had been limited before the development of the personal computer and the privatization of computer networks in the mid 1980s. Presciently, however, in the 1970s artists had begun to employ various networks to establish communication among remote participants. With the support of NASA (National Aeronautical and Space Administration) in 1977, Kit Galloway and Sherie Rabinowitz produced *Satellite Arts Project: A Space with No Boundaries*, a collaborative performance involving four dancers, two in Maryland and two in California, their performances unified by satellite composite imagery. *A Hole in Space*, a satellite link between two storefronts, one in New York and one in Los Angeles, followed in 1980. In contrast to the first project, conceived as an art performance, *A Hole in Space* facilitated access to expensive satellite technology to people on the street. Arranged as part of the cityscape with no special signage or previous advertisements, a passerby who happened on the piece could communicate with people in the other city and see their images projected on the storefront. Building on this experience, in 1984 Galloway and Rabinowitz established the *Electronic Café*, initially a telecommunications project linking six distinct communities in Los Angeles. The customers exchanged images, played music, and wrote poetry.

Already in 1980, a network for artists had been founded by Robert Adrian and Bill Barlett under the auspices of I. P. Sharp Associates (IPSA), a timesharing system based in Toronto that provided network computer services to businesses via telephone. The first prototype of this network, ARTBOX, was launched as ARTEX (Artists' Electronic Exchange System) in 1982. It remained in operation until 1990. In 1982, Adrian also organized "The World in 24 Hours," a multimedia event connecting artists in 24 cities using fax, e-mail, and slow-scan video.

The following year, Roy Ascott, an early subscriber to ARTBOX, presented *Plissure du Texte* (*The Pleating of the Text*) at the exhibition Electra, organized by Frank Popper at the Museé de l'art moderne de la ville de Paris. Inspired by Roland Barthes' 1973 book, *Pleasure of the Text*, Ascott's piece linked involved artists in 11 cities via computer network; the artists, working through what Ascott called "distributive authorship," created a collaborative text illustrated with ASCII images.[44] For Ascott this kind of creative networking was "an unending process. . . . In this sense art itself becomes, not a discrete set of entities, but rather a web of relationships between ideas and images in constant flux to which no single authorship is attributable, and whose meanings depended on those who enter the network. . . . The observer of the 'artwork' is a participator who, in accessing the system, transforms it." Ascott also envisioned networks as live entities. He declared: "The creative use of networks makes them organisms."[45]

All of these early telematic works utilized technology that would not become popularly available for yet a few years and were to that extent futuristic. In 1973, most computers were mainframes. In fact, it was that year that the first international e-mails in the military network ARPANET made their appearance. By 1979, only 16 ARPANET sites were located on campuses, the remaining 46 were in the military industrial complex. Alternative networks, including CSNET, were not financially stable until the mid 1980s.[46] Sharing the belief that the exchange of music, images, and text via a network and among people of various socioeconomic backgrounds, cultures, and languages exemplified "communication," many early telematic works unwittingly reinscribed Shannon and Weaver's notion of communication as data sent, encoded, and received.

Interactive Installations

Process, communication, and embodied interaction have continued to be central to artists working in the 1990s and beyond. Roy Ascott's employment of telematics and his notion of "distributed authorship" find new instantiations in online multi-user environments, which multiple artists have used to produce collaborative visual, literary, and theatrical works as well as game spaces.

Eduardo Kac and Ikuo Nakamura's *Essay on Human Understanding* of 1994 linked a plant in New York and a canary in Kentucky via a telephone line. Circuit boards, a speaker, and a microphone located on top of the canary's cage were wired to the phone system to transmit the bird's songs to the plant, while an electrode placed on one of the plant's leaves sensed its response to the singing of the bird. In turn, the micro voltage from the plant was then fed to a computer and analyzed by a program designed to interpret human brain waves. Another Macintosh computer transformed this information into sound.[47] According to Kac, the work explored communication between two different species. Although more complex, *Essay on Human Understanding* is reminiscent of Shannon's *Squat* in the interconnection of organic and inorganic systems.

In *Telematic Dreaming*, first exhibited in 1992 at the Kiasma Museum in Finland, British artist Paul Sermon explored affective dimensions of telematics. A video camera situated above a bed in one location sent a video image of the bed and a participant lying on it via a telephone line to the second location where another participant lay; a video camera in this second location sent the image of the projection of both participants interacting to a series of monitors placed around the bed at the first location. As in Krueger's *Video Place*, the participants reacted strongly to advances on their personal space and to the other participant's touch of their virtual images. The obligatory intimacy required by the piece was especially poignant at a time when AIDS was identified as an epidemic of worldwide proportions.[48]

Two artists influential in the development of immersive, responsive environments were Australian Jeffrey Shaw and Hungarian-born Agnes Hegedus.

Practicing in Amsterdam in the late 1960s Shaw unified virtual and physical environments by projecting images on inflatable structures, as in his *Corpocinema* (1967) and *Movie Movie* (1967). Shaw's monumental interactive installations from the late 1980s and 1990s allowed participants to explore virtual environments using familiar objects as interfaces. In his celebrated *Legible City* (1988–91) textual narratives were superimposed on three city plans (for Manhattan, Amsterdam, and Karlsruhe) to constitute virtual cityscapes where giant letters replaced architecture. The participant could explore these "legible" cities by riding a stationary bicycle located in the exhibition space. The coalescence of virtual and real space is a recurrent motif in Shaw's work.[49]

Agnes Hegedus's installation *Handsight*, exhibited at Ars Electronica (a prestigious festival of electronic art in Linz, Austria) in 1992, invited the viewer to reflect on the interactions of technology, perception, corporeality, identity, and memory (Figure 27.3). The work was conceptually far more complex than most digital art of its time. The installation consisted of three main parts arranged in the front of a darkened room: a large circular screen onto which real-time computer imagery was projected; an interface in the form of a large eyeball, which the participant manipulated; and a Plexiglas sphere with a hole into which the participant could insert the eyeball, which contained a sensing device that transmitted its position and orientation, to explore the interior. As the eyeball traveled inside the sphere, images of the virtual environment were projected on the screen and the eyeball thus functioned as an extension of the viewer's body. By making perception of the virtual environment dependent on the viewer's movement, the work exemplified the embodiment of vision. The literalness of having to hold the eyeball with one's hand in order to see delicately parodied the enthusiasm of contemporary artists and theorists – from novelist William Gibson, to artificial intelligence expert Hans Moravec and Australian artist Stelarc – for the obsolescence of the fleshed body.[50] *Handsight* suggested the interdependence of the virtual and the corporeal, an argument later developed by theorists such as Elizabeth Grosz, George Lakoff, and Mark Johnson, and most recently by Brian Massumi and Mark Hansen.[51]

Virtual Reality (VR), a technology with multiple origins that became viable in the mid 1980s, can be described as the real-time coordination of stereographic display with the user's viewpoint in physical space. In one technical manifestation, this is achieved via HMD (head mounted display), with one screen for each eye and a head-mounted tracking sensor. In most cases, a second sensor tracks the position of the user's hand through a glove or pointer interface and renders the movement of the hand accurately with respect to the viewpoint of the user in the rendered image. VR allows the user to explore visually a three-dimensional virtual world by head movement. CAVE (Computer Automated Virtual Environment) is a three-meter cube in which three walls and the floor are stereographic projection surfaces. The users wear LCD shutter glasses synchronized to the frame-rate of the imagery. This results in persuasive stereoscopic illusion. The primary differences between CAVE and the HMD technology are

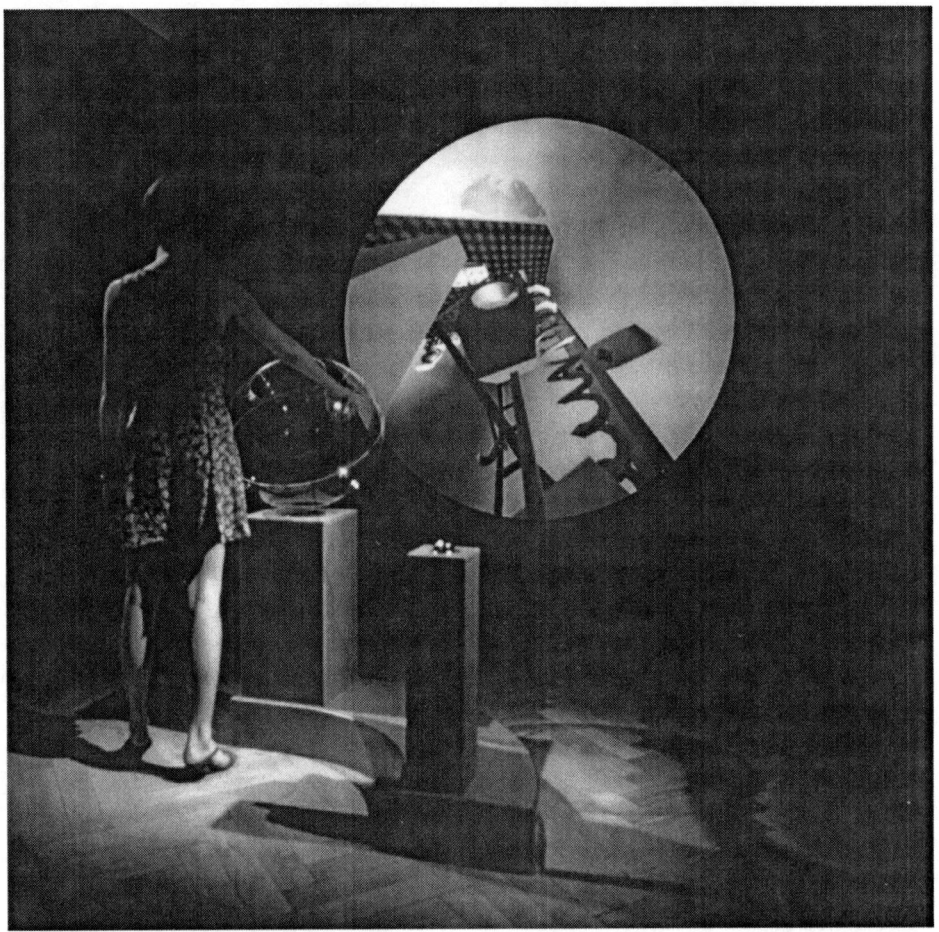

FIGURE 27.3 Agnes Hegedus, *Handsight*, Ars Electronica, Linz, 1992. Photograph courtesy of the artist

that the user can see her or his own physical body immersed in this illusory space in CAVE and is able to move freely. In the CAVE, a head tracker is usually used to determine viewpoint and the user often employs a pointer, mouse, or "wand."[52]

French artist Maurice Benayoun's installation *World Skin* exploited the immersive capabilities of the CAVE to stimulate the participant's reflection on the relation of individuals to complex systems such as world politics and the media. Exhibited at Ars Electronica in 1998, *World Skin* situated the viewer in a war zone, which she/he was invited to explore in three dimensions by walking around soldiers, tanks, and architectural ruins. Cameras dangling from the ceiling allowed the participant to photograph the virtual world of the CAVE. Taking a photograph had the visual effect of erasing the selected slice of this world from the landscape and transforming it into a shadow, making the participant into a virtual tourist of destruction. By letting the viewer experience a war zone, *World*

Skin anticipated recent digital art work, such as two games developed by the artists' collaborative SWEAT™ under the direction of Rafael Fajardo – *Crosser* (2000), and *La Migra* (2002) – which offer viewers the possibility of virtually experiencing politically charged and violent situations.

Artificial Life Art

In the last two decades, artists have engaged modes of artificial life to create works that behave, evolve, mutate, and form complex systems. In contrast to Artificial Intelligence, a-life, which separates life from its material substrate by focusing on organization and behavior, abandons centralized control in favor of distributed processes characteristic of the functioning of living organisms. A-life techniques include (but are not limited to): utilization of genetic algorithms that simulate genetic and evolutionary dynamics in digital computation; development of software agents that behave individually and with each other in an artificial-life world; and cellular automata – simple planar cell-based computer graphic systems which display emergent global behaviors.[53]

Although the discipline of a-life is less than 20 years old, its roots extend backward. Already in the mid 1940s John von Neumann developed a theory of self-reproducing automata based on a biological model.[54] In 1971, German scientist and philosopher Max Bense wrote an essay entitled "The Project of Generative Aesthetics," in which he described an evolving aesthetic based on mathematical and linguistic models. Anticipating a-life art, Bense differentiated the "material carrier" of a work of art and the organization or "aesthetic state" achieved by the carrier.[55] The concept of agents could be traced back to mathematical linguistic models from the turn of the twentieth century.[56]

In the late 1980s and early 1990s artist William Latham, in collaboration with programmer Stephen Todd, developed art evolution software that allowed the artist to create "ghost" sculptures (sculptures made of data which were then exhibited as prints or film). The program, "FormGrow," was based on a previous framework consisting of an evolutionary grammar that enabled the artist to build complex forms though the accumulation and transformation of simple elements. The resulting images resemble shells, coral, or plants distorted by the addition of extraneous parts. A subsequent program, "Mutator" (1991), offers the user a set of forms to be selected for further evolution, translating the trajectory of the user through form-space and producing the impression of evolutionary mutations.[57] The resulting images display aspects of the selection process and evolutionary procedures, not representations of physical or imaginary forms.

In 1993, artificial life scientist/artist Karl Sims constructed an art evolution system that allowed infinite numbers of mutations. In *Genetic Images* (1993), 15 video screens linked to a supercomputer displayed 15 images – each produced by a complex mathematical equation – which shifted every 30 seconds. Via a pressure-sensitive mat the visitors selected an image or pair of images to lead the next cycle of mutations. Metaphorically, the images bred other images, thus the work reproduced as a living organism, exemplifying a computer simulation of evolution.[58] Sims' later works apply these evolutionary principles to creatures that interact and reproduce in a digital environment.[59]

In *TechnoSphere* (1995), British artist Jane Prophet built an artificial-life system accessible to viewers through the Internet. The visitor constructed a synthetic creature from a series of elementary three-dimensional shapes and then released the creature into a virtual world. Unlike previous a-life environments *TechnoSphere* directly explored the ability of artificial-life forms to stimulate affective responses from users. The system regularly e-mailed the user to inform her or him of the creature's activities (including eating and mating) in the virtual world such that the owner could follow the progress of the creature from birth to death. *TechnoSphere* was tremendously popular, receiving between 70,000 and 80,000 hits per day. In addition to its affective qualities, this work shares with Pask's *Musicolour* and *Colloquy of Mobiles* a focus on agency and interaction.

After Inhatowicz's *Senster* other artists also have critically engaged the discipline of artificial intelligence through robotics and artificial life. Australian artist and theorist Simon Penny has investigated the affective capacities of real-time human–machine interaction through gesture and movement since the mid-1980s. Penny's robot *Petit Mal* (1992–5) was predicated on bottom-up concepts of reactive robotics exemplified by the work of roboticist Rodney Brooks. It navigated interior spaces and interacted with people through ultrasonic and pyroelectric sensors without the centralized mapping typical of traditional robotics and artificial intelligence. As with Schoffer's *CYSP* series and Ihnatowicz's *Senster*, users quickly ascribe emotive qualities to *Petit Mal* and treat it as if it were a child or pet.

From 1995, Penny has collaborated with software engineer Andre Bernhardt in the design of machine vision systems capable of constructing three-dimensional models of users in an interactive space derived from multiple camera images, often under infrared light. This custom-made vision system was a central component of subsequent works such as *Traces* (1999) and *Fugitive II* (2004). *Traces*, presented at Ars Electronica and designed in collaboration with Jaime Schulte, Andre Bernhardt, Jeffrey Smith, and Phoebe Sengers, is an immersive environment with an infrared vision system designed for CAVE. *Traces* creates a real-time three-dimensional model of the user derived from data from the vision system. The behavior of the user in the space elicits behaviors from the system, which manifests as three-dimensional forms that coexist with the user in the space of interaction. By means of a custom three-dimensional cellular automaton, the visual traces exhibit simple behaviors of their own – for example, throwing motions generate flocks of spheres arranged in serpentine formations loosely resembling Chinese dragons. These semi-autonomous agents interact with each other and respond to the user by gathering around her body.

Traces offers an alternative to other forms of immersive experience such as the goggle-and-glove form of Virtual Reality much publicized in the early 1990s. The participant needs no previous training, nor does he or she require any

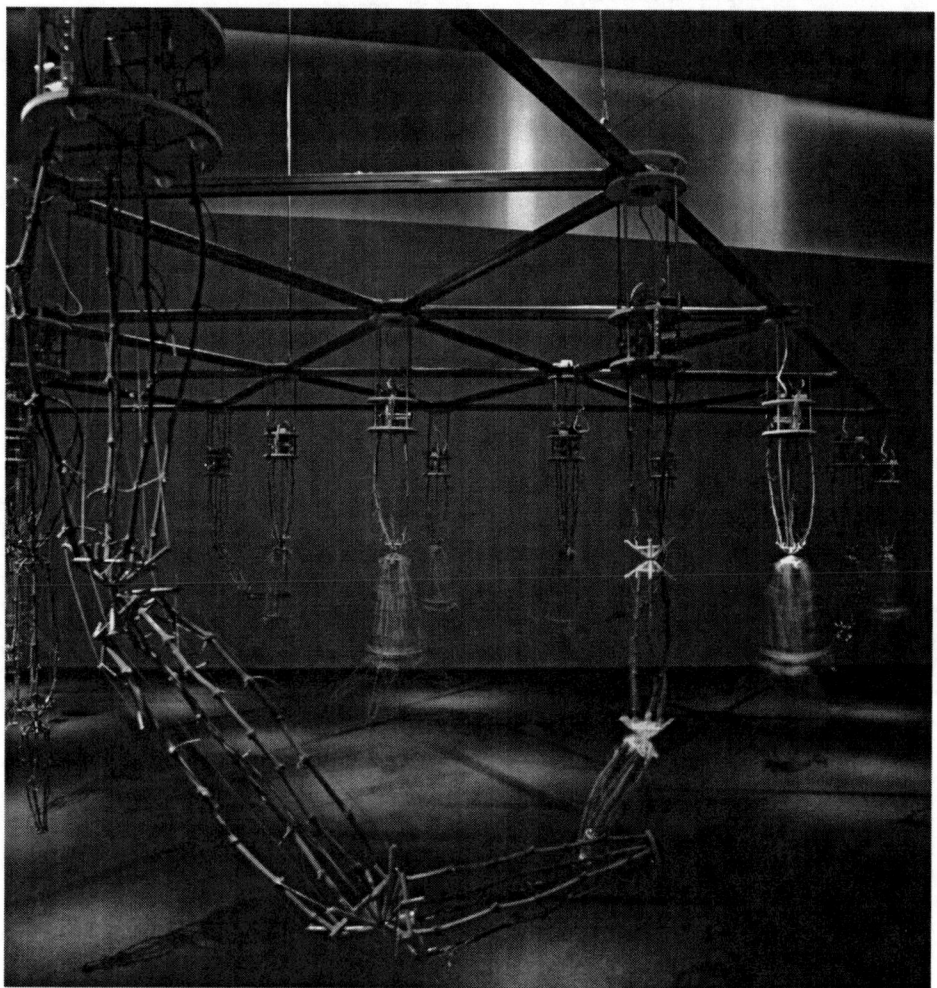

FIGURE 27.4   Ken Rinaldo, *Autopoiesis*, 2000. *Alien Intelligence* exhibition, Museum of Contemporary Art Kiasma, Helsinki. Photographer: Central Art Archives/Petri Virtanen

restrictive equipment to use the system. Dynamic forms are generated by moving the body as one does in everyday life. As the system responds to large body movement, it encourages the user to engage in active physical behavior. As Penny put it, the experience of *Traces* marks one of the few instances in which people leave an interactive work sweating and panting.[60]

American artist Ken Rinaldo has consistently explored emergent and self-organizing behavior as well as intra- and inter-species communication. *Autopoiesis*, the title of which refers to a concept originated by biologists Humberto Maturana and Francisco Varela, was commissioned by the Kiasma Museum in Finland in 2000 (Figure 27.4).[61] Maturana and Varela's 1980 book *Autopoiesis and Cognition* advanced the notion that a system's reality is determined by its internal, self-managing organization rather than its material structure. An autopoietic system recursively re-produces the elements and conditions of its organization to maintain its identity. To that end, Rinaldo's *Autopoiesis* consists of 15 robotic sculptures that interact musically and kinetically with each other and with the public, and modify their behaviors according to the actions and sounds of the participants and of other sculptures. Telephone tones enable the arms to talk to each other and allow the group to communicate with the viewer, while infrared sensors inform the sculptures of the position of the viewer and direct their movements. "Lipstick cameras" mounted at the tip of two of the arms project images of their surroundings on the walls of the space, suggesting that the sculptures survey the participants. Rinaldo describes the behavior of *Autopoiesis* as "a cybernetic ballet of experience."[62]

Conclusion

The practices and the projects discussed here represent only a small fraction of the history of technologically-based art, but they suffice to demonstrate that a consideration of "process" has been central to artistic practices for *at least* 50 years. While notions of process and procedurality are integral to contemporary digital art, it is seldom acknowledged that these concepts are less determined by technologies themselves than they are preoccupations of experimental art practices now absorbed into new media art practices. Contemporary critical theories enrich our understanding of this kind of work, yet theory alone is insufficient to understand its complex meanings. Theoretical knowledge must be paired with historical knowledge of both technology and art. Otherwise sophisticated pronouncements about the potential of contemporary art risk predicting developments that are already historical.

Notes

1   de Landa (2000), 21.
2   Lynn (1999), 10.
3   Massumi (2002), 5.
4   Ibid., 192. See de Landa (2001) and de Landa (2003); in the latter he extends his argument to cover varied artistic practices.
5   Langton (1999), 261.
6   Some of these investigations were indebted to Turing (1950).
7   Clarke "From Thermodynamics to Virtuality," in Clarke and Dalrymple (2002), 19, 20.
8   Ibid., 26.
9   For a succinct account of these developments see Gere (2002), 17–47. For a more extensive history see Winston (1998).

10   Wiener (1954/1988), 16.
11   Ibid., 24.
12   Ibid., 21.
13   von Bertalanffy (1972), 12, 92–3.
14   In his Nobel Prize acceptance speech in 1977, physicist/chemist Ilya Prigogine stated that his fascination with time drove him to research irreversible processes in the mid 1940s and dissipative structures in the 1960s. These studies were vital to the later development of chaos theory. Prigogine credited computer science pioneers Alan Turing and John von Neumann, as well as the philosopher Henri Bergson, among his sources. The philosopher Gilles Deleuze also employed scientific ideas of irreversibility, nonlinearity, transformation, and instability. See Deleuze (1968). Links between science and philosophy continue to be vital to the theory and practice of digital arts.
15   Popper (1977), 140.
16   Ibid.; plates 236 and 238 and 239 illustrate several of these works included in the exhibition *Bewogen Beweging* at the Moderna Museet Stockholm in 1961.
17   Agam worked with computers during his tenure at the Carpenter Center for the Visual Arts at Harvard University in 1968 where he taught a seminar entitled Advanced Exploration in Visual Communication.
18   See Benthall (1972), 106.
19   Pask (1971), 78.
20   See Shanken (2002a), 1–97 (Ascott's early work is discussed in pages 26–35); and Shanken (2002b), 257.
21   Ascott (2002b), 97, and (2002a), 110.
22   Ibid.
23   Penny (1994), 231–48; Hansen (2004).
24   See Reichardt (1968).
25   For a critical analysis of a-life narratives, see Hayles (1996), 146–64, and Whitelaw (2004), 181–205.
26   Davis (1974), 77.
27   Burnham (1973), 313.
28   Ibid., 320.
29   Burnham (1974), 16.
30   Burnham (1973), 347–9.
31   Medalla (2000), 299.
32   Ibid., 299–70.
33   See the Defense Advanced Research Projects Agency website (http://www.darpa.mil/ipto/programs/sdr/) and also the anonymous article "Insects Help in Developing Military Hardware," *Sydney Morning Herald* (8 August 2004), available at http://www.smh.com.au/articles/2004/08/25/1093246580311.html?oneclick=true. Scientists have built several kinds of robotic birds including "hummingbirds" developed by Dr Sunil Agrawal of the University of Delaware in 2003.
34   Burnham (1973), 357.
35   Kluver and Rauschenberg credited engineers as much as artists in the creation of technological works of art. This attitude was never embraced by the art world. Recently, theorist Lev Manovich proposed that a radical history of culture would acknowledge that "the true cultural innovators of the last decades of the twentieth

century were interface designers, computer game designers, music video directors and DJs-rather than painters, filmmakers or fiction writers." Manovich (2003), 16.

36 For an extensive and informative description of the building, see Garmire (1972), 173–246. The sound quotation is from Experiments in Art and Technology (1972), 275.

37 Kluver in ibid., x, xiii.

38 Gere (2002), 108. For another view on the marginalization of electronic art, see Maxwell (1991).

39 See Davis (1974), 84–91; Shanken (2002a), 54–9; and Youngblood (1970).

40 On the liveliness of electronic images, see Marks (2002), 161–75.

41 Cited in Davis (1974), 89.

42 Krueger (2001), 113–14.

43 Nora and Minc (1978).

44 See Shanken (2002a), 65. ASCII is the standard code for representing English characters as numbers.

45 Ascott (2002c), 199.

46 Winston (1998), 330–1.

47 The piece employed Max/MSP, a set of graphical programming tools that has a broad range of artistic application from electronic music to media installations. David Zicarelly, an engineer specializing in interactive media software, developed MAX at IRCAM (the computer music institute at the Centre Georges Pompidou in Paris) in the late 1980s. MIDI (musical instrument digital interface) is a standard adopted by the electronic music industry for controlling devices, such as synthesizers and sound cards, that emit music. MIDI files contain not sounds but encoded information that describes the instruments, notes, pitch, and timing of the music, which can then be recreated on MIDI-capable devices.

48 See Springer (1996).

49 Duguet (1997), 44.

50 See Moravec (1988).

51 Grosz (1994); Lakoff and Johnson (1999); Massumi (2002); Hansen (2004).

52 CAVE was developed by Thomas Defantic and Dave Sandin at the Electronic Visualization Laboratory at the University of Illinois at Chicago in 1991.

53 See Whitelaw (2004), 8–9.

54 This research was published in von Neumann (1966).

55 Bense (1971), 57.

56 See Weibel (2003).

57 See Whitelaw (2004), 32–4.

58 See Ibid., 27.

59 See ibid., 30–1 and Sims (2003), 512–15.

60 Penny (1999).

61 Maturana and Varela (1980).

62 Rinaldo (2004).

References and further reading

Ascott, Roy (2002a). "Behaviouristic Art and the Cybernetic Vision." 109–56.
—— (2002b). "The Construction of Change." 97–107.

—— (2002c). "Art and Telematics: Towards a Network Consciousness." 185–201.

Ascott, Roy, and Edward Shanken (2002). *Telematic Embrace*. Berkeley: University of California Press.

Bender, Gretchen, and Timothy Druckrey, eds. (1994). *Culture on the Brink: Ideologies of Technology*. Seattle: Bay Press.

Bense, Max (1971). "The Project of Generative Aesthetics." In *Cybernetics, Art and Ideas*, ed. Jasia Reichardt. Greenwich, CT: New York Graphic Society. 57–60.

Benthall, Jonathan (1972). *Science and Technology in Art Today*. New York: Praeger Publishers.

Bertalanffy, Ludwig von (1972). *General Systems Theory: Foundations, Development, Applications*. New York: George Braziller.

Burnham, Jack (1973). *Beyond Modern Sculpture: The Effects of Science and Technology on the Sculpture of this Century*. New York: George Braziller.

—— (1974). "Systems Esthetics." In *Great Western Salt Works: Essays on the Meaning of Post-Formalist Art*. New York: George Braziller. 15–25.

Clarke, Bruce, and Linda Dalrymple, eds. (2002). *From Energy to Information*. Stanford, CA: Stanford University Press.

Davis, Douglas (1974). *Art and the Future*. New York: Praeger Publishers.

Deleuze, Gilles (1968). *Différence et Répétition*. Paris: Presses Universitaires de France.

Druckrey, Timothy, with Ars Electronica, ed. (1999). *Ars Electronica: Facing the Future*. Cambridge, MA: MIT Press.

Duguet, Anne Marie (1997). "Jeffrey Shaw: From Expanded Cinema to Virtual Reality." In *Jeffrey Shaw – A User's Manual: From Expanded Cinema to Virtual Reality*, ed. Anne-Marie Duguet, Heinrich Klotz, and Peter Weibel. Karlsruhe: ZKM/ Zentrum fur Kunst und Medientechnologie.

Experiments in Art and Technology (1972). *Pavilion*. New York: E. P. Dutton.

Garmire, Elsa (1972). "An Overview." In Experiments in Art and Technology (1972). 173–246.

Gere, Charlie (2002). *Digital Culture*. London: Reaktion Books.

Grosz, Elizabeth (1994). *Volatile Bodies: Toward a Corporeal Feminism*. St. Leonards, Australia: Allen and Unwin.

Hansen, Mark B. N. (2004). *New Philosophy for New Media*. Cambridge, MA: MIT Press.

Hayles, Katherine (1996). "Narratives of Artificial Life." In *Future Natural: Nature, Science, Culture*, ed. George Robertson et al. London: Routledge. 146–64.

Krueger, Myron (2001). "Responsive Environments." In *Multimedia: From Wagner to Virtual Reality*, ed. Randall Packer and Ken Jordan. New York: W. W. Norton and Company. 104–20.

Lakoff, George, and Mark Johnson (1999). *Philosophy in the Flesh: The Embodied Mind and its Challenge to Western Thought*. New York: Basic Books.

Landa, Manuel de (2000). *A Thousand Years of Nonlinear History*. New York: Swerve Editions.

—— (2001). "Deleuze and the Use of the Genetic Algorithm in Architecture." http://boo.mi2.hr/~ognjen/tekst/delanda2001.html.

—— (2003). "Deleuze y el uso del algoritmo genético en la arquitectura." Lecture delivered at Laboratorio de Arte Alameda, Mexico City, May 27.

Langton, Christopher (1999). "Artificial Life" in Druckrey, with Ars Electronica (1999), 126–268.

Lynn, Greg (1999). *Animate Form*. New York: Princeton Architectural Press.

Manovich, Lev (2003). "New Media from Borges to HTML." In The *New Media Reader*, ed. Noah Wardrip-Fruin and Nick Monfort. Cambridge, MA: MIT Press. 13–25.

Marks, Laura (2002). "How Electrons Remember." In *Touch: Sensuous Theory and Multisensory Media*. Minneapolis: University of Minnesota Press. 161–75.

Massumi, Brian (2002). *Parables for the Virtual: Movement, Affect, Sensation*. Durham, NC: Duke University Press.

Maturana, Humberto R., and Francisco J. Varela (1980). *Autopoiesis and Cognition: The Realization of the Living*. Boston: D. Reidel.

Maxwell, Delle (1991). "The Emperor's New Art?" In *Computers in Art and Design. SIGGRAPH 91 Art and Design Show*. July to August 1991. Las Vegas, Nevada and New York: Association for Computing Machinery.

Medalla, David (2000). "New Projects." *Signals*, vol. 1, London, August 1964. Repr. in *Force Fields; Phases of the Kinetic*, exhibition catalogue. Barcelona: Museu d'Art Contemporani de Barcelona (MACBA), and London: The Hayward Gallery. 299–300.

Moravec, Hans (1988). *Mind Children: The Future of Robot and Human Intelligence*. Cambridge, MA: Harvard University Press.

Neumann, John von (1966). *Theory of Self-Reproducing Automata*. Urbana: University of Illinois Press.

Nora, Simon, and Alain Minc (1978). *L'Informatisation de la Société. Rapport à M. le Président de la République*. Paris: La documentation Française.

Pask, Gordon (1971). "A Comment, a Case History and a Plan." In *Cybernetics, Art and Ideas*, ed. Jasia Reichardt. Greenwich, CT: New York Graphic Society. 76–99.

Penny, Simon (1994). "Virtual Reality as the Completion of the Enlightenment Project." In Bender and Druckrey (1994). 231–48.

—— (1999). *Traces, An Embodied Immersive Project for CAVE with Multicamera Machine Vision*. Videotape, courtesy of the artist.

Popper, Frank (1977). *Agam*. New York: Harry N. Abrams.

Reichardt, Jasia, ed. (1968). *Cybernetic Serendipity: The Computer and the Arts, A Studio International Special Issue*. London: Studio International.

Rinaldo, Ken (2004). *Interactive Robotic Sculptures 1990–2004*. Videotape, courtesy of the artist.

Shanken, Edward (2002a). "From Cybernetics to Telematics: The Art, Pedagogy and Theory of Roy Ascott." In Ascott and Shanken (2002). 1–97.

—— (2002b). "Cybernetics and Art: Cultural Convergence of the 1960s." In Clarke and Dalrymple (2002). 255–77.

Sims, Karl (2003). "Evolved Virtual Creatures." In Weibel and Shaw, eds. (2003), 512–15.

Springer, Claudia (1996). *Electronic Eros: Bodies and Desire in the Postindustrial Age*. Austin: University of Texas Press.

Turing, Alan (1950). "Computing Machinery and Intelligence." *Mind: A Quarterly Review of Psychology and Philosophy*, vol. 59(236), October:433–60.

Weibel, Peter (2003). "The Intelligent Image: Neuro Cinema or Quantum Cinema." In Weibel and Shaw (2003). 594–601.

Weibel, Peter, and Jeffrey Shaw, ed. (2003). *Future Cinema: The Cinematic Imaginary after Film*. Exhibition catalogue. Cambridge, MA: MIT Press and Karlsruhe: ZKM.

Whitelaw, Mitchell (2004). *Metacreation: Art and Artificial Life*. Cambridge, MA: MIT Press.

Wiener, Norbert (1954/1988). *The Human Use of Human Beings*. New York: Da Capo Press.

Winston, Brian (1998). *Media Technology and Society. A History from the Telegraph to the Internet*. New York: Routledge.

Youngblood, Gene (1970). *Expanded Cinema*. New York: E. P. Dutton.

Index

Note: page numbers in italics refer to illustrations